LANGENSCHEIDT'S UNIVERSAL TURKISH DICTIONARY

TURKISH-ENGLISH
ENGLISH-TURKISH

Edited by the
Langenscheidt Editorial Staff

L

LANGENSCHEIDT

NEW YORK · BERLIN · MUNICH
VIENNA · ZURICH

Compiled by Prof. Dr.
H.-J. Kornrumpf

Contents

İçindekiler

Abbreviations Used in this Dictionary —
Bu Sözlükte Kullanılan Kısaltmalar 5

American Spelling — *Amerikan İngilizcesinin
Yazımı* 7

Pronunciation of the Turkish Alphabet —
Türkçe Alfabesinin Söylenişi 9

Guide to English Pronunciation —
İngilizce Söylenişinin Temelleri 11

Turkish-English Vocabulary —
Türkçe-İngilizce Sözlük 15

English-Turkish Vocabulary —
İngilizce-Türkçe Sözlük 185

British and American Abbreviations —
İngilizce'de Kullanılan Kısaltmalar 437

Turkish Abbreviations —
Türkçe'de Kullanılan Kısaltmalar 440

Irregular Verbs — *İngilizce' deki Kuralsız Fiiller* 442

Numbers — *Sayılar* 446

© 1979 Langenscheidt KG, Berlin und München
Printed in Germany

Abbreviations Used in this Dictionary

Bu Sözlükte Kullanılan Kısaltmalar

The tilde (~, when the initial letter changes:2) stands for the catchword at the beginning of the entry or the part of it preceding the vertical bar (|). Examples: **birth ... ~day = birthday; approv|al ... ~e = approve; Bibl|e ... ℓiography = bibliography.**

(~) işareti — yazım değişikliği varsa: (2) — ya esas sözcüğün tümünü veya onun çizgiye (|) kadar olan kısmını gösterir; örneğin: **birth ... ~day = birthday; approv|al ... ~e = approve; Bibl|e ... ℓiography = bibliography.**

a. also dahi

adj. adjective sıfat

adv. adverb zarf, belirteç

Am. American English Amerikan İngilizcesi

an. anatomy anatomi

arch. architecture mimarlık

astr. astronomy astronomi, gökbilim

av. aviation havacılık

b. bir(i) someone

bot. botany botanik

chem. chemistry kimya

coll. colloquial konuşma dili

conj. conjunction bağlaç

-de ismin de-hali locative

-den ismin den-hali ablative

-e ismin e-hali dative

ec. economy iktisat, ekonomi

el. electricity, electrical engineering elektrik, elektroteknik

fig. figuratively mecazî

geo. geography, geology coğrafya, jeoloji

gr. grammar gramer, dilbilgisi

-i ismin i-hali accusative

-in ismin in-hali genitive

inf. infinitive mastar, eylemlik

intj. interjection ünlem

jur. jurisprudence hukuk, türe

math. mathematics matematik

med. medicine tıp

mil. military terminology askerlikle ilgili
mus. music müzik

n. noun isim, ad
naut. nautical terminology denizcilik
neg. negative sense olumsuz anlam

phot. photography fotoğrafçılık
phys. physics fizik
pl. plural çoğul
pol. politics siyaset, politika
prp. preposition ön edat, ilgeç

rel. religion din

ş. şey(i) something
sg. singular tekil
sl. slang argo
so. someone biri
sth. something bir şey(i)

tech. technology teknik
tel. telephone, telegraph telefon, telgraf
thea. theatre tiyatro

v/i verb intransitive geçişsiz fiil
v.s. ve saire and so on
v/t verb transitive geçişli fiil
vulg. vulgar kaba, bayağı

zo. zoology zooloji

American Spelling

Amerikan İngilizcesinin Yazımı

İngiltere'de konuşulan İngilizcenin yazımından farklı olarak Amerikan İngilizcesinin (*Am.*'nin) yazımında başlıca şu özellikler vardır:

1. İki sözcüğü birbirine bağlayan çizgi çoğu kez kaldırılır, örneğin co-operate yerine cooperate.

2. **...our** ekindeki u harfi kaldırılır, örneğin: color, humor.

3. **...re** yerine **...er** yazılır, örneğin: center, theater; fakat **...cre** eki değişmez.

4. **...l** ve **...p** ile biten fiillerin türetmelerinde son ünsüz harf ikilenmez, örneğin: travel — traveled — traveling — traveler, worship — worshiped — worshiping — worshiper. Diğer bazı sözcüklerde dahi iki ünsüz harfin birisi kaldırılır, örneğin: waggon yerine wagon, woollen yerine woolen.

5. **...ence** eki yerine **...ense** yazılır, örneğin: defense, offense.

6. Fransızcadan gelen ekler çoğu kez kaldırılır veya kısaltılır, örneğin: dialog(ue), program(me), envelop(e).

7. **ae** ve **oe** yerine çoğu kez yalnız **e** yazılır, örneğin: an(a)emia, man(o)euvers.

8. **...xion** yerine **...ction** kullanılır, örneğin: connection.

9. Söylenmiyen **e**, abridg(e)ment, judg(e)ment v.s. gibi sözcüklerde kaldırılır.

10. **en...** öneki yerine **in...** daha çok kullanılır, örneğin: inclose.

11. *Am.*'de diğer özel yazım biçimleri: staunch yerine stanch, mould yerine mold, moult yerine molt, plough yerine plow, moustache yerine mustache, cheque yerine check, grey yerine gray, gypsy yerine gipsy, sceptic yerine skeptic, skilful yerine skillful, tyre yerine tire.

12. although, all right, through yerine altho, alright, thru biçimleri de kullanılabilir.

Pronunciation of the Turkish Alphabet

Türkçe Alfabesinin Söylenişi

A. Vowels and Diphthongs

The vowels are usually short or of medium length though, however, there is still a number of foreign, mostly Arabic, words with long vowels.

a as **u** in but, sometimes long as **a** in far.
e as **e** in bed.
ı similar to the **a** in along.
i as in hit.
o as in doll or god.
ö as French **œu** in œuvre.
u as in bull.
ü as French **u** in plume.

The diphthongs are as follows:

ay as **uy** in buy.
ey as **a** in make.
oy as **oi** in boil.
uy as French **oui** in Louis.

B. Consonants

The consonants are as in English, except:

c as **j** in jam.
ç as **ch** in chalk.
g as in English, but when followed by **â** or **û** it is palatalized; thus **gâ** is very nearly gya, **gû** like gyoo.
ğ with soft vowels (e, i, ö, ü) is a consonantal **y**; with hard vowels (a, ı, o, u) it is a very guttural but hardly perceptible g and very little more than a lengthening of the preceding vowel.
h is always pronounced.

j	as French **j** in journal.
k	with soft vowels is frontal like the **k** in kill; with hard vowels it is backward like the **c** and **ck** in cuckoo; when followed by **â** or **û** it is highly palatalized: thus **kâ** is almost like **kya**.
l	is much like the English **l**, but before soft vowels and **â** and **û** it is frontal and similar to the German **l**.
r	is much like a slight Scottish **r**, but at the end of a word it is practically unvoiced.
ş	as **sh** in she.
v	as in vile; after a vowel it may change to the English **w** in we: e.g. levha, lavta.

C. Circumflex and Apostrophe

The circumflex (düzeltme işareti) denotes:

1. on **a** and **u** the frontal pronunciation of the preceding consonants **g**, **k** and **l** (ikametgâh, kâtip; lûtfen, lûgat are often replaced by lütfen, lügat).

2. the lengthening of a vowel when two words are spelled in the same way: alem (flag), âlem (world).

The apostrophe (kesme işareti) denotes:

1. the separate pronunciation of two syllables: kat'etmek, san'at; in modern spelling, however, it is mostly dispensed with;

2. the separation of suffixes from a proper name or a number: İngiltere'de, 1978'de.

D. Stress

The stress is usually on the final syllable; important exceptions to this rule are:

1. The stress lies always on the final syllable before the interrogative and negative particles mı, mi, mu, mü and ma, me: geldi mi? Yápma!

2. The suffix -le (from ile) is never stressed: bu surétle.

3. The syllables denoting the tense of the verb (like -yor-, -ir-, etc.) are usually stressed: geliyórum, gidérsin, etc.

Guide to English Pronunciation

İngilizce Söylenişinin Temelleri

İngilizcede 45 ses (fonem) vardır. Bunlardan 12 tanesi ünlü, 9'u iki ünlü ve 24'ü ünsüzdür. Halbuki bunları yazıya çevirmek için alfabede yalnız 26 harf vardır. Bundan dolayı bir harf, bazı durumlarda birden fazla ses için kullanılır; örneğin: far, match, warm, watch, make, arrive gibi sözcüklerde a harfi, birbirlerinden ayrı altı biçimde söylenir. Öte yanda bir ses, birbirlerinden ayrı harflerle gösterilebilir; örneğin: her, girl, fur, learn, worse, colonel sözcüklerindeki ünlü harf aynı biçimde yani uzun ö (ô) gibi söylenir.

Bu sözlüğü kullananlara İngilizce söylenişini kolaylaştırmak için sözlüğün İngilizce-Türkçe bölümünde her maddenin başında ilgili olan sözcüğün söylenişi, fonetik bir yönteme göre köşeli ayraçlar içinde gösterilir. Bu yöntemin işaretleri çoğunlukla Türkçe alfabesi harflerinin aynıdır ve Türkçede olduğu gibi söylenir.

Bu sözlükte kullanılan fonetik işaretler şunlardır:

Ses	Türkçesi	İngilizce örnekler
Ünlüler:		
â, aa	lâle, kaabil	far, father
a	a	nut, much
ä	çok açık a'ya benzer yayık bir e	man, mad
e	e	pen, egg
î	î	me, feel
i	i	ship, hint
ı	ı	the, above
ô	uzun o gibi söylenir	all, form
o	o	not, song

12

(Ses	Türkçesi	İngilizce örnekler)
ö	uzun ö gibi söylenir	her, girl
û, uu	tufan'daki u'ya benzer	do, shoe
u	u	put, pull

İki ünlüler:

ay	ay	by, life
au	au	out, how
äı	a'ya benzer e ile ı	care, chair
ey	ey	late, may
iı	iı	cheer, fear
iu	iu; ou da söylenir	go, foam
oy	oy	boy, voice
uı	uı	sure, poor
yû	yû	new, beauty

Ünsüzler:

b	b	born, rubber
p	p	path, happy
d	d	die, sad
t	t	tie, matter
g	g	gold, dig
k	k	cold; kill
v	v	very, brave
f	f	fine, safe
z	z	zero, maze
s	s	so, gas
j	j	pleasure, occasion
ş	ş	shine, fish
c	c	joke, bridge
ç	ç	church, each
dh	dili üst kesicidişlere dokundurarak söylenen d	that, with
th	dili üst kesicidişlere dokundurarak söylenen t	thank, nothing
h	h	happy, adhere
m	m	make, swim
n	n	name, finish
ŋ	dili damağa dokundurarak genizden söylenen n	sing, English

(Ses	Türkçesi	İngilizce örnekler)
r	r (dil ağızda yuvarlanarak damağa hafifçe dokundurulur	red, very
l	sözcüğün başında ince, ortasında veya sonunda ise art damaktan çıkarılarak kalın söylenen l	leave; full
w	dudakları yuvarlıyarak söylenen v	will, away
y	y	yellow, year

Vurgulanan heceden önce (') işareti vardır.

Fazla yer harcamamak için İngilizce'de en çok kullanılan eklerin söylenişleri aşağıdaki listede gösterilmiştir. Bir farklılık olmadığı sürece söylenişler, sözlükte bir daha tekrarlanmamıştır.

-ability [-ıbiliti]
-able [-ıbl]
-age [-ic]
-al [-ıl]
-ally [-ıli]
-an [-ın]
-ance [-ıns]
-ancy [-ınsi]
-ant [-ınt]
-ar [-ı]
-ary [-ıri]
-ation [-eyşın]
-cious [-şıs]
-sy [-si]
-dom [-dım]
-ed [-d; -t; -id]
-edness [-dnis; -tnis; -idnis]
-ee [-î]
-en [-n]
-ence [-ıns]
-ent [-ınt]
-er [-ı]

-ery [-ıri]
-ess [-is]
-fication [-fikeyşın]
-ful [-ful]
-fy [-fay]
-hood [-hud]
-ial [-ıl]
-ian [-iın; yın]
-ible [-ıbl]
-ic(s) [-ik(s)]
-ical [-ikıl]
-ily [-ili]
-iness [-inis]
-ing [-iŋ]
-ish [-iş]
-ism [-izım]
-ist [-ist]
-istic [-istik]
-ite [-ayt]
-ity [-iti]
-ive [-iv]
-ization [-ayzeyşın]

-ize [-ayz]
-izing [-ayziŋ]
-less [-lis]
-ly [-li]
-ment(s) [-mınt(s)]
-ness [-nis]
-oid [-oyd]
-or [-ı]
-ory [-ıri]
-our [-ı]
-ous [-ıs]

-ry [-ri]
-ship [-şip]
-(s)sion [-şın]
-sive [-siv]
-some [-sım]
-ties [-tiz]
-tion [-şın]
-tious [-şıs]
-trous [-trıs]
-try [-tri]
-y [-i]

Turkish-English Vocabulary

A

-a (*dative suffix*) to, towards
aba (*coarse woollen cloth*)
abajur lampshade
abanmak -e lean against
abanoz ebony
abartmak *s.* **obartmak**
abes useless, trifle
abıhayat water of life; elixir
abi (*for* **ağabey**) elder brother
abide monument
abla elder sister
abluka blockade; ~ etm. ~ya almak *v/t* blockade
abone subscriber; subscription; ~ olm -e subscribe to; -in ~liğinden vazgeçmek discontinue the subscription of
abstre abstract
abuk sabuk inconsiderate, rash
acaba I wonder if ...?
acar clever, cunning; enterprising
acayip strange, wonderful
acele haste, hurry; hasty, urgent; ~ etm. *v/i* haste, hurry
acemi inexperienced; ~lik inexperience
acente agent; ~lik agency
acı bitter, sharp

acık grief, sorrow; ~lı tragic, touching; sentimental
acıkmak feel hungry
acı|lık bitterness; ~mak feel pain, hurt; -e take pity on; ~nmak -e be pitied
âciz incapable, impotent; ~ kalmak (*or* olm.) -den be incapable of, be unable to
acuze old woman; hag
aç hungry; ~gözlü covetous, avaricious
açı *math.* angle
açık open, uncovered; clear; light (*colour*); deficit; ~ğa vurmak *v/t* reveal, disclose; ~ hava open air; ~ça *adv.* openly, clearly; ~göz wide awake, cunning; ~lama explanation, statement; ~lamak *v/t* make public, explain; ~lık open space, interval
açıl|ış opening, inauguration; ~mak be opened; -e open out to
açlık hunger
açmak *v/t* open, begin, unfurl; turn on, switch on, start
ad name, reputation; ~ı geçen afore-mentioned; ~ına in the name of, for
ada island; ~ tavşanı rabbit

adak vow; votive offering

adale muscle

adalet justice; **~siz** unjust; **~sizlik** injustice

adam man, human being

adamak v/t promise, vow

adaş of the same name, namesake

adavet hostility; hate

aday candidate

adçekme designation by lot

addetmek -*i* ... **olarak** consider, regard *so.* to be *sth.*

Âdem Adam

adet number

âdet custom, habit; *med.* menstruation; **~a** *adv.* nearly, almost; simply, merely

adım step, pace; **~ ~** step by step

adi common; mean

adil just

adilik commonness; vulgarity, baseness

adlandırmak v/t name, call

adlı named

adli judicial; **~iye** (administration of) justice

adres address; **~ rehberi** address book

Adriyatik (denizi) Adriatic Sea

af pardon; **~ dilemek** apologize

afacan unruly, undisciplined

afaki superficial; objective

aferin *intj.* bravo!, well done!

âfet disaster, calamity; *fig.* bewitching person

affetmek v/t pardon, forgive; **~edersiniz!** I beg your pardon!

afiyet health; **~ olsun!** may it do you good!, your health!

aforoz *rel.* excommunication

Afrika Africa

afsun spell, charm, incantation; **~cu** sorcerer

afyon opium

agraf clip; paper-clip

agrandisman *phot.* enlargement

ağ net, web

ağa master, gentleman; **~bey** elder brother

ağaç tree; timber; **~lık** wooded; wood

ağarmak become white or pale; **~tmak** v/t whiten, clean

ağda syrup

ağı poison

ağıl sheep fold; halo

ağılamak v/t poison

ağır heavy, weighty; serious; strong; **~ yağ, ~ yakıt** heavy oil, Diesel oil; **~başlı** grave, serious; **~laşmak** become heavier, more serious, more mature; **~lık** weight, heaviness; *fig.* nightmare

ağıt lament, mourning

ağız mouth; opening; dialect, manner of speaking; **~lık** mouthpiece; cigarette holder

ağla|mak weep (-e or için over); **~tmak** v/t cause to weep
ağmak v/i rise
ağrı pain, ache; pains of childbirth
Ağrı dağı Mount Ararat
ağrı|mak v/i ache, hurt; **~sız** without pain
ağu s. ağı
ağustos August
ah intj. ah!, oh!
ahali pl. inhabitants, people
ahbap friend, acquaintance
ahçı s. aşçı
ahdetmek -e promise solemnly, take an oath on
ahenk accord, harmony; **~li** harmonious, in accord; **~siz** inharmonious
ahır stable
ahiret s. ahret
ahize tel. receiver
ahlâk pl. morals; character; **~î** pertaining to morals; moral; **~sız** immoral, amoral
ahmak silly, idiotic
ahret rel. next world, future life
ahşap wood; wooden
ahu gazelle; **~dudu** raspberry
aid|at pl. contribution sg.; allowance; **~iyet** interest, concern
aile family; wife; **~vî** regarding the family, domestic
ait -e concerning, belonging to
ajan agent; **~s** news agency

ak white, clean
akademi academy
akalliyet minority
akarsu running water
akasya acacia
ak|baba vulture; **~ciğer** lung(s)
akça whitish, pale; asper; money
Akdeniz the Mediterranean
akdetmek v/t bind, tie; conclude
âkıbet end, consequence, result
akıcı liquid; fluent
akıl reason, intelligence; sense; **aklı başına gelmek** come to one's senses; **aklına gelmek** come to one's mind; **~lı** clever, intelligent, reasonable; **~sız** stupid, unreasonable
akı|m flowing; current; **~ntı** current, stream; **~tmak** v/t make flow, let flow; smelt
akide[1] faith, creed
akide[2] sugar candy
akis contrary, reflex, reflection
akit contract, treaty; marriage
aklî pertaining to mind or reason, reasonable
akmak v/i flow, drip, ooze
akortetmek v/t tune
akraba relative(s)
akreditif ec. letter of credit
akrep scorpion; hour-hand of the clock
aksa|k limping; **~mak** v/i limp

akset|mek -e be reflected to; come to the hearing of; ~tirmek v/t reflect, echo

aksır|ık sneeze; ~mak v/i sneeze

aksi contrary, opposite; adverse; ~ takdirde otherwise, else; ~lik contrariness; obstinacy, adverseness; ~ne adv. on the contrary; -in contrary to

aksiyon ec. share, stock

aksülâmel reaction

akşam evening; ~ üstü towards evening; ~leyin in the evening

aktarma transhipment; change of train etc.; ~ yapmak change the train etc.; ~k v/t move, transfer

akt|ör actor; ~ris actress; ~üalite (film) news-reel

akümülâtör tech. accumulator

al red, crimson

âlâ very good, excellent; pek ~! very good!, all right! [motley)

alaca of various colours,)

alacak ec. money owing, credit, claims; ~lı creditor

alafranga in the European fashion

alâimisema rainbow

alâka connection, relationship, interest; ~dar ile connected with, interested in; ~dar etm. -i interest (ile in); ~lı ile interested in, concerned with

alâmet sign, mark, symbol; ~i farika ec. trademark

alan plain, space

alarm alarm

alaşım chem. alloy

alaturka in the Turkish fashion

alay¹ crowd, procession; mil. regiment

alay² joke, derision; ~ etm. make fun (ile of)

alaz flame

albay mil. colonel

albüm album

albümin albumen

alçak low, vile, base; ~gönüllü humble, modest; ~lık lowness, baseness, meanness

alçal|mak become low; degrade oneself; ~tmak v/t lower, reduce; abase

alçı gypsum, plaster of Paris

alda|nmak be deceived; be mistaken; ~tılmak be cheated, be defrauded; ~tmak v/t deceive, dupe, cheat

aldırmak -e take notice of, pay attention to, mind

alel|âde adv. as usual, ordinarily; ~umum adv. in general, generally

alem flag; peak of a minaret

âlem world, universe; ~şümul universal

alenî public, openly

alerji med. allergy

alet tool, instrument

alev flame; ~lenmek flame up, flare

aleyh|- against; -in ~inde bulunmak be against so. or sth.; ~tar opponent

ana

alfabe alphabet
algı perception
alıcı buyer, customer; *tech.* receiver
alık crazy, imbecile
alıko(y)mak *v/t* keep back, detain
alım taking; purchase; **~ satım** purchase and sale
alın forehead
alın|dı *ec.* receipt; **~mak** be taken; take offense (*-den* at)
alış taking, buying
alış|kan, **~kın** tamed, familiar; **~mak** *-e* be accustomed to, become familiar with; **~tırmak** *v/t* accustom, tame; **~veriş** buying and selling, trade
âli high, exalted
âlim scholar
alkım rainbow
alkış applause; **~lamak** *v/t* acclaim; **~lanmak** be greeted with applause
alkol alcohol; **~izm** alcoholism; **~suz** non-alcoholic, soft
Allah God; **~!** good Lord!; **~aşkına!** for God's sake!; **~a ısmarladık!** goodbye!
almak *v/t* take, get, obtain, receive; buy
Alman German; **~ca** German (*language*); **~ya** Germany
Alp dağları, **Alpler** *pl.* Alps
alt *n.* lower part, underside; *adj.* lower, inferior; *-in* **~ına**, **~ında** under; **~ taraf** underpart, underside

alternatif alternative; **~ (akım)** *el.* alternating current
altı six
altın gold; golden
altmış sixty
altüst etm. *v/t* turn topsy-turvy
alüminyum aluminium
ama but
amaç target, object, aim
aman pardon, mercy; **~ ~!** for goodness sake!; **~sız** pitiless, without mercy
amatör amateur
ambalaj packing, wrapping
ambar granary, storehouse, magazine
amca paternal uncle; **~ kızı** girl cousin; **~ oğlu** male cousin; **~zade** cousin
amel action, deed; **~e** worker(s); **~î** practical; **~iyat** *pl.* practical deeds, operations; *med.* surgical operation
Amerika America; **~ Birleşik Devletleri** United States of America, U.S.A.; **~lı**, **~n** American
amil doing, active; factor
amir commander, superior
amiral admiral
amortis|man *ec.* amortization; **~ör** *tech.* shock absorber
amper *el.* ampere
ampul *el.* light bulb
amudî perpendicular, vertical
an moment, instant; **bir ~ evvel** as soon as possible
ana mother; **~ baba** parents *pl.*; **~ okulu** kindergarten

Anadolu Anatolia, Asia Minor

anafor eddy, back current; *fig.* illicit gain

anahtar key; switch

analiz analysis

anamal *ec.* capital

anane tradition; **~vî** traditional

anarşi anarchy

anason *bot.* aniseed

anatomi anatomy

ana|yasa constitution; **~yurt** mother country

ancak but, only, however

ançüez anchovy

and|aç gift, souvenir; **~ır-mak** *v/t* bring to mind

angaj|e etm. *v/t* engage, amploy; **~man** engagement, employment

angarya|, ~e forced labour

Anglikan Anglican; **~izm** Anglicanism

anık *-e* apt, ready to

anıt monument, memorial

ani sudden, unexpected

anket enquiry

aula|m meaning; **~mak** *v/t* understand; conceive

anlaş|ılır comprehensible, clear, intelligible; **~ma** agreement, understanding; **~mak** *-in* hususunda (or hakkında) come to an agreement on; **~mazlık** misunderstanding

anla|tmak *v/t* explain, expound, narrate; **~yış** understanding; intelligence

anmak *v/t* call to mind, remember

anne mother

anonim anonymous; **~ or-taklık, ~ şirket** *ec.* joint-stock company

anormal abnormal

ansızın *adv.* suddenly, without warning

ansiklopedi encyclopedia

ant oath, vow; **~içmek** take an oath

anten *zo.*, *tech.* antenna

antepfıstığı *bot.* pistachio

antifriz *tech.* antifreeze

antika antique(s)

antlaşma pact, treaty

antre entrance-hall, vestibule

antren|man training; **~ör** trainer

antrepo bonded warehouse

apandisit *an.* appendicitis

apartman apartment house; **~ (dairesi)** apartment, flat

apse *med.* abcess

aptal silly, stupid

aptes *rel.* ablution; **~ almak** perform ablution; **~ boz-mak** relieve nature; **~ane** latrine

ara interval; relation, understanding; **~ vermek** *-e* stop, cease; **bu ~da** in the meantime; **~da bir** here and there, sometimes; **~mız iyidir** we are on good terms; **~sına, ~sında** between, among; **~ya gir-mek** meddle, intervene

araba carriage; cart; car; **~ vapuru** ferry-boat; **~cı** coachman; driver

aracı mediator; **~lık** mediation

araç means

aralık space, interval

ara|mak v/t seek, look for; **~nmak** be sought, be searched

Arap Arab; Negro; **~ça** Arabic

arasıra adv. sometimes, now and then

araştırma research, investigation; **~k** v/t search, investigate

aratmak v/t make so. search (-e)

arazi pl. estates; land sg.

arbede riot, tumult

ardıç bot. juniper; **~ kuşu** zo. fieldfare

ardınca adv. shortly afterwards

ardiye warehouse; storage rent

arduvaz slate

aren arena

argo slang; technical language

arı¹ clean, innocent

arı² bee; **~ kovanı** beehive

arıza accident; defect; **~lı** defective, full of obstacles

arızî accidental

arife eve

arka n. back, back part; -in **~sına, ~sında** behind; **~ya** one after the other; **~daş** companion, friend; **~lık** back of a chair, etc.

arkeoloji archaeology; **~ müzesi** archaeological museum

arma naut. rigging; armorial bearings pl.

armağan present, gift

armut pear

Arnavut Albanian; **~ça** Albanian (language); **~luk** Albania

arpa barley; **~cık** sty; foresight of a gun

arsa building-ground, building-site

arsız impudent, insolent

arslan s. aslan

arşın (Turkish yard, ab. 27 in./72 cm)

arşiv archives

art n. back, back part; **~çı** mil. rearguard; **~ı** math. plus

artık n. rest, remnant; adj. remaining, left over; adv. finally; more; **~yıl** leap-year

artır|ım economy, frugality; **~ma** ec. sale by auction; **~mak** v/t increase, augment

art|ış increase, augmentation; **~mak** v/i increase, rise

artist artist

arz¹ earth, land

arz² width, breadth; representation; petition; **~etmek** v/t present, submit; express

arzu wish, desire; **~ etm.** v/t wish, desire

arzuhal petition

asa stick, baton

asab|î nervous; **~iyet** nervousness

asal sayı odd number

asansör lift, elevator

asayiş repose; public peace

aseton *chem.* acetone

asfalt asphalt; asphalt highway

asgari smallest, minimum; ~ **fiat** minimum price

asıl *n.* foundation, base; source, origin; *adj.* essential, real

asıl|ı hanging, suspended; ~**mak** -*e* be hung on, be suspended to

asılsız without foundation

asılzade nobleman, aristocrat

asır century; age, time, epoch

asi rebellious; rebel, insurgent

asil noble

asistan assistant

asit *chem.* acid

asker soldier; ~**î** military; ~**lik** military service

askı hanger; ribbon

asla (with *negation*) never, in no way

aslan lion

aslî fundamental; essential

asma hanging, suspending; vine; ~ **kilit** padlock; ~**k** *v/t* hang (-*e* upon), suspend; put off

asrî modern, up-to-date

astar lining; ~**lamak** *v/t* line

asteğmen *mil.* second lieutenant

astronomi astronomy

Asya Asia

aş food; ~ **kabı** mess-tin

aşağı *adv.* down, below; *adj.* low, inferior; ~ **yukarı** more or less, about; ~**da** below; ~**ya** down(wards); ~**lamak** *v/t* lower, degrade

aşçı cook

aşı inoculation; graft; vaccine

âşık in love (-*e* with); lover

aşıkkemiği knuckle-bone

aşılamak *v/t* inoculate, vaccinate; infect

aşın|dırmak *v/t* wear out, corrode; ~**mak** wear away, be corroded

aşır|ı excessive; exaggeration; beyond; every second; ~**mak** -*den* pass over; steal, rob from

aşikâr clear, evident

aşk love, passion; **Allah ~ına!** for God's sake!, is that true?; ~**ınıza!** your health!

aşmak *v/t* pass over *or* beyond; exceed, surpass

aşure (sweet *dish of cereals, sugar, etc.*)

at horse; ~ **meydanı** hippodrome; ~**a binmek** ride a horse

ata father; old man; ~**lar sözü** proverb

atak reckless; boastful

atalet idleness, inertia

atamak *v/t* appoint

atardamar *an.* artery

atasözü proverb

ataşe attaché

atelye studio; workshop

ateş fire; heat, fever; ~ **al-**

mak catch fire; ~ **etm.** *v/t*
fire; ~**e vermek** *v/t* set on
fire; ~**böceği** firefly, glow-
worm; ~**çi** stoker, fireman;
~**leme** *el.* ignition; ~**lemek**
v/t light; ~**lenmek** catch
fire

atfetmek *v/t* attribute (-**e**
to)

atıl|gan dashing, bold; ~
mak be thrown (-**e** at), be
discharged; attack (-**e** *so.*)

atı|m discharge, shot; ~**ş**
firing

Atina Athens

atkı shawl

atlamak *v/i* jump (-**den**
over); *v/t* skip, omit

atlas atlas; satin

atlayış jump

atlet athlete; undershirt

atlı mounted on horseback;
rider

atmak *v/t* throw, throw
away, drop; fire, discharge

atmosfer atmosphere

atom atom; ~ **bombası**
atomic bomb

av hunting, shooting, fishing; game, prey

avadanlık artificer's set of
tools

avam *pl.* common people;
 ♀ **Kamarası** the House of
Commons

avan|s *ec.* advance *of money*;
~**taj** profit, gain

avare vagabond, good-for-
nothing

avarya *naut.* average

avcı hunter; *mil.* rifleman;
~**lık** hunting

---

aydın

avdet return; ~ **etm.** *v/i*
return

avize chandelier

avlamak *v/t* hunt, shoot,
fish for

avlu courtyard

Avrupa Europe; ~**lı** *n.*, *adj.*
European; ~**lılaşmak** be-
come Europeanized

avuç hollow of the hand;
handful

avukat advocate, lawyer

avunmak be consoled (**ile**
with)

Avustralya Australia; ~**lı**
n., *adj.* Australian

Avusturya Austria; ~**lı** *n.*,
adj. Austrian

avutmak *v/t* distract; delude; quieten

ay moon, crescent; month

ayak foot, leg; ~ **parmağı**
toe; ~**ta** on foot, standing;
~**kabı** footwear; shoe; ~
landırmak *v/t* stir up, incite to rebellion; ~**lanmak**
rise in rebellion; ~**lı** having
feet; ~**sız** having no feet;
~**takımı** rabble, mob; ~
yolu latrine

ayar standard *of fineness*,
accuracy; regulating, ad-
justing; ~ **etm.**, ~**lamak**
v/t test, regulate, adjust

ayartmak *v/t* lead astray,
seduce

ayaz dry cold; clearness *of
the air*; ~**lamak** become
cold

ayazma *rel.* sacred spring

aybaşı *an.* menstruation

aydın bright, clear; ~**lan-**

mak brighten up, become clear; **~latmak** v/t illuminate; explain; **~lık** light; clearness, brightness

ayet rel. verse of the Koran

aygır stallion

aygıt apparatus

ayı zo. bear

ayık sober; **~lamak** v/t clean off; select

ayılmak recover from fainting, etc.

ayıp shame, disgrace; **~lamak** v/t find fault with, censure

ayır|mak v/t separate, sever; divide; select; **~t etm.** v/t distinguish, discern (-den from); **~tmak** v/t put aside, reserve

ayin rel. rite, ceremony

aykırı -e contrary to, not in accordance with

aylak unemployed, idle

aylık monthly; n. monthly salary

ayna mirror; **~lı** having a mirror

ayn|en adv. without any change, textually; **~ı** identical; the same

ayraç gr. bracket

ayran (drink made with yoghurt and water)

ayrı apart, separate; different; **~ca** adv. separately, in addition; **~k** separate; **~lmak** -den separate oneself from, depart from, leave; **~m** difference

ayşekadın (fasulyesi) French beans

aytutulması eclipse of the moon

ayva bot. quince

ayyaş drunkard; **~lık** drunkenness

az little; few; seldom; **~** kaldı all but, almost

aza pl. limbs, members; sg. member

azal|mak diminish, be reduced; **~tmak** v/t diminish, reduce

azam greater, greatest

azamet greatness, grandeur; **~li** magnificent, imposing

azami greatest, maximum; **~** sürat maximum speed

azar reproach, reprimand; **~lamak** v/t scold, reproach

Azeri belonging to Azerbaijan; Turk of Azerbaijan

azgın furious, wild

azık provisions pl.

azınlık minority

azışmak grow vehement

azil dismissal, removal

aziz dear, precious

azletmek v/t dismiss

azmak¹ n. dry well, puddle

azmak² v/i be in flood; be unmanageable

azmetmek -e resolve upon

azot chem. nitrogen

B

baba father; **~lık** paternity; **~yiğit** brave, virile

Babıâli the Sublime Porte

baca chimney, funnel

bacak an. leg, shank

bacanak brother-in-law (husband of one's wife's sister)   [sister]

bacı negro nurse; elder]

badana whitewash; **~ etm., ~lamak** v/t whitewash

badem almond; **~ şekeri** sugar almonds; **~cik** an. tonsil

bagaj luggage, baggage

bağ¹ bond, bandage; gr. conjunction

bağ² vineyard; **~bozumu** vintage; **~cılık** viniculture

bağdaş sitting cross-legged; **~mak ile** agree, get along with

bağım dependence; **~lı -e** dependent on; **~sız** independent; **~sızlık** independence

bağıntı relation(ship) (-e to)

bağır breast, bosom

bağırmak shout, yell

bağırsak intestine

bağış gift, donation; **~lamak** v/t donate; forgive

bağlaç gr. conjunction

bağla|ma connecting, coupling; **~mak** v/t tie, bind, connect, fasten; **~n-mak -e** be tied to; be obliged to; **~ntı** connection; liaison

bağlı -e bound to, tied to; dependent on

bahane pretext, excuse

bahar¹ spring

bahar² spice; **~at** pl. spices; **~lı** spiced, aromatic

bahçe garden; **~li** having a garden

bahçıvan gardener

bahis discussion; inquiry; **~konusu** theme, subject of discussion

bahrî maritime, naval, nautical

bahriye navy; **~li** sailor

bahsetmek -den discuss, speak of

bahş|etmek v/t give; **~iş** tip, bakhshish

baht|iyar lucky, happy; **~sız** unfortunate, unhappy

bakan minister; **~lar kurulu** cabinet, council of ministers; **~lık** ministry

bakı|cı attendant; **~lmak -e** be attended to, be looked after

bakım attention, upkeep; point of view; **bu ~dan** from this point of view; **~sız** neglected

bakınmak v/i look about

bakır copper

bakış look; care

baki permanent, everlasting

bakir virgin, untouched; **~e** virgin, girl

bakiye remainder; ec. arrears, balance

bakkal grocer; **~iye** grocery shop

bakla broad-bean, horse bean

baklava (*sweet pastry made of flake pastry, nuts, and honey*)

bakmak *-e* look at, examine; look after, see to; **bana bak!** look here! hi!

bakteri bacterium; **~yoloji** bacteriology

bal honey; **~ arısı** bee

balast ballast

balçık clay

baldır *an.* calf

baldız sister-in-law (*sister of the wife*)

balgam *med.* mucus, phlegm

balık fish; **~ ağı** fishing-net; **~ tutmak** *v/i* fish; **~ yumurtası** hard roe; **~çı** fisherman

baliğ olm. *-e* amount to, reach

balina whale

Balkan yarımadası the Balkan Peninsula

balkon balcony

ballı honeyed

balo ball, dance

balon balloon

balotaj *pol.* ballotage

balta axe; **~lamak** *v/t* cut down with an axe; cut away; *fig.* sabotage

Baltık denizi the Baltic Sea

balya *ec.* bale, packet

balyoz sledge-hammer

bambaşka utterly different

bambu bamboo

bamya *bot.* gumbo

bana me, to me; **~ gelince** as to me; **~ kalırsa** as far as I am concerned

bandıra flag

bando *mus.* band

bank *ec.* bank; bench; **~a** *ec.* bank; **~not** banknote

banliyö suburb; **~ treni** suburban train

bant *el., med.* band, tape; **~ izole** *el.* insulating tape

banyo bath; **~ yapmak, ~ almak** take a bath

bar bar

baraj barrage, dam

baraka hut, shed

barbunya *zo.* red mullet; *bot.* (*a kind of bean*)

bardak glass, goblet

barem *pol.* classification of salaries

barfiks (*sport*) horizontal bar

barın|ak shelter; **~mak** *-e* take refuge in, take shelter in

barış peace, reconciliation; **~çı** peace-loving; **~mak** make peace; **~tırmak** *v/t* reconcile

barikat barricade

bariz prominent, manifest

baro *jur.* bar

barometre barometer

barsak *s.* bağırsak

barut gunpowder

bas|amak step, stair; tread; round; **~ı** *tech.* printing; **~ıcı** printer; **~ık** low

basım printing, impression; **~ evi** printing house

basın press, newspapers; ~ **toplantısı** press conference; ~**ç** *phys.* pressure

basiret understanding, insight; caution

basit simple, plain, elementary

basketbol basketball

bas|kı press, stamp; oppression; ~**kın** sudden attack, raid; ~**ma** printed cotton; printed goods; ~**mak** -*e* press on, tread on; *v/t* print; ~**tırmak** *v/t* have printed; suppress, crush

baston stick

basur *med.* haemorrhoids

baş head, top; beginning; main; ~ **ağrısı** headache; ~ **göstermek** appear, arise; **~ vurmak** *s.* **başvurmak**; **tek ~ına** *adv.* alone; tek *e* at the head, at the top; ~**tan** again, from the beginning; ~**tan ~a** entirely, completely

başak *bot.* ear

başar|ı success; ~**ılı** successful; ~**mak** -*i* succeed in, accomplish

başbakan Prime Minister; ~**lık** Prime Ministry

başıboş untied, free

başka other, another; different (-*den* from); **bundan** ~ besides this

başkan president, chief; ~**lık** presidency

baş|kent capital; ~**komutan** commander-in-chief; ~**konsolosluk** Consulate General; ~**kumandan** *s.*

~**komutan**; ~**lamak** -*e* start, begin; ~**langıç** beginning, start; ~**lıca** main, principal; ~**lık** headgear; headline; *arch.* capital; ~**parmak** thumb; ~**piskopos** archbishop; ~**şehir** *s.* ~**kent**

başvur|mak -*e* apply to; ~**u** application, referring (-*e* to)

batak *n.* bog, marsh; *adj.* marshy; ~**hane** gambling den; ~**lık** marshy place

batarya *mil., el.* battery

batı west

batıl false, vain, useless

batılı *pol. adj., n.* Western (-*er*)

bat|ırmak *v/t* sink, submerge; ~**mak** *v/i* sink (-*e* into), go to the bottom; penetrate

battaniye woollen blanket

bavul suitcase, trunk

bay gentleman; Mr.

bayağı common, ordinary; mean

bayan lady; Mrs., Miss

bayat stale, not fresh

baygın faint; unconscious; ~**lık** swoon, fainting

bayılmak faint, swoon

bayındır prosperous, developed; ~**lık** prosperity; **2lık Bakanlığı** Ministry of Public Works

bayır slope; hill

bayi vendor

baykuş *zo.* owl

bayrak flag, standard; **bayrağı çekmek** hoist the

flag; **bayrağı indirmek** lower the flag; **~tar** standard-bearer.

bayram religious festival; holiday; **~lık** adj. fit for a festival; n. present given on a festival

baytar veterinary surgeon

baz chem. base

baz|an, ~en sometimes; **~ı** some, a few; **~ı defa, ~ı kere** sometimes

be! hi! I say!

bebe baby; **~k** baby; doll; an. pupil of the eye

becerik|li capable, clever; **~siz** incapable, clumsy

becermek v/t do skillfully

bedava gratis, for nothing

bed|baht unfortunate, unhappy; **~bin** pessimistic; **~dua** curse, malediction; **~dua etm.** -e curse

bedel substitute, equivalent (-e for); price

beden trunk, body; **~ eğitimi** physical training; **~î** bodily, corporal

bedhah malevolent, malicious

beğenmek v/t like, approve; admire

beher to each, for each, per

bek (football) back

bekâr bachelor; unmarried

bek|çi watchman, sentry; night-watchman; **~lemek** v/t await; watch; hope for **~len(il)mek** be expected; **~letmek** v/t cause to wait

bel[1] waist; loins

bel[2] spade

belâ trouble, misfortune, calamity

Belçika Belgium; **~lı** adj., n. Belgian

beled|î municipal; local; **~iye** municipality

belge document, certificate, **~lemek** v/t confirm, prove

belir|lemek v/t determine; **~li** determined; **~mek** v/i appear, become visible; **~siz** indefinite, undetermined; **~ti** sign, symptom; **~tmek** v/t state, make clear

belki perhaps, maybe

bel|lemek v/t 1. commit to memory, learn by heart; 2. dig with a spade; **~li** evident, clear; **~li başlı** clear, definite

ben[1] an. mole

ben[2] I; **~cil** selfish; **~cilik** ego(t)ism [spotted]

benek spot, speck; **~li**

benim my; mine; **~semek** v/t make one's own; identify oneself with

benlik egotism; personality

bent paragraph; arch. dam, aqueduct

benze|mek -e resemble, be like; **~şmek** resemble each other; **~tmek** v/t compare (-e with); mistake (for)

benzin petrol, gasoline, benzine; **~ borusu** petrol pipe; **~ pompası** pump feeding petrol into carburetor

beraber together

beraet acquittal; **~ etm.** be acquitted

berat patent, warrant; ~ **gecesi** rel. (Moslem feast, celebrating the night of the revelation of his mission to Mohammed)

berbat ruined, spoilt; filthy

berber barber

bere[1] beret

bere[2] bruise, dent

bereket blessing; abundance; ~**li** fertile; fruitful; ~**siz** infertile; bringing no good luck

berelemek -i cause bruises on

berhava destroyed, annihilated; ~ **etm.** v/t destroy; blow up

beri the near side, this side; ~ **-den** since; ~**de** on this side

berk hard, firm

berrak clear, limpid, transparent

bertaraf aside, apart, out of the way; ~ **etm.** v/t put aside, do away with

berzah geo. isthmus

besi nourishing, nutrition; fattening

besle|me feeding, nourishing; foster-child; ~**mek** v/t feed, nourish; ~**yici** nutritious

bestekâr mus. composer

beş five

beşeriyet human nature; humanity; mankind

beşik cradle

betimlemek v/t describe

beton concrete; ~**arme** tech. reinforced concrete

bey gentleman; Mr. (used after the first name); husband

beyan declaration, explanation; ~ **etm.** v/t declare, explain; ~**name** manifesto, declaration

beyaz white; ~**latmak** v/t whiten, bleach

beyefendi sir

beygir horse; ~**gücü** tech. horsepower

beyhude (yere) adv. in vain

beyin brain; intelligence; ~ **sarsıntısı** med. concussion of the brains; ~**sektesi** med. cerebral apoplexy

beyit verse

bez[1] cloth, duster

bez[2] an. gland

bezelye bot. pea(s)

bıçak knife; ~**lamak** v/t stab, knife

bıçkı two-handed saw

bık|kın disgusted, bored; ~**mak** -den tire of, get bored with

bırakmak v/t leave, quit, abandon; put off

bıyık moustache; zo. whiskers

biber pepper; **kara** ~ black pepper; **kırmızı** ~ red pepper (pod); ~ **dolması** stuffed peppers

biçare poor, wretched

biçim cut, form, shape; ~**siz** ill-shaped

biç|ki n. cutting-out; ~**mek** v/t cut, cut out; reap

bidon can

biftek beefsteak

bilakis on the contrary

bilanço ec. balance sheet

bilardo billiards

bilcümle all; in all; totally

bildir|i communiqué; **~im** declaration; **~mek** v/t make known (-e to)

bile even; together with

bileği (taşı) whetstone

bilek wrist

bilemek v/t sharpen, whet

bileş|ik composed; **~ik faiz** math. compound interest; **~mek** chem. be compounded (**ile** with)

bilet ticket; **~ gişesi** ticket window; **~çi** conductor, ticket collector

bilezik bracelet

bilgi knowledge; **~n** learned man, expert; **~siz** ignorant

bilhassa adv. especially, in particular

bili|m knowledge, learning; science; **~nç** conscience; **~nmek** be known; **~rkişi** jur. expert

billur cristal, cut-glass

bilmece riddle, enigma; **~k** v/t know, recognise; be able to inf.

bin thousand; **~ bir gece** the Arabian Nights

bina building, edifice; **~en** -e on account of, according to; **~enaleyh** consequently, therefore

binbaşı mil. major; commander

bin|dirmek v/t cause to mount; load; -e collide with, run into; **~ici** rider,

horseman; **~mek** -e mount, ride; go on

bir one; **~den** adv. suddenly; together; **~denbire** adv. suddenly; **~i(si)** one of them; someone

bira beer

birader brother

birahane beer-house

bir|az a little; **~ine**, **~birine** one another; **~çok** many, a lot; **~den(bire)** s. **bir**; **~er** one each; **~ey** n. individual

birik|inti accumulation, heap; **~mek** v/i assemble, collect; **~tirmek** v/t collect, amass; save up

birkaç a few, some

birleş|ik united; **~mek** v/i unite, meet (**ile** with); **~tirmek** v/t unite, connect

birlik unity, union; association; **~te** adv. together, in company

birtakım a quantity, some

bisiklet bicycle; **~ yolu** cycle track

bisküvit biscuit

bit louse

bitap exhausted, feeble

bitaraf impartial, neutral

bitevi(ye) adv. all of a piece, uninterruptedly

bit|ik exhausted; **~im** ending, end; **~irmek** v/t finish, complete, terminate, eat up; **~işik** touching, neighbouring; **~iştirmek** v/t join, unite, attach; **~ki** plant

bitlenmek be infested with lice; get lice

bitmek come to an end; be completed; be exhausted

bitpazarı rag-fair

biyoloji biology

biz we; ～**im** our

Bizans Byzantium

bizzat in person, personally

blok block; *pol.* bloc

blöf bluff

bluz blouse

bobin *phys.*, *el.* reel, spool, coil

bodrum cellar

bodur short, dwarf

boğa bull

boğaz throat; mountain pass; strait; 2**içi** the Bosphorus; ～**lamak** -*i* cut the throat of; 2**lar** the Straits (*Bosphorus and Dardanelles*)

boğma|ca *med.* whooping-cough; ～**k 1.** *n.* node, joint; **2.** *v/t* choke, strangle

boğu|k hoarse; ～**lmak** be choked, be drowned; ～**m** node; knot; ～**şmak** fly at one another's throats

bohça wrapping cloth, bundle

bok excrement; ordure

boks boxing; ～ **maçı** boxing match; ～**ör** boxer

bol wide, loose; ample; ～**laşmak** become wide or loose; be abundant; ～**luk** wideness, looseness, abundance

Bolşevik Bolshevist

bomba bomb; ～**lamak** *v/t*

bomb; ～**rdıman** bombardment, bombing

bomboş quite empty

bonbon bonbon, sweet-meat

boncuk bead

bon|file sirloin steak; ～**marşe** department store; ～**o** bond; cheque; ～**servis** certificate of good service, written character

bora tempest, hurrican

borazan trumpeter; trumpet

borç debt; obligation; ～ **almak** -*den* borrow from; ～ **vermek** lend (-*e* -*i so. sth.*); ～**lu** -*e* indebted to, under obligation

borda ship's side

bordro payroll

borsa *ec.* bourse, stock-exchange; ～**cı** *ec.* stock-broker

boru tube, pipe; trumpet

bostan vegetable garden

boş empty; unoccupied; unemployed; ～ **una** *adv.* in vain; ～ **vakit**, ～ **zaman** free time; ～**almak** be emptied; become free; ～**altmak** *v/t* empty, pour out

boşa|mak *v/t* divorce; ～**n-mak** be divorced (-*den* from)

boşboğaz garrulous, indiscreet; ～**lık** idle talk

boşluk emptiness; vacuum

botanik *n.* botany; *adj.* botanic(al)

boy length; stature; size; **~unca** along

boya dye; paint, colour; **~cı** shoe-black; dyer; **~hane** dye-house; **~lı** dyed; painted; **~mak** v/t paint; dye

boykot boycott; **~ etm.** v/t boycott

boy|lam geo. longitude; **~lu** of high stature

boynuz zo. horn

boyun neck; geo. pass; **~duruk** yoke

boyut math. dimension

boz grey

boza (drink made of fermented millet)

boz|durmak v/t cause to spoil, cause to deteriorate; money: have changed; **~gun(luk)** defeat, rout

bozkır steppe

bozmak v/t spoil, ruin, destroy; money: change

bozuk destroyed, spoilt, broken; **~ para** small change

boz|ulmak be spoilt, be destroyed; break down; **~uşmak** break with one another

böbrek an. kidney

böbürlenmek be arrogant, boast

böcek insect, bug

böğür side, flank of the body

böğürmek bellow

böğürtlen bot. blackberry

bölge zone, district; **~sel** regional

bölme partition; dividing

wall; **~k** v/t separate, divide (-e into)

böl|ü math. divided by; **~ük** mil. company, squadron; **~üm** dividing; chapter; **~ünmek** -e be divided into

bön silly; naive

börek (pastry or pie)

böyle so; thus; such; in this way; **~ce**, **~likle** thus, in this way

branş branch, department, field of work

briket briquette

bronşit med. bronchitis

broş brooch

bu this; **~ kadar** that much; that's all; **~nlar** pl. these; all this; **~nun için** for that reason, therefore; **~nunla beraber** however, inspite of this

bucak corner, angle; pol. sub-district

buçuk half (after numerals); **bir ~** one and a half

budak twig, knot in timber

budala silly, imbecile; **~lık** stupidness

budamak v/t lop, trim

bugün today; **~kü** of today; **~lük** for today

buğday wheat

buğu steam, vapour; **~lanmak** be misted over

buhar steam, vapour; **~ makinesi** steam-engine; **~lı** steamy, vaporous

buhran crisis

buhur incense

buji tech. spark plug

buket bouquet

bukle lock, curl

bulan|dırmak v/t render turbid or muddy; turn the stomach; **~ık** turbid; cloudy, overcast; **~mak** become cloudy; **midesi ~tı** nausea

bulaş|ık smeared over, soiled; med. contagious; n. dirty kitchen utensils; **~mak** become dirty; **~tır-mak** v/t smear; infect

Bulgar Bulgarian; **~istan** Bulgaria

bulgur boiled and pounded wheat

bul|maca crossword puzzle; **~mak** v/t find; invent; **~undurmak** v/t make available; **~unmak** be found; be present; be; **~uş** finding, invention, idea; **~uşmak** meet

bulut cloud; **~lanmak** become cloudy; **~lu** cloudy, overcast

bulvar boulevard

bunak dotard

bunal|ım crisis; **~mak** be stupefied, be suffocated (-den with)

bunun s. bu

bura|da here; **~dan** from here; **~sı** this place, here; **~ya** to this spot, here

burç[1] tower

burç[2] astr. sign of the Zodiac

burgu orger, gimlet; corkscrew; **~lamak** v/t drill, bore

burjuvazi pol. bourgeoisie

burkmak v/t sprain, twist

burmak v/t twist; castrate; **burun ~e** sneer at

burnuz bathrobe

burs scholarship

burun nose; geo. promontory, cape

buruş|mak be wrinkled, creased; **~turmak** v/t crease, wrinkle; **~uk** puckered, wrinkled

buse kiss

but thigh

buy|ruk order, command; **~rultu** order, decree; **~ur-mak** v/t order; condescend to inf.; **~urun(uz)**! please!

buz ice; frozen; **~ dolabı** refrigerator; **~dağı** iceberg; **~kıran** ice-breaker; **~lu** iced; **~ul** glacier

büfe buffet, bar

bük|lüm n. twist, curl, fold; **~mek** v/t twist, spin, curl; **~ülmek** be twisted, be bent; **~ülü** bent, twisted

bülbül nightingale

bünye structure, constitution

bürç s. burç

büro office, bureau; **~krasi** bureaucracy, red tape

bürü|mcük raw silk gauze; **~mek** v/t wrap, cover up

bürünmek -e be filled with; wrap oneself in

büsbütün altogether, quite

büst bust; portrait.

bütçe ec. budget

bütün adj. whole, entire; all; n. whole; **~lük** entirety, universality

büyü incantation, sorcery; **~cü** sorcerer, magician

büyük great; large; high; elder; **⌾ Millet Meclisi** *pol.* Grand National Assembly; **~anne** grandmother; **~baba** grandfather; **~elçi**

pol. ambassador; **~lük** greatness; largeness

büyülemek *v/t* bewitch

büyü|mek *v/i* grow, grow up; **~tmek** *v/t* bring up; enlarge

büzülmek contract, shrink

C

cadde main road, street

cadı witch, hag

cahil ignorant

caiz lawful, permitted

cam glass, pane; **~cı** glazier

camekân *s.* **camlık**

cami mosque

cam|lamak *v/t* cover with glass; **~lı** glass-covered; **~lık** hotbed, hothouse; shop-window

can soul; life; darling, friend; **~ı sıkılmak** be bored (-*e* by); be annoyed

canavar monster, brute

can|kurtaran life-belt; **~landırmak** *v/t* animate, invigorate; **~lanmak** come to life, become active; **~lı** alive; lively; **~sız** lifeless; dull

cari *adj.*, *ec.* current

casus spy; **~luk** espionage

cavlak bald, naked

cay|dırmak *v/t* cause to renounce, make *so.* change his purpose; **~mak** change one's mind; renounce (-*den sth.*)

cazibe attractiveness, attraction; **~li** attractive

cazip *s.* **cazibeli**

cebbar tyrannical; tyrant

cebir 1. *math.* algebra; 2. force, violence; **~ kullanmak** use force

cebr|en *adv.* by force; **~î** 1. compulsory, forced; 2. *math.* algebraic

cefa ill-treatment, cruelty

cehennem *rel.* hell

ceket jacket, coat

celbetmek *v/t* attract; summon

celp(name) *jur.* summons

celse sitting, session

cem|aat community, group, congregation (*a. rel.*); **~etmek** *v/t* collect; add up (*a. math*); **~i** *math.* addition; *gr.* plural; **~iyet** meeting; association; society

cenaze corpse; funeral; **~ alayı** funeral procession

cendere press, roller press

cengâver warlike, brave

cengel jungle

cennet *rel.* paradise

centilmen gentleman; **~ce** gentleman-like

cenu|bî southern; **~p** south

cep pocket; **~ sözlüğü** pocket dictionary

cephane *mil.* ammunition

cephe front; forehead

cerahat *med.* pus

cereyan flowing, current, course; ~ **etm.** happen, flow, pass   [*gery*]

cerrah surgeon; ~**lık** sur-ſ

cesaret boldness, daring; ~ **etm.** *-e* dare

ceset corpse

cesur bold, daring, courageous

cetvel list, schedule; ruler

cevahir *pl.* jewel(s); ~**ci** jeweller

cevap answer, reply; ~ **vermek** *-e* answer to, reply to; ~**landırmak** *v/t* answer *sth.*

cevher essence, substance, nature; ~**li** talented; set with jewels

ceviz *bot.* walnut

ceylan *zo.* gazelle, antilope

ceza punishment, fine; ~ **çekmek** serve a sentence (*-den* for); ~**evi** prison; ~**landırmak** *v/t* punish; ~**lanmak** be punished

cezbetmek *v/t* attract, draw

cezir *geo.* ebb

cezve *pot for making Turkish coffee*

cılız thin, delicate

cılk rotten; inflamed

cırıldamak, cırlamak creak, screech

cıvata bolt, screw

cıvık wet, sticky; ~**lanmak** become wet *or* sticky

cıvıldamak twitter, chirp

cızıldamak, cızırdamak sizzle

cibinlik mosquito-net

cici 1. good, pretty, nice; **2.** toy, plaything

cidd|**î** earnest, serious; ~**i-yet** seriousness

ciğer *an.* liver; lung(s); darling

cihan world, universe

cihaz apparatus, equipment; *an.* system; trousseau

cihet side, direction

cilâ polish; varnish; ~**la-mak** *v/t* polish

cilt skin, hide; volume; ~**çi** bookbinder; ~**lemek** *v/t* bind *a book*; ~**li** bound (*book*); in ... volumes; ~**siz** unbound

cilve coquettery, charm; ~**li** graceful; coquettish

cimnastik gymnastics

cimri parsimonious

cin genie, demon, spirit

cinas play upon words, pun

cinayet crime

cins species, class, kind; sex; ~**el,** ~**î** generic, sexual; ~**iyet** sex; sexuality

ciro *ec.* endorsement

cisim body, substance

cismanî corporeal, material   [silver]

civa *chem.* mercury; quick-ſ

civar neighbourhood, environs

civciv chicken

coğrafya geography

conta *tech.* joint

coş|**kun** boiling over; exuberant; excited; ~**luk** overflowing; enthusiasm

coş|**mak** become violent;

be enthusiastic; **~turmak**
v/t inspire, fill with enthusiasm

cömert generous; **~lik** generosity [day]

cuma Friday; **~rtesi** Satur-∫

cumhur people, populace; **~başkanı** President of the Republic; **~iyet** republic; **~iyetçi** republican; **~reisi** *s.* **~başkanı**

cüce dwarf

cülûs accession *to the throne*

cümle total, whole; system; *gr.* phrase, sentence

cüppe *robe with full sleeves and long skirts*

cüret boldness, daring; **~kâr**, **~li** bold, daring

cürüm crime, felony; **cürmü meşhut** *jur.* caught in the act

cüz part, section

cüzam *med.* leprosy

cüzdan wallet, portfolio

cüzî trifling, partial

Ç

çabalamak strive, struggle

çabucak quickly

çabuk quick, agile; **~laştırmak** *v/t* accelerate; **~luk** speed, haste

çadır tent; **~ direği** tentpole; **~ kurmak** pitch a tent

çağ time, epoch, age; **~daş** contemporary

çağıldamak burble, murmur

çağırmak *v/t* call, invite (-e to)

çağl|amak burble, murmur; **~ıyan** cascade

çağrı invitation; **~lmak** -e be invited to

çakal *zo.* jackal

çakı pocket-knife

çakıl pebble; **~ döşemek** pave with pebbles

çakır|diken burdock, burr; **~keyif** half-tipsy

çakmak¹ *v/t* drive in with blows; light; *fig.* know (-den

abouth *sth.*); be 'ploughed' (*in an examination, etc.*); **şimşek ~** flash (*lightning*)

çakmak² *n* pocket-lighter; **~taşı** flint

çal|ar saat alarm clock; **~dırmak** *v/t* cause to play *or* steal; loose by theft; **~gı** musical instrument

çalı bush, shrub; **~lık** thicket [stolen]

çalınmak be struck *or* ∫

çalış|kan industrious, hard working; **~ma müsaadesi** working permit; **~mak** work, strive; study (-e *sth.*); **~tırmak** *v/t* make work, make run

çalka(la)mak *v/t* shake; rinse, wash out; churn; stir

çalmak *v/i* ring, strike; -e knock on, give a blow to; ring; *v/t* steal; *instrument*: play; **zili ~** ring the bell

çam *bot.* fir; pine; **~ fıstığı** pine kernel

çamaşır underclothing; washing; ~hane laundry room

çamur mud, clay; ~lu muddy; ~luk gaiter; (auto) mudguard

çan bell; ~ kulesi belfry

çanak eartenware pot

çangırdamak clang, jangle

çanta bag, case; el ~sı handbag

çap diameter, bore, calibre

çapa hoe, mattock; anchor; ~lamak v/t hoe

çapkın vagabond, rascal; rake; ~lık profligacy; debauchery

çapraşık intricate, tangled

çapraz crossing, crosswise

çapul booty, spoil; raid, sack

çardak hut, pergola

çare remedy, means; ~ bulmak find a remedy

çark wheel of a machine

çarmıh cross for crucifying; ~a germek v/t crucify

çarp|ı math. ... times; ~ık crooked, bent; slanting; ~ınmak struggle; ~ıntı palpitation; ~ışma collision, clash; ~ışmak collide; fight; ~ma blow, stroke; math. multiplication; ~mak -e strike, knock against; collide with; math. multiply (-i ile sth. with)

çarşaf sheet of a bed; veiled dress

çarşamba Wednesday

çarşı bazaar, street with shops

çatal fork; forked; ~lanmak bifurcate, fork

çatana naut. small steamboat

çatı framework; roof; ~ arası, ~ katı attic

çatır|damak v/i chatter, clatter; ~datmak v/t make chatter; ~tı clattering; chattering

çatışmak clash, collide (ile with)

çatla|k split, cracked; ~mak v/i crack, split; ~tmak v/t split, crack

çatmak v/t fit together; sew coarsely; animal: load; -e scold, rebuke; -e win the favour of so.

çavdar bot. rye

çavuş mil. sergeant

çay[1] stream

çay[2] tea; ~danlık teapot

çayır meadow, pasture; ~lanmak v/i graze, pasture

çehre face, countenance

çek ec. cheque

çek|ecek shoehorn; ~ici attractive

çekiç hammer

çeki|liş drawing of lots, etc.; ~lmek withdraw, retire (-den from); ~m gr. inflection, declination, conjugation; ~nmek -den beware of; refrain from

çekirdek stone, pip

çekirge zo. grasshopper, locust

çekişmek v/i quarrel; dispute

çekme phys. attraction; ~

halatı tow rope; **~ taşıdı** recovery vehicle; **~(ce)** drawer, till; **~k** v/t pull, draw; suffer; send *a telegramme*; take *a photograph*
çelebi adj. educated; gentleman
çelenk wreath
çelik steel
çelim form, shape
çelişmek be in contradiction
çeltik bot. rice
çember yoop, ring, circle; **~lemek** v/t hoop; mil. encircle
çene an. jaw; chin
çengel hook
çent|ik notch; **~mek** v/t notch; mince
çepel gloomy, dull; muddy
çerçeve frame; **~lemek** v/t frame, put in a frame
çerez tidbits, snack
Çerkez Circassian; **~ tavuğu** (chicken with walnut)
çeşit sort, variety, sample; **~li** various, assorted
çeşme fountain
çeşni taste, flavour
çete band; **~ harbi** guerilla warfare
çetin difficult; harsh
çetrefil confused; bad (*language*)
çevik nimble, agile
çevir|en translator; **~mek** v/t turn round; change, translate (*-e* into)
çevr|e circumference; surroundings; **~elemek** v/t surround, encircle; **~i** forced interpretation;

whirlpool, whirlwind; **~il-mek** be turned round; be changed, be translated (*-e* into)
çeyiz bride's trousseau
çeyrek quarter *of an hour*
çıban boil, abscess
çığ avalanche; **~ır** track left by an avalanche; *fig.* path, way
çığlık cry, scream
çık|ar yol way out; **~ar-mak** v/t take out, extract; remove, take off; derive, deduce; **~artmak** v/t let remove, let extract; **~ıntı** projection; **~ış** exit, sortie; leaving; **~ış vizesi** pol. exit visa; **~mak** come out; appear; get about; be dislocated; *-e* start; mount; **~maz** blind, dead end
çıl|dırmak v/i go mad; **~gın** mad, insane
çınar plane-tree
çın|gırak small bell; **~la-mak** ring; sing
çıplak naked, bare
çırak apprentice; **~lık** apprenticeship
çırp|ınmak flutter, struggle; **~mak** v/t strike, tap, pat; rinse
çıt|çıt snap fastener; **~ır-damak, ~lamak** v/i crackle; **~latmak** v/t cause to crackle
çiçek flower, blossom; *med.* small-pox; **~lenmek** bloom, blossom
çift pair; couple; **~ sayı** even number; **~ priz** *el.*

two-pin plug; ~ sürmek plow; ~çi farmer; ~e paired, doubled; ~leşmek v/i mate; ~lik farm

çiğ¹ raw, unripe

çiğ² s. çiy

çiğdem bot. crocus

çiğnemek v/t crush; chew

çiklet chewing-gum

çikolata chocolate

çil spot, freckle; speckled

çile¹ trial, sufferance

çile² hank, skein

çilek strawberry

çilingir locksmith

çimdik pinch; ~lemek v/t pinch

çimen turf, grass plot; ~lik lawn, meadow

çimento cement

Çingene gypsy

çini tile; tiled

çinko chem. zinc

çiriş paste, size; ~lemek v/t smear with paste

çirkin ugly; unseemly

çiş urine

çit¹ fence

çit² chintz

çivi nail; ~lemek v/t nail

çiy dew

çizgi line, mark, scratch; ~li marked with lines; striped

çizme top boot; ~k v/t draw; sketch; strike off

çoban chepherd

çocuk infant, child; ~luk childhood; childishness

çoğal|mak v/i increase, multiply; ~tmak v/t increase, augment

çoğu|l gr. plural; ~nluk majority

çok much, many; very; ~ taraflı multilateral; ~luk abundance; crowd

çolak with one arm; crippled in one hand

çoluk çocuk household, family; pack of children

çorak arid, barren

çorap stocking(s)

çorba soup

çök|ertmek v/t make kneel; cause to collapse; ~mek collapse, fall down; diz ~mek kneel; ~üntü debris; sediment, deposit

çöl desert, wilderness

çömlek earthen pot

çöp dust, rubbish; ~ tenekesi dustbin, garbage can; ~çü dustman

çörek (a kind of sweetened cake); disc

çöz|mek v/t untie; solve; ~ülmek be untied; mil. withdraw

çözüm solution; ~lemek v/t analyze

çubuk shoot, twig; cigarette holder

çukur hole, hollow, ditch, cavity

çul hair-cloth; ~luk zo. woodcock

çuval sack

çünkü, çünki because

çürük rotten, spoilt; ~lük rottenness, putrefaction

çürü|mek rot, decay; ~tmek v/t cause to rot, let decay

D

da, de, ta, te also, too

-da, -de, -ta, -te in; on; at

dadı nurse

dağ[1] brand, mark, cautery

dag[2] mountain; **~cı** alpinist

dağı|lmak scatter, be dispersed; be distributed; **~tım** distribution; **~tmak** v/t scatter, disperse; distribute [terize]

dağlamak v/t brand, cau-]

dağlı[1] branded, scarred

dağlı[2] mountaineer; **~k** mountainous

daha more (-*den* than); further; yet; **bir ~** once more

dahi also, too

dâhi genius

dahil inside; included

dahili internal, inner

daim|a always, perpetually; **~î** constant, permanent

dair -*e* concerning; about; **~e** circle; department, office; limit

dakika minute

daktilo typist; typewriting; **~ (makinesi)** typewriter

dal branch, bough

dalamak v/t bite

dalavere trick, intrigue

daldırmak v/t plunge; layer

dalga wave; undulation; **~-kıran** breakwater; **~lan-mak** become rough; wavy; **~lı** covered with waves; rough

dalgı|ç diver; **~n** plunged in thought, absentminded

dalkavuk sycophant, parasite

dallanmak become branched, ramify

dalmak -*e* plunge, dive into

dalya dahlia

dam roof

dama game *of draughts*

damacana large bottle, demijohn

damak palate

damar an. vein; *geo.* seam

damat son-in-law

damga stamp, mark; **~ pulu** revenue stamp; **~la-mak** v/t mark with a stamp; **~lı** stamped, marked

damıtmak v/t distil

damla drop; **~lık** dropper; **~mak** v/i drip; **~tmak** v/t pour out drop by drop; distil

-dan, -den, -tan, -ten from; than

dana zo. calf; **~ eti** veal

danış|ma information; **~-mak** consult (*-e -i so.* about *sth.*), ask for; **Stay** Council of State

Danimarka Denmark; **~lı** n., adj. Danish

dans dance; **~ etm.** dance; **~ör** dancer

dantel(a) lace

dar narrow, tight; with difficulty

dara *ec.* tare

darağacı gallows

daral|mak become narrow; shrink; **~tmak** *v/t* make narrower, reduce

darb|e blow, stroke; **~imesel** proverb

darboğaz *fig.* bottle-neck

dargın angry, irritated

darı *bot.* millet

darıl|gan easily offended; **~mak** be offended (*-e* with); get cross

darla|ştırmak, **~tmak** *v/t* make narrow, restrict

darmadağan in utter confusion

darphane *n.* mint

dava *jur.* lawsuit; trial; claim; **~ açmak** bring a suit of law (*-e* against); **~cı** claimant, plaintiff; **~lı** defendant

davar sheep *or* goat(s)

davet invitation; summons; **~ etm.** *v/t* invite, summon (*-e* to); **~iye** card *of invitation*; **~li** guest

davran|ış behaviour, attitude; **~mak** behave, take [pains]

davul drum

dayak prop, support; beating; **~ yemek** get a thrashing

dayamak *v/t* support, lean (*-e* against)

dayanık|lı lasting; enduring; **~sız** not lasting, weak

dayan|ışma solidarity; **~mak** *-e* endure; lean on; rely on

dayı maternal uncle

de *s.* **da**; **-se** *de* even if, although

-de *s.* **-da**

debdebe pomp, display

dede grandfather

dedikodu tittle-tattle, gossip

defa time, turn; **birkaç ~** on several occasions; **çok ~** often

defetmek *v/t* drive away, expel

defile fashion show

defin burial, interment

defne *bot.* bay-tree, laurel

defnetmek *v/t* bury

defolmak go away

defter register; book; list; **~dar** accountant

değer *n.* value, worth, price; *adj.* *-e* worthy of; **~lendirmek** *v/t* appraise; estimate; utilize; **~li** valuable; **~siz** worthless

değil not

değin *-e* until

değirmen mill; **~ci** miller

değiş exchange

değişik changed, different; varied; **~lik** alteration; variation

değiş|mek *v/i* change, alter, vary; **~tirmek** *v/t* change, exchange, alter

değme every, any; **~k** be worth; reach, touch (*-e sth.*)

değnek stick, rod

dehşet terror; **~li** terrible

dek *-e s.* **değin**

dekar (*measure of land:* 0.247 *acres*)

deklanşör trigger (*photo*)

dekor *thea.* stage scenery

dekovil narrow gauge railroad

delâlet guidance; indication; ~ **etm.** -*e* guide to; show, indicate

deli mad, insane

delik hole, opening

delikanlı youth, young man

delil guide; proof, evidence; ~ **göstermek** adduce proofs

deli|lik madness; ~**rmek** go mad, become insane

delmek *v/t* pierce, hole

dem breath; time; alcoholic drink

demeç statement, speech

demek say, tell; mean; ~ **ki** this means to say that

demet sheaf, bunch, faggot; ~**lemek** *v/t* tie in bunches

demir iron; anchor; ~ **almak** weigh anchor; ~ **atmak** cast anchor; ~**baş** furnishings, inventory; ~**ci** blacksmith; ~**lemek** *v/i* anchor; *v/t* bolt and bar *a door*; ~**yolu** railwayman; ~**yolu** railway

dem|lenmek be steeped (*tea*); ~**lik** teapot

demokra|si democracy; ~**t** democrat; ~**tik** democratic

-den *s.* **-dan**

denaet meanness, baseness

deneme trial, test; ~**k** *v/t* test, trial

denet|(im) control; ~**lemek** *v/t* control

deney *chem.* test

denge equilibrium; ~**li** balanced; ~**siz** out of balance

denilmek be said; be called

deniz sea; ~ **böceği** *zo.* shrimp; ~**altı** submarine; ~**aşırı** overseas; ~**ci** şeaman, sailor; ~**cilik** navigation; sailing

denk bale; balance; ~**lem** *math.* equation; ~**leştirmek** *v/t* bring into balance

denmek *s.* **denilmek**

densiz lacking in manners, tactless

depo depot, warehouse; ~**zito** *ec.* deposit, security

deprem earthquake

depreşmek *s.* **tepreşmek**

derbent defile, pass

dere valley; stream; ~**beyi** feudal lord; ~**otu** *bot.* dill

derece step, stair; degree

dergi magazine, periodical

derhal *adv.* at once, immediately

deri skin, hide, leather

derin deep, profound; ~**leştirmek** *v/t* deepen (*a. fig.*); ~**lik** depth, profundity

derkenar marginal note

derlemek *v/t* gather, collect

derman strength, energy; ~**sız** week, feeble

dernek association

ders lecture, lesson; ~**hane** class-room

dert pain, suffering; grief, trouble

deruhte etm. *v/t* undertake, take upon oneself

deruni internal; cordial

derviş beggar, dervish

derya sea

desen design; drawing

desise trick, intrigue

destan story, legend, epic

deste handle; hilt; bunch; packet

destek beam; prop, support; **~lemek** v/t prop up; support

destur permission; **~!** by your leave! make way!

deşelemek v/t scratch up

dev giant; demon

deva medicine, remedy

devam continuation, permanence; **~ etm.** last; **-e** continue; follow; **~lı** continuous; **~sız** inconstant, not persevering

deve camel; **~kuşu** ostrich

develope etm. v/t develop (photo)

devran rotation; circulation

devir rotation, cycle, circuit; period, epoch

devirmek v/t overturn, reverse

devlet state, government; **~çi** favouring state control; **~leştirmek** v/t nationalize

devr|e cycle; generation; period; **~en** adv. by continuation of the present contract; **~etmek** v/t transfer (-e to)

devri|k turned over; **~lmek** be overturned; **~m** revolution; transformation

devriye police round, patrol

deyi|m phrase, expression; **~ş** way of speaking

dezenfekte etm. v/t disinfect

dılı an. rib; math. side of a triangle

dış outer, exterior; outside; **~ taraf** outside

dışarı outside; exterior; out; **~da** outside; abroad; **~dan** from the outside; from abroad; **~ya** abroad; towards the outside

Dışişleri pl. pol. External Affairs

Dicle geo. Tigris

didiklemek v/t tear to pieces; search

didinmek toil, wear oneself out

didişmek quarrel, bicker (ile with)

diferansiyel tech. differential gear

difteri diphtheria

diğer other, another; different; next

dik upright, straight; steep; **~ kafalı** obstinate

diken thorn, sting; **~li** thorny, prickly; **~li tel** barbed wire

dikey math. vertical

diki|li sewn, stitched; set up; **~lmek** be sewn, be planted; stand stiff; **~ş** sewing, stitching; seam; **~ş makinesi** sewing machine

dikkat attention; care; **~ etm.** -e pay attention to; be careful with; **~le** adv. with care; **~li** attentive, careful; **~siz** careless; **~siz-lik** carelessness

dikmek v/t sew, stitch; set up; plant

diktatör dictator; **~lük** dictatorship

dikte dictation; **~ et(tir)-mek** v/t dictate

dil tongue; language; **~ balığı** zo. sole; **~bilgisi** grammar; **~bilim** linguistics

dilek wish, desire; request; **~çe** petition, formal request

dilemek v/t wish, desire; **özür ~** ask pardon

dilen|ci beggar; **~mek** beg

dilim slice, strip

dilsiz dumb, mute

dimağ brain, intelligence

din religion, faith

dinç vigorous, robust; **~leş-tirmek** v/t strengthen, invigorate; **~lik** robustness, good health

din|dar pious; **~daş** co-religionist

dindirmek v/t cause to cease, cause to stop

dingil axle

dini pertaining to religion

dinle|mek v/t listen to, hear, pay attention to; **~n-me yeri** road house; **~n-me yurdu** recreation home; **~nmek** rest; become quiet; **~yici** listener

dinmek cease; leave off

dinsiz without religion

dip bottom, lowest part; **~çik** butt of a rifle

diploma diploma, certifi-

cate; **~si** diplomacy; **~t** diplomate

dipsiz bottomless

dirayet comprehension, intelligence

direk pole, pillar, mast

direk|siyon steering-wheel; **~tör** director

diren|iş resistance; **~mek** insist (-de on)

diri alive, fresh; **~lmek** come to life; **~ltmek** v/t bring to life; **~m** life

dirsek elbow; bend

disiplin discipline

disk tech. disk; discus; **~ atma** throw the discus

dispanser med. dispensery

distribütör el. distributor

diş tooth; cog, clove; **~ fır-çası** toothbrush; **~ macu-nu** toothpaste; **~çi** dentist; **~çilik** dentistry

dişi female; **~l** gr. feminine

dişli toothed; cogged

divan 1. sofa, divan; 2. collection of poems; 3. pol. council of state

divane insane; crazy

diyafram an., phys. diaphragm

diyanet religious affairs pl.

diye saying; **~lek** dialect

diz an. knee; **~ çökmek** kneel; **~ kapağı** knee cap

dizanteri med. dysentery

dizel Diesel

diz|i line, row, string; **~il-mek** -e be arranged in; be strung on; **~mek** v/t arrange in a row; string

doçent lecturer, assistant professor

doğa nature; **~l** natural

doğan *zo.* falcon

doğma birth; by birth; **~k** be born; *astr.* rise

doğrama work of a carpenter; **~cı** carpenter; **~k** *v/t* cut into pieces

doğru straight, upright; right, true, honest; **~dan ~ya** directly; **~ca** direct, straight; **~lamak** *v/t* confirm; **~lmak** become straight; **~ltmak** *v/t* put straight; correct; **~luk** straightness; honesty, truth

doğu east; eastern

doğum birth; **~ günü** birthday; **~lu** *-de* born in

doğur|**mak** *v/t* give birth to, bring forth; **~tmak** *v/t* assist delivery

dok *naut.* dock

doksan ninety

doktor doctor; physician; **~a** doctorate

doku tissue

dokuma weaving; woven; **~cı** weaver; **~k** *v/t* weave

dokun|**aklı** touching, biting, harmful; **~mak 1.** be woven; **2.** *-e* touch, injure; **~ulmazlık** *pol.* immunity

dokuz nine

dola|**mak** *v/t* twist, wind (*-e* on); **~mbaç(lı)** winding, sinuous

dolandırıcı swindler; **~lık** swindle

dolandırmak *v/t* cheat, swindle, defraud

dolap cupboard; waterwheel; merry-go-round

dolaş|**ık** tortuous, confused; **~mak** go around, walk about, make a roundabout way; **~tırmak** *v/t* make *so.* go around; **-i -e** show *so.* over *sth.*

dolayı *-den* on account of, due to; *conj.* as, because

dol|**durmak** *v/t* fill; complete; fill up; **~gun** full; filled; high (*wages*); **~ma** stuffed, filled; **~ma kalem** fountain-pen; **~mak** become full; be completed; **~muş** filled, stuffed; a taxi all seats of which use to be engaged; **~u** *adj.* full, filled; solid; *n.* hail; **~unay** full moon

domates tomato(es)

domuz pig, swine

don¹ frost

don² pair of drawers

donanma fleet; navy; illumination; **~k** be illuminated

donat|**ım** *mil.* outfit, equipment; **~mak** *v/t* ornament, illuminate

dondurma ice-cream; **~cı** ice-cream vendor; **~k** *v/t* freeze

don|**mak** *v/i* freeze; set; **~uk** matt, dull

dopdolu chockful

dost friend; lover; **~ane**, **~ça** friendly; **~luk** friendship; favour

dosya dossier, file

doy|**mak** be satiated; **~maz**

insatiable; **~urmak** *v/t* satiate; satisfy

dök|me casting; cast; **~mek** *v/t* pour; scatter; cast; **~ülmek** be poured; be cast; fall out; disintegrate; drop off

döküm dropping; cast; enumeration *of an account;* **~hane** *tech.* foundry

döküntü remains; debris

döl seed, germ; race, stock; **~lemek** *v/t* inseminate, fertilize

dön|dürmek *v/t* turn round, reverse; **~em** period *of time;* **~er kebap** meat roasted on a revolving vertical spit; conversion; *rel.* Jewish convert to Islam; **~mek** *v/i* turn back; return; change; **~ük** turned (-*e* to); **~üm 1.** turn, revolution; **2.** (*surface measure: 0.23 acre or 920 m²*); **~üş** return(ing); **~üştürmek** *v/t* change, transform (-*e* into)

dört four; **~gen** *kenar* quadrangle; **~nala** at a gallop

döşe|k mattress; **~me** floor covering, pavement; **~meci** upholsterer; **~mek** *v/t* spread; pave

döviz slogan, device; *ec.* foreign currency

döv|mek *v/t* beat; hammer; thrash; **~üşmek** fight, struggle with one another

dram *thea.* drama

dua prayer, blessing; **~ etm.** pray, bless

duba *naut.* barge, pontoon

dubara trick, fraud; **~cı** trickster, cheat

duçar olm. -*e* be subject to, be exposed to

dudak lip

duhuliye entrance fee, ticket

duka duke; **~lık** duchy, dukedom

dul widow(er); widowed

duman smoke, mist; **~lanmak** become smoky *or* cloudy (*a. fig.*); **~lı** smoky, misty

durak *n.* stop, halt; **~lamak** *v/i* stop, pause

dur|durmak *v/t* stop, cause to wait; **~gun** stagnant; stationary; **~gunluk** stagnation, standstill; **~mak** *v/i* stop; cease; stand; remain; **~um** position; attitude; **~uş** posture, attitude; **~uşma** *jur.* hearing of a case

duş shower-bath; **~ yapmak** take a shower

dut mulberry

duvar wall; **~cı** mason, bricklayer

duygu perception; feeling; sense; **~lu** sensitive, impressionable; **~suz** insensitive, apathetic

duy|mak *v/t* feel; perceive; learn; hear; **~um** perception; sensation; **~urmak** -*e* -*i* let *so.* hear *or* learn *sth.*; **~uş** impression; feeling

düdük whistle, pipe, flute

düello duell

düğme button; knob; **~lemek** v/t button up

düğüm knot, bow; **~lemek** v/t knot

düğün feast (*wedding or circumcision*)

dükkân shop; **~cı** shopkeeper

dülger carpenter, builder

dümen *naut.* rudder; **~ci** helmsman

dün yesterday; **~den, ~kü** of yesterday

dünür father-in-law (*as a relation between the fathers of a married couple*)

dünya world; earth; this life

dürbün telescope; field-glasses

dürmek v/t roll up

dürt|mek v/t prod, goad; **~üşmek** push *or* prod one another   [honest)

dürüst straightforward,)

düstur principle, code of laws

düş dream

düş|ey perpendicular; **~kün** fallen, decayed; addicted (-*e* to); **~künlük** decay; poverty

düşman enemy, foe; **~lık** enmity, hostility

düş|mek fall down (-*e* upon); fall to one's lot; **~ük** fallen, drooping; low (*price*); *gr.* misconstrued

düşünce thought, reflection; anxiety; **~li** thoughtful; worried; **~siz** thoughtless, inconsiderate

düşün|mek v/t think of; remember; ponder over; **~ülmek** be thought *or* planned

düşürmek v/t cause to fall, cause to drop; bring down

düz flat, level, smooth; **~elmek** be arranged; be improved; **~eltmek** v/t make smooth; put in order; arrange

düzen order, regularity, trick, lie; **~lemek** v/t put in order; **~li** orderly, tidy; **~siz** out of order

düzgün smooth, level; regular

düzine dozen

düz|lem *math.* plane; **~lemek** v/t smooth, flatten; **~lük** flatness, plainness; **~mek** v/t arrange; invent; forge

E

-e *s.* **-a**

ebe midwife

ebed|î eternal, without end; **~iyet** eternity

ebeveyn parents

ebleh imbecile, stupid

ebru(lu) marbled (*paper*)

ecel *rel.* appointed hour of death; appointed term

ecnebi foreign; foreigner

eczacı chemist, druggist; **~lık** pharmacy (*profession*)

ecza(ha)ne pharmacy, chemist's shop

eda payment, execution; tone, manner

edat *gr.* particle

edeb|i literary; **~iyat** literature

edep|li well-behaved, with good manners; **~siz** ill-mannered, rude

edi|lgen *gr.* passive; **~lmek** be done, be made; **~nmek** *v/t* get, procure

Edirne Adrianople

efe elder brother; village hero

efendi master; Mr. (*after the first name*); **~m** yes, sir! I beg your pardon?

efsane fable; idle tale

ege master, guardian; **~menlik** sovereignty

egzos(t) *tech.* exhaust

eğe file; *an.* rib; **~lemek** *v/t* file

eğer if, whether; when

eğil|im inclination; **~mek** *v/i* bend, incline

eğirmek *v/t* spin

eğit|im education; **~mek** *v/t* educate; **~men** educator

eğlen|ce diversion, amusement; **~celi** amusing, diverting; **~dirmek** *v/t* amuse, divert; **~mek** be amused, amuse oneself

eğmek *v/t* bend, incline

eğreltiotu *bot.* bracken, fern

eğreti false, artificial; makeshift, temporary

eğri crooked; bent; **~lik** crookedness, dishonesty; **~lmek** become bent, incline; **~ltmek** *v/t* make crooked, bend, twist

ehemmiyet importance; **~li** important; **~siz** unimportant

ehil family, household; *-in* **ehli olm.** be endowed with, be versed in

ehli tame, domesticated

ehliyet capacity, competence; **~name** certificate of competence; driving license; **~siz** incapable, incompetent

ehven cheap(est)

ejder(ha) dragon

ek joint; addition, supplement; *gr.* suffix, affix, prefix

eki|li planted; sown; **~m** sowing; October

ekin crops; **~ biçmek** reap, harvest

ekip team, crew, gang

ekle|m *an.* joint; **~mek** *v/t* join, add (*-e* to); **~nmek** *-e* be joined to, be added to; **~nti** annex

ekmek[1] *v/t* sow; scatter

ekmek[2] *n.* bread; **~çi** baker

ekonomi economy

ekran *tech.* screen

eksantrik mili *tech.* excentric rod

ekselans Excellency

ekser[1] large nail, spike

ekser[2] majority; **~i** most; **~iya** *adv.* generally, mostly; **~iyet** majority

eksi *math.* minus

eksik deficient, lacking; ~ **olmayın!** thank you very much!; ~**lik** deficiency, defectiveness; ~**siz** without defect; complete, perfect

eksil|mek *v/i* decrease; be absent; ~**tmek** *v/t* diminish, reduce

ekser expert

ekspres express train *or* steamer

ekstra extra, first quality

ekşi sour, acid; ~**mek** become sour; be upset (stomach); *sl.* be disconcerted; ~**msi** sourish

ekvator *geo.* equator

el[1] country; people

el[2] hand; forefoot; handle; ~ **çantası** hand-bag; ~ **koymak** *-e* seize; monopolize; ~ **topu** hand-ball; ~ **yazısı** handwriting; manuscript; ~**de etm.** get hold of, obtain; ~**e almak** *v/t* take charge of; ~**e geçmek** come into one's possession; ~**i açık** generous; ~**ine bakmak** depend on (*-in so.*)

elastik(**i**) elastic [edly]

elbet(**te**) certainly, decid-

elbise *pl.* clothes; clothing; ~ **askısı** coat-hanger

elçi envoy, ambassador; ~**lik** embassy

eldiven glove

elebaşı ringleader, captain

elek sieve

elektrik electricity; ~**akımı** electric current; ~**li** electric

elem pain, suffering

eleman element; personnel

elemek *v/t* sift, sieve

eleştir|ici *n.* critic; *adj.* critical; ~**im**, ~**me** criticism; ~**mek** *v/t* criticize

elhasıl *adv.* in short, in brief

ellemek *v/t* feel with the hand

elli fifty

elma apple; ~ **ağacı** apple tree

elmas diamond

elti sister-in-law (relationship between the wives of two brothers)

elveda farewell, good-by

elver|işli sufficient; useful; profitable; ~**mek** suffice; be suitable

elzem indispensable

emanet peace, anything entrusted *to so.*; ~**etm.** *v/t* entrust (*-e* to)

emare sign, mark; token

emcik teat, nipple

emek work, labour; trouble; ~**li** retired; pensioner; ~**liye ayrılmak** retire, be pensioned off; ~**lilik** retirement; ~**siz** free from labour; easy; ~**tar** old and faithful, veteran

emel longing, desire

emin safe, secure; sure; ~ **olm.** *-e* be sure of

emir order, command

emlâk *pl.* lands, possessions, real estates; ~ **alım vergisi** purchase tax on real estate

emmek *v/t* suck

emniyet security, safety; police; **~li** safe, reliable; **~siz** insecure, unsafe; **~sizlik** lack of confidence

emprime print fabric

emretmek *v/t* order, command

emsal *pl.* similars, equals; **~siz** peerless, unequalled

emtia *pl. ec.* goods

emzi|k nipple, teat; baby's bottle; **~rmek** *v/t* suckle

en¹ *n.* width, breadth

en² *adv.* most (*superlative*); **~ az(dan)** at least; **~ güzel** most beautiful

encam end; conclusion, result

endam body, shape, figur

endaze (*linear measure, ab. 65 cm*)

endişe throught, anxiety; **~li** thoughtful, anxious

endüstri industry

enerji energy; **~k** energetic

enfes delightful, delicious

enflasyon *ec.* inflation

engebe unevenness of ground; **~li** steep and broken

engel obstacle; difficulty; **~ olm. -e** hinder, prevent; **~lemek** *v/t* hinder, hamper

engerek *zo.* adder, viper

engin¹ ordinary, common

engin² vast, boundless; **~ deniz** the open sea

enginar *bot.* artichoke

enik whelp, cub, puppy

enişte husband *of an aunt or sister*

enkaz *pl.* ruins, debris; wreck

enl|em *geo.* parallel; **~i** wide, broad

ense back of the neck, nape

ensiz narrow

enstantane snapshot

enstitü institute

entari loose robe

entegrasyon integration

enteresan interesting

enterne *etm. v/t* intern

entrika intrigue; **~cı** schemer, trickster

epey(ce) a good many; fairly

er¹ early; soon

er² man, male; *mil.* private; **~at** *pl.* non-commissioned officers and private soldiers

erbap expert, specialist

erbaş *mil.* non-commissioned officer

erdem virtue

erg|en marriageable; unmarried; **~in** mature, adult; ripe

erguvan judas-tree; purple; **~i** purple

erik plum

eril *gr.* masculine

erimek *v/i* melt, fuse; pass away

erişmek *-e* arrive, attain; reach the age of marriage

eritmek *v/t* melt, dissolve; squander

erk power; authority

erkek man, male; husband; **~lik** masculinity; manliness

erken early

erkin free, independent

ermek *-e* reach, attain

Ermeni Armenian; **~ce** Armenian (*language*)

ersiz without husband

ertelemek *v/t* postpone

ertesi the following *day, etc.*; **~ gün** the following day

erzak *pl.* provisions; food

esans *chem.* essence, perfume

esas *n.* foundation; principle; *adj.* basic; **~en** fundamentally, in principle; **~î** fundamental, essential; **~lı** based, founded; sure; **~sız** baseless, unfounded

esen hearty, robust; **~lik** health, soundness

eser sign, trace; work *of art, etc.*

esham *ec.* share

esir captive, prisoner of war

esirge|mek *v/t* protect, spare; **Allah ~sin!** may God protect us!

esirlik captivity

eski old; ancient; out of date; **~ püskü** old and tattered things; **~ci** old-clothes man, cobbler; **~mek** be worn out; **~tmek** *v/t* wear out

eskrim (*sport*) fencing; **~ci** fencer

esmek *v/i* blow; *fig.* come into the mind (*-e so.*)

esmer brunette, dark complexioned

esna|da: o ~da at that time;

-diği ~da *conj.* while; **~sında** in the course of, during

esnaf *pl.* tradesmen, artisans

esnek elastic; **~lik** elasticity

esnemek yawn

esrar hashish

esrimek become ekstatic; get drunk

estağfurullah! don't mention it!, not at all!

eş one of a pair; husband; wife; partner

eşek donkey; ass; **~ arısı** wasp, hornet

eşik threshold; bridge of a violine, etc. [equality]

eşit equal, equivalent; **~lik**

eşkıya *sg. u. pl.* brigand(s)

eşsiz matchless, peerless

eşya *pl.* things, objects; luggage; furniture

et meat; flesh

etek skirt; *geo.* foot of a mountain; **~lik** skirt of a woman

eter *chem.* ether

etiket label, ticket; etiquett

etiket label, ticket; etiquette; **~lemek** *v/t* label

etimoloji etymology

etken *gr.* active

etki effect; **~lemek** *v/t* affect, influence; **~li** effective, influential

etkin active; effective; **~lik** activity; efficiency

etmek do, make

etraf *pl.* sides, ends; surroundings; *-in* **~ında** around; **~lı** detailed

et|siz without meat; weak; **~suyu** gravy, meat broth

ettir|gen *gr.* causative (*verb*); **~mek** *v/t* cause to do

etüt study, essay

ev house, home, dwelling; **~ idaresi** household; **~ kadını** housewife; **~cil** domesticated

evet yes

evkaf *pl. rel.* pious foundations; estates in mortmain

evlât child(ren), descendant(s)

evlen|dirmek *v/t* marry, give in marriage (*-e* to); **~me** marriage; **~mek** marry (**ile** *so.*)

evli married

evrak *pl.* documents, papers; **~ çantası** brief-case, portfolio

evren universe

evvel ago; first; *-meden* **~** *conj.* before; **bir an ~** as

soon as possible; **~â** firstly; **~ce** previously, formerly; **~ki, ~si** first, former; **(~si) gün** the day before yesterday

eyalet province

eyer saddle

eylem action

eylemek *s.* **etmek**

eylül September

eyvah alas!

eyvallah thank you!; good bye!; all right!

ezan *rel.* call to prayer

ezber by heart; **~lemek** *v/t* learn by heart

ezcümle for instance

ezelî without beginning, eternal

ezilmek be crushed, oppressed

eziyet injury, pain, torture; **~li** fatiguing, painful

ezme something crushed, paste, purée; **~k** *v/t* crush, pound, bruise

F

faal active, industrious; **~iyet** activity, energy

fabrika factory; **~cı, ~tör** manufacturer

facia tragedy, disaster

fahişe prostitute

fahri honorary

faide *s.* **fayda**

fail agent; *gr.* subject

faiz *ec.* interest; **birleşik ~** compound interest; **~e vermek** *v/t* lend at interest

fakat but, only

fakir poor, pauper; **~lik** poverty

fakülte faculty *of a university*

fal omen; fortune; **~a bakmak** tell a fortune

falaka bastinado

falan so and so, such and such; and so on

falcı fortune-teller

familya family (*a. bot.*)

fanila flannel; undershirt

fantezi fancy (goods)

faraz|a supposing that; **~î** hypothetical

fare mouse; rat; **~ kapanı** mouse-trap

farfara empty-headed, braggart; **~lık** idle brag, frivolity

fark difference, distinction; **-in ~ına varmak** become aware of, perceive; **-in ~ında olm.** be aware of; **~etmek** v/t distinguish; perceive; **~lı** different, changed; **~sız** indistinguishable, without difference

farmason s. **mason**

farz rel. precept; supposition; **~etmek** v/t suppose; **~edelim** let us

Fas Morocco [suppose]

fasıl chapter, section

fasıla separation; interval, interruption; **~ vermek -e** interrupt; break; **~sız** continuous, uninterrupted

fasikül fascicule, section of a book

fasulye bot. bean; **taze ~** string beans

faşi|st Fascist; **~zm** Fascism

fatih conqueror

fatura ec. invoice

favori whiskers

fayans tile

fayda use, profit, advantage; **~lanmak -den** profit by, make use of; **~lı** useful, profitable; **~sız** useless, in vain

fayton phaeton

fazilet merit, superiority; **~kâr**, **~li** virtuous, excellent

fazla remainder; superfluous; more, too much; **~laşmak** v/i increase

feci painful, tragic

fecir dawn

feda ransom; sacrifice; **~ etm.** v/t sacrifice; **~kâr** self-sacrificing; devoted; **~kârlık** self-sacrifice, devotion

federa|l federal; **~syon** federation, association; **~tif** s. **~l**

felâket disaster, catastrophe; **~zede** victim of a disaster

felç med. paralysis; **çocuk felci** infantile paralysis

felek firmament; destiny

Felemenk Holland; **~li** n., adj. Dutch

felsef|e philosophy; **~î** philosophical

fen technics, art; natural sciences

fena bad, unpleasant; **~laşmak** become worse, deteriorate; **~laştırmak** v/t make worse, worsen; **~lık** evil, bad action

fener lantern, street-lamp, lighthouse

fennî scientific, technical

feragat abandonment, renunciation; **~ etm. -den** renounce, give up

ferah spacious, open; joy, pleasure; **~lanmak** become spacious, cheerful; **~lık** spaciousness, cheerfulness

ferdî individual

fer'î secondary; accessory

feribot *naut.* train or car ferry

fermejüp snap-fastener

fermuar zip-fastener

fert person, individual

feryat cry, wail

fes fez

fesat depravity, corruption; **~çı** mischief-maker, conspirator

feshetmek *v/t* annul, cancel

fesih abolition, cancellation

fethetmek *v/t* conquer

fetih conquest

fetva *rel.* decision on religious matter given by a mufti [cence]

feveran boiling, effervescence

fevkalâde extraordinary

feyezan overflowing, flood

feza *astr.* space, universe

fıçı cask, barrel; **~cı** cooper

fıkara *pl.* the poor; **~lık** poverty

fıkırdamak *s.* fokurdamak

fıkra paragraph; passage

fındık *bot.* hazel-nut; **~ faresi, ~ sıçanı** *zo.* common house-mouse

Fırat Euphrates

fırça brush; paint-brush; **~lamak** *v/t* brush, dust

fırıldak ventilator; spinning-top; **~(n)mak** spin round

fırın oven; bakery; **~cı**

baker; who looks after a furnace

fırka *pol.* party; *mil.* division

fırla|mak *v/i* fly off, fly out; **~tmak** *v/t* hurl, shoot

fırsat opportunity, chance

fırtına gale, storm; **~lı** stormy

fısıl|damak *v/t* whisper; **~tı** whisper [tain]

fıskıye jet of water, fountain

fıstık *bot.* pistachio nut

fışırdamak gurgle, rustle

fışkır|mak *v/i* gush out, spurt out; **~tmak** *v/t* spurt, splash

fıtık *an.* hernia, rupture

fıtr|at creation, nature; **~î** natural, innate

fiat *s.* fiyat

fidan *bot.* plant, sapling; **~lık** nursery

fide *bot.* seedling plant

figüran *thea.* super

fihrist index, catalogue, list

fiil act, action, deed; *gr.* verb; **~î** actual, real

fikir thought, idea; mind, opinion; **~siz** thoughtless

fil elephant

filan *s.* falan

fildişi ivory

file net

fileto fillet

filim *s.* film

filinta carbine, short gun

Filistin Palestine

filiz tendril, young shoot; **~lenmek** sprout, send forth shoots

film film; movie; *-in* **~ini**

almak film; X-ray; ~ **yıldızı** film star

filo *naut.* fleet, squadron; ~**tilla** flotilla

filozof philosopher

filtre filter, sieve; ~ **etm.** *v/t* filter

final *n* final (*sport*); *mus.* finale

finanse etm. *v/t* finance

fincan cup; *el.* porcelain insulator

fingirdemek behave coquettishly

firar flight, desertion

firkete hair-pin

fiske flip *with the fingers*; pinch; ~**lemek** *v/t* give a flip to

fistül fistula

fiş slip of paper, card; *el.* plug

fişek cartridge, rocket

fitil wick, fuse

fitne instigation, disorder

fiyat price, value

fizik physics

flama *naut.* pennant

flaş flash-light

flavta flute

fleş *s.* **flaş**

flört flirt

flüt flute

fodra lining, padding

fokurdamak *v/i* boil up, bubble

folklor folklore

folye foil

fonksiyon *math.* function

for forward (*football*)

forma forme, folio; uniform, colours; ~**lite** formality; red tape

formül formula; ~**er** formulary

forvet *s.* **for**

fosfor phosphorus

fotoğraf photograph; ~ **makinesi** camera; *-in* ~**ını çekmek** *v/t* photograph; ~**çı** photographer

frak tail-coat

francala white bread; roll

Frans|a France; ~**ız** French; ~**ızca** French (*language*)

fren brake

frengi syphilis

Frenk (Western)European; **üzümü** *bot.* red currant

frenlemek *v/t* brake

frikik free kick (*football*)

friksiyon friction

fuar *ec.* fair, exposition

fukara(lık) *s.* **fıkara(lık)**

funda shrub, thicket

furgon luggage-van

futbol football; ~ **maçı** football match

fuzuli meddling, superfluous

füme smoked; ~ **etm.** *v/t* smoke

füze rocket, missile

G

gaddar cruel, perfidious; **~lık** cruelty, perfidy

gafil careless, inattentive; **~avlamak** v/t catch unawares

gaga beak; **~lamak** v/t peck

gâh sometimes

gaile anxiety, trouble; **~li** worried; **~siz** carefree

gaip absent; invisible

galebe victory; **~ etm., ~ çalmak** -e conquer, overcome

galeri gallery

galib|a probably, presumably; **~iyet** victory

galip victorious, superior

gam¹ mus. scale

gam² anxiety, grief

gammaz sneak, informer; **~lamak** v/t calumniate, denounce; **~lık** spying

gangren med. gangrene

ganimet spoils, booty

gar railway station

garaj garage

garanti guarantee

garaz malice, grudge; **~kâr** selfish, spiteful; **~siz** unprejudiced, unbiased

garbi western

gardı|fren brakeman (railway); **~rop** wardrobe, cloakroom

gardiyan guard, attendant

gargara gargling, gargle; **~ yapmak** gargle

garip strange; curious

garnizon mil. garrison

garp West; Europe

garson waiter

gaseyan med. vomiting

gasıp usurpation

gaspetmek v/t seize by force

gâvur n. Non-Moslem, giaour; adj. obstinate, merciless; **~luk** quality of being a Non-Moslem; fanacism, cruelty

gaye aim, object, end; **~t** end, limit; extremely

gayret zeal, energy; **~li** zealous, persevering; **~siz** slack, without enthusiasm

gayrı now; neg. no longer

gayri (negative prefix); **~ kabil** impossible

gaz¹ gas, petroleum

gaz² gauze

gazete newspaper; **~ci** journalist; news-vendor; **~cilik** journalism

gazi rel. fighter for Islam; victorious Moslem general

gazino casino, restaurant

gazlı containing gas

gazometre gasometer

gazoz fizzy lemonade

gebe pregnant; **~lik** pregnancy

gebermek perish, die

gebre bot. caper-tree

gece night; **~ gündüz** day and night; **~ yarısı** midnight; **~kondu** house set up in one night without permission; shanty; **~leyin** by

gerçek

night; **~lik** pertaining to the night; night-dress

gecik|me delay; retardment; **~mek** be late; **~tirmek** *v/t* delay, be slow in doing *sth.*

geç late; **~ kalmak** be late

geçe -*i* past (*time*); üçü on ~ 10 minutes past three

geç|en past; last; **~en(ler)de** recently; **~er** current (*money*, etc.); **~erli** valid; **~ici** passing, temporary; **~ilmek** -*den* be passable

geçim getting on with one another; livelihood; **~siz** unsociable, quarrelsome

geçin|dirmek *v/t* support, maintain; **~inmek ile** live by, exist, subsist on

geçirmek *v/t* infect (-*e* with); transport; spend, pass

geçiş change, transfer; **~li** *gr.* transitive; **~siz** *gr.* intransitive

geç|it pass, ford; **~mek** *v/i* pass (-*den* along, over, etc.); expire, pass away; *v/t* skip, leave out; **~miş** past; *gr.* past tense; **~miş olsun!** I wish you a speedy recovery!

gedik breach, notch, gap; **~li** *mil.* regular non-commissioned officer

geğirmek belch, eructate

gelecek future; **~ zaman** *gr.* future tense

gelenek tradition

gelgit tide, flood-tide

gelin bride; daughter-in-law

gelince -*e* as for, regarding

gelincik *bot.* poppy

gelir income, revenue; **~ vergisi** income tax

geliş coming, happening; **~igüzel** *adv.* by chance, at random; **~me** development; **~mek** *v/i* develop, grow up; **~mekte olan ülke** developing country; **~miş** developed; **~tirmek** *v/t* develop

gel|mek come; -*e* suit, fit; seem, appear; **~ip almak** *v/t* fetch, pick up

gem bit of a horse; **~ vurmak** -*e* curb

gemi ship; **~ci** sailor

gen broad, vast; untouched (*ground*)

genç young; youngster; **~leşmek** become youthful; **~leştirmek** *v/t* rejuvenate; **~lik** youth

gene again, moreover

genel general; **~ af** amnesty; **~ge** circular; **~kurmay** General Staff; **~leşmek** become general; **~likle** *adv.* generally

general *mil.* general

geniş wide, vast, extensive; **~le(n)mek** *v/i* widen, extend, become spacious; **~letmek** *v/t* expand, enlarge; **~lik** width; abundance

gensoru *pol.* interpellation

geometri geometry

gerçek true, actual; really;

~ten truly, really; **~leşmek** turn out to be true; **~leştirmek** v/t certify, verify; **~lik** truth, reality

gerçi conj. although

gerdan neck, throat; **~lık** necklace, neckband

gereç necessaries, material

gereğince in accordance with

~erek necessary, needed; requisite; **~ ... ~** whether ... or; **~çe** statement of reasons; **~li** necessary, required; **~lik** necessity; **~mek** be necessary; be suitable (-e for); **~tirmek** v/t necessitate, require

gergef embroidery frame

gergin stretched, strained; **~lik** tension

geri behind, back, backward; **~ye bırakmak** v/t put off, postpone; v/i reactionary; **~lemek** recede, be slow

gerili stretched, taut

gerilik backwardness

geril|im phys., el. tension; **~mek** be tightened; be spread

gerinmek stretch oneself

germek v/t stretch, tighten

getir|mek v/t bring, produce; **meydana ~mek** v/t create; **~tmek** v/t cause to be brought

geveze talkative, chattering; **~lik** babbling, gossip

gevrek brittle, crackly; biscuit

gevşe|k loose, slack; **~mek**

become loose, become slack; **~tmek** v/t loosen, slacken

geyik zo. deer, stag; **~ boynuzu** antlers pl.

gez¹ mil. back-sight

gez² plumbline

gez|dirmek v/t lead about, conduct, cause to walk about; **~gin** widely travelled; **~i** excursion; **~inmek** go about, stroll; **~inti** walk, stroll; **~mek** go about, travel; v/t inspect

gıcıklamak v/t tickle; fig. make suspicious

gıcırda|mak v/i creak, rustle; **~tmak** v/t make creak, gnash

gıda food, nourishment; **~lı** nutritious; **~sız** not nutricious

gıdıkla|mak v/t tickle; **~nmak** v/t tickle

gıpta longing, envy

gırtlak throat

gıyaben adv. by default

gıybet backbiting; **~çi** slanderer, backbiter

gibi similar, like; **bunun ~** like this

gid|er ec. expenditure, expense; **~ermek** v/t remove, cause to go; **~ilmek** be frequented, visited; **~iş** going, leaving; **~işmek** itch

gidon handlebar of a bicycle

girdap whirlpool

girinti recess, indentation

giriş entry, entrance; **~mek** -e set about, undertake

Girit (adası) geo. Crete

girmek -e enter, go into; begin, join, participate

gişe ticket-window, pay-desk

git|gide adv. gradually; **~mek** -e go to; suit, fit; **hoşuna ~mek** like, be fond of; **~tikçe** adv. by degrees, gradually

giy|dirmek v/t clothe, dress so.; **~im** clothing, dress; **~inmek** dress oneself; **~mek** v/t wear, put on

giz|lemek v/t hide, conceal; **~lenmek** hide oneself; **~li** hidden, secret; **~lice** secretly; **~lilik** secrecy

gliserin glycerine

glüten chem. gluten

gol goal; **~ atmak** kick a goal

goril zo. gorilla [goal]

göbek navel; belly; **~lenmek** become paunchy

göç migration; **~ebe** nomad; **~mek** move off; **~men** immigrant; refugee; **~menlik** immigration; **~ürmek** v/t cause to move off (-e to)

göğüs breast, chest

gök sky, heavens; **~ gürlemek** v/i thunder; **~ gürlemesi,** **~ gürültüsü** n. thunder; **~çe** blue; pleasant; **~deldi, ~delen** skyscraper; **~taşı** turquoise; **~yüzü** firmament

göl lake, pond

gölge n. shadow, shade; **~lendirmek** v/t shade; **~li** shaded, shady; **~lik** shady spot; arbour

gömlek shirt; skin of a snake

gömmek v/t bury, hide by burying, inter

gömülü buried, underground

gönder|en sender; **~ilmek** -e be sent to; **~mek** v/t send (-e to)

gönenç comfort, luxury

gönül heart; feelings; affection; **~lü** willing; volunteer; **~süz** unwilling; without pride; **~süzlük** disinclination; modesty

gör|e -e according to, respecting, considering; **~enek** custom, fashion

görev duty, obligation; **~lendirmek** v/t charge, entrust (ile with)

gör|gü experience; good manners pl.; **~mek** v/t see; visit; **~ü** view, panorama; **~ülmek** be seen or visited or examined

görümce sister of the husband; sister-in-law

görün|mek appear, be visible; **~üm** outward appearance; **~ürde** adv. in appearance; in sight; **~üş** appearance, view

görüş mode of seeing, point of view

görüşmek ile meet, become acquainted with; discuss (-i sth.)

göster|ge tech. indicator; **~i** show, demonstration

gösteriş appearance, aspect; demonstration; **~li** stately,

imposing; **~siz** poor looking

göster|mek v/t show (**-e** to
so.); **Allah ~mesin!** God
forbid!

göt vulg. behind, arse

götür|mek v/t take away,
carry off; **~ü** adv. in a
lump sum; **~üm** endur-
ance, patience

gövde body, trunk; whole
carcass

göynük burnt; ripe

göz eye; hole, opening;
drawer; **~den düşmek** fall
into disesteem; **~e almak**
v/t venture, risk; **~e çarpmak** strike the eye; **~ akı**
the white of the eye; **~ alıcı**
striking, dazzling; **~ kapağı** eyelid; **~ kararı** judgement by the eye; **~ yaşı**
tear; **~altı** police supervision; **~bebeği** an. pupil
of the eye; **~cü** watchman,
sentinel; **~de** favourite, pet

gözet|im watch, super-
vision; **~lemek** v/t observe,
spy upon

göz|etmek v/t mind, look
after; watch; **~evi** eye-
socket; **~lemek** v/t watch
for, wait for

gözlük spectacles; **~ camı**
spectacle lens; **~cü** optician

göz|süz blind; **~taşı** copper
sulphate; **~üpek** brave,
bold, daring

gram gram(me)

gramer grammar

grev strike; **~ hakkı** freedom of strike; **~ci** striker

gre(y)pfrut bot. grapefruit

gri grey

grip influenza

grup group

gudde an. gland

guguk zo. cuckoo

gurbet absence from home

gurul|damak v/i rumble;
~tu rumbling

gurur pride, vanity; **~lu**
arrogant, vain

gûya s. güya

gübre dung, manure; **~le-
mek** v/t dung, manure

gücenmek -e to be offended
with, hurt by

güç[1] strength, force

güç[2] difficult; **~leşmek** v/i
grow difficult; **~leştirmek**
v/t render difficult, complicate, impede

güçlü strong, powerful

güçlük difficulty, pain

güçsüz weak, feeble

güdü motive, incentive

güdümlü controlled

güherçile chem. saltpetre

gül rose; **~ fidanı** rose-
bush; **~ yağı** attar of roses

güldürmek v/t make laugh

güllâç (sweet made with
wafers, cream, etc.)

gül|mek laugh, smile;
~ümsemek smile; **~ünç**
ridiculous; **~üşmek** laugh
together

gümbür|demek v/i boom,
thunder; **~tü** booming
noise, crash, thunder

gümeç honeycomb

gümrük customs; **~ kontrolü** customs control; **~**

memuru, ~çü customs officer

gümüş silver; ~**lemek** v/t silver plate

gün day; sun; light; ~**den** ~**e** from day to day; ~**ün birinde** one day

günah sin, fault; ~**kâr** sinner, culpable; ~**sız** without sin

gün|aşırı every other day; ~**aydın!** good morning!; ~**batısı** west; ~**çiçeği** sunflower; ~**delik** adj. daily; n. daily wage; ~**dem** agenda; ~**doğusu** southeast wind; east; ~**dönümü** astr. solstice

gündüz daytime, by day; ~**ün** adv. by day

güneş sun; ~**lenmek** bathe in the sun; ~**lik** sunny place; sunshade

gün|ey south; ~**lük 1.** daily; ... days old; sufficient for ... days; **2.** chem. francincense, myrrh

gür abundant; strong (voice); rank; ~**büz** sturdy, healthy

güreş wrestling; ~çi wrestler; ~**mek** wrestle (ile with)

gürlemek v/i make a loud noise, thunder

güruh group, lot

gürüldemek thunder

gürültü loud noise, uproar; ~**lü** noisy, tumultuous; ~**süz** noiseless, quiet

gütmek v/t drive an animal

güve clothes-moth

güveç earthenware cooking pot; vegetables and meat cooked in this pot

güven confidence, reliance; ~**lik** security; ~**mek** -e trust in, rely on; ~**sizlik** lack of confidence

güvercin pidgeon

güverte naut. deck

güvey bridegroom, son-in-law

güya as if, as though

güz autumn, fall

güzel beautiful, pretty, nice; ~**leşmek** become beautiful, nice; ~**leştirmek** v/t beautify; ~**lik** beauty, goodness

H

habbe grain, seed

haber knowledge, information; ~ **almak** -den receive information, learn from; ~ **vermek** -e inform, give notice; ~**ci** messenger; ~**dar olm.** -den know, possess information about; ~**leşmek ile** correspond with; ~**siz** not informed (-den about)

hac rel. pilgrimage to Mecca

hacet need, necessity

hacı Hadji (one who made the pilgrimage to Mecca); ~**laryolu** astr. the Milky Way

hacim volume, capacity

hacir *jur.* putting under restraint

haciz *jur.* seizure

haczetmek *v/t jur.* seize

haç cross, crucifix; **~lamak** *v/t* crucify; **~lılar** *pl.* the Crusaders

had limit, boundary; **~dini bilmek** know one's place

hâd sharp; acute (*illness*)

hadde wire-drawer's plate; **~hane** *tech.* rolling-mill

hademe servant *at an office, etc.*

hadım eunuch

hadi *s.* **haydi**

hadise event, incident

hadsiz unbounded, unlimited

haf half-back (*sport*)

hafıza memory

hafif light; easy; flighty; **~lemek** become light, easier; **~leştirmek, ~letmek** *v/t* make lighter, easier; **~lik** lightness, ease of mind; **~meşrep** flighty, frivolous

hafiye detective, spy

hafriyat *pl.* excavations

hafta week; **~larca** for weeks on end; **~lık** weekly, per week; *n.* weekly wages

haham *rel.* Rabbi; **~başı** Chief Rabbi

hain traitor; treacherous; **~leşmek** become *or* act treacherous, **~lik** treachery, perfidy

haiz olm. *-i* possess, obtain

hak¹ truth, right, justice; right, true; ♀ God

hak² engraving, erasing

hâk earth, soil

hakaret insult, contempt; **~ etm.** *-e* insult

hakem arbitrator, umpire

hakikat truth, reality; truly, really; **~en** *adv.* in truth, really

hakikî true, real; sincere

hâkim judge; ruler; ruling, dominating; **~ olm.** *-e* rule over, dominate; **~iyet** sovereignty, domination; **~lik** the office of a judge

hakketmek *v/t* engrave, erase

hakkı|nda concerning, with regard to; **~yle** *adv.* properly, rightfully

haklı right, who is right

haksız unjust, wrong; **~lık** injustice, wrong

hal¹ condition; state; quality, attribute; present time; *gr.* case; **o ~de, şu ~de** in this case, therefore, consequently; **-diği ~de** *conj.* although

hal² melting; solution

hal³ covered market-place

hala paternal aunt

hâlâ at the present time; now, just

halâs salvation; **~kâr** saviour, deliverer

halat rope

halbuki *conj.* however, nevertheless, whereas

halef successor

halel defect, injury

halen *adv.* now, at present
Halep Aleppo
hal'etmek *v/t* dethrone
halı carpet; **~cı** carpet maker; **~cılık** manufacturing of carpets
hâli *-den* free from
haliç *geo.* strait, estuary; ♀ the Golden Horn
halife Caliph
halim mild, gentle
halis pure, genuine
halita alloy
halk people, crowd
halka ring, hoop, circle; link; **~lı** ringed, linked
halkçı *pol.* populist; **~lık** populism
halkoyu *pol.* plebiscite
halletmek *v/t* solve, dissolve, analyse
halojen lambası halogen reflector
halsiz weak, exhausted
halter bar-bell (*sport*); **~ci** weight-lifter
ham unripe; raw, crude
hamak hammock
hamal porter, carrier
hamam Turkish bath
hamarat hard-working
hamd|etmek *-e* give thanks to God; **~olsun!** Thank God!
hamız acid   [God!]
hami protector; guarding
hamil bringing, bearer; **~e** pregnant
hamle attack, onslaught
hammadde raw material
hamur dough, leaven; quality *of paper*; **~suz** unleavened (*bread*)

han[1] Khan, sovereign
han[2] caravanserai; commercial building
hançer dagger
hançere *an.* larynx
hane house; subdivision; square *of a chessboard*; **~dan** family, dynasty
hangar hangar
hangi which?; **~si** which of them?
hanım lady; **~efendi** madam
hani where?; you know!; well
hantal clumsy, coarse
hap pill
hapis confinement, prison; **~hane** prison
hapsetmek *v/t* imprison, confine
harabe ruin
haraç tribute
haram *rel.* forbidden by religion
harap ruined, devastated; **~ olm.** be devastated, fall into ruin
hararet heat; fever; **~li** heated, feverish
harbiye *mil.* war academy
harc|amak *v/t* expend, spend, use; **~ırah** travelling expenses
harç[1] mortar, plaster
harç[2] expenditure; customs duty; **~lı** liable to duty; **~lık** pocket-money; allowance
hardal mustard
hareket movement, act, behaviour; departure; **~**

etm. *-den* depart from; **∼siz** motionless

harem the women's apartments, harem

harf letter; **∼i ∼ine** *adv.* word for word

harıltı loud and continuous noise

harici external, foreign

hariç *n.* outside, exterior; *adj.* excluded

harika wonder, miracle

haris greedy, avaricious

harita *s.* **harta**

harman threshing *of grains;* harvest time; threshing floor; blend; **∼ dövmek** thresh; **∼lamak** *v/t* blend

harmoni *mus.* harmony

harp war; battle; fight; **∼ gemisi** warship; **∼ malulü** invalid, disabled soldier; **∼ okulu** military college

hars culture, education

harta map, plan; **∼cılık** cartography

hartuç cartridge

has *-e* special, peculiar to

hasar damage, loss; **∼a uğramak** suffer loss *or* damage; **∼at** *pl.* losses

hasat reaping; harvest

hasebiyle by reason of, because of

haset envy, jealousy; **∼çi** envious, jealous

hâsıl resulting; **∼ olm.** result, be obtained *(-den* from); **∼ı** *adv.* in a word

hasır rush mat; **∼ koltuk** wicker chair

hasis stingy, vile; **∼lik** stinginess, vileness

hasret regret, longing

hasretmek *v/t* restrict, consecrate *(-e* to)

hassas sensitive, delicate; **∼iyet** sensibility, touchiness

hasta sick; ill; **∼ düşmek** fall ill; **∼bakıcı** hospital attendant; nurse; **∼lanmak** fall ill

hastalık illness, disease; **∼lı** ailing, in ill health

hastane hospital

haşarat *pl.* insects, vermin

haşarı dissolute, naughty

haşhaş *bot.* poppy

haşin harsh, rough

haşiş hashish

haşiye marginal note, postscript

haşlama boiled *(meat);* **∼k** *v/t* boil; sting *(insect)*

haşmet majesty, pomp; **∼li** majestic

hat line, mark

hata mistake, fault; **∼ya düşmek** err

hatır thought, idea, memory; consideration; *-in* **∼ına gelmek** occur *to one's* mind; **∼ından çıkmak** pass out of one's mind

hatıra memory, remembrance; souvenir; **∼t** *pl.* memories; memoirs

hatırla|mak *v/t* remember; **∼tmak** *-e -i* remind *so.* of

hatırşinas considerate, obliging

hatip preacher, orator

hatta adv. even, to the extent that

hattat calligrapher

hav down (feather); nap

hava air, weather, wind, atmosphere; desire, whim, fancy; ~ alanı airport; ~ korsanı hijacker; ~ kuvvetleri pl. Air Force; ~cı aviator, airman; ~cılık aviation; ~dar airy; ~gazı coal-gas; ~î aerial; fanciful; ~î fişek rocket; ~küre atmosphere; ~lanmak be aired, ventilated; fly

havale assignment, bill of exchange; ~ etm. v/t transfer, refer (-e to); ~name order for payment, money order [bourhood)

havali environs, neigh-}

havan mortar; ~ eli pestle; ~ topu mortar, howitzer

havari rel. Apostle

hava|sız airless, badly ventilated; ~yolu airline

havi -i containing; ~ olm. -i contain

havlamak bark

havlu towel

havra Rel. synagogue

havuç bot. carrot

havuz artificial basin, pond dock; ~lamak v/t dock

havyar caviare

havza river-basin; sphere, domain

hayal spectre, phantom, fancy, imagination; ~î fantastic, imaginary

hayat¹ covered court; courtyard

hayat² life, living; ~ sürmek live a life

haydi! come!; be off!

haydut brigant; ~ yatağı brigands' den; ~luk brigandage

hayhay! certainly!; by all means!

hayır¹ no!

hayır² good, prosperity, excellence; ~ dua blessing, benediction; ~hah benevolent; ~lı good, auspicious; ~lı olsun! good luck to it!; ~sız good-for-nothing; ill-omened

haykır|ış shouting, bawling; ~mak shout, cry out

haylaz idle, lazy; ~lık laziness

hayli much, many; fairly

hayran astonished, perplex; ~ olm. be astonished, perplexed; -e admire

hayret amazement, stupor, admiration; ~te bırakmak v/t astound; ~te kalmak be lost in amazement

haysiyet honour, dignity; ~li self-respecting; ~siz without dignity

hayvan animal; ~at bahçesi zoological garden; ~ca adv. bestially; stupidly; ~î animal, bestial

Hazer denizi Caspian Sea

hazım digestion; ~sız indigestible; irritable

hazır present, ready, prepared; ~ ol! mil. attention!; ~dan yemek live on one's capital; ~cevap quick at reply; **~lamak** v/t prepare; **~lanmak** prepare oneself; be prepared; **~lık** readiness, preparation; **~lop** hardboiled (*egg*)

hazin sad, melancholy.

hazine s. hazne

haziran June

hazmetmek v/t digest; *fig.* swallow

hazne treasure, treasury; reservoir, cistern; **~dar** treasurer

hazret *rel.* Saint; 2i **Peygamber** the Holy Prophet (Muhammed); **~leri** (*after a title*) His Excellency

hece syllable; **~lemek** v/t spell; **~li** having ... syllables

hecin *zo.* dromedary

hedef mark, target; object, aim; **~ tutmak** -*i* aim at

hediye present, gift; **~ etm.** v/t give as a present (-*e* to)

hekim doctor, physician; **~lik** profession of a doctor

helâ closet, privy

helâk destruction, death

helâl *rel.* permitted, lawful

hele above all, especially; at least

helezon snail, spiral

helikopter *av.* helicopter

helva (*sweetmeat made of sesame oil and honey*)

hem and also, too; **~ ... ~ (de)** both ... and, as well as; **~en** at once; just now; about, nearly; exactly; **~en ~en** almost, very nearly; **~şeri** fellow townsman;

compatriot; **~şire** sister; hospital nurse

hendek ditch, moat, trench

hendese geometry

hengâme uproar, tumult

henüz yet, still

hep all, the whole; **~si** all of it *or* them

her every, each; **~ biri** each one; **~ gün** every day; **~ halde** in any case; for sure; **~ hangi** anybody; **~ ne** whatever; **~ ne kadar** however much; although; **~ yerde** everywhere; **~ zaman** every time, always

hercümerç confused, disordered

herhangi s. her hangi

herif fellow, rascal

herkes everyone

hesap counting, reckoning, calculation; account; bill; **~ etm.** v/t calculate; count; **~ tutmak** keep accounts; **~ vermek** -*e* give *so.* an account (*hakkında* of *sth.*); **hesaba katmak** -*i* take into account; **~lamak** v/t reckon, estimate; **~laşmak** settle accounts; **~lı** calculated; **~sız** countless, uncertain

heves desire, inclination; **~kâr, ~li** -*e* desirous of, eager for

heybet awe, majesty

heyecan excitement, enthusiasm; **~lı** excited, enthusiastic

heyet commission, committee

heyhat! alas!

heykel statue; **~tıraş** sculptor

hezeyan talking nonsense

hezimet utter defeat, rout

hıçkırık hiccough, sob; **~mak** have the hiccoughs, sob

hıdrellez beginning of summer (May 6th)

hıfzıssıhha hygiene

hınç hatred, grudge

hır sl. row, quarrel; **~çın** ill-tempered

hırdavat small wares, ironmongery; **~çı** pedlar, ironmonger

hırıl|damak growl, purr; **~tı** growling, snarling

Hıristiyan Christian; **~lık** Christianity

hırlamak growl, snarl

hırpalamak v/t ill-treat, misuse

hırpani in tatters

hırs inordinate desire, greed

hırsız thief; **~lık** theft, thieving

hırs|lanmak -den get angry at; get greedy of; **~lı** angry; avaricious

hısım relative, kin

hışıldamak v/i rustle

hışır unripe (melon)

hışırdamak v/i rustle, rasp

hıyanet treachery, perfidy

hıyar bot. cucumber

hız speed, impetus; **~ almak** get up speed; **~landırmak** v/t accelerate; **~lanmak** gain speed; **~lı** quick, fast; violent

hibe jur. gift, donation

hicr|et emigration; rel. the Hegira; **~i** of the Hegira era

hiç no, nothing; never; (without negation) ever; **~olmazsa** at least; **~bir şey** nothing at all; **~bir yerde** nowhere; **~biri** nobody, none

hiddet violence; anger; **~lenmek** -e be angry with; **~li** angry

hidrojen chem. hydrogen

hikâye narration, story; **~etm.** v/t narrate, tell

hikmet wisdom; inner meaning

hilâf contrary, opposite; -in **~ına** contrary to, against

hilâl crescent

hile trick, wile; fraud; **~ci, ~kâr** wily, deceitful; **~li** fraudulent

himaye protection, defence

himmet effort, zeal; benevolence

hindi zo. turkey

Hindistan India; **2 cevizi** bot. coconut

Hint|li n., adj. Indian; **2yağı** chem. castor oil

his sense, perception

hisar castle, fortress

hisse share; allotted portion; **~dar** shareholder; **~li** having shares, divided into portions

hissetmek v/t feel, perceive

hitabe address, speech; **~t** oratory

hitam conclusion, completion; ~ **bulmak** come to an end

hitap addressing, address; ~ **etm.** -*e* address *so.*

hiyerarşi hierarchy; ~**k** hierarchic(al)

hiza line, level

hizmet service, duty, employment; ~ **etm.** -*e* serve, render service; ~**çi** servant; ~**li** employee

hoca hodja; teacher; ~**lık** teaching

hodbin selfish, egotistical

hokka inkpot; ~**baz** conjurer, cheat; ~**bazlık** cheating, trickery

Hollanda Holland; ~**lı** Dutch

homo|gen homogeneous; ~**seksüel** homosexual

homurdanmak grumble (-*e at*)

hoparlör loudspeaker

hoplamak jump about(-*den* for)

hoppa flighty, flippant; ~**lık** levity, flightiness

hor contemptible; ~ **görmek** -*i* look down upon

horlamak[1] *v/t* treat with contempt

horlamak[2] snore

horoz zo. cock, rooster; ~**i-biği** cockscomb (*a. bot.*); ~**lanmak** strut about

hortlak specter, ghost

hortum zo. trunk; *tech.* hose

horuldamak snore

hostes hostess

hoş pleasant, agreeable; ~

geldiniz! welcome!; ~ **bulduk!** (*answer*) thank you!; ~**lanmak** -*den* like; ~**nut** contented, pleased

hovarda spendthrift; rich lover; ~**lık** dissoluteness

hoyrat coarse and clumsy

hörgüç zo. hump

höyük hill, mound

hububat *pl.* cereals

hudut limits; frontier

hukuk *jur.* law; **Roma** ~**ü** Roman Law; **ticaret** ~**u** commercial law; ~ **devleti** constitutional state; ~**çu** jurist; ~**î** legal, juridicial

hulâsa extract; summary; ~**ten** *adv.* in short

hulul entering, penetrating

hulya day-dream

humma fever; typhus; ~**lı** feverish (*a. fig.*)

huni funnel *for pouring liquids*

hurafe silly tale, superstition; ~**perest** superstitious

hurda old iron, scrap metal; ~**cı** scrap dealer

hurma *bot.* date; ~ **ağacı** date palm

husul occuring, appearance; ~ **bulmak**, ~**e gelmek** be accomplished, attained

husumet enmity, hostility

husus particularity; matter; **bu** ~**ta** in this matter; ~**unda** with reference to; ~**î** special; private; ~**iyet** peculiarity [*the mosque*]

hutbe *rel.* Friday sermon *in*]

huy disposition, temper,

habit; **~lu**, **~suz** bad-tempered   [*etc.*}

huzme *phys.* bunch *of rays,*}

huzur presence; repose; *-in*
　~unda in the presence of

hüccet argument, proof

hücre cell

hücum attack, assault; **~**
　etm. *-e* attack

hüküm|etmek *v/t* rule, dominate; decide on; believe,
assume; **~i** judicial; nominal

hüküm rule, authority;
command, edict; *jur.* sentence; decision; **~ giymek**
be condemned; **~ sürmek**
reign; prevail; **~dar** monarch, ruler

hükümet government,
state, authority

hükümsüz no longer in
force, null

hüner skill, ability, talent;
~li skilful, talented

hüngürdemek *v/i* sob

hür free

hürmet respect, veneration;
~ etm. *-e* respect, honour;
~li venerable, respectable;
~sizlik irreverence, want
of respect

hürriyet freedom, liberty

hüsnü|hal good conduct;
~niyet good intention,
goodwill

hüviyet identity; **~ cüzdanı** identity card

I

ıhlamur *bot.* lime-tree; **~**
　çiçeği lime-blossom

ıkınmak *v/i* grunt, moan

ıklim *s.* iklim

ılgar gallop; foray, raid

ılgın *bot.* tamarisk

ılı|ca hot spring; **~k** tepid;
~m moderation, temperance; **~nmak** become lukewarm

ırak[1] distant (*-den* from)

Irak[2] Irak

ırgat workman

ırk race, lineage; **~çılık**
racialism

ırmak river

ırz honour, chastity; *-in*
　~ına geçmek violate

ısı heat; warm; **~nmak**
grow warm

ısır|gan *bot.* nettle; **~mak**
v/t bite (*-den* into)

ısıtma heating; **~k** *v/t* heat

ıskala *mus.* scale

ıskarta discard (*in card
games*)

ıskat annulment; rejection

ıskonto *ec.* discount

ıslah improvement, reform;
~ etm. *v/t* improve, reform

ısla|k wet; **~nmak** become
wet, be wetted; **~tmak** *v/t*
wet; *vulg.* flog, beat

ıslık whistle; **~ çalmak**
whistle; **~lamak** *v/t* boo

ısmarlama ordered; **~k** *v/t*
order; **Allaha ısmarladık!** good-bye!

ıspanak *bot.* spinach

ısrar insistence; ~ **etm.** *-de* insist on

ıssız lonely, desolate; ~**lık** desolate place, desolation

ıstampa inking-pad

ıstavroz *rel.* cross, sign of the cross; ~ **çıkarmak** cross oneself

ıstakoz *zo.* lobster

ıstılah technical term

ıstırap distress, anxiety

ıstok *ec.* stock, store

ışık light, lamp; ~**landır-mak** *v/t* illuminate, light up; ~**ölçer** photometer

ışılda|k searchlight; ~**mak** shine, sparkle

ışın gleam, flash

ıtır perfume, aroma; ~ **çiçe-ği** *bot.* geranium

ıtriyat *pl.* perfumes

ızgara *n.* grill, grate; *adj.* grilled

ızrar causing harm

I

iade restauration, giving back; ~ **etm.** *v/t* give back, return

iane help, subsidy, donation; ~ **toplamak** collect subscriptions

ibadet worship, prayer; ~ **etm.** *-e* worship

ibare sentence, clause; ~**t olm.** *-den* consist of

ibik *zo.* comb

iblis *rel.* Satan, devil

ibra discharge, acquitting

ibraz display, presentation; ~ **etm.** *v/t* document: present

ibre needle, pointer [sent]

ibret example, warning

ibrik kettle, ewer

ibrişim silk thread

icap requiring, demand; **icabında** in case of necessity; ~ **etm.** *v/i* be necessary; *v/t* necessitate, require

icar letting, leasing; ~ **etm.**, ~**a vermek** *v/t* let out, lease

icat invention; fabrication; ~ **etm.** *v/t* invent, fabricate

icbar compelling, constraining; ~ **etm.** *v/t* compel

icmal summary, resumé

icra execution, performance; ~ **etm.** *v/t* carry out, perform; ~**at** *pl.* performances; acts

iç inside, interior; inner; ~**inde** in, within; ~**ine** into; ~**bükey** *math.* concave

içecek drinkable; drink

içeri inside, interior; in; ~**de** in; ~**den** from the inside; ~**ye** to the inside; ~**si** its interior; ~ **girmek** *v/i* enter

içgüdü instinct

içim mouthful; taste; ~**li** pleasant to the taste

için for, on account of; in order to; **bunun** ~ for this reason

içindekiler *pl.* contents

içirmek *v/t* cause to drink

İçişleri *pl. pol.* Internal Affairs

içki drink, liquor; **~li** licensed to sell alcoholic drinks

içlenmek *-den* be affected, overcome by

içmek *v/t* drink; **tütün ~** smoke *tobacco*

içten *adv.* sincere, from the heart

içtima assembly; **~i** social

içtinap avoidance; **~ etm.** *-den* avoid; abstain from

iç|tüzük statutes; **~yüz** inner meaning, real truth

idam execution; **~ etm.** *v/t* execute, put to death

idame continuance

idare management; administration; economizing; **~ etm.** *v/t* administer, manage, handle; **~ci** good manager, organizer; **~hane** office; **~li** economical; efficient; **~siz** wasteful

idbar adversity

iddia claim, pretension; **~ etm.** *v/t* claim; **~cı** obstinate; **~lı** pretentious; disputed

idman training, sport

idrak perception, intelligence; **~ etm.** *v/t* perceive;

idrar urine [reach, attain]

ifa performance, fulfilment; **~ etm.** *v/t* execute, fulfil

ifade explanation, expression; **~ etm.** *v/t* express, explain

iffet chastity; **~li** chaste; honest

iflâs bankruptcy; **~ etm.** go bankrupt

ifrat excess

ifraz separating; secretion

ifşa divulgation, disclosure; **~ etm.** *v/t* devulge, reveal

iftar *rel.* breaking one's fast

iftihar laudable pride

iftira slander, forgery; **~ etm.** *-e* slander

iğ spindle

iğde *bot.* wild olive, oleaster

iğilmek *s.* eğilmek

iğmek *s.* eğmek

iğne needle, pin; thorn; injection; **~lemek** *v/t* fasten with a pin (*-e* to)

iğren|ç disgust, loathing; repulsive; **~mek** *-den* feel aversion against

iğreti *s.* eğreti

iğri *s.* eğri

iğril|mek, ~tmek *s.* eğrilmek, eğriltmek

ihale *ec.* adjudication

ihanet treachery; **~ etm.** *-e* betray

ihata surrounding; **~ etm.** *v/t* surround, comprehend

ihbar communicating, notification; **~ etm.** *v/t* convey (*-e* to); notify (of)

ihlâl spoiling, infraction

ihmal negligence; **~ etm.** *v/t* neglect; **~ci** negligent, careless

ihracat *pl.* exports

ihraç *ec.* exportation; **~ etm.** *v/t* export

ihraz etm. *v/t* obtain, attain

ihsan kindness, favour

ihtar reminding, warning; **~ etm.** v/t remind, warn of; **~da bulunmak** -e warn, remind so.

ihtifal commemorative ceremony

ihtikâr profiteering; **~cı** profiteer

ihtilâf difference, disagreement

ihtilâl rebellion, revolution

ihtilâs embezzlement; **~ etm.** v/t embezzle

ihtimal probability, possibility

ihtimam care, carefulness

ihtira invention; **~ etm.** v/t invent

ihtiras passion, greed

ihtiraz precaution, avoidance; **~ etm.** -den guard against, avoid

ihtisas[1] sentiment; affection

ihtisas[2] specialization; **~ sahibi** specialist

ihtişam pomp

ihtiva etm. v/t contain, include

ihtiyaç want, necessity; **~cı olm.** -e be in need of

ihtiyar[1] old

ihtiyar[2] choice, selection; **~î** optional, voluntary

ihtiyar|lamak grow old; **~lık** old age

ihtiyat precaution; reserve; **~î** precautionary; **~sız** incautious, imprudent

ihtizaz vibration

ihya bringing to life; **~ etm.** v/t animate; enliven

ikame setting up; establishing; substitution

ikamet residence, dwelling; **~ etm.** -de dwell, stay in; **~ tezkeresi** residence permit; **~gâh** place of residence, domicile

ikaz rousing, warning

ikbal good fortune, success

iken conj. while; when

iki two; **~de bir** one in two, every other; frequently; **~si** both of them; **~lemek** v/t make two, make a pair; **~lik** consisting of two; disunion; **~ncil** secondary

ikindi rel. the time of the afternoon prayer

iki|yüzlü having two faces; hypocrite; **~z** twins; twin

iklim geo. climate, region

ikmal completion; **~ etm.** v/t complete, finish

ikna etm. v/t convince, persuade

ikram showing honour, kindness; **~ etm.** -e show honour to; v/t offer sth. (-e to); **~iye** bonus, gratuity; prize in a lottery

ikrar declaration, confession

ikraz loan; **~ etm.** v/t lend

iktibas quotation, adaptation

iktidar power, ability; pol. party in power, government [with)]

iktifa etm. be content (ile)

iktisadî economic

iktisap acquisition, gain; **~ etm.** v/t acquire, gain

iktisat economy

il province; country

ilâ up to, towards, until

ilâç remedy; medicine

ilâh god; ~e goddess; ~î divine; ~iyat theology

ilâm *jur.* decree in writing

ilân declaration, notice; advertisement; ~ etm. *v/t* declare, announce

ilâve addition, supplement; ~ etm. *v/t* add (-e to)

ilçe prov. district

ile with; by means of; and

ileri forward part, front; forward; fast (*clock*); advanced; ~ci progressive

iler(i)de in front; in future

ilerigelenler *pl.* notables

ilerle|mek *v/i* advance, progress; ~tmek *v/t* cause to advance; ~yiş progress

ilet|ken tranferring; *phys.* conducting; ~mek *v/t* carry off, send; *phys.* conduct

ilga abolition, annulment

ilgi interest; ~lendirmek *v/t* arouse one's interest; ~lenmek be interested (ile in); ~li ile interested in, connected with; ~nç interesting; ~siz not interested

ilhak annexation; ~ etm. *v/t* annex

ilham inspiration

ilik[1] marrow

ilik[2] buttonhole; ~lemek *v/t* button up

ilikli[1] buttoned

ilikli[2] containing marrow

ilim knowledge; science

iliş|ik -e connected with, attached to; connexion, relation; ~ki relation, connection; ~kin -e concerning, regarding; ~mek -e interfere with; be fastened to; ~tirmek *v/t* fasten (-e to); attach

ilk first, initial; ~ defa (for) the first time; ~bahar spring; ~çağ ancient times *pl.*; ~e substance; principle; ~el elementary; primitive; ~okul primary school

illâ, ille whatever happens; by all means; or else

illet disease, defect; cause,

ilmî scientific [reason]

ilmik loop, noose

ilmühaber identity papers; certificate

iltica etm. -e take refuge in

iltifat favour

iltihak joining, adherence

iltihap *med.* inflamation; ~lanmak become inflamed

iltimas request; protection, patronage; ~lı who gets a job by favouritism, favoured

iltizam favouring; *pol.* farming of *revenues*; ~ etm. *v/t* take the part of, favour

ima allusion, hint; ~ etm. -e allude to, hint at

imal manufacture; ~ etm. *v/t* make, produce; ~âthane factory, workshop

imam *rel.* leader of the ritual prayer, Imam; ~bayıldı (a dish of eggplants with oil and onions)

iman belief, faith; **~sız** unbelieving; atheist

imar improvement, cultivation; **~ etm.** v/t improve, render prosperous

imaret soup-kitchen *for the poor*

imbik retort, still

imdat help, assistance; **~ freni** emergency brake; **~ kapısı** emergency exit

imge image

imha distruction, effacement; **~ etm.** v/t obliterate, destroy

imkân possibility, practicability; **~sız** impossible

imlâ spelling, orthography

imparator Emperor; **~içe** Empress; **~luk** Empire

imrenmek -e long for, desire

imsak temperance, diet; *rel.* hour at which the daily Ramazan fast begins

imtihan trial, test; examination; **~ etm.** v/t examine

imtiyaz privilege, concession; **~lı** privileged, autonomous

imza signature; **~ etm.** v/t, **~ atmak** -e sign; **~lamak** v/t sign

in den, lair

inadına adv. out of obstinacy

inak dogma

inan belief, trust; **~ç** belief, confidence; **~dırmak** -i -e cause so. to believe sth.; **~lır** credible; **~mak** -e believe, trust

inat obstinacy; **~çı** obstinate, pig-headed

ince slender, thin, fine, slight; **~lemek** v/t examine; **~ltmek** v/t make fine, slender, refine; **~saz** mus. Turkish orchestra of stringed instruments

inci pearl; **~ çiçeği** bot. lily of the valley

incik[1] an. shin

incik[2] bruised; sprain

İncil rel. Gospel, New Testament

incinmek be sprained; be hurt, offended (-den by)

incir bot. fig; **~ ağacı** fig-tree

incitmek v/t hurt; touch; offend

indî subjective, arbitrary

indir|im lowering, reduction; **~mek** v/t cause to descend, lower

inek cow [out)

infaz execution, carrying)

infilâk explosion

İngiliz English(man); **~ anahtarı** spanner; **~ce** English (language)

İngiltere England

inha memorandum

inhina curving, bend

inhiraf deviation

inhisar monopoly

inhitat decline, degradation

inil|demek echo, resound; **~ti** echo; moan, groan

inisiyatif initiative

iniş descent, slope; landing

inkâr denial, refusal; **~ etm.** v/t deny, refuse

inkılâp revolution; **~çı** revolutionary

inkıraz decline, extinction

inkişaf development; **~ etm.** *v/i* develop

inlemek moan, groan

inme descending; fall *of the tide*; *med.* apoplexy, stroke; **~k** *v/i* descend, land; fall (*price*)

insaf justice, fairness; **~lı** just, equitable; **~sız** unjust, unfair

insan human being; man; **~iyet**, **~lık** humanity; humankind; **~üstü** superhuman

insicam coherence, harmony

insiyak instinct

insiyatif *s.* **inisiyatif**

inşa construction, creation; **~ etm.** *v/t* construct, build; **~at** *pl.* building *sg.*; works

inşallah if God pleases; I hope that

intibak adaptation, adjustment

intihap choice; *pol.* election; **~ etm.** *v/t* choose; *pol.* elect

intihar suicide; **~ etm.** commit suicide

intikal transition, transfer

intikam revenge; **~almak -den** take revenge on

intişar publication, dissemination

intizam regularity, order; **~sız** irregular, disordered; **~sızlık** disorder

intizar expectation; curse

inzibat disciplin; *mil.* military police

ip rope, cord, string

ipek silk; silken; **~ böceği** *zo.* silkworm; **~li** of silk

iplik thread, sewing-cotton

ipotek mortgage

iptal rendering null and void; **~ etm.** *v/t* annul

iptida beginning; **~î** primitive, elementary

iptilâ addiction (-e to)

irade will, command; decree

İran Persia; **~lı** Persian

irat income, revenue

irfan knowledge, culture

iri huge, voluminous; **~baş** *zo.* tadpole; **~leşmek** become large; **~lik** largeness; size

irin pus, filth; **~lenmek** suppurate

irk|**ilmek** become stagnant; *med.* swell, tumefy; **~inti** stagnant pool

İrlanda Ireland; **~lı** Irish

irmik semolina

irs inheritance

irsal sending; **~ etm.** *v/t* send

irsî hereditary

irtibat connection; communication

irtica going back, reaction

irtidat *rel.* apostasy *from Islam*

irtifa elevation; altitude

irtikâp bribery, corruption; **~ etm.** *v/t* commit, perpetrate

is soot

İsa Jesus
isabet hitting the mark; thing done right; ~ **etm.** *-e* hit; fall to *one's share*
is'af compliance
ise however, as for; when, if; ~ **de** although
ishal purging, diarrhoea
isim name; *gr.* noun; ~**lendirmek** *v/t* name, call
iskambil playing card; *(kind of card game)*
iskân settling, inhabiting; ~ **etm.** *v/t* settle, inhabit
iskandil *naut.* sounding-lead
iskarpela carpenter's chisel
iskarpin low shoe
iskele *naut.* landing-place, quay; port; larboard
iskelet skeleton
iskemle chair, stool
İskender|iye Alexandria; ~**un** Alexandrette
İskoç Scotch; ~**ya** Scotland; ~**yalı** Scottish, Scotsman
iskonto *ec.* discount
iskorbüt scurvy
İslâm Islam; ~**iyet** the Moslem world
İslanda Iceland
islenmek become black with soot
islim steam
ismet chastity, innocence
isnat imputation; ~ **etm.** *v/t ile* accuse *so.* of, charge *so.* with
İspanya Spain; ~**lı** Spanish
İspanyol Spanish; Spaniard; ~**ca** Spanish *(language)*

ispat proof, confirmation; ~ **etm.** *v/t* prove, confirm
ispinoz *zo.* chaffinch
ispirto alcohol
İsrail Israel
israf wasteful expenditure; ~ **etm.** *v/t* waste, squander
istasyon station
istatistik statistics
istavroz *s.* **ıstavroz**
istek wish, longing; ~**li** interested; bidder; candidate; ~**siz** unwilling; apathetic
iste|m volition; *ec.* demand; ~**mek** *v/t* wish for, desire, want
isteri *med.* hysteria
istibdat despotism, absolute rule
isticar hiring; ~ **etm.** *v/t* take on hire
isticvap interrogation
istida demand, petition; ~ **etm.** *v/t* demand, request
istif stowage, arrangement of goods; ~ **etm.** *v/t* pack, stow
istifa resignation; ~ **etm.** *-den* resign from
istifade profit, advantage; ~ **etm.** *-den* benefit, profit by
istif|çi packer, stevedore; ~**lemek** *v/t* stow, pack; hoard
istihbar asking for information; ~**at bürosu** information office [pursue]
istihdaf etm. *v/t* aim at,
istihdam employment; ~ **etm.** *v/t* take into service, employ

istihkâm fortification; military engineering
istihlâk consumption
istihsal producing; production; ~ **etm.** *v/t* produce, obtain
istihza ridicule, mockery
istikamet direction
istikbal future
istiklâl independence; 2 **Marşı** the Turkish National Anthem
istikrar stability
istikraz loan; ~ **etm.** *v/t* borrow
istilâ invasion; ~ **etm.** -**e** invade
istim steam
istimal using, making use of
istimdat asking for help
istimlâk *jur.* expropriation; ~ **etm.** *v/t* expropriate
istinaden -**e** based on
istinat relying (-**e** upon); ~ **etm.** -**e** rely on, lean on
istintak *jur.* interrogation cross-examination; ~ **etm.** *v/t* interrogate
istirahat repose; ~ **etm.** rest, take one's ease
istirdat restitution
istirham asking a favour; petition; ~ **-den** -**i** petition, ask *so.* for *sth.*
istiridye *zo.* oyster
istismar *etm. v/t* exploit
istisna exception; ~ **etm.** *v/t* exclude; **~î** exceptional
istişare consultation; ~ **kurulu** advisory council
istizah *pol.* interpellation; ~

etm. *v/t* ask for an explanation, question
İsveç Sweden; **~li** Swedish
İsviçre Switzerland; **~li** Swiss [rebel]
isyan rebellion; ~ **etm.** ⌡
iş work, action; business, occupation; affair; ~ **başında** at one's work; **~im var** I am busy; **~alan** employee
işaret sign, signal, mark; ~ **zamiri** *gr.* demonstrative pronoun; ~ **etm.** -**e** mark; indicate; **~lemek** *v/t* mark, denote
iş/başı foreman; **~birliği** cooperation; **~bölümü** division of labour
işbu this, the present
işçi workman, labourer; **~lik** occupation *or* pay of a workman
işemek *v/i* urinate
işgal occupation; ~ **etm.** *v/t* keep busy; *mil.* occupy
işgüder *pol.* chargé d'affaires
işgüzar efficient
işit/ilmek be heard; **~mek** *v/t* hear, listen to
işkembe paunch, tripe
işkence torture; ~ **etm.** -**e** torture
işkil doubt; suspicion
işle/k good flowing; busy; **~me** handiwork; embroidery; **~mek** *v/t* work, manipulate, work up; carve, engrave; -**e** penetrate; **~meli** embroidered; **~n-mek** be worked up; **~r** functioning

işletme working, running; administration, management; **~k** v/t cause to work, run, operate

işporta open basket; **~cı** peddler

işsiz unemployed; **~lik** unemployment

iştah appetite, desire; **~sız** without appetite

işte look!; here!; now, thus

iştikak derivation; **~ ettirmek** v/t derive (-den from)

iştirak participation; **~ etm. -e** participate in

iştiyak longing

işveren employer

it dog

itaat obedience; **~ etm. -e** obey; **~li** obedient; **~siz** disobedient

İtalya Italy; **~n** Italian; **~nca** Italian (language)

itfaiye fire-brigade

ithaf dedication; **~ etm.** v/t dedicate (-e to)

ithal import; **~ etm.** v/t import; **~ gümrüğü** import duty; **~ât** pl. imports

itham imputation, accusation; **~ etm.** v/t accuse (ile of)

itibar esteem, regard, credit; **~ etm. -e** esteem, show consideration; **~ nazarına almak** -i consider, take into account; **~dan düşmek** to be discredited; **~en** -den from, dating from; **~î** nominal, theoretical

itikat belief, creed

itilâf agreement, understanding

itimat confidence, reliance; **~ etm. -e** rely on, have confidence in; **~name** pol. letter of credentials

itina care, attention; **~sız** careless, inattentive

itiraf confession, admission; **~ etm.** v/t confess, admit

itiraz objection; **~ etm. -e** object to

itişmek push one another

itiyat habit

itizar apologizing, excuse

itlâf destruction; waste

itmek v/t push

ittifak concord; alliance

ittihat union

ittihaz etm. v/t procure; take

ittisal being in contact

ivdirmek v/t hasten; **~edi(lik)** haste; **~mek** be in a hurry

iye possessor, owner; **~lik zamiri** gr. possessive pronoun

iyi good, well; the good; **en ~si** the best of it; **~ce** well, rather good; **~leşmek** get better, improve; **~leştirmek** v/t improve; **~lik** goodness, kindness; **~mser** optimistic

iyot chem. iodine

iz footprint, track, trace

izaf|et (terkibi) gr. nominal compound; **~î** relative; nominal

izah explanation; **~ etm.**

v/t manifest, explain; **~at** *pl.* explanations

izale removing

izci tracker; boy-scout

izdiham crowd

izdivaç matrimony

izhar display, manifestation; **~ etm.** *v/t* show, display

izin permission, leave; **~ vermek** *-e* grant leave, give permission; **~li** on leave; with permission; **~siz** without permission

izlemek *v/t* trace

izole etm. *v/t* el., *phys.* insulate, isolate

izzet might, glory, honour

J

jambon ham

jandarma police soldier, gendarme

jant *tech.* rim of a *wheel*

Japon Japanese; **~ca** Japanese (*language*); **~ya** Japan

jelatin gelatine

jeolo|g geologist; **~ji** geolo-)

jest gesture   [gy]

jet *av.* jet-plane

jilet safety-razor; razorblade

jimnastik *s.* cimnastik

jüri *jur.* jury

K

kaba large, coarse, rough, vulgar; **~dayı** rough fellow, bully

kabahat fault; offence; **~li** guilty; **~siz** innocent

kabak 1. *bot.* pumpkin; marrow; **2.** *fig.* bald, close-shaven; worn out (*tyre*)

kaba|kulak *med.* mumps; **~laşmak** become coarse or vulgar; **~lık** sponginess; coarseness

kabar|cık *med.* bubble, pimple, pustle; **~ık** swollen, blistered, puffy; **~ma** flood-tide, high-water; **~mak** swell, become fluffy, be raised; **~tı** swelling; **~tma** *adj.* embossed, in relief; *n.* relief

kabız *med.* constipation

kabil *-e* capable of, possible)

kabile tribe   [for]

kabiliyet capability, possibility; **~li** intelligent, skilful; **~siz** incapable

kabine *pol.* cabinet; small room

kabir grave, tomb

kablo *el.* cable

kabotaj *naut.* cabotage, coast navigation

kabristan cemetery

kabuk bark, rind, peel, skin, shell, crust; **~unu soymak** peel, skin; **~lu** having a shell, *etc.*

kabul acceptance; reception; consent; **~ etm.** *v/t* accept, receive, consent to

kaburga *an.* thorax; rib; *naut.* frame of a ship

kâbus nightmare

kabz|a handle, hilt; **~ımal** *ec.* middleman

kaç how many?; how much?; **saat ~?** what is the time?; **~a?** what is the price?

kaçak fugitive, deserter; contraband; **~çı** smuggler; **~çılık** smuggling

kaçamak flight, evasion, subterfuge; **~lı** evasive

kaçık crazy; ladder *in a stocking*; **~lık** craziness

kaç|ınılmaz inevitable; **~ınmak** *-den* abstain from, avoid; **~ırmak** *v/t* make or let escape, drive away; miss; smuggle; **~ışmak** *v/i* disperse, flee in confusion; **~mak** flee, run away (*-den* from); escape

kadar 1. as much as, as big as; like, about; **beşyüz ~** about five hundred; **2. -e** up to, until; *-ınceye* **~** *conj.* until; **yarına ~** until to-morrow

kadastro land survey

kadavra corpse, carcass

kadayıf (*various kinds of sweet pastry*)

kadeh glass, cup; wineglass

kadem foot; pace

kademe step, stair, rung; degree; **~li** stepped

kader destiny, fate, providence

kadı Moslem judge, Cadi

kadın woman; matron; **~-**

budu (*meat ball with eggs and rice*); **~göbeği** (*sweet dish made with semolina and eggs*)

kadife velvet

kadim old, ancient

kadir¹ *adj.* powerful, capable (*-e* of)

kadir² worth, value

kadran *tech.* face, dial

kadro staff, roll, cadre

kafa head; nape; intelligence; **~dar** intimate, like-minded; **~lı** having a head; intelligent

kafes cage, lattice, grating; **~li** latticed

kâfi sufficient, enough (*-e* for)

kafile caravan, convoy

kâğıt paper; letter; **~ para** paper money

kağnı two-wheeled ox-cart

kâhin soothsayer, seer

kahkaha loud laughter

kahraman hero, gallant; **~lık** heroism

kahr|etmek *v/t* overpower; *v/i* be distressed; **~olmak** be depressed; **~olsun!** to hell with him!

kahvaltı breakfast

kahve coffee; Oriental coffee-house; **~ değirmeni** coffee-mill; **~ci** coffee-maker; **~rengi** brown

kâhya steward, majordomo

kaide base, rule, principle
kâinat universe
kak¹ dried fruit
kak² puddle, pool
kakao cocoa
kakırdamak rattle, rustle, crackle; *sl.* die
kakışmak keep nudging (**ile** *so.*)
kakma repoussé work; **~k** *v/t* push, nail, encrust
kaktüs *bot.* cactus
kala *-e* to (*time*); **saat ona beş ~** five minutes to ten
kalabalık crowd, throng, confused mass
kalafatlamak *v/t* caulk, careen
kalas beam, plank
kalay tin; **~cı** tinsmith; **~lamak** *v/t* tin; **~lı** tinned
kalbî cardiac; cordial
kalbur sieve; **~dan geçirmek**, **~lamak** *v/t* sieve, sift
kalça *an.* hip
kaldır|aç *tech.* lever; **~ım** pavement, causeway; **~mak** *v/t* raise, erect, lift; remove; abolish
kale fortress, castle; goal; **~ci** goalkeeper
kalem reed; pen; paintbrush; office; **~e almak** *v/t* write, draw up; **~tıraş** pencil-sharpener
kalender unconventional
kalfa assistant master; qualified workman
kalın thick, stout, coarse; **~laşmak** become thick *or* stout; **~lık** thickness

kalınmak stay, stop
kalıntı remnant, remainder
kalıp mould, form, model; **~lamak** *v/t* form
kalıt inheritance
kalifiye qualified
kalite quality
kalkan shield
kalkın|dırmak *v/t* cause to recover; lead towards progress; **~ma** recovery; progress, development; **~mak** *v/i* recover, rise
kalkış rising; departure
kalkışmak *-e try to do sth.*
kalkmak rise, get up
kalmak remain, be left
kalori calory; **~fer** central heating
kaloş galosh
kalp¹ 1. *n.* change, transformation; 2. *adj.* false, spurious, forged
kalp² *an.* heart; **~ sektesi** heart attack
kalpak fur cap
kalpazan counterfeiter
kama dagger, wedge
kamara ship's cabin; 2 House *of Lords or Commons*
kamaş|mak be dazzled; **~tırmak** *v/t* dazzle
kambiyo *ec.* foreign exchange (office)
kambur *n., adj.* hunchback(ed)
kamçı whip; **~lamak** *v/t* whip; *fig.* stimulate
kamer *astr.* moon; **~ yılı** lunar year; **~iye** arbour
kamış reed, cane

kâmil perfect, complete

kamp camp; camping; ~ **yeri** camping place; ~**anya** cropping-season

kamu everybody; public; ~ **hizmeti** public service; ~ **oyu** public opinion; ~ **yararı** public interest; ~**laştırmak** v/t nationalize; **2tay** pol. National Assembly

kamyon truck; ~**et** small truck, station-car

kan blood; ~ **gütmek** continue blood feud; -in ~**ına dokunmak** make one's blood boil

kanaat contentment, conviction; opinion; ~ **getirmek** come to the conclusion (-e that); ~**kâr** contented

Kanada Canada; ~**lı** Canadian

kanal canal; ~**izasyon** canalization

kanama bleeding; ~**k** bleed

kanarya zo. canary-bird

kanat wing (a. zo., tech.), leaf of a door; ~**lanmak** take wing, fly away; ~**lı** winged, folded

kanatmak v/t make bleed

kanca large hook; ~**lamak** v/t put on a hook; grapple with a hook

kançılar pol. head of the registry office of a consulate; ~**ya** consular office

kandırmak v/t satisfy, convince; take in, cheat

kandil oil-lamp; ~ **gecesi** rel. the nights of four Moslem feasts when the minarets are illuminated with oil-lamps

kanepe sofa

kangal coil, skein

kanı conviction, opinion

kanık content, satisfied; ~**samak**, ~**sımak** -e be satiated by; become inured to

kanıt proof, evidence; ~**lamak** v/t prove

kanlanmak become soiled with blood; increase one's blood; ~**lı** bloody

kanmak be satiated with; believe

kanser med. cancer

kansız med. anaemic; ~**lık** anaemia

kantar weighing-machine

kantin canteen

kanun[1] mus. (a zither-like instrument)

kanun[2] rule, law; code of laws; ~**i**, ~**lu** legal, legislative; ~**iyet**, ~**luluk** legality; ~**suzluk** lawlessness

kanyak brandy

kap[1] cape, mantle

kap[2] receptacle; vessel; cover

kapak cover, lid; ~**lanmak** v/i fall on one's face; capsize

kapa|lı shut, covered, closed; ~**mak** v/t shut, close, cover up; ~**n** trap; ~**nış** closing; ~**nmak** be shut, closed, covered up

kaparo ec. earnest money

kapatmak v/t shut, close; get very cheap

kapı door, gate; ~cı doorkeeper

kapılmak -e carried away by

kapışmak v/t snatch, scramble for; v/i get to grips (**ile** with)

kapital capital; ~ist capitalist; ~izm capitalism

kapitalisyon pol. capitulation

kaplamak v/t cover (-e with); bind, line

kaplan zo. tiger

kaplıca thermal spring

kaplumbağa zo. tortoise

kapmak v/t snatch, seize, carry off

kaporta bonnet, hood (auto); naut. skylight

kapot s. **kaput**

kapsa|m contents pl.; ~mak v/t comprise, contain

kapsül capsule

kaptan captain

kaptıkaçtı minibus

kaput mil. cloak; bonnet, hood (auto)

kar snow; ~ topu snowball; ~ yağmak snow

kâr gain, profit

kara[1] n. mainland, shore; ~ya çıkmak go ashore; ~ya oturmak naut. run aground, be stranded

kara[2] black, gloomy; ~ağaç bot. elm; ~basan nightmare; ~biber bot. black pepper; ~borsa black market; ~ca zo. roe, deer;

~ciğer liver; ♀deniz Black Sea; ~fatma zo. cockroach; ~göz Turkish shadow-play; Turkish Punch; ~kol police-station; ~koncolos bogy, vampire

karakter character; ~istik characteristic

kara|**kuş** zo. eagle; ~lamak v/t blacken, dirty

karanfil bot. pink

karanlık darkness, dark

karantina quarantine

karar decision, resolution, agreement; firmness; ~ vermek decide (hakkında upon); ~a varmak reach a decision; ~gâh headquarters

kararlaş|mak be agreed (hakkında upon); ~tırmak v/t decide, resolve on

kararlı settled, decided; ~lık stability

kararmak become black, dark

karar|name decree; ~sız unstable, restless; ~sızlık instability, indecision

karartmak v/t blacken, black-out

karavan caravan, trailer; ~a mil. mess tin; meal

karayolu overland route

karbon chem. carbon; ~ kâğıdı carbon paper

karbüratör tech. carburator [shaft]

kardan mili tech. cardan

kardeş brother; sister; ~çe brotherly, fraternal; ~lik brotherhood

kare square; ~li in squares, chequered

karga zo. crow; ~burun who has a prominent nose

kargaşa(lık) disorder, tumult

kargı pike, javelin

kargı|mak v/t curse; ~ş cursing

karı wife; woman; ~ koca wife and husband, couple

karık n. snow-blindness; adj. snow-blind

karın belly, stomach

karınca zo. ant

karış span

karışık mixed, confused; ~lık confusion, disorder

karış|mak -e interfere, meddle with; ~tırmak v/t mix; confuse

karina bottom of a ship

karlı covered with snow

kârlı profitable, advantageous

karma mixed; ~ eğitim co-education

karmak v/t knead; mix; thrust (-e into)

karmakarışık adj. in utter disorder

karnabahar bot. cauliflower

karne schoolboy's report; book of tickets

karpuz bot. water-melon

karşı -e opposed to, against; -in ~sına, sında opposite to, in front of; ~ya face to face

karşıla|mak v/t meet; reply to; oppose; ~nmak be

met; ~şmak meet face to face; ~ştırmak v/t confront; compare

karşılık reply, retort; equivalent; ~lı equivalent; reciprocal

karşıt adj. opposite, contrary (-e to)

kart[1] old, hard, dry

kart[2] card

kartal zo. eagle

karton cardboard

kart|postal postcard; ~vizit visiting-card

karyola bedstead

kasa chest, safe; cashier's office

kasaba small town

kasadar cashier

kasap butcher

kâse bowl, basin

kasık an. groin

kasım November

kasınmak shrink; be conceited

kasırga whirlwind, cyclone

kasıt intention, endeavour

kasket cap

kasmak v/t tighten, curtail; oppress

kasnak rim, hoop

kastarlamak v/t bleach

kast|en adv. intentionally, deliberately; ~etmek v/t purpose, intend; mean; ~i adj. deliberate

kasvet depression, gloom; ~li oppressive; gloomy

kaş eyebrow; something curved

kaşar sheep cheese

kaşık spoon

kaşı|mak v/t scratch; **~n-mak** scratch oneself; itch

kâşif discoverer, revealer

kaşkaval soft cheep cheese

kat fold, layer; coating; story *of a building*

katalog catalogue

katar file *of camels, etc.*; train

kategori category

katetmek v/t cut, traverse

katı hard, violent, strong; **~ yürekli** strong-hearted

katılaş|mak become hard or heavy; **~tırmak** v/t make hard or strong

katılık hardness, severity

katılmak -e be added to, join

katır zo. mule

katıyağ solid oil, paraffin

katî definite, decisive

katil[1] killing, murder

katil[2] murderer

kâtip clerk, secretary

katiye|n adv. definitely, absolutely; **~t** definiteness

katkı addition, supplement; **~da bulunmak** -e be added to

katla|mak v/t fold, pleat; **~nmak** -e be folded into; undergo, suffer, endure

katl|etmek v/t kill, murder; **~iam** general massacre

katma addition; **~değer vergisi** surplus value tax; **~k** v/t add (-e to), join, mix

katman layer, stratum

katmer a kind of pastry; multiplicity; **~li** manifold, multiplied

Katolik Catholic; **~lik** Catholicism

katran tar; **~lamak** v/t tar; **~lı** tarred

kauçuk caoutchouc, unvulcanized rubber

kav tinder

kavak bot. poplar

kaval shepherd's pipe

kavalye cavalier; male partner *in a dance*

kavanoz jar, pot

kavas guard or attendant *of an embassy or consulate*

kavga brawl, quarrel, fight; **~cı** quarrelsome; **~lı** quarreling, angry

kavis bow, arc, curve

kavla|k barkless, peeled off; **~mak** peel off, fall off

kavra|m concept, idea; **~mak** v/t seize, grasp; **~yış** conception, understanding

kavşak junction, crossroads

kavuk quilted turban

kavun bot. muskmelon

kavurmak v/t fry; roast

kavuşak s. **kavşak**

kavuş|mak -e reach, attain, touch, meet; **~turmak** v/t bring together, unite, join; **~um** astr. conjunction

kay med. vomiting

kaya rock

kayak ski

kayalık rocky place

kayb|etmek v/t lose; **~ol-mak** be lost, disappear

kayd|etmek v/t enrol, register; **~ol(un)mak** -e be registered in

kaygan slippery; polished

kaygana omelet

kaygı care, anxiety; **~lanmak** be worried; **~lı** worried, anxious

kaygın polished, slippery

kaygısız carefree; **~lık** freedom from care

kayık 1. n. boat, caique; **2.** adj. displaced

kayın¹ beech

kayın² brother-in-law; **~baba** father-in-law; **~birader** brother-in-law; **~peder** s. **~baba**; **~valide** mother-in-law

kayıp 1. n. loss; **2.** adj. lost

kayırmak v/t protect, care)

kayısı bot. apricot [for]

kayış¹ slipping

kayış² strap, belt

kayıt registration, enrolment; restriction; **~ sildirme** cancellation, deletion of a record; **~lamak** v/t restrict, limit; **~lı** registered; restricted; **~sız** unregistered; carefree; **~sızlık** indifference, carelessness

kaymak¹ v/i slip, slide

kaymak² n. cream

kaymakam head official of a district

kaynak 1. spring, fountain; source; **2.** tech. weld, welding

kaynamak v/i boil, spout up

kaynana mother-in-law

kaynaş|mak v/i unite, weld (**ile** with); **~tırmak** v/t weld together

kaynata father-in-law

kaynatmak v/t cause to boil; boil, weld

kaypak slippery; stolen

kaytan cotton or silk cord

kaz goose; **~ beyinli** stupid, silly

kaza 1. accident, mischance; **2.** jur. office and functions of a Cadi; **3.** pol. district; **~en** adv. by accident

Kazak Cossack

kazalı dangerous

kazan couldron; boiler

kazan|ç gain, profits; **~dırmak** v/t cause to win sth.; **~mak** v/t earn, win, gain

kazazede ruined, shipwrecked

kazı excavation; **~cı** excavator; engraver

kazık stake, peg, pile; trick, swindle; **~çı** swindler; **~lamak** v/t cheat, play a trick on

kazımak v/t scratch, eradicate, erase

kazma digging; pickaxe, mattock; **~k** v/t dig, excavate; engrave

kebap roast meat

kebze an. shoulder-blade

keçe felt; mat

keçi goat

keder care, grief, affliction; **~lenmek** be sorrowful, anxious; **~li** sorrowful, grieved

kedi zo. cat; **~otu** bot. valerian

kefalet jur. bail, security

kefaret rel. atonement

kefe scale *of a balance*

kefen shroud

kefil *jur.* bail, guarantor; ~ olm. stand as surety (*-e* for); ~lik bail, security

kehle louse; ~lenmek become lousy

kehlibar amber

kek cake

keke stammering; ~lemek *v/i* stammer, stutter; ~me having a stammer

kekik *bot.* thyme

kekre acrid, sharp

kel *n. med.* ringworm; *adj.* bald, scabby

kelebek *zo.* butterfly

kelek *adj.* partly bald, immature; *n.* unripe melon

kelepçe handcuffs; *tech.* pipe clip

kelepir bargain

keler *zo.* lizard; reptile

kelime word

kelle head

kemal perfection, maturity; value, price

keman violine; *arch.* bow; ~cı violinist; ~e *mus.* bow *for a violine, etc.*

kemer belt, girdle; *arch.* arch, vault; aqueduct

kemik bone; ~li having bones, bony

kemir|**gen** *zo.* rodent; ~mek *v/t* gnaw, nibble

kemiyet quantity

kenar edge, border; shore; ~lı having an edge *or* margin; having a hem

kendi self; ~ ~ne by himself, all alone; ~ni beğen-

mek be arrogant, conceited; ~si himself; ~liğinden of one's own accord, spontaneous; ~lik personality

kene *zo.* tick

kenet *tech.* metal clamp; ~lemek *v/t* clamp together

kenevir *bot.* hemp

kent town, city

kepaze vile, contemptible; ~lik vileness, degradation

kepçe skimmer, ladle

kepek *bot.* bran

kepenk pull-down shutter, wooden cover

keramet *rel.* miracle

kere time; üç ~ three times

kerempe *naut.* rocky promontory

kereste timber; material for making shoes

kerevet wooden bedstead

kereviz *bot.* celery

kerhane brothel

kerpeten pincers

kerpiç sun-dried brick

kerte notch, score; degree

kertenkele *zo.* lizard

kert|**ik** notch, gash; ~mek *v/t* notch, scratch, gash

kervan caravan; ~saray caravanserai

kesbetmek *s.* kesp etm.

kese purse, small bag; coarse cloth bath glove; ~ kâğıdı paper bag

keser adze   [paper bag]

kesif dense, thick

kesi|**k** cut, broken; curdled; ~lmek be cut; cease; be exhausted; be cut off; ~m cutting; section, sector

kesin definite, certain; **~leşmek** become certain or definite; **~ti** deduction; interruption

kesir breaking, fracture; math. fraction

kesişmek conclude an agreement, settle an account (**ile** with)

keski bill-hook, coulter

keskin sharp, keen; **~leşmek** become sharp, severe; **~lik** sharpness, incisiveness

kesme adj. cut; fixed(price); **~k** v/t cut, cut off; interrupt; define; diminish; coin

kesp etm. v/t earn, acquire

kestane bot. chestnut

kestirmek v/t cause to cut, shorten; cause to cease; decide

keşfetmek v/t uncover, discover

keşide drawing in a lottery

keşif discovery

keşiş rel. Christian priest; monk

keşke, keşki would that ...!

keşkül sweetened milk with pistachio nuts and almonds

keten flax; linen

ketum discreet, keeping a secret

keyfletmek amuse, enjoy oneself; **~i** arbitrary, capricious; **~iyet** condition; quality

keyif health; inclination, whim; tipsy; **~ çatmak** enjoy oneself; **~li** merry, happy; **~siz** indisposed;

~sizlik indisposition; depression

kez time; **bu ~** this time

keza(lik) thus, too

kıble rel. direction of Mecca to which a Moslem prays

Kıbrıs Cyprus; **~lı** Cypriote

kıç hinder part, behind

kıdem priority, seniority; **~li** senior in service

kıkırda|k an. cartilage, gristle; **~mak** rustle, rattle; sl. die

kıl hair, bristle

kılavuz guide; naut. pilot; **~luk** profession of a guide

kılçık fish-bone; string of a bean

kılıç sword; **~ balığı** zo. sword-fish

kılıf case; sheath

kılık shape, appearance, costume

kılınmak be done, performed

kılmak v/t render, make; perform

kımılda|(n)mak v/i move, shake; **~tmak** v/t move,}
kın sheath   [shake}

kına henna; **~lı** dyed with henna

kına|mak v/t reproach; **~msımak** v/t find fault with

kınnap yarn; twine

kıpır|da(n)mak move slightly, vibrate; **~tı** slight quiver

kıp|kırmızı, ~kızıl bright red

k**ır 1.** *n.* country, wilderness; **2.** *adj.* grey

kıraathane reading room, coffee-house

kıraç parched, sterile

kırağı white frost

kıral king; **~içe** queen; **~lık** kingdom, kingship

kırat carat; value

kırba water-skin, leather-bottle [whip]

kırbaç whip; **~lamak** *v/t*

kırç hoar-frost, rime

kırçıl sprinkled with grey

kırgın disappointed

kırık 1. *adj.* broken, cracked; **2.** *n.* fragment, splitter; **~lık** physical weariness, weakness

kırılmak break, be broken; be offended (*-e* by)

Kırım (yarımadası) the Crimea

kırıntı crumb, fragment

kırıtmak *-e* behave coquettishly towards

kırk forty

kırk|ı shears, scissors; **~mak** *v/t* shear, clip

kırlangıç swallow, martin

kırma *n.* pleat, fold; *adj.* folding (*gun, etc.*); **~k** *v/t* break, split, fold, lower, destroy; **~lı** pleated

kırmızı red; **~biber** *bot.* red pepper

kırp|ık clipped; **~ıntı** clippings; **~mak** *v/t* clip, trim, shear; wink

kırtasiye stationery; **~cilik** selling of stationery; *fig.* bureaucracy, red tape

kısa short; **~ca** *adv.* shortly, briefly; **~lık** shortness; **~lmak** become short, shrink; **~ltma** abbreviation; **~lt-mak** *v/t* shorten

kısas *jur.* retaliation

kısık pinched; hoarse, choked; **~lık** hoarseness

kısılmak be pinched; become hoarse

kısım part, portion, piece

kısıntı restriction

kısır barren, sterile; **~laş-tırmak** *v/t* render sterile; **~lık** sterility

kısıt *jur.* putting under restraint

kıskaç pincers; pair of folding steps

kıskanç jealous, envious; **~lık** jealousy, envy

kıskanmak envy, grudge (*-den -i so. sth.*)

kısmak *v/t* pinch, cut down, diminish

kısm|en *adv.* partly, partially; **~et** destiny, lot, fate; **~î** partial

kısrak mare

kıstırmak *v/t* cause to be pinched, crush

kış winter; **~ lastiği** winter tyre; **~ın** *adv.* in the winter

kışkırt|ıcı inciter, provoker; **~mak** *v/t* incite, excite

kışla *mil.* barracks; **~k** winter quarters; **~mak** pass the winter

kışlık suitable for the winter

kıta

kıta continent; *mil.* detachment

kıtık *n.* tow

kıtır maize grains cracked over a fire, popcorn; **~damak** *v/i* crack(le)

kıt|laşmak become scarce; **~lık** scarcity, dearth

kıvanç pleasure, joy; **~mak** be proud (**ile** of)

kıvılcım spark

kıvır|cık curly, crisp; **~mak** *v/t* curl, twist, coil

kıvra|k brisk, alert; **~anmak** writhe (**-den** with); **~ılmak** *v/i* curl up, twist about; **~ım** twist; fold

kıyafet appearance; dress

kıyamet *rel.* Resurrection of the Dead; tumult

kıyas comparison

kıyı edge, shore, bank

kıy|ık, **~ımlı** minced, chopped up; **~ma** minced meat; **~mak** *-i* mince, chop up; **-e** sacrifice; do an injury to

kıymet value, price, esteem; **~li** valuable, precious; **~siz** worthless

kıymık splinter

kız girl, daughter; virgin; **~ kardeş** sister

kızak sledge, slide

kızamık *med.* measles

kızar|mak turn red, blush; be roasted; **~tma** roasted, roast meat; **~tmak** *v/t* roast, grill

kızdırmak *v/t* heat, anger, annoy

kızgın hot; angry, excited; **~lık** heat, excitement

kızıl red; **2ay** *pol.* Red Crescent; **~cık** *bot.* cornelian cherry

kızışmak get angry, excited

kızlık maidenhood, virginity; **~ adı** maiden name

kızmak get hot; **-e** be angry with

ki that, in order that; who

-ki (**-kü**) in; of; **Türkiyede'ki İngilizler** the English in Turkey; **bugünkü Türkiye** Turkey of to-day

kibar noble, rich; **~lık** gentility, nobility

kibir pride, haughtiness; **~lenmek** be proud *or* haughty; **~li** proud, haughty

kibrit *chem.* sulphur; match

kifayet sufficiency; **~ etm.** be contented (**ile** with); **~li** adequate

kil clay

kiler store-room; pantry

kilim woven matting, kilim

kilise church

kilit lock; **~lemek** *v/t* lock; **~li** furnished with a lock; locked

kiliz *bot.* reed

kilo|(gram) kilogram(me); **~metre** kilometre; **~vat** [kilowatt]

kils limestone

kim who?; whoever

kimlik identity; **~ cüzdanı** identity card

kimse someone, anyone; **~siz** without relations *or* friends

kimya| chemistry; **~ager** chemist; **~evî** chemical

kimyon *bot.* cummin

kin malice, grudge, hatred; ~ **beslemek** nourish a grudge

kinaye allusion, hint

kinin *med.* quinine

kip *gr.* form, voice

kir dirt

kira hire, rent; ~**ya vermek** *v/t* let; ~**cı** tenant; ~**lamak** *v/t* rent, hire; ~**lık** for hire, to let

kiraz *bot.* cherry

kireç lime

kiremit tile

kiriş violine string; rafter

kir|lemek *v/t* dirty, soil; ~**lenmek** become dirty; ~**letmek** *v/t* dirty, soil; ~**li** dirty, soiled

kirpi *zo.* hedgehog

kirpik eyelash

kişi person, human being; one; ~**lik** special to ... persons; personality; ~**sel** personal

kişnemek neigh

kitabe inscription; ~**t** art of writing, style

kitabevi bookshop

kitap book; ~**çı** bookseller; ~**lık** library

kit|lemek *v/t* lock; ~**li** locked

klakson motor horn

klasik classic, classical

klasör file

klavye keyboard

klinik clinical hospital

kliring *ec.* clearing

klişe cliché (*a. fig.*)

klor *chem.* chlorium

klüp club

koalisyon *pol.* coalition

koca 1. husband; 2. large, great; old; ~**başı** village headman; ~**lı** having a husband; ~**(l)mak** grow old; ~**man** huge, enormous; ~**sız** unmarried; widow

koç ram

koçan corncob, stump; heart *of a vegetable*

kodeks official list of pharmaceutical formulas

kof hollow, rotten; stupid

koğuş dormitory

kok coke

kok|ak smelling, fetid; ~**lamak** *v/t* smell; ~**mak** *v/i* smell, stink; ~**muş** putrid, rotten, *fig.* lazy, dirty

kokoroz *bot.* ear of maize; maize plant

kokoz *sl.* poor, hard up

kokteyl cocktail

koku smell, scent; *-in* ~**sunu almak** perceive the smell of; ~**lu** having a special smell, perfumed; ~**suz** having no smell

kol arm, foreleg; wing, branch; *tech.* handle, bar; ~ **saati** wrist watch

kola starch; ~**lamak** *v/t* starch and press; ~**lı** starched

kolan band, belt, girth

kolay easy; ~**laştırmak** *v/t* make easy, facilitate; ~**lık** easiness; means

kolej collage

koleksiyon collection

kolektif collective; ~ **or-**

kolektivizm

taklık (*or* **şirket**) private firm

kolektivizm collectivism

kolera *med.* cholera

koli parcel

kol|lamak *v/t* search, keep under observation; **∼luk** cuff

Kolonya Cologne; **∼ suyu** Eau-de-Cologne

kolordu army corps

koltuk armpit; arm-chair; **∼ değneği** crutch; **∼çu** old--clothes man; **∼lu** having arms (*chair*)

kombin|a *ec.* combine, factories *pl.*; **∼e** combined

komedi comedy

komik comic; ridiculous

komiser superintendent of police

komisyon commission; **∼cu** commission-agent

komit|a a secret society; **∼e** committee

komodin bed-side table

kompartıman compartment

komplike complicated, complex

komplo plot, conspiracy

komposto stewed fruit

komşu neighbour; **∼luk** being a neighbour

komuta command

komutan *mil.* commander, commandant; **∼lık** command, authority

komüni|st communist; **∼zm** communism

konak halting-place, stage; mansion, government

house; **∼lamak** stay for the night

konca bud

konç leg *of a boot or stocking*

kondoktor, kondüktör conductor

konferans lecture; *pol.* conference; **∼ vermek** give a lecture

konfor comfort

kongre congress

koni cone; **∼k** conic

konmak *-e* be placed on; stop during night at; camp in; be added to

konser concert

konserv|atuvar *mus.* conservatory; **∼e** canned food; can

konsey *pol.* council

konsolos consul; **∼luk** consulate

kont count

kontenjan *ec.* quota

kontes countess

kontrat(o) contract

kontrol control; **∼ etm.** *v/t* control

konu subject, matter, theme; **∼k** guest; **∼ksever** hospitable; **∼lmak** *-e* be put, placed in

konuş|ma lecture; talk; **∼mak** talk (*-i ile* about *sth.* with *so.*); **∼ulmak** be discussed (**ile** with)

konut residence, house

kooperatif *ec.* co-operative (organization); **∼çilik** co--operative system

koparmak *v/t* pluck, break off

kopça hook-and-eye; **~lamak** v/t fasten with hook-and-eye

kopmak v/i break in two; break out

kopya, kopye copy; **~ etm.** v/t, **-in ~sını (~sini) çıkarmak** copy

kor[1] mil. army corps

kor[2] ember; redhot cinder

koramiral naut. vice admiral

kord|ele ribbon; **~on** cord, cordon

korgeneral mil. Lieutenant-General

koridor corridor

korkak timid; coward; **~lık** cowardice; timidity

korkmak -den be afraid of, fear

korku fear, alarm; **~lu** frightening, dangerous; **~luk** scare-crow; banister; **~nç** terrible; **~suz** fearless; **~tmak** v/t frighten, threaten

korna horn of a car, atc.

korner corner (football)

koro mus. chorus

korsa, korse corset

kort tennis court

koru small wood; **~cu** forest watchman

koru|mak v/t defend, watch over; **~nma** defence; **~nmak** -den defend oneself against, avoid; **~yucu** defender

koskoca enormous

koş|mak v/i run; v/t harness, put to work; **~tur-**

~mak v/t cause to run, dispatch; **~u** race; **~ucu** runner

koşul condition, stipulation

kota ec. quota

kotra naut. cutter

kova bucket; **~lamak** v/t pursue

kovan hive; cartridge-case

kovmak v/t drive away, repel, persecute

kovuk hollow, cavity

kovuşturmak v/t jur. prosecute

koy geo. small bay

ko(y)mak v/t put, place (-e in), add (-e to); **yoluna ~** v/t put right, set going

koyu thick, dense; dark; **~laşmak** become dense or dark; **~luk** density; depth of colour

koyun[1] sheep

koyun[2] bosom

koy(u)vermek v/t let go

koz bot. walnut

koza cocoon

koza(la)k cone of a tree

kozmetik cosmetics

köçek zo. camel foal; boy dancer

köfte meat ball

köhne old, worn, antiquated

kök root, base; origin; **-in ~ünden koparmak** v/t eradicate; **-in ~ünü kurutmak** exterminate; **~lemek** v/t uproot; **~lenmek, ~leşmek** take root; **~lü** having roots, rooted

köle slave; **~lik** servitude

kömür charcoal; coal; **~**

ocağı coal-mine; **~cü** charcoal burner; coal-dealer; **~leşmek** v/i char, carbonize; **~lük** coal-cellar; naut.)
köpek dog [bunker)
köprü bridge
köpü|k froth, foam; **~rmek** v/i froth, foam
kör blind; **~bağırsak** an. appendix
körfez geo. gulf
kör|lenmek, ~leşmek become blind, blunt; **~leştirmek, ~letmek** v/t blind; blunt; **~lük** blindness, bluntness
körpe fresh, tender
körük bellows; **~lemek** v/t fan with bellows
köse with no beard
kösele stout leather
kösnü lust
köstebek zo. mole
köstek fetter, hobble
köşe corner, angle; **~ başı** street-corner; **~bent** tech. angle-iron; **~li** having corners or angles
köşk pavillon, summer-house
kötü bad; **~ye kullanmak** v/t misuse; take advantage of; **~leşmek** become bad; **~lük** badness; **~msemek** v/t think ill of; **~mser** pessimistic
kötürüm paralysed, crippled; **~lük** paralysis
köy village; **~lü** peasant, fellow villager
kral, ~içe, ~lık s. kıral, kıraliçe, kırallık

kramp med. cramp, convulsion
krank tech. crank; **~ mili** crank-shaft
krater geo. crater
kravat tie
kredi credit
krem cosmetic cream; **~a** cream of milk; whipped cream; **~şanti(yi)** whipped cream
kriko tech. lifting-jack
kriz crisis
kroki sketch
krom chem. chromium
kruvazör naut. cruiser
kuaför s. kuvaför
kubbe dome, cupola
kucak breast, embrace; lap; **~lamak** v/t embrace; include
kudret power, strength; **~li** powerful; **~siz** powerless, incapable
kudu|rmak go mad; **~z** med. hydrophobia, rabies
Kudüs Jerusalem
kuğu zo. swan
kukla doll; puppet
kuku zo. cuckoo
kukulete hood, cowl
kul slave, creature
kulaç fathom
kulak ear; **~ vermek** listen (-e to); **~ memesi** lobe of the ear; **~lık** tech. earpiece, earphone
kule tower, turret
kullanış method of using; **~lı** serviceable, handy
kullanmak v/t use, employ; drive a car, etc.

kulluk slavery, servitude

kulp handle

kuluçka broody hen; ~**ya oturmak** sit on the eggs

kulunç colic, cramp

kulübe hut, shed; *mil.* sentry-box

kulüp s. **klüp**

kum sand; gravel (*a. med.*)

kumanda *mil.* command; ~**n** commander

kumar gambling; ~**baz** gambler; ~**hane** gambling casino

kumaş tissue, fabric; cloth, texture

kumbara money-box; bomb shell

kumlu sandy, gravelly; ~**k** sandy (place)

kumral light brown

kumru *zo.* turtle-dove

kumsal sand-beach

kundak swaddling clothes; bundle of rags; ~**çı** incendiary; ~**lamak** *v/t* swaddle; set fire to

kundura shoe; ~**cı** shoemaker

kunduz *zo.* beaver

kupa[1] cup, wine-glass

kupa[2] hearts (*cards*)

kupkuru bone-dry

kupon coupon

kur[1] *ec.* rate of exchange

kur[2] courtship, flirtation; ~ **yapmak** *-e* pay court to, flirt with

kur'a lot; ~ **çekmek** draw lots

kurabiye *cake made with almonds, nuts, etc.*

kurak dry, arid; ~**lık** draught

kural *gr.* rule

Kur'an *rel.* the Koran

kurbağa *zo.* frog

kurban sacrifice; victim; ~ **bayramı** *rel.* The Moslem Festival of Sacrifices; ~ **kesmek** *rel.* kill an animal for sacrifice; ~ **olayım!** I beseech you!

kurcalamak *v/t* scratch, rub; meddle with

kurdela *s.* **kordele**

kuriye courier

kurmak *v/t* set up, establish; pitch *the tent*; lay *the table*

kurmay *mil.* staff

kurna basin of a bath *under the tap*

kurnaz cunning, shrewd; ~**lık** cunning, shrewdness

kurs[1] disk

kurs[2] course of lessons, *etc.*

kurşun lead; bullet; ~ **kalem** lead pencil; ~**î** lead-coloured

kurt[1] wolf

kurt[2] worm, maggot

kurtar|ılmak be saved, rescued; ~**mak** *v/t* save, rescue

kurt|lanmak become maggoty; *fig.* become impatient; ~**lu** wormy; *fig.* uneasy, fidgety

kurtul|mak *-den* escape from, be saved from, get out of; ~**uş** liberation, escape

kuru dry, dried, bare; ~ **-**

fasulye kidney beans; ~ **kahve** roasted *or* ground coffee; ~ **meyva** dried fruit(s)

kurul commission, committee

kurula|mak *v/t* wipe dry, dry; **~nmak** be wiped dry, dried

kurul|mak be founded, established; *-e* settle oneself comfortably on; **~tay** assembly, congress

kurulu established; composed (*-den* of)

kuruluk dryness

kuruluş foundation

kurum[1] soot

kurum[2] association, society

kurum[3] pose, conceit

kuruma|k *v/i* dry, wither up

kurum|lanmak be puffed-up; **~lu** conceited, puffed-up (illusion)

kuruntu strange fancy; }

kuruş piastre (*the 100th part of a lira*); **~luk** being worth ... piastres

kurut|maç blotter; **~mak** *v/t* dry, cause to shrivel

kus|mak *v/t* vomit; **~turucu** emetic

kusur defect, fault; **~a bakmayınız!** I beg your pardon!; Excuse me!; **~lu** defective, incomplete; **~suz** without defect; complete

kuş bird

kuşa|k sash, girdle; **~nmak** *v/t* put on, gird on; **~tmak** *v/t* surround; besiege

kuşbaşı *adj.* in small pieces (meat, *etc.*)

kuşet couchette, bed

kuşkonmaz *bot.* asparagus

kuşku suspicion, nervousness; **~lanmak** feel nervous *or* suspicious

kuştüyü feather

kut luck, prosperity; **~lamak** *v/t* celebrate *sth.*; congratulate *so.*; **~lanmak** be celebrated; **~lu** lucky, happy; **~lulamak** *v/t* offer congratulations to *so.*

kuts|al, ~î sacred; **~allık, ~iyet** sanctity

kutu box, case

kutup *geo.* pole; ~ **yıldızı** *astr.* Pole-Star

ku(v)aför ladies' hairdresser

kuvve potency, faculty; strength

kuvvet strength, force, power; **~ten düşmek** weaken, lose strength; **~lendirmek** *v/t* strengthen; **~lenmek** become strong; **~li** strong, powerful; **~siz** weak

kuyruk tail; queue; **~ta beklemek** stand in line

kuyruklu having a tail; ~ **piyano** *mus.* grand piano; ~ **yıldız** *astr.* comet

kuytu snug, hidden, remote

kuyu well, pit, borehole

kuyumcu jeweller, goldsmith

kuzen male cousin

kuzey north

kuzgun *zo.* raven

kuzin female cousin

kuzu lamb; **~m** my dear; **~dişi** milk-tooth

kübik cubic

küçük small, young; ♀**ayı** *astr.* Ursa minor

küçül|mek become small, be reduced; **~tme** *gr.* diminutive; **~tmek** *v/t* diminish, reduce

küçümsemek *v/t* belittle

küf mould, mouldiness; **~ bağlamak, ~ tutmak** become mouldy

küfe large basket

küf|lenmek turn mouldy; *fig.* become out-of-date; **~lü** mouldy; out-of-date

küfretmek **-e** curse, blaspheme

küfür unbelief, blasphemy

kükremek foam with rage; roar (*lion*)

kükürt *chem.* sulphur; **~lü** sulphurous

kül¹ the whole, all

kül² ashes; **~ etm.** *v/t* reduce to ashes; ruin

külâh conical hat; anything conical; trick, deceit

külçe metal ingot, heap

külek tub with handles

külfet trouble, inconvenience; **~li** troublesome, laborious; **~siz** easy

külhan stoke-hold of a bath; **~beyi** rowdy, idle youngster

külliyet totality, entirety; **~li** abundant

küllü containing ashes

külot riding-breeches *pl.*;

knickers *pl.*; **~lu çorap** tights *pl.*

külrengi ash-coloured

kültive etm. *v/t* cultivate

kültür culture; **~el** cultural; **~lü** civilized, educated

kümbet *arch.* cupola, dome

küme heap, mass; hut, hide

kümes poultry-house, coop

künde fetter, hobble

künk eartenware water-pipe

künye personel data

küp¹ large eartenware jar

küp² cube

küpe ear-ring; *an.* dewlap

kür health cure

kürdan tooth-pick

Kürdistan Kurdistan

küre¹ globe, sphere

küre² furnace

kürek shovel; oar; **~ çekmek** row; **~ kemiği** *an.* shoulderblade

küre(le)mek *v/t* clear away, shovel up

kürk fur; fur-coat; **~lü** fur, adorned with fur

kürsü reading-stand, pulpit; professorial chair

Kürt Kurd; **~çe** Kurdish (*language*)

küskü *tech.* crow-bar; iron wedge

küskün disgruntled; **~lük** vexation

küsmek **-e** be offended with

küstah insolent; **~lık** insolence

küt *adj.* blunt, not pointed; *n. the noise of knocking on a door, etc.*

kütle heap, block, mass
kütük tree-stump; baulk, log; ledger, register
kütüphane library

kütürdemek *v/i* crash, crunch
küvet basin, sink; bath-tub

L

laboratuvar laboratory
lacivert lapis-lazuli; dark-blue
laf word, talk; empty words, boasting; ~ **atmak** *-e* make insinuating remarks to
lağım underground tunnel; sewer; ~**la atmak** *v/t* blast
lahana *bot.* cabbage
lâhika appendix, additional note
lahit tomb
lahmacun *kind of meat pizza*
lahza instant, moment
lakap cognomen; nickname
lake lacquered
lakırdı word, talk, gossip
lâkin but; nevertheless
lâl *n.*, *adj.* ruby
lala servant *put in charge of a boy*, tutor
lâle *bot.* tulip
lamba cornice, mortise; lamp
lânet curse, imprecation; damnable; ~ **okumak** swear and curse; ~**lemek** *v/t* curse
lap flop!, flap!
lapa mush, pulp
lastik *adj.* of rubber; *n.* rubber; galoshes; tyre; ~**li** made of rubber; elastic

lata lath
latarna *mus.* barrel-organ
latif fine, slender, elegant
latife joke, witticism; ~**ci** fond of making jokes
Latin Latin; ~**ce** Latin (*language*)
lâubali free-and-easy, careless
lav *geo.* lava
lavabo hand-basin
lavanta lavender-water
lavta¹ *mus.* lute
lavta² *med.* obstetric forceps; doctor, mid-wife
lâyık *-e* suitable for, worthy
lâyiha *jur.* explanatory document, bill
layik lay, secular; ~**lik** secularism
lâzım *-e* necessary for; requisite
leblebi roasted chick-peas
leğen bowl, basin
Leh Pole; Polish
leh- in favour of, for; *-in* ~**inde** (~**ine**) **olm.** be in favour of
lehçe¹ dialect; language
Lehçe² Polish (*language*)
lehim solder; ~**lemek** *v/t* solder; ~**li** soldered
Leh|istan Poland; ~**li** Polish; Pole
leke stain, mark, spot (*a.*

fig.); ~ etm. v/t stain; ~le-mek v/t stain; try to dis-honour; ~li spotted, stained; ~siz spotless, im-maculate

lenf(a) lymph
lenger large deep dish; naut. anchor
leş carcass
letafet charm, grace
letarji lethargy
Levanten Levantine
levazım(at) pl. materials, supplies, provisions
levha signboard
levrek zo. sea bass
leylak bot. lilac
leylek zo. stork
lezzet taste, flavour; pleas-ure; ~li pleasant to the taste; delightful; ~siz tasteless
liberal liberal; ~izm liber-alism
libre pound (500 gramme)
lider pol. leader; ~lik leadership
lif fibre; loofah
lig league, union
liman harbour
limon lemon; ~ata lem-onade; ~lu flavoured with lemon
linç lynching
linyit lignite
lira Turkish lira; ~lık of the value of ... liras
liret Italian lira
lisan language, tongue
lisans diploma; license
lise high-school
liste list

litre litre (1.76 pint); ~lik holding ... litres
liyakat merit, suitability; ~li able, qualified; ~siz [unqualified]
lobut club
loca box at the theatre, etc.; Masonic lodge
lodos south-west wind
loğusa woman after child-birth; ~lık childbed
lojman lodging for workers and employees
lokanta restaurant; ~cı restaurant keeper
lokavt ec. lock-out
lokma mouthful, morsel; kind of sweet fritter
lokomotif locomotive, en-gine
lokum Turkish delight
lonca guild
Londra London
lop round and soft; ~ yu-murta hard-boiled egg
lor cheese of goat's milk
lort lord; ~lar Kamarası the House of Lords
lostra shoe polish
losyon lotion; Eau-de-Cologne
loş dark, gloomy, dim
lök awkward, clumsy
lökün putty
lûgat word; dictionary
lûtf|en please!, ~etmek v/t have the kindness of -ing; allow
lûtuf kindness, favour; ~kâr kind, gratious
Lübnan Lebanon
lüfer zo. bluefish
lügat s. lûgat

lüks n. luxury; adj. luxurious

Lüksemburg Luxemburg

lüle curl, fold, paper-cone;
~**taşi** meerschaum

lüp; ~**e konmak** get something gratis

lütf|en, ~**etmek** s. lûften, lûtfetmek

lütuf, ~**kâr** s. lûtuf, lûtufkâr

lüzum necessity; need; ~**lu** necessary, needed; ~**suz** unnecessary, useless

M

maada -**den** besides, except; **bundan** ~ besides this, furthermore

maalesef unfortunately, with regret

maarif education, public instruction

maaş salary; allowance

mabet place of worship, temple

mabeyin interval; relation; **mabeynimizde** between us

mablak spatula; putty knife

Macar Hungarian; ~**ca** Hungarian (language); ~**istan** Hungary

macera event; adventure; ~**cı**, ~**perest** adventurous, adventurer

macun putty; paste

maç match

maça spade at cards

maçuna tech. steam-crane

madalya medal

madd|e matter, substance, material; paragraph; ~**î** adj. material

madem(ki) while, since, as

maden mine; mineral; metal; ~ **kömürü** coal, pit-coal; ~**istan** mine; ~ **suyu** mineral water; ~**î** metallic, mineral

madrabaz ec. middleman

madun adj., n. subordinate

mafiş a kind of very light pastry [fritter]

mafsal joint

magazin magazine

magneti|k magnetic; ~**zma** magnetism

mağara cave, pit

mağaza large store; storehouse

mağdur wronged, victim

mağlubiyet defeat

mağlup defeated; ~ **etm.** v/t defeat

mağrur proud (-e of); conceited

mahalle quarter of a town

mahallebi sweet dish made with rice and milk

mahallî local

maharet skill, proficiency

mahcubiyet bashfulness, modesty

mahcup ashamed, bashful

mahdut limited; definite

mahfaza case, box

mahfil place of resort, club; rel. private pew in a mosque

mahfuz protected, looked after

malul

mahir skilful

mahiyet reality; nature, character

mahkeme *jur.* court of justice

mahkûm sentenced, subject (*-e* to); **~ etm.** *v/t* sentence, condemn; **~iyet** condemnation, sentence

mahluk created; creature

mahlut mixed

mahmuz spur; *naut.* ram *of a ship;* **~lamak** *v/t* spur

mahpus imprisoned

mahreç outlet; origin, source

mahrem confidential, secret

mahrukat *pl.* combustibles; fuel *sg.*

mahrum deprived (*-den* of)

mahrut cone; **~î** conical

mahsul product, produce; crop; **~dar** productive, fertile

mahsus *-e* special, peculiar to, reserved for

mahun mahogany

mahv|edici destroying, crushing; **~etmek** *v/t* destroy, abolish; **~olmak** be destroyed, ruined

mahya *lights strung between minarets during Ramazan to form words or pictures*

mahzen underground store-house, cellar

mahzur objection, inconvenience

maişet means of subsistence, livelihood

maiyet suite, following

majör *mus.* major

makale article *in a newspaper, etc.*

makam place, abode; office

makara *tech.* pulley, reel spule

makarna macaroni

makas scissors, shears *pl.*; *tech.* switch, points; **~çı** pointsman; **~tar** cutter-out

makbul accepted; liked

makbuz receipt *for payment, etc.*

makine machine; engine; **~ inşaatı, ~ yapımı** mechanical engineering; **~li** fitted with a machine; **~li tüfek** machine-gun

makinist engin-driver; mechanic

maksat aim, purpose

maksure private pew in a mosque

maktu cut off; fixed (*price*)

maktul killed

makul reasonable, wise

makyaj make-up

mal property, possession; wealth, goods; **~ sahibi** owner

malarya *med.* malaria

malî financial

malik olm. *-e* possess, own

maliye finance; ♀ **Bakanlığı (Bakanı)** Ministry (Minister) of Finance; **~ci** financier; economist

Malta Malta; ♀ **eriği** *bot.* loquat

maltız[1] brazier

Maltız[2] *n.* Maltese

malul ill; invalid

malum known; **~unuzdur ki** you know that

malumat information, knowledge; **~ vermek -e** inform *so*. (**hakkında** of *sth*.); **~ım yok** I have no knowledge; **~lı** learned, informed

malzeme necessaries *pl.*; materials

mamafih nevertheless

mamul made (-*den* of); manufactured; **~ât** *pl.* manufactures, goods

mamur prosperous, flourishing

mana meaning, sense; **~lı** significant; allusive; **~sız** senseless, without significance

manastır monastery

manav fruiterer

manda¹ *zo.* water buffalo

manda² *pol.* mandate

mandal latch; catch; clothes-peg; tuning-peg *of a violin, etc.*

mandalina *bot.* mandarin

mandallamak *v/t* shut with a latch; hang up with a peg

mandıra small dairy

manevi moral, spiritual

maneviyat morale

manevra manoeuvre(s); trick

manga *mil.* squad; *naut.* mess

mangal brazier; **~ kömürü** charcoal

mangan(ez) *chem.* manganese

mani obstacle, impediment; **~ olm. -e** prevent, hinder

mânia obstacle, difficulty; **~lı koşu** hurdle race

manifatura textiles *pl.*; **~cı** draper

manikür manicure

manivela *tech.* lever, crank

manken mannequin; tailor's dummy

manolya *bot.* magnolia

mansap *geo.* river-mouth

mantar *bot.* mushroom; cork

mantık logic; **~î** logical

manto woman's cloak, mantle

manya mania

manzara view, panorama; **~lı** having a fine view

manzum written in rhyme and metric; **~e** row, series; poem

marangoz joiner, cabinetmaker; **~luk** joinery, cabinet-making

mareşal *mil.* Marshal

margarin margarine

marifet knowlege, skill; **~iyle** by means of

marka mark, trademark; **konulan ~** trademark; **~lı** trade-marked

marksizm Marxism

marmelat jam; marmalade

maroken Morocco leather

marş *mus.* march; starter (*auto*)

marşandiz goods train

mart March (*month*)

martaval lie; **~ atmak** talk nonsense

martı zo. gull

maruf well known

maruz exposed (-e to); ~ **kalmak** -e to be exposed to

marya zo. female animal

masa table, desk; ~ **örtüsü** table-cloth; ~ **tenisi** table tennis, ping-pong

masaj massage

masal story, tale, myth

maskara adj. funny; ridiculous; n. buffoon; mask; ~**lık** buffoonery; shame

maske mask; ~**li** masked

maslahat business, affair; ~**güzar** pol. chargé d'affaires

maslak stone trough

mason freemason; ~**luk** freemasonry [pensive]

masraf expense; ~**lı** ex-/

mastar gr. infinitive

masum innocent

masun guarded, safe; ~**iyet** inviolability, immunity

maşa tongs; pincers

maşallah wonderful!; What wonders God hath willed!

mat[1] matt, faint

mat[2] check-mate

matara waterbottle

matbaa printing-office; ~**cı** printer

matbu printed; ~**a(t)** printed matter

matem mourning

matematik mathematics

materyalizm materialism

matine thea. matinée

matkap drill

matlubat pl. demands, debts due

matlup n. debt due; adj. demanded

matrah category of taxed goods, standard

matuf directed, aiming (-e at)

mavi blue; ~**msi**, ~**mtırak** bluish

mav(u)na barge, lighter

maya ferment, yeast; fig. essence, origin; ~**lanmak** ferment; ~**lı** fermented, leavened

maydanoz bot. parsley

mayhoş slightly acid, bitter-sweet

mayın mil. floating mine

mayıs May (month); ~ **böceği** zo. cockchafer

maymun zo. monkey; ~**cuk** tech. picklock

mayo bathing suit

mayonez mayonnaise

mazbata official report, protocol, minutes pl.

mazgal embrasure, loophole

mazı bot. gall-nut; arbor vitae

mazi past, bygone; the past

mazlum oppressed, suffered injure

maznun accused, suspected (ile of)

mazot Diesel oil

mazur excused, excusable; ~ **görmek**, ~ **tutmak** v/t hold excused

meal meaning, purport

meblağ sum, amount

mebni -e based on; because of

mebus *pol.* deputy, member of parliament

mebzul abundant, lavish

mecal power, ability; **~siz** powerless, exhausted

mecaz metaphor, figurative expression; **~î** figurative, metaphorical

mecbur compelled; **~ olm.** *-e* be compelled to; **~ etm.** *v/t* compel; **~î** obligatory, forced; **~iyet** compulsion, obligation

meccan|en *adv.* gratis; **~î** *adj.* free, gratis

meclis sitting; assembly, council

mecmua review, periodical

mecnun mad, insane

mecra watercourse, canal

meçhul unknown

meddah story-teller

meddücezir *geo.* ebb and flow, tide

medenî civilised; civil; **~ hal** state of being married or unmarried; **~ kanun** *jur.* civil law

medeniyet civilisation; **~siz** uncivilised

medih praise

medrese *rel.* Moslem theological school

mefhum sense; concept, idea

mefkûre ideal

mefruş furnished; **~at** *pl.* furniture

meftun *-e* madly in love with, admiring

meğer but, however, only; **~ki** unless; **~se** *s.* meğer

mehaz source, authority *of a book*

mehenk touchstone; test

Mehmetçik the Turkish 'Tommy'

mehtap moonlight

mekanik mechanics; **~zma** mechanism

mekkâre pack-animal

mektep school

mektup letter; **~laşmak** correspond by letter (**ile** with)

mekûlât *pl.* comestibles, provisions

melankoli *n.* melancholy; **~k** *adj.* melancholy, gloomy

melek angel

melemek *v/i* bleat

melez cross-bred, half-bred; mixed; **~leme** *bot.* cross-breeding

melfuf enclosed (*-e* in)

melhem ointment, salve

melodi melody

memba spring; source, origin

meme teat, nipple; udder; *tech.* burner, nozzle; **~ vermek** *-e* nurse; **~den kesmek** *v/t* wean; **~liler** *pl. zo.* mammals

memleha salt-pit, salt-works

memleket country; home district; **~li** inhabitant, fellow countryman

memnu forbidden

memnun pleased, glad (*-den* at); **~ etm.** *v/t* please, make happy

memnuniyet pleasure, gratitude; **~le** *adv.* gladly, with pleasure

memur official, employee; **~iyet** official post, duty, appointment; quality and duties of an official

mendil handkerchief

mendirek *naut.* artificial harbour

menekşe *bot.* violet

menetmek *v/t* prevent, forbid

menfaat use, advantage, profit; **~li** useful, advantageous; **~perest** self-seeking

menfez hole; vent

menfi exiled, banished; negative

mengene press, clamp, vice

menkul transported; **~at** *pl.* movables

mensucat *pl.* textiles

mensup *-e* related to, connected with; **~ olm.** *-e* belong to

menşe place of origin

menteşe hinge

menzil halting-place, stage; range *of a gun*

mera pasture

merak curiosity, whim, great interest; **~ etm.** *-i* be anxious about; be curious about; *-e* be interested in; **~lı** curious; interested (*-e* in); **~sız** uninterested, indifferent

meram desire, intention

merasim *pl.* ceremonies

merbut *-e* attached to; **~iyet** dependence

mercan *zo.* coral

mercek *phot.* lense

merci reference, competent authority

mercimek *bot.* lentil

merdane *tech.* cylinder, roller

merdiven ladder, steps, stairs

merhaba Good-day!, hello!

merhale day's journey, stage

merhamet mercy, pity; **~ etm.** *-e* pity; **~li** merciful, tender-hearted; **~siz** merciless, cruel; **~sizlik** cruelness

merhum deceased

mer'i *jur.* in force

meridyen *geo.* meridian

Merih *astr.* Mars

meriyet being in force, validity

merkep donkey

merkez centre; **~cilik** centralization; **~kaç** centrifugal; **~lenmek** be concentrated, centralized (*-e* in)

Merkür *astr.* Mercury

mermer marble

mermi projectile, missile

merserize *chem.* mercerized

mersi thank you!

mersin *bot.* myrtle

mert manly, brave

mertebe degree, rank, grade

mertlik manliness, courage

mesafe distance, space

mesaha measurement, measure *of* land

mesai *pl.* efforts, pains; ~ **saatleri** *pl.* working hours

mesaj message

mesam|at *pl.* pores; ~**e** pore

mescit small mosque

meselâ *adv.* for instance, for example

mesele question, problem

meshetmek *v/t* stroke, rub lightly

Mesih *rel.* the Messiah; **2î** Christian

mesken dwelling

meskûkât *pl.* coins

meskûn inhabited

meslek career, profession; ~**î** professional; ~**siz** without a career; unprincipled; ~**taş** colleague

messetmek *v/t* occur, rise; -*e* touch

mest[1] drunk

mest[2] light soleless boot

mesul responsible, answerable (-*den* for)

mesuliyet responsibility; ~ **sigortası** liability insurance

meşakkat hardship, trouble

meşale torch

meşe *bot.* oak

meşgul busy; occupied; ~ **etm.** *v/t* keep busy, engage; ~**iyet** occupation, work [known]

meşhur famous, well-

meşhut *jur.* witnessed

meşin leather

meşrep character

meşru *jur.* legal, legitimate

meşrubat *pl.* drinks

meşrutiyet *pol.* constitutional government

met *geo.* high-tide

meta merchandise, good

metal metal

metanet firmness, solidity

meteor *astr.* meteor; ~**oloji** meteorology

methal entrance; beginning

methetmek *v/t* praise

metin[1] text

metin[2] solid, firm

metod method, system

metre metre

metres mistress, kept woman

metris *mil.* entrenchment

metro underground railway, subway; ~**polit** *rel.* Greek Metropolitan

metruk left, abandoned

mevcudiyet existence, presence

mevcut existing, present

mevduat *pl. ec.* deposits

mevki place, position; class *on a train, etc.*

mevkuf arrested, detained

mevlit, mevlut *rel.* the birthday of the Prophet Mohammad

mevsim season; ~**lik** seasonal; ~**siz** untimely, out of place

mevsuk reliable, authentic

mevzi place, position

mevzu subject, proposition; ~**(u)bahis** subject under discussion, theme

meyan middle; **bu ~da** among them

meydan open space, public square, ground; opportunity; **~ okumak** *-e* challenge; **~a çıkarmak** *v/t* expose to view, publish, discover; **~a çıkmak** come forth, show oneself; **~a getirmek** *v/t* form, create, bring into view; **~a koymak** *v/t* produce, bring forward

meyhane wine-shop, tavern

meyil inclination, slope; **~li** inclined (*-e* towards)

meyletmek be inclined; *-e* have a liking for

meyus hopeless, despairng

meyve fruit; (**~li**) made of fruit; **~ suyu** fruit-juice

meyyal *-e* inclined towards, fond of

meyzin *s.* müezzin

mezar grave, tomb; **~cı** grave-digger; **~lık** cemetery

mezat *ec.* auction

mezbaha slaughterhouse

meze snack, appetizer

mezhep *rel.* creed; school of thought

meziyet excellence, virtue; talent; value

mezkûr mentioned, aforesaid

mezun *-den* graduate of; excused from; on leave; authorized; **~ olm.** *-den* be graduated from; **~iyet** leave; authorization

mı *s.* mi

mıh nail; **~lamak** nail *v/t* (*-e* on)

mıknatıs magnet; **~lamak** *v/t* magnetize

mıntaka zone, district

mırıl da(n)mak mutter, grumble; **~tı** muttering, grumbling

Mısır Egypt; ♀ *bot.* maize; **~lı** Egyptian

mıskala burnisher

mısra line of poetry

mızıka *mus.* band; toy trumpet; mouth-organ

mızmız hesitant; querulous

mızrak lance

mi, mı, mu, mü *interrogative particle, sometimes adding emphasis*

mide *an.* stomach

midye *zo.* mussel

miğfer helmet

mihanikî mechanical (*a. fig.*)

mihmandar host; **~lık** hospitality

mihnet trouble, affliction

mihrak *phys.* focus

mihrap niche in a mosque *indicating the direction of Mecca*

mihver pivot, axis, axle

mikâp cube

mikro|fon microphone; **~p** microbe; **~skop** microscope

miktar quantity, amount

mikyas measuring instrument; scale

mil¹ silt

mil 108

mil² pin, peg, pivot
mil³ *geo.* mile
milâdî pertaining to the birth of Christ, A.D.
milât *rel.* birth of Christ
mili|gram milligram; **~metre** millimetre
millet nation; people; **~ meclisi** *pol.* national assembly; **~lerarası** international; **~vekili** *pol.* deputy
millî national; **~ bayram** national holiday
milliyet nationality; **~çi** nationalist; **~çilik** nationalism
milyar milliard; *Am.* billion, a thousand million
milyon million; **~er** millionaire
mimar architect; **~lık** architecture
mimber pulpit *in a mosque*
minare minaret
minder mattress
mine enamel; dial *of a clock*; **~lemek** *v/t* enamel
mineral mineral
mini|k small and sweet; **~mini** very small, tiny
minkale *math.* protractor
minnet obligation, taunt; **~tar** grateful, indebted (-*e* to)
minör *mus.* minor
minyatür miniature
miraç ascent to heaven; **~ gecesi** *rel.* night of Mohammad's ascent to heaven
miras inheritance; **~çı** heir (-*ess*)

miri belonging to the state
misafir guest, visitor; **~hane** public guesthouse *in villages*; **~perver** hospitable
misal model, precedent
misilleme *jur.* retortion; retaliation
misk musk
miskin poor, wretched; abject; *med.* leprous; **~ hastalığı** leprosy
misli ... times as much (*or* many)
misyon mission; **~er** missionary
miting meeting
miyavlamak miaow
miyop *med.* short-sighted
mizaç temperament, disposition
mizah jest, joke, humour; **~çı** humorist
mobilya furniture
moda fashion
model pattern, model
modern modern
mola rest, pause; **~ vermek** *v/i* rest, pause
molekül *phys.* molecule
moloz rough stone; rubble
monarşi monarchy
monoton monotonous
montaj *tech.* mounting, fitting
mor violet, purple; **~armak** become bruised
morfin *med.* morphine
morg mortuary
Mosko|f Russian; **~va** Moscow
mostra pattern, sample

motel motel

motif *mus., etc.* pattern, motif

motor motor; motorboat; **~lu** having a motor

motosiklet motor cycle

motör, ~lü *s.* motor, motorlu

mozaik mosaic-work; floor made of concrete mixed with marble splinters

mu *s.* mi

muadil equivalent (**-e** to)

muaf *-den* excused from; exempt from; **~iyet** exemption, immunity

muahede pact, treaty

muaheze censure, criticism; **~ etm.** *v/t* blame, criticize [sequent]

muahhar posterior; sub-

muamele dealing; transaction; procedure, formality; **~ etm.** *-e* treat

muamma mystery; riddle

muariz opponent; **-e** against, opposing

muasır contemporary

muaşeret social intercourse

muattal disused; idle

muavenet help, assistance; **~ etm.** *-e* help

muavin assistant

muayene inspection, examination; **~ etm.** *v/t* inspect, examine; **~hane** *med.* consulting-room

muayyen definite, determined

muazzam great, esteemed

mubah *rel.* tolerated, permissible

mubayaa purchase; **~cı** *ec.* stockbroker

mucibince according to requirements, as necessary

mucip causing, cause, motive; **~ olm.** *v/t* cause

mucir who lets or hires out

mucize miracle, wonder

mudi *ec.* depositor, investor

mufassal detailed, lengthy

muğlak abstruse, obscure

muhabere correspondence by letters; *mil.* signals *pl.*

muhabir correspondent

muhaceret emigration

muhacir emigrant, refugee

muhafaza protection, preservation; **~ etm.** *v/t* protect, take care of; **~kâr** conservative; **~kârlık** conservatism

muhafız guard, defender; commander of *a fort*

muhakeme *jur.* hearing of a case, trial; judgement

muhakkak certain, without doubt

muhalefet opposition; **~ etm.** *-e* oppose, disagree with; **~ partisi** *pol.* opposition party

muhalif *-e* opposing, contrary to

muharebe battle, war

muharip warrior, combatant

muharrik stirring up; moving

muharrir writer, editor, author

muhasara siege; **~ etm.** *v/t* besiege

muhasebe

muhasebe book-keeping, accountancy; **~ci** accountant

muhasım opponent

muhatap: ~ olm. be addressed in speech; be reproached (-e with)

muhatara danger; **~lı** dangerous, risky

muhavere conversation; *thea.* dialogue

muhayyile imagination, fancy

muhbir who gives information; reporter

muhit surrounding; milieu

muhkem firm, strong, tight

muhlis sincere

muhrip *naut.* destroyer

muhtaç: ~ olm. -e be in want, in need of

muhtar headman *of a village or quarter;* ~iyet autonomy; **~lık** office of a headman

muhtasar abridged

muhtekir profiteer

muhtelif diverse, various

muhtemel possible, probable

muhterem respected, honoured

muhteşem magnificent, majestic

muhteva contents; **~i** -i containing

muhtıra note; memorandum; ~ **defteri** note-book

mukabele reward, retaliation; confronting; **~bilmisil** *jur.* retortion; retaliation

mukabil opposite, facing; -e in return for; **buna** ~ on the other hand; **~inde** opposite, in return

mukadderat *pl.* destiny *sg.*

mukaddes sacred, holy

mukavele agreement, contract; **~name** written agreement, deed; pact

mukavemet resistance, endurance; ~ **etm.** -e resist, endure

mukavva cardboard

mukayese comparison

mukim who dwells *or* stays; stationary

muktedir capable, powerful; ~ olm. -e be able to, capable of

mum wax; candle

mumaileyh aforementioned

mumya mummy

munis sociable; tame

muntazam regular, orderly; **~an** *adv.* orderly, regularly

munzam extra, additional

murabaha usury; **~ci** usurer

murabba square; squared

murahhas delegated; delegate, plenipotentiary

murakabe control, supervision; meditation

murakıp controller

murat wish, intention

musallat: ~ **etm.** -i -e bring down *sth.* upon *so.;* ~ olm. -e fall upon, infest

musannif compiler of a book; classifier

Musevî Jew, Jewish

musibet calamity, evil

musiki music

muska amulet, charm

musluk tap; spigot; ~ **taşı** stone basin *under a tap*

muş *naut.* steam launch

muşamba tarpaulin; mackintosh, waterproof

muştu good news

mut luck; happiness

mutaassıp fanatical, bigoted

mutabakat conformity, agreement

mutabık agreeing (*-e* with)

mutaf maker of goat-hair goods

mutat customary, habitual

muteber esteemed, of good repute; *jur.* valid

mutedil moderate

mutemet reliable; fiduciary

mutfak kitchen; cuisine

mutlak absolute, autocratic; **~a** *adv.* absolutely, certainly; **~iyet** absolutism

mutlu lucky, fortunate

muttasıl *-e* joined to; *adv.* continuously

muvafakat agreement, consent; ~ **etm.** *-e* agree, consent to

muvaffak successful; ~ **olm.** succeed

muvaffakıyet success; **~li** successful; **~siz** without success; **~sizlik** lack of success, failure

muvafık agreeable, suitable (*-e* for)

muvakkat temporary, provisory

muvasala communication; **~t** arrival

muvazene(t) equilibrium, balance

muvazzaf *mil.* regular

muz *bot.* banana

muzaf *-e* added, appended to

muzır harmful, detrimental

muzip plaguing, tormenting; mischievous; **~lik** teasing; practical joke

mü *s.* **mi**

mübadele exchange; barter

mübalâğa exaggeration; ~ **etm.** exaggerate; **~lı** exaggerated [bountiful)

mübarek blessed, sacred;}

mübaşir *jur.* process-server, usher *of a court*

mücadele dispute, struggle

mücahit *rel.,fig.* champion

mücavir neighbour(ing)

mücellit bookbinder

mücerret bare; abstract

mücevher jewel; **~at** *pl.* jewels, jewellery

mücmel concise; summary

mücrim guilty; criminal

müdafaa defence, resistance; ~ **etm.** *v/t* defend

müdafi defender

müdahale interference, intervention; ~ **etm.** *-e* meddle with, interfere in

müddeiumumî *jur.* public prosecutor

müddet space of time, period, interval; **-diği ~çe** *conj.* as long as, while

müderris teacher; professor

müdevver round, spherical; transferred

müdür director, administrator; **~lük** directorate, head-office

müebbet perpetual, for life

müellif author

müessese foundation, establishment, institution

müessir touching; effective, influential

müeyyide confirming statement; *pol.* sanction

müezzin *rel.* muezzin, the one who calls Moslems to prayer

müfettiş inspector; **~lik** inspectorship, inspectorate

müflis bankrupt, penniless

müfreze *mil.* detachment

müfrit excessive; extremist

müfteri slanderer, calumniator

müftü *rel.* Mufti, expounder of Islamic law; **~lük** office and rank of a Mufti

mühendis engineer; **~lik** engineering

mühim important, urgent; **~mat** *pl.* ammunition *sg.*

mühlet respite, delay

mühtedi *rel.* who converted to Islam

mühür seal, signet-ring; **~lemek** *v/t* stamp with a seal; **~lü** sealed

müjde good news

mükâfat recompense, reward; prize; **~landırmak** *v/t* reward, recompense

mükellef obliged, liable

(**ile** to); **~iyet** obligation, liability

mükemmel complete, perfect, excellent

mülâhaza consideration, reflection; **~ etm.** *v/t* observe; consider

mülâkat meeting, interview

mülâyim suitable; gentle

mülhak *-e* added, annexed to; dependent on

mülk possession, property, landed property

mülkiyet possession, property; **~ zamiri** *gr.* possessive pronoun

mülteci refugee

mümarese skill; training

mümbit fertile, productive

mümessil representative

mümeyyiz distinctive

mümkün possible; **~ olduğu kadar** as far as possible

mümtaz distinguished, priviledged; autonomous

münadi herald, public crier

münakalât *pl.* transport, communication *sg.*

münakaşa dispute; **~ etm.** *v/t* discuss, dispute

münasebet fitness; proportion; relation; connection; opportunity; **~siz** unseemly, unreasonable

münasip suitable, proper; **~ görmek** *v/t* think proper, approve of

münavebe alternation, turn

münderecat *pl.* contents *of* a book, *etc.*

müneccim astrologer

müşavir

münevver enlightened, educated
münferit separate
münhal solved; vacant
münhani bent, curved
münhasır -e restricted to
münzevi retiring to a solitary place; hermit
müphem vague, indefinite
müptelâ -e subject to, having a passion for
müracaat application; reference; ~ **etm.** -e refer, apply to
mürai hypocrite; ~**lik** hy-[pocrisy]
mürebbiye governess
mürekkep 1. adj. -den composed of; **2.** n. ink; ~**li** inky; filled with ink
mürettebat pl. naut. crew sg.
mürettip compositor, typesetter
mürteci pol. reactionary
mürtekip corrupt, taking bribes
mürur passage, lapse of time; ~**uzaman** jur. limitation
müsaade permission; favour; ~ **etm.** v/t permit, consent to; ~ **ederseniz**, ~**nizle** with your permission, if you don't mind
müsabaka competition; race; ~**ya girmek** compete
müsademe collision, encounter
müsadere confiscation; ~ **etm.** v/t confiscate
müsait -e favourable to, convenient for

müsamaha indulgence, tolerance; ~ **etm.** -e be indulgent towards, tolerate; ~**kâr**, ~**lı** tolerant
müsav|at equality; ~**i** equal, equivalent
müseccel officially registered; notorious
müsekkin med. sedative
müshil med. purgative
müskirat pl. intoxicants
Müslüman rel. Moslem; ~**lık** the Religion of Islam; the Moslem world
müspet proved; positive
müsrif extravagant
müstahdem adj. employed; n. employee
müstahkem fortified
müstakil independent; apart
müstakim straight; upright
müstecir who rents; tenant
müstehcen obscene
müstehzi jeering, mocking
müstemleke pol. colony
müstenit -e based on, relying on
müstesna excluded (-den from); exceptional
müsteşar pol. councillor; undersecretary
müsvedde draft, rough copy
müşahede witnessing; observation
müşahhas personified; concrete
müşavere consultation; deliberation
müşavir counsellor

müşerref honoured

müşkül adj. difficult; n. difficulty; ~**ât** pl. difficulties; ~**ât çıkarmak** raise difficulties

müştak derived, derivative

müştemilât pl. contents; annexes, outhouses

müşterek common, joint

müşteri customer, purchaser, client

müşür mil. field-marshal

mütalaa studying, observation; opinion; ~ **etm.** v/t read, study

mütareke pol. armistice

müteahhit contractor; purveyor

müteakıp -i following after; subsequent

müteallik -e dependent on, concerning

mütecaviz -i exceeding, transgressing

müteessir -den sorry for, regretful of; influenced by

mütehassıs specialist

mütemadiyen adv. continuously, continually

mütenakız contradictory

mütenasip proportional, symmetrical

müteradif synonymous

mütercim translator

müteveccih -e turned towards, facing; ~**en** -e adv. in the direction of

müthiş terrible, fearful; enormous

müttefik agreeing; allied

müttehem accused, suspected (ile of)

müverrih historian, chronicler

müvezzi distributor; postman

müzakere discussion, conference, negotiation

müzayede ec. auction

müze museum

müzehhep gilded, gilt

müzik Western style music

müzmin chronic; ~**leşmek** become chronic

N

nabız pulse; -in **nabzını ölçmek** veya **tutmak** feel one's pulse

nacak short handled axe

nadan tactless, uneducated

nadir rare, unusual; ~**en** adv. rarely

nafaka livelihood; jur. alimony

nafia public works pl.

nafile useless, in vain

nağme tune, song

nahif thin, weak, fragile

nahiye an. region; pol. sub--district

nahoş unpleasant; unwell

nakarat refrain, repetition

nakd|en adv. in cash; ~**î** cash, in ready money; ~**î ceza** jur. fine

nakıs deficient; math. minus

nakız annulment; violation

nakil transport, removal, transfer

nakl|etmek v/t transport, transfer; narrate; **~i** traditional; **~iyat** pl. transport sg.; **~iye** transport expenses pl.

nakzetmek v/t jur. annul

nal horseshoe; **~bant** shoeing-smith; blacksmith; **~bur** hardware dealer

nalın pattens, clogs

nallamak v/t shoe

nam name, reputation; **~ına** in the name of

namaz rel. the Moslem ritual prayer; **~ kılmak** perform the ritual prayer; **~gâh** open space devoted to prayer

nam|dar, ~lı famous, celebrated

namlu barrel of a gun, etc., blade

namus honour, good name; **~lu** honourable, honest; **~suz** without honour, dishonest; **~suzluk** dishonesty [candidacy]

namzet candidate; **~lik**

nane bot. mint; peppermint; **~ şekeri** peppermint drop

nankör ungrateful; **~lük** ingratitude

nar bot. pomegranate

narcıl bot. coconut

nargile water-pipe, narghile

narh ec. officially fixed price

narin slim, slender, delicate

narkotik narcotic drug

nasbetmek v/t nominate, appoint (-e to)

nasıl how?, what sort?; **~sa** in any case

nasıp appointment, nomination

nasır wart, corn

nasihat advice, admonition; **~ etm. -e** advise

nasip lot, share, portion; **~ olm. -e** fall to one's lot

naşir publisher

natıka eloquence

natura nature, constitution

navlun naut. freight, chartering expenses

naylon nylon

naz coquetry; whims

nazar look, regard, consideration; the evil eye; **~ı itibara almak** v/t take into consideration; **~ boncuğu** bead worn to avert the evil eye; **~an -e** according to, with regard to; seeing that; **~î** theoretical; **~iye** theory

nazım versification, verse

nazır adj. -e overlooking, facing; n. pol. Minister

nazik delicate; polite; courteous; **~âne** adv. politely

naz|lanmak be coy; feign reluctance; **~lı** coqhettish, coy; reluctant

ne¹ what?, what, whatever, how; **~ güzel!** how nice; **~ ise** anyway; **~ kadar** how much?; **~ kadar zaman** how long?; **~ var ki** but; in fact; **~ zaman** when?

ne² not; nor; **~ ... ~ ...** neither ... nor

nebat plant; **~at bahçesi**

botanical garden; **~î** vegetable

necat salvation, safety

neceftaşı rock-cristal

nedamet regret, remorse

neden for what reason?, why?; *n.* reason; **~se** for some reason or other

nefer individual, person; *mil.* private

nefes breath; **~ almak** breathe, take a breath; **~ çekmek** take a whiff; *sl.* smoke hashish; **~ vermek** breathe out; **~li çalgı** *mus.* wind-instrument

nefis[1] soul, life, self, essence

nefis[2] excellent, exquisite

nefiy banishment, exile; negation

nefret aversion (-*den* for), disgust

nefrit *med.* nephritis

neft naphta

nefyetmek *v/t* banish

negatif negative (*a. phot.*)

nehir river

nekes mean, stingy

nem moisture; damp; **~len-mek** become damp; **~let-mek** *v/t* moisten; **~li** damp, humid

Neptun *astr.* Neptune

nere, **~si** what place?; whatsoever place; **~de** where?; **~den** from where?; **~ye** whither?; to what place?; **~li** from what place?

nergis *bot* narcissus

nesep family, genealogy

nesiç weaving; tissue

nesil generation; family

nesir prose

nesne thing; anything; *gr.* object

neşe gaiety, merriment, joy; **~lendirmek** *v/t* render merry; **~li** merry, in good humour; **~siz** sad, in bad humour

neşet origin [tion]

neşir publishing, publica-⌡

neşr|etmek *v/t* publish; **~i-yat** *pl.* publications

net net (*weight*); clear, distinct

netice consequence, effect, result; **~lenmek** come to a conclusion; close (**ile** with); **~siz** without success, result

nevi species, sort, variety

nevralji *med.* neuralgia

nevruz the Persian New Year's Day (*March 22nd*)

ney *mus.* reed, flute

neye *s.* **niye**

nezafet cleanliness

nezaket delicacy; politeness; **~li** refined; polite; **~siz** impolite

nezaret supervision, superintendence; Ministry; **etm.** -*e* superintend, direct, inspect

nezif *med.* haemorrhage

nezle cold in the head; **~ olm.** catch a cold

nıkris *med.* gout

nışadır *chem.* sal ammoniac; ammonia

nice how many?, many a ...; **~lik** state, quantity

niçin why?
nida cry, shout
nifak discord, strife
nihaî final
nihayet n. end, extremity;
adv. at last, finally; ~siz
endless, infinite
nikâh betrothal, marriage
~lı married; ~sız unmar-
ried, out of wedlock
nikbin optimistic
nikel nickel
nikotin nicotine
nilüfer bot. water-lily
nine grandmother
ninni lullaby
nirengi geo. triangulation
nisan April
nispet relation, proportion;
spite; ~en adv. relatively;
spitefully
nispî proportional; relative
nişan sign, mark; indica-
tion; scar; target; engagement; pol. decoration, order; ~ almak -i take aim
at; ~ yüzüğü engagement
ring; ~gâh backsight of a
gun; butt, target; ~lı engaged
nişasta chem. stark
nite|kim just as; as a mat-
ter of fact; ~le(ndir)mek
v/t qualify; ~lik quality
niyaz entreaty, supplication
niye why?
niyet resolve, intencion; ~
etm. -e, -mek ~inde olm.
intend
niza quarrel, dispute
nizam order, regularity;
system; ~î, ~lı legal; regu-

lar; ~name regulation; ~-
sız in disorder, illegal
Noel Christmas; ~ ağacı
Christmas tree; ~ baba
Father Christmas
nohut bot. chick-pea
noksan adj. deficient, defective; n. deficiency, defect
nokta point, dot; full stop;
spot, speck; mil. sentry,
post; ~ı nazar point of
view; ~lamak v/t dot,
mark, punctuate; ~lı vir-
gül gr. semicolon
norm standard; ~al nor-
mal
Norveç Norway; ~li n., adj.
Norwegian
not note; mark in school; ~
almak -den take a note of;
~ vermek -e pass judge-
ment on, think of; ~a pol.,
mus. note
noter jur. notary; ~lik office of a notary
nöbet turn of duty, etc.;
watch; med. onset, fit; ~
beklemek mount guard;
~çi adj. on guard, on duty;
n. watchman; ~leşe adv. in
turn, by turns
nöt(ü)r chem., gr. neutral
numara number; note,
mark; item; event; ~lamak
v/t number; ~lı numbered
numune sample, pattern,
model
nur light, brilliance
nutuk speech, discourse
nüans nuance
nüfus pl. people, souls; in-

habitants; ~ cüzdanı identity card; ~ kütüğü register of births and deaths; ~ sayımı census; ~lu having ... inhabitants

nüfuz penetration; influence; ~lu influential

nükleer nuclear

nükte subtle point, witty remark; ~li witty

nümayiş show, pomp; demonstration

nümune s. numune

nüsha specimen, copy

O

o he, she, it; that, those

oba large nomad tent; nomad family; nomad camp

obartmak v/t exaggerate

objektif phot. lens, objective; adj. objective

obruk phys. concave; n. pit

observatuvar observatory

obur gluttonous, greedy

ocak¹ January

ocak² furnace, kiln, hearth, fireplace; quarry, mine; family; club, local branch of a party, etc.; ~çı stoker, chimney-sweep

oda room, office; chamber; ~cı servant at an office or public building

odak phys. focus

oditoryum auditorium

odun firewood, log; ~cu wood-cutter; seller of firewood

ofis office

oflamak say 'ugh'

ofsayt offside (football)

Oğlak astr. Capricorn; 2 zo. kid

oğlan boy; knave at cards; ~cı pederast

oğul¹ son

oğul² zo. swarm of bees

ok arrow; beam, pole

okaliptüs bot. eucalyptus

okçu archer

oklava rolling-pin

oksijen oxygen; ~t chem. oxyde

okşamak v/t caress, fondle

oku|l school; ~ma yazma reading and writing; ~mak v/t read; learn, study; ~muş educated, learned

okunak|lı legible; ~sız difficult to read

oku|nmak be read or recited; ~tmak -e -i cause so. to read sth.; instruct so. in sth.; teach so. sth.; ~tman lecturer; ~yucu reader

okyanus geo. ocean

olacak which will happen

olağan commonly happening, frequent; ~üstü extraordinary

olanak possibility; ~lı possible

olanca utmost, all

olası probable; ~lık probability

olay event, incident

oldukça adv. rather, pretty

olgu fact

olgun ripe, mature; **~laş-mak** become ripe; mature; **~luk** ripeness, maturity

olimpiyat olympic games *pl.*

olmadık unprecedented

olmak *v/i* be, become; happen; ripen, mature

olma|**mış** not ripe, immature; **~z** impossible

olmuş ripe, mature

olta fishing-line; ~ **iğnesi** fish-hook; ~ **yemi** bait

oluk gutter-pipe, groove; **~lu** grooved

olum|**lu** *gr.* positive; **~suz** *gr.* negative

olunmak become, be

olur all right; possible; ~ **olmaz** anybody

oluş nature, condition; genesis, formation; **~um** formation

omlet omelette

omurga *an.* backbone; *naut.* keel

omuz shoulder; ~ **silkmek** shrug the shoulders; **~la-mak** *v/t* shoulder

on ten

ona to him, her, it

onamak *v/t* approve

onar|**ım** repair, restauration; **~mak** *v/t* repair

onay suitable, convenient; **~lamak** *v/t* approve, ratify

onbaşı *mil.* corporal

onda tenth; **~lık** tenth; decimal [perous)

ongun flourishing, pros-∫

onikiparmak (**bağırsağı**) *an.* duodenum

ons ounce *(28.35 gramme)*

onu him, her, it; **~n** his, hers, its

onur dignity, honour

opera *mus.* opera; **~tör** *med.* surgeon

ora; **~sı** that place; **~da** there; **~dan** from there; thence; **~ya** thither, there

orak sickle; harvest; **~çı** reaper

oralı of that place

oramiral *naut.* vice-admiral

oran measure, scale; proportion; **~lı** proportioned; **~tı** *math.* porportion

ordinaryüs professor holding a chair

ordu *mil.* army; **~evi** officers' club; **~gâh** military camp

org *mus.* organ

organ *an.,* *pol.* organ; **~ik** organic; **~izma** organism

orgeneral *mil.* full general

orijinal original

orkestra *mus.* orchestra

orkide *bot.* orchid

orkinos *zo.* tunny fish

orman forest, wood; **~cı** forester; **~lık** woodland

orospu prostitute, whore

orta middle, centre; central; ~ **parmak** middle finger; -*in* **~sından** through; **~dan kaldırmak** *v/t* remove; **~ya çıkmak** arise, come into being; **~ya koymak** *v/t* put forward; **~çağ** the Middle Ages *pl.*; **~elçi** Minister Plenipotentiary

ortak partner, associate; accomplice; **~laşa** adv. in common, jointly; **~lık** partnership; **ec.** joint-stock company

orta|lamak v/t reach the middle of; divide in the middle; **~m** environment; **~nca 1.** middle, middling; **2.** bot. hydrangea; **~okul** secondary school

Ortodoks orthodox; **~luk** the Orthodox Church

oruç rel. fasting, fast; **~ tutmak** fast; **~lu** fasting

Osmanlı Ottoman; **~ca** the Ottoman Turkish language

ot grass, herb; fodder

otel hotel; **~ci** hotel-keeper; **~cilik** hotel industry

otla|k pasture; **~mak** graze

oto motor-car; **~büs** motorbus; **~krasi** autocracy

otomat automaton; **~ik** automatic

oto|mobil s. oto; **~nomi** autonomy; **~park** car park; **~rite** authority

otur|ak chamberpot; seat, foot, bottom; **~mak** -e sit down on; run aground on; -de sit on, dwell in; settle; **~tmak** v/t seat, place; **~um** sitting, session

otuz thirty

ova grassy plain, meadow

ovalamak s. uvalamak

ov|mak, ~uşturmak s. uvmak, uvuşturmak

oy opinion; vote; **~ vermek** -e vote for

oya pinking, embroidery; **~lamak** v/t **1.** pink, embroider; **2.** fig. distract one's attention

oydaş who has the same opinion, like-minded

oylama voting, poll; **~k** v/t vote on

oylaş|ım deliberation; **~mak** v/t discuss, deliberate on

oyma sculpture, craving, engraving; **~cı** sculptor, engraver

oymak¹ v/t scoop out; engrave, carve

oymak² n. subdivision, tribe

oyna|k playful; unstable; tech. loose, having much play; **~mak** play, dance; be loose; **~tmak** v/t cause to play, move, dance

oysa(ki) yet, however, whereas

oyuk adj. hollowed out; n. cave

oyulga tacking; **~(la)mak** v/t tack together

oyun game, play, jest; **~ bozan** spoil-sport, kill-joy; **~cak** toy, plaything; **~cu** player, gambler; dancer

Ö

öbek heap; group
öbür the other; the next but one
öç revenge
öde|mek v/t pay, indemnify; **~nce** jur. damages pl., compensation; **~nek** appropriation, allowance; **~nmek** be paid; **~nti** subscription, fee
ödev duty
ödlek cowardly, timid
ödün compensation
ödünç loan; **~ almak** -den borrow from; **~ vermek** lend (-i -e sth. to)
öfke anger, rage; **~lendirmek** v/t anger, bring into a rage; **~lenmek** -e grow angry at; **~li** choleric, hotheaded
öge element
öğle noon; **~nde** at noon, about midday; **~(n)den önce** in the morning; **~(n)den sonra** in the afternoon; **~yin** s.
öğren|ci pupil; **~im** study, education; **~mek** v/t learn; become familiar with; hear
öğret|i doctrine; **~im** instruction; lessons; **~mek** v/t teach (-e to so.); **~men** teacher
öğün portion of a meal
öğür of the same age; familiarized
öğüt advice; **~ vermek** -e, **~lemek** v/t advise

ökçe heel of a boot
ökse birdlime; **~otu** bot. mistletoe
öksür|mek v/i cough; **~ük** cough
öksüz motherless; orphan; without friends [arnica]
öküz zo. ox; **~gözü** bot.]
ölç|ek measure, scale; **~mek** v/t measure
ölçü measure; dimensions; **~lü** moderate, temperate; **~süz** unmeasured; immoderate; **~t** criterion
öldür|mek v/t kill; **~tmek** v/t order to be killed; **~ücü** mortal, fatal
öl|mek die, fade, wither; **~mez** undying, immortal; **~ü** dead; corpse
ölüm death; **~ tehlikesi** danger of life
ömür life, existence
ön front; foremost; in the front; before; **~ümüzde** in front of us; -in **~ünde, ~üne** in front of; **~tekerlek** front wheel
önce in front, first; -den before; **ilk ~, ~den** first of all; **~lik** payment in advance
öncü mil. vanguard
öndelik precedence, priority
önder leader; **~lik** leadership
önek gr. prefix
önem importance; **~li** important; **~siz** unimportant

öner|ge proposal, motion; **~i** offer; **~mek** v/t propose, motion

öngör|mek v/t provide for; **~ü** far-sightedness

ön|lemek v/t resist, face, prevent; **~lük** apron; **~söz** preface; **~takı** gr. preposition; **~yargı** prejudice; **~yüzbaşı** mil. lieutenant-commander

öp|mek v/t kiss; **~ücük** kiss; **~üşmek** kiss one another

ördek zo. duck; med. urinal for use in bed

örf common usage; sovereign right; **~î** conventional; **~i idare** jur. state of siege

örgen organ

ör|gü plaited or knitted thing; tress of hair; **~güt** organization; **~mek** v/t plait, knit; darn

örne|ğin adv. for instance; **~k** specimen, sample, model, pattern; example

örs anvil

örselemek v/t handle roughly, spoil, rumple

örtmek v/t cover, wrap, veil

örtü cover, wrap; blanket; **~lmek** be covered, wrapped; **~lü** roofed; covered, wrapped up; concealed; **~nmek** cover, veil oneself

örümcek zo. spider; (**~ ağı**) cobweb

öt an. gall, bile

öte the farther side; other, farther; **~beri** this and that, various things; **~denberi** from of old; **~ki** the other, the farther

ötmek v/i sing; crow

ötürü -den by reason of, on account of, because of

öv|gü eulogy; **~mek** v/t praise; **~ülmek** be praised; **~ünmek** boast (ile with)

övüt|mek v/t grind; fig. eat heartily; **~ülmek** be ground

öyle so, such, like that; **~ki** such as to inf., so that; **~likle** adv. in such a manner; **~yse** if so, in that case

öyük artificial hill, mound

öz adj. own, real, genuine, essential; n. marrow; essence; pith; cream; self; **~ad** Christian name; **~dek** matter; **~deş** identical

özel personal, private special; **~ ad** gr. proper name; **~ hayat** private life; **~lik** peculiarity; **~likle** adv. particularly, specially

özen care, pains pl.; **~mek** -e take pains about, desire ardently; **~siz** careless, superficial (**~lik** autonomy)

özerk pol. autonomous; **~~)

özet extract; summary; **~lemek** v/t sum up, summarize

öz|gü -e peculiar, to; **~gün** specific, peculiar

özgür free, independent

özle|m longing; inclination; **~mek** v/t wish for, long for; **~tmek** -e -i make so. long for

özlü having kernel, pith, *etc.*; pulpy, substantial

özne *gr.* subject

özümlemek *v/t bot.* assimilate

özür defect; apology; ~ **dilemek** ask pardon; **~lü** having an excuse

özveri self-sacrifice, self-denial

P

pabuç shoe, slipper; *arch.* base(ment); **~çu** shoe-maker

paça lower part of the trouser leg; *zo.* trotters

paçavra rag; **~cı** rag-picker

padavra shingle, thin board

padişah sovereign, Sultan

pafta metal plate; large coloured spot; *geo.* section of a map

paha price

pahalı expensive; **~laşmak** become high-priced; **~lık** dearth

pak clean, pure

paket packet, parcel; package; **~ yapmak** *-den*, **~lemek** *v/t* pack up, make into a parcel

pakt *pol.* pact

palamar *naut.* hawser, cable

palamut¹ *zo.* tunny, pelamid

palamut² *bot.* valonia

palanka *mil.* redoubt

palavra idle talk, boast

palaz *n. zo.* young

palmiye *bot.* palm-tree

palto overcoat

pamuk cotton; **~lu** of cotton; wadded

panayır fair

pancar *bot.* beet

pancur outside shutter

pandül pendulum

panik panic

pankart placard

panorama panorama

pansıman *med.* dressing

pansiyon boarding-house; **~er** boarder

pantolon trousers

pantufla felt slipper

panzehir antidote

papa *rel.* Pope

papağan *zo.* parrot

papalık *rel.* Papacy, the Holy See

papatya *bot.* camomile; daisy

papaz *rel.* priest; king *at cards*

papiyon bow-tie

papyekuşe surface-coated paper, art paper

para money; Para (40th part of a Piastre); ~ **bozmak** change money; ~ **cezası** *jur.* fine; ~ **etm.** be worth; ~ **kırmak** earn a lot of money

parabol parabola

parafe etm. *v/t* initial

paragraf paragraph

parakete *naut.* log; long fishing-line

parala|mak v/t tear, cut in pieces; **~nmak** be torn in pieces; become rich
paralel adj. parallel; n. geo. parallel; parallel bars pl. (sport)
paralı rich; expensive; requiring payment
parantez parenthesis; bracket
parapet naut. bulwarks; parapet
para|sal ec. monetary; **~sız** without money; gratis
paraşüt parachute; **~çü** parachutist
paratoner lightning conductor
paravana folding screen
parazit parasite; atmospherics pl. (radio)
parça piece, bit; segment; **~lamak** v/t break or cut into pieces; **~lanmak** be broken into pieces; **~lı** in parts; allusive, sarcastic
pardesü light overcoat
pardon I beg your pardon!
parıl|damak gleam, glitter; **~tı** glitter, gleam, flash
park park; car park; **~ saati** parking meter; **~ yapmak** park a car; **~ yeri** parking place; Am. parking lot
parke parquet; small paving stones pl.
parla|k bright, shining; successful; **~mak** shine, flare; become distinguished
parlamento parliament
parlatmak v/t cause to shine, polish

parmak finger, toe; spoke of a wheel; **~ izi** fingerprint; **~lık** railing, balustrade, grating
parola password
pars zo. leopard
parsa money collected from the crowd
parsel plot of land; **~lemek** v/t divide into plots of land, subdivide
parşömen parchment
parti pol. political party; match, game; **~li** party member; **~zan** partisan
pas¹ rust, tarnish, dirt; **~ tutmak** rust
pas² stake at cards; pass (sport)
pasaj passage; arcade
pasak dirt; **~lı** dirty, slovenly
pasaport passport
pasif adj. passive; n. ec. liability, debt
paskalya rel. Easter; **~ ekmeği** a kind of sweet bread
pas|lanmak become rusty; **~lanmaz** stainless; **~lı** rusty, dirty
paso pass on a railway, etc.
paspas doormat
pasta¹ fold, pleat
pasta² cake, pastry, tart; **~cı** pastry-cook, confectioner; **~(ha)ne** confectioner's shop, pastry-shop
pastırma pressed meat
pastörize pasteurized
paşa Pasha (former title of generals and governors of a province).

paşmak shoe, slipper
pat[1] *adj.* flat, snub
pat[2] *bot.* aster
pat[3] thud
patak whacking, beating; **~lamak** *v/t* give a whacking to
patates *bot.* potato
patavatsız tactless
paten skate; roller skate
patenta patent; *naut.* bill of health; *pol.* letters of naturalisation
patır|damak make the noise of footsteps; **~tı** noise; row, tumult
patik child's shoe; **~a** footpath
patinaj skating, slipping
patla|k burst, torn open; **~mak** *v/i* burst, explode; **~ngaç, ~ngıç** fire-cracker; toy torpedo; **~tmak** *v/t* blast, blow up
patlıcan *bot.* aubergine, egg-plant
patrik *rel.* Patriarch; **~hane** Patriarchate; **~lik** the office of a patriarch
patron head of a firm *or* business, employer
paviyon pavilion
pay share; lot, portion; *math.* divident; **~da** *math.* divisor; **~daş** participator, partner
paydos cessation from work; break, rest
paye rank, dignity
payitaht residence, capital
payla|mak *v/t* scold; **~şmak** *v/t* share, divide up

paytak *adj.* knock-kneed; *n.* pawn *at chess*
payton *s.* **fayton**
pazar[1] Sunday
pazar[2] open market, market-place; **~laşmak** bargain (**ile** with); **~lık** bargaining; **~lık etm.** *s.* **~laşmak**
pazartesi Monday
peçete napkin
pehlivan wrestler; *fig.* hero, champion
pehpeh! bravo!
pehriz abstinence, continence; *med.* diet; **~ tutmak** fast; observe a diet
pek hard, firm, violent; very much; **~âlâ!** very good!; all right!; **~i!** very good!; very well!
pek|işmek become firm; **~mez** boiled grape-juice
peksimet hard biscuit
pelerin cape
pelesenk *s.* balm, balsam
pelte jelly, gelatine
peltek lisping
pembe rose colour, pink
penaltı penalty kick (*football*)
pencere window
pençe paw; strength, violence; sole of *a shoe;* **~lemek** *v/t* grasp, claw; **~leşmek** be at grips (**ile** with)
penisilin *med.* penicillin
pens penny
pens(e) *tech.* pliers, tweezers *pl.*
pepe stammering; **~lemek** stammer

perakende *ec.* retail; **~ci** retailer

perçin *tech.* rivet; **~lemek** *v/t* rivet, clench; **~li** riveted

perdah polish, gloss; **~ vurmak** *-e*, **~lamak** *v/t* polish, burnish; **~lı** polished, shining; **~sız** unpolished, dull; matt

perde curtain, screen, veil; membrane; *thea.* act; **~lemek** *v/t* screen, veil; **~li** veiled, curtained; having ... acts; **~siz** without veil, shameless

perende somersault; **~ atmak** turn a somersault

perese mason's plumb-line; *fig.* state, condition

pergel pair of compasses

perhiz *s.* pehriz

peri fairy; good genius

perişan scattered, routed; wretched, ruined; **~ etm.** *v/t* scatter; rout; **~ olm.** be scattered, routed; **~lık** disorder, wretchedness

perma(nant) permanent wave, perm

permi pass *at the railway*; *ec.* permit

peron platform

persenk refrain, word continually repeated in speech

personel personnel, staff

perşembe Thursday

pertavsız *phys.* magnifying-glass

peruka wig

pervane *zo.* moth; *tech.* propeller, screw

pervasız fearless, without restraint

pervaz cornice, fringe

pesek tartar *of the teeth*

pestil pressed and dried fruit pulp

peş the space behind; *-in* **~inde dolaşmak (gezmek)** pursue *sth.*; *-in* **~inden koşmak** run after

peşin *adv.* in advance, formerly; *adj.* paid in advance, ready

peşkeş gift

peşkir napkin

peştamal large bath-towel

petek honeycomb; circular disk

petrol petroleum

pey money on account; **~ vermek** pay a deposit

peyda existent, manifest; **~ olm.** appear

peygamber *rel.* prophet

peyk *astr., pol.* satellite

peylemek *v/t* reserve for oneself

peynir cheese

peyzaj landscape (picture)

pezevenk *vulg.* pimp, procuror

pıhtı coagulated, liquid; **~laşmak** clot, become coagulated

pınar spring, source

pırasa leek

pıratika *naut.* clean bill of health

pırıl|damak gleam, glitter; **~tı** gleam, flash

pırlangıç humming-top

pırlanta *n.* brilliant

pırtı (worn-out) things *pl.*
pıtır|damak make a tapping sound; **~tı** tapping, crackling sound

piç bastard, offshoot, sucker
pide *a kind of* flat bread
pijama pyjamas *pl.*
pikap *mus.* record-player; pick-up, small truck
pike[1] piqué, quilting
pike[2] *av.* diving
piknik picnic
pil *el.* battery
pilaki stew of beans or fish *with oil, onions, etc.*
pilav pilaf
piliç chick
pilot *av., naut.* pilot
pineklemek slumber, doze
pingpong ping-pong, table tennis
pinti stingy
pipo tobacco pipe
pir patron saint
pire flea; **~lenmek** become infested with fleas
pirinç[1] rice
pirinç[2] brass
piruhi stewed dough *with cheese or ground meat*
pirzola cutlet
pis dirty; foul; obscene; **~boğaz** greedy
piskopos *rel.* bishop
pis|lemek *-e* relieve oneself on, make a mess on; **~lenmek** become dirty; **~letmek** *-i* make dirty, soil; **~lik** dirtiness, dirt, mess
pist running track
piston *tech.* piston; **~ kolu** connecting rod, piston-rod

piş|irim(lik) amount to be cooked at one time; **~irmek** *v/t* cook, bake; learn very well; **~kin** well-cooked, well-baked; *fig.* self-assured
pişman: **~ olm.** *-e* be sorry for, regretful of; **~lık** regret; penitence
pişmek be cooked, baked; ripen, mature
piyade *mil.* foot-soldier; infantry; pedestrian; pawn *at chess*
piyango lottery
piyano *mus.* piano; **~ çalmak** play the piano
piyasa promenading; *ec.* market, market price
piyaz onions and parsley *added to a stew*; salad of beans, onions, oil, *etc.*
piyes *thea.* play
plaj strand, beach
plak gramophone record; **~a** number plate *of a car*
plan plan; **~lamak** *v/t* plan; **~ör** *av.* glider; **~ya** carpenter's plane
plasman *ec.* investment
plastik plastic
platin platinum
plebisit *pol.* plebiscite
plise pleated
Plüton *astr.* Pluto
podra powder
podüsüet suède
pohpohlamak *v/t* flatter
poker poker
polarmak *v/t phys.* polarize
polemik polemics

poliçe *ec.* bill of exchange; insurance policy

poligon *mil.* artillery range

polis police; policeman

politika politics; policy; **~cı** politician; who knows when to flatter

Polon|ez *tech.* Pole, Polish; **~ya** Poland

pompa *tech.* pump; **~ lamak** *v/t* pump

ponksiyon *med.* puncture

ponza pumice (stone)

porselen porcelain

porsiyon portion, plate

porsuk *zo.* badger

portakal *bot.* orange

portatif portable

Portekiz Portugal

portmanto coat-stand, coat-hanger

portre portrait

posa sediment; tartar

post skin, hide *with the fur on*

posta post, postal service; passenger-train, mail train; **~ pulu** postage stamp; **~cı** postman

pot: ~ gelmek go wrong; **~ yeri** difficulty

postane post-office

potin boot

potrel *tech.* iron support

potur pleat, fold; pleated; Turkish breeches

poyra *tech.* hub; axle end

poyraz *geo.* north-east wind

poz pose; *phot.* exposure; **~ vermek** *-e phot.* expose

pozitif positive

pörsük shrivelled up; withered

pösteki sheep *or* goat skin; **~ saydırmak** *-e* give tiresome but useless work to do

pratik *adj.* practical; *n.* practice; **~a** *s.* **piratika**

piratika

prens prince; **~es** princess

prensip principle

prevantoryum sanatorium *for tuberculosis suspects*

prim premium

priz *el.* wall-socket

profes|ör professor; **~yonel** professional

program program(me)

proje project

projek|siyon projection; **~tör** search-light

prolet|arya proletariat; **~er** proletarian

propaganda propaganda; **~cı** propagator

protestan *rel.* Protestant; **~lık** Protestantism

protesto protest; **~ etm.** *v/t* protest against

protokol protocol

prova trial, test, rehearsal; printer's proof

pruva *naut.* prow, bow

psik|analiz psychoanalysis; **~oloji** psychology

puan *s.* **puvan**

puding *geo.* conglomerate; pudding

pudra *s.* **podra**

pul thin round disk; scale for fishing; stamp; **~cu** vendor of stamps; stamp collector; **~lamak** *v/t*

stamp; **~lu** bearing stamps;
~suz without stamps
pupa *naut.* stern
puro cigar
pus mist, haze; blight,
mildew; **~arık** hazy; mirage; **~armak** become
hazy
pusat equipment
puse kiss
puslanmak be misty,
hazy
pus|mak crouch down, lie
in ambush; **~u** ambush;
~uya yatmak lie in wait
pusula¹ *naut.* compass
pusula² short letter *or*
note

put idol; cross; **~perest**
idolator
puvan point, score
püf puff *of wind, etc.*;
~kürmek, ~lemek *v/t* blow
out, puff
pünez drawing-pin
pürçek curl, curly
püre purée, mash
pürtük knob, protuberance
pürüz roughness, unevenness; **~lü** rough, uneven;
~süz even, smooth
püskül tuft, tassel
püskür|mek *tech.* atomizer;
~mek *v/t* blow out, spray,
splutter; **~tmek** *v/t* scatter,
beat off

R

Rabbi: Ya ~! My God!
rabıt connection, bond
rabıta tie, bond, connection, conformity; **~lı** in
good order, regular; **~sız**
disordered, irregular
radar radar
radyatör *tech.* radiator
radyo radio, wireless
radyum radium
raf shelf
rafadan soft-boiled (*egg*)
rağbet desire, inclination;
~li desirous (*-e* for); in
demand, sought after; **~-
siz** feeling no inclination
rağmen *-e* in spite of
rahat *n.* rest, ease, comfort;
adj. at ease, comfortable;
~ etm. rest, make oneself
comfortable; **~sız** unquiet,

uneasy; indisposed, ill; **~-
sızlık** uneasiness; indisposition
rahibe *rel.* nun
rahim *an.* womb
rahip *rel.* monk
rahle low reading-desk
rahmet mercy, compassion;
fig. rain; **~li(k)** the deceased, the late
rakam figure, number
raket tennis-racket
rakı raki, arrack
raks dance, dancing
rakik tender, softhearted
rakip rival; **~siz** unrivalled
rakkas pendulum; **~e** woman dancer
raksetmek dance, play
ramazan Ramazan (*the
month of Moslem fasting*)

rampa 1. *naut.* boarding; **2.** ramp; loading platform

randevu rendezvous, meeting, date; **~ evi** secret brothel; **~cu** keeper of a secret brothel

randıman *ec.* yield, profit, output

rapor report; medical certificate; **~tör** reporter

raptiye paper-clip

rasat *astr.* observation; **~hane** observatory, meteorological station

raspa *tech.* scraper; grater; **~ etm.** *v/t* scrape

rastge|le met by hazard; by chance, at random; **~lmek** *-e* meet by chance, come across; **~tirmek** *v/t* succeed in meeting

rastla|mak *-e* meet by chance; **~ntı** chance, coincidence

raşiti|k *med.* rachitic, rickety; **~zm** rickets

ravent *bot.* rhubarb

ravnt round (*sport*)

ray rail *of the railway, etc.*

rayiç *ec.* market price, current value

rayiha smell, aroma

razı *-e* satisfied, contented with, agreeing to; **~ etm.** *v/t* satisfy

realite reality

reçel fruit preserve, jam

reçete recipe, prescription

reçin|a, ~e *bot.* resin

reddetmek *v/t* reject, repel, refute

redingot frock-coat

refah comfort, luxury

refakat accompaniment; **~ etm.** *-e* accompany

referandum *pol.* referendum

refetmek *v/t* raise, remove, annul

refik companion; **~a** wife

reform reform

rehber guide; guide-book; **~lik** guiding

rehin pawn, pledge, security

rehine hostage

reis head, chief, president

rejim *pol.* regime; *med.* diet

rejisör *thea.* stage-manager

rekabet rivalry, competition; **~ etm.** compete (**ile** with)

reklam advertisement

rekolte harvest, crop

rekor record; **~cu** record-breaker

rektör rector *of a university*; **~lük** rectorship

relatif relative

remiz sign, nod; allusion

ren[1] *zo.* reindeer

Ren[2]: **~ nehri** the Rhine

rencide hurt, annoyed

rençper workman, farm-hand

rende carpenter's plane; grater; **~lemek** *v/t* plane, grate

rengârenk multicoloured

renk colour; **~li** coloured; **~siz** colourless, pale

repertuvar *thea.* repertoire, program(me)

resif *geo.* reef

resim design, drawing, picture; ceremony; tax, toll; **~ çekmek** (or **çıkarmak**) take a photo; **~li** illustrated

resmî official, formal; **~ elbise** evening dress; uniform; **~ gazete** official gazette

ressam designer, artist; **~lık** the art of painting

reşit *jur.* adult

ret rejecting; repudiation

retuş s. **rötuş**

reva lawful, permissible

revaç ec. being in demand, being current

revani a kind of sweet made with semolina

revanş s. **rövanş**

reverans bow, courtesy

revir infirmary

rey opinion; vote; **~ vermek** -e vote for

rezalet vileness, baseness

reze hinge

rezene *bot.* fennel

rezil vile, base

rıhtım *naut.* quay; wharf

rıza consent, acquiescence; **~ göstermek** -e consent to, resign oneself to

riayet observance; respect, consideration; **~ etm.** -e treat with respect, pay attention to; **~sizlik** disrespect, irreverence

rica request; **~ etm.** *v/t* request (-den from so.)

ringa zo. herring

risale treatise, pamphlet

---

ruhsat

risk risk; **~e etm.** *v/t* risk

ritim *mus.* rhythm

rivayet narrative, tale

riya hypocrisy; **~kâr** hypocritical

riyaset presidency, chairmanship

riziko risk

roket rocket

rol role, part

roman novel; **~cı** novelist; **~tik** romantic

Romanya R(o)umania

romatizma *med.* rheumatism

Romen Roman; **~ rakamları** *pl. math.* Roman numbers

rop robe, dress

rosto roasted; roast meat

rota *naut.* ship's course

rozbif roast beef

rozet rosette

rölöve registration

römork trailer; **~ör** tractor; *naut.* tugboat

Rönesans Renaissance

röportaj report of a newspaperman

rötuş *phot.* retouching

rövanş revenge (*sport*)

rugan varnish; patent leather

ruh soul; spirit; essence; energy

ruhan|i spiritual; **~iyet** spirituality

ruhban *rel.* clergy

ruh|bilim psychology; **~î** psychic; **~lu** animated, lively

ruhsat permission, permit;

5*

~name permit; credentials

ruhsuz inanimate, lifeless

Rum Greek *living in Moslem countries;* **~ca** Modern Greek *(language);* **~en** Rumanian; **~î** *adj. (Turkish modification of the Julian calendar)*

Rus Russian; **~ça** Russian *(language);* **~ya** Russia

rutubet dampness, humidity; **~li** damp

rüsum *pl.* customs, taxes

rüşvet bribe; **~ almak, ~ yemek** accept bribes

rütbe degree, grade; rank

rüya dream; **~ görmek** *v/i* dream; **~sında görmek** *-i* see in a dream

rüyet seeing, vision

rüzgâr wind; **~li** windy

S

saadet happiness

saat hour; time; watch; clock; **~ kaç?** what is the time?; **~ beştir** it is five o'clock; **~çi** watchmaker

sabah morning; **~ları** every morning; **~leyin** in the morning, early; **~lık** morning dress

saban plough

sabık former, previous, foregoing

sabıka *jur.* previous conviction; **~lı** previously convicted

sabır patience; **~lı** patient; **~sız** impatient; **~sızlık** impatience

sabih havuz *naut.* floating dock

sabit fixed, stationary, firm; proved

sabotaj sabotage

sabretmek be patient; *-e* endure

sabun soap; **~cu** soap-maker, soap-seller; **~lamak** *v/t* soap; **~luk** soap-dish

saç¹ sheet-iron, iron plate; *adj.* made of sheet-iron

saç² hair

saçak eaves of a house; fringe; **~bulut** fleecy cloud, cirrus; **~lı** having eaves; fringed

saç|kıran *med.* alopecia; **~lı** having hair, hairy

saçma scattering; small shot; *adj.* nonsensical; **~k** *v/t* scatter, sprinkle; **~lamak** talk nonsense, say incongruous things

sada sound; echo

sadaka alms; charity

sadakat fidelity, devotion; **~li** faithful, devoted (*-e* to)

sadaret Grand Vizierate

sade mere, simple; unmixed, pure; plain; **~ce** *adv.* merely, simply; **~dil** guileless, naive; **~leştirmek** *v/t* simplify; **~lik** ingenuousness

sadık faithful, honest (*-e* to)

sadme collision; explosion

sadrazam Grand Vizier

saf[1] row, line, rank

saf[2] pure; sincere

safa enjoyment, pleasure; peace, ease

safdil simple-hearted, naive

safha phase

safi clear, pure; sincere; net

safiha leaf, sheet, plate

safra[1] *naut.* ballast

safra[2] *an.* bile, gall

safran *bot.* saffron

safsata false reasoning; sophistry

sağ 1. alive, safe, sound; **2.** right, right-handed; **~a dönmek** turn to the right

sağanak rainstorm, downpour

sağcı *pol.* rightist, right-wing sympathizer

sağduyu common sense

sağı bird excrement

sağım quantity milked

sağır deaf; giving out a dull sound; **~lık** deafness

sağ|lam sound, whole, trustworthy; **~lamak** v/t secure, ensure; **~lamlaş-tırmak** v/t put right, make sound or firm

sağlık life; health

sağmak v/t milk; take honey from

sağmal, sağman giving milk; **~inek** milch cow

sağrı rump of an animal

sağu eulogy; lamentation

saha space, field area

sahaf dealer in secondhand books

sahan copper pan; **~lık** landing on a staircase, platform

sahi sound, true, correct; **~ mi?** is that really so!?

sahibe female owner

sahife s. **sayfa**

sahih s. **sahi**

sahil shore, coast, bank

sahip owner, possessor; **~ olm.** -e possess, own; **~siz** ownerless, abandoned

sahne *thea.* stage

sahra open place; desert

sahte false, counterfeit; **~ci, ~kâr** who counterfeits or forges; **~kârlık** forgery, counterfeiting

sahur *rel.* meal before dawn during Ramazan

sair other; that remains; **~filmenam** somnambulist

sakal beard; whiskers; **~ı koyvermek** (or **uzatmak, salıvermek**) let the beard grow; **~lı** bearded; **~sız** having no beard

sakar[1] white blaze on a horse's forehead

sakar[2] ill-omened, unlucky

sakarin saccharine

sakat defected; disabled, invalid; **~lamak** v/t injure, mutilate; **~lık** infirmity; defect

sakın beware!, don't!; **~ca** objection; danger; **~gan** timid; cautious; **~mak** -den guard oneself from, beware of; be cautious

sakır|damak shiver; **~tı** shivering

Sakıt *astr.* Mars

sakız mastic

sakin adj. stationary; n. in-habitant

sakit silent; taciturn

sak|lamak v/t hide, keep secret; keep, store; **~lam-baç** hide-and-seek; **~lan-mak** hide oneself; be kept; be concealed

saklı hidden, secret; pre-served

saksağan zo. magpie

saksı flower-pot

saksonya Dresden china

sal naut. raft

salâhiyet authority, com-petence; **~ vermek** -e au-thorize; **~tar** authoritative; competent (-e for)

salak silly, doltish

salam salami

salamura brine for pickling

salapurya naut. small lighter

salata salad, lettuce; **~lık** cucumber

salça sauce; tomato sauce

saldır|gan aggressor; **~ım** aggression, attack; **~mak** -e attack, make an attack on; **~mazlık** pol. non-ag-gression

salep bot. salep; hot drink made of salep

salgın 1. adj. contagious, epidemic; n. contagion; **2.** pol. temporary tax

salı Tuesday

salık information

salıncak swing; a kind of hammock; **~lı koltuk** rocking-chair

salınmak sway from side to

side; be thrown (-e at, into); tech. be turned on

salıvermek v/t let go, set free, release

salih -e suitable for

salim sound, healthy

salip rel. cross, crucifix

salkım hanging bunch, cluster; bot. acacia, wist-aria

salla|mak v/t swing, shake, wave; **~nmak** swing about; fig. totter, loiter about

salmak v/t throw, spread, cast (-e on); impose; -e at-tack

salon guest-room, dining-room, hall

salt adj. mere, simple; adv. merely, solely

salta¹ standing on the hind legs (dog, etc.)

salta² slackening of a rope

saltanat sovereignty, rule; fig. pomp, magnificence

saltçılık absolutism, auto-cracy

salya an. saliva

salyangoz zo. snail

saman straw; **~ kâğıdı** tracing-paper; **~ nezlesi** med. hey fever; **~kapan** amber; **~lık** barn, granary; **~yolu** astr. the Milky Way

samim|î sincere, cordial; **~iyet** sincerity

samur zo. sable

samyeli poisonous wind, simoon

san reputation, esteem

sana to you, you

sanat trade, craft; art; skill,

ability; ~ **okulu** trade school; ~**cı**, ~**kâr** artisan; artist; actor; ~**lı** artistic

sanatoryum sanatorium

sanayi pl. industries; ~**leştirmek** v/t industrialize

sancak flag, standard, pol. sub-province

sancı stomach-ache, gripes, stitch; ~**mak** ache

sandal[1] sandalwood

sandal[2] sandal (shoe)

sandal[3] naut. rowing-boat; ~**cı** boatman

sandalye chair; fig. office, post [cash-box)

sandık chest, coffer, box;}

sandviç sandwich

sangı confused, stupefied

sanı idea, imagination; ~**k** suspected, accused

saniye second, moment

sanki supposing that; ~ -**miş gibi** as if, as though

sanmak v/t think, suppose

sansar zo. pine-marten; polecat

sansör pol. censor; ~**ür** censureship

santigram centigram(me); ~**m(etre)** centimetre

santral telephone exchange; power-station

santrfor centre forward (sport); ~**haf** centre half (sport)

sap stem, handle, stalk

sapa adj. off the road

sapak unnatural, abnormal

sapan sling, catapult

sapık abnormal, perverted; crazy

sapılmak turn off (-e into)

sapıtmak v/i go crazy; talk nonsense

saplamak v/t thrust, pierce (-e into); ~**lı** having a handle or stem

sapmak -e deviate, turn to; get into

sapsarı bright yellow; very pale

saptamak v/t fix, establish; ~**nmak** be fixed

saptırmak v/t make deviate, turn (-e to)

sara med. epileptic fit

saraç saddler, leather-worker

sarahat explicitness

sararmak turn yellow or pale

saray palace, mansion; government house

sardalya zo. sardine

sarf expenditure, use; ~ **etm.** v/t spend, expend; ~**ınazar etm.** -**den** disregard, relinquish; ~**iyat** pl. expenses

sargı bandage

sarhoş -**den** drunk with; ~**luk** drunkenness

sarı yellow; pale; ~**çalı** bot. barberry

sarık turban; ~**lı** wound, surrounded; ~**lmak** -e be wound or wrapped in; throw oneself upon; clasp, embrace

sarılık yellowness; med. jaundice

sarım bandage; el., phys. turn of winding

sarı|sabır bot. aloe; **~şın** fair-haired, blond

sarih clear, explicit

sark|aç pendulum; **~ık** pendulous, hanging; **~ınmak** lean over; -e molest, worry; **~ıntı** robbery; molestation; **~mak** -den hang down from, lean out of; -e come down on, attack

sarmak v/t wind; surround; wrap (-e into); -e climb (vine)

sarman huge

sarmaş|ık bot. ivy; **~mak** embrace one another

sarmısak bot. garlic

sarnıç cistern, tank

sarp steep, inaccessible; **~laşmak** become steep

sarraf money-changer

sars|ak palsied, quivering; **~ı** shock of an earthquake; **~ık s.~ak**; **~ılmak** -den be shaken by; **~ıntı** shock, concussion; **~mak** v/t shake, agitate, upset

sataşmak -e annoy, seek a quarrel with, tease

sathî superficial

satıcı salesman, seller

satıh upper surface, face

sat|ılık on sale, for sale; **~ılmak** -e be sold to; **~ım** sale; **~ın almak** v/t buy

satır¹ line of writing; **~ başı** paragraph (indentation)

satır² large knife

sat|ış selling, sale; **~mak** v/t sell (-e to)

satranç chess

Satürn astr. Saturn

satvet force, power

sav word; thesis

savana savanna

savaş struggle, fight; war; **~çı** combatant; **~kan** warlike, brave; **~mak** struggle, fight (ile with)

savat engraving in black on silver, Tula work

savcı public prosecutor; **~lık** office of the prosecutor

savmak v/t drive away, dismiss; get over an illness; pass away

savruk awkward, clumsy

savsa|k negligent, dilatory; **~lamak** v/t put off with pretexts

savsamak v/t neglect

savunma defence; **Millî 2 Bakanlığı** Ministry of National Defence; **~k** v/t defend

savurmak v/t toss about; blow violently

savuş|mak pass, cease; slip away; **~turmak** v/t escape, avoid

sây endeavour, effort

saya upper part of a shoe

sayaç tech. meter, counter

saydam transparent

saye shadow, shade; **~sinde** thanks to; **bu ~de** by this, here by

sayfa page; **~yı çevirmek** turn over the leaf

sayfiye summer house, villa

saygı respect, esteem, consideration; **~larımla** yours faithfully; **~lı** respectful, considerate

saygın esteemed, respected; ~**lık** esteem, credit

saygısız disrespectful; ~**lık** disrespect

sayı number

sayıklamak talk in one's sleep *or* delirium

sayı|lama statistics; counting; ~**lı** counted, limited; ~**lmak** be counted, numbered, esteemed; ~**m** census; ~**n** esteemed; dear (*in a letter*); ~**sız** innumerable

sayış|mak settle accounts (**ile** with); 2**tay** *pol.* the Exchequer and Audit Department

say|lav *pol.* deputy, member of parliament; ~**mak** *v/t* count, number; count as, respect, esteem; suppose

sayrı ill; ~**msak** sham patient

saz[1] *mus.* musical instrument; Oriental music

saz[2] *bot.* rush, reed; ~**lık** place covered with rushes

sebat stability; perseverance; ~**kâr**, ~**lı** enduring, persevering; ~**sız** unstable, fickle

sebebiyet vermek -*e* cause, occasion

sebep cause, reason; source; ~ **olm.** -*e* cause; ~**siz** without any reason *or* cause

sebil public fountain

sebze vegetable

seccade prayer rug

seciye character, natural disposition; ~**li** of high moral character; ~**siz** untrustworthy

seçilmek be picked, chosen

seçim election; ~ **hakkı** *pol.* suffrage, franchise

seçkin choice, distinguished

seçme|k choose, select, elect; ~**n** elector

sedef mother-of-pearl

sedir[1] *a kind of* divan

sedir[2] *bot.* cedar

sedye stretcher

sefahat dissipation

sefalet poverty, misery

sefaret *pol.* ambassadorship; embassy, legation; ~**hane** embassy, legation (*building*)

sefer 1. voyage; campaign; 2. time, occurance; ~**ber** mobilized for war; ~**berlik** mobilization; ~**tası** food box *with several dishes fastened together*

sefih spendthrift; dissolute

sefil poor, miserable

sefir *pol.* ambassador

seğir|mek tremble, twitch nervously; ~**tmek** -*e* run, hasten to

seher time before dawn

sehpa tripod; three-legged stool; gallow

sehven *adv.* inadvertently

Sekendiz *astr.* Saturn

seki pedestal; stone seat

sekiz eight

sekmek hop, ricochet

sekreter secretary

seksen eighty

seksü|alite sexuality; ~**el** sexual

sekte pause, interval

sektirmak v/t cause to rebound, ricochet

sektör sector

sel torrent, inundation, flood

selâm greeting, salutation, salute; ~ **söylemek** -e give one's regards to; ~ **vermek** -e greet, salute

selâmet safety, security, soundness

selâmla|ma salutation, welcome; **~mak** v/t salute, greet; **~şmak** exchange greetings (ile with)

selâm|lık the part of a Moslem house reserved for men; **~(ün)aleyküm!** Peace be on you! (formal greeting of Moslems)

self predecessor, ancestor

selim safe, sound

selüloit celluloid

selüloz cellulose

selvi s. servi

semafor signal

semaver samovar

semavî celestial, heavenly

sembol symbol

semer pack-saddle

semere fruit, profit, result

semir|mek v/i grow fat; **~tmek** v/t fatten; manure

semiz fat, fleshy; **~lik** fatness; **~otu** bot. purslane

sempati sympathy; **~k** sympathetic

semt region, quarter; **~ürres** astr. zenith

sen you, thou

sena praise, eulogy

senaryo thea. scenario

senat|o senate; **~ör** senator

sendelemek v/i totter, stagger

sendika trade union; **~cılık** trade unionism

sene year; **~lik** lasting ... years

senet written proof, document, title-deed; **~li** based on written proof

senfoni mus. symphony

seni you; thee; **~n** thine, your, of you

senli benli familiar, intimate

sentetik chem. synthetic

sepet basket; wickerwork; **~çi** maker or seller of baskets; **~lemek** v/t put in a basket; sl. get rid of

sepi dressing for hides; **~ci** tanner; **~lemek** v/t tan, prepare

serbest free, independent; **~çe** adv. freely; **~î, ~lik** liberty

serçe zo. sparrow

ser|dar mil. general, commander-in-chief; **~dengeçti** who sacrifices his life

sere span

seren naut. yard

sergi anything spread for sale; exhibition; **~lemek** v/t exhibit

sergüzeşt adventure

seri[1] n. series

seri[2] adj. quick, swift

serilmek -e be spread out on; fall, drop on

serin cool; **~leşmek** become cool; **~letmek** *v/t* cool, refresh; **~lik** coolness

serkeş unruly, rebellious

serlevha title, heading

sermaye *ec.* capital, stock; **~dar** capitalist

sermek *v/t* spread (**-e** on, over)

serpelemek *v/i* drizzle

serp|ilmek fall as if sprinkled; grow; **~inti** drizzle, spray; repercussion; **~mek** *v/t* sprinkle, scatter (**-e** on)

sersem stunned, bewildered; **~letmek** *v/t* stunn, stupefy; **~lik** stupefaction, confusion

serseri vagrant; loose

sert hard, harsh, severe, violent; **~leşmek** become hard, severe; **~lik** hardness, harshness, violence

servet wealth

servi *bot.* cypress

servis service, waiting

ses sound, noise, voice, cry; **~ çıkarmak** speak; **~ vermek** give out a sound; **~lemek** *v/t* hearken, listen to; **~lenmek** *-e* call out to; answer a call

sesli voiced; **~ (harf)** *gr.* vocal

sessiz quiet, silent; **~ (harf)** *gr.* consonant

set barrier, dam, bank

sevap good deed, meritorious action

sevda love, passion; intense longing; **~lı** madly in love

sevgi love, affection, compassion; **~li** beloved, dear

sev|ici Lesbian; **~ilmek** be loved, lovable

sevim love, affability; **~li** lovable, sympathetic

sevinç joy, delight; **~li** joyful

sevin|dirmek *v/t* make happy; cheer, comfort; **~mek** *-e* be pleased with

Sevir *astr.* Taurus

sevişmek love one another

seviye level, rank, degree

sevk driving; dispatch; **~ etm.** *v/t* drive; send; **~ıyat** *pl.* dispatch *sg.*

sevmek *v/t* love, like, fondle

seyahat journey, travelling; **~ etm.** *v/i* travel

seyir movement, voyage; looking on; **~ci** spectator, onlooker

seylâp flood, torrent

seyran pleasure trip, excursion

seyrek rare, sparse

seyr|etmek *v/t* see, look on; *v/i* move, go along; **~üsefer** traffic

seyyah traveller

seyyar mobile, portable; **~e** *astr.* planet

sez perception; intuition; **~mek** *v/t* perceive, feel, discern

sezon season

sıcak hot, warm; heat; **~lık** heat

sıçan *zo.* rat; mouse; **~otu** *chem.* arsenic

sıçra|mak spring, jump (**-e** on); **~tmak** *v/t* make jump, spring (**-e** on)

sıfat quality, attribute; *gr.*

adjective; **~iyle** in the capacity of

sıfır zero, nought

sığ shallow

sığamak v/t tuck or roll up

sığın|ak shelter; **~mak** -e take refuge or shelter with

sığır ox, cow; buffalo; **~ eti** beef; **~tmaç** herdsman, drover

sığ|ışmak fit into a confined place; **~mak** -e go into, be contained by

sıhhat health; truth; **~li** healthy, sound

sıhh|i hygienic; **~iye** public health

sık close together, dense, tight; **~ı** tight, strict, severe; necessity; **~ıcı** tiresome, boring

sıkıl|gan bashful, shy; **~mak** be bored; be ashamed (-e from); be pressed (-e into); **canı ~lmak** be bored

sıkıntı annoyance, boredom; lack

sıkış|ık pressed together; **~mak** be pressed together, crowded; **~tırmak** v/t press, squeeze (-e into); force, oppress

sıklaşmak be frequent, close together

sıklet heaviness, weight

sıklık density, frequency

sıkma squeezing; **~k** v/t press, squeeze, tighten

sımsıkı very tight, narrow

sına|at trade, craft; **~î** industrial

sınamak v/t try, test

sınav examination; **~lamak** v/t examine

sındırmak v/t defeat, rout

sınıf class; sort, category; **~ta kalmak** fail in one's class

sınır frontier; limit; **~lamak** v/t limit; determine; **~lı** limited; determined

sır[1] glaze; silvering

sır[2] secret, mystery

sıra row, file, rank; order, series; turn; **~dığı ~da** conj. while; as; **~sı gelmek** -e have one's turn; **~sına göre** according to circumstances; **~ca** med. scrofula; **~lamak** v/t arrange in a row, set up in order; **~lanmak** stand in line; **~lı** in a row, in due order; **~sız** out of order, improper

sırça glass

sırf adv. pure; mere; sheer

sırık pole, stick; **~lamak** v/t sl. carry off, steal

sırıt|kan given to grinning; **~mak** v/i grin; fig. show up

sırma silver-thread

sırnaşık worrying, pertinacious

sırsıklam wet to the skin

sırt back; ridge; **~armak** pile up (clouds); arch its back (cat); **~lamak** v/t take on one's back

sırtlan zo. hyena

sıska dropsical; thin and weak

sıtma med. malaria; **~lı** malarial

sıva plaster

sıvalı¹ plastered, stuccoed

sıvalı² with sleeves rolled up

sıvamak¹ plaster (-e -i sth. with)

sıvamak² v/t tuck up, roll up

sıvazlamak v/t stroke, caress

sıvı adj. liquid; ~ndırmak v/t phys. liquify, turn into a fluid

sıvışık sticky; importunate

sıyanet preservation, protection

sıyga gr. tense, mood

sıyırmak v/t tear or peel off, strip off, skim off

sıyrı|k adj. brazenfaced; n. abrasion; ~ntı scrapings pl.; scratch

-sız s. -siz

sızdırmak v/t cause to ooze out, squeeze

sızı ache, pain; ~ltı complain, lamentation

-sızın s. -sizin

sızıntı oozings, tricklings pl.

sızla|mak suffer sharp pain; ~nmak moan, lament

sızmak ooze, leak

sicil register; ~li registered; previously convicted

sicim string, cord

sidik an. urine; ~kavuğu bladder

sigara cigarette; ~lık cigarette-holder

sigorta insurance; el. fuse; ~ etm. v/t insure; ~lı insured

sinema

sihir magic, sorcery, charm; ~baz magician, sorcerer; ~li bewitched

sikke coin

sikmek v/t vulg. have sexual intercourse with

silâh weapon, arm; ~ başına! to arms!; ~landırmak v/t arm; ~lanmak arm oneself; ~lı armed; ~sız unarmed; ~sızlanma pol. disarmament

sil|ecek large bath-towel; ~gi duster; sponge, eraser; ~giç wind-screen wiper; ~ik rubbed out, worn

silindir cylinder; roller; top hat [oneself]

silinmek be scraped; rub]

silk|elemek v/t shake off; ~inmek shake oneself; ~inti shaking, trembling; ~mek v/t shake, shake off

sille box on the ear, slap

silmek v/t wipe, scrub, rub down, erase; burnunu ~ blow the nose

silsile chain, line; dynasty

sima face; figure, personage

simge symbol

simit cracknel in the shape of a ring; naut. life-belt

simsar ec. broker; commission agent

simsiyah jet black

sincap zo. squirrel

sindir|im digestion; ~mek v/t digest, swallow

sine bosom, breast

sinek zo. fly; ~lik fly-whisk

sinema cinema

sinir an. sinew, nerve; **~lendirmek** v/t irritate; **~lenmek** -e become irritated at; **~li** on edge, nervous; **~lilik** nervousness

sinmek -e crouch down into, be hidden in; penetrate; fig. be cowed, humiliated

sinüs math. sine

sinyal signal; blinker (auto)

sipahi mil. cavalry

sipariş ec. order, commission; **~ almak** take orders; **~ etm.** v/t order

siper shield, shelter; peak of a cap

sirayet contagion, infection

sirk circus

sirke[1] vinegar

sirke[2] nit

sirküler circular

siroko sirocco

sis fog, mist; **~lenmek** become damp, foggy; **~li** foggy, misty

sistem system

sistire scraper

sitem reproach

sivil civilian

sivilce pimple

sivri sharp-pointed; **~lik** sharp-pointedness; **~lmek** become pointed; fig. make rapid progress in one's career; **~ltmek** v/t make pointed at the end; **~sinek** zo. mosquito

siyah black; **~lanmak** become black

siyasa|l political; **~et** politics, policy; **~î** political

siyoni|st Zionist; **~zm** Zionism

siz you

-siz, -sız, -suz, -süz without; ... -less

sizin your; of you

-sizin, -sızın without, before

Skandinavya Scandinavia

skeç thea. sketch

smokin dinner-jacket

snop snob

soba stove; **~cı** maker or installer of stoves

soda soda; **~ (suyu)** soda-water

sofa hall, ante-room

sofra dining-table; meal; **~yı kaldırmak** clear away; **~yı kurmak** lay the table

softa rel. theological student; fanatic, bigot

sofu religious, devout; fanatic

soğan bot. onion

soğuk cold; frigid; **~ almak** catch a cold; **~kanlı** calm, coolheaded; **~luk** coldness; cold sweat

soğumak get cold

soğutma|c tech. cooling system; **~k** v/t cool, render cold

sohbet chat, conversation; **~ etm.** have a chat

sokak road, street

sokmak v/t drive in, insert; sting, bite; injure, calumniate

sokul|gan sociable, quick to make friends; **~mak** -e push into; steel in

sokuşturmak v/t push, slip (-e into)

sol left, left-hand side; **~ak** left-handed; **~cu** pol. leftist

sol|gun faded, withered; **~mak** fade, wither

solucan zo. worm; **bağırsak ~ı** tapeworm; **yer ~ı** earthworm

soluk¹ faded, withered, pale

soluk² breath; **~a** out of breath

solu|mak -den snort, pant with; **~ngaç** zo. gill; **~nmak** breathe

som¹ solid, massive

som² zo. salmon

somaki porphyry

somun round loaf; tech nut

somurt|kan sulky; **~mak** frown, sulk

somut concrete

somye spring mattress

son end, result; last, final; afterbirth; **~ derece** the uttermost; extremely; **~bahar** autumn, fall

sonda tech. bore; med. catheter; **~j** tech. test bore; fig. sounding, exploration; **~lamak** v/t bore, sound

sonek gr. suffix

sonra afterwards, in future; -den after; **~dan** later, recently; **~dan görme** parvenue; **~ları** adv. later; **~sız** eternal, without end

sonsuz endless, eternal

sonuç end, result; **~la(ndır)mak** v/t conclude; cause; **~lanmak** result (ile in)

sop clan

sopa thock stick; fig. beating; **~ atmak** -e give a beating to; **~ yemek** get a beating

sorgu interrogation; **~ya çekmek** v/t cross-examine, interrogate

sorguç plum, crest

sormak¹ ask (-e -i so. about sth.); -i inquire about

sormak² v/t suck

soru question, interrogation; **~lmak** be asked

sorum responsibility; **~lu** responsible

soru|n problem, question, matter; **~şturmak** v/t inquire about

sosis sausage

sosyal social; **~ sigorta** social insurance; **~ist** socialist; **~izm** socialism

sosyoloji sociology

Sovyetler Birliği Soviet Union

soy family, lineage; **~adı** family name, surname

soygun pillage, spoliation

soylu of good gamily

soymak v/t strip, peel, undress; rob, sack

soysuz degenerate; good-for-nothing

soytarı clown, buffoon

soy|ulmak be stripped, peeled; **~unmak** undress oneself; **~ut** abstract, incorporeal

söbe oval

söğüt bot. willow

sök|mek v/t tear down, rip

open; *fig.* surmount; **~tür-mek** *v/t* cause to tear down or rip open; read with difficulty; **~ük** unstitched, ripped

sömestr semester, half-year

sömür|ge colony; **~mek** *v/t* devour; *fig.* exploit

sön|dürmek *v/t* extinguish, disconnect, switch off; **~mek** go out (*fire*); be deflated; **~ük** extinguished, deflated

söv|gü curse; **~mek** *-e* curse, swear at; **~üşmek** swear at one another

söylemek *v/t* say, explain (*-e* to)

söylen|iş pronunciation; **~mek** be spoken *or* said; **~ti** rumour

söyle|mek *-e -i* make so. say *sth.*; **~v** speech, discourse

söz word, speech, rumour; **~ atmak** *-e* make improper remarks to; **~cü** speaker, spokesman; **~cük** word; **~ gelişi** *adv.* for instance

sözleşme agreement, contract; **~k** agree (**ile** with)

sözlü agreed together; verbal

sözlük dictionary, vocabulary

sözümona so-called

spatül spatula

spekülasyon speculation

spiker speaker

spor sport, games; **~ alanı** sports field, athletic

ground; **~cu**, **~tmen** sportsman, athlete

stadyum stadium (*sport*)

staj apprenticeship; **~iyer** apprentice

sterlin Sterling

stilo fountain-pen

stok s. **ıstok**

stratejik *mil.* strategics

stüdyo studio

su water, fluid, sap, broth; stream; **~ almak** leak; **~ya düşmek** fail, come to nought; **~ bendi** water reservoir

sual question, inquiry

subay *mil.* officer

sucu water-seller

sucuk 1. sausage (*esp. in the Turkish way*); **2.** sweetmeat *made of grape juice, nuts, etc.*

suç fault; crime; **~lamak** *v/t* accuse (**ile** of); **~landırmak** *v/t* find guilty; **~lanmak** be accused (**ile** of); **~lu** criminal, offender; **~suz** innocent; **~üstü** *adv. jur.* red-handed

sugeçirmez waterproof

sui|istimal misuse, abuse; **~kast** criminal attempt

sukut fall, lapse; **~u hayal** disappointment

sula|k watery, marshy; water-trough; **~ma** irrigation; **~mak** *v/t* water, irrigate; **~ndırmak** *v/t* mix with water

sulh peace, reconciliation; **~çu**, **~perver** peace-loving

sulp hard, solid

sürgün

sultan 1. ruler, sovereign, sultan; **2.** daughter of a sultan, princess

sulu watery, moist, juicy; *fig.* importunate; ~ **boya** water-colour

sumen writing-pad

suni artificial, false

sun|mak *v/t* offer, present (-*e* to); ~**u** ec. offer; ~**ul-mak** -*e* be presented to

supap *tech.* valve

sur city wall, rampart

surat face, mien; ~ **asmak** make a sour face

sure *rel.* Chapter *of the Koran*

suret form, shape, manner; copy; -*in* **ini çıkarmak** make a copy of; **bu ~le** in this way   [Syrian]

Suriye Syria; ~**li** *n, adj.*

susak *adj.* thirsty; *n* wooden drinking cup

susam *bot.* sesame

susa|mak be thirsty; -*e* thirst for; ~**mış** thirsty

sus|mak be silent, cease speaking; ~**malık** hush-money; ~**turmak** *v/t* silence

susuz waterless, arid; ~**luk** lack of water

sutyen brassière

suvare evening show, soirée

su|varmak *v/t* water *an animal*; ~**yolu 1.** water-mark *in a paper*; **2.** water conduit

-suz *s.* **-siz**

sübye sweet drink *made with pounded almonds, etc.*

sühulet being easy, facility

sühunet heat; temperature

sükût silence

sülâle family, line

sülük *zo.* leech; *bot.* tendril

sülün *zo.* pheasant

sümbül *bot.* hyacinth; ~**î** cloudy, overcast

sümkürmek expel mucus from the nose

sümük *an.* mucus; ~**lü** slimy, snivelling; ~**lü böcek** slug

sünger sponge; ~ **kâğıdı** blotting-paper; ~**taşı** pum-ice-stone

süngü bayonet

sünnet *rel.* **1.** the habits of the Prophet Muhammad; **2.** circumcision; ~**çi** cir-cumciser; ~**li** circumcised

sünnî *rel.* Sunnite

süprüntü sweepings, rub-bish

süpür|ge broom, brush; ~**mek** *v/t* sweep, brush

sürat speed, velocity; ~**li** quick, hurried

sürç slip, mistake; ~**mek** stumble

süre period, extension; ~**ce** *conj.* as long as, while; ~**ç** process

sürek duration; ~**li** lasting, prolonged; ~**siz** transitory

süreli periodic(al)

Süreyya *astr.* the Pleiades *pl.*

sürfe *zo.* caterpillar, maggot

sürgü harrow; bolt; trowel; ~**lemek** *v/t* harrow; bolt

sürgün 1. *pol.* exile, banishment; exiled person; **2.** *bot.* shoot, sucker; **3.** *med.* diarrhoea

sürme 1. kohl, collyrium *for painting the eyelids;* **2.** bolt

sürmek *v/t* drive; banish (*-e* to); rub (*-e* on); *v/i* continue; pass

sürme|lemek *v/t* bolt; **~li** having a bolt, bolted

sürpriz surprise

sürşarj surcharge

sürt|mek *v/t* rub (*-e* against); *v/i* loiter, wander about; **~ünme** *tech.* friction

sürü herd, flock, drove; **~cü** drover, driver

sürüklemek *v/t* drag, involve (*-e* in)

sürülmek be rubbed; *-e* be driven to

sürüm *ec.* sale, demand; **~lü** in great demand

sürün|gen *zo.* reptile; **~mek** *v/t* rub in or on; *v/i*

drag oneself along the ground, live in misery

süs ornament, decoration; **~lemek** *v/t* adorn, embellish; **~lenmek** adorn oneself; **~lü** ornamented, decorated, carefully dressed

süt milk; **~ana, ~anne** wet-nurse, foster-mother; **~çü** milkman

sütlaç rice-pudding

süt|leğen *bot.* euphorbia; **~lü** milky in milk; **~nine** wet-nurse

sütun column (*a.* in a news-*paper*); pillar

süvari *mil.* cavalryman; cavalry [Suez Canal]

Süveyş Suez; **~ kanalı**⌐

~süz *s.* **-siz**

süz|geç, ~gü filter, sieve, strainer; **~mek** *v/t* strain, filter; *fig* look attentively at; **~ülmek 1.** be filtered; **2.** glide; **3.** become weak

S

şadırdamak bubble, murmur

şadırvan reservoir with a jet or taps

şafak twilight; dawn

şaft *tech.* shaft

şah¹ Shah

şah²: ~a kalkmak rear up (*horse*)

şahadet witnessing, testimony; *rel.* death in battle of a Moslem; **~ getirmek** pronounce the Moslem

creed; **~ parmağı** index finger; **~name** certificate

şah|ane royal; magnificent; **~damarı** *an.* aorta; **~eser** masterpiece

şahıs person, individual; **~ zamiri** *gr.* personal pronoun

şahin *zo.* peregrine falcon

şahit witness; example; **~lik** testimony

şahlanmak rear up (*horse*)

fig. become angry and threatening

şahmerdan *tech.* beetle; battering-ram

şahs|en *adv.* personally, in person; ~**î** personal, private; ~**iyet** personality

şair poet

şaka fun, joke, jest; ~ **söylemek**, ~ **yapmak** jest, joke; ~**cı** joker, jester

şakak *an.* temple

şaka|laşmak joke (**ile** with); ~**sız** earnest(ly)

şakır|damak rattle, jingle; ~**tı** clatter, rattle

şaki brigand, robber

şaklaban mimic, buffoon

şaklatmak *v/t* crack a whip, *etc.*

şakul plumb-line; ~**î** perpendicular, vertical

şal shawl

şalgam *bot.* turnip

şallak naked

şalter *el.* switch

şalupa *naut.* sloop

şalvar baggy trousers

şamandıra float *for a wick*; *naut.* buoy

şamar slap, box on the ear

şamata great noise, uproar

şamdan candlestick

şamfıstığı *bot.* pistachio nut

şâmil -*i* comprising, including

şamme (sense of) smell

şampanya Champagne

şampiyon champion; ~**a** championship

şan fame, glory, reputation

şangırdamak crash, make the noise of breaking glass

şanjman *tech.* gear, shift

şanlı glorious, famous

şans chance, luck

şansız without renown, unknown

şans|lı lucky; ~**sız** unhappy

şansölye *pol.* chancellor

şantaj *jur.* blackmail, extortion; ~**cı** blackmailer

şantiye building-site; *naut.* wharf, dockyard

şantöz female singer

şap *chem.* alum

şapır|damak make a smacking noise; ~**tı** smacking noise *of the lips*

şapka hat; truck *of a mast*; cowl *of a chimney*; ~**sını çıkarmak** take off one's hat; ~**sını giymek** put on one's hat; ~**cı** hatter; ~**lık** wardrobe

şaplamak make a smacking noise

şarap wine

şarıl|damak flow *with a splashing noise*; ~**tı** gurgling, splashing

şarjör cartridge clip *or* drum

şark east; Orient

şarkı song; ~ **söylemek** sing; ~**cı** song-writer; singer

şark|î eastern; ~**iyat** Orientalism]

şarlatan charlatan

şart condition; ~**lı** stipulated; having a condition attached; ~**name** list of conditions; ~**sız** unconditional

şasi *tech.* chassis

şasi *tech.* chassis

şaşaa glitter; splendour

şaşalamak be bewildered, confused

şaşı squinting, squint-eyed; **~lamak** squint

şaşır|mak *v/t* be confused about; lose, miss; **~tmak** *v/t* confuse, bewilder, mislead

şaşkın bewildered, confused; **~lık** bewilderment

şaşmak *-e* be perplexed, astonished at; *-i* lose, miss; deviate *(-den* from)

şato castle

şatranç chess

şayan *-e* deserving, suitable for; **~ı dikkat** notable, worth attention

şayet perhaps; if

şayia rumour

şaz irregular, exceptional

şeamet evil omen

şebboy *bot.* wallflower

şebek *zo.* baboon

şebeke net; network; gang

şecere genealogical tree

şef chief, leader

şefaat intercession

şeffaf transparent

şefkat compassion, affection; **~li** compassionate, affectionate

şeftali *bot.* peach

şehir town, city; **~lerarası** interurban; **~li** townsman, citizen

şehit *rel.* martyr; Moslem who dies in battle *or* during an accident; **~lik** martyrdom

şehriye *bot.* vermicelli

şehv|ani lustful, sensual; **~et** lust, sensuality

şehzade prince

şekavet brigandage

şeker sugar; candy; a sweet; *fig.* darling; **~ bayramı** *rel.* Moslem feast after the Ramazan fast; **~ hastalığı** *med.* diabetes; **~ci** sweet-seller; confectioner; **~ kamışı** sugar-cane; **~leme** candied fruit; doze, nap; **~li** sugared, sweetened; **~pare** pastry *over which syrup had been poured*

şekil form, shape; plan; kind; feature; **~ vermek** *-e* form, shape; **~siz** shapeless, without form

şekli formal

şelâle waterfall

şema outline, sketch, plan

şemsiye parasol, umbrella; **~lik** umbrella-stand

şen joyous, cheerful; **~el-mek** become inhabited; **~lendirmek** *v/t* cheer, enliven; **~lenmek** become cheerful, gay, joyous; become inhabited; **~lik** gaiety, cheerfulness; public rejoicings

şerbet sweet drink, sherbet; liquid manure

şeref honour; glory; distinction

şerefe *arch.* gallery of a minaret

şerefiye tax on the increase of land value

şereflen|dirmek *v/t* honour, do honour to; **~mek** acquire honour, be honoured [mentary]

şerh explanation; com-ſ

şeriat *rel.* the Moslem religious law; **~çı** upholder of the religious law

şerik partner, shareholder

şerit ribbon, tape; film

şev *n.* slope; *adj.* sloping

şevk desire, yearning

şevket majesty, pomp

şey thing; what's his name; **bir ~** something

şeyh sheikh; *rel.* head of a religious order; **~ülislâm** Sheikhulislam (*the highest religious dignitary of the Ottoman Empire*)

şeytan *rel.* Satan, devil; *fig.* crafty man; **~lık** devilry

şezlong chaise longue

şık¹ chic, smart

şık² one of two alternatives

şıkır|damak rattle, jingle; **~tı** jingling

şıklık elegance, smartness

şımar|ık spoilt, saucy, impertinent; **~mak** be spoilt, get above oneself; **~tmak** *v/t* spoil

şıngır|damak crash, make the noise of breaking glass; **~tı** the noise of breaking glass

şıp noise *of a drop falling;* **~ diye** all of a sudden

şıra must, unfermented grape-juice

şırıl|damak make the noise of gently running water; **~tı** splashing

şırlop eggs served with yogurt

şırvan(ı) loft *over a shop or beneath a roof*

şiar badge, sign; habit

şiddet strength, violence, severity; **~lenmek** become severe *or* intensified; **~li** violent, severe

şifa restoration to health, healing; **~ bulmak** recover health

şifah|en *adv.* orally, verbally; **~î** oral, verbal

şifalı wholesome, healing

şifre cipher, code; **-in ~sini açmak** decipher, decode; **~li** in cipher

Şiî *rel.* Shiite; **~lik** Shiism

şiir poetry; poem

şikâyet complaint; **~ etm.** complain (*-den* about, *-e* to); **~çi** complainant

şile *bot.* marjoram

şilep *naut.* cargo boat *or* steamer

şilin Shilling

şilte thin mattress, quilt

şimal north; **~î** northern, north

şimdi *adj.* at present, now; **~den** henceforth; already; **~ki** the present, actual; **~lik** *adv.* for the present

şimşek lightning; **~ çakmak** lighten, flash

şimşir *bot.* box-tree

şinitsel cutlet, schnitzel

şirin sweet, affable

şirk *rel.* polytheism

şirket *ec.* company, partnership

şirpençe *med.* carbuncle, anthrax

şirret *adj.* malicious, tartar

şiryan *an.* artery

şiş¹ spit, skewer; rapier; ~ **kebap**, ~ **kebabı** meat roasted on a spit *or* skewers

şiş² *n.* swelling; *adj.* swollen

şişe bottle; lamp-glass

şiş|irmek *v/t* cause to swell, inflate, pump up; **~kin** swollen, puffed up; **~ko** *sl.* very fat

şişlemek *v/t* spit, skewer, stab

şişman fat; **~lık** fatness

şişmek swell, become inflated, swollen

şive accent; idiom; **~siz** with a bad accent

şlep *s.* şilep

şnitsel *s.* şinitsel

şoför chauffeur, driver

şose macadamized road, highway

şoven *pol.* chauvinistic; **~lik** chauvinism

şöhret fame, reputation; pseudonym

şölen feast, banquet

şömine fireplace

şövalye knight

şöyle *adv.* in that manner, so; just; such; ~ **böyle** so so, not too well; roughly)
şu that; this   [speaking∫
şua ray *of* light

şubat February

şube section, branch (office)

şuh lively; coquettish

şura, **~sı** that place, this place; **~da** there, here; **~dan** from there, from here; **~ya** there, thither

şûra council; **Devlet Şsı** *pol.* Council of State

şurup syrup; sweet medicine

şuur comprehension, intelligence; conscience; **~suz** unconscious

şükran thankfulness, gratitude

şükür thanks, gratitude

şümul comprehending; **~ü olm. -e** include, embrace; **~lü** comprehensive

şüphe doubt, suspicion; **~lenmek** have a suspicion *or* doubt (-**den** about); **~li -den** suspicious of, suspected of; doubtful; **~siz** doubtless

şüt shot (*football*)

T

ta¹ even; until; ~ **-e kadar** even until; ~ **ki** so that;)
ta² *s.* **da**   [order that∫
-ta *s.* **-da**

taahhüt undertaking, engagement; **~lü** registered (*letter*)

taalluk -e connection with, relation to; ~ **etm. -e** concern

taarruz attack, assault; ~ **etm. -e** attack, assault

taassup *rel.* bigotry, fanaticism

tabak¹ plate, dish

tabak² tanner

tabaka¹ layer; class; sheet

tabaka² tobacco *or* cigarette box

tabaklamak *v/t* tan

taban sole; floor, base; bed of a river

tabanca pistol

tabanvay: ~**la gitmek** *sl.* go on foot

tabela sign of a shop, *etc.*; list of food; card of treatments [print, edition]

tab|etmek *v/t* print; ~**ı**

tabi -e following; dependent on, subject to

tabi|at nature; character, quality; ~**î** natural, normal; *adv.* naturally

tabiiyet dependence; *pol.* nationality

tabip doctor, physician

tabir phrase, expression

tabiye *mil.* tactics

tabla circular tray, disk; ash-tray

tabl|et tablet; ~**o** picture; tableau; *math.* table

tabur *mil.* battalion; ~**cu** *mil.* discharged from hospital

tabure footstool

tabut coffin; large egg-box

tabya *mil.* bastion, redoubt

taciz bothering, worrying; ~ **etmek** *v/t* annoy, disturb

taç crown, diadem; *bot.* corolla; *zo.* crest of a bird

tadım the faculty of taste

tadil adjustment; modification (*pl.* ~**ât**)

taflan *bot.* cherry laurel

tafsil, *pl.* ~**ât** detail; ~**ât vermek** -*e* explain all details to; ~**âtlı** detailed

tağşiş *ec.* adulteration of a product

tahakkuk verification; ~ **etm.** *v/i* prove true, be realized; ~ **ettirmek** *v/t* certify, verify, realize

tahakküm arbitrary power; oppression

tahammül endurance; ~ **etm.** -*e* endure, support

tahammür *chem.* fermentation

taharri search; ~ (**memuru**) detective, plain-clothes policeman

tahayyül imagination, fancy; ~ **etm.** *v/t* fancy, imagine

tahdit limitation; definition; ~ **etm.** *v/t* limit, circumscribe

tahıl cereals

tahin sesame oil

tahkik verification; investigation; ~ **etm.** *v/t* verify, investigate; ~**at** *pl.* investigations; research *sg.*

tahkim fortifying; ~ **etm.** *v/t* strengthen, fortify

tahkir insult; ~ **etm.** *v/t* despise, insult

tahlil *chem.* analysis

tahlis (**iye**) rescuing; ~**iye sandalı** *naut.* lifeboat

tahliye emptying, evacuation; ~ **etm.** *v/t* empty, discharge

tahmin estimate, conjec-

tahminen 152

ture; ~ **etm.** v/t estimate, calculate; ~**en** adv. approximately; ~**î** approximate

tahribat pl. destructions

tahrif distortion, falsification; ~ **etm.** v/t falsify, misrepresent

tahrik incitement; ~ **etm.** v/t incite, instigate, provoke

tahrip destruction, devastation; ~ **etm.** v/t destroy, ruin

tahrir writing, essay; ~**en** adv. in writing

tahsil collection; study, education; ~ **etm.** v/t acquire; study; ~**ât** pl. payments; taxes; ~**dar** collector of taxes, etc.

tahsis assignment; ~ **etm.** v/t assign (-e to); ~**at** pl. allowance, appropriation sg.

taht throne; ~**a çıkmak** succeed to the throne; ~**tan indirilmek** be dethroned

tahta board, plank; wood; adj. wooden; ~**biti**, **kurusu** zo. bed-bug

tahterevalli see-saw

tahvil transforming, conversion, draft; ~ **etm.** v/t convert, transmute; ~**ât** pl. ec. securities

taife s. tayfa

tak arch, vault

takas ec. clearing

takat strength, power; ~**siz** powerless, exhausted

takdim presentation, offer;

~ **etm.** v/t present, offer, introduce (-e to)

takdir appreciation, supposition; ~ **etm.** v/t appreciate, understand, estimate; -diği ~**de** in case, if

takdis rel. sanctification, consecration

tak|ı gr. particle, postposition; ~**lmak** -e be affixed to, attach oneself to; deride, ridicule

takım set, lot; service, suit; squad, team, gang; ~**adalar** pl. geo. archipelago sg.; ~**yıldız** astr. constellation

takınmak v/t attach to oneself; put on, assume an attitude

takır|damak make a tapping or knocking noise; ~**tı** tapping, knocking

takibat pl. jur. persecution sg.

takip pursuit, persecution; ~ **etm.** v/t follow, pursue

takke scull-cap

takla(k) somersault

taklit imitation, counterfeiting; ~ **etm.** v/t imitate, feign

takma attached; false; ~ **diş** false tooth; ~ **saç** false hair [(to), put on]

takmak v/t affix, attach (-e)

takoz wooden wedge

takrib|en adv. approximately, about; ~**î** adj. approximate

takrir statement, report; jur. notification of transference of real property

taksa tax, due

taksi taxicab

taksim division, partition, distribution; ~ **etm.** v/t divide; distribute; ~**at** pl. divisions, parts

taksimetre taximeter

taksir jur. default, omission; ~**li** imprudent, guilty

taksit instalment; ~**le** adv. by instalments

takt tact

taktik mil. tactics

taktir etm. v/t distil

takunya clog

takvim calendar, almanac

takviye reinforcement; ~ **etm.** v/t strengthen, rein-force

takyit restriction [force]

talâk divorce

talaş sawdust, filings

talaz wave, billow; a being ruffled up (silk)

talebe student, pupil

talep request, demand; ~ **etm.** v/t request, ask for

tali secondary, subordinate

talih luck, good fortune; ~**li** lucky; ~**siz** unlucky

talik etm. v/t suspend, put off; attach (-e to)

talim instruction, drill; ~ **etm.** teach, drill sth. (-e to so.); ~**atname** regulations pl.

talip(li) -e desirous for

talk talc

taltif etm. v/t show favour to; confer on (ile ile.)

tam adj. complete, entire; perfect; adv. completely; exactly

tamah greed, avarice; ~**kâr** greedy, avaricious (-e for)

tamam n. completion, end; whole; adj. complete, ready; that's right!; ~**en**, ~**iyle** adv. completely, entirely; ~**lamak** v/t complete, finish; ~**lanmak** be completed, finished

tambur mus. oriental guitar

tamim circular letter; generalization

tamir repair, restoration; ~ **etm.** v/t repair, mend; ~**at** pl. repairs

tamla|ma gr. compound word; ~**nan** gr. the part of a compound in the nominative; ~**yan** gr. genitive

tampon med. wad, plug; buffer (railway); bumper (auto) [ber]

tamsayı math. whole num-[

tan dawn

-tan s. -dan

tandır oven made in a hole in the earth

tane grain, seed, berry; piece; ~**cik** granule; ~**lemek** v/t granulate; ~**li** having grains or berries

tanı med. diagnosis; ~**dık** acquaintance

tanık jur. witness; ~**lamak** v/t prove by witnesses; ~**lık** evidence

tanı|lamak v/t med. diagnose; ~**mak** v/t know, recognize; acknowledge

tanım definition; ~ **harfi** gr. article; ~**lamak** v/t describe, define

tanın|mak be known *or* recognized; **~mış** well-known, famous

tanış|ıklık acquaintance; **~mak** make acquaintance (ile with); **~tırmak** *v/t* introduce (ile to)

tanıt proof, evidence; **~mak** *v/t* introduce (-e to)

tank *mil.* tank

Tanrı God; **♀** god; **♀sız** godless, atheist

tansık miracle, wonder

tansiyon *an.*blood-pressure

tantana pomp, magnificence

tanzifat *pl.* town scavenging service *sg.*

tanzim putting in order, organizing; **~ etm.** *v/t* organize, arrange; **♀at** *pl.* the political reforms in *1839 and the time following*

tapa fuse; cork

tapan harrow, roller

tap|ı worshipped idol; **~ınak** *rel.* temple; **~ınmak**, **~mak** *-e* worship, adore

tapon second-rate, worthless

tapu title-deed; **~lamak** *v/t* register with a title-deed

taraça terrace

taraf side, direction, part, end; party; **~ından** by, from the direction of (-e); **~gir** partial, biased; **~lı** having sides *or* supporters; **~sız** neutral; **~sızlık** neutrality; **~tar** partisan, supporter

tarak comb; rake, harrow; weaver's reed; crest *of a*

bird; gills *of a fish;* **~lamak** *v/t* comb; rake

tara|mak *v/t* comb, rake; search minutely; **~nmak** comb oneself; be combed

tarassut watching, observation

taraz combings, fibres *pl.*

tarçın *bot.* cinnamon

tardetmek *s.* tart etm.

tarh¹ flower-bed

tarh² imposition *of taxes;* substraction

tarhana preparation of yogurt and flour *dried in the sun*

tarım agriculture; **~sal** agricultural

tarif description, definition; **~ etm.** *v/t* describe, define

tarife time-table; price-list

tarih history; date; **~çi** historian; **~î** historical; **~li** dated

tarik way, road; method; **~at** *rel.* religious order

tarla arable field; **~ kuşu** *zo.* lark

tart expulsion; repulsion; **~ etm.** *v/t* expel; degrade

tartı weighing, weight; balance; **~lı** weighed, balanced; **~lmak** be weighed

tartışma dispute; **~k** *v/i* argue, dispute

tartmak *v/t* weigh; ponder well

tarz form, shape, manner

tarziye apology; **~ vermek** *-e* give satisfaction to

tas bowl, cup

tasa worry, anxiety, grief

tasar project, plan; **~1** *pol.* bill, draft law; **~lamak** *v/t* plan, project

tasarruf possession; economy, saving; *-in* **~unda olm.** be in the possession, at the disposal of; **~ sandığı** savings bank

tasavvuf *rel.* mysticism

tasavvur imagination, idea; **~ etm.** *v/t* imagine

tasdik confirmation, ratification; **~ etm.** *v/t* confirm, affirm, ratify; **~name** certificate

tasfiye cleaning, liquidation; **~ etm.** clean, clear up, liquidate; **~hane** *tech.* refinery

tashih correction; **~ etm.** *v/t* correct

tasım syllogism; **~lamak** *v/t* plan, project

tasla|k draft, sketch, model; **~mak** *v/t* make a show of, pretend to

tasma collar *of a dog, etc.*, strap

tasnif classification; **~ etm.** *v/t* classify; compile

tasrif *gr.* declension, conjugation

tasvip approval; **~ etm.** *v/t* approve

tasvir design, picture; **~ etm.** *v/t* depict, draw

taş stone; hard as stone; **~çı** stonemason, quarryman

taşı|mak *v/t* carry, transport, bear; **~nmak** *-e* be carried to; move to, go very often to; **~t** vehicle

taşkın overflowing

taş|kömür coal, pitcoal; **~-lamak** *v/t* stone; grind; **~lı** stony, rocky; **~lık** stony place

taşmak *v/i* overflow, boil over

taşra the outside; the provinces *pl.*

tat taste, flavour, relish; *-in* **tadına bakmak** taste

tatarcık *zo.* sandfly

tatbik adaptation, application; **~ etm.** *v/t* apply, adapt; **~î** practical; applied

tatil suspension of work, holiday, vacation

tatlı *adj.* sweet, drinkable, agreeable; *n.* dessert, sweet; **~laştırmak** *v/t* sweeten; **~lık** sweetness, kindness; **~msı** sweetish

tatmak *v/t* taste, try

tatmin etm. *v/t* satisfy, calm, appease

tatsız tasteless; disagreeable [-apple]

tatula *bot.* datura, thorn-

taun *med.* pest, plague

tav *tech.* proper heat or condition

tava frying-pan; *tech.* ladle; trough *for slaking lime*

tavan ceiling

tavassut mediation

tavır mode, manner, attitude

tavla¹ backgammon

tavla² stable

tavlamak *v/t* bring to its best condition; *fig.* deceive, swindle

tavlamak *(header)*

tavsif description; ~ **etm.** *v/t* describe

tavsiye recommendation; ~ **etm.** *v/t* recommend (-e to)

tavşan *zo.* hare; **~cıl** *zo.* vulture, eagle

tavuk hen; **~göğsü** *sweet dish made with milk and the pounded breast of a fowl*

tavus *zo.* peacock

tay *zo.* foal

tayfa band, troup, crew

tayfun typhoon

tayın *mil.* ration

tayin appointment, designation; ~ **etm.** *v/t* appoint; decide, fix

tayyör tailor-made costume

taze fresh; new; young; **~leşmek** become young or fresh; **~lik** freshness, youth

tazı greyhound

tazim honouring, respect

taziye condolence

tatmin indemnification (*pl.* **~at**); ~ **etm.** *v/t* indemnify

tazyik pressure; oppression; ~ **etm.** *v/t* put pressure on; oppress

te *s.* **da**

-te *s.* **-da**

teati exchange

tebaa *pol.* subject *of a state*

tebarüz etm. become manifest *or* prominent

tebdil change, exchange

teberru gift, donation; ~ **etm.** offer *as a* free gift

tebessüm smile

tebeşir chalk

tebliğ communication,

communiqué; ~ **etm.** *v/t* transmit, communicate

tebrik congratulation; ~ **etm.** *v/t* congratulate (-den dolayı on)

tebriye etm. *v/t* acquit

tecavüz transgression, aggression; ~ **etm.** -e transgress; attack; -i pass, exceed

tecdit renewal

tecessüs search; inquisitiveness

tecil etm. *v/t* defer, postpone

tecrit separation, isolation; ~ **etm.** *v/t* free, isolate (-den from); ~ **kampı** *pol.* isolation *or* concentration camp

tecrübe trial, test, experiment; ~ **etm.** *v/t* try, test, experiment; **~li** experienced; **~siz** inexperienced

teçhiz equipping; ~ **etm.** *v/t* equip, fit out

tedafüi defensive

tedarik preparation, provision; ~ **etm.** *v/t* procure, obtain, provide

tedavi *med.* treatment, cure

tedavül circulation

tedbir precaution, measure; ~ **almak** take the necessary measures

tedfin interring, burial

tedhiş terrifying; **~çi** terrorist; **~çilik** terrorism

tedirgin irritated, troubled; ~ **etm.** *v/t* disturb, trouble

tediy|at *pl.* payments, deposits; **~e** payment

tedric|en adv. gradually; **~î**
adj. gradual

teessüf regret, being sorry;
~ etm. -e regret, be sorry
for

teessür emotion, grief

teessüs being founded or
established

tefe tech. machine for winding silk; **~ci** ec. usurer; **~**
cilik usury

tefekkür reflection

teferruat pl. details

tefrik separation, distinction; **~ etm.** v/t separate,
distinguish (-den from)

tefrika discord

tefsir interpretation

teftiş investigation, inspection; **~ etm.** v/t inspect

teğmen mil. lieutenant

tehdit threat, menace; **~**
etm. v/t threaten

tehir delay, postponement;
~ etm. v/t defer, postpone

tehlike danger; **~li** dangerous; **~siz** without danger

tek n. a single thing; adj.
single, alone; **~ başına**
apart; on one's own; **~ sayı**
math. odd number; **~ tük**
here and there

tekâmül evolution

tekaüt retirement, pension;
~ maaşı retirement pay,
pension   [shrimp]

teke zo. 1. he-goat; 2. ⎰

tekel monopoly

teker|(lek) tr. wheel; **~li**
circular, round; **~leme**
the use of similarly sounding
words in folk narratives

tekerrür recurrence; relapse

tekil gr. singular

tekin empty, deserted; **~**
olmıyan haunted; **~siz**
taboo

tekit confirmation; **~ etm.**
v/t confirm, repeat

tekke rel. Dervish Convent

teklif proposal, offer; obligation; **~ etm.** v/t pro-
pose, offer, submit (-e to);
~siz without ceremony;
free and easy; **~sizlik** un-
ceremoniousness

tekme kick; **~lemek** v/t
kick

tekne trough; hull

teknik technique; **~çi, ~er,**
teknisyen technician

tekrar repetition; again; **~**
etm., ~lamak v/t repeat

teksif making dense

teksir multiplication; **~**
etm. v/t multiply; dupli-
cate; **~ makinesi** multi-
plying machine, hecto-
graph

tekstil textiles pl.

tekzip contradiction, denial; **~ etm.** v/t deny, contradict

tel wire; fibre; thread; hair;
string; **~ çekmek** send a
wire; -e enclose with wire;
~ örgü barbed-wire fence

telâffuz pronunciation

telâfi compensation; **~ etm.**
v/t make up for, compen-
sate

telakki interpretation, view

telâş confusion, alarm, anxiety; **~a düşmek**, **~lanmak** be confused, flurried; **~lı** flurried, upset

telef ruin, perdition; death; **~at** pl. losses of life

teleferik tech. telpher, cable ropeway

telefon telephone; **~ etm.** -e telephone; **~ kabinesi** telephone-box

teles threadbare

televiz|ör television set; **~yon** television

telgraf telegraph; telegram; **~ çekmek** send a wire

telif composition; reconciling; **~ etm.** v/t write, compile; **~ hakkı** copyright

telkih inoculation, vaccination

telkin suggestion, inspiration; **~ etm.** v/t suggest (-e to)

tellal broker, middleman

tel|lemek v/t adorn with gold wire or thread; wire; **~siz** adj. wireless; n. wireless telegraphy

teltik deficiency; defect; **~siz** complete, whole; round (sum)

telve coffee-grounds

temas contact; **~ touch**, touch on; **~ta bulunmak** be in touch (ile with)

temaşa walking about to see things; scene, show; **~ etm.** v/t look on at

temayül inclination, tendency (-e towards)

temayüz etm. be distinguished

tembel lazy; **~lik** laziness

tembih warning; stimulation; **~ etm.** v/t excite; warn

temdit prolongation, extension

temel n. foundation, base; adj. basic; **~ atmak** lay a foundation; **~ hak** jur. constitutional right; **~leşmek** become firmly established, settle down; **~li** fundamental; permanent; **~siz** without foundation, baseless

temenni desire, wish; **~ etm.** v/t desire, request

temerküz concentration; **~ kampı** pol. concentration camp

temettü ec. profit; dividend

temin making sure, assurance; **~ etm.** v/t assure, secure; **~at** pl. security sg.; deposit, guarantee sg.

temiz clean, pure; honest; **~lemek** v/t clean; clean up; clear away; **~lik** cleanliness, purety; honesty

temkin self-possession; dignity; **~li** grave, dignified

temlik jur. disposal, alienation

temmuz July

tempo time, measure, pace

temsil representation; thea. performance; **~ etm.** v/t represent; thea. present; **~ci** agent

temyiz distinguishing; jur.

appeal; ~ **etm.** v/t distinguish; jur. appeal; ~ **mahkemesi** court of appeal

ten the body; ~ **rengi** flesh-colour

-ten s. **-dan**

tenakuz contradiction

tenasül reproduction, generation

tencere saucepan, pot

tender tender (railway)

teneffüs respiration; rest; ~ **etm.** v/i breathe; pause

teneke tin, tinplate; **~ci** tinsmith

tenezzüh pleasure walk, excursion

tenezzül fig. condescension

tenha solitary, lonely; **~lik** solitude, lonely place

tenis tennis; ~ **alanı** tennis-court [inge]

tenkıye med. cyster, syr-

tenkit criticism; ~ **etm.** v/t criticize; **~çi** critic

tensikat pl. reorganisation sg.; combing out of officials, staff reduction

tente awning

tentene lace

tentür chem. tincture, **~diyot** tincture of iodine

tenvir illumination; ~ **etm.** v/t illumine; **~at** pl. lighting of a street, etc.

tenzilât pl. ec. reductions of prices, etc.; **~lı** reduced in price

teori theory; **~k** theoretical

tepe hill; summit; **~lemek** v/t thrash unmercifully; fig. kill; **~li** crested (bird)

tepinmek v/i kick and stamp

tepir hair sieve

tepki reaction; power of repulsion; **~li uçak** av. jet aeroplane; **~mek** v/i react

tepmek v/t kick

tepreşmek med. return and cause a collapse

tepsi small tray

ter sweat, perspiration

terakki advance, progress; **~perver** progressive

terane tune; fig. yarn, story

teras s. **taraça**

teravi rel. prayer special to the nights of Ramazan

terazi balance, pair of scales; astr. Libra

terbiye 1. education, training; 2. sauce; flavouring; ~ **etm.** v/t educate, train; **~li** 1. educated, goodmannered; 2. flavoured; **~siz** uneducated, ill-mannered; **~sizlik** bad manners pl.

tercih preference; ~ **etm.** prefer v/t (-den to)

tercüman interpreter, translator

tercüme translation; ~ **etm.** v/t translate (-e into); **~ihal** biography

tereddüt hesitation; ~ **etm.** hesitate

tereke jur. heritage; legacy

terementi turpentine

terennüm singing

tereyağı fresh butter

terfi promotion, advancement; ~ **etm.** v/i be promoted

terfih etm. v/t bring prosperity to

terhin pawning, pledging

terhis mil. discharge of a soldier

terim (technical) term

terk abandonment; ~ etm. v/t abandon, leave; renounce

terkip composition, compound; gr. s. **izafet**

ter|lemek sweat, perspire; **~li** sweating, perspiring

terlik slipper

terminal terminal (station)

termo|metre thermometre; **~s** thermos flask; **~stat** tech. thermostat

ters¹ excrement of an animal

ters² back, reserve; opposite, wrong; contrary; ~ **gelmek** to appear to so. to be in the wrong way; ~ **gitmek** go wrong, turn out badly; **~ine** adv. in the reverse way

tersane naut. dockyard

tersim etm. v/t picture, design, draw

terslik contrariness, vexatiousness

tertemiz absolutely clean

tertibat pl. installations

tertip arrangement, order, plan; composition; **~ etm.,** v/t organize; arrange; compose; **~çi** planner, organizer; **~lemek** s. ~ **etm.**

terzi tailor

tesadüf chance event, coincidence; ~ **etm.** -e meet by chance, come across; **~en** adv. by chance

tesanüt solidarity

tesbit s. **tespit**

tescil registration

teselli consolation

teshin heating; ~ **etm.** v/t heat

tesir effect, impression, influence; ~ **etm.** -e affect, influence; **~li** impressive

tesis laying a foundation; ~ **etm.** v/t found, establish, institute; **~at** pl. institutions, establishments

teskere stretcher; bier

teskin etm. v/t pacify, calm

teslim delivery; surrender, submission; ~ **etm.** v/t hand over, deliver (-e to); ~ **olmak** v/i surrender

tespih rel. rosary

tespit establishing; proving; ~ **etm.** v/t establish, confirm, prove

testere tech. saw

testi pitcher, jug

tesviye making level; payment; free pass given to travelling soldiers; ~ **etm.** v/t level, smooth, plane

teşbih comparison, simile

teşebbüs effort, initiative; ~ **etm.** -e start, undertake; **~e geçmek** set to work

teşekkül formation, organization

teşekkür thanks, giving thanks; ~ **etm.** -e thank; ~ **ederim!** thank you!

teşhir exhibiting; ~ **etm.**

v/t exhibit; **~ salonu** show-room

teşhis recognition, identification; *med.* diagnosis

teşkil formation, organization; **~ etm.** *v/t* form, organize; **~ât** *pl.* organization *sg.*

teşri *jur.* legislation

teşrif conferring honour, arrival; **~ etm.** *v/t* honour by visiting; **~at** *pl.* ceremonies; protocol *sg.*

teşrih *med.* anatomy; dissection

teşrii *jur.* legislative

teşrik: ~i mesai joint effort, co-operation

teşvik encouragement, incitement; **~ etm.** *v/t* encourage, incite (-*e* to)

tetik¹ trigger

tetik² *adj.* agile, quick; prompt

tetkik examination; **~ etm.** *v/t* investigate, examine

tevali etm. *v/i* follow *in an uninterrupted succession*

tevcih etm. *v/t* direct, confer (-*e* to)

tevdi entrusting; **~ etm.** *v/t* entrust, deposit

tevellüt birth [with]

tevfikan -*e* in conformity∫

tevkif detention, arrest; **~ etm.** *v/t* detain, arrest; **~hane** place of custody

Tevrat *rel.* Pentateuch

tevsi etm. *v/t* enlarge, extend

tevsik etm. *v/t* prove *by documentary evidence*

tevzi distribution, delivery; **~at** *pl.* postal deliveries

teyel coarse sewing, tacking; **~lemek** *v/t* sew coarsely, tack; **~li** tacked

teyit confirmation; **~ etm.** *v/t* strengthen; confirm

teyp tape recorder

teyze maternal aunt

tez¹ *adj.* quick; *adv.* quickly

tez² *n.* thesis

tezahür manifestation; **~at** *pl.* demonstration *sg.*

tezat contrast

tezek dried dung

tezgâh loom, work-bench; counter; *naut.* ship-building yard; **~tar** who serves at a counter

tezhip gilding, inlaying with gold

tezkere note; certificate

tez|lemek *v/t* hasten, accelerate; **~lenmek** make haste; **~lik** speed, haste

tezvir willful misrepresentation; deceit

tezyin (*pl.* **~at**) adorning, decoration

tıbb|i medical; **~iye** medical school

tığ crochet-needle, bodkin, awl; **~lamak** *v/i* give a piercing pain

tıka|ç plug, stopper; **~lı** stopped up, plugged; **~mak** *v/t* stop up, plug; **~nık** *s.* **~lı**; **~nmak** be stopped up; choke, suffocate

tıkır|damak clink, rattle; **~tı** rattling, clinking

162

tıkış|ık crammed, squeezed together; **~mak** be squeezed together
tıkız hard, tight
tıkmak v/t thrust, squeeze, cram (*-e* into)
tıknaz plump
tıksırmak sneeze *with the mouth shut*
tılsım talisman, charm
tımar[1] military fief
tımar[2] dressing *of wounds*; grooming *of a horse*; pruning; **~hane** lunatic asylum
tıngıldamak, **tıngırdamak** tinkle, clink, clang
tın|ı tone, timbre; **~lamak** tinkle, ring (*metal*)
tıp medicine
tıpa stopper, plug, cork
tıpır|damak walk with little noise; tap, throb; **~tı** tapping; tripping noise
tıpkı adj. same; **~ ... gibi** adv. exactly like; **~ basım** facsimile
tırabzan hand-rail, banister
tıraş shaving; sl. boring talk; bragging; **~ etm.** v/t shave; **~ olm.** get a shave; **~çı** boring talker, braggart; **~lı 1.** shaved; **2.** needing a shave
tırıldamak sl. be 'broke'
tırkaz bar behind the door
tırmalamak v/t scratch
tırmanmak *-e* climb
tırmık scratch; rake, harrow; **~lamak** v/t scratch, rake, harrow
tırnak finger-nail, toe-nail,

claw, hoof; *naut.* fluke *of an anchor*
tırpan scythe; **~lamak** v/t mow
tırtıkçı sl. pickpocket
tırtıl zo. caterpillar; **~lı traktör** tech. crawler tractor
tıslamak hiss (*goose*); spit (*cat*)
ticaret trade, commerce; **~ odası** ec. chamber of commerce; **~hane** business house, firm
ticarî commercial
tifo med. typhoid fever
tiftik mohair
tifüs med. typhus
tik twitching; mannerism
tike piece, patch
tiksinmek *-den* be disgusted with, loathe
tilki zo. fox
timsah zo. crocodile
timsal symbol, image
tin soul, spirit
tip type
tipi blizzard, snow-storm
tirbuşon corkscrew
tire sewing cotton
tirfil bot. clover
tirit bread soaked in gravy
tiriz lath, batten; piping *of clothes*
tiryaki addicted (*-in* **~si** to *sth.*)
titiz peevish, captious, hard to please; **~lik** peevishness, pedantry
titre|k trembling; **~mek** shiver, tremble; **~şim** vibration

tiyatro theatre

tiz high-pitched

tohum seed, grain, semen; **∼luk** kept for seed

tok satiated; closely woven, thick; ∼ **gözlü** contented, not covetous

toka[1] buckle

toka[2] shaking hands, clinking glasses; **∼laşmak** shake hands (**ile** with)

tokat slap; **∼lamak** v/t slap

tokmak mallet; door-knocker; wooden pestle

tokurdamak bubble

tokuş|mak collide (**ile** with); **∼turmak** v/t cause to collide (**ile** with); clink (glasses); cannon (billiard-balls)

tolga helmet

tomar roll, scroll

tombak chem. copper-zinc alloy

tombaz naut. barge; pontoon

tomruk heavy log, square boulder

tomurcuk bot. bud; **∼lanmak** put forth buds

ton[1] ton

ton[2] mus. note

ton[3] (**balığı**) zo. tunny

tonilato naut. tonnage

tonoz arch. vault

top ball, any round thing; gun, cannon; roll of cloth or paper; the whole; ∼ **yekûn** total; **∼aç** top (plaything)

topal lame; cripple; **∼lamak** limp

toparla|k round; n. mil. limber; **∼mak** v/t collect together, pack up

top|atan bot. an oblong kind of melon; naut. **∼çeker** gunboat; **∼çu** mil. artillery; artilleryman

toplam total, sum

toplama math. addition; ∼ **kampı** concentration camp; **∼k** v/t collect, gather, sum up; clear away; put on weight

toplan|mak v/i assemble; come together; **∼tı** assembly, meeting

toplatmak v/t seize, confiscate

toplu having a knob or round head; collected, in a mass; ∼ **iğne** pin; ∼ **sözleşme** collective agreement; **∼ tabanca** revolver; **∼luk** compactness; community

toplum community; **∼bilim** sociology; **∼sal** social

toprak earth, soil, land; ∼ **altı** being in the earth; **∼sız** landless

toptan ec. wholesale; **∼cı** wholesaler

topuk heel, ankle

topuz mace, knob

tor net

torba bag; an. scrotum

torik zo. large bonito

torna tech. (turning-) lathe; **∼cı** turner; **∼vida** screw-driver

torpido(bot) naut. torpedo-boat

torpil *naut.* mine; torpedo; **~lemek** *v/t* torpedo

tortu dregs, sediment

torun grandchild

tos blow *with the head*; **~lamak** *v/t* butt

toto pools *pl.*

toy¹ banquet

toy² *zo.* great bustard

toy³ *adj.* inexperienced, "green"

toygar *zo.* crested lark

toyluk inexperience

toynak hoof

toz dust; powder; **-in ~unu almak** dust; **~armak** raise the dust; **~lu** dusty; **~luk** gaiter

töhmet suspicion; guilt

töre custom(s); **~l** moral; ethical; **~n** ceremony, celebration

törpü rasp, file; **~lemek** *v/t* rasp, file

tövbe *rel.* repentance; **~kâr, ~li** penitent

trafik traffic

trahom *med.* trachoma

trajedi tragedy

traktör tractor

Trakya Thrace

trampa *ec.* barter, exchange

trampete *mus.* side drum

tramplen spring-board

tramvay tram, streetcar

transfer transfer

transistor *tech.* transistor; **~lu** equipped with transistor(s)

transit transit

travers sleeper (*railway*)

tren train (*railway*, etc.)

tribün tribune

trişin trichina

troleybüs trolley-bus

trompet trumpet

tropika *geo.* tropical zone; tropic; **~l** tropical

tröst *ec.* trust

trup *thea.* troupe

tufan *rel.* the Flood; violent rainstorm

tugay *mil.* brigade

tuğ horse-tail, plume; **~amiral** *naut.* rear-admiral; **~bay** *mil.* brigadier; **~general** *mil.* brigadier-general

tuğla brick

tuğra monogram *of the Sultan*

tuğyan overflowing; *fig.* rebellion

tuhaf uncommon, curious, odd, comic; **~iye** millinery, clothing accessories *pl.*; **~lık** being odd *or* funny

tul lenght; *astr.* longitude

tulum skin *for holding water, etc.*; tube; overall; *mus.* bagpipe

tulumba pump; fire-engine

tumturak bombast, pompous speech

Tuna (nehri) Danube

tunç bronze

tur tour

turba turf; peat

turfa *rel.* not kosher

turfanda early (*fruit, etc.*), not in its proper season

turi|st tourist, traveller; **~zm** tourism, travelling

turna *zo.* crane

turn|e *thea.* tour; ~ike turnstile; ~uva tourney, tournament

turp *bot.* radish

turşu pickle

turta tart, cake

turunç *bot.* Seville orange

tuş key *of a piano, typewriter, etc.*

tuta|k 1. handle; 2. hostage; ~m small handful; ~mak 1. handle; 2. proof, evidence; ~nak protocol, report; ~r total, sum; ~rak, ~rık *med.* seizure, fit

tutkal glue; ~lamak *v/t* glue; ~lı glued

tut|ku passion (-e for); ~kun -e affected by, given to; ~mak *v/t* hold, hold on to; catch, seize; stop; hire, rent; amount to; *v/i* take root; adhere; ~sak *mil.* prisoner, captive; ~turmak *v/t* begin, start; run his mind on

tutuk embarassed, tonguetied; ~lamak *v/t* detain, arrest; ~lu arrested, detained; ~luluk confinement

tutulma *astr.* eclipse; ~k -e be struck with, be mad about

tutum conduct; economy

tutuş|mak catch fire; ~e start, meddle into; ~turmak *v/t* set on fire; -i -in eline press *sth.* into *someone's* hand

tutya *chem.* zinc

tuvalet toilet; dressing-table; lavatory

tuz salt

tuzak trap; ~ kurmak -e lay a trap for

tuz|la salt-pan; ~lamak *v/t* salt, pickle; ~lu salted, pickled; ~luk saltcellar; salt-shaker; ~ruhu *chem.* hydrochloric acid, spirit of salt; ~suz unsalzed, insipid

tüberküloz *med.* tuberculosis

tüccar merchant

tüfek gun, rifle

tüken|mek be exhausted, give out; ~mez 1. inexhaustible; 2. *n. a kind of* syrup; ~mez kalem ball-point pen

tüket|im consumption; ~mek *v/t* exhaust, use up

tükür|mek *v/t* spit (-e on); ~ük spittle, saliva

tül tulle

tüm the whole; ~admiral *naut.* Vice-Admiral; ~en great number, 10.000; division; ~general *mil.* Major-General; ~leç *gr.* object, complement; ~lemek *v/t* complete

tümsek *geo.* small mound

tün night; ~aydın! good evening!

tünel tunnel

tüp tube

tür species

türbe *arch.* tomb, mausoleum

türbin turbine

türe *jur.* law

türedi

türedi upstart, parvenu
türel legal, juridical
türe|mek appear, come into existence; **~tici** inventor; **~tmek** v/t produce, invent
Türk Turk; Turkish; **~çe** Turkish (language); **~çülük** pol. Panturkism
Türkiyat Turkology
Türkiye Turkey; **~ Cumhuriyeti** the Turkish Republic
Türk|leşmek become like a Turk; **~lük** the quality of being a Turk; **~men** Turcoman; **2oloji** turkology
türkü mus. folk song

türlü adj. various, of many sorts; n. sort, kind, variety; **bir ~** somehow; **iki ~** in two ways
türüm genesis, creation
tüt|mek v/i smoke; **~sü** fumigant, incense
tütün tabacco; **~ içmek** smoke (tobacco); **~cü** grower or seller of tobacco
tüy feather; hair; **~lenmek** grow feathers; fig. grow rich; **~lü** feathered; **~süz** without feathers; young
tüzel jur. legal; **~ kişi** juristic person, corporation
tüzük regulations, statutes pl.

U

ucuz cheap; **~luk** cheapness
uç tip, point, extremity; end; frontier
uçak aeroplane; **~ bileti** air-travel ticket; **~ faciası** air disaster; **~savar (topu)** mil. anti-aircraft gun
uç|kun spark; **~kur** belt, band for holding up trousers; **~lu** pointed
uçmak fly; evaporate; fade away, disappear
uçsuz without a point
uçucu flying; volatile
uçur|mak v/t cause to fly; cut off; **~tma** kite (toy); **~um** precipice; abyss
uçuş flight, flying; **~ hattı** flight route
uçuşmak fly about
ufacık very small, tiny

ufak small; **~ para** small change; **~ tefek** small, of no account; **~lık** small change
ufa|lamak v/t break up, crumble; **~lmak** diminish, become smaller
ufki horizontal
uflamak say 'oof'
ufuk horizon
uğra|k frequented place or region; **~mak** -e stop, touch at; meet with, suffer; undergo; **~şmak** be busy, fight (ile with); **~t-mak** -i -e cause so. to stop at; expose so. to; -i -den dismiss so. from
uğul|damak hum, buzz; howl; **~tu** humming, buzzing

uğur good omen; **uğrun(d)a** for the sake of, on account of; **~lu** lucky, suspicious; **~suz** inauspicious; **~suzluk** ill omen

uhde obligation, charge

uhrevî *rel.* pertaining to the next world

ulaç *gr.* gerund

ulak courier

ulamak *v/t* join (*-e* to)

ulan hi! man alive!

ulaşım communication, contact; **~mak** *-e* reach, arrive at

ulaştır|ma communication; **2ma Bakanlığı** Ministry of Transport; **~mak** *v/t* cause to reach (*-e a place, etc.*)

ulema *pl. rel.* doctors of Moslem religious law

ulu great, high; **~lamak** *v/t* honour

ulumak howl (*dog, etc.*)

uluorta *adv.* rashly, recklessly, without reserve

ulus people, nation; **~al** national; **~lararası** international

ulvî high, sublime

umacı bogy man

um|madık unexpected; **~mak** *v/t* hope, expect

umum *adj.* general, universal, all; *n.* the public; **~î** general, universal; public

umumiyet generality; **~le** *adv.* in general

umut hope; **~suz** hopeless, desperate

un flour

unmak heal, get well

unsur element

unut|kan forgetful; **~mak** *v/t* forget

unvan title; superscription

Uranus *astr.* Uranus

uranyum *chem.* uranium

urgan rope

us state of mind, reason, intelligence

usan|ç boring, boredom; **~dırıcı** boring, tedious; **~dırmak** *v/t* bore, disgust; **~mak** become bored, disgusted (*-den* with)

uskumru *zo.* mackerel

uskur *naut.* screw, propeller; **~u** *tech.* skrew thread, worm

us|lanmak become sensible, well-behaved; **~lu** well-behaved, sensible

usta *n.* master; master workman; *adj.* skilled, clever; **~lık** mastery, proficiency

ustura razor

usturuplu *sl.* striking, hitting the target, right

usul method, system, manner; **~üne göre** *adv.* duly, in due form; **~cacık, ~la(cık)** *adv.* slowly, gently, quietly

uşak boy, youth; servant, assistant; **~kapan** *zo.* lammergeier

utan|ç shame, modesty; **~dırmak** *v/t* make ashamed, cause to blush; **~gaç, ~gan** bashful, shy; shamefaced; **~mak** be ashamed (*-den* of); **-e** recoil at, be ashamed of *doing*

Utarit *astr.* Mercury

uvalamak *v/t* press with the hand, crumble

uv|mak *v/t* press with the hand, massage, polish; **~uşturmak** *v/t* rub against each other

uyan|dırmak *v/t* awaken, revive, stir; **~ık** awake, vigilant; **~mak** awake, wake up, come to life

uyar conformable; **~lamak** *v/t* accomodate, adjust (**-e** to)

uyarmak *v/t* awaken, arouse; *fig.* remind, warn

uydurma invented, false, made-up; **~k** *v/t* make to fit, adapt; **~syon** *sl.* invention, fable

uygar civilized; **~lık** civilization

uygulamak *v/t* apply

uygun *-e* conformable, in accord to, fitting; **~ bulmak, ~ görmek** *v/t* agree to, approve of; **~ gelmek** *-e* suit; **~luk** being appropriate, fitting; **~suz** unsuitable

uyku sleep; **~ya dalmak** fall asleep; **~suz** sleepless

uyluk *an.* thigh

uymak *-e* conform, fit to; follow, listen to; harmonize with

uyruk *pol.* subject, citizen; **~luk** nationality

uysal conciliatory, easy-going

uyuklamak *v/i* doze

uyum harmony, conformity

uyu|mak sleep; **~rgezen** somnambulist

uyuşmak[1] come to an agreement (**ile** with)

uyuş|mak[2] become numb, insensible; **~turmak** *v/t* benumb, deaden; **~uk** numbed, insensible

uyut|mak *v/t* send to sleep; *fig.* ease, allay; put off; **~ucu** soporific

uyuz *med. n.* itch, mange; *adj.* mangy, scabby

uz good, able

uzak distant, remote (**-den** from); **~tan** from far-off; **~laşmak** retire, be far away (**-den** from); **~laştırmak** *v/t* remove, take away (**-den** from); **~lık** distance, remoteness

uza|m largeness, extent; **~mak** grow long, extend, be prolonged; **~nmak** *-e* be extended to, stretch oneself out on, extend to; **~tmak** *v/t* extend, prolong; **~y** *astr.* space

uzlaşmak come to an agreement *or* understanding

uzman expert, specialist

uzun long; **~luk** length, lengthiness

uzuv *an.* member, organ

Ü

ücret pay, wage, fee, cost, price; **~li** paid, employed for pay; **~li memur** employee; **~siz** unpaid; gratis
üç three; **~ köşeli** triangular, three-cornered; **~gen** *math.* triangle; **~üz** triplets *pl.*; triplet
üflemek -e blow upon; -i blow out
üfür|mek -i blow; -e cure by breathing on; **~ükçü** sorcerer *who claims to cure by breathing on*
üleş|mek divide, share (**ile** with); **~tirmek** *v/t* distribute, share out (-e to)
ülfet familiarity, friendship
ülke country
Ülker *astr.* the Pleiades
ülkü ideal
ülser *med.* ulcer
ültimatom *pol.* ultimatum
ümit hope, expectation; **~ etm.** *v/t* hope, expect; **~lendirmek** *v/t* make hopeful; **~li** full of hope; **~siz** hopeless; desperate
ün fame, reputation
üni|forma uniform; **~versite** university
ünlem cry, shout; *gr.* interjection; **~ işareti** *gr.* exclamation mark
ünlemek -e call out to
ünlü famous; *gr.* vowel
ünsiyet familiarity (**ile** with)
ünsüz *gr.* consonant

üre|m *ec.* interest; **~mek** *v/i* multiply, increase; **~tim** *ec.* production; **~tmek** *v/t* multiply, breed, raise
ürkek timid, fearful; **~lik** timidity
ürk|mek -den start with fear from, be frightened of; **~ütmek** *v/t* startle, scare
ürpermek stand on end (*hair*)
ürümek howl; bay
ürün product
üs base, basis
üsçavuş *mil.* sergeant
üslup manner, form, style
üst *n.* upper surface, top; outside; -in **~ün(d)e** in, upon, over; -in **~ünden** from above, over; **~ ~e** one on top of the other
üstat master, teacher
üstderi *an.*, *bot.* epidermis
üsteğmen *mil.* first lieutenant
üste|lemek -e be added to; recur (*illness*); **~lik** *adv.* furthermore, in addition
üstün superior (-den to); victorious; **~körü** superficial; **~lük** superiority
üstüvane *tech.* cylinder
üşen|ç, **~geç**, **~gen** lazy, slothful; **~iklik** laziness, sloth; **~mek** -e be too lazy to *inf.*, do with reluctance
üşmek -e flock to
üşü|mek catch cold; **~tmek**

v/t cause to catch cold; *v/i* catch cold

ütü flat-iron; **~lemek** *v/t* iron; singe; **~lü** ironed, singed; **~süz** not ironed

üvey step-; **~ baba** stepfather; **~ evlât** stepchild

üye member *of a council, etc.*; *an.* organ

üzengi stirrup

üzere *-mek* at the point of *-ing*, just about to *inf.*

üzeri|nde *-in* on, over, above; *-in* **~ne** on, upon; about

üzgeç rope ladder

üzgü oppression; cruelty; **~n** weak, invalid

üz|mek *v/t* strain, break; hurt the feelings of; **~ülmek** be worn out; *-e* be sorry for, regret

üzüm *bot.* grape

üzüntü anxiety; dejection; **~lü** tedious; anxious

V

vaat promise; **~ etm.** *v/t* promise

vacip necessary

vade fixed term, date; **~li** having a fixed term

vadetmek *s.* **vaat etm.**

vadi valley

vaftiz *rel.* baptism; **~ etm.** *v/t* baptize

vagon railway car; **~ restoran** dining-car

vah vah! *intj.* how sad!; what a pity!

vahe oasis

vahim serious, dangerous

vahiy *rel.* inspiration, revelation

vahş|et wildness, savageness; **~î** wild, savage, brutal

vaiz *rel.* sermon

vaiz *rel.* preacher

vaka event, occurence

vakar gravity, dignity; **~lı** grave, dignified, calm

vakf|etmek *v/t* devote, dedicate (*-e* to); **~iye** *rel.* deed of trust *of a pious foundation*

vakıa *adv.* in fact; indeed

vakıf pious foundation, wakf

vâkıf *-e* aware, cognizant of

vakit time; *-diği* **~** *conj.* when; **~siz** inopportune, untimely

vakt|aki *conj.* when, at the time that; **~inde** in due time; **~iyle** *adv.* in due time; at one time

vakum *phys.* vacuum

valf *tech.* valve

vali *pol.* governor *of a province*

valide mother

valiz suit-case

vallahi! *intj.* By God!

vals waltz

vanilya *bot.* vanilla

vantilatör ventilator, fan; **~ kayışı** ventilator-belt

vapur steamer

var there is, there are; ~ **olm.** exist; ~ **ol!** may you live long!; bravo!

varak leaf; sheet of paper; ~**a** leaf; note, letter

varda! intj. keep clear! make way!

var|dırmak v/t cause to reach (~**e** a place or condition); ~**ılmak** be reached (~**e** place); ~**ış** arrival

varidat pl. revenues

varil small cask

vâris heir

varlık existence, presence, self; wealth; ~ **vergisi** property tax

varmak ~**e** arrive at, reach, attain; result, end in

varoş suburb

varta great peril

varyete thea. variety theatre

varyos sledge-hammer

vasat middle; average; ~**î** adj. middle, average

vasıf quality; ~**landırmak** v/t qualify, describe

vasıl olm. ~**e** arrive at, reach

vasıta means; intermediary; vehicle; ~**sıyle** by means of; ~**lı** indirect; ~**sız** direct

vasi jur. executor; trustee

vasiyet will, testament; ~**name** written will

vaşak zo. lynx

vat el. Watt

vatan native country; ~**daş** compatriot; ~**daşlık** citizenship; ~**perver** patriot

vatman tram-driver

vay! intj. oh! woe!

vazgeç|irmek -i -den make so. give up or abandon sth.; ~**mek** -den give up, cease from, abandon

vazıh clear, manifest

vazife duty, obligation; home-work (school); ~**len-dirmek** v/t charge, entrust (**ile** with)

vaziyet position, situation

vazo vase

ve and; ~ **saire** and so on

veba med. plague, pestilence

vecibe obligation

vecih face; direction; s. **veçhile**

veçhile: bir ~ in some way; **bu ~** in this way

veda farewell; ~ **etm.** -**e** bid farewell to; ~**laşmak** say farewell (**ile** to)

vefa fidelity, loyality; ~**dar**, ~**lı** -**e** faithful, loyal to; ~**sız** faithless, untrustworthy

vefat death; ~ **etm.** die

vehim groundless fear

vekâlet attorneyship, representation; pol. Ministry; ~**name** jur. power of attorney

vekil agent, representative; pol. Minister of State; ~ **harç** major-domo

velense a kind of thick blanket

velet child; bastard

velev (ki) conj. even if

velhasıl in short

veli jur. guardian; rel. saint; ~**aht** pol. heir to the throne;

~nimet benefactor, patron

velvele noise, clamour

Venüs *astr.* Venus

veraset inheritance

verecek debt

verem *n. med.* tuberculosis; *adj.* (~li) tuberculous

veresi(ye) *adv.* on credit

verev oblique

vergi tax; gift; **~ beyannamesi** income-tax return; **~li** generous

verilmek *-e* be given, delivered to

verim produce, profit, output; **~li** profitable, productive; **~siz** yielding little produce, unfruitful

vermek *v/t* give, deliver, attribute (*-e* to); pay

vernik varnish

vesika document

vesile cause, pretext

vesselâm so that's well!

vestiyer cloak-room

veteriner *med.* veterinary surgeon

vetire process

veto veto

veya(hut) or

vezin weighing; weight; metre (*poetry*)

vezir Vizier; minister

vezne treasury, pay-office; **~dar** treasurer, cashier

vıcıklamak *v/t* make sticky

vınlamak buzz, hum

vırılda(n)mak talk incessantly; grumble, nag

vızıl|damak buzz, hum; **~tı** buzzing noise

vicdan conscience; **~lı** conscientious, honest; **~sız** unscrupulous

vida *tech.* screw; **~lamak** *v/t* screw; **~lı** having screws; screwed

vilâyet *pol.* province

villa villa

vinç *tech.* crane, winch

viraj curve of *a road*

viran ruined; **~e** *n.* ruin

virgül *gr.* comma

virüs *med.* virus

visamiral *naut.* vice-admiral

viski whisky [miral)

viskonsolos *pol.* vice-consul

vişne *bot.* morello cherry

vites *tech.* gear; **~ kolu** gearlever

vitrin shop-window

Viyana Vienna

vize *pol.* visa

vizita *med.* visit; doctor's fee

voleybol volleyball

volkan *geo.* volcano

volt *el.* volt; **~aj** voltage

votka vodka

vuku occurrence; event; **~ bulmak, ~a gelmek** happen, take place; **~at** *pl.* events, incidents

vukuf *-e* knowledge of, information about

vulkanize etm. *v/t tech.* vulcanize

vurgu *gr.* accent, stress; **~lu** stressed

vurgun(culuk) *ec.* profiteering

vur|mak *v/t* hit (*-e* against);

apply (**-e** to); kill; steal, swindle; **~uş** blow; **~uş-mak** fight (**ile** with)

vusul arrival

vuzuh clearness

vücu|t existence, being; the human body; **~da gelmek** arise, come into existence

Y

ya¹ *intj.* oh!

ya² (*at the beginning of a sentence*) well; yes, but ...; (*at the end of a sentence*) indeed; there!; after all

ya³ or; **~ ... ~ ...** either ... or ...

-ya *s.* **-a**

yaba wooden fork

yaban desert, wilderness; stranger; **~ domuzu** *zo.* wild boar; **~ kedisi** *zo.* wild cat; **~cı** strange; foreign; **~î** untamed, wild; **~î gül** bot. wild rose

yadırgamak *v/t* regard as a stranger, find strange

yadigâr souvenir; *fig.* scoundrel

yadsımak *v/t* deny

yafta label

yağ oil, fat, grease; **~dan(lık)** grease-pot; oil-can

yağdırmak *v/t* let rain (**-e** upon); *ec.* glut with

yağış rain; **~lı** rainy

yağ|lamak *v/t* grease, oil; **~lı** fat, greasy, oily; *fig.* profitable

yağma booty; loot; **~ etm.** *v/t* plunder; **~cı** plunderer, pillager

yağmak *v/t* rain (**-e** upon)

yağmur *n.* rain; **~ yağmak**

rain; **~lu** rainy; **~luk** rain-coat

yahni meat stew with onions

yahşi pretty

yahu! *intj.* see here!; say!; my goodness!; please!

Yahudi *n.* Jew; *adj.* Jewish; **~lik** Judaism; quality of a Jew

yahut or

yaka collar; bank, shore

yakacak fuel; combustibles *pl.*

yakala|mak *v/t* collar, seize; **~nmak** be seized; be held responsible

yakı *med.* cautery, plaster

yakıcı burning, biting

yakın *adj.* near (**-e** to); *n.* nearby place, neighbourhood; **~da** *adv.* near; in the near future; recently; **~dan** *adv.* closely, from the near; **~laşmak** *-e* approach; **~lık** nearness, proximity

yakışık suitability; **~sız** unsuitable, unbecoming

yakışmak be suitable, proper (**-e** for)

yakıt fuel

yakinen *adv.* for certain, doubtless

yaklaş|ık approximate; **~mak** *-e* approach, approximate; **~tırmak** v/t bring near

yakmak v/t light, set on fire; apply

yakut ruby

yalak trough; stone basin

yalamak v/t lick, sweep over

yalan lie; false; **~ söylemek** lie; **~cı** lier; imitated, false; **~cılık** lying, mendacity; **~lamak** v/t deny, contradict

yalçın bare, slippery, steep

yaldız gilding; **~lamak** v/t gild; **~lı** gilt; false

yalı shore, beach; water-side residence

yalım 1. flame; **2.** blade, edge

yalın single; bare, naked; **~ hal** gr. nominative case; **~ayak** barefoot

yalıt|kan phys., el. isolating, insulating; **~mak** v/t isolate, insulate

yalnız alone; only; **~lık** solitude, loneliness

yalpa naut. rolling

yaltak|(çı) fawning, cringing; **~lanmak** fawn, flatter; **~lık** flattery

yalvaç messenger, prophet

yalvarmak -e entreat, implore, beg

yama patch

yamaç side, slope of a hill

yamak assistant

yama|(la)mak v/t patch; **~lı** patched

yaman strong, violent

yamanmak -e be patched

on; fig. be imposed on; foist oneself on

yamuk bent, crooked; math. trapezoid

yamyam cannibal; **~lık** cannibalism

yan side, flank; direction; **~ sokak** side street; **~a** side by side; **-in ~ına** towards, to; **-in ~ında** beside; with; **-in ~ından** from

yanak an. cheek

yanardağ geo. volcano

yanaş|ma approaching; hireling; **~mak** -e draw near, approach, come alongside; **~tırmak** v/t bring near, let come alongside

yanay profile, side-face

yandaş partisan, supporter

yandık bot. camel-thorn

yangı inflammation; **~lanmak** become inflamed

yangın fire, conflagration; **~ muhbiri** fire-alarm; **~ sigortası** fire insurance

yanık burned, scorched; piteous; burn, scald

yanıl make a mistake; go wrong; **~tmak** v/t lead into error [v/t answer)

yanıt n. answer; **~lamak)**

yani that is, namely

yankesici pickpocket

yankı echo; reaction

yanlış n. mistake, error; adj. wrong, incorrect; **~lık** mistake, blunder

yanmak burn, be alight; catch fire; be burnt

yansı reflection; **∼lamak, ∼tmak** reflect

yansız neutral, impartial

yapa|ğı, ∼k wool *shorn in spring*

yapı construction, edifice; **∼cı** *n.* maker, constructor; *adj.* constructive; **∼lı** made, built

yapıl|ış construction; structure; **∼mak** be built, be constructed

yapım construction, building; manufacture; **∼evi** factory, workshop

yapınmak *v/t* make or have made for oneself; *-e* try to *inf.*

yapış|kan sticky, adhesive; **∼mak** *-e* stick to, hang on; **∼tırmak** *v/t* attach, fasten (*-e* to)

yapıt work *of art, etc.*

yapma *n.* imitation; *adj.* false; **∼k** *v/t* do, make, construct

yaprak leaf; sheet *of paper*; **∼lanmak** come into leaf

yaptırmak *v/t* cause to be made, order

yar precipice, abyss

yara wound; *fig.* pain

yara|dan *rel.* Creator; **∼dılış** creation; nature, constitution

yara|lamak *v/t* wound, hit; **∼lanmak** be wounded; **∼lı** wounded

yara|mak *-e* be useful, suitable for; **∼maz** useless, naughty; **∼mazlık** naughtiness

yaranmak offer one's services (*-e* to)

yarar *adj. -e* useful, serviceable for; *n.* advantage; **∼lık** capability, courage

yarasa *zo.* bat

yaraş|ıklı suitable; **∼mak** *-e* harmonize, go well with

yarat|ıcı creative, creating; **∼mak** *v/t* create

yarbay *mil.* lieutenant-colonel

yarda yard

yardak assistant

yardım help, assistance; **∼ etm.** *-e* help; **∼cı** helper, assistant; *adj.* auxiliary; **∼cı fiil** *gr.* auxiliary verb

yargı *jur.* decision; lawsuit; **∼ yetkisi** judicial power; **∼ç** judge; **∼lamak** try, judge; **∼tay** Court of Appeal

yarı half; **∼ya** *adv.* fifty-fifty; **∼k** split, cleft, crack, fissure

yarım half; **∼ada** *geo.* peninsula

yarın tomorrow; **∼ değil öbür gün** the day after tomorrow

yarış race, competition; **∼ma** competition; **∼mak** race, compete (*ile* with)

yarmak *v/t* split, cleave, break through

yas mourning; **∼ tutmak** be in mourning

yasa law

yasak *n.* prohibition; *adj.* forbidden, prohibited; **∼ etm.** *v/t* forbid

yasama: ~ **yetkisi** *jur.* legislative power; ~**k** *v/t* arrange

yasemin *bot.* Jasmin

yaslı in mourning

yassı flat and wide; ~**lık** flatness, planeness; ~**lt-mak** *v/t* flatten, plane

yastık pillow, cushion, bolster; nursery-bed (*garden*)

yaş[1] *adj.* wet, damp; *n.* tears

yaş[2] age; **yirmi** ~**ında** 20 years old

yaşa|m life; ~**mak** *v/i* live; ~**ntı** way of life; experience of life

yaşarmak become wet

yaşayış way of living, life

yaşlanmak grow old

yaşlı[1] wet

yaşlı[2] aged

yat *naut.* yacht

yatağan heavy curved knife

yatak bed, lair, berth; orebed; *tech.* bearing; ~ **odası** bedroom; ~ **takımı** bedclothes; ~**lı vagon** sleeping-car

yata|lak bedridden; ~**y** horizontal

yatı halting place *for the night*; ~**lı okul** boarding-school; ~**rım** *ec.* deposit; investment; ~**rmak** *v/t* cause to lie down; deposit; ~**şmak** calm down, become quiet

yat|mak -*e* lie down on, lean towards; go *to bed*; ~**sı** time two hours after sunset

yavan with little fat; tasteless

yavaş slow; low, soft (*voice*); gentle, mild; ~ ~ *adv.* gently, steadily; ~**lamak** become slow; ~**latmak** *v/t* slacken, slow down

yave foolish talk

yaver assistant; *mil.* aide-de-camp

yavru young; cub, chick

yavuklanmak -*e* become engaged to

yavuz ferocious, resolute

yay bow; *tech.* spring; *astr.* Sagittarius

yaya on foot; pedestrian; ~ **gitmek** go on foot; ~ **kaldırımı** foot pavement; ~**n** on foot; *fig.* without skill

yaygara shout, outcry

yaygın widespread

yayık[1] churn

yayı|k[2] spread out; wide; ~**lmak** -*e* be spread on

yayım publishing; publication; ~**lamak** *v/t* publish

yayın publication; ~**evi** publishing house

yayla high plateau; ~**k** summer pasture; ~**mak** graze *on a high plateau*

yaylı having springs

yaymak *v/t* spread, scatter; broadcast

yayvan broad

yaz summer

yaz|ar writer, author; ~**dırmak** *v/t* cause to be written, have registered; ~**gı** destiny

yazı writing; handwriting;

written article; **~ makinesi** typewriter; **~hane** desk; office

yazık pity; shame; deplorable; what a pity!

yazılı[1] written; inscribed; **~mak** be written; be registered (*-e* in)

yazım orthography, spelling

yazın[1] literature

yazın[2] *adv.* in summer

yazışmak correspond (**ile** with)

yazıt inscription

yazlık suitable for the summer

yazma writing; **~ kitap** manuscript; **~k** *v/t* write; register, enrol (*-e* in)

-ye *s.* **-a**

yedek in reserve, spare; **~ parça** spare part; **~ subay** *mil.* reserve conscript officer

yedi seven

yediemin *jur.* depositary, trustee

yedirmek *v/t* cause to eat, feed

yegâne sole, unique

yeğen nephew; niece

yek|nesak uniform, monotonous; **~pare** in a single piece

yekûn total, sum

yel wind

yele mane

yelek waistcoat

yelken sail; **~ açmak** hoist sails; **~li** *adj.* fitted with sails; *n.* sailing ship

yelkovan minute-hand; weather-cock

yellemek *v/t* blow upon, fan

yelpaze fan; **~lemek** *v/t* fan

yelpik asthma

yem food, fodder; bait

yemek 1. *n.* meal, food, dish; banquet; 2. *v/t* consume, eat, spend; bite; suffer; **~lik** serving as a food, edible

yemin oath; **~ etm.** swear, take an oath (*-in üzerine* by); **~li** sworn in

yemiş 1. fruit; 2. *zo.* fig(s)

yem|lemek *v/t* bait; feed; entice; **~lik** *adj.* suitable for food; *n.* trough, manger; *fig.* bribe

yemyeşil very green

yen sleeve

yençmek *v/t* crush, smash

yenge the wife of one's uncle *or* brother

yengeç *zo.* crab; ♀ *astr.* Cancer

yengi victory

yeni new; recent; **~den** anew, once again; **~bahar** *bot.* allspice; **~çeri** Janissary; **~lemek** *v/t* renew, renovate; **~lenmek** be renewed, renovated; **~lik** newness; renovation, reform

yenilmek[1] be eaten

yenilmek[2] be overcome, lose

yenmek[1] *v/t* overcome, conquer

yenmek[2] be edible

yepyeni brand new

yer earth, ground, place; space, room; ~ **bulmak** take place; ~**de** on the ground; ~**inde** in its place, suitable; ~**ine** instead of; ~**ine getirmek** v/t carry out

yer|altı underground, subterranean; ~**el** local; ~**fıstığı** bot. peanut

yerleş|mek -de settle down in, become established in; ~**tirmek** v/t put into place, settle

yer|li local, indigenous, native; ~**siz** out of place; ~**yüzü** geo. face of the earth

yeşil green, fresh; ~**lenmek** become green; ~**lik** greenness; meadow; greens

yetenek ability, capacity

yeter sufficient, enough; ~**li** competent, qualified; ~**lik** competence, qualification; ~**siz** inadequate

yetim orphan

yetinmek be contented (**ile** with)

yetiş|mek -e reach, attain; catch (train, etc.); be brought up; suffice; ~**tir-mek** v/t cause to reach; bring up, educate

yetki competence, qualification; ~**li** competent, qualified; ~**n** perfect

yetmek -e suffice, reach; attain

yetmiş seventy

yevmiye daily pay

yığılı heaped, piled up

yığın heap, pile; ~**ak** mil. concentration; ~**tı** accumulation, heap

yığ|ışmak v/i crowd together; ~**mak** v/t collect, pile up

yıka|mak v/t wash; ~**nmak** wash oneself

yıkı|cı destructive; ~**k** demolished, ruined; ~**lmak** be demolished, fall down; ~**m** bankruptcy; ~**ntı** ruins, debris

yık|mak v/t pull down, demolish; ~**tırmak** v/t cause to be pulled down

yıl year

yılan zo. snake; ~**balığı** zo. eel; ~**cık** med. erysipelas; ~**kavi** adj. spiral, winding

yılbaşı New Year's Day

yıldırak shining; ♀ astr. Canopus

yıldırım lightning; ~ **harbi** mil. blitzkrieg

yıldız star; ~ **çiçeği** bot. dahlia

yıldönümü anniversary

yılgı horror, dread; ~**n** cowed, frightened

yılış|mak importunate; ~**mak** grin impudently

yıl|la(n)mak take on. years; grow old; ~**lık** n. annual, yearbook; adj. one year old; for one year

yılma|k -den be afraid of, dread; ~**z** undaunted

yıpra(n)mak wear out, be worn out, grow old

yırtıcı: ~ **hayvan** beast of prey

yırt|ık torn, rent, tattered; *fig.* shameless; **~ılmak** be torn, rent; **~mak** *v/t* tear, rend; break in (*horse*)

yiğit hero; young man; *adj.* courageous, **~lik** courage, heroism

yine *s.* gene

yirmi twenty

yit|irmek *v/t* lose; **~mek** be lost; go astray

yiv groove; *tech.* thread

yiyecek food

yobaz *rel.* fanatic; **~lık** fanaticism

yoğalt|ım consumption; **~mak** *v/t* consume, use up

yoğun thick, dense; **~luk** density, thickness

yoğurmak *v/t* knead

yoğurt yogurt, yaourt; **~cu** maker or seller of yogurt

yok there is not; non-existent, absent; no; **~ etm.** *v/t* annihilate

yoklama roll-call; *mil.* call-up; examination; **~k** *v/t* search, examine, try, test

yok|luk absence, lack, non-existence; **~sa** if not, otherwise; but not

yoksul destitute; **~luk** destitution

yoksun deprived (*-den* of)

yokuş rise, ascent; **~ aşağı** down-hill; **~ yukarı** up-hill

yol road, way, street; manner, method; rule; law; **~ açmak** *-e* cause; **~ vermek** *-e* make way to; discharge; **~a çıkmak** start, depart; **~una koymak** *v/t* set right; **~unda** in order, going well; **~unu şaşırmak** lose the way; **~ kesici** brigand

yolcu traveller, passenger; **~luk** travelling

yol|daş comrade; **~lamak** *v/t* send, dispatch (*-e* to); **~lu** striped; having *such and such* roads *or* manners; **~luk** provisions for a journey

yolmak *v/t* pluck, tear out, strip

yolsuz roadless; contrary to law; **~luk** irregularity; abuse, misuse

yonca *bot.* clover, trefoil

yonga chip, chipping

yontmak *v/t* cut, sharpen; chip

yordam agility, dexterity

yorgan quilt; **~cı** quilt-maker

yorgun tired, weary; **~luk** fatigue, weariness

yormak[1] *v/t* tire, fatigue

yormak[2] *v/t* attribute (*-e* to)

yortu *rel.* Christian feast

yorulmak[1] be tired

yorulmak[2] be attributed (*-e* to)

yorum commentary, interpretation; **~lamak** *v/t* explain, comment on

yosma pretty, attractive; coquette

yosun *bot.* moss; **~lu** mossy, covered with moss

yoz virgin (*soil*), wild

yön direction; **~eltmek** v/t direct, turn (-e towards)

yönet|im administration, management; **~mek** v/t direct, administer; **~melik** regulation; **~men** director

yöntem method, way

Yörük Turcoman nomad

yörünge astr. orbit

yudum mouthful

yufka n. thin layer of dough; adj. thin, weak

Yugoslavya Yugoslavia

yuha intj. shame on you!; **~lamak** v/t hoot down or off

yukarı n. top, upper part; adj. high, upper, top; **~da** above, overhead; **~dan** from above; **~ya** upward

yulaf bot. oats

yular halter

yumak[1] v/t wash

yumak[2] ball of wool, etc.

yummak v/t shut, close

yumru round thing, boil

yumruk fist; blow with the fist; **~lamak** v/t hit with the fist

yumu|k closed, half-shut; **~lmak** become closed

yumurta egg; roe, spawn; **~ akı** the white of an egg; **~ sarısı** the yolk of an egg; **~lık** egg-cup

yumurtlamak v/t lay eggs; fig. invent

yumuşak soft, mild; **~lık** softness, mildness

yumuşa|mak v/i become soft; **~tmak** v/t soften

Yunan Greek; **~istan**

Greece; **~lı** Greek; **~ca** Greek (language)

yunusbalığı dolphin

yurdu eye of a needle

yurt native country; home for students, etc.; **~sever** patriotic; **~taş** fellow countryman

yut|kunmak v/i swallow one's spittle, gulp; **~mak** v/t swallow, gulp down

yuva nest, home; socket; **~lamak** v/t make a nest

yuvar an. blood-corpuscle; **~lak** round, spherical; roundness; **~lamak** v/t roll, make round, swallow greedily; **~lanmak** v/i revolve, roll; topple over

yüce high, exalted; **2 Divan** jur. High Court; **~lik** height, loftiness

yük load, burden; **~ gemisi** naut. cargo-steamer, freighter

yükle|m gr. predicate; **~mek** load v/t (-e on); attribute (-e to); **~nmek** -e shoulder; throw oneself against; **~tmek** v/t place, impose (-e on) [drunk]

yüklü loaded; pregnant; sl.J

yüksek high; loud (voice); **~ mühendis** graduated engineer; **~ öğretim** higher education; **~lik** height, elevation

yüksel|mek rise; **~tmek** v/t raise; fig. praise

yüksük thimble

yüküm obligation; **~lü** charged (ile with)

yün wool; woollen; ~lü woollen

yürek heart; *fig.* courage, boldness; ~li stout-hearted, bold; ~siz timid

yürü|k fast, fleet; 2k *s.* Yörük; ~mek walk, advance, march; ~lük *jur.* being in force, validity

yürüt|me: ~me görevi *jur.* executive power; ~mek *v/t* cause to walk; put into force; put forward; ~üm execution *of an order*, etc.

yürüyüş *n.* march, walk

yüz[1] one hundred

yüz[2] face; surface; motive, cause; bu ~den for this reason; ~ünden on account

of; ~ çevirmek turn away (-den from); ~ kızartıcı shameful; ~ tutmak -e begin, turn towards; ~ vermek give encouragement, be indulgent (-e to)

yüzbaşı *mil.* captain

yüzey face, surface

yüzgeç swimming, floating

yüz|leşmek be confronted (ile with); meet face to face; ~lü with *such and such* a face *or* surface

yüzmek[1] *v/t* flay, skin

yüzmek[2] *v/i* swim

yüzsüz shameless; ~lük effrontery, shamelessness

yüzük ring

yüzyıl century

Z

zabıt seizure; protocol; ~name protocol; minutes *pl.*

zafer success, victory

zağ keen edge

zahife *zo.* reptile

zahir outward, external; clear, evident; ~i external, outward

zahmet trouble; difficulty; ~ çekmek suffer trouble *or* fatigue; ~ etmeyiniz! don't trouble yourself!; ~li troublesome, difficult; ~siz easy

zaika the faculty of taste

zakkum *bot.* oleander

zalim tyrannical, unjust

zam addition, increase; ~

yapmak -e raise the price of

zaman time, period; -diği ~ *conj.* when; o ~ then; bir ~(lar) once, at one time; ~aşımı *jur.* prescription; ~sız untimely, inappropriate

zambak *bot.* lily

zamir *gr.* pronoun

zamk gum; ~lamak *v/t* gum; ~lı gummed

zammetmek *v/t* increase, add {women, rake}

zampara who runs after}

zan opinion

zanaat craft, handicraft

zangırdamak tremble, clank

zani adulterer

zannetmek *v/t* think, suppose

zapt|etmek *v/t* seize, take possession of; restrain, master; **~urapt** discipline

zar¹ membrane, film; thin skin

zar² dice

zarar damage, injury, harm; **~ vermek** *-e* cause harm *or* loss; **~ı yok!** never mind!, it doesn't matter!; **~lı** harmful (*-e* to); **~sız** harmless; not so bad

zarf envelope; cover; cupholder; case; *gr.* adverb; **~ında** during, within

zarif elegant, graceful; witty; **~lik** elegance

zarp striking, blow; **~ musluğu** main cock *of* pipes

zarur|et need, necessity; want, poverty; **~î** necessary, indispensable

zat essence; person, individual; **~en** *adv.* in any case, as a matter of fact; **~î** essential; personal

zavallı unlucky, miserable

zaviye corner, angle

zayıf weak, thin; slim, slender; **~lamak** become thin *or* weak; **~latmak** *v/t* weaken, enfeeble; **~lık** weakness, debility

zayi lost; **~at** *pl.* losses

zayiçe horoscope

zebir *zo.* zebra

zebun weak, powerless

Zebur *rel.* the Psalms of David

zecir compulsion

zecrî compulsory; coercive

zedelemek *v/t* bruise; maltreat

zehir poison; **~lemek** *v/t* poison; **~li** poisonous; poisoned

zekâ intelligence, quickness of mind

zekât *rel.* alms *prescribed by Islam*

zeki quick-qitted, intelligent

zelil low, base

zelzele *geo.* earthquake

zemberek spring *of a watch, etc.*

zemin earth, ground (*a.* of *a design*); *fig.* subject, theme; **~ katı** ground-floor

zencefil *bot.* ginger

zenci negro

zencir *s.* zincir

zengin rich; **~le(ş)mek** become rich; **~lik** wealth

zeplin *av.* Zeppelin airship

zerdali *bot.* wild apricot

zerde *sweetened rice coloured with saffron*

zerdeva *zo.* beech marten

zerre atom; molecule

zerzevat *pl.* vegetables; **~çı** greengrocer

zeval decline, decadence; **~î** reckoned from noon; **~siz** everlasting, permanent

zevce wife

zevk taste, flavour; enjoyment, pleasure; good taste; **-in ~ine varmak** appreciate; **~lenmek ile** mock at, make fun of; **~li** pleasant, amusing; **~siz** tasteless; unpleasant

zevzek giddy, talkative; **~lenmek** say stupid things; **~lik** senseless chatter, silly behaviour

zeyil appendix, addendum

zeyrek intelligent

zeytin *bot.* olive; **~ yağı** olive-oil; **~lik** olive grove

zeytunî olive-green

zıddiyet contrast; *fig.* detestation

zıh edging, border

zıkkım unpleasant food

zımba drill; file-punch; **~lamak** *v/t* punch

zımbırtı twanging noise; *fig.* worthless thing

zımn|en *adv.* tacitly, by implication; **~î** implied, tacitly understood

zımpara emery; **~ kâğıdı** emery paper

zıngı|ldamak, ~rdamak tremble; rattle

zıpkın *naut.* harpoon

zıplamak jump, skip about

zıpzıp marble *for playing*

zırdava s. **zerdeva**

zırdeli raving mad

zırh armour; **~lı** armoured; *n. naut.* battleship

zırıl|damak chatter continuously; **~tı** chatter, squabble

zırnık *chem.* yellow arsenic

zırva silly chatter; nonsense

zıt the contrary, opposite; *-in* **zıddına gitmek** get on

one's nerves; **~ gitmek** oppose (**ile** *so.*)

zıvana short tube; mouthpiece *for a cigarette*

zıya loss

zifos splash of mud

zift pitch; **~lemek** *v/t* daub with pitch

zihin mind, intelligence, memory

zihniyet mentality

zikir remembrance, recollection; *rel.* recitation of litanies *by dervishes*

zikretmek *v/t* mention

zikzak zigzag

zil cymbal; bell; **~i çalmak** ring the bell; **~zurna** blind drunk

zimmet *ec.* debit side *of an account*; *-in* **~ine geçirmek** *v/t* place to *one's* debit; **kendi ~ine geçirmek** *v/t* embezzle

zina adultery, fornication

zincir chain, fetters; **~lemek** *v/t* chain; **~li** chained; provided with a chain

zindan dungeon; **~cı** jailer

zinde alive, active

zira *conj.* because, for

zira|at agriculture; **~î** agricultural

zirve summit, peak

ziya light

ziyade more; surplus; too much; **~siyle** *adv.* to a great degree, largely

ziyafet feast, banquet

ziyan loss, damage; **~ı yok!** no matter!

ziyaret visit; pilgrimage; ~ **etm.** *v/t* pay a visit to; ~**çi** visitor; ~**gâh** *rel.* place to which a pilgrimage is made

ziynet ornament, decoration

zoka artificial bait

zonklamak *v/i* throb with pain

zooloji zoology

zor *n.* compulsion; strength; *adj.* difficult; ~**aki** *adv.* under compulsion; by force; ~**la** *adv.* with difficulty; by force

zorba who uses force, bully; ~**lık** violence, bullying

zorla *s.* **zor**

zorla|mak *v/t* force (-*e* to *inf.*); use force against; try to open; ~**şmak** grow difficult; ~**ştırmak** *v/t* render difficult, complicate; ~**yıcı** compelling

zor|lu strong, violent; ~**luk** difficulty; ~**unlu** necessary

zuhur appearance, happening; ~ **etm.** appear

zulüm wrong, oppression

zurna *mus. a kind of* shrill pipe

zücaciye glassware, porcelain

züğürt *sl.* bankrupt, 'stony-broke'

Zühal *astr.* Saturn

Zühre *astr.* Venus; ♀**vî** *med.* venereal

zülüf love-lock, tassel

zümre party, group

zümrüt emerald

züppe fop, affected person

zürafa *zo.* giraffe

zürriyet issue, progeny

English-Turkish Vocabulary

A

a [ey, ı] bir
aback [ı'bäk]: **be taken ~** şaşalamak, şaşırıp kalmak
abandon [ı'bändın] v/t terketmek, bırakmak; **~ment** jur. terk
abash [ı'bäş] v/t utandırmak
abate [ı'beyt] v/t indirmek, azaltmak, hafifletmek; v/i azalmak
abb|ess ['äbıs] rel. başrahibe; **~ey** ['ʌ-i] manastır; **~ot** ['ʌıt] başrahip
abbreviat|e [ı'brīviyet] v/t kısaltmak; **~ion** kısaltma
ABC ['eybī'sī] alfabe
abdicat|e ['äbdikeyt] vazgeçmek, istifa etm. **-den**; **~ion** istifa
abdomen ['äbdımen] an. altkarın, karın
abduct [äb'dakt] v/t kaçırmak
abeyance [ı'beyıns]: **in ~** henüz karara bağlanmamış
abhor [ıb'hô] nefret etm. **-den**; **~rence** [ʌorıns] nefret, tiksinme; **~rent** tiksindirici
abide [ı'bayd] v/i kalmak, durmak
ability [ı'biliti] kabiliyet, yetenek

abject ['äbcekt] alçak, sefil
able ['eybl] muktedir, güçlü; **be ~ to** inf. muktedir olm. **-e**, yapabilmek **-i**
ablution [ı'blūuşın] aptes
abnormal [äb'nômıl] anormal [miye)
aboard [ı'bôd] gemide; ge-J
abode [ı'bud] s. abide; n. ikametgâh, oturulan yer
aboli|sh [ı'boliş] kaldırmak, iptal etm.: **~tion** [äbıu'lişın] kaldırılma, ilga
A-bomb ['eybom] atom bombası
abominable [ı'bominıbl] iğrenç, nefret verici
abortion [ı'bôşın] med. çocuk düşürme
abound [ı'baund] v/i bol olm.
about [ı'baut] aşağı yukarı, hemen hemen; prp. hakkında; **-in** etrafında; **be ~ to** inf. **-i** yapmak üzere olm.
above [ı'bav] yukarıda, **-in** üstünde; **-den** yukarı, **-den** fazla; **~ all** her şeyden önce
abreast [ı'brest] yan yana
abridge [ı'bric] v/t kısaltmak, özetlemek; **~ment** kısaltma; özet
abroad [ı'brôd] yabancı ülkede, dışarıda

abrupt [ɪ'brapt] anî; sert

abscess ['äbsis] *med.* çıban

absence ['äbsıns] yokluk, bulunmayış; **~ of mind** dalgınlık

absent ['äbsınt] yok, bulunmıyan; **~-minded** dalgın

absolute ['äbsıluut] katî, kesin

absolut|ion [äbsı'luuşın] günahların affı; **~ism** istibdat, mutlakçılık

absolve [ıb'zolv] *v/t* beraet ettirmek (**from** *-den*)

absorb [ıb'sôb] *v/t* emmek, içine çekmek

abstain [ıb'steyn] çekinmek (**from** *-den*)

abstention [~'stenşın] çekinme

abstinen|ce ['äbstinıns] perhiz, sakınma; **~t** perhizkâr

abstract ['äbsträkt] anî; mücerret, soyut; nazarî; *n.* özet; *v/t* çıkarmak, ayırmak

absurd [ıb'söd] gülünç, manasız

abundan|ce [ı'bandıns] bolluk, zenginlik; **~t** çok, bol

abus|e [ı'byûs] *n.* suiistimal, kötüye kullanma; *v/t* kötüye kullanmak; **~ive** tahkir edici

abyss [ı'bis] uçurum

acacia [ı'keyşı] *bot.* akasya

academ|ic [äki'demik] akademik, üniversiteye ait; **~y** [ı'kädimi] akademi

accelerat|e [ık'selıreyt] *v/t*

hızlandırmak; **~or** *tech.* gaz pedalı

accent ['äksınt] vurgu, aksan; şive, ağız

accept [ık'sept] *v/t* kabul etm.; **~able** kabul edilebilir; **~ance** kabul

access ['äkses] giriş; *med.* nöbet; **~ road** giriş yolu; **have ~ to** girebilmek *-e*; **~ary** *s.* ~ory; **~ible** ['äk'sesıbl] erişilebilir, tırmanılabilir; **~ion** [äk'seşın] ulaşma; tahta çıkma; **~ory** ['äk'sesiri] *jur.* ferî fail; ferî, ikinci derecede

accident ['äksidınt] tesadüf; kaza, arıza; **~al** [-'dentl] tesadüfî, arızî

acclimatize [ı'klaymıtayz] *v/t* alıştırmak

accomodat|e [ı'komıdeyt] *v/t* uydurmak, yerleştirmek; **~ion** uyma; yerleşme

accompan|iment [ı'kampınimınt] refakat; **~y** refakat etm. *-e*

accomplice [ı'komplis] suç ortağı

accomplish [ı'kompliş] *v/t* bitirmek, başarmak; **~ed** hünerli, usta; **~ment** başarı

accord[1] [ı'kôd] *v/t* uzlaştırmak; *v/i* uymak (**with** *-e*)

accord[2] uygunluk; ahenk; anlaşma; akort; **of one's own ~** kendiliğinden; **~ance** uygunluk; **~ing to** *-e* göre

account [ı'kaunt] *v/i* hesap vermek; sorumlu olm. (**for**

-*den*); *n.* hesap; rapor; hikâye; sebep; **on no** ~ hiçbir suretle, asla; **on** ~ **of** sebebiyle, -*den* dolayı; **take** ~ of hesaba katmak -*i*; ~**ant** *ec.* muhasebeci; ~**ing** muhasebe

accredit [ı'kredit] *v/t* tasdik etm.; yetki vermek -*e*

accrue [ı'kruu] *v/i* hâsıl olm., gelmek

accumulat|e [ı'kyûmyuleyt] *v/t* artırmak, toplamak; *v/i* artmak, toplanmak; ~**ion** toplama, yığın; ~**or** *el.* akümülatör

accura|cy ['âkyurisi] doğruluk, sıhhat; tam vaktinde olma; ~**te** ['~it] doğru, tam

accursed [ı'kösid] melûn

accus|ation [âkyu'zeyşın] suçlama, itham; ~**ative** [ı'kyûzitiv] *gr.* -*i* hali; ~**e** [ı'kyûz] suçlamak, itham etm. (*so.* **of** *sth. b-i b. ş. ile*); ~**er** *jur.* davacı

accustom [ı'kastım] *v/t* alıştırmak (**to** -*e*); ~**ed to** alışık, alışkın -*e*

ace [eys] birli; *fig.* çok cesur savaş havacısı

ache [eyk] *n.* ağrı, sızı; *v/i* ağrımak, sızlamak

achieve [ı'çîv] *v/t* icra etm., meydana çıkarmak, elde etm.; ~**ment** başarı

acid ['âsid] *chem. n.* asit; *adj.* ekşi

acknowledge [ık'nolic] *v/t* kabul etm., tanımak; itiraf etm.; *b. ş-in alındığını* bil-

dirmek; ~**ment** kabul; tasdik; itiraf [palamudu)

acorn ['eykôn] *bot.* meşe]

acoustic|(al) [ı'kuustik(ıl)] akustiğe ait; ~**s** *pl.* akustik *sg.*

acquaint [ı'kweynt] bildirmek, tanıtmak (*so.* **with** *b-e b. ş-i*); ~**ance** tanışma; malumat; tanıdık; **be** ~**ed with** bilmek -*i*, haberdar olm. -*den*

acquire [ı'kwayı] *v/t* elde etm., kazanmak; ~**ment** edinme; edinilen bilgi, hüner

acquisition [âkwi'zişın] edinme, elde edilen şey, kazanç

acquit [ı'kwit] *v/t* jur. beraet ettirmek; ~**tal** beraet

acre ['eykı] İngiliz dönümü (*0.40 hektar*)

acrid ['âkrid] buruk, acı

acrobat ['âkrıbât] akrobat, cambaz

across [ı'kros] karşıdan karşıya, öbür tarafa; çapraz

act [âkt] *n.* fiil, hareket, iş, yapılan şey; *jur.* kanun; *thea.* perde; *v/i* hareket etm., davranmak (**upon** -*e* göre); *thea.* rol yapmak; ~**ion** fiil, hareket, iş; faaliyet; etki; *jur.* dava; *mil.* muharebe

activ|e ['âktiv] faal, enerjik, canlı; *gr.* geçişli; ~**ity** faaliyet, çeviklik

act|or ['âktı] aktör, artist, rol oynayan; ~**ress** aktris, kadın aktör

actual ['äkçul] gerçek, hakikî; **~ity** [äktyu'äliti] hakikat; gerçek durum; **~ly** *adv.* gerçekten

acute [ı'kyût] şiddetli, keskin; keskin akıllı

adapt [ı'däpt] *v/t* uydurmak, tatbik etm.; **~able** uyabilir

add [äd] *v/t* katmak, eklemek, ilâve etm.; *math.* toplamak

addict ['ädikt] düşkün; **~ed** [ı'diktid] **to** -e düşkün, -in tiryakisi

addition [ı'dişın] ilâve, ek, zam; *math.* toplama; **in ~ to** -*den* başka; **~al** eklenilen

address [ı'dres] *n.* adres; hitabe; *v/t* -*in* üstüne adres yazmak; hitap etm. -*e*; **~ oneself to** girişmek -*e*; **~ee** [ädre'si] alacak olan

adept ['ädept] usta, mahir

adequa|cy ['ädikwısi] kifayet, yeterlilik; **~te** ['~wit] uygun, münasip

adhe|re [ıd'hiı] yapışmak, yapışık kalmak (**to** -*e*); **~sive** [~'hisiv] yapışkan, yapışıcı; **~sive tape**, **~sive plaster** plaster, bant

adjacent [ı'ceysınt] bitişik, komşu

adjective ['äciktiv] *gr.* sıfat

adjoin [ı'coyn] *v/t* bitişik olm. -*e*

adjourn [ı'cön] *v/t* ertelemek, tehir etm.; **~ment** tehir

adjudicate [ı'cuudikeyt] *v/i jur.* karar vermek (**upon** -*e*)

adjust [ı'cast] *v/t* doğrultmak, düzeltmek; ayar etm., uydurmak (**to** -*e*); **~ment** uydurma, ayarlama, düzeltme

administ|er [ıd'ministı] *v/t* idare etm., tatbik etm.; **~ration** idare, yönetim; hükümet; **~rator** [~treytı] idareci, müdür; *jur.* tereke idare memuru

admirable ['ädmırıbl] takdire değer

admiral ['ädmırıl] *naut.* amiral

admir|ation [ädmı'reyşın] hayranlık, takdir; **~e** [ıd-'mayı] *v/t* takdir etm., çok beğenmek; **~er** hayran olan kimse; âşık

admissi|ble [ıd'misıbl] kabul olunabilir; **~on** itiraf; kabul; giriş; **~on fee** duhuliye, girmelik

admit [ıd'mit] *v/t* itiraf etm.; içeriye almak, kabul etm.; **~tance** kabul; giriş; **~tedly** *adv.* itiraf edildiği gibi, gerçekten

admoni|sh [ıd'moniş] *v/t* ihtar etm., tembih etm.; **~tion** [ädmı'nişın] ihtar, tembih

ado [ı'duu] telâş, gürültü

adolescent [ädıu'lesnt] genç, delikanlı

adopt [ı'dopt] *v/t* benimsemek, kabul etm.; evlâtlığa kabul etm.; **~ion** kabul; evlât edinme

ador|able [ı'dôrıbl] tapılacak; **~ation** [ädô'reyşın]

tapma; aşk; ~e [ı'dô] tapmak -e
adorn [ı'dôn] v/t süslemek;
~ment süs
Adrianople ['eydrı'nıupl]
Edirne
adrift [ı'drift] sularla sürük-
lenen
adroit [ı'droyt] becerikli,
usta
adult ['ädalt] büyük, reşit,
ergin
adulter|ate [ı'daltıreyt] v/t
karıştırmak, bozmak; ~a-
tion karıştırma; ~er jur.
zina işliyen, zâni; ~ess zina
işliyen kadın; ~y zina
advance [ıd'vâns] n. ilerleme, terakki; terfi; ec.
avans, peşin; v/t ilerletmek; v/i ilerlemek; in
adv. peşin olarak; ~ book-
ing önceden rezervasyon;
~d ilerlemiş, ileri; ~ment
ilerleme; terfi
advantage [ıd'vântic] avan-
taj, yarar, fayda; take ~ of
faydalanmak -den; ~ous
[ädvın'teycıs] faydalı, yararlı
advent ['ädvınt] gelme; rel.
Noel yortusundan önceki
dört hafta
adventur|e [ıd'vençı] ma-
cera, sergüzeşt; ~er avan-
türiye, maceracı; ~ous
maceraya düşkün, cesaret-
li; tehlikeli
adverb ['ädvöb] gr. zarf
advers|ary ['ädvısırı] düş-
man, muhalif; ~e ['~ôs] zıt,
ters, karşı gelen

advertise ['ädvıtayz] v/t
ilân etm.; ~ment [ıd'vötis-
mınt] ilân, reklam; ~r ilân
eden veya reklam yapan
kimse; ilân gazetesi
advice [ıd'vays] nasihat,
öğüt; tavsiye; take ~ sözünü dinlemek
advis|able [ıd'vayzıbl] tav-
siye edilir, makul, uygun;
~e v/t nasihat etm., haber
vermek -e; ~er müşavir;
~ory board istişare kurulu
advocate ['ädvıkeyt] n. avukat; v/t tavsiye etm.
aerial ['äırıl] adj. havaî; n.
anten
aero|drome [äırı'drıum]
hava alanı; ~nautics [~-
'nôtiks] pl. havacılık sg.; ~-
plane uçak
aesthetics [îs'thetiks] pl.
estetik sg.
afar [ı'fâ] uzak(ta)
affair [ı'fäı] iş, mesele, olay
affect [ı'fekt] v/t tesir etm.,
dokunmak -e; ~ation yap-
macık, gösteriş; ~ed yap-
ma, yapmacıklı; tutulmuş
(**with** -e); ~ion sevgi; düşkünlük; ~ionate [~şnit]
şefkatli, sevgi gösteren
affinity [ı'finiti] yakınlık,
benzeşme
affirm [ı'föm] v/t tasdik
etm.; ~ation [äfö'meyşın]
tasdik, teyit; ~ative [ı'fö-
mıtıv] müspet, olumlu
affix [ı'fiks] v/t bağlamak,
takmak, yapıştırmak
afflict [ı'flikt] v/t vermek
-e, eziyet etm. -i; ~ed tu-

tulmuş (**with** -*e*); **~ion** dert, keder

affluen|ce ['æfluıns] bolluk; **~t** bol

afford [ı'fôd] *v/t* meydana getirmek, vermek; bütçesi müsait olm. -*e*

affront [ı'frant] hakaret, tahkir [nan]

afire [ı'fayı] tutuşmuş, ya-ʃ

afloat [ı'flıut] su üzerinde dolaşan

afraid [ı'freyd] korkmuş, korkar; **be ~ of** korkmak -*den*

afresh [ı'freş] yeniden, tekrar

Africa ['æfrıkı] Afrika; **~n** Afrikalı

after ['âftı] -*den* sonra; -*e* göre; -*e* rağmen; sonra; **~ all** bununla birlikte; **~ that** bundan sonra; **~-effect** sonra görülen sonuç; **~-noon** ikindi, öğleden sonra; **good ~noon!** günaydın!, merhaba!; **~thought** sonradan gelen düşünce; **~wards** ['~wıdz] sonra (-dan)

again [ı'gen] tekrar, gene, bir daha; bundan başka; **~ and ~, time and ~** bazan, arasıra

against [ı'genst] -*e* karşı, -*e* rağmen; -*in* aleyhinde

age [eyc] yaş; çağ, devir; **of ~** reşit, ergin; **under ~** küçük, reşit olmıyan; **~d** ['eycid] yaşlı; yıllanmış; **~ fifty** [eycd-] elli yaşında; **~less** eskimez

agen|cy ['eycınsi] ajans, acentalık, vekillik; **~da** [ı'cendı] gündem, ruzname; **~t** ['eycınt] acente, vekil; casus; amil

agglomeration [ıglomı-'reyşın] yığılma, toplanma, yığın

aggrandize [ı'grændayz] *v/t* büyütme

aggravat|e ['ægrıveyt] *v/t* zorlaştırmak, fenalaştırmak; kızdırmak; **~ion** zorlaştırma; hiddet

aggregate ['ægrigit] *adj.* toplu, bütün; *v/t* toplamak

aggress|ion [ı'greşın] saldırma, tecavüz; **~ive** saldırgan; **~or** saldıran

agile ['æcayl] çevik, faal

agitat|e ['æciteyt] *v/t* sallamak, tahrik etm., karıştırmak; **~ion** heyecan; tahrik; **~or** kışkırtıcı, tahrikçi

ago [ı'gıu] önce, evvel; **long ~** uzun zaman önce

agon|izing ['ægınayzin] ezijet verici; **~y** ıstıraptan kıvranma, şiddetli acı

agrarian [ı'grärin] ziraî, tarımsal

agree [ı'grî] *v/i* razı olm., aynı fikirde olm., muvafakat etm.; **~ to** razı olm. -*e*, kabul etm. -*i*; **~ with** anlaşmak, bir fikirde olm. *b.* ile; **~able** [~î-] uygun, münasip; hoş, nazik; **~ment** [~î-] anlaşma, sözleşme

agricultur|al [ægri'kalçırıl] ziraî, tarımsal; **~e** ziraat, tarım

aground [ı'graund] karaya oturmuş

ague ['eygyû] *med.* sıtma

ahead [ı'hed] önde, ilerde; ileriye

aid [eyd] *n.* yardım, muavenet; *v/t* yardım etm. *-e*

ailing ['eyliŋ] rahatsız

aim [eym] hedef, amaç; nişan alma; ~ **at** amaçlamak *-i*; nişan almak *-i*; ~**less** gayesiz, hedefsiz

air [âı] **1.** *n.* hava; tavır, eda; melodi; **2.** *v/t* havalandırmak; **in the open** ~ açıkta, ~**base** *mil.* hava üssü; ~**bed** deniz yatağı; ~**brake** *tech.* hava freni; ~**conditioned** otomatik ısıtma ve soğutma tesisatı olan; ~**craft** uçak; ~**craft carrier** uçak gemisi; ~**cushion** şişirme yastık; ~**field** hava alanı; ~ **force** hava kuvvetleri *pl.*; ~ **hostess** hostes; ~**lift** hava köprüsü; ~**line** hava yolu; ~**liner** yolcu uçağı; ~ **mail** uçak postası; ~**man** havacı; ~**pipe** *tech.* hava borusu; ~**plane** uçak; ~**port** hava alanı; ~ **raid** hava hücumu; ~ **raid shelter** sığınak; ~ **route** hava yolu; ~**ship** hava gemisi; ~**sick** hava tutmuş; ~ **terminal** *hava yollarının* şehir bürosu; ~**tight** hava geçmez; ~**y** havalı, hafif

aisle [âıl] yan yol, geçit

ajar [ı'câ] yarı açık, aralık

akin [ı'kin] **to** akraba *-e*

alabaster ['älıbâstı] ak mermer

alacrity [ı'läkriti] çeviklik; isteklilik

alarm [ı'lâm] *n.* alarm, tehlike işareti; korku, telaş; *v/t* tehlikeyi bildirmek *-e*; korkutmak *-i*; ~**clock** çalar saat

alas! [ı'lâs] vay!, yazık!

Albania [äl'beynı] Arnavutluk

alcohol ['älkıhol] alkol, ispirto; ~**ic** alkolik, ispirtolu

alderman ['öldımın] kıdemli belediye meclisi üyesi

ale [eyl] *bir çeşit* bira

alert [ı'löt] uyanık; **be on the** ~ tetikte olm.

algebra ['älcibrı] cebir

Algeria [äl'cırîı] Cezayir

alibi ['älibay] *jur.* suç işlendiği *anda* başka yerde bulunduğunu ispat etmesi

alien ['eylyın] yabancı

alight [ı'layt] *adj.* ateş, içinde, yanan; *v/i av.* inmek

alike [ı'layk] benzer, aynı

aliment ['älimınt] yiyecek, gıda; ~**ary** [~'mentırı] besleyici, yiyeceğe dair

alimony ['älimıni] nafaka

alive [ı'layv] hayatta, canlı

all [ôl] bütün, hep, hepsi, her; **after** ~ nihayet, bununla birlikte; **not at** ~ asla, hiç; ~ **of us** hepimiz; ~ **right** iyi, pekâlâ, tamam; ~ **the better** daha iyi ya

alleg|ation [äle'geyşın] ileri sürme, iddia; **~e** [ı'lec] v/t ileri sürmek, iddia etm.; **~ed** sözde, diye

allegorical [äle'gorikl] alegorik

alleviate [ı'lîvieyt] v/t azaltmak

alley ['äli] dar sokak; iki tarafı ağaçlı yol; **blind ~** çıkmaz yol

alli|ance [ı'layıns] ittifak, birlik; **~ed** [ı'älayd] müttefik

alligator ['äligeytı] zo. Amerika timsahı

allocate ['älikeyt] v/t tahsis etm., dağıtmak

allot [ı'lot] v/t ayırmak

allow [ı'lau] v/t müsaade etm., kabul etm.; razı olm. **-e**; vermek **-i**; v/i hesaba katmak (**for -i**); **~ance** müsaade; tahsisat; cep parası

alloy ['äloy] chem. alaşım

all|-round çok cepheli; **£ Saints' Day** rel. Azizler günü (1 kasım); **~weather** her havaya dayanan

allude [ı'luud] to **ima** etm. **-i**

allure [ı'lyuı] v/t çekmek, cezbetmek; **~ment** çekicilik

allusion [ı'luujın] ima

ally ['älay] n. müttefik; [ı'lay] v/i birleşmek

almighty [ôl'mayti] her şeye kadir [dem)

almond ['âmınd] bot. ba-∫

almost ['ôlmıust] hemen hemen, az kaldı

alms [âmz] pl. sadaka

aloft [ı'loft] yukarıda

alone [ı'lıun] yalnız, tek başına; **leave ~** kendi haline bırakmak **-i**; **let ~** şöyle dursun

along [ı'lon] boyunca; **all ~** öteden beri; her zaman; **come ~!** haydi gel!; **~side** yan yana

aloud [ı'laud] yüksek sesle

alphabet ['älfıbit] alfabe; **~ical** [~'betikıl] alfabe sırasına göre

already [ôl'redi] şimdiden, zaten

also ['ôlsıu] dahi, da (de, ta, te); bir de; ayrıca

altar ['ôltı] kilise mihrabı

alter ['ôltı] v/t değiştirmek; v/i değişmek; **~ation** değişiklik

alternat|e [ôl'tönit] adj. nöbetleşe değişen; ['~tı-neyt] v/t nöbetleşe değiştirmek; **~ing** current dalgalı akım; **~ion** değişme; **~ive** [~'tönıtiv] ikinci şık

although [ôl'dhu] her ne kadar, -diği halde, bununla birlikte, gerçi

altitude ['ältityûd] yükseklik

altogether [ôltı'gedhı] hep birlikte, tamamen

alum ['älım] chem. şap

alumin|ium [älyu'min-yım], Am. **~um** [ı'luumin-ım] alüminyum

always ['ôlweyz] daima, her zaman

am [äm, ım]: **I ~** ben -im

amalgamat|e [ı'mälgı-meyt] v/t karıştırmak; v/i bileşmek; **~ion** karışma; alaşım

amass [ı'mäs] v/t yığmak, toplamak

amateur ['ämitö] amatör

amaz|e [ı'meyz] v/t hayrette bırakmak, şaşırtmak; **~e-ment** şaşkınlık, hayret; **~ing** şaşırtıcı

ambassador [äm'bäsıdı] pol. büyük elçi

amber ['ämbı] kehribar

ambiguous [äm'bigyuıs] müphem, şüpheli

ambiti|on [äm'bişın] ihtiras; büyük istek; **~ous** hırslı, çok istekli

ambulance ['ämbyulıns] hasta arabası; **~ station** ilk yardım istasyonu

ambush ['ämbuş] n. pusu; v/t pusuda beklemek

ameliorat|e [ı'mîlyıreyt] v/t iyileştirmek, düzeltmek; **~ion** iyileşme

amen ['â'men] rel. âmin

amend [ı'mend] v/t düzeltmek, ıslah etm.; v/i iyileşmek; **~ment** düzeltme, tadil; **~s** pl. tazminat; **make ~s** kusurunu düzeltmek

America [ı'merikı] Amerika; **~n** Amerikalı, Amerikan [tatlı]

amiable ['eymyıbl] hoş,]

amicable ['ämikıbl] dostça, dostane

amid(st) [ı'mid(s)t] -in ortasında

amiss [ı'mis] eksik, yanlış; bozuk; **take ~** fenaya almak -i

ammunition [ämyu'nişın] cephane, mühimmat

amnesty ['ämnisti] genel af

among(st) [ı'maŋ(st)] -in arasında, arasına; içinde

amortization [ımôti'zeyşın] ec. amortisman

amount [ı'maunt] n. miktar, meblâğ, tutar, yekûn; v/i varmak (**to** -e)

amphitheatre ['ämfithiıtı] amfiteatr

ampl|e ['ämpl] geniş, bol; **~ifier** ['~ifayı] tech. amplifikatör; **~ify** ['~ifay] v/t genişletmek, büyütmek

amputate ['ämpyuteyt] med. v/t kesmek

amuck [ı'mak]: **run ~** kudurmuş gibi etrafa saldırmak

amulet ['ämyulit] tılsım

amuse [ı'myûz] v/t eğlendirmek, güldürmek; **~ment** eğlence

an [ân, ın] bir

anachronism [ı'näkrınizım] bir olayı ait olmadığı tarihte gösterme

an(a)emia [ı'nîmyı] med. kansızlık

an(a)esthesia [änis'thîzyı] med. anestezi

analog|ous [ı'nälıgıs] benzer, kıyas yoluyle olan; **~y** [**~**ci] kıyas; benzerlik

analy|se, Am. **~ze** ['änı-layz] v/t çözümlemek; **~sis**

anarchy

[ı'nälısis] analiz, çözümleme

anarchy ['änıki] anarşi

anatomy [ı'nätımi] anatomi

ancest|or ['änsıstı] ata, dede; **~ry** ecdat, dedeler *pl.*

anchor ['änkı] *n.* çapa, gemi demiri; *v/i* demir atmak, demirlemek

anchovy ['änçıvi] ançüez

ancient ['eynşınt] eski, kadim

and [änd, ınd] ve, ile; daha; **~ so on** ve saire

anecdote ['änıkdut] fıkra, hikâye

anew [ı'nyû] yeniden, tekrar

angel ['eyncıl] *rel.* melek

anger ['ängı] hiddet, öfke

angina [än'caynı] *med.* anjin, boğak

angle¹ ['ängl] köşe, açı; *fig.* görüş noktası

angle² *n.* olta; *v/i* balık tutmak

Angl|ican ['änglikın] Anglikan; **~o-Saxon** ['änglıu'säksın] Anglosakson, İngiliz

angry ['ängri] öfkeli, kızgın; darılmış (**at**, **about** *-den* dolayı); gücenmiş (**with** *-e*)

anguish ['ängwiş] ıstırap, keder

angular ['ängyulı] köşeli

animal ['änimıl] hayvan

animat|e ['änimeyt] *adj.* canlı; *v/t* canlandırmak; **~ed cartoon** canlı resim-

lerden ibaret film; **~ion** canlılık, heyecan

animosity [äni'mositi] düşmanlık

anise ['änis] *bot.* anason

ankle ['änkl] *an.* topuk, ayak bileği

annex ['äneks] *n.* ek; müştemilât *pl.*; *v/t* ilhak etm., eklemek, katmak; **~ation** [~'seyşın] ilhak

annihilate [ı'nayıleyt] *v/t* yoketmek

anniversary [äni'vösıri] yıldönümü.

annotation [änıu'teyşın] haşiye, not

announce [ı'nauns] *v/t* bildirmek, ilân etm.; **~ment** bildiri, ilân; **~r** sözcü, spiker

annoy [ı'noy] *v/t* taciz etm., kızdırmak; **be ~ed** kızmak; **~ance** canını sıkma

annual ['änyuıl] yıllık

annul [ı'nal] feshezmek, iptal etm.

anodyne ['änıudayn] uyuşturucu (ilâç)

anomalous [ı'nomılıs] anormal

anonymous [ı'nonimıs] anonim

another [ı'nadhı] başka, diğer, öbür; **with one ~** birbirini

answer ['änsı] *n.* cevap, yanıt; *v/t* cevap vermek *-e*, yanıtlamak *-i*; sorumlu olm. (**for** *-den*); uymak (**to** *-e*)

ant [änt] karınca

antagonis|m [ân'tägını-zım] düşmanlık; **~t** düşman, muhalif

Antarctic [ânt'âktik] Antarktika

antelope [ântilup] *zo.* ceylan

antenna [ân'tenı] *zo.* duyarga; *tech.* anten

anthem [ânthım] ilâhi; millî marş

anti|-aircraft gun *mil.* uçaksavar topu; **~biotic** ['~bay'otik] antibiyotik

anticipat|e [ân'tisipeyt] *v/t* önceden görmek, beklemek; **~ion** önceden görme, tahmin, bekleme

anti|cyclone ['ânti'sayk-liun] yüksek basınç alanı; **~dote** ['~diut] panzehir; **~freeze** antifriz

Antioch [ântiak] Antakya

antipathy [ân'tipıthi] antipati, sevişmezlik

antiqu|arian [ântikwâ-riın] *adj.* antikaya ait; *n.* antikacı, antika meraklısı; **~ary** ['~wırı] antikacı; **~e** [ân'tîk] çok eski, kadim; **~ity** ['~tikwiti] eskilik; eski zamanlar *pl.*

antiseptic [ânti'septik] antiseptik

antler ['ântlı] *zo.* geyik boynuzu

anvil ['ânvil] örs

anxi|ety [ân'zayıti] endişe, kuruntu, merak; **~ous** ['ânkşıs] endişeli, meraklı; **be ~ous** to *inf.* arzu etm. *-i,* can atmak *-e*

any ['eni] bir; her hangi, her bir; bazı, birkaç; hiç; **~ more** artık; daha fazla; **~body** her hangi bir; **~how** her nasılsa; her halde; **~one** *s.* **~body; ~thing** her hangi bir şey, her şey; hiçbir şey; **~way** *s.* **~how; ~where** her hangi bir yer(d)e; hiçbir yer(d)e

apart [ı'pât] ayrı, bir tarafta; başka (**from** *-den*); **~ment** apartman dairesi

apathetic [âpı'thetik] hissiz, ilgisiz

ape [eyp] *zo.* maymun

aperture ['âpıtyuı] aralık, delik, açık

apex ['eypeks] zirve, tepe

apiece [ı'pîs] her biri; beher

A-plant [ey–] nükleer elektrik fabrikası

apolog|ize [ı'polıcayz] özür dilemek (**for** *-den*); **~y** özür dileme, itizar

apoplexy ['âpıupleksi] *med.* inme, felç

apostasy [ı'postısi] *rel.* irtidat, dininden dönme

apostle [ı'posl] *rel.* havari, misyoner

apostrophe [ı'postrıfi] *gr.* kesme işareti [eczacı]

apothecary [ı'pothikri]

appal(l) [ı'pôl] *v/t* korkutmak, ürkütmek

apparatus [âpı'reytıs] cihaz, makine

apparel [ı'pârıl] elbise

apparent [ı'pârınt] açık belli; görünüşte olan

appeal

appeal [ı'pîl] yalvarma, n. başvurma; jur. temyiz; v/i başvurmak (**to** -e); beğenmek (-i); ~**ing** yalvaran; sevimli, cazip

appear [ı'pîı] v/i görünmek, gözükmek, meydana çıkmak; ~**ance** görünüş; gösteriş

appease [ı'pîz] v/t yatıştırmak, teskin etm.

append|icitis [ıpendı'saytis] med. apandisit; ~**ix** [ı'pendiks] ek, zeyil

appeti|te ['äpitayt] iştah; ~**zing** iştah verici

applau|d [ı'plôd] v/t alkışlamak; ~**se** [ˌz] alkış

apple ['äpl] elma; ~-**pie** üstü hamurlu elma turtası

appliance [ı'playıns] alet, cihaz

applica|ble ['äplikıbl] uygulanabilir; ~**nt** istekli; ~**tion** tatbik; dilekçe, istida

apply [ı'play] v/i müracaat etm., başvurmak (**to** -e, **for** için)

appoint [ı'poynt] v/t tayin etm., atamak; kararlaştırmak; ~**ment** tayin, memuriyet, iş; randevu

apportion [ı'pôşın] v/t paylaştırmak

appreciat|e [ı'prişieyt] v/t takdir etm., -in kıymetini anlamak; ~**ion** değerlendirme, kıymet bilme; ec. kıymet artması

apprehen|d [äpri'hend] v/t yakalamak, tevkif etm.; anlamak; korkmak -den;

~**sion** tevkif; anlama; korku; ~**sive** çabuk kavrayan; korkan (**of** -den)

apprentice [ı'prentis] çırak; stajiyer; ~**ship** [ˌişip] çıraklık; staj

approach [ı'pruç] n. yaklaşma, yanaşma; müracaat; v/t yaklaşmak, yanaşmak, -e; ~ **road** giriş yolu

appropriat|e [ı'pnupriit] adj. uygun, münasip; v/t tahsis etm., ayırmak; ~**ion** tahsis

approv|al [ı'pruuvil] tasvip, uygun görme; ~**e** v/t beğenmek, uygun görmek

approximate [ı'proksimit] takribî, aşağı yukarı

apricot ['eyprikot] bot. kayısı; zerdali

April ['eyprıl] nisan

apron ['eyprın] önlük

apt [äpt] uygun; yerinde; zeki; **be ~ to** inf. -mek eğilimde olm.; ~**itude** ['äptityûd] kabiliyet; uygunluk

aqua|rium [ı'kwärıım] akvaryum; ~**tic** [ı'kwätik] suda yaşar; ~**tic sports** pl. su sporları

aquaeduct ['äkwidakt] su kemeri

aquiline ['äkwilayn] kartal gibi; gaga burunlu

Arab ['ärıb] Arap; ~**ia** [ı'reybyı] Arabistan; ~**ian** Arabistan'a ait; ~**ic** ['ärıbık] Arapça

arable ['ärıbl] sürülebilir

arbitra|ry ['äbitrıri] keyfî;

arrears

~te [~treyt] *hakem sıfatıyla* karar vermek; **~tion** hakem kararı

arbo(u)r ['âbı] kameriye, çardak

arc [âk] yay, kavis; **~ade** [â'keyd] kemeraltı yolu

arch¹ [âç] kemer, tak

arch² *adj.* saklaban, açıkgöz

arch(a)eology [âki'olıci] arkeoloji

archaic [â'keyik] kadim, eski

arch|angel ['âk-] başmelek; **~bishop** *rel.* başpiskopos; **~duchess** arşidüşes; **~duke** arşidük

archer ['âçı] okçu; **~y** okçuluk

archipelago [âki'peligıu] *geo.* adalar grubu

architect ['âkitekt] mimar; **~ure** mimarlık

archives ['âkayvz] *pl.* arşiv

archway kemeraltı yolu

Arctic ['âktik] kuzey kutbunda bulunan (bölge)

ard|ent ['âdınt] ateşli, heyecanlı; **~o(u)r** ateşlilik, gayret

are [â] *s.* **be**

area ['âırıı] saha, alan, bölge; yüzölçümü

Argentina [âcın'tînı] Arjantin

argu|e ['âgyû] *v/t* ileri sürmek, ispat etm.; münakaşa etm.; **~ment** delil; münakaşa; **~mentation** delil gösterme

arid ['ârid] kurak, çorak

arise [ı'rayz] *v/i* kalkmak,

çıkmak, doğmak (**from** *-den*)

aristocra|cy [âris'tokrısı] aristokrasi; **~t** ['~tıkrät] aristokrat

arithmetic [ı'rithmıtik] aritmetik

ark [âk] tahta sandık; **Noah's** ♀ *rel.* Nuh'un gemisi

arm¹ [âm] kol

arm² *n.* silah; *v/t* silahlandırmak; *v/i* silahlanmak

armament ['âmımınt] teçhizat *pl.*, silahlanma; **~race** silahlanma yarışı

armchair koltuk

Armenia [â'mînyı] Ermenistan

armistice ['âmistis] mütareke

armo(u)r ['âmı] zırh; **~ed** zırhlı; **~ed car** zırhlı otomobil

armpit koltuk altı

arms [âmz] *pl.* silahlar

army ['âmi] *mil.* ordu; **~corps** kolordu

arnica ['ânikı] *bot.* arnika, öküzgözü

aroma [ı'rıumı] güzel koku

around [ı'raund] *-in* etrafın(d)a; orada burada, oraya buraya

arouse [ı'rauz] *v/t* uyandırmak, canlandırmak

arrange [ı'reync] *v/t* tanzim etm., düzenlemek; **~ment** tertip, sıralama, düzenleme

arrears [ı'rîız] *pl.* geri kalan *sg.*; ödenmemiş bo ç

arrest [ı'rest] *n.* tutuklama, tevkif; durdurma; *v/t* tevkif etm., tutuklamak, durdurmak

arriv|al [ı'rayvıl] varış, geliş; gelen kimse; **~e** varmak, vâsıl olm. (at *-e*)

arrogan|ce ['ärugıns] kibir, gurur; **~t** kibirli, mağrur

arrow ['ärıu] ok

arsenal ['âsınl] tersane

arsenic ['âsnik] *chem.* arsen(ik)

arson ['âsn] kundakçılık

art [ât] sanat; hüner, maharet; **fine ~s** *pl.* güzel sanatlar

arter|ial [â'tiriıl] *an.* atardamara ait; **~ial road** anayol; **~y** ['âturi] atardamar

artesian [â'tizyın] artezyen

artful kurnaz

artichoke ['âtiçuk] *bot.* enginar

article [â'tikl] makale; madde; *gr.* tanım edatı

articulate [â'tikyuleyt] *v/t* dikkatle telaffuz etm.; *adj.* açık, seçkin

artificial [âti'fişıl] sunî, yapma

artillery [â'tilıri] *mil.* topçuluk

artisan [âti'zän] zanaatçı

artist ['âtist] artist, sanatkâr; **~ic** [â'tistik] artistik

artless sade, saf

as [äz, ız] gibi, kadar; iken; *-diği* gibi; *-den* dolayı; *-mekle* beraber; çünkü; **~ a rule** genellikle; **~ if** sanki;

güya; **~ soon ~** *-ince*; *-ir* *-mez*; **~ well ~** gibi

ascen|d [ı'send] *v/i*, *v/t* çıkmak, tırmanmak *-e*; **~dancy** [~dınsı] üstünlük; nüfuz; **~sion Day** *rel.* İsa'nın göğe çıkışı yortusu; **~t** çıkış, tırmanma

ascertain [äsı'teyn] *v/t* soruşturmak, öğrenmek

ascetic [ıs'setik] *rel.* zahit, münzevi

ascribe [ıs'krayb] *v/t* atfetmek (to *-e*)

aseptic [ä'septik] aseptik

ash[1] [äş] *bot.* dişbudak

ash[2] *pl.* **~es** ['äşiz] kül

ashamed [ı'şeymd]: **be ~ of** utanmak *-den*

ash|-bin, **~-can** çöp tenekesi

ashore [ı'şô] karada; karaya

ash-tray kül tablası

Asia ['eyşı] Asya; **~ Minor** Küçükasya, Anadolu; **~tic** [eyşi'ätik] Asyalı

aside [ı'sayd] bir tarafa, yana; başka (from *-den*)

ask [âsk] *v/t* sormak *-e*; rica etm. *-den*; **~ for** sormak *-i*, istemek *-i*

asleep [ı'slîp]: **be ~** uyumak; **fall ~** uykuya dalmak

asparagus [ıs'pärıgıs] *bot.* kuşkonmaz (rünüş)

aspect ['äspekt] görüş, gö-

asphalt ['äsfält] asfalt

aspir|ation [äspı'reyşın] istek, iştiyak; nefes alıp verme; **~e** [ıs'payı] şiddetle arzu etm., elde etmeğe çalışmak (after *or* to *-i*)

aspirin ['äspirin] *med.* aspirin

ass [äs] eşek

assail [ı'seyl] *v/t* saldırmak, hücum etm. *-e*; **~ant** saldıran

assassin [ı'säsin] katil; **~ate** [~eyt] *v/t* öldürmek; **~a-**tion suikast, katil

assault [ı'sôlt] *n.* saldırı, taarruz; *v/t* saldırmak *-e*

assembl|age [ı'semblic] *tech.* montaj; **~e** [~bl] *v/t* toplamak, birleştirmek, kurmak; *v/i* toplanmak, birleşmek; **~y** toplantı; montaj; **~y line** *tech.* sürekli iş bandı

assent [ı'sent] *n.* muvafakat; *v/i* muvafakat etm. (**to** *-e*)

assert [ı'sôt] *v/t* ileri sürmek, iddia etm.; **~ion** öne sürme, iddia

assess [ı'ses] *v/t* tarh etm.; takdir etm.; **~ment** vergi (takdiri)

assets ['äsets] *pl. ec.* aktifler

assiduous [ı'sidyus] çalışkan, gayretli

assign [ı'sayn] *v/t* ayırmak, tahsis etm. (**to** *-e*); **~ment** tayin, atama; *jur.* feragat

assimilate [ı'simileyt] *v/t* benzetmek, uydurmak (**to** *-e*)

assist [ı'sist] *v/t* yardım etm. *-e*; *v/i* hazır bulunmak (**at** *-de*); **~ance** yardım; **~ant** yardımcı, muavin; asistan

assizes [ı'sayziz] *pl.* jüri mahkemesi *sg.*

associat|e [ı'sıuşieyt] *v/t* birleştirmek *-i*; *v/i* ortak olm. (**with** *-e*), katılmak (*-e*); [~iit] *n.* ortak; **~ion** birleşme; kurul; ortaklık

assort|ed [ı'sôtid] çeşitli; **~ment** tasnif; çeşitler *pl.*

assume [ı'syuum] *v/t* üstüne almak; farzetmek

assumption [ı'sampşın] üstüne alma; farz, zan; kibir, gurur; gasıp; 2 *rel.* Meryem'in göğe kabulü

assur|ance [ı'şuurıns] temin; güven; söz; sigorta; **~e** [~uu] *v/t* temin etm. *-i*; vermek *-e*; sigorta etm. *-i*; **~ed** sigortalı olan

asthma ['äsmı] *med.* astma, yelpik

astir [ı'stö] harekette, heyecanlı

astonish [ıs'toniş] *v/t* şaşırtmak, hayrete düşürmek; **be ~ed** şaşmak, hayret etm.; **~ment** şaşkınlık, hayret

astray [ıs'trey]: **lead ~** *v/t* baştan çıkarmak

astride [ıs'trayd] bacakları ayrılmış

astro|loger [ıs'trolıcı] müneccim; **~naut** [~'ästrınôt] astronot; **~nomy** [ıs'tronımi] astronomi

astute [ıs'tyût] kurnaz; zekâlı   [rılmış]

asunder [ı'sandı] ayrı, ay-}

asylum [ı'saylım] sığınak, barınak

at [ät, ıt] -da, -de; -a, -e; *-in* üstün(d)e; yanın(d)a; ha-

linde; ~ **five o'clock** saat
beşte; ~ **home** evde; ~ the
age of yaşında
ate [et] s. **eat**
atheism ['eythiizım] ateizm,
tanrısızlık
Athens ['äthinz] Atina
athlet|e ['äthlit] atlet, spor-
cu; **~ic** [~'letik] atletik,
kuvvetli; **~ics** atletizm
Atlantic [ıt'läntik]: **the ~
Ocean** Atlas Okyanusu
atlas ['ätlıs] atlas
atmosphere ['ätmısfiı] atmosfer; *fig.* hava, çevre
atom ['ätım] atom; **~ bomb**
atom bombası
atomic [ı'tomik] atomla ilgili; **~ age** atom çağı; **~
energy** atom enerjisi; **~
pile** reaktör
atone [ı'tiun] *v/i* tarziye
vermek (**for** için)
atroci|ous [ı'truşıs] vahşi,
tüyler ürpertici; **~ty** [~o-
siti] gaddarlık
attach [ı'täç] *v/t* bağlamak,
yapıştırmak, takmak (**to
-e**); **~ oneself to** iltiham
etm., takılmak *-e*; **~ed to**
bağlı *-e*; **~ment** bağlılık;
sevgi
attack [ı'täk] *n.* hücum,
saldırma; *med.* nöbet; *v/t*
hücum etm., saldırmak *-e*
attain [ı'teyn] *v/t* ermek *-e*,
elde etm. *-i*; *v/i* varmak,
yetişmek (**to -e**)
attempt [ı'tempt] *n.* teşebbüs, gayret; suikast; *v/t*
teşebbüs etm. *-e*, kasdet-
mek *-e*; denemek *-i*

atten|d [ı'tend] *v/t* hazır
bulunmak *-de*, refakat etm.
-e, bakmak *-e*; *v/i* dikkat
etm. (**to -e**), dinlemek (*-i*);
~dance bakım, hizmet;
maiyet; **~dant** hizmetçi;
~tion dikkat; nezaket;
~tion! *mil.* hazır ol!; **~tive**
dikkatli; nazik
attest [ı'test] *v/t* tasdik etm.;
~ation [ätes'teyşın] tasdik
attic ['ätik] çatı arası
attitude ['ätityûd] davranış, tavır
attorney [ı'töni] *jur.* avukat, vekil; **power of ~** ve-
kâletname; **~-general** baş-
savcı
attract [ı'träkt] *v/t* çekmek,
cezbetmek; **~ion** çekme
gücü; çekim, alımlılık; **~ive**
çekici, alımlı
attribute ['ätribyût] *n.* sıfat; remiz, simge; *gr.* yükle-
lem; [ı'tribyut] *v/t* atfetmek (**to -e**)
auburn ['öbın] kestane
rengi
auction ['ökşın] *n.* artırma
ile satış; *v/t* artırma ile
satmak; **~eer** [ökşı'nii] tellal
audaci|ous [ö'deyşıs] kor-
kusuz; küstah; **~ty** [ö'dä-
siti] pervasızlık; küstahlık
audi|ble ['ödibl] işitilebilir;
~ence ['~yıns] dinleyiciler
pl.; huzura kabul; **~to-
rium** [~i'törium] konferans
salonu; dinleyiciler *pl.*
aught [öt]: **for ~ I care**
bana ne

augment [ôg'mɪnt] v/t artırmak; v/i artmak; **~ation** art(ır)ma

August¹ ['ôgɪst] ağustos

august² [ô'gast] yüce, aziz

aunt [ânt] teyze; hala; yenge

auspic|es ['ôspɪsɪs] pl. uğurlu fal; fig. himaye; **~ious** [ôs'pɪşɪs] uğurlu

auster|e [os'tiɪ] sert; sade; **~ity** [~'teritɪ] sertlik; sadelik, süssüzlük

Australia [os'treylɪɪ] Avustralya; **~n** Avustralyalı

Austria ['ostrɪ] Avusturya; **~n** Avusturyalı

authentic [ô'thentɪk] sahih, güvenilir

author ['ôthɪ] yazar; sebep; **~itative** [ô'thoritɪtiv] otoriter; yetkili; **~ity** otorite; yetki; etki; uzman; makam, daire; **~ize** [~'ırayz] v/t yetki vermek -e; **~ship** yazarlık; asıl

autocracy [ô'tokrɪsɪ] otokrasi, istibdat

auto|graph ['ôtɪgrâf] otoğraf; imza; **~matic** [~'mâtik] otomatik; **~mation** tech. otomasyon; **~nomous** [ô'tonɪms] pol. özerk; **~nomy** özerklik, muhtariyet; **~psy** ['ôtɪpsi] med. otopsi

autumn ['ôtɪm] sonbahar, güz   [dɪmcɪ]

auxiliary [ôg'zilyɪri] yar-

avail [ɪ'veyl] v/t faydalı olm., yaramak -e; **~able** mevcut, elde edilebilir; geçer(li)

avalanche ['âvılânş] çığ

avaric|e ['âvɪris] hırs, tamah; **~ious** [~'rişɪs] haris, tamahkâr

avenge [ɪ'venc] v/t -in intikamını almak

avenue ['âvinyû] cadde, iki taraflı ağaçlı yol

average ['âvɪric] n. orta, ortalama, vasat; adj. ortalama; v/t -in ortasını bulmak; -in ortalaması olm.

aver|se [ɪ'vö:s] muhalif, karşı (**to**, **from** -e); **~sion** nefret, hoşlanmayış; **~t** v/t çevirmek; önlemek

aviat|ion [eyvi'eyşɪn] havacılık; **~or** ['~tɪ] havacı

avoid [ɪ'voyd] v/t sakınmak, çekinmek -den; **~ance** sakınma

avow [ɪ'vau] v/t itiraf etm., kabul etm.; **~al** itiraf

await [ɪ'weyt] v/t beklemek

awake [ɪ'weyk] adj. uyanık; v/t uyandırmak; v/i uyanmak; **be ~ to** -in farkında olm.; **~n** v/t uyandırmak

award [ɪ'wôd] n. hüküm, karar; ödül, mükâfat; v/t (mükâfat olarak) vermek -e

aware [ɪ'weɪ]: **be ~ of** bilmek -i, haberdar olm. -den; **become ~ of** öğrenmek -i; -in farkına varmak

away [ɪ'wey] uzakta; uzağa

aw|e [ô] n. korku, sakınma; saygı; v/t korkutmak; **~ful** ['ôful] korkunç, müthiş; berbat

awhile [ɪ'wayl] bir müddet

awkward ['ôkwɪd] beceriksiz, biçimsiz; sıkıntılı
awning ['ôniŋ] tente
awoke [ı'wɪuk] s. **awake**
awry [ı'ray] eğri, yanlış, ters
axe [äks] balta

axiom ['äksiım] aksiyom
ax|is ['äksis] pl. **∼es** ['∼îz] mihver, eksen; **∼le(-tree)** ['äksl-] tech. dingil
ay(e) [ay] evet, hayhay
azure ['äzı] mavi

B

babble ['bäbl] v/i saçmalamak; n. saçma sapan konuşma
babe [beyb] s. **baby**
baboon [bı'buun] zo. Habeş maymunu
baby ['beybi] bebek; **∼ carriage** Am. çocuk arabası; **∼hood** bebeklik çağı
bachelor ['bäçılı] bekâr
back [bäk] n., adj. arka; ri(ye); yeniden, tekrar; v/t geri yürütmek; himaye etm.; desteklemek; para yatırmak -e; v/i geri gitmek; **∼ tyre** arka lastik; **∼ wheel** arka tekerlek; **∼bite** v/t iftira etm. -e; **∼bone** an. omurga, belkemiği; fig. karakter, metanet; **∼fire** geri tepme; **∼ground** arka plan; fig. muhit, görgü; **∼side** kıç; **∼stairs** pl. arka merdiven sg.; **∼ward** geri, arkaya doğru; isteksiz; gelişmemiş
bacon ['beykın] domuz pastırması
bacteri|um [bäk'terium] pl. **∼a** [∼ı] bakteri
bad [bäd] fena, kötü, zararlı, kusurlu; **he is ∼ly off**

malî durumu pek fenadır; **want ∼ly** v/t çok istemek
bade [bäd] s. **bid**
badge [bäc] nişan, rozet
badger ['bäcı] zo. porsuk
badminton ['bädmintın] badminton
baffle ['bäfl] v/t şaşırtmak, bozmak
bag [bäg] torba, çuval, kese; çanta; kese kâğıdı
baggage ['bägic] bagaj; **∼ check** Am. bagaj kâğıdı
bag|gy ['bägi] çok bol; **∼pipe(s** pl.) gayda; **∼piper** gaydacı; **∼snatcher** el çantaları çalan hırsız
bail [beyl] jur. n. kefalet; kefil; **∼ (out)** v/t kefil olm. -e
bailiff ['beylif] çiftlik kâhyası; jur. mübaşir
bait [beyt] yem (a. fig.)
bak|e [beyk] v/t (fırında) pişirmek; v/i pişmek; **∼er** fırıncı, ekmekçi; **∼ery** fırın, ekmekçi dükkânı; **∼ing powder** toz mayası
balance ['bälıns] v/t tartmak, dengelemek; n. terazi; bakıye; bilanço, denge; **∼ of payments** ec. ödemeler dengesi

balcony ['bälkını] balkon

bald [bôld] saçsız, kel; çıplak

bale [beyl] balya, denk

balk [bôk] n. kiriş; engel; v/t mâni olm. -e; kaçırmak -i

Balkans ['bôlkıns] pl. Balkan (yarımadası) sg.

ball [bôl] top; küre; yumak; balo

ballast ['bälıst] balast; safra

ball-bearings pl. tech. bilyalı yatak pl.

ballet ['bäley] balet

ballistics [bı'listiks] balistik

balloon [bı'luun] balon

ballot ['bälıt] n. oy (kâğıdı); v/i oy vermek (**for** için); ~-**box** oy sandığı

ball(-point)-pen tükenmez kalem

ballroom dans salonu

balm [bâm] n. yasak; fig. teselli; ~y ['~i] yatıştırıcı

balsam ['bôlsım] pelesenk

Baltic Sea ['bôltik-] Baltik denizi

balustrade [bälıs'treyd] tırabzan, parmaklık

bamboo [bäm'buu] bot. bambu

ban [bän] n. yasak; rel. aforoz; v/t yasaklamak

banana [bı'nânı] bot. muz

band [bänd] bağ, şerit, kayış; topluluk, güruh; bando, müzik takımı

bandage ['bändic] n. sargı; v/t. bağlamak, sarmak

bandmaster mus. bando şefi

bang [bäŋ] n. çat, pat, gürültü; v/t gürültü ile kapamak

banish ['bäniş] v/t pol. sürgüne göndermek; ~**ment** sürgün

banisters ['bänistız] pl. tırabzan sg.

bank [bäŋk] n. kenar, kıyı; bayır; yığın; ec. banka; v/t bankaya yatırmak; ~(**ing**) **account** banka hesabı; ~**er** bankacı; ~-**holiday** bankaların kapalı olduğu tatil günü; ~**ing** bankacılık; ~-**note** banknot; ~-**rate** ıskonto haddi; ~**rupt** ['~rapt] müflis, iflâs etmiş

banner ['bänı] bayrak, sancak

banns [bänz] pl. evlenme ilânı sg.

banquet ['bäŋkwit] şölen, ziyafet

bapti|sm ['bäptizım] rel. vaftiz; ~**ze** [~'tayz] v/t vaftiz etm.; ad koymak -e

bar [bâ] n. sırık, çubuk, kol; engel, mania; kalıp, parça; bar; jur. baro; v/t kapamak; önlemek

barb [bâb] oku ucu, diken; ~**ed wire** dikenli tel

barbar|ian [bâ'bäriın] barbar; ~**ous** ['~bırıs] barbarca, vahşi

barber ['bâbı] berber

bare [bâı] çıplak, açık; boş; sade; çıplak yüzsüz, utanmaz; ~**foot(ed)** yalınayak; ~**headed** başı açık, şapkasız; ~**ly** adv. sadece; ancak

bargain 204

bargain ['bâgin] *n.* anlaşma; pazarlık, kelepir; *v/i*
pazarlık etm. (**for** için)
barge [bâc] *naut.* mavna,
salapurya
bark[1] [bâk] ağaç kabuğu
bark[2] *v/i* havlamak
barley ['bâli] *bot.* arpa
barn [bân] ambar; ahır
barometer [bɪ'romitɪ] barometre
barracks ['bärıks] *pl. mil.*
kışla *sg.*
barrage ['bâric] baraj, bent
barrel ['bärıl] fıçı, varil;
namlu; (*163,7l; Am. 119,2
l*); **~organ** latarna
barren ['bârın] kısır; kurak,
çorak
barricade [bäri'keyd] *n.*
barikat; *v/t* barikatla kapamak   [nia; çit]
barrier ['bärin] engel, ma-┘
barring ['bârin] *prp.* hariç,
-den maada
barrister ['bärıstı] *jur.* avukat, dava vekili
barter ['bâtı] *ec. n.* trampa;
v/t trampa etm.
basalt ['bâsôlt] bazalt
base [beys] *n.* temel, esas;
taban, kaide; *mil.* üs; *chem.*
baz; *adj.* bayağı, alçak; *v/t*
kurmak (**upon** üstüne);
~ball beysbol; **~less** te-
melsiz, esassız; **~ment**
temel; bodrum katı; **~ness**
aşağılık, alçaklık
bashful ['bäşful] utangaç,
sıkılgan
basic ['beysik] *adj.* esas,
temel

basin ['beysn] leğen; havuz;
havza
basis ['beysis] esas, temel,
dayanak
bask [bâsk] *v/i* güneşlen-
mek
basket ['bâskit] sepet, küfe;
zembil; **~ball** basketbol
bass [beys] *zo.* levrek; *mus.*
baso
bastard ['bâstıd] piç
baste [beyst] *v/t -in* üzerine
erimiş yağ dökmek; teyel-
lemek *-i*; *fig.* dayak atmak
-e
bat[1] [bät] yarasa
bat[2] sopa, çomak
bath [bâth] *n.* banyo; hamam; *v/i* banyo yapmak;
~e [beydh] *v/i* (denizde) yı-
kanmak; yüzmek; **~ing
suit** ['beydhiŋ-] mayo; **~-
robe** bornuz; **~room** banyo (odası); **~towel** hamam
havlusu; **~tub** küvet
battalion [bɪ'tälyın] *mil.*
tabur
batter ['bätı] *v/t* şiddetle
vurmak *-e*; **~ed** çarpık; eskimiş
battery ['bätıri] *m il.* batarya; *el.* pil
battle ['bätl] muharebe,
savaş; **~field** savaş alanı;
~ship zırhlı savaş gemisi
baulk [bôk] *s.* **balk**
bawdy ['bôdi] açıksaçık
bawl [bôl] *v/i* bağırmak,
haykırmak
bay[1] [bey] *geo.* koy, körfez
bay[2] *bot.* defne
bay[3] doru (*horse*)

beetle

bay⁴ havlamak; **keep at ~** sıkıştırmak

baza(a)r [bı'zâ] çarşı

be [bi, bî] olmak, bulunmak; **there is** or **are** vardır; **~ to** inf. -meğe mecbur olm.

beach [bîç] kumsal, plaj; **~wear** plaj elbisesi

beacon ['bîkın] fener

bead [bîd] boncuk; inci

beak [bîk] gaga; ağız

beam [bîm] n. kiriş, mertek; terazi kolu; ışın; v/t yaymak; v/i parlamak

bean [bîn] bot. fasulye

bear¹ [bäı] zo. ayı

bear² v/t taşımak; tahammül etm., katlanmak -e; doğurmak -i; üstüne almak -i; **in mind** aklında tutmak; **~ out** desteklemek; **~ up** dayanmak (**against** -e)

beard [bîıd] sakal; **~ed** sakallı

bear|er ['bäırı] taşıyan; hamil; **~ing** tavır, davranma; ilgi; tahammül; tech. yatak; **~ings** pl. yol, yön sg.

beast [bîst] hayvan; canavar; **~ of prey** yırtıcı hayvan

beat [bît] n. vuruş, darbe; devriye; v/t dövmek, vurmak; çalmak; çalkamak; yenmek; **~ it!** defol!; **~en** s. beat; **~ing** dövme, dmak

beaut|iful ['byûtıful] güzel, latif; **~ify** ['~tifay] v/t güzelleştirmek; **~y** güzellik; güzel kimse; **~y parlo(u)r** güzellik salonu;

~y-spot (yüzdeki) ben; güzel manzaralı yer

beaver ['bîvı] zo. kunduz; kunduz kürkü

because [bi'koz] çünkü, zira, -diği için; **~ of** -den dolayı, sebebiyle, yüzünden

beckon ['bekın] v/t işaret etm. -e

becom|e [bi'kam] v/i olmak; v/t yakışmak -e; **what has ~e of him?** o ne oldu? o şimdi ne halde?; **~ing** uygun; yakışık

bed [bed] v/t yatırmak, yerleştirmek; n. yatak, karyola; dip; bahçe tarhı; **~ and breakfast** yatak ve kahvaltı ve yatacak yer; **~-bug** tahtakurusu; **~-clothes** pl. yatak takımı sg.; **~ding** yatak; **~linen** yatak takımı; **~rid (-den)** yatalak; **~room** yatak odası; **~side table** komodin; **~spread** yatak örtüsü; **~stead** karyola, kerevet; **~time** yatma zamanı

bee [bî] zo. arı

beech [bîç] bot. kayın ağacı

beef [bîf] sığır eti; **~eater** Londra kalesi bekçisi; **~steak** biftek; **~ tea** sığır eti suyu

bee|hive arı kovanı; **~keeper** arıcı; **~line** en kısa yol

been [bîn, bin] s. **be**

beer [bî] bira

beet [bît] bot. pancar

beetle ['bîtl] bot. böcek

beetroot pancar; **~ sugar** pancar şekeri

befall [bi'fôl] *v/i* vuku bulmak; *v/t -in* başına gelmek

before [bi'fô] önde; önce; *-in* önünde, önüne; *-in* huzurunda, huzuruna; *-den* önce; **~hand** önceden; **~ long** çok geçmeden, az zamanda

befriend [bi'frend] *v/t* dostça hareket etm., yardım etm. *-e*

beg [beg] *v/i* dilenmek; *v/t* dilemek, istemek (**of** *-den*); **I ~ your pardon** özür dilerim, affedersiniz

began [bi'gän] *s.* **begin**

beggar [′begı] dilenci; *pop.* çapkın

begin [bi'gin] *v/t* başlamak *-e*; meydana gelmek; **to ~ with** ilk olarak; **~ner** yeni başlayan, başlayıcı; **~ning** başlangıç

begone [bi'gon] *intj.* defol!

begun [bi'gan] *s.* **begin**

behalf [bi'hâf]: **on ~ of** adına, namına; lehinde

behav|e [bi'heyv] *v/i* davranmak, hareket etm.; **~io(u)r** [~yı] davranış, tavır

behead [bi'hed] *v/t -in* başını kesmek

behind [bi'haynd] arkada; *-in* arkasında, arkasına; geri

behold [bi'hıuld] *v/t* görmek; bakmak *-e*

being [′bîiŋ] *n.* oluş, varlık

belated [bi'leytid] gecikmiş

belch [belç] *v/i* geğirmek; *v/t* püskürtmek

belfry [′belfri] çan kulesi (sahanlığı)

Belgi|an [′belcın] Belçikalı; **~um** [′~ım] Belçika

belie|f [bi'lîf] inanç; iman; itikat; güven; **~ve** [~v] *v/t* inanmak *-e*; zannetmek *-i*; *v/i* güvenmek, inanmak (**in** *-e*); **make ~ve** *v/t* inandırmak (*so. -e*); **~ver** inanan, inançlı, mümin

belittle [bi'litl] *v/t* küçültmek

bell [bel] zil, çıngırak, çan, kampana; **~flower** *bot.* çançiçeği

belligerent [bi'licırınt] muharip; kavgacı

bellow [′belu] *v/i* böğürmek; **~s** [~z] *pl.* körük *sg.*

bell|-pull zil kordonu; **~push** zil düğmesi

belly [′beli] karın

belong [bi'loŋ] *v/i* ait olm. (**to** *-e*); **~ings** *pl.* eşya; pılı pırtı

beloved [bi'lavd] sevilen; sevgili

below [bi'lıu] aşağıda; *-in* altında; *-den* aşağı

belt [belt] kuşak, kemer; kayış; bağ; bölge

bench [benç] sıra, bank; tezgâh

bend [bend] *n.* kavis, döneme ç; viraj; *v/t* bükmek, eğriltmek, kıvırmak; *v/i* bükülmek, eğilmek, çevrilmek

beneath [bi'nîth] *s.* **below**

bene|diction [beni'dikşın] hayır dua, takdis; **~factor** ['~fäktı] iyilik eden, velinimet; **~ficent** [bi'nefisınt] hayır sahibi, lütufkâr; **~ficial** [~fişıl] yararlı; hayırlı; **~fit** ['~fit] n. yarar, fayda, menfaat; hayır; v/t yaramak, faydalı olm. -e; v/i faydalanmak (**by** -den); **~volent** [bi'nevılınt] iyi dilekli, hayırhah

bent [bent] s. **bend**; **be ~ on** azmetmek -e, çok istemek -i

benzene ['benzîn] chem. benzol

benzine ['benzîn] benzin

beque|ath [bi'kwîdh] v/t vasiyet etm., terketmek; **~st** [~'kwest] vasiyet; bağışlama

ber|eave [bi'rîv] v/t çalmak -den; (of sth. -i); **~eft** [~'reft] s. **bereave**

beret ['berey] bere

berry ['beri] bot. tane

berth [böth] yatak; ranza

beseech [bi'sîç] v/t yalvarmak -e

beside [bi'sayd] -in yanına, yanında; -in dışında; **~ oneself** çılgın; **~s** -den başka; adv. bundan başka

besiege [bi'sîc] v/t kuşatmak

besought [bi'sôt] s. **beseach**

best [best] en iyi(ler); **at ~** olsa olsa; **make the ~ of** mümkün olduğu kadar yararlanmak -den; **~ man**

sağdıç; **to the ~ of my knowledge** benim bildiğime göre

bestial ['bestyıl] hayvanca, vahşi

bestow [bi'stıu] v/t vermek, hediye etm.; bağışlamak (**upon** -e)

bet [bet] n. bahis; v/i bahse girmek

betray [bi'trey] v/t ele vermek; ağzından kaçırmak; **~al** hıyanet, ele verme; **~er** hain

betroth [bi'trıudh] nişanlamak (so. to AD); **~al** nişan(lama)

better ['betı] daha iyi; üstün; **get the ~ of** yenmek -i, üstün olm. -den; **get ~** iyileşmek; **so much the ~** daha iyi

between [bi'twîn] -in arasına, arasında; arada, araya; **~-decks** pl. naut. ara güverte

beverage ['bevırıc] içecek

bewail [bi'weyl] ağlamak -e

beware [bi'wäı] v/i sakınmak, korunmak (**of** -den); intj. dikkat, sakın!

bewilder [bi'wildı] v/t şaşırtmak; **~ment** şaşkınlık, hayret

bewitch [bi'wiç] v/t büyülemek, teşhir etm.

beyond [bi'yond] ileri, ötede, öteye; -in ötesine, ötesinde; -den ötede; -in dışında, üstünde; **~ doubt** adv. şüphesiz; **it is ~ me** buna aklım ermez

bias

bias ['bayıs] *n.* meyil; peşin yargı; *v/t* etkilemek; ~(s)ed peşin yargı sahibi

Bibl|e ['baybl] *rel.* Mukaddes Kitap, Tevrat, Zebur ve İncil; **~ical** ['biblikl] Mukaddes Kitaba ait; **~ography** [bibli'ogrıfi] bibliyografya

bicycle ['baysikl] bisiklet

bid [bid] *n.* teklif; *v/t* emretmek; davet etm.; ~ **farewell** vedalaşmak (to ile); **~den** *s.* bid; **~ding** artırma; emir; davet

bier [bɪı] cenaze teskeresi

big [big] büyük, kocaman; iri; ~ **business** *ec.* büyük sermayeli ticaret; ~ **shot** *sl.* kodaman

bigamy ['bigımi] *jur.* çok karılı evlenme

bigot|ed ['bigıtid] mutaassıp, dar kafalı; **~ry** dar kafalılık

bike [bayk] bisiklet

bilateral [bay'lätırıl] iki taraflı

bilberry ['bilbırı] *bot.* ya- bile [bayl] *an.* safra

bilingual [bay'liŋwıl] iki dilli

bilious ['bilyıs] safralı

bill[1] [bil] **1.** *zo.* gaga

bill[2] hesap pusulası; fatura; *jur.* kanun tasarısı; *Am.* banknot; *ec.* poliçe; ~ **of exchange** poliçe; ~ **of health** sağlık raporu

billfold *Am.* cüzdan

billiards ['bilyıdz] *pl.* bilardo *sg.*

billion ['bilyın] bin milyar; *Am.* milyar

billow ['bilu] *n.* büyük dalga; *v/i* dalgalanmak; **~y** dalgalı

bimonthly ['bay'manthli] iki ayda bir (teneke)

bin [bin] kutu, sandık,

bind [baynd] *v/t* bağlamak; sarmak; ciltlemek; mecbur etm.; *v/i tech.* katılaşmak, donmak; **~ing** *adj.* yapıştırıcı; kesin; *n.* cilt (-leme); bağlama tertibatı

binoculars [bi'nokyulız] *pl.* dürbün *sg.*

biography [bay'ogrıfi] hal tercümesi

biology [bay'olıci] biyoloji

birch [böç] *bot.* huş ağacı

bird [böd] kuş; ~ **of passage** *zo.* göçmen kuş; ~ **of prey** *zo.* yırtıcı kuş; **~'s eye view** kuş bakışı görünüş

birth [böth] doğum; soy; başlangıç; **give** ~ **to** doğurmak *-i*; **date of** ~ doğum tarihi; **~control** doğum kontrolü; **~day** doğum günü; **~place** doğum yeri; **~rate** doğum oranı

biscuit ['biskit] bisküvit

bishop ['bişıp] *rel.* piskopos

bit [bit] **1.** gem; **2.** parça, lokmacık; **3.** *s.* bite

bitch [biç] *zo.* dişi köpek

bite [bayt] *n.* ısırım; lokma; diş yarası, sokma; *v/t* ısırmak; sokmak; yakmak, acıtmak; ~ **at** ısırmağa çalışmak *-i*

biting ['baytıŋ] keskin; acı

bitten ['bitn] *s.* **bite**

bitter ['bitı] acı, keskin; sert; **~ness** acılık; sertlik

bitumen ['bityumin] zift, katran

blab [bläb] *v/i* boşboğazlık etm.

black [bläk] *adj.* siyah, kara, karanlık; uğursuz; *v/i* kararmak; *v/t* karartmak, boyamak; **~berry** *bot.* böğürtlen; **~bird** *zo.* karatavuk; **~board** yazı tahtası; **~en** *v/t* karartmak; *fig.* lekelemek; **~head** (yüzde siyah) benek; **~ing** ayakkabı boyası; **~mail** *n. jur.* şantaj; *v/t* şantaj yapmak *-e*; **~market** kara borsa; **~ marketeer** kara borsacı; **~ness** siyahlık; kötülük; **~smith** demirci, nalbant

bladder ['blädı] *an.* mesane, sidik torbası; kavuk

blade [bleyd] bıçak ağzı; ot yaprağı; kürek palası

blame [bleym] *v/t* ayıplamak, sorumlu tutmak; *n.* kabahat, kusur; sorumluluk; **be to ~** suçlu olm. (**for** ile); **~less** kabahatsiz, kusursuz

blank [bläŋk] boş; yazısız; manasız; şaşkın; *n.* boş kur'a

blanket ['bläŋkit] battaniye

blasphemy ['bläsfimi] küfür

blast [blâst] *n.* (şiddetli ve

---

anî) rüzgâr esmesi; boru sesi; patlama; *v/t* berhava etm., yakmak, patlatmak; **~furnace** *tech.* yüksek fırın; **~ing** berhava etme; patlama

blaze [bleyz] *n.* alev; parlaklık; yangın; *v/i* parlamak, yanmak, ışık saçmak; **~r** spor ceketi

bleach [bliç] *v/t* ağartmak, beyazlatmak

bleak [blîk] çıplak; soğuk

blear [blii] *adj.* çapaklı (*göz*); *v/t* kamaştırmak

bleat [blît] melemek

bled [bled] *s.* **bleed**

bleed [blîd] *v/i* kanamak, kanını dökmek; *v/t fig. -in* parasını sızdırmak; **~ing** kanama

blemish ['blemiş] *n.* kusur; leke; *v/t* lekelemek

blend [blend] *n.* alaşım; harman; *v/t* karıştırmak; *v/i* karışmak

blent [blent] *s.* **blend**

bless [bles] *v/t* kutsamak; hayır dua etm. *-e*; **~ my soul!** aman ya Rabbi!; **~ed** ['...id] mübarek, kutlu; **~ing** hayır dua

blew [bluu] *s.* **blow**

blight [blayt] yanma, pas, küf

blind [blaynd] *adj.* kör; *fig.* kısa görüşlü; çıkmaz (*yol*); *n.* perde; kepenk; **~alley** çıkmaz yol; **~fold** *adj.* gözleri bağlı; *v/t -in* gözlerini bağlamak; **~ness** körlük

blink [bliŋk] *v/i* göz kırpmak; **~ the facts** gerçeğe
gözlerini yummak

bliss [blis] saadet, bahtiyar-
lık   [yakı]

blister ['blistı] kabarcık;

blizzard ['blizıd] tipi, kar
fırtınası

bloat [blıut] *v/t* şişirmek;
tütsülemek; **~ed** ['~id]
göbeği yağ bağlamış; **~er**
tütsülenmiş ringa balığı

block [blok] *n.* kütük, kaya
parçası; engel; blok; *v/t*
tıkamak, kapamak: **~ letters** *pl.* kitap yazısı; **~ up**
v/t kapatmak, tıkamak

blockade [blo'keyd] *n.* abluka; *v/t* ablukaya almak

blockhouse blokhavz

blond(e) [blond] sarışın

blood [blad] kan; soy;
cause bad ~ aralarını
bozmak; **in cold ~** soğukkanlı; **~curdling** tüyler
ürpertici; **~less** kansız;
fig. renksiz; **~poisoning**
kan zehirlenmesi; **~shed**
kan dökme; **~shot** kanlan-
mış; **~vessel** *an.* kan
damarı; **~y** kanlı

bloom [bluum] *n.* çiçek;
fig. gençlik, tazelik; *v/i*
çiçek açmak

blossom ['blosım] *n.* bahar
çiçeği; *v/i* çiçek açmak

blot [blot] *an.* leke; ayıp;
v/t lekelemek, kirletmek,
karartmak; **~ out** silmek;
~ter kurutma kâğıdı tam-
ponu; **~ting-paper** sünger kâğıdı

blouse [blauz] bluz

blow[1] [blıu] vuruş, darbe;
come to ~s kavgaya tutuşmak

blow[2] *v/i* esmek, üflemek;
v/t üflemek; *mus.* çalmak;
~ in çıkagelmek, uğramak;
~ one's nose sümkürmek;
~ out *v/t* üfleyip söndürmek; *v/i* dinmek; **~ up**
havaya uçurmak; **~n** *s.*
blow[2]

blue [bluu] mavi; *fig.* kede-
li; **~bell** *bot.* yabanî sümbül; **~bottle** *bot.* peygamber çiçeği; *zo.* mavi sinek;
~s *pl. fig.* melankoli *sg.*

bluff [blaf] *n.* blöf; *v/t* blöf
yapmak **~e**

bluish ['blu(u)iş] mavimsi

blunder ['blandı] *n.* hata,
gaf; *v/i* hata yapmak; *v/t*
berbat etm.

blunt [blant] *adj.* kesmez,
kör; *fig.* sözünü sakınmaz;
v/t körletmek, körleştirmek

blur [blö] *n.* leke; bulaşık
şey; *v/t* bulaştırmak, silmek

blurt [blöt]: **~ out** *v/t*
ağzından kaçırmak

blush [blaş] *n.* kızarma,
utanma; *v/i* utanmak, kızarmak

boar [bö] *zo.* erkek domuz

board [böd] *n.* tahta, levha;
mukavva; masa; yiyecek;
kurul; idare; *v/t* döşemek,
kaplamak; yedirip içirmek;
binmek **~e**; **~ and lodging** yiyecek ve yatacak;
2 of Trade Ticaret Odası

veya Bakanlığı; **full** ~ tam pansiyon; **notice** ~ ilân tahtası; **on** ~ gemide; trende; ~**er** pansiyon kiracısı; yatılı öğrenci; ~**ing-house** pansiyon; ~**ing-school** yatılı okul

boast [biust] *n.* övünme; *v/i* övünmek, yüksekten atmak; ~**ful** övüngen, palavracı

boat [but] sandal, kayık, gemi; ~**ing** sandal *v.s.nin* eğlence için kullanılması; ~**man** sandalcı, kayıkçı; ~**race** kayık yarışı

bob [bob] *v/t* hafifçe hareket ettirmek; *v/i* oynamak, kımıldamak

bobbin ['bobin] makara, bobin

bobby ['bobi] *coll.* polis memuru

bob-sleigh ['bob-] kızak

bodi|ce ['bodis] korsaj, korse; ~**ly** bedeni; *adv.* büsbütün

body ['bodi] vücut, beden; ceset; kurul, heyet, grup; karoseri; ~**guard** hassa askeri

bog [bog] batak, bataklık

bogus ['biugıs] sahte, yapma

boil [boyl] *n.* çıban; *v/i* kaynamak; *v/t* kaynatmak, haşlamak; ~**over** *v/i* taşmak; ~**ed egg** rafadan yumurta; ~**er** kazan

boisterous ['boystırıs] şiddetli, gürültülü

bold [biuld] cesur, atılgan; arsız, küstah; ~**ness** atılganlık; küstahlık

bolster ['biulstı] yastık

bolt [biult] *n.* cıvata, sürme; yıldırım; ok; *v/t* sürmelemek; yutmak; *v/i* kaçmak; **make a** ~ **for** -e doğru atılmak; ~**upright** dimdik

bomb [bom] *n.* bomba; *v/t* bombalamak; ~**ardment** [~'bâdmınt] bombardıman; ~**er** ['~ı] bombardıman uçağı

bond [bond] bağ, rabıta; bono; *ec.* tahvil; **in** ~ antrepoda; ~**age** esirlik, serflik

bone [biun] kemik; kılçık

bonfire ['bonfayı] şenlik ateşi

bonnet ['bonit] başlık, bere; motor kapağı, kaporta

bonn|ie, ~**y** ['boni] güzel, zarif; gürbüz

bonus ['biunıs] ikramiye

bony ['biuni] kemikleri görünen, zayıf; kılçıklı

book [buk] *n.* kitap; defter; *v/t* ısmarlamak, tutmak, kaydetmek; ~**ed up** hepsi satılmış; yer kalmamış; ~**binder** ciltçi; ~**case** kitap dolabı; ~**ing-clerk** gişe memuru; ~**ing-office** bilet gişesi; ~**keeper** defter tutan, muhasebeci; ~**keeping** defter tutma; ~**let** broşür; ~**seller** kitapçı; ~**shop** kitabevi

boom [buum] *ec.* fiatların

yükselmesi, piyasada canlılık

boor [buɪ] kaba adam

boost [buust] v/t arkasından itmek; artırmak

boot [buut] bot, potin, çizme; **~ee** [ˈ-tɪ] kadın botu

booth [buudh] kulübe, baraka [yağma)

booty [ˈbuuti] ganimet,∫

border [ˈbôdɪ] n. kenar, pervaz; sınır; v/t sınırla(ndır)mak; v/i bitişik olm.; (on, upon -e)

bore[1] [bô] s. **bear**

bore[2] n. çap, delgi, boru kutru, sonda; can sıkıcı adam, can sıkıcı iş; v/t delmek, sondalamak; -in canını sıkmak; **~hole** sonda deliği

boric [ˈbôrik]: **~ acid** chem. bor asidi

born [bôn] s. **bear**[2]; doğmuş; **be ~** doğmak; **~e** s. **bear**[2]

borough [ˈbarɪ] kasaba, küçük şehir

borrow [ˈborɪɪ] v/t ödünç almak, borç almak

bosom [ˈbuzɪm] göğüs, koyun

Bosphorus [ˈbosforɪs] Boğaziçi

boss [bos] patron, şef

botan|ic(al) [bɪˈtänik(ıl)] botaniğe ait; **~y** [ˈbotni] botanik

botch [boç] n. kaba iş; v/t kabaca yamamak, bozmak

both [bɪuth] her iki(si); **~ ...**
and hem ... hem de

bother [ˈbodhı] n. canını sıkma, sıkıntı; v/t -in canını sıkmak; v/i endişelenmek (about -den)

bottle [ˈbotl] n. şişe, biberon; v/t şişeye koymak; **~neck** şişe boğazı; fig. dar geçit

bottom [ˈbotım] dip, alt; kıç; temel; **~less** dipsiz

bough [bau] dal

bought [bôt] s. **buy**

boulevard [ˈbuulvâ] bulvar

boulder [ˈbɪuldı] çakıl, kaya parçası

bounce [bauns] n. sıçrama; v/i sıçramak

bound[1] [baund] s. **bind**; **~ for** -e gitmek üzere olan; **~ to** inf. -meğe mecbur

bound[2] v/t sınırlamak

bound[3] v/i atlamak, sıçramak

bound|ary [ˈbaundıri] sınır; **~less** sınırsız, sonsuz; **out of ~s** yasak bölge

bounty [ˈbaunti] cömertlik; ec. ikramiye, prim

bouquet [buˈkey] buket, demet; koku (şarap)

bout [baut] med. nöbet; yarış

bow[1] [bɪu] yay, kavis

bow[2] [bau] naut. pruva

bow[3] [bau] n. reverans; v/t eğmek; v/i reverans yapmak [saklar)

bowels [ˈbaulz] pl. bar-∫

bower [ˈbauɪ] çardak, kameriye

bowl[1] [bɪul] kâse, tas, kadeh; pipo ağzı

bowl² *n.* top; *v/t* yuvarlamak, atmak

bowler ['bıulı] melon şapka

box [boks] *n.* kutu, sandık;
loca; arabacı yeri; kulübe;
tech. yuva; *v/i* boks yapmak; *v/t* tokatlamak; **~er**
boksör; **~ing** boks; **♀ing
Day** 26 aralık; **~ing-
-match** boks maçı; **~-
office** tiyatro gişesi

boy [boy] erkek çocuk,
oğlan; **♀ Scout** izci

boycott ['boykıt] *n.* boykot;
v/t boykot etm.

boy|-friend erkek arkadaş;
~hood çocukluk çağı; **~ish**
(erkek) çocuk gibi

bra [brâ] sutyen

brace [breys] *n.* kuşak,
köşebent; *pl.* pantolon askısı; *v/t* sağlamlaştırmak;
~ up sıkmak; **~let** ['~lit]
bilezik

bracket ['bräkit] *n.* kol,
destek; raf; *gr.* ayraç, parantez; *v/t* birleştirmek,
birbirine bağlamak

brackish ['bräkiş] tuzlum-
su, acı

brag [bräg] *v/i* yüksekten
atmak, övünmek; **~gart**
['~ıt] palavracı

braid [breyd] *n.* saç örgüsü;
kurdele, örgülü şerit; *v/t*
örmek; kurdele takmak *-e*

brain [breyn] beyin, dimağ;
~less akılsız; **~wave** birdenbire gelen fikir

brake [breyk] *n.* fren; *v/i*
fren yapmak; *v/t* frenlemek

bramble ['brämbl] *bot.*
böğürtlen çalısı

branch [brânç] *n.* dal; kol,
şube; *v/i* dallanmak, kollara ayrılmak

brand [bränd] *n.* yanan
odun; kızgın demir, dağ,
damga; marka, cins; *v/t*
dağlamak, damgalamak;
~-new yepyeni; **~y** kanyak

brass [brâs] pirinç; **~ band**
bando, mızıka

brassière ['bräsiı] sutyen

brave [breyv] *adj.* cesur,
yiğit; *v/t* göğüs germek *-e*;
~ry kahramanlık

brawl [brôl] kavga, gürültü

brazier ['breyzıı] mangal

Brazil [brı'zil] Brezilya;
~ian Brezilyalı; **~-nut** *bot.*
Brezilya kestanesi

breach [briç] *n.* delik, kırık;
bozulma; *v/t* kırmak, bozmak

bread [bred] ekmek; **~-
-and-butter letter** teşekkür mektubu

breadth [bredth] genişlik,
en

break [breyk] *n.* kırık; ara;
arası kesilme; (*day*) ağartı;
v/t kırmak, koparmak, parçalamak; dağıtmak; aç-
mak, yarmak; alıştırmak;
mahvetmek; *promise:* tut-
mamak; ara vermek *-e*; *v/i*
parçalanmak, kırılmak,
kuvvetten düşmek; (*day*)
ağarmak; **~ away** ayrılmak; **~ down** *v/t* yıkmak;
v/i bozulmak; **~ off** *v/i*
ayrılmak *v/t* ayırmak; **~ up**

breakable 214

v/t parçalamak, kırmak;
v/i dağılmak; **~able** kırılacak; **~down** yıkılma,
bozulma; **~fast** ['brekfıst]
kahvaltı; **~through** fig.
başarı

breast [brest] göğüs; meme; **~stroke** kurbağalama
yüzüş

breath [breth] nefes, soluk;
out of ~ soluğu kesilmiş;
~e [brîdh] nefes almak;
~ing ['~îdhiŋ] nefes (alma); **~less** ['~ethlis] nefesi
kesilmiş

bred [bred] s. **breed**

breeches ['briçiz] pl. pantolon, külot sg.

breed [brîd] n. soy, ırk; v/t
doğurmak, üretmek, yetiştirmek; **~er** yetiştirici;
~ing üreme, yetiştirme

breeze [brîz] hafif rüzgâr,
meltem

brevity ['breviti] kısalık

brew [bruu] v/t yapmak,
hazırlamak; v/i basturmak
üzere olm.; **~ery** bira
fabrikası

bribe [brayb] n. rüşvet; v/t
rüşvet vermek; **~ry** rüşvet verme veya alma

brick [brik] tuğla; **~layer**
duvarcı; **~work** tuğla işi;
pl. tuğla ocağı

bridal ['braydl] gelinlik,
geline ait

bride [brayd] gelin; **~groom** güvey; **~smaid**
düğünde geline refakat
eden kız

bridge [bric] n. köprü;

briç oyunu; v/t köprü kurmak -e; **~ over** atlatmak

bridle ['braydl] n. at başlığı; dizgin; v/t gem vurmak,
dizgin takmak -e; **~path**,
~road atlılara mahsus yol

brief [brîf] kısa; **~case**
evrak çantası

briga|de [bri'geyd] mil. tugay; **~dier** [,~ı'dıı] tuğbay

bright [brayt] parlak, berrak; neşeli, canlı; zeki; **~en**
v/t parlatmak, neşelendirmek; v/i parlamak; **~ness**
parlaklık; uyanıklık

brillian|ce, **~cy** ['brilyıns,
'~si] parlaklık, pırıltı; **~t**
adj. çok parlak; çok zeki;
n. pırlanta

brim [brim] kenar, ağız;
~ful(l) ağzına kadar dolu

bring [briŋ] v/t getirmek; **~
about** v/t sebep olm.; **~ an
action** dava açmak; **~
along** yanında getirmek;
~ forth meydana çıkarmak;
~ up yaklaştırmak; yetiştirmek; **~ to an end** sona
erdirmek

brink [briŋk] kenar

brisk [brisk] faal, canlı,
işlek

bristle ['brisl] n. sert kıl;
v/t tüyleri ürpermek

Brit|ain ['britn] Britanya;
~ish Britanyalı, İngiliz;
~on ['britn] İngiliz

brittle ['britl] kolay kırılır,
gevrek

broach [brıuç] v/t delik
açmak -e; fig. girişmek -e

broad [brôd] geniş, enli;

açık, belli; erkinci, liberal; **~cast** n. radyo yayımı; v/t yayımlamak; **~en** v/t genişletmek; **~minded** açık fikirli

brocade [brı'keyd] brokar

broil [broyl] gürültü, kavga

broke [bruk] s. **break**; **~n** s. **break**; **~er** simsar, komisyoncu [med. bronşit]

bronchitis [broŋ'kaytis]

bronze [bronz] tunç, bronz

brooch [bruuç] broş

brood [bruud] n. yumurtadan çıkan civciler veya kuş yavruları pl.; v/i kuluçkaya yatmak

brook [bruk] dere, çay

broom [brum] süpürge

broth [broth] etsuyu

brothel ['brothl] genelev

brother ['bradhı] kardeş, birader; **~hood** kardeşlik; **~-in-law** kayınbirader, bacanak, enişte; **~ly** kardeşçe

brought [brôt] s. **bring**

brow [brau] an. kaş; alın

brown [braun] kahverengi, esmer; **~ paper** ambalaj kâğıdı

bruise [bruuz] n. bere, çürük; v/t berelemek, çürütmek

brush [braş] n. fırça; çalı; tüylü kuyruk; v/t fırçalamak, süpürmek; hafifçe dokunmak -e; **~ up** tazelemek

Brussels ['brıslz] Brüksel; **~-sprouts** ['~l'sprauts] bot. frenk lahanası

brut|al ['bruutl] hayvanca, vahşi; **~ality** [~'täliti] vahşet, canavarlık; **~e** [bruut] hayvan, canavar

bubble ['babl] n. hava kabarcığı; v/i köpürmek, kaynamak

buck [bak] n. erkek karaca, geyik v.s.; Am. sl. dolar; v/i sıçramak

bucket ['bakit] kova

buckle ['bakl] n. toka, kopça; v/t tokalamak, kopçalamak; **~ on** tokalamak, takmak

buckskin güderi

bud [bad] n. tomurcuk, konca; v/i konca vermek

buddy ['badi] sl. arkadaş

budget ['bacit] bütçe

buffalo ['bäfılu] manda

buffer ['bafı] tech. tampon

buffet ['bafit] büfe

buffoon [ba'fuun] soytarı, maskara

bug [bag] tahtakurusu; Am. böcek; **~gy** Am. hafif yay arabası; çocuk arabası

bugle ['byûgl] borazan, boru

build [bild] v/t inşa etm., kurmak, yapmak; **~ upon** güvenmek -e; **~er** inşaatçı; inşaat ustası; **~ing** bina, yapı

built [bilt] s. **build**; **~-in** gömme; yerleşmiş

bulb [balb] bot. soğan; el. ampul

Bulgaria [bal'gäırı] Bulgaristan; **~n** Bulgar; Bulgarca

bulge 216

bulge [balc] *n.* bel verme, şiş; *v/i* bel vermek, kamburlaşmak

bulk [balk] hacım, kütle; en büyük kısım; ~y hacımlı, büyük

bull [bul] *zo.* boğa; ~dog buldok köpeği

bullet ['bulit] kurşun, mermi

bulletin ['bulitin] günlük haber, tebliğ; ~ board *Am.* ilân tahtası

bullion ['bulyın] altın *veya* gümüş külçesi

bully ['buli] *v/t* korkutmak

bum [bam] *sl.* serseri, başıboş

bumble-bee ['bambl-] *zo.* hezen arısı

bump [bamp] *n.* vuruş, çarpma; *v/i* çarpmak (**against** -*e*); *v/t* vurmak; ~er tampon; ağza dolmuş bardak

bun [ban] kuru üzümlü çörek

bunch [banç] demet, deste, salkım

bundle ['bandl] *n.* bağ, bohça, paket; *v/t* (**up**) çıkınlamak, sarmalamak

bungalow ['bangılıu] tek katlı köşk

bungle ['bangl] *n.* kötü iş, bozma; *v/t* bozmak, bulaştırmak

bunk [bank] yatak yeri, ranza

bunny ['bani] tavşan(cık)

buoy [boy] şamandıra; ~ant yüzebilir; *fig.* neşeli.

burden ['bödn] *n.* yük, ağır iş; ana fikir; nakarat; *v/t* yüklemek (*so.* **with** -*e* -*i*)

bureau ['byuırıu] büro, yazıhane; *Am.* çekmeceli dolap

burglar ['böglı] gece hırsızı; ~y ev soyma

burial ['beriıl] gömme; ~-ground mezarlık

burly ['böli] iriyarı

burn [bön] *n.* yanık; *v/t* yakmak; *v/i* yanmak; ~er gaz ocağı memesi; ~ing yanan; ~t *s.* **burn**

burst [böst] *n.* patlama; patlak, yarık; *v/i* patlamak, yarılmak; *v/t* patlatmak; ~ **into flames** alevlenmek; ~ **into tears** ağlamağa başlamak

bury ['beri] *v/t* gömmek; saklamak

bus [bas] otobüs; **miss the** ~ *fig.* fırsatı kaçırmak

bush [buş] çalı, çalılık

bushel ['buşl] İngiliz kilesi. (*36, 37 l*)

bushy çalılık; fırça gibi

business ['biznis] iş, görev, meslek; ticaret; mesele; ~ **hours** *pl.* iş saatleri; ~**like** ciddî, düzenli; ~**man** iş adamı; ~ **tour**, ~ **trip** iş yolculuğu

bust [bast] büst; göğüs

bustle ['basl] *n.* faaliyet; telâş; *v/i* acele etm.; telâşlanmak

busy ['bizi] faal, iş gören, meşgul; işlek; **be** ~ -**ing**,

~ **oneself with** meşgul olm., uğraşmak *-mekle*
but [bat, bıt] ama, fakat; ancak; bilakis; şu kadar ki; halbuki; *-den* başka; **the next ~ one** birinci değil ikinci
butcher ['buçı] *n.* kasap; *v/t* kesmek [racı]
butler ['batlı] *n.* kâhya; sof-
butt [bat] fıçı; dipçik; hedef; tos; ~ **in** *sl.* karışmak *-e*
butter ['batı] *n.* tereyağı; *v/t* tereyağı sürmek *-e*; ~**cup** *bot.* düğünçiçeği; ~**fly** *zo.* kelebek; ~**milk** yayık ayranı
buttocks [batıks] *pl.* kıç *sg.*
button ['batn] *n.* düğme; konca; *v/t* (**up**) düğmelemek, iliklemek; ~**hole** ilik
buttress ['batris] payanda, destek

buy [bay] *v/t* satın almak, almak; ~**er** alıcı
buzz [baz] *n.* vızıltı, gürültü; *v/i* vızıldamak
buzzard ['bazıd] *zo. bir cins* şahin
by [bay] *-in* yanında, yakınında; ile, vasıtasiyle; tarafından; *-e* göre; ~ **and** ~ yavaş yavaş; az sonra; ~ **and large** genellikle; ~ **day** gündüz; ~ **far** çok daha fazla; ~ **God!** vallahi!; ~ **itself** kendi kendine; **day** ~ **day** her gün; ~**e-bye** ['bay'bay] **s. good-bye**; ~**gone** geçmiş; ~**election** *pol.* ara seçim; ~**name** lakap; ~**pass** dolaştırma; ~**product** yan ürün; ~**stander** seyirci; ~**street** yan sokak
Byzantium [bay'zantıym] Bizans

C

cab [käb] kira arabası
cabaret ['käbırey] kabare
cabbage ['käbic] *bot.* lahana
cabin ['käbin] kamara; kulübe; **three-berth** ~ üç yataklı kamara
cabinet ['käbinit] dolap; *pol.* kabine, bakanlar kurulu; ~**maker** ince iş yapan marangoz
cable ['keybl] *n.* kablo, palamar; telgraf; *v/i* telgraf çekmek; ~**car** teleferik; ~**gram** telgraf

cab|man taksi şoförü; ~**stand** taksi durağı
cackle ['käkl] *v/i* gıdaklamak
cact|us ['käktıs], *pl.* ~**uses** ['~sız], ~**i** ['~tay] *bot.* atlasçiçeği, kaktüs
café ['käfey] pastahane
cafeteria [käfi'tiırıı] kafeterya
cage [keyc] kafes; asansör odası
Cairo ['kayırıu] Kahire
cake [keyk] kurabiye, pasta, kek, çörek; kalıp; ~ **of soap**

sabun parçası; **~-tin** kek kalıbı

calamity [kı'lämiti] felâket, afet

calculat|e ['kälkyuleyt] v/t hesaplamak, tahmin etm., saymak; **~tion** hesap, tahmin

calendar ['kälındı] takvim

calf [kaaf], pl. **calves** [~vz] **1.** zo. dana; buzağı; **2.** an. baldır

calib|re, Am. **~er** ['kälibı] çap

call [kôl] n. çağırma; çağrı, davet; uğrama; telefon etme; v/t çağırmak; bağırmak; uyandırmak; adlandırmak; demek; ~ **at** uğramak -e; ~ **back** geri çağırmak; ~ **for** istemek -i; icabetmek -i; ~ **on** ziyaret etm. -i, uğramak -e; ~ **up** mil. silah altına çağırmak; **~-box** telefon hücresi; **~er** ziyaret eden kimse; telefon eden kimse; **~ing** meslek, iş

callous ['kälıs] sertleşmiş, hissiz

calm [kaam] adj. sakin, durgun; n. sakinlik; v/t yatıştırmak; ~ **down** v/i yatışmak; **~ness** sakinlik, durgunluk

calor|ie, Am. **~y** ['kälıri] kalori

cambric ['keymbrik] patiska

came [keym] s. **come**

camel ['kämıl] zo. deve

camera ['kämırı] fotoğraf makinesi, kamera

camomile ['kämıumayl] bot. papatya

camouflage ['kämuflâj] n. kamuflaj; v/t kamufle etm., gizlemek

camp [kämp] n. kamp; mil. ordugâh; v/i kamp kurmak; **~aign** sefer, savaş; **~er** kamp yapan kimse; **~ ground** Am. s. **~ing-ground**; **~ing** kamp yapma; **~ing-ground** kamp yeri

campus ['kämpıs] üniversite veya okul arazisi

can[1] [kän] kap, kutu; konserve kutusu

can[2] inf. -ebilmek

Canad|a ['känıd] Kanada; **~ian** [kı'neydyın] Kanadalı

canal [kı'näl] kanal, mecra

canary [kı'näıri] zo. kanarya

cancel ['känsıl] v/t silmek, çizmek; kaldırmak, iptal etm.; **be ~(l)ed** iptal olunmak

cancer ['känsı] kanser

candid ['kändid] samimî, açık

candidate ['kändidit] namzet, aday

candied ['kändid] şekerle kaplanmış

candle ['kändl] mum; **~ stick** şamdan

candy ['kändi] şekerleme, bonbon

cane [keyn] baston, değnek

cann|ed [känd] Am. kutulanmış; **~ery** Am. konserve fabrikası

cannibal ['känibıl] yamyam

cannon ['känın] *mil.* top

cannot ['känot] *inf.* -ememek

canoe [kı'nuu] hafif sandal, kano

canopy ['känıpi] gölgelik, tente

cant [känt] ikiyüzlülük, riyakârlık; argo

can't [kaant] *s.* **cannot**

canteen [kän'tîn] kantin; *mil.* aş kabı; *Am.* matara

canvas ['känvıs] keten bezi, kanava; tual, yağlı boya resim; ~s *v/t -i* dolaşarak oy *veya* sipariş toplamak

cap [käp] kasket, başlık; kapak

capa|bility [keypı'biliti] kabiliyet, yetenek; **~ble** muktedir, kabiliyetli, ehliyetli; kabil (**of** *-e*)

capacity [kı'päsiti] istiap; yetenek; verim; kabiliyet

cape[1] [keyp] *geo.* burun

cape[2] kap, pelerin

caper[1] ['keypı] *bot.* kebere

caper[2] *v/t* sıçramak

capital ['käpitl] *n.* başkent, hükümet merkezi; *ec.* sermaye, kapital; *gr.* büyük harf; *adj.* en büyük, mükemmel; ~ **crime** *jur.* cezası olan suç; **~ism** kapitalizm; **~ist** anamalcı, kapitalist

capitulation [kıpityu'leyşın] teslim; *pol.* kapitülasyon

capricious [kı'prişıs] kaprisli

Capricorn ['käprikôn] *astr.* keçi burcu

capsize [käp'sayz] *naut. v/t* devirmek; *v/i* devrilmek

capsule ['käpsyûl] kapsül

captain ['käptin] *naut.* kaptan; *mil.* yüzbaşı

caption ['käpşın] başlık, serlevha; yazılı tercüme (*film*)

captiv|ate ['käptiveyt] *v/t* cezbetmek; **~e** tutsak, esir; **~ity** [~'tiviti] tutsaklık

capture ['käpçı] *n.* yakalama, esir alma; *v/t* tutmak, yakalamak

car [kaa] otomobil, araba; vagon; ~ **ferry** araba vapuru

caravan ['kärıvän] kervan; treyler; **~serai** [~'sıray] kervansaray

carbine ['kaabayn] karabina

carbohydrate ['kaabıu'haydreyt] *chem.* karbonhidrat

carbon ['kaabın] *chem.* karbon; (~ **paper**) kopya kâğıdı; **~ic** [kaa'bonik] karbonik

carbuncle ['kaabaŋkl] çıban, şirpençe

carbure|tter, ~t(t)or ['kaabyureti] *tech.* karbüratör

carca|se, ~ss ['kaakıs] leş; oyun kağıdı; ~ **index** klasör; fişler *pl.*; **~board** karton, mukavva (kalçle ilgili)

cardiac ['kaadiäk] *med.*

cardigan ['kaadıgın] yün ceket

cardinal

cardinal ['kaadinl] *rel.* kardinal; *adj.* baş, esaslı; ~ **number** asıl sayı

care [käı] *n.* dikkat, bakım; ilgi; merak, üzüntü; *v/i* ilgilenmek (**for** ile); endişelenmek (*-den*); bakmak (*-e*); **take** ~ **of** muhafaza etm. *-i*; bakmak, dikkat etm. *-e*; **with** ~ dikkatle; ~ **of** evinde, eliyle

career [kı'rıı] meslek hayatı, kariyer

care|free kaygısız; ~**ful** dikkatli; ~**less** dikkatsiz, ihmalci, kayıtsız

caress [kı'res] *n.* okşama; *v/t* okşamak

care|taker kapıcı; ev yöneticisi; ~**worn** kederden bitkin

cargo ['kaagıu] yük, hamule

caricature [kärikı'tyuı] karikatür

caries ['kärüiz] *med.* diş çürümesi

carnal ['kaanl] cinsi, şehvani; dünyevi

carnation [kaa'neyşın] *bot.* karanfil

carol ['kärıl]: **Christmas** ~ Noel şarkısı

carp [kaap] *zo.* sazan

car-park park yeri

carpenter ['kaapıntı] marangoz, dülger, doğramacı

carpet ['kaapıt] halı

carriage ['käric] araba, vagon; taşıma, nakil; nakliye ücreti; davranış; ~**free** nakliyesiz; ~**way** araba yolu

carrier ['kärıı] taşıyan; nakliyeci; **aircraft** ~ uçak gemisi; ~ **bag** alışveriş torbası

carrion ['kärın] leş; *adj.* leş gibi

carrot ['kärıt] *bot.* havuç

carry ['kärı] *v/t* taşımak, götürmek, nakletmek; ~ **on** devam ettirmek; ~ **out** yerine getirmek

cart [kaat] iki tekerlekli yük arabası; **put the** ~ **before the horse** bir işi tersinden yapmak

cartoon [kaa'tuun] karikatür; (**animated**) ~ miki filmi; ~**ist** karikatürcü

cartridge ['kaatric] hartuç; *phot.* kartuş, kaset

cart-wheel araba tekerleği; takla

carv|e [kaav] *v/t* oymak, hakketmek; *meat:* sofrada kesmek; ~**er** oymacı, hakkâk

cascade [käs'keyd] çağlayan

case[1] [keys] kutu, kasa

case[2] hal, husus, olay; **in that** ~ o takdirde; **in** ~ **of** halinde; **in any** ~ her halde

casement ['keysmınt] pencere kanadı

cash [käş] *n.* para, nakit; *v/t* paraya çevirmek; bozmak; ~ **down** peşin para; ~ **on delivery** ödemeli; ~**and-carry** *adj.* peşin para ile alınan; ~**ier** [kä'şiı] kasadar, veznedar

casing ['keysın] kaplama

cask [kaask] fıçı, varil; ~**et**

celery

[`~it] değerli eşya kutusu; *Am.* tabut

Caspian Sea [`käspłın -] Hazer denizi

cassock [`käsık] papaz cüppesi

cast [kaast] *n.* atma, atış; dökme, kalıp; tip, kalite; *v/t* atmak, saçmak; *tech.* dökmek; **be ~ down** yüreği kararmak; **~ iron** *tech.* dökme demir; **~ steel** dökme çelik

caste [kaast] kast, birbirine karşı kapalı sınıf

castle [`kaasl] kale; şato

castor [`kaastı] tuzluk, biberlik

castor oil hintyağı

castrate [käs`treyt] *v/t* hadım etm.

casual [`käyuıl] tesadüfî, rastgele; **~ty** kaza; kayıp

cat [kät] kedi

catalog(ue) [`kätılog] katalog, liste

cataract [`kätıräkt] çağlayan

catarrh [kı`tâ] *med.* nezle

catastrophe [kı`tästrıfi] felâket, facia

catch [käç] *v/t* tutmak, yakalamak; kavramak; yetişmek -*e*; *n.* tutma; av; tuzak; kilit dili; **~ a cold** nezle olm., üşümek; **~ up** yetişmek (**with** -*e*); **~-as-catch-can** serbest güreş; **~ing** çekici; *med.* bulaşıcı; **~word** parola; slogan

category [`kätıgıri] cins, kategori

cater [`keytı] *v/i* tedarik etm., hazırlamak (**for** -*i*)

caterpillar [`kätıpilı] tırtıl

cathedral [kı`thîdrıl] katedral

Catholic [`käthılik] Katolik; **~ism** [kı`tholisizım] Katoliklik

cattle [`kätl] sığır, davar

Caucasus [`kôkısıs] Kafkas (dağları *pl.*)

caught [kôt] *s.* catch

ca(u)ldron [`kôldrın] kazan

cauliflower [`koliflauı] *bot.* carnabahar

cause [kôz] *n.* neden, sebep; dava; *v/t* sebep olm. -*e*; *fig.* doğurmak *v/t*; **~less** sebepsiz

caution [`kôşın] *n.* dikkat, ihtar; sakınma; *v/t* uyarmak, ihtar etm.; **~ous** ihtiyatlı, çekingen

cavalry [`kävılri] *mil.* süvari

cav|e [keyv], **~ern** [`kävın] mağara, in

caviar [`käviâ] havyar

cavity [`käviti] çukur, boşluk

cease [sîs] *v/i* bitmek, durmak; *v/t* bitirmek; **~less** sürekli, durmadan

cedar [`sîdı] *bot.* sedir

cede [sîd] *jur.* terketmek

ceiling [`sîlin] tavan; azami sınır

celebrat|e [`selibreyt] *v/t* kutlamak; şenlik yapmak; **~ion** kutlama

celebrity [si`lebriti] şöhret kazanmış şahıs

celery [`selıri] *bot.* kereviz

celibacy ['selibısı] bekârlık; *rel.* evlenme yasağı

cell [sel] hücre; *el.* pil

cellar ['selı] kiler, bodrum

Celtic ['keltik] Keltlere ait; Keltçe

cement [si'ment] *n.* çimento; tutkal; *v/t* yapıştırmak

cemetery ['semitri] mezarlık

censor ['sensı] *v/t* sansür etm.; ~ship sansür

censure ['sensı] *n.* azar (-lama); *v/t* azarlamak, tenkit etm.

census ['sensıs] nüfus sayımı

cent [sent] doların yüzde biri; per ~ yüzde; ~enary [~'tineri], ~ennial [~'tenyıl] yüz yıllık; *n.* yüzüncü yıldönümü

centi|grade ['sentigreyd] santigrat; ~metre santimetre

central ['sentrıl] orta, merkezî; ~ heating kalorifer; ~ize *v/t* merkezîleştirmek

cent|re, *Am.* ~er ['sentı] *n.* orta, merkez; *v/t* ortaya koymak, merkeze toplamak; *v/i* merkezlenmek; ~re-forward santrfor; ~re-half santrhaf

century ['sençuri] yüzyıl

cereals ['siırılz] *pl.* hububat; zahire *sg.*

cerebral ['seribrıl] *an.* beyne ait

ceremon|ial [seri'mıunyıl] resmî; *n.* tören; ~ious törensel; ~y ['~mıni] tören;

rel. ayin; *pol.* protokol, teşrifat

certain ['sôtn] muhakkak; kesin; emin; belirli; bazı; ~ly *adv.* elbette, tabiî; ~ty kesinlik

certi|ficate [sı'tifikit] tasdikname; ruhsat; belge; ilmühaber; ~fy ['sôtifay] *v/t* tasdik etm., onaylamak; ~tude ['~tyûd] kesinlik

chafe [çeyf] *v/t* sürtmek, sürterek berelemek; *v/i* sürtünmek; sinirlenmek; ~r böcek

chaff [çâf] saman tozu

chaffinch ['çâfinç] *zo.* ispinoz

chagrin ['şâgrin] iç sıkıntısı

chain [çeyn] *n.* zincir; silsile; *v/t* zincirlemek

chair [çäı] iskemle, sandalye; başkanlık makamı; kürsü; ~lift telesiyej; ~man başkan

chalk [çôk] tebeşir

challenge ['çâlinc] *n.* meydan okuma, davet; *v/t* çağırmak; meydan okumak

chamber ['çeymbı] oda; salon; meclis; ♀ of Commerce Ticaret Odası; ~maid kadın oda hizmetçisi

chamois ['şâmwâ] *zo.* dağ keçisi; ~leather ['şâmi-güderi

champagne [şâm'peyn] şampanya (şarabı)

champion ['çâmpyın] şampiyon, kahraman; ~ship şampiyonluk

chance [çâns] şans, talih; tesadüf; fırsat; ihtimal; **by ~** tesadüfen; **take one's ~** talihe bırakmak

chancellor ['çânsılı] rektör; şansölye

chandelier [şândi'lii] avize

change [çeync] *n.* değiş(tir)me, değişiklik; bozulan para, bozukluk; *v/t* değiştirmek; boz(dur)mak; *train:* aktarma yapmak; *v/i* değişmek; **for a ~** değişiklik olsun; **~ one's mind** fikrini değiştirmek; **~able** kararsız; değişebilir; **~less** değişmez

channel ['çânl] kanal; yol; **the ~** *geo.* Manş Denizi

chaos ['keyos] karışıklık; kaos

chap [çâp] çocuk, arkadaş

chapel ['çâpıl] küçük kilise; **~lain** ['lin] papaz

chapter ['çâptı] bölüm, kısım

charakter ['kâriktı] karakter, seciye; şöhret; vasıf; harf; *thea.* şahıs; **~istic** karakteristik, tipik; **~ize** *v/t* tanımlamak; vasıflandırmak

charcoal ['çâkıul] mangal kömürü

charge [çâc] *n.* yük, hamule; şarj; hamle; görev, memuriyet; bedel, ücret; itham; *v/t* yüklemek, doldurmak; suçlamak (**with** ile); *price:* istemek; hücum etm. *-e;* **free of ~** karşılıksız; **in ~ of** ile vazifeli;

take ~ of yüklenmek, üstüne almak *-i*

chariot ['çârit] iki tekerlekli araba

charit|able ['çâritıbl] hayırsever; **~y** hayırseverlik

charm [çâm] *n.* büyü; muska; *fig.* çekicilik; *v/t* büyülemek; teshir etm.; **~ing** çekici

chart [çât] *naut.* harita

charter ['çâtı] *n.* berat, imtiyaz; *v/t* kiralamak; **~ plane** charter uçağı

charwoman ['çâwumın] temizleyici kadın

chase [çeys] *n.* av, takip, kovalama; *v/t* avlamak, kovalamak

chasm ['kâzım] yarık, uçurum

chassis ['şâsi] şasi

chast|e [çeyst] iffetli, temiz; **~ity** ['çâstiti] iffet, saffet

chat [çât] *n.* sohbet; *v/i* sohbet etm., konuşmak; **~ter** *v/i* çene çalmak, çatırdamak; **~terbox** boşboğaz, geveze

chauffeur ['şıufı] şoför

cheap [çîp] ucuz; değersiz; bayağı; **~en** *v/t* ucuzlatmak; *v/i* ucuzlamak; **~ness** ucuzluk

cheat [çît] *n.* hile, düzen; hileci; *v/t* aldatmak, dolandırmak

check [çek] *n.* engel, durdurma; kontrol; fiş, marka; *Am.* çek; *v/t* önlemek, durdurmak; karşılaştırmak, kontrol etm.; **~ in** *Am.* otel

defterine kaydolmak; **~out**
Am. otelden ayrılmak; **~ed**
kareli; **~-room** gişe; *Am.*
vestiyer

cheek [çîk] yanak; yüzsüzlük; **~y** yüzsüz

cheer [çîn] *n.* alkış, 'yaşa!'
sesi; neşe; *v/t* alkışlamak,
neşelendirmek; **~ (on)** yü-
reklendirmek; **~ (up)** teselli etm.; **~ful** neşeli, şen;
~io! ['..ri'iu] Allaha ısmarladık!; **~less** neşesiz; kederli; **~y** neşeli

cheese [çîz] peynir

chemical ['kemikıl] kimyasal; **~s** *pl.* kimyasal mad-
deler

chemist ['kemist] kimya-
ger; eczacı; **~ry** kimya

cheque [çek] çek

chequered ['çekıd] kareli

cherish ['çeriş] *v/t* aziz tutmak; gütmek

cherry ['çeri] *bot.* kiraz

chess [çes] satranç oyunu;
~board satranç tahtası; **~-
man** satranç taşı

chest [çest] sandık, kutu;
an. göğüs

chestnut ['çesnat] kestane;
kestane renginde

chew [çuu] *v/t* çiğnemek;
~ing-gum çiklet

chicken ['çikin] piliç, civciv; **~-pox** ['..poks] *med.*
su çiçeği hastalığı

chief [çîf] büyük, en önemli; *n.* baş, şef; **~tain** ['..tın]
kabile reisi

chilblain ['çilbleyn] *med.*
soğuk şişliği

child [çayld], *pl.* **~ren** ['çil-
drın] çocuk; **~hood** çocuk-
luk; **~ish** çocukça; **~less**
çocuksuz; **~like** çocuk ruh-
lu

chill [çil] *n.* soğukluk algın-
lığı; soğuk; *v/t* soğutmak;
üşütmek; **~y** soğuk, serin

chime [çaym] *n.* ahenkli
çan sesi; *v/t* çal(ın)mak;
in with uymak *-e*

chimney ['çimni] baca; **~-
sweep(er)** baca temizleyici

chin [çin] çene

China ['çaynı] Çin; $\mathbb{2}$ porselen, çini

Chinese ['çay'nîz] Çinli;
Çince

chink [çink] yarık, çatlak

chip [çip] *n.* çentik; küçük
parça, kırıntı; *v/t* yontmak,
çentmek

chirp [çöp] cıvıldamak

chisel ['çizl] *n.* çelik kalem;
v/t oymak, yontmak

chivalr|ous ['şivılrıs] mert,
kibar; **~y** şövalyelik, mertlik

chlorine ['klôrîn] klor

chocolate ['çokılit] çikolata

choice [çoys] seçme, tercih;
tercih hakkı

choir ['kwayı] koro

choke [çuk] *v/t* tıkamak,
boğmak; *v/i* tıkanmak, boğulmak

cholera ['kolırı] kolera

choose [çuuz] *v/t* seçmek;
tercih etm.

chop [çop] *n.* darbe; parça;
pirzola; *v/t* doğramak, yarmak

chord [kôd] kiriş, tel

chose [çıuz], ~n s. **choose**

Christ [krayst] Hazreti İsa; ℓen [′krisn] v/t rel. vaftiz etm., isimlendirmek; ℓening vaftiz

Christian [′kristyın] Hıristiyan; ~ **name** öz ad; ~ity [~i′äniti] Hristiyanlık

Christmas [′krismıs] Noel; ~ **Eve** Noel arifesi; ~tree Noel ağacı

chronic [′kronik] med. müzmin, süreğen; ~le tarih, vakayiname

chuck [çak]: ~ **out** v/t kapı dışarı etm.

chuckle [′çakl] kendi kendine gülmek

chum [çam] arkadaş

church [çöç] kilise; ~yard kilise avlusu; mezarlık

churn [çön] n. yayık; v/t yayıkta çalkamak; köpürtmek [paraşüt}

chute [şuut] çağlayan;}

cider [′saydı] elma şarabı

cigar [si′gaa] yaprak sigarası, puro; ~ette [sigı′ret] sigara

cinder [′sındı] kor, köz; ℓella [~′relı] Sinderella; ~track atletizm pisti

cine|-camera [′sini-] film çekme makinesi; ~ma [′sinımı] sinema

cinnamon [′sınımın] tarçın

cipher [′sayfı] n. sıfır; şifre; v/t şifre ile yazmak

circle [′sökl] n. daire, halka, çevre; grup; thea. balkon; v/t devretmek, kuşatmak

circuit [′sökit] dolaşma; dolaşım; devre; **short** ~ el. kontak

circular [′sökyulı] dairevî; ~ (**letter**) sirküler

circulat|e [′sökyuleyt] v/i dolaşmak; v/t dağıtmak; ~ion dolaşma; deveran; dağıtım mikdarı

circum|cise [′sökımsayz] v/t sünnet etm.; ~cision sünnet; ~ference [sı′kamfırıns] çevre; ~flex [′sökımfleks] gr. düzeltme işareti; ~scribe [~skrayb] v/t -in etrafını çizmek; sınırlamak -i; ~stance hal, durum, keyfiyet

circus [′sökıs] sirk; meydan

cistern [′sistın] sarnıç

citadel [′sitıdl] kale, hisar

cite [sayt] v/t jur. celbetmek; zikretmek, anmak

citizen [′sitizn] hemşerî; vatandaş; ~ship vatandaşlık

city [′siti] şehir; site; ~ **guide** şehir planı; ~ **hall** belediye dairesi

civil [′sivl] sivil; nazik; iç, dahilî; ~ **rights** pl. vatandaşlık hakları; ~ **service** devlet hizmeti; ~ **war** iç savaş; ~ian sivil şahıs; ~ity nezaket; ~ization medenîyet; ~ized uygar, medenî

clack [kläk] tıkırtı

clad [kläd] s. **clothe**

claim [kleym] n. iddia; istek, talep; v/t iddia etm., istemek; ~ant iddiaî

clammy

226

clammy ['klämi] soğuk ve ıslak, yapışkan

clamo(u)r ['klämı] gürültü, patırtı; **~ous** gürültülü

clamp [klämp] *n.* kenet, köşebent

clan [klän] *n.* kabile, klan

clandestine [klän'destin] gizli, el altından

clank [kläŋk] *n.* tınlama, çınlama; *v/i* tınlamak, çınlamak

clap [kläp] *n.* vuruş, el çırpma; *v/t* çırpmak

claret ['klärıt] kırmızı şarap

clari|fy ['klärifay] *v/t* tasfiye etm.; aydınlatmak; **~ty** açıklık

clash [kläş] *n.* çarpışma (sesi); *v/i* çarpışmak

clasp [kläsp] *n.* toka; el sıkma; *v/t* sıkmak, yakalamak, bağlamak; **~-knife** çakı

class [klâs] *n.* sınıf, tabaka; kategori; tasnif etm.

classic ['kläsik] klasik yazar; *adj.* klasik; mükemmel; **~al** klasik

classif|ication [kläsifi'keyşın] tasnif, sınıflandırma; **~y** ['~fay] *v/t* sınıflandırmak

class|-mate sınıf arkadaşı; **~room** dersane; **~-struggle**, **~-war** sınıflar mücadelesi

clatter ['klätı] *n.* takırtı; *v/i*

clause [klôz] madde, şart; *gr.* cümlecik

claw [klô] hayvan pençesi; pençe tırnağı

clay [kley] kil, balçık

clean [klîn] *adj.* temiz, pak; *v/t* temizlemek; **~ out** temizlemek; **~ up** düzenlemek; bitirmek; **~(li)ness** ['klenlinis, 'klînnis] temizlik; **~se** [klenz] *v/t* temizlemek

clear [klii] *adj.* berrak, açık, sarih, aşikâr; *ec.* net; *v/t* temizlemek, açmak; kurtarmak; boşaltmak; **~ away** kaldırmak; **~ up** *v/t* halletmek; *v/i* açılmak; **~ing** açık saha; *ec.* kliring; **~ness** berraklık, açıklık

cleave [klîv] *v/t* yarmak; *v/i* çatlamak; bağlı olm. (**to** ~e)

clef [klef] *mus.* anahtar

cleft [kleft] yarık; *s.* **cleave**

clemency ['klemınsi] şefkat, yumuşaklık

clench [klenç] *v/t* sıkmak

clergy ['klöci] *rel.* rahipler sınıfı; **~man** papaz, rahip

cleric ['klerik] rahip; **~al** rahiplere ait; kilisenin siyasete karışmasına taraftar

clerk [klâk] kâtip

clever ['klevı] akıllı, becerikli, marifetli; zarif

cliché ['klîşey] klişe

click [klik] *n.* şıkırtı, çatırtı; *v/i* şıkırdamak

client ['klaynt] müşteri

cliff [klif] kayalık; uçurum

clima|te ['klaymit] iklim; **~x** ['~mäks] dönüm noktası, zirve

climb [klaym] *n.* tırmanma;

v/i, v/t tırmanmak (-*e*); **~er** dağcı; *bot.* sarmaşık

clinch [klinç] kucaklama

cling [kliŋ] yapışmak (**to** -*e*)

clinic ['klinik] klinik

clink [kliŋk] *v/t* tokuşturmak

clip [klip] *n.* kırkım; klips; pens; mandal; *v/t* kırpmak; **~ping** gazete kupürü

cloak [kluk] manto, palto, pelerin; **~-room** vestiyer; bagaj gişesi

clock [klog] *n.* masa saati; duvar saati; **two o'~** saat iki; **~wise** saat yelkovanlarının döndüğü yönde

clod [klod] toprak parçası, kesek

clog [klog] *n.* kütük; engel; *v/t* engel olm. -*e*

cloister ['kloysti] manastır

close [klus] *adj.* yakın, bitişik, dikkatli, sık, sıkı, dar; *n.* son; *v/t* kapamak, bitirmek; *v/i* kapanmak, sona ermek; **~ down** *v/t* kapamak; *v/i* kapanmak; **~ in on** -*in* etrafını çevirmek; **~d** kapalı

closet ['klozit] oda; dolap; helâ

clot [klot] *n.* pıhtı; *v/i* pıhtılaşmak

cloth [kloth] kumaş; bez; masa örtüsü; **lay the ~** sofrayı kurmak; **~e** [kluodh] *v/t* giydirmek, örtmek; **~es** [~z] *pl.* elbise(ler); **~es- -hanger** elbise askısı; **~es- -line** çamaşır ipi; **~ing** giyim; elbise

cloud [klaud] *n.* bulut; *v/t* bulutla örtmek; bulandırmak; *v/i* bulutlanmak; **~y** bulutlu; bulanık

clove[1] [kluv] karanfil (*bahar*)

clove[2], **~n** *s.* **cleave**

clover ['kluvı] yonca, tirfil

clown [klaun] palyaço, soytarı

club [klab] **1.** çomak, değnek; **2.** kulüp; **~(s** *pl.*) ispati, sinek

clue [kluu] *fig.* ipin ucu

clumsy ['klamzi] beceriksiz, acemi

clung [klaŋ] *s.* **cling**

cluster ['klastı] *n.* demet; salkım; küme; *v/i* toplanmak

clutch [klaç] *n.* tutma, kavrama; *tech.* debriyaj; *v/t* yakalamak, tutmak

coach [kouç] *n.* vagon; araba; hoca, antrenör; *v/t* hazırlamak, alıştırmak

coagulate [kou'ägyuleyt] *v/i* koyulaşmak, pıhtılaşmak

coal [kıul] kömür

coalition [kou'lışın] *pol.* koalisyon [(ocağı)

coal|-mine, ~-pit kömür⌋

coarse [kôs] kaba; bayağı

coast [kust] *n.* kıyı, sahil; *v/i* sahil boyunca gitmek; **~guard** sahil muhafızı

coat [kıut] *n.* ceket; kat, tabaka; palto, manto; hayvan postu; *v/t* kaplamak, örtmek; **~ of arms** arma; **~ing** kaplama; boya tabakası

coax [kuoks] *v/t* kandırmak
cob [kob] *bot.* mısır koçanı
cobble ['kobl] arnavut kaldırım taşı
cobra ['kıubrı] *zo.* kobra yılanı
cobweb ['kobweb] örümcek ağı
cocaine [kı'keyn] kokain
cock [kok] horoz; erkek kuş; musluk; tetik; **~chafer** *zo.* mayısböceği; **~ney** ['~ni] Londralı adam; **~pit** *av.* pilot yeri; **~roach** ['~ruç] *zo.* hamamböceği; **~scomb** ['~skuam] horoz ibiği; **~sure** kendinden fazla emin; **~tail** kokteyl
coco ['kuıkuı] *bot.* Hindistan cevizi ağacı; **~a** ['kuıkuı] kakao; **~nut** ['kuıkınat] Hindistan cevizi
cocoon [kı'kuun] koza
cod [kod] morina balığı
code [kud] *n.* kanun; şifre; *v/t* şifre ile yazmak
cod-liver oil balık yağı
co|-education ['kuuedyu-'keyşın] karma öğretim; **~erce** [kuu'ös] *v/t* zorlamak; **~existence** ['~ig'zistıns] bir arada var oluş
coffee ['kofi] kahve; **~-bean** kahve çekirdeği; **~-grounds** kahve telvesi; **~-mill** kahve değirmeni; **~-pot** kahve ibriği; cezve
coffin ['kofin] tabut
cog ['kog] çark dişi
cognac ['kunyäk] kanyak
cog-wheel dişli çark
cohe|re [kıu'hiı] *v/i* yapış-

mak, tutmak; **~rence, ~rency** tutarlık; **~rent** yapışık; uygun; **~sive** [~'hísiv] yapışık
coiffure [kwä'fyuı] saç biçimi
coil [koyl] *n.* kangal, roda; *el.* bobin; **~ (up)** *v/t* sarmak; *v/i* kıvrılmak, burulmak
coin [koyn] *n.* maden para, sikke; *v/t* basmak; uydurmak; **~age** para basma; para sistemi
coincide [kıuin'sayd] *v/i* tesadüf etm., uymak (**with -e**); **~nce** [ku'insidns] tesadüf; rastlantı
coke [kıuk] kok kömürü; *sl.* kokain
cold [kıuld] soğuk; soğukkanlı; nezle; **catch a ~** nezle olm., üşümek; **~ness** soğukluk; **~-storage room** soğuk hava deposu
colic ['kolik] *med.* sancı, kolik
collaborat|e [kı'läbıreyt] işbirliği yapmak; **~ion** işbirliği
collaps|e [kı'läps] *n.* çökme, yıkılma; *v/i* çökmek, düşmek, yıkılmak; **~ible** açılır kapanır
collar ['kolı] *n.* yaka; tasma; *v/t* yakalamak; **~-bone** *an.* köprücük
colleague ['koliğ] meslektaş
collect [kı'lekt] *v/t* toplamak, tahsil etm., biriktirmek; *v/i* birikmek, toplanmak; **~ed** aklı başında;

~ion topla(n)ma; koleksiyon; **~ive** toplu; **~or** koleksiyon sahibi, toplayan; tahsildar

college ['kɔlic] kolej; üniversite

collide [kɪ'layd] çarpmak (**with** -e); ['çarpışma (ile)

colliery [kɪ'kɔlyɪri] maden kömürü ocağı

collision [kɪ'lijɪn] çarp(ış)ma

colloquial [kɪ'lɪukwiɪl] konuşma diline ait

colon ['kɪulɪn] gr. iki nokta

colonel ['kɔnl] mil. albay

colonial [kɪ'lɪunyɪl] sömürgelere ait; **~ism** sömürgecilik

colon|ist ['kɔlnist] sömürgede yerleşen insan; **~ize** v/t sömürge kurmak -de; yerleşmek -e; **~y** sömürge; koloni

colo(u)r ['kʌlı] n. renk; boya; v/t boyamak; kızarmak; fig. olduğundan başka göstermek; **~ bar** ırk ayrımı; **~ed** renkli; zenci; beyaz ırka mensup olmıyan; **~s** pl. bayrak, bandıra; **~ful** renkli, canlı; **~ing** renk; **~less** renksiz

colt [kɪult] zo. tay, sıpa

column ['kɔlım] sütun, direk; gazete sütunu; mil. kol

coma ['kʌumɪ] med. koma

comb [kɪum] n. tarak; ibik; v/t taramak, taraklamak

combat ['kɔmbɪt] n. savaş, çarpışma; v/i dövüşmek, çarpışmak; **~ant** savaşçı

combin|ation [kɔmbi'neyşın] birleş(tir)me; kasa şifresi; **~e** [kɪm'bayn] v/t birleştirmek; v/i birleşmek; **~e-harvester** biçer-döver makinası

combusti|ble [kɪm'bʌstıbl] tutuşabilir; **~bles** pl. yanacak, yakıt sg.; **~on** [~stʃın] yanma

come [kʌm] gelmek (**to** -e); **to ~** gelecek; **~ about** olmak; **~ across** rast gelmek -e; **~ along** ilerlemek; acele etm.; birlikte gelmek; **~ at** varmak -e; **~ by** geçmek; **~ for** alıp götürmek -i; **~ in** girmek; **~ loose** çözülmek, gevşemek; **~ off** kopmak, olmak; **~ on!** Haydı gel!; **~ round** ayılmak; uğramak; **~ upon** rast gelmek -e; **~-back** thea. sahneye dönüş

comed|ian [kɪ'mīdyın] komik aktör; **~y** ['kɔmidi] komedi, komedya

comet ['kɔmit] astr. kuyruklu yıldız

comfort ['kʌmfıt] n. konfor, rahat(lık), refah; teselli; v/t teselli etm.; **~able** rahat, konforlu

comic|(al) ['kɔmik(ıl)] komik, gülünç; **~ strips** pl. karikatür şeklinde hikâye serisi sg.

comma ['kɔmı] gr. virgül

command [kɪ'mând] n. emir, komuta; otorite; v/t emretmek; kumanda etm.; hâkim olm. -e; **~er** komutan, kumandan; **~er-in- -chief** başkumandan; **~ment** *rel.* Allahın emri

commemorat|e [kɪ'memɪreyt] *v/t* kutlamak *-i*, *-in* hatırasını anmak; **~ion** kutlama, anma

commence [kɪ'mens] *v/t* başlamak *-e*; **~ment** başlangıç

commend [kɪ'mend] *v/t* övmek; emanet etm. (**to** *-e*)

comment [′koment] *n.* düşünce; tefsir, yorum; *v/i* tefsir etm., yorumlamak (**upon** *-i*); **~ary** ['~ɪntɪri] tefsir, şerh; **~ator** ['~enteyti] yorumcu, eleştirmeci

commerc|e [′komôs] ticaret; **~ial** [kɪ'môşıl] ticarî

commiseration [kɪmɪzı'reyşın] acıma

commission [kɪ'mişın] *n.* görev, vazife; emir, sipariş; komisyon; kurul; *v/t* yetki vermek *-e*; hizmete koymak *-i*; **~er** [~şnı] delege; komiser

commit [kɪ'mit] *v/t* teslim etm., tevdi etm.; işlemek; **~ment** taahhüt; **~tee** [~ti] komite; komisyon, kurul

commodity [kɪ'moditi] mal, ticaret eşyası

common [′komın] genel, ortak; bayağı; mutat; **in ~** ortaklaşa; **~ law** *jur.* örf ve âdete dayanan hukuk; **~ market** *ec.* ortak pazar; **~ sense** sağduyu; **~er** burjuva; **~place** adî, olağan; basma kalıp şey; **House of**

~s Avam Kamarası; **the British ~wealth** İngiliz Milletler Topluluğu

commotion [kɪ'muşın] heyecan, ayaklanma

commun|al ['komyunl] toplumsal; **~e** [′~yûn] komün

communicat|e [kɪ'myûnikeyt] *v/t* bildirmek; *v/i* haberleşmek (**with** ile); **~ion** tebliğ, haber; *pl.* ulaştırma *sg.*; **~ive** [~tiv] konuşkan

communion [kɪ'myûnyın] cemaat, birlik; *rel.* şarap içme ve yemek yeme ayini

communis|m ['komyunizm] komünizm; **~t** komünist

community [kɪ'myûniti] topluluk, cemaat

commute [kɪ'myût] *v/t* değiştirmek; *jur.* hafifletmek

compact ['kompäkt] sıkı, kesif; pudralık

companion [kɪm'pänyın] arkadaş; eş; ortak; **~ship** arkadaşlık; ortaklık

company ['kampını] grup; arkadaşlar, misafirler *pl.*; *ec.* kumpanya, ortaklık; *mil.* bölük

compar|able ['kompırbl] karşılaştırılabilir; **~ative** [kım'pärıtiv] orantılı; **~e** *v/t* karşılaştırmak; **beyond** (**without, past**) **~** eşsiz, üstün; **~ison** [~'pärisn] mukayese

compartment [kım'pâtmınt] bölme; kompartıman

compass ['kampıs] çevre; hacım; pusula; **(pair of)** **~es** *pl.* pergel *sg.*

compassion [kım'päşın] merhamet, acıma; **~ate** [~it] şefkatli

compatible [kım'pätıbl] uygun

compatriot [kım'pätriıt] vatandaş, yurttaş

compel [kım'pel] *v/t* zorlamak

compensat|e ['kompenseyt] *v/t* tazmin etm., telâfi etm.; **~ion** tazmin, telâfi; bedel, karşılık

compete [kım'pît] boy ölçüşmek, müsabakaya girmek **(for** için)

competen|ce [kım'kompitıns], **~cy** yetki; yeterlik; **~t** yetkili; yeterli

competit|ion [kompi'tişın] yarışma, rekabet; **~ive** [kım'petitiv] rekabet edilebilir; rakip olan; **~or** rakip

compile [kım'payl] *v/t* derlemek, toplamak

complacent [kım'pleysnt] kendini beğenmiş

complain [kım'pleyn] *v/i* şikâyet etm. **(about, of** *-den*); **~t** şikâyet; hastalık; dert

complet|e [kım'plît] *adj.* tam, tamam; eksiksiz; *v/t* tamamlamak, bitirmek; **~ion** tamamlama, bitirme

complex ['kompleks] karışık; bileşik; kompleks; **~ion** [kım'plekşın] ten, cilt

compliance [kım'playıns] rıza

complicate ['komplikeyt] *v/t* karıştırmak, güçleştirmek

compliment ['komplimınt] *n.* kompliman, iltifat; *v/t* kompliman yapmak **-e**, övmek *-i*

comply [kım'play] razı olm. **(with** *-e)*

component [kım'punınt] parça, unsur

compos|e [kım'pıuz] *v/t* yazmak, bestelemek; dizmek; **~ed** kendi halinde; ibaret **(of** *-den)*; **~er** *mus.* bestekâr; **~ition** [kompı'zişın] kompozisyon; terkip, bileşim; eser; **~ure** [kım'pıuji] sakinlik

compote ['kompot] komposto

compound ['kompaund] *adj.* bileşik; *n.* bileşim, alaşım; [kım'paund] *v/t* birleştirmek; **~ interest** *ec.* bileşik faiz

comprehen|d [kompri'hend] *v/t* anlamak, kavramak; içine almak; **~sible** anlaşılır; **~sion** anlayış, idrak; **~sive** şümullü, etraflı

compress [kım'pres] *v/t* sıkmak; *n. med.* kompres

comprise [kım'prayz] *v/t* kapsamak, ihtiva etm.

compromise ['komprımayz] *n.* uzlaşma; *v/t -in* şerefini tehlikeye atmak

compuls|ion [kım'palşın] zorlama; **~ory** mecburî

compunction [kım'paŋk-şın] vicdan azabı; pişmanlık

compute [kım'pyût] v/t hesaplamak; ~r tech. kompütür

comrade ['komrid] arkadaş; yoldaş; ~ship arkadaşlık

conceal [kın'sîl] v/t gizlemek, saklamak

conceit [kın'sît] kendini beğenmişlik, kibir; ~ed kibirli

conceiv|able [kın'sîvıbl] düşünülebilir; akla gelecek; ~e v/t düşünmek, kavramak; gebe olm. -den

concentrat|e ['konsıntreyt] v/t bir yere toplamak; v/i bir yere toplanmak; ~ion topla(n)ma; ~ion camp toplama kampı

conception [kın'sepşın] fikir, görüş; gebe olma

concern [kın'sön] n. ilgi; endişe; ec. firma, ortaklık; v/t ilgilendirmek; endişeye düşürmek; ~ed ilgili; endişeli; ~ing hakkında; dair -e

concert ['konsıt] konser

concession [kın'seşın] teslim; imtiyaz

conciliat|e [kın'silieyt] v/t uzlaştırmak, barıştırmak; ~ory [~ıtıri] barıştırıcı

concise [kın'says] muhtasar, kısa

conclu|de [kın'klûud] v/t bitirmek; sonuçlandırmak; akdetmek; ~sion [~jın] son, sonuç; akdetme; ~sive [~siv] son, kesin

concord ['koŋkôd] uygunluk; barış

concrete ['konkrît] beton; somut; belirli

concur [kın'kö] uymak, razı olm. (with -e)

concussion [kın'kaşın] (of the brain) med. sadme

condemn [kın'dem] v/t mahkûm etm.; ~ation [kondem'neyşın] mahkûmiyet

condense [kın'dens] v/t koyulaştırmak; kısaltmak; ~r el. kondansatör

condescend [kondi'send] tenezzülde bulunmak; ~ing tenezzül eden

condition [kın'dişın] durum, hal; koşul, şart; ~al şartlı, şarta bağlı; ~al clause gr. şart cümlesi; ~al (mood) gr. şart kipi

condole [kın'dul] taziyede bulunmak (with -e); ~nce taziye

conduct ['kondakt] n. davranış, tavır; [kın'dakt] v/t idare etm., yürütmek; nakletmek; ~ oneself davranmak; ~or [kın'daktı] orkestra şefi; biletçi; kondoktor

cone [kıun] koni, mahrut; bot. kozalak

confection [kın'fekşın] şekerleme; ~er [~ksı] şekerci, pastacı; ~ery şekerlemeler pl.; pastahane

confedera|cy [kın'fedırısı] pol. birlik; ~te [~it] adj. birleşmiş; ~eyt] v/i birleşmek; **~tion** birlik, konfederasyon

confer [kın'fö] v/i danışmak, görüşmek; v/t vermek **(on** -e); **~ence** ['konfırıns] müzakere, konferans

confess [kın'fes] v/t itiraf etm., ikrar etm.; **~ion** itiraf, ikrar; rel. günah çıkarma

confide [kın'fayd] v/t emanet etm. **(to** -e); v/i güvenmek **(in** -e); **~ence** ['konfidens] güven; emniyet; **~ent** emin, güvenli; **~ential** [~'denşıl] gizli, mahrem

confine [kın'fayn] v/t sınırlamak; hasretmek; **be ~d** yatakta yatmak; loğusa olm.; **~ment** hapis; loğusalık

confirm [kın'föm] v/t teyit etm., saptamak; **~ation** [konfı'meyşın] tasdik

confiscate [kın'fiskeyt] v/t müsadere etm.; **~ion** müsadere

conflagration [konflı'greyşın] yangın

conflict ['konflikt] n. aykırılık; çatışma; mücadele; [kın'flikt] v/i zıtlaşmak **(with** ile); muhalif olm. (-e)

conform [kın'föm] v/t uydurmak **(to** -e); v/i uymak **(to** -e); **~ity** uygunluk; **~ity with** uygun -e; mucibince

confound [kın'faund] v/t karıştırmak; **~ it!** Allahın cezası!

confront [kın'frant] v/t karşılaştırmak

confus|e [kın'fyûz] v/t karıştırmak, şaşırtmak; **~ed** karışık; şaşkın; **~ion** [~jın] karışıklık; şaşkınlık

congeal [kın'cîl] v/t dondurmak; v/i donmak

congestion [kın'cesçın] med. kan birikmesi; tıkanıklık

congratulat|e [kın'grätyuleyt] v/t tebrik etm.; **~ion** tebrik, kutlama

congregat|e ['kongrigeyt] v/i toplanmak, birleşmek; **~ion** rel. cemaat; toplantı

congress ['kongres] kongre; 2 Am. Millet Meclisi; **~man** Am. Millet Meclisi üyesi

conjecture [kın'cekçı] n. zan, sanı; v/t tahmin etm.

conjugal ['koncugıl] evlilikle ilgili

conjugat|e ['koncugeyt] gr. çekmek; **~ion** fiil çekimi

conjunct|ion [kın'cankşın] birleşme; gr. bağlaç; **~ive (mood)** gr. şart kipi

conjuncture [kın'cankçı] hal, durum; ec. konjonktür

conjure[1] [kın'cuı] v/t yalvarmak -e

conjure[2] ['kancı] **(up)** v/t büyü yolu ile çağırmak

connect [kın'nekt] v/t bağlamak, birleştirmek; **~ion** bağlantı; ilgi; **in this ~ion** bu münasebetle

connexion [kı'nekşın] s. **connection**

conque|r ['koŋkı] v/t fethetmek, zaptetmek; **~ror** fatih, galip; **~st** [~kwest] fetih; başarı

conscien|ce ['konşıns] vicdan; **~tious** [~şi'enşıs] vicdanının sesini dinliyen; temiz iş yapan; **~tious objector** pol. askerlik hizmetini reddeden kimse

conscious [~şıs] bilinçli, şuurlu; ayık; **be ~ of** -*in* farkında olm.; **~ness** bilinç, şuur, idrak

conscription [kın'skripşın] askere çağırma

consecrate ['konsikreyt] v/t takdis etm.

consecutive [kın'sekyutiv] art arda gelen; ardıl

consent [kın'sent] *n.* müsaade, muvafakat; v/t razı olm., muvafakat etm. (**to, in** -*e*)

consequen|ce ['konsikwıns] sonuç, akıbet; **~tly** adv. sonuç olarak

conservat|ion [konsö'veyşın] koruma, muhafaza; **~ive** [kın'sövıtiv] muhafazakâr

conserve [kın'söv] v/t muhafaza etm., korumak; **~s** pl. konserve sg.

consider [kın'sıdı] v/t addetmek, saymak; hesaba almak; düşünmek; incelemek; **~able** hayli; çok; önemli; **~ably** adv. oldukça; **~ate** [~rıt] saygılı, nazik; **~ation** itibar; saygı, nezaket; karşılık

consign [kın'sayn] v/t göndermek, teslim etm.; **~ment** sevk, teslim

consist [kın'sist] ibaret olm., mürekkep olm. (**of** -*den*); **~ency** koyuluk, kesafet; birbirini tutma; **~ent** birbirini tutan

consol|ation [konsı'leyşın] teselli; **~e** [kın'sıul] v/t teselli etm., avundurmak

consolidate [kın'solideyt] v/t sağlamlaştırmak; birleştirmek

consonant ['konsınınt] gr. sessiz harf

consort ['kon'sôt] eş

conspicuous [kın'spikyuıs] göze çarpan, âşikâr

conspir|acy [kın'spirısi] jur. gizli anlaşma; **~ator** suikastçı; **~e** [~'spayı] fesat maksadı ile anlaşmak

constable ['kanstıbl] polis memuru

constant ['konstınt] devamlı, sabit

consternation [konstö'neyşın] donup kalma, hayret

constipation [konsti'peyşın] *med.* peklik

constituen|cy [kın'stityuınsi] *pol.* seçim çevresi, seçmenler pl.; **~t** seçmen; öğe, unsur

constitut|e [kın'stityût] v/t teşkil etm.; tayin etm., atamak; kurmak; **~ion** terkip; bünye; *pol.* anayasa; **~ional** nel anayasaya uygun

constrain [kın'streyn] v/t zorlamak; **~t** zorlama, cebir

construct [kın'strakt] *v/t*
inşa etm., kurmak; **~ion**
yapı, bina; **~ive** yapıcı;
~or kurucu, yapıcı

consul ['konsıl] *pol.* konsolos; **~general** başkonsolos;
~ate ['~yulit] konsolosluk

consult [kın'salt] *v/t* başvurmak, müracaat etm. *-e*;
danışmak *-e*; **~ation** danışma; *med.* konsültasyon; **~ing hours**
pl. med. muayene saatleri

consum|e [kın'syûm] *v/t*
yiyip bitirmek, yoğaltmak;
~er yoğaltıcı; **~mate** [~'samit] *adj.* tam, mükemmel; ['konsımeyt] *v/t* tamamlamak; **~ption** [kın-'sampşın] yoğaltım; *med.*
verem

contact ['kontäkt] *n.* temas,
dokunma; *v/t* temasa geçmek (ile); **~ lense** kontakt
mercek   [bulaşıcı]

contagious [kın'teycıs] *adj.*

contain [kın'teyn] *v/t* ihtiva
etm., içine almak; **~er** kap;
konteyner

contaminat|e [kın'tämineyt] *v/t* kirletmek; bulaştırmak; **~ion** bulaştırma

contemplat|e ['kontempleyt] *v/t* seyretmek; düşünmek, tasarlamak; **~ion**
düşünme; **~ive** dalgın

contemporary [kın'tempırıri] çağdaş

contempt [kın'tempt] nefret, küçük görme; **~ible** alçak, rezil; **~uous** [~yuıs]
küçük gören, kibirli

contend [kın'tend] çarpışmak; müsabakaya girmek
(for için)

content [kın'tent] *n.* öz;
hacim; *adj.* memnun, razı;
v/t memnun etm.; **be ~**
yetinmek **(with** ile); **~ed**
memnun; **~s** ['kontents] *pl.*
içindekiler

contest ['kontest] *n.* yarışma, müsabaka; *v/t* itiraz
etm. *-e*; *v/i* müsabakaya
girmek

context ['kontekst] sözgelişi, münasebet

continent ['kontinınt] *geo.*
kıta; *adj.* [~'nentl] kıtaya
ait; Avrupa kıtasına ait

continu|al [kın'tinyul] devamlı, sürekli; **~ance** devam; *adj.* devam, uzatma; **~e** [~û] *v/t* devam etm.
-e; *v/i* devam etm., sürmek;
to be ~d arkası var; **~ous**
devamlı, sürekli

contort [kın'tôt] *v/t* burmak, bükmek

contour [,kontuı] dış hatlar
pl.   [çak mal·ı]

contraband [kontrı'-] ka-ʃ

contraceptive [kontrı'septiv] *med.* gebeliği önleyici

contract ['konträkt] *n.* sözleşme; [kın'träkt] *v/t* daraltmak, kısaltmak; *disease:* tutulmak *-e*; *v/i* daralmak, büzülmek; **~or** [kın-'träktı] mütaahhit

contradict [kontrı'dikt] *v/t*
yalanlamak, *-in* aksini söylemek; **~ion** yalanlama;
~ory aykırı

contrary ['kontrıri] ters, zıt; aykırı; karşı (**to** -*e*); **on the** ~ bilakis, tersine

contrast ['kontrâst] *n.* tezat, ayrılık; [kın'trâst] *v/t* karşılaştırmak; *v/i* ~ **with** -*in* tezadı olm.

contribut|e [kın'tribyut] *v/t* bağışlamak; *v/i* yazı vermek (**to** -*e*); ~**ion** [kontri'byûşın] yardım; iane; yazı; ~**or** [kın'tribyutı] yardım eden; yazı veren

contriv|ance [kın'trayvıns] buluş; hüner; tertibat, cihaz; ~**e** *v/t* icat etm., bulmak; başarmak

control [kın'trıul] *n.* kontrol, denetleme; *v/t* kontrol etm., denetlemek; ~**ler** murakıp

controvers|ial [kontrı'vöşıl] çekişmeli; ~**y** ['~vösi] çekişme, münakaşa

contus|e [kın'tyûz] *v/t* berelemek; ~**ion** [~jın] bere, çürük

convalesce [konvı'les] iyileşmek; ~**nce** nekahet; ~**nt** iyileşen, şifa bulan

convenience [kın'vînyıns] uygunluk, rahatlık; **at your earliest** ~ müsait en yakın zamanınızda; **public** ~ umumî helâ

convenient [kın'vînyınt] uygun; rahat

convent ['konvınt] manastır; ~**ion** [kın'venşın] toplantı; anlaşma; ~**ional** göreneksel

convers|ation [konvı'sey-

şın] konuşma, sohbet; ~**e** [kın'vös] konuşmak, görüşmek (**with** ile)

conver|sion [kın'vöşın] değiş(tir)me; *rel.* ihtida; ~**t** *n. rel.* dönme, mühtedi; *v/t* değiştirmek; ~**tible** değiştirilebilir; kabriyole

convey [kın'vey] *v/t* taşımak, götürmek; ifade etm.; ~**ance** taşıma, nakil; taşıt; ~**or** (**belt**) *tech.* taşıma bandı

convict ['konvikt] *n.* mahkûm, suçlu; *v/t* suçlandırmak (**of** ile); ~**ion** inanç; suçlandırma

convince [kın'vins] *v/t* inandırmak ~**e** (**of** -*i*)

convoke [kın'vıuk] *v/t* toplantıya çağırmak

convoy [k'konvoy] *n.* konvoy; *v/t* rehberlik etm.

convuls|ion [kın'valşın] ihtilâç, çırpınma; ~**ive** ihtilâç gibi

cook [kuk] *n.* aşçı; *v/t* pişirmek; *v/i* pişmek; ~**ing** pişirme (sanatı)

cool [kuul] *adj.* serin, soğuk; soğukkanlı; *v/t* soğutmak, serinletmek; *v/i* serinleşmek; ~**er** *tech.* soğutma cihazı; ~**ness** serinlik; soğukkanlılık

co-op ['kuop] *s.* **co-operative** (**society**)

co(-)operat|e [kıu'opıreyt] *v/i* işbirliği yapmak, birlikte çalışmak; ~**ion** işbirliği; ~**ive** [~ıtiv] *n.* kooperatif; *adj.* işbirliği yapan; ~**ive**

society tüketim koopera-
tifi; **~or** iş arkadaşı
co(-)ordinate [kuˈôdineyt]
v/t ayarlamak; düzeltmek
cop [kop] *vulg.* polis memuru
co-partner ['kɪuˈpâtnɪ] ortak
cope [kup] boy ölçmek
(**with** ile)
co-pilot ['kɪuˈpaylɪt] *av.*
ikinci pilot
copious ['kɪupyɪs] bol, mebzul
copper ['kopɪ] bakır; kazan;
bakır para
copy ['kopi] *n.* kopya, nüsha; örnek; *v/t* kopya etm.,
-*in* suretini çıkarmak; **~-
book** defter; **~right** telif
hakkı
coral ['korɪl] mercan
cord [kôd] *n.* ip, sicim, şerit; *v/t* iple bağlamak
cordial ['kôdyɪl] samimî,
candan; **~ity** [~iˈâliti] sami-
miyet [kadife\
corduroy ['kôdɪroy] fitilli\
core [kô] iç, öz; *bot.* göbek
cork [kôk] *n.* mantar; tapa;
v/t mantarla kapamak; **~-
screw** tirbuşon, tapa bur-
gusu
corn [kôn] *n.* hububat; buğday; *Am.* mısır; *med.* nasır;
v/t tuzlayıp kurutmak; **~-
cob** mısır koçanı
corner ['kônɪ] *n.* köşe, köşe-
başı; *v/t* çıkmaza sokmak;
~ed köşeli
cornet ['kônit] *mus.* kornet;
kâğıt külâh

---

corrupt

coronation [korɪˈneyşın]
taç giydirme
coroner ['korɪnɪ] *jur.* şüpheli ölüm vakalarını tahkik
eden memur
corpor|al ['kôpırıl] bedenî;
mil. onbaşı; **~ate** [~rit] or-
taklığa ait; birlik olmuş,
toplu; **~ation** birlik; *jur.*
tüzel kişi; anonim ortaklık
corps [kô] *mil.* kolordu;
Diplomatic ♀ kordiplo-
matik
corpse [kôps] ceset
corpulent ['kôpyulınt] şişman
corral [kôˈrâal, *Am.* kıˈrâl]
ağıl
correct [kɪˈrekt] *adj.* doğru,
sahih; dürüst; münasip;
v/t düzeltmek; cezalandırmak; **~ion** tashih; cezalan-
dırma
correspond [korisˈpond]
mektuplaşmak (**with** ile);
uymak, uygun gelmek (**to**
-*e*); **~ence** mektuplaşma;
~ent muhabir
corridor ['koridô] koridor
corrigible ['koricıbl] düzel-
tilebilir
corroborate [kɪˈrobıreyt]
v/t doğrulamak
corro|de [kɪˈrıud] *v/t* aşın-
dırmak, çürütmek; **~sion**
[~jın] aşınma; paslanma;
~sive *tech.* aşındırıcı madde
corrugated iron ['koru-
geytid -] *tech.* oluklu demir
levha
corrupt [kɪˈrapt] *adj.* çürü-

müş; rüşvet yiyen; *v/t* bozmak, ayartmak; **~ion** rüşvet yeme

corset ['kôsit] korsa

cosmetic [koz'metik] makiyaja ait; kozmetik

cosm|ic ['kozmik] kozmik; **~onaut** ['~minôt] kozmonot; **~os** ['~mos] kozmos, acun

cost [kost] *n.* fiat, değer; zarar, masraf; *v/t* -*in* fiatı olm., malı olm.; **~ly** değerli; pahalı

costume ['kostyûm] kostüm, elbise; kıyafet

cosy ['kuzi] rahat, keyifli

cot [kot] yatak, portatif karyola [köşk\

cottage ['kotic] küçük ev,∫

cotton ['kotn] pamuk, pamuk bezi; pamuklu; **~ wool** hidrofil pamuk; *Am.* ham pamuk

couch [kauç] *n.* yatak; divan; *v/i* yatmak; çömelmek

cough [kof] *n.* öksürük; *v/i* öksürmek

could [kud] *s.* **can**

council ['kaunsl] meclis, divan, konsey; **~(l)or** ['~silı] meclis üyesi

counsel ['kaunsl] *n.* danışma; nasihat; *jur.* avukat, dava vekili; *v/t* öğüt vermek -*e*; **~(l)or** ['~slı] müşavir

count¹ [kaunt] kont

count² *n.* sayma, hesap; *v/t* saymak, hesap etm., hesaba katmak; **~-down** hazırlık devresi

countenance ['kauntinıns] yüz, çehre

counter¹ ['kauntı] tezgâh; sayaç; marka

counter² *adj.* karşı, aykırı (**to** -*e*); *v/t* karşılamak, önlemek; **~act** *v/t* [\~'äkt] karşılamak, önlemek; **~balance** [\~'bälıns] *v/t* denkleştirmek; **~espionage** karşı casusluk; **~feit** ['~fit] *adj.* sahte; *n.* taklit; *v/t* taklit etm.; **~foil** ['~foyl] makbuz koçanı; **~intelligence** ['~rintelicıns] *s.* **~espionage**

countess ['kauntis] kontes

count|ing-house *ec.* muhasebe dairesi; **~less** sayısız, hesapsız

country ['kantri] memleket, yurt, vatan; taşra, kır; **in the ~** kırda, köyde; **~ house** yazlık; **~man** yurttaş, vatandaş; **~side** kır, kırlık; **~-town** kasaba

county ['kaunti] kontluk; vilâyet, il; *Am.* kaza, ilçe

coupl|e ['kapl] *n.* çift; *v/t* birleştirmek, bağlamak; **~ing** *tech.* kavrama

coupon ['kuupon] kupon

courage ['karic] cesaret, mertlik; **~ous** [kı'reycıs] cesur, yiğit

courier ['kurıı] haberci, kuriye

course [kôs] yol, rota; yön; pist; *ec.* rayiç; kurs, ders; **in due ~** sırası gelince; **of ~** tabiî, elbette; **matter of ~** tabiîlik

court [kôt] *n.* avlu; alan,
kort; *jur.* mahkeme; saray;
v/t kur yapmak -e; ~ **of
justice** mahkeme; **~eous**
['kôtyıs] nazik, kibar; **~esy**
['kôtisi] nezaket, saygı; **~ier**
['kôtyı] saraylı; **~martial**
askerî mahkeme; **~ship** kur
yapma; **~yard** avlu

cousin ['kazn] kuzen, kuzin,
amca (*veya* dayı, hala,
teyze) çocuğu

cover ['kavı] *n.* kap, örtü,
kılıf; zarf; sığınak, siper;
v/t kaplamak, örtmek; saklamak; gizlemek; yazmak;
distance: almak, katetmek;
damage: karşılamak; **~age**
olayın takip edilip yazıl-
ması; **~ing** örtü

covet ['kavit] *v/t* şiddetle
arzu etm.; **~ous** açgözlü

cow [kau] inek, dişi
manda

coward ['kauıd] korkak,
yüreksiz; **~ice** ['~is] korkak-
lık; **~ly** korkak, alçak

cowboy kovboy

cower ['kauı] *v/i* çömelmek

cow|-hide sığır derisi; **~slip**
bot. çuhaçiçeği; *Am.* mer-
zagı nergis

cox|comb ['kokskıum] züp-
pe, hoppa; **~swain** ['~
sweyn, 'koksn] dümenci

coy [koy] çekingen, ürkek

crab [kräb] *zo.* yengeç

crack [kräk] *n.* çatlak, yarık,
çatırtı; şaklama; darbe; *v/t*
kırmak, yarmak; çatlatmak;
şaklatmak; *v/i* kırılmak,
çatlamak; şaklamak; **~er**

gevrek bisküvit; patlangaç;
~le *v/i* çatırdamak

cradle ['kreydl] *n.* beşik; *v/t*
beşiğe yatırmak

craft [kräft] hüner; sanat;
hile; *mar.* gemi; **~sman**
sanat erbabı, sanatkâr, usta;
~y kurnaz

crag [kräg] sarp kayalık

cram [kräm] *v/t* doldurmak, tıkmak

cramp [krämp] *n. med.*
kramp; *tech.* mengene, kenet; *v/t* kenetlemek; kısıtlamak

cranberry ['kränbıri] *bot.*
kırmızı yaban mersini

crane [kreyn] *n. zo.* turna
kuşu; *tech.* maçuna; *v/t
boynunu* uzatmak

crank [kränk] *tech.* manivela, kol; garip adam; **~ up**
v/t hareket ettirmek; **~
shaft** *tech.* krank mili

crape [kreyp] krep; siyah
tül

crash [kräş] *n.* çatırtı; şan-
gırtı; *av.* düşüp parçalan-
ma; *ec.* iflâs; *v/t* kırmak;
v/i kırılmak; *av.* düşüp
parçalanmak; **~helmet**
motosikletçi miğferi; **~
-landing** *av.* mecburî iniş

crate [kreyt] kafesli sandık

crater ['kreytı] *geo.* krater;
huni şeklinde çukur

crav|e [kreyv] şiddetle arzu
etm. (**for** -*i*); **~ing** şiddetli
arzu

crawl [krôl] sürünmek,
emeklemek; krol yüzmek

crayfish 240

crayfish ['kreyfiş] zo. kerevides

crayon ['kreyın] renkli kalem

crazy ['kreyzi] çılgın, deli

creak [krîk] gıcırdamak

cream [krîm] n. krema, kaymak; krem; fig. kalbur üstü; v/t -in kaymağını almak; ~ cheese yumuşak peynir; ~y kaymaklı; krem gibi

crease [krîs] n. kırma; ütü çizgisi; v/t buruşturmak

create [krî'eyt] v/t yaratmak, meydana getirmek; ~ion yaradılış, yaratma; evren; ~ive adj.; ~or n. yaratıcı; ~ure ['krîçı] yaratık

credentials [kri'denşılz] pl. itimatname sg.

credible ['kredıbl] inanılabilir

credit ['kredit n. ec. kredi; güven, itibar; v/t inanmak -e; ec. matluba geçirmek -i; letter of ~ ec. akreditif; on ~ veresiye; ~ card kredi kartı; ~able şerefli; ~or alacaklı

credulous ['kredyulıs] her şeye inanan

creed [krîd] iman, itikat

creek [krîk] koy; Am. dere, çay

creep [krîp] sürünmek; ürpermek; sarılmak; ~er sürüngen; ~y tüyler ürpertici

cremate [kri'meyt] v/t ölüyü yakmak; ~ion yakma

crept [krept] s. creep

crescent ['kresnt] dilim ay, ayça

cress [kres] bot. tere

crest [krest] ibik; miğfer püskülü; tepe, zirve; ~fallen üzgün, yılgın

Crete [krît] Girit adası

crevasse [kri'väs] buzul yarığı; ~ice ['krevis] çatlak, yarık

crew¹ [kruu] tayfa, takım

crew² s. crow

crib [krib] yemlik; çocuk yatağı

cricket ['krikit] zo. cırcırböceği; kriket oyunu

crime [kraym] cinayet, suç, cürüm

Crimea [kray'mîı] Kırım

criminal ['kriminl] n. suçlu, cani; adj. ağır cezalarla ilgili

crimson ['krimzn] fes rengi

cringe [krinc] v/i köpeklemek

cripple [kripl] adj. sakat, topal, kötürüm; v/t sakatlamak

crisis ['kraysis] pl. ~es ['~îz] buhran, kriz

crisp [krisp] kıvırcık; gevrek

criterion [kray'tiırin] ölçüt

critic ['kritik] eleştirici, münekkit; ~al tenkitçi; vahim, tehlikeli; ~ism ['~sizm] tenkit; ~ize ['~sayz] v/t eleştirmek; kusur bulmak -de [bağırmak]

croak [kruak] vak vak etmek

Croat, ~ian ['kruat, kru'eyşın] Hırvat

crochet ['krıuşey] *v/i* kroşe yapmak

crockery ['krokıri] çanak çömlek

crocodile ['krokıdayl] *zo.* timsah

crocus ['kruıkıs] *bot.* çiğdem

crook [kruk] *n.* kanca; değnek; *sl.* dolandırıcı; *v/t* bükmek; **~ed** ['~id] eğri, çarpık

crop [krop] *n.* kursak; ekin, ürün; *v/t* kesmek, biçmek; **~ up** meydana çıkmak

cross [kros] *n.* haç, salip; çarmıh, ıstavros; çapraz işareti; *v/t* geçmek, aşmak; karıştırmak; çapraz koymak *-e*; *adj.* dargın, öfkeli; **~ off** *or* **out** *v/t* çizmek, silmek; **~ oneself** ıstavroz çıkarmak; **~-examination** *jur.* sorgu; **~ing** geçit; **~-road** yan yol; *pl.* dört yol ağzı; **~word (puzzle)** çapraz bilmece

crouch [krauç] çömelmek, eğilmek

crow [krıu] *zo.* karga; *v/i* ötmek; **~bar** *tech.* kaldıraç

crowd [kraud] *n.* kalabalık; halk; yığın; *v/t* doldurmak, sıkıştırmak; *v/i* toplanmak, birikmek; **~ed** kalabalık, dolu

crown [kraun] *n.* taç; kuron; tepe; *v/t* taç giydirmek *-e*

crucial ['kruuşıl] kesin, önemli

cruci|fix ['kruusifiks] çar-

mıh; **~fixion** [~'fikşın] çarmıha ger(il)me; **~fy** *v/t* çarmıha germek

crude [kruud] ham; kaba

cruel [kruil] zalim, gaddar; **~ty** zulüm, gaddarlık

cruise [kruuz] *n.* deniz gezintisi; *v/i* gemi ile gezmek; **~r** kruvazör

crumb [kram] ekmek kırıntısı; **~le** ['~bl] *v/t* ufalamak, parçalamak; *v/i* ufalmak

crumple ['krampl] *v/i* buruşmak; **~ (up)** *v/t* buruşturmak

crunch [kranç] *v/t* çiğnemek, ezmek

crusade [kruu'seyd] Haçlılar seferi; **~r** Haçlı

crush [kraş] *n.* kalabalık; ezme; *v/t* ezmek, sıkıştırmak

crust [krast] *n.* kabuk; *v/t* kabukla kaplamak; **~y** kabuklu; huysuz

crutch [kraç] koltuk değneği

cry [kray] *n.* bağırma; ağlama; *v/i* bağırmak; ağlamak

crypt [kript] *arch.* yeraltı kemer *veya* türbe

crystal ['kristl] kristal, billur; **~lize** *v/t ir* billurlaştırmak   [rusu]

cub [kab] *zo.* hayvan yav-

cub|e [kyûb] küp; **~e root** *math.* küp kök; **~ic** kübik

cubicle ['kyûbikl] odacık

cuckoo ['kukuu] *zo.* guguk kuşu

cucumber [kyûkambı] *bot.* hıyar, salatalık

cuddle ['kadl] v/t kucaklamak

cudgel ['kacıl] n. sopa, değnek; v/t dövmek

cue [kyuı] işaret; isteka

cuff [kaf] kolluk, yen; tokat;
~link kol düğmesi

culminat|e ['kalmineyt]
zirvesine ermek, sonuçlanmak; ~ion en yüksek de-
rece   [mücrim]

culprit ['kalprit] suçlu,]

cult [kalt] ibadet, tapınma;
~ivate ['~iveyt] v/t işlemek, yetiştirmek; ~ivation
tarım; toprağı işleme; yetiştirme; ~ivator çiftçi

cultur|al ['kalçırıl] kültü-
rel; uygarlığa ait; ~e ['~çı]
kültür; ~ed kültürlü

cum(m)in ['kamin] bot.
kimyon

cumul|ative ['kyumyulıtiv]
birikmiş, biriken; ~us ['~
lıs] yığın; höyük

cunning ['kanin] kurnaz,
açıkgöz; kurnazlık, şeytan-
lık

cup [kap] fincan, kâse, bardak; kupa; ~board ['ka-
bıd] dolap; ~ful fincan
dolusu

cupola ['kyüpılı] kubbe

cura|ble ['kyuırıbl] tedavisi
kabil; ~te ['~rit] papaz
muavini; ~tor ['~'reytı]
müdür

curbstone [köb-] s. kerb-
stone

curd [köd] kesilmiş süt,
beyaz peynir; ~le v/i süt:
kesilmek; v/t kesmek

cure [kyuı] n. tedavi, şifa;
v/t tedavi etm.; tuzlamak,
tütsülemek

curfew ['köfyü] jur. sokağa
çıkma yasağı

curio|sity [kyuuri'ositi] me-
rak; az bulunan veya tuhaf
şey; ~us ['~ıs] meraklı; tuhaf

curl [köl] n. büküm; bukle;
v/t kıvırmak; v/i kıvrılmak;
~y kıvırcık

currant ['karınt] bot. frenk-
üzümü

curren|cy ['karınsi] revaç;
döviz; ~t akıntı, cereyan;
akım; cari; bugünkü

curricul|um [kı'rikyulım]
pl. ~a [~ı] müfredat pro-
gramı; ~um vitae [~'vaytî]
hal tercümesi

curse [kös] n. lânet, beddua,
küfür; v/t lânetlemek

curt [köt] kısa, sert

curtail [kö'teyl] v/t kısaltmak, kısmak

curtain ['kötn] perde

curts(e)y ['kötsi] diz büke-
rek reverans

curve [köv] n. kavis, eğri,
viraj; v/t eğmek; v/i eğilmek; ~d kavisli; virajlı

cushion ['kuşın] n. yastık;
minder; v/t kıtıkla doldurmak

custody ['kastıdi] muhafaza; nezaret

custom ['kastım] âdet, örf,
görenek; pl. gümrük; ~ary
alışılmış, âdet olan; ~er
müşteri; ~house gümrük
dairesi

cut [kat] *n.* kesim, kesme; kesinti; tenzilât; yara; biçim; kalıp; *adj.* kesik, kesilmiş; *v/t* kesmek, biçmek; kısaltmak; selâm vermek *-e;* **power** ~ *el.* akımın kesilmesi; **short** ~ kestirme yol; **~ down** kesip devirmek; **~ off** kesip koparmak; ayırmak; **~ out** kesip çıkarmak; **~ up** doğramak; **~ back** kesinti

cute [kyút] açıkgöz; zarif, hoş

cuticle ['kyútikl] *an.* üstderi; tırnakları çevreliyen ölü deri   [mı]

cutlery ['katlıri] sofra takı-⌡

cutlet ['katlit] pirzola

cut|off *Am.* kestirme yol; **~**

purse yankesici; **~ter** kesici; *naut.* kotra; **~ting** keskin, kesici; kesilip çıkarılmış gazete makalesi

cycl|e ['saykl] *n.* devir, devre; bisiklet; *v/i* bisikletle gitmek; **~ist** bisikletçi

cyclone ['sayklun] siklon, kiklon

cylinder ['silindi] silindir

cynic ['sinik] *n.,* **~al** *adj.* kötü gözle gören, alaycı; **~ism** kinizm

cypress ['saypris] *bot.* servi

Cypr|iot ['sipriot] Kıbrıslı; **~us** ['sayprıs] Kıbrıs

cyst [sist] *med.* kist

Czech [çek] Çek; **~oslovakia** ['çekuıslu'väkıı] Çekoslovakya

D

dab [däb] *v/t* hafifçe vurmak *-e*

dad|(dy) [däd(i)] baba, babacık; **~dy-longlegs** *zo.* sivrisinek; *Am. uzun bacaklı örümcek çeşidi*

daffodil ['däfıdil] *bot.* fulya, zerrin, nergis

dagger ['dägı] hançer, kama

dahlia ['deylyı] *bot.* dalya, yıldız çiçeği

daily ['deyli] günlük, her gün

dainty ['deynti] nefis; ince; lezzetli

dairy ['däıri] süthane; sütçü dükkânı

daisy ['deyzi] *bot.* papatya

dale [deyl] vadi, dere

dam [däm] *n.* baraj, bent; *v/t* bentle durdurmak

damage ['dämic] *n.* zarar; *pl.* tazminat; *v/t* zarar vermek *-e,* bozmak *-i*

Damas|cus [dı'mâskıs] Şam; **2k** ['dämisk] damasko

damn [däm] *v/t* lânetlemek; **~ation** [~'neyşın] lânet, kargıma

damp [dämp] *adj.* rutubetli, nemli; *n.* rutubet; *v/t* ıslatmak; **~en** *v/t* söndürmek, azaltmak

danc|e [dâns] *v/t, v/i* dansetmek; *n.* dans; **~er** danseden; dansöz

dandelion 244

dandelion ['dändilayın]
bot. kara hindiba

dandruff ['dändraf] an. kepek, konak

Dane [deyn] Danimarkalı

danger ['deynci] tehlike;
~ous ['~crıs] tehlikeli

dangle ['dängl] v/i asılıp
sallanmak; v/t sallamak

Danish ['deyniş] Danimar-
kalı

dar|e [däı] v/i (inf.) cesaret
etm., kalkışmak -(meğ)e; I
~e say diyebilirim ki; her
halde; ~ing cüretli; cesaret

dark [dâk] karanlık; koyu;
~ brown esmer; ~en v/t
karartmak; v/i kararmak;
~ness karanlık; koyuluk

darling ['dâlin] sevgili

darn [dân] v/t örerek tamir
etm.

dart [dât] n. cirit, kargı;
hızla atılma; v/t fırlatmak;
v/i hızla atılmak (at, on -e)

dash [däş] n. saldırma;
hamle; darbe, vuruş; az
miktar; çizgi; v/i atılmak,
fırlamak (at -e); v/t fırlatmak; hope: kırmak; ~board
tech. kontrol paneli; ~ing
atılgan

data ['deytı] pl. veriler;
bilgi sg.

date¹ [deyt] bot. hurma

date² n. tarih, zaman; randevu; v/t tarih koymak -e;
v/i tarihli olm.; out of ~
modası geçmiş; up to ~
modern, modaya uygun

dative ['deytiv] (case) gr. -e
hali, datif

daub [dôb] v/t bulaştır-
mak

daughter ['dôtı] kız, kız
evlât; ~-in-law gelin

dawdle ['dôdl]: ~(away) v/t
avare geçirmek

dawn [dôn] n. fecir, tan,
gün ağarması; v/i gün ağarmak

day [dey] gün; gündüz; zaman; ~ off boş gün; the
other ~ geçenlerde; ~ by ~
günden güne; ~break tan,
şafak; ~labo(u)rer gün-
delikçi; ~light gün ışığı,
aydınlık; ~time gündüz

daze [deyz] v/t kamaştır-
mak, sersemletmek

dazzle ['däzl] v/t -in gözünü
kamaştırmak

dead [ded] ölü, ölmüş; solgun; duygusuz; the ~ pl.
ölüler; ~ tired çok yorgun,
bitkin; ~end çıkmaz yol;
~line son teslim tarihi;
~lock çıkmaz; durgunluk;
~ly öldürücü; ölüm derece-
sinde

deaf [def] sağır; ~en v/t sağır etm.; ~ness sağırlık

deal [dîl] n. miktar; alışveriş; anlaşma; v/t dağıtmak;
v/i meşgul olm., uğraşmak
(with ile); ~ in ... ticareti
yapmak; a great ~ of bir
hayli; ~er tüccar, satıcı;
~ings pl. ilişkiler; ~t [delt]
s. deal

dean [dîn] dekan

dear [dir] sevgili; pahalı; ♀
Sir Sayın Bay ...

death [deth] ölüm, vefat;

deduce

~ly öldürücü; **~rate** ölüm oranı

debar [di'bâ] v/t mahrum etm. **(from** *-den)*

debase [di'beys] v/t alçaltmak

debate [di'beyt] n. tartışma; v/t tartışmak

debauchery [di'bôçıri] sefahat

debit ['debit] n. ec. borç, açık; v/t *-in* zimmetine geçirmek

debris ['deybrî] enkaz pl.

debt [det] borç; **~or** borçlu

decade ['dekeyd] on yıl

decadence ['dekıdıns] inhitat, çöküş

decapitate [di'käpiteyt] v/t *-in* başını kesmek

decay [di'key] n. çürüme, bozulma; v/i çürümek, bozulmak

decease [di'sîs] n. vefat; v/i vefat etm.

deceit [di'sît] hile(kârlık), yalan; **~ful** aldatıcı, hilekâr

deceive [di'sîv] v/t aldatmak; yalan söylemek *-e*

decelerate [di'selıreyt] v/i yavaşlamak

December [di'sembı] aralık (ayı)

decen|cy [di'dînsi] terbiye; iffet; **~t** edepli, terbiyeli

deception [di'sepşın] aldatma, hile

decide [di'sayd] v/t kararlaştırmak; karar vermek (hakkında); **~d** kesin

decimal ['desimıl] math. ondalık

decipher [di'sayfı] v/t *-in* şifresini çözmek

decisi|on [di'sijın] karar, hüküm; sebat; **~ve** [di'saysiv] katî, kesin

deck [dek] naut. güverte; **~chair** şezlong

declar|ation [deklı'reyşın] beyanname; bildiri; **~e** [di'klä] v/t bildirmek, ilân etm., beyan etm.

declension [di'klenşın] gr. isim çekimi

decline [di'klayn] n. inme; inhitat; v/i azalmak, kuvvetten düşmek; v/t reddetmek, kabul etmemek; gr. çekmek

declivity [di'kliviti] iniş, meyil

decode [di'kıud] v/t *-in* şifresini çözmek

decorat|e [di'dekıreyt] v/t süslemek, donatmak; nişan vermek *-e*; **~ion** süs, nişan, madalya; **~ive** ['~ırıtiv] süsleyici; **~or** dekoratör

decoy ['dîkoy] n. tuzak, yem; v/t tuzağa düşürmek

decrease [di'krîs] n. azalma; [di'krîs] v/t azaltmak; v/i azalmak

decree [di'krî] n. hüküm, karar; v/t kararlaştırmak

decrepit [di'krepit] dermansız, zayıf

dedicat|e ['dedikeyt] v/t vakfetmek, adamak **(to** *-e)*; **~ion** tahsis, ithaf

deduce [di'dyûs] v/t anlamak, sonuç çıkarmak **(from** *-den)*

deduct

deduct [di'dakt] v/t hesaptan çıkarmak; **~ion** çıkarılan miktar; sonuç

deed [dîd] iş, eylem; hareket; belge

deep [dîp] adj. derin; koyu (colour); tok (voice); n. derinlik; **~en** v/t derinleştirmek; artırmak; v/i derinleşmek; **~-freeze** dipfriz; **~ness** derinlik; tokluk

deer [dii] zo. geyik, karaca

deface [di'feys] v/t bozmak

defame [di'feym] v/t iftira etm. -e

defeat [di'fît] n. yenilgi, bozgun; v/t yenmek

defect [di'fekt] kusur, eksiklik; **~ive** kusurlu, noksan

defen|ce, Am. **~se** [di'fens] müdafaa, savunma; **~d** v/t müdafaa etm., savunmak; **~dant** jur. davalı; **~er** koruyucu; **~sive** müdafaa; savunmalık

defer [di'fö] v/t ertelemek

defian|ce [di'fayns] meydan okuma; **~t** karşı gelen, serkeş

deficien|cy [di'fişnsi] eksiklik; açık; **~t** noksan, eksik

deficit ['defisit] ec. açık

defile ['dîfayl] geçit, boğaz

defin|e [di'fayn] v/t tanımlamak; sınırlamak; **~ite** ['definit] kesin; belirli; **~ition** tarif; tanım; **~itive** [di'finitiv] kesin; son

deflat|e [di'fleyt] v/t -in havasını boşaltmak; **~ion** ec. deflasyon

deflect [di'flekt] v/t saptırmak, çevirmek

deform [di'fôm] v/t bozmak, çirkinleştirmek; **~ed** biçimsiz, çirkin

defrost [di'frost] v/t -in buzlarını çözmek

defy [di'fay] v/t -in alnını karışlamak; dayanmak -e

degenerat|e [di'cenirit] adj. soysuzlaşmış; [.reyt] v/t soysuzlaşmak; **~ion** [.'reyşın] soysuzlaşma

degrade [di'greyd] v/t alçaltmak, -in rütbesini indirmek

degree [di'gri] derece, mertebe; **by ~s** derece derece, gittikçe

dejected [di'cektid] kederli

delay [di'ley] n. gecikme, tehir; v/t geciktirmek; v/i gecikmek

delegat|e ['deligit] n. delege; [.'geyt] v/t göndermek, delege etm.; **~ion** [.'gey-şın] delegasyon

deliberat|e [di'librit] adj. kasti, kasıtlı; [.eyt] v/t düşünmek, tartmak; **~ion** [.'reyşın] düşünme; tartışma

delica|te [di'delikit] nazik, ince; **~tessen** [.'tesn] mezeci dükkânı

delicious [di'lişıs] nefis, hoş

delight [di'layt] n. zevk, sevinç; v/t sevindirmek; zevk vermek -e; v/i sevinmek; **~ful** hoş, zevkli

delinquen|cy [di'linkwınsi] kabahat; suçluluk; **~t** suçlu

deliver [di'livı] *v/t* kurtartarmak; teslim etm., vermek; dağıtmak; **be ~ed of** doğurmak *-i*; **~ance** kurtuluş; **~y** teslim; dağıtım; doğurma   [mak]
delude [di'luud] *v/t* aldat-]
deluge ['delyuc] tufan, sel
delusi|on [di'luujın] aldatma, aldanma; vehim; **~ve** [~siv] aldatıcı
demand [di'mând] *n.* talep, istem; istek; *v/t* istemek; gerektirmek
demeano(u)r [di'mînı] tavır, davranış
demi- ['demi] yarı
demilitarize [~'di'mîlıtırayz] *v/t* askersiz hale getirmek
demise [di'mayz] *jur.* vefat, ölüm
demobilize [di'mıubilayz] *v/t mil.* terhis etm.
democra|cy [di'mokrısı] demokrasi; **~t** ['demıkrät] demokrat; **~tic** [~'krätik] demokratik
demoli|sh [di'moliş] *v/t* yıkmak; **~tion** [demı'lişın] yıkma, tahrip
demon ['dîmın] şeytan, cin
demonstrat|e ['demınstreyt] *v/t* ispat etm. göstermek; *v/i* nümayiş yapmak; **~ion** ispat, gösterme; nümayiş; **~ive** [di'monstrıtiv] işaret eden, gösteren; **~or** [~'demınstreytı] nümayişçi
demoralize [di'morılayz] *v/t -in* ahlâkını bozmak

den [den] in, mağara; küçük oda
denial [di'nayıl] inkâr, yalanlama; ret
Denmark ['denmâk] Danimarka
denomination [dinomi'neyşın] ad(landırma); *rel.* mezhep
denote [di'nıut] *v/t* göstermek
denounce [di'nauns] *v/t* suçlamak; *-in* feshini bildirmek
dens|e [dens] sık, kesif; **~ity** kesafet, sıklık
dent [dent] *n.* çentik; *v/t* çentmek
dent|al ['dentl] dişlere ait, dişçiliğe ait; **~ist** dişçi, diş doktoru; **~ure** [~çı] takma dişler *pl.*
deny [di'nay] *v/t* inkâr etm., yalanlamak; reddetmek
depart [di'pât] ayrılmak (**from** *-den*); **~ment** şube, daire; *Am.* bakanlık; **~ment store** büyük mağaza; **~ure** [di'pâçı] gidiş kalkış
depend [di'pend] bağlı olm.; güvenmek (**on, upon** *-e*); **~ence** bağlılık; **~ent** bağlı (**on, upon** *-e*); bağımlı
deplor|able [di'plôrıbl] acınacak; **~e** *v/t* acımak *-e*
deport [di'pôt] *v/t* yurtdışı etm.; **~ation** [~'teyşın] yurtdışı etme
depose [di'pıuz] *v/t* azletmek

deposit [di'pozit] *n.* tortu;
ec. depozito; pey; *v/t* yatırmak, tevdi etm.; **~or** para
yatıran

depot ['depɪu] depo, ambar

depraved [di'preyvd] ahlâkı bozuk

depress [di'pres] *v/t* indirmek, alçaltmak; **~ed** kederli; **~ion** *ec.* durgunluk; çukur; alçak basınç bölgesi

deprive [di'rayv] *v/t* mahrum etm. (**of** *-den*)

depth [depth] derinlik

deputy ['depyuti] vekil;
muavin; *pol.* milletvekili

derail [di'reyl] *v/t* raydan
çıkarmak

derange [di'reync] *v/t* karıştırmak

deri|de [di'rayd] alay
etm. (ile); **~sion** [~'ijın]
alay; **~sive** [~'aysiv] alaylı

derive [di'rayv] *v/t* çıkarmak, türetmek (**from**
-den)

derogatory [di'rogıtıri] zararlı (**to** *-e*)

descend [di'send] *v/i* inmek, alçalmak; **be ~ed**
nesebi olm. (**from** *-den*);
~ant torun, hafit

descent [di'sent] iniş; yokuş; soy, nesil

descri|be [dis'krayb] *v/t*
tanımlamak, vasıflandır-
mak; anlatmak; **~ption**
[~'kripşn] tanımlama, tarif

desert[1] ['dezıt] *geo.* çöl

desert[2] [di'zöt] *v/t* bırakmak, terketmek; *v/i* askerlikten kaçmak; **~ed** ıssız;

~er asker kaçağı; **~ion**
terk; askerlikten kaçma

deserve [di'zöv] *v/t* ...
hakkı olm.

design [di'zayn] *n* resim,
plan, proje, model; maksat;
v/t tasarlamak, hazırlamak;
çizmek

designate ['dezigneyt] *v/t*
belirtmek; seçmek

designer [di'zaynı] teknik
ressam

desir|able [di'zayrıbl] iste-
nilir; makbul; **~e** [~ayı] *n*
arzu, istek; *v/t* arzu etm.,
istemek; **~ous** istekli

desk [desk] yazı masası;
okul sırası

desolat|e ['desılit] *adj.* ha-
rap; ıssız, tenha; perişan;
['~leyt] *v/t* perişan etm.; boş
bırakmak; **~ion** viranlık;
perişanlık

despair [dis'päı] *n* ümitsizlik; *v/i* ümidi kesmek
(**of** *-den*)

desperat|e ['despırit] ümit-
siz; deliye dönmüş; **~ion**
ümitsizlik

despise [dis'payz] *v/t* hakir
görmek

despite [dis'payt], **in ~ of**
-e rağmen [ümitsiz]

despondent [dis'pondınt]∫

despot ['despot] despot,
müstebit; **~ism** istibdat

dessert [di'zöt] yemiş,
tatlı

destin|ation [desti'neyşın]
gidilecek yer; **~e** [~in] *v/t*
ayırmak, tahsis etm. (**for**
-e); **~y** kader; talih

destitute ['destityût] yoksul, mahrum

destroy [dis'troy] v/t yıkmak, bertaraf etm.; **~er** naut. destroyer

destructi|on [dis'trakşın] yıkım, imha; **~ve** yıkıcı

detach [di'täç] v/t ayırmak, kopmak; **~ed** ayrı; tarafsız; **~ment** ayırma; mil. müfreze, kol

detail ['diteyl] ayrıntı; **~ed** mufassal, ayrıntılı

detain [di'teyn] v/t alıkoymak; geciktirmek

detect [di'tekt] v/t meydana çıkarmak, keşfetmek; **~ion** keşif, bulma; **~ive** sivil polis; dedektif

detention [di'tenşın] alıkoyma; tevkif

deter [di'tö] v/t vazgeçirmek

detergent [di'töcınt] deterjan

deteriorat|e [di'tiiriireyt] v/t fenalaştırmak; v/i fenalaşmak; **~ion** fenalaşma

determin|ation [ditömi'neyşın] tespit, sınırlama; azim; hüküm, karar; **~e** [di'tömin] v/t sınırlamak, belirtmek; kararlaştırmak

deterrent [di'terınt] caydıran

detest [di'test] v/t nefret etm. -den; **~able** iğrenç, berbat

detonation [detıu'neyşın] patlama, infilâk

detour ['dituı] dolambaçlı yol

---

devalu|ation [dîvalyu'eyşın] ec. devalüasyon, para değerinin düşürülmesi; **~e** ['~'välyû] v/t -in değerini düşürmek

devastate ['devisteyt] v/t harap etm.

develop [di'velıp] v/t geliştirmek; phot. develope etm.; v/i gelişmek; **~ment** gelişme; phot. developman

deviat|e [dî'vieyt] sapmak (from -den); **~ion** sapma

device [di'vays] icat; cihaz; hile, oyun

devil ['devıl] şeytan, iblis; **~ish** şeytanca

devise [di'vayz] v/t tasarlamak

devoid [di'voyd]; **~ of** -den mahrum [terk]

devolution devir, havale;

devot|e [di'viut] v/t vakfetmek, adamak (to -e); **~ed** sadık, bağlı (to -e); **~ion** bağlılık, fedakârlık

devour [di'vauı] v/t yutmak

devout [di'vaut] dindar; sadık

dew [dyû] çiğ; **~y** çiğle kaplı

dexter|ity [deks'teriti] beceriklik, ustalık; **~ous** ['~rıs] becerikli

diabetes [dayı'bîtîz] med. şeker hastalığı

diagnosis [dayıg'nıusis] med. teşhis

dial ['dayıl] n kadran; tel. kurs; v/t telefon numaralarını çevirmek

dialect 250

dialect ['dayılekt] şive, lehçe

dia|log(ue) ['dayılog] *thea.* diyalog; **~meter** [day'ämıtı] çap

diamond ['dayımınd] elmas; *(pl.)* karo

diaper ['dayıpı] *Am.* kundak bezi

diaphragm ['dayıfräm] *an.* diyafram

diarrh(o)ea [dayı'rıı] *med.* ishal, amel

diary ['dayıri] muhtıra defteri

dice [days] **1.** *pl.* oyun zarları; **2.** *v/i* zar oynamak

dict|ate [dik'teyt] *v/t* yazdırmak, dikte etmek; zorla kabul ettirmek; **~ation** emir; dikte; **~ator** diktatör; **~atorship** diktatörlük

dictionary ['dikşınri] sözlük

did [did] *s.* **do** [lük]

die¹ [day] zar

die² ölmek; şiddetle arzu etm. (**for** *sth.*, **to** *inf.* **-i**)

diet ['dayıt] *n* perhiz, rejim; *pol.* diyet, meclis; *v/i* perhiz etm., rejim yapmak

differ ['difı] farklı olm., ayrılmak (**from** *-den*); **~ence** ['difrıns] ayrılık, fark; ihtilâf; **~ent** farklı, ayrı, başka; çeşitli; **~ential** [difı'renşıl] *tech.* diferansiyel

difficult ['difikılt] zor, güç; titiz, inatçı; **~y** güçlük

diffident ['difidınt] çekingen

diffuse [di'fyûz] *v/t* yaymak, dağıtmak

dig [dig] *v/t* kazmak

digest ['daycest] *n* özet; [di'cest] *v/t* hazmetmek, sindirmek; **~ible** [di'cestibl] hazmı kolay; **~ion** [di'cestşın] hazım, sindirim

digni|fied [dignifayd] ağırbaşlı, vakur; **~ty** vakar; değer

digress [day'gres] ayrılmak (**from** *-den*); **~ion** ayrılma

dike [dayk] set, bent; hendek

dilapidated [di'läpideytid] harap

dilate [day'leyt] *v/t* genişletmek; *v/i* genişlemek

diligen|ce ['dilicens] gayret; **~t** gayretli, çalışkan

dill [dil] *bot.* dereotu

dilute [day'lyût] *v/t* sulandırmak

dim [dim] bulanık, donuk; *v/t* bulandırmak; *v/i* kararmak

dime [daym] *Am.* on sentlik para

dimension [di'menşın] ebat, boyut

dimin|ish [di'miniş] *v/t* azaltmak; *v/i* azalmak; **~utive** [-'yutiv] ufak; *gr.* küçültme

dimple ['dimpl] çene *veya* yanak çukuru, gamze

dine [dayn] *v/i* akşam yemeğini yemek; **~r** vagon restoran

dining-|car ['dayniŋ-] vagon restoran; **~room** yemek odası

dinner ['dinı] esas yemek;

akşam yemeği; **~jacket** smokin

dip [dip] *n.* dal(dır)ma; yokuş, iniş; *v/t* daldırmak, batırmak; ışıkları körletmek; *v/i* dalmak

diphtheria [dif'thirıı] *med.* difteri   [diftong)

diphthong ['difthon] *gr.*

diploma [di'plumı] diploma; **~cy** diplomasi; **~t** ['-ı-māt] diplomat; **~tic** [~ı-'mätik] diplomatik

direct [di'rekt] *adj.* doğru, vasıtasız; *v/t* doğrultmak, yöneltmek; idare etm.; **~ current** *el.* doğru akım; **~ion** yön, cihet; emir; *pl.* tarifname, kullanış tarzı *sg.*; **~ly** *adv.* doğrudan doğruya

director [di'rektı] müdür, direktör; **board of ~s** idare kurulu; **~y** rehber, adres kitabı

dirigible ['diricıbl] güdümlü

dirt [döt] kir, pislik, çamur; **~-cheap** sudan ucuz; **~y** *adj.* kirli, pis; iğrenç; *v/t* kirletmek, pisletmek

disable [dis'eybl] *v/t* sakatlamak; **~d** sakat, malul

disadvantage [disıd'vântic] mahzur, aleyhte oluş; **~ous** [disädvân'teycıs] mahzurlu, zararlı

disagree [disı'gri] uyuşamamak; anlaşamamak (**with** ile); uygun gelmemek (**with** *-e*); **~able** [~ıbl] hoş olmıyan; **~ment** uyuşmazlık, çekişme

disappear [disı'pıı] kaybolmak; **~ance** gözden kaybolma

disappoint [disı'poynt] *v/t* hayal kırıklığına uğratmak; **~ment** hayal kırıklığı

disapprov|al [disı'pruuvıl] beğenmeyiş, ayıplama; **~e** *v/t* beğenmemek, uygun görmemek

disarm [dis'âm] *v/t* silâhsızlandırmak; **~ament** [~mınt] silâhsızlanma

disarrange ['disı'reync] *v/t* karıştırmak, *-in* düzenini bozmak   [lık)

disarray ['disı'rey] karışık-

disaste|r [di'zâstı] felâket, belâ; **~rous** feci

disband [dis'bând] *v/t* terhis etm., dağıtmak

disbelie|f ['disbi'lîf] imansızlık; güvensizlik; **~ve** ['-'lîv] *v/t* inanmamak *-e*

disc [disk] disk; plak; **~ jockey** diskcokey

discern [di'sön] *v/t* ayırt etm.

discharge [dis'çâc] *n.* boşaltma, salıverme; terhis; işten çıkarılma; ateş etme; *v/t* boşaltmak; terhis etm., işten çıkarmak; ödemek; *duty:* yerine getirmek

discipl|e [di'saypl] öğrenci; *rel.* havari; **~ine** ['disiplin] disiplin

disclaim [dis'kleym] *v/t* inkâr etm.; feragat etm. *-den*

disclose [dis'kluuz] *v/t* ifşa etm.

discolo(u)r 252

discolo(u)r [dis'kʌlǝ] v/t -in rengini bozmak

discomfort [dis'kʌmfǝt] rahatsızlık

discompose [diskǝm'pǝuz] v/t şaşırtmak

disconcert [diskǝn'sö:t] v/t şaşırtmak, karıştırmak

disconnect ['diskı'nekt] v/t ayırmak

discontent ['diskǝn'tent] hoşnutsuzluk; ~ed hoşnutsuz

discontinue [dis'kǝn'tinyu] v/t kesmek; devam etmemek -e

discord ['diskôd], ~ance [~'kôdıns] anlaşmazlık, ahenksizlik; ~ant uyumsuz

discotheque ['diskutek] diskotek

discount ['diskaunt] ec. iskonto; ~ house Am. uzuca mal satılan mağaza

discourage [dis'karic] v/t -in cesaretini kırmak, vazgeçirmek -i (from -den)

discourse [dis'kôs] söylev, nutuk

discover [dis'kʌvǝ] v/t keşfetmek, bulmak; ~er bulucu; ~y keşif, buluş

discredit [dis'kredit] güvensizlik; şüphe; v/t kötülemek, itibardan düşürmek

discreet [dis'krît] ketum, ağzı sıkı

discrepancy [dis'krepǝnsi] ayrılık

discretion [dis'kreşǝn] ketumiyet; akıllılık; naziklik; yetki

discriminat|e [dis'krimineyt] v/t ayırmak; v/i ayırım yapmak; ~ion [~krimi'neyşǝn] ayırım, temyiz

discuss [dis'kas] v/t görüşmek, müzakere etm.; ~ion görüşme, tartışma

disdain [dis'deyn] n hakaret; v/t aşağısamak

disease [di'zîz] hastalık; ~d hasta

disembark ['disim'bâk] v/t karaya çıkarmak; v/i karaya çıkmak

disengage ['disin'geyc] v/t ayırmak, çözmek; ~d serbest, boş

disentangle ['disin'tängl] v/t çözmek

disfavo(u)r ['dis'feyvı] gözden düşme

disfigure [dis'figı] v/t çirkinleştirmek

disgrace [dis'greys] n gözden düşme, yüzkarası; v/t gözden düşürmek; ~ful ayıp, yüz kızartıcı

disguise [dis'gayz] n kıyafet değiştirme; v/i kıyafet değiştirmek; v/t gizlemek

disgust [dis'gast] n nefret, tiksinme (at -den); v/t tiksindirmek, bıktırmak A; ~ing iğrenç

dish [diş] tabak; yemek

dishevel(l)ed [di'şevıld] karmakarışık

dishonest [dis'onist] namussuz; ~y namussuzluk

dishono(u)r [dis'onı] m namussuzluk, leke; v/t -in namusuna leke sürmek; -in

ırzına geçmek; *bill:* **kabul etmemek** -*i;* **~able namussuz**

dish-washer bulaşık yıkama makinesi

disillusion [disi'luujın] *v/t* hayal kırıklığına uğratmak

disinfect [disin'fekt] *v/t* dezenfekte etm.; **~ant** antiseptik ilâç

disinherit ['disin'herit] *v/t* mirastan mahrum etm.

disintegrate [dis'intigreyt] *v/t* parçalara ayırmak; *v/i* parçalanmak

disinterested [dis'intristid] tarafsız, menfaat düşünmiyen

disk [disk] *s.* **disc**

dislike [dis'layk] *n* beğenmeyiş; *v/t* beğenmemek, sevmemek

dislocate ['dislıkeyt] *v/t* yerinden çıkarmak

dismal ['dizmıl] kederli; sönük

dismantle [dis'mäntl] *v/t* sökmek [dehşet]

dismay [dis'mey] korku,⌐

dismember [dis'membı] *v/t* parçalamak

dismiss [dis'mis] *v/t* işten çıkarmak; yol vermek -*e*; **~al** yol verme

dismount [dis'maunt] *v/t* sökmek; *v/i* attan inmek

disobedience [disı'bidyıns] itaatsizlik; **~t** itaatsiz

disobey [disı'bey] *v/t* itaat etmemek -*e*

disobliging ['disı'blaycin] nezaketsiz

---

disorder [dis'ôdı] karışıklık; hastalık; **~ly** düzensiz; itaatsiz; çapaçul

disown [dis'un] *v/t* inkâr etm., tanımamak

disparage [dis'päric] *v/t* kötülemek

dispassionate [dis'päşnit] tarafsız

dispatch [dis'päç] *n.* acele; gönderme; rapor; haber; telgraf; *v/t* göndermek; tamamlamak

dispens|able [dis'pensıbl] vaz geçilebilir; **~ary** dispanser; **~e** *v/t* dağıtmak; *v/i* vazgeçmek (**with** -*den*)

disperse [dis'pôs] *v/t* dağıtmak, yaymak; *v/i* dağılmak

displace [dis'pleys] *v/t* yerinden çıkarmak, götürmek

display [dis'pley] *n.* gösteriş, nümayiş, teşhir; *v/t* göstermek, teşhir etm., sermek

displeas|e [dis'plîz] *v/t* gücendirmek; **~ed** dargın; **~ure** [~ejı] gücenme

dispos|al [dis'pıuzıl] tertip, düzen; tasarruf; bertaraf etme; **~e** *v/t* düzenlemek; **~e of** -*in* tasarrufunda olm.; kullanmak -*i;* bertaraf etm. -*i;* **~ed** hazır (**to** -*e*); **~ition** [~ı'zişın] düzen; eğilim; tabiat

disproportionate [disprı'pôşnit] nispetsiz

dispute [dis'pyût] *n.* münakaşa, tartışma; *v/t* tartışmak, kabul etmemek

disqualify

254

disqualify [dis'kwolifay] *v/t* diskalifiye etm.

disregard ['disri'gaad] *v/t* ihmal etm., saymamak

disreputable [dis'repyu- tıbl] rezil; itibarsız

disrespectful [disris'pekt- ful] hürmetsiz

disrupt [dis'rapt] *v/t* yarmak, ayırmak

dissatisf|action ['dissätis- fäkşın] hoşnutsuzluk; ~y ['di'sätisfay] *v/t* memnun etmemek

disseminate [di'semineyt] *v/t* saçmak, yaymak

dissen|sion [di'senşın] ihti- lâf, çekişme; ~t *bir hususta* ayrılmak (**from** *–den*)

dissimilar ['di'similı] farklı (**to** *–den*)

dissipate ['disipeyt] *v/t* dağıtmak; israf etm.; ~ion [~'peyşın] sefahat

dissociate [dis'siuşieyt]: ~ **oneself** ayrılmak (**from** *–den*)

dissol|ute ['disiluut] ahlâk- sız, sefih; ~ution [~'luuşın] eri(t)me; ~ve [di'zolv] *v/t* eritmek; feshetmek; *v/i* erimek

dissuade [di'sweyd] *v/t* vazgeçirmek, caydırmak (**from** *–den*)

distan|ce ['distıns] mesafe; uzaklık; ara; ~t uzak; soğuk, mesafeli

distaste [dis'teyst] tiksin- me, nefret; ~ful [~'teystful] iğrenç

distinct [dis'tiŋkt] ayrı,

farklı; belli; ~ion ayırma, ayırt etme, temayüz, üstün- lük; nişan; ~ive ayıran, özellik belirten

distinguish [dis'tiŋgwiş] *v/t* ayırmak, ayırt etm.; ~ed seçkin, mümtaz, kibar

distort [dis'tôt] *v/t* bük- mek, bozmak, tahrif etm.

distract [dis'träkt] *v/t* baş- ka tarafa çekmek; ~ed deli, çılgın; ~ion karışıklık; eğ- lence; çılgınlık

distress [dis'tres] *n.* sıkıntı, zaruret; *v/t* sıkıntıya sok- mak; ~ed endişeli; sıkıntı çeken

distribut|e [dis'tribyut] *v/t* dağıtmak, yaymak; ~ion [~'byûşın] dağıtım; yayılma

district ['distrikt] bölge; il- çe, kaza

distrust [dis'trast] *n.* güven- sizlik, şüphe; *v/t* gü- venmemek *-e*

disturb [dis'tôb] *v/t* karış- tırmak; rahatsız etm.; ~ance karışıklık; rahatsız- lık

disuse [dis'yûs] kullanıl- mayış; ~d [~'yûzd] eski, vaktini doldurmuş

ditch [diç] hendek

dive [dayv] *n.* dalış; *av.* pike; *v/i* dalmak (**into** *–e*); pike yapmak; ~r dalgıç

diverge [day'vôc] birbirin- den ayrılmak

divers|e [day'vôs] çeşitli, değişik; ~ion başka tarafa çevirme; eğlence; ~ity fark, başkalık

divert [day'vöt] *v/t* başka tarafa çevirmek; eğlendirmek

divide [di'vayd] *v/t* bölmek, ayırmak; *v/i* ayrılmak

divin|e [di'vayn] ilâhî, kutsal; **~ity** [di'viniti] tanrılık niteliği; ilâhiyat

division [di'vijın] bölme; ayrılma; kısım, daire; *mil.* tümen

divorce [di'vôs] *n.* boşanma; *v/t* boşamak; *v/i* boşanmak

dizzy ['dizi] baş döndürücü

do [duu] *v/t* yapmak; etmek; hazırlamak; bitirmek; **that will ~** yeter; **how ~ you ~?** nasılsınız?; **~ you like London?** Londra'dan hoşunuza gider mi?; **we ~ not know** bilmiyoruz; **~ shut up!** sus yahu!; **~ well** işi iyi gitmek; iyi para kazanmak; **~ with** ihtiyacı olm. *-e;* **~ without** muhtaç olmamak *-e*

docile [di'dusayl] uslu, uysal

dock [dok] *naut.* havuz, dok; **~er** liman işçisi; **~yard** tersane

doctor [dokti] doktor; hekim; **~ate** [~rit] doktora

doctrine [doktrin] doktrin, öğreti

document ['dokyumınt] belge; **~ary** [~'mentri] belgelere dayanan, yazılı

dodge [doc] *n.* oyun, kurnazlık; *v/i* kaçamak bulmak

doe [du] *zo.* dişi geyik *veya* tavşan

dog [dog] köpek; **~eared** kıvrılmış; **~ged** ['~id] inatçı [inak]

dogma ['dogmı] dogma,

doings ['duuŋz] *pl.* işler

dole [dul] sadaka; işsizlere verilen haftalık

doll [dol] bebek, kukla

dollar ['dolı] dolar

dolorous ['dolırıs] kederli, elemli

dolphin ['dolfin] *zo.* yunusbalığı

domain [dı'meyn] mülk, arazi; alan

dome [dum] kubbe

domestic [dı'mestik] *adj.* eve ait, ehli, evcil; yerli; *n.* hizmetçi; **~ animal** evcil hayvan; **~ation** [~mesti-'keyşın] alıştırma

domicile ['domisayl] oturma yeri

domin|ant ['domınınt] hâkim, üstün; **~ate** [~neyt] *v/t* hâkim olm. *-e;* **~ation** [~'neyşın] egemenlik

domineer [domi'niı] *v/t* tahakküm altında tutmak; zorbalık etm.; **~ing** otoriter

dominion [dı'minyın] *pol.* dominyon

donat|e [du'neyt] *v/t* bağışlamak; **~ion** bağış

done [dan] *s.* do; **be ~** yapılmak; bitkin olm.

donkey ['doŋki] eşek

donor ['dunı] veren, verici

doom [duum] *n.* kader; kıyamet; *v/t* mahkûm etm. **(to -e);** **~sday** *rel.* kıyamet günü

door [dô] kapı; **~handle** kapı mandalı; **~keeper**, **~man** kapıcı; **~way** kapı yeri, giriş

dope [düup] *n.* esrar, afyon; *v/t* ilâçla sersemletmek

dorm|ant ['dômint] uyuyan; **~er (window)** çatı penceresi; **~itory** ['dômitri] yatakhane, koğuş

dose [dıus] doz

dot [dot] *n.* nokta; benek; *v/t* noktalamak

dote [düt] bunamak; düşkün olm. **(on, upon** *-e)*

double ['dabl] çift, iki misli, iki kat; *n.* eş; dublör; çift iki misli olm.; *v/t* iki kat etm.; **~ bed** iki kişilik yatak; **~ room** çift yataklı oda; **~cross** *v/t* aldatmak; **~faced** ikiyüzlü

doubt [daut] *n.* şüphe; *v/i* şüphelenmek **(about** *-den)*; **~ful** şüpheli, kararsız; **~less** şüphesiz

douche [düuş] *med.* şırınga

dough [dıu] hamur; **~nut** çörek

dove [dav] *zo.* güvercin

down¹ [daun] *geo.* kumul, eksibe

down² *n.* ince tüy

down³ *adv.* aşağı(ya); *v/t* indirmek; **~cast** üzgün; **~fall** düşüş; **~hearted** cesareti kırılmış; **~hill** yokuş aşağı; **~pour** sağanak; **~right** kesin; tamamiyle; **~stairs** aşağıda; aşağıya; **~town** *Am.* şehrin merke-

zi; **~ward** ['~wıd] aşağıya doğru

dowry ['dauırı] çeyiz

doze [dıuz] *v/i* uyuklamak; *n.* hafif uyku

dozen ['dazn] düzine

drab [dräb] gri

draft [drâft] *n.* police; taslak; *mil.* mecburî askerliğe alma; *v/t* tasarlamak, çizmek; *mil.* silâh altına çağırmak; *s.* **draught**; **~sman** *s.* **draughtsman**

drag [dräg] *v/t* sürüklemek, çekmek

dragon ['drägın] ejderha; **~fly** *zo.* yusufçuk

drain [dreyn] *n.* lağım, su yolu; *v/t* akıtmak, kurutmak; **~age** akaçlama, drenaj; kanalizasyon

drake [dreyk] *zo.* erkek ördek

drama ['drâmı] dram, tiyatro eseri; **~tic** [drı'mätik] dramatik; heyecanlı

drank [dränk] *s.* **drink**

drape [dreyp] *v/t* kumaşla kaplamak; *-in* kıvrımlarını düzeltmek; **~r** kumaşçı

drastic ['drästik] şiddetli; açık

draught [drâft], *Am.* **draft** çekme, içme, yudum; hava cereyanı; **~sman** teknik ressam; **~y** cereyanlı

draw [drô] *n.* kur'a çekilişi; çok rağbetli şey; beraberе biten oyun; *v/t* çekmek, celbetmek; germek; çizmek; *money:* çekmek; **~ near** *v/i* yaklaşmak; **~ out**

v/t uzatmak; ~ **up** *v/t* tasarlamak, hazırlamak; *v/i* yaklaşıp durmak; ~**back** mahzur, engel; ~r çekmece, göz; ressam; *pl.* don

drawing ['drôiŋ] resim; çekme; ~**pin** pünez; ~**room** salon, misafir odası

drawn [drôn] *s.* draw; berabere

dread [dred] korku, dehşet; *v/t* korkmak -*den*; ~**ful** korkunç

dream [drîm] *n.* rüya; hulya; *v/i* rüya görmek; ~**t** [dremt] *s.* dream; ~**y** dalgın

dreary ['driıri] can sıkıcı, ıssız

dredge [drec] *v/t* taramak; *n.* tarak; ~**r** tarak dubası

dregs [dregz] *pl.* tortu, telve *sg.*

drench [drenç] *v/t* ıslatmak

dress [dres] *n.* elbise, kıyafet; *v/t* giydirmek; süslemek; hazırlamak; düzenlemek; *v/i* giyinmek; ~ **designer** moda desinatörü

dressing ['dresiŋ] giy(in)me; *med.* pansuman; salça; terbiye; ~**cubicle** soyunma kabinası; ~**gown** sabahlık; ~**table** tuvalet masası

dress-maker kadın terzisi

drew [druu] *s.* draw

dried [drayd] *s.* dry; kuru

drift [drift] *n.* sürüklenme; kar yığıntısı; hedef, eğilim; *v/t* sürüklemek; *v/i* sürüklenmek

drill [dril] *n.* delgi, matkap; *mil.* talim; tohum dizisi; *v/t* delmek; talim etm.

drink [driŋk] *n.* içki; içecek; *v/t* içmek; ~**ing water** içecek su

drip [drip] *v/i* damlamak; ~**dry** buruşmaz; ~**ping** erimiş yağ

drive [drayv] *n.* gezinti; işleme; teşebbüs, gayret; *v/t* sürmek; kullanmak; götürmek; sevketmek; ~ **away** *v/t* kovmak; ~ **on** *v/t* gitmeğe devam etm.; ~ **out** kovmak, çıkarmak; ~**in** müşterilerine araba içinde servis yapan

drive|n ['drivn] *s.* drive; ~**r** ['drayvı] şoför

driving ['drayviŋ] sürme, kullanma; ~ **license** şoförlük ehliyetnamesi; ~ **school** şoförlük okulu

drizzle ['drizl] *n.* çiseleme; *v/i* çiselemek

dromedary ['drɑmıdıri] *zo.* hecin devesi

drone [drıun] *zo.* erkek arı

droop [druup] *v/t* indirmek; *v/i* sarkmak, bükülmek

drop [drop] *n.* damla; düşme, sukut; *v/t* düşürmek, atmak; damlatmak; *v/i* damlamak; ~ **a line** kısa bir mektup yazmak; ~ **in** uğramak (**at** -*e*)

drought [draut] kuraklık

drove [drıuv] *s.* drive

drown [draun] *v/t* boğmak; *v/i* boğulmak; **be ~ed** boğulmak

drowsy 258

drowsy ['drauzi] uykusu basmış; uyutucu

drudge [drac] ağır işler yapmak

drug [drag] *n.* ilâç; esrar; *v/t* ilâçla uyutmak; ~ **addict** esrarkeş; ~**gist** ['~gist] eczacı; bakkal; ~**store** *Am.* bakkaliye; eczane

drum [dram] *n.* davul; trampete; *v/i* davul çalmak

drunk [draŋk] *s.* **drink**; sarhoş; ~**ard** ['~əd] ayyaş, sarhoş; ~**en** sarhoş

dry [dray] *adj.* kuru, kurak; susuz; *v/t* kurutmak, kurulamak; *v/i* kurumak; ~ **goods** *pl. Am.* manifatura *sg.*; ~ **up** tamamen kurumak; ~**cleaning** kuru temizleme

dual ['dyul] çift, iki kat

dubious ['dyûbyıs] şüpheli

duch|ess ['daçis] düşes; ~**y** dukalık

duck [dak] *n. zo.* ördek; *v/i* dalmak, başını eğmek; *v/t* daldırmak

dudgeon ['dacın] öfke

due [dyû] *adj.* gerekli; ödenmesi gerekli; *n.* hak; vergi; ~ **to** yüzünden, -*den* dolayı; **in** ~ **time** zamanı gelince; **be** ~ -*mesi* gerekli olm.

duel ['dyul] düello

dug [dag] *s.* **dig**; ~**out** *mil.* sığınak

duke [dyûk] duka, dük

dull [dal] donuk, sönük; sıkıcı; durgun; cansız

duly ['dyûli] *adv.* gereğince; tam zamanında

dumb [dam] dilsiz, sessiz; *Am.* aptal, budala; ~**founded** hayret içince; ~**-waiter** seyyar masa; mutfak asansörü

dummy ['dami] taklit; manken; kukla adam

dump [damp] *v/t* boşaltmak, atmak; ~**ing** *ec.* damping [(turmak)]

dun [dan] *v/t borçluyu sıkış-}*

dune [dyûn] kumul, eksibe

dung [daŋ] *n.* gübre; *v/t* gübrelemek

dungeon ['dancın] zindan

dupe [dyûp] *v/t* aldatmak

dupl|ex ['dyûpleks] çift; ~**icate** ['~likit] *n.* eş; kopya, nüsha; ['~likeyt] *v/t* -*in* suretini çıkarmak

dura|ble ['dyuırıbl] dayanıklı, devamlı; ~**tion** [~'reyşın] devam, süre

duress(e) [dyuı'res] cebir, baskı

during ['dyuırıŋ] esnasında, zarfında

dusk [dask] akşam karanlığı

dust [dast] toz; çöp; *v/t* -*in* tozunu silkmek; ~**bin** çöp tenekesi; ~**man** çöpçü; ~**pan** faraş; ~**y** tozlu, toz gibi

Dutch [daç] Holandalı, Felemenkli; Felemenkçe; ~**man** Felemenkli

dutiful ['dyûtiful] görevini bilen

duty ['dyuti] ödev, görev, hizmet; gümrük resmi; **off** ~ izinli; **on** ~ vazife başında; ~**free** gümrüksüz

dwarf [dwôf] cüce, bodur
dwell [dwel] v/i oturmak; durmak (**on** üzerinde); ~ **ing** oturma yeri
dwelt [dwelt] s. **dwell**
dye [day] n. boya; v/t boya-⌉
dying ['dayin] s. **die** [mak⌋
dyke [dayk] s. **dike**

dynam|ic [day'nämik] di- namik; enerjik; ~**ics** dina- mik; ~**ite** ['~ımayt] dina- mit; ~o ['~ımıu] et. dinamo
dynasty ['dinısti] hanedan, soy
dysentery ['disntri] med. dizanteri, kanlı basur

E

each [iç] her biri, her; be- her; ~ **other** birbiri
eager ['igı] hevesli; istekli, sabırsız; ~**ness** istek, gayret
eagle ['igl] zo. kartal, kara- kuş
ear [iı] kulak; başak; ~ **-drum** an. kulak zarı
earl [ôl] kont
early ['ôli] erken(den); eski, ilk
earn [ôn] v/t kazanmak
earnest ['ônist] ciddî; **in** ~ ciddî olarak
earnings ['ôninz] pl. ka- zanç sg.
ear|-phone et. kulaklık; ~ **-ring** küpe; ~**shot** kulak erimi
earth [ôth] n. toprak; kara; yeryüzü; dünya; v/t et. top- rağa bağlamak; ~**en** top- raktan yapılmış; ~**enware** çanak çömlek; ~**quake** geo. deprem; ~**worm** zo. yer solucanı
ease [iz] n. rahat; refah; kolaylık; v/t hafifletmek, yatıştırmak; **at** ~ rahat, hoş
east [ist] doğu; **Near** ⌒ Yakın Doğu

Easter ['istı] rel. paskalya
east|ern ['istın] doğu(da); ~**ward** ['~wıd] doğuya doğru
easy ['izi] kolay, rahat, sı- kıntısız; **take it** ~! acele etmeyiniz!; darılmayınız!; ~**chair** koltuk; ~**going** kayıtsız, kaygısız
eat [it] v/t yemek; ~ **up** v/t yiyip bitirmek; ~**en** s. **eat**
eaves [ivz] çıkıntı; ~**drop** v/i gizlice dinlemek
ebb(-tide) ['eb('-)] geo. ce-⌉
ebony ['ebıni] abanoz [zir⌋
eccentric [ik'sentrik] ek- santrik, dışmerkezli; fig. garip, tuhaf
ecclesiastical [iklzi'ästikl] kiliseye ait
echo ['ekıu] n. yankı; v/i yansımak; v/t yansıtmak
eclipse [i'klips] ay tutulma- sı, güneş tutulması
econom|ic [iku'nomik] ikti- sadî; pl. iktisat bilimi; ~ **ical** idareli, tutumlu
econom|ist [i'konmist] ikti- satçı; ~**ize** idareli kullan- mak (**in, on** -i); ~**y** iktisat, ekonomi; tutum, idare

ecstasy ['ekstsı] vecit

edge [ec] *n.* kenar, sırt; bıçak ağzı; *v/t* bilemek; kenar geçirmek *-ê*; **on** ~*e* sinirli; ~**ing** kenarlık, şerit; ~**y** sinirli

edible ['edibl] yenir

edif|ice ['edifis] bina; ~**ying** ['~fayin] yüksek duygulara ulaştıran

edit ['edit] *v/t* yayımlamak; ~**ion** [i'dişın] baskı; ~**or** ['editı] yayımlayan; yazı işleri müdürü; ~**orial** [edi'tôriıl] başyazı; yazı işleri müdürlüğüne ait

educat|e ['edyukeyt] *v/t* eğitmek, yetiştirmek; ~**ed** okumuş, aydın; ~**ion** eğitim, öğretim; ~**or** eğitmen

eel [îl] *zo.* yılan balığı

effect [i'fekt] *v/t* başarmak; etkilemek; *n.* sonuç, etki; gösteriş; *pl.* mallar, eşya; **take** ~ yürürlüğe girmek; ~**ive** etkili

effeminate [i'feminit] kadın gibi, yumuşak

effervescent [efı'vesnt] köpüren

efficien|cy [i'fişınsi] kifayet, ehliyet; etki; verim; ~**ient** ehliyetli; verimli; etkili

effort ['efıt] gayret, çaba

effusive [i'fyûsiv] taşkın; bol

egg [eg] yumurta; ~**cup** yumurta kabı; ~**plant** *bot.* patlıcan; ~**head** *Am.* sl. aydın kimse; ~**shell** yumurta kabuğu

egois|m ['eguizm] bencilik; ~**t** bencil, hodbin

egress ['îgrıs] çıkış

Egypt ['îcipt] Mısır; ~**ian** [i'cipşın] Mısırlı

eight [eyt] sekiz; ~**een** ['ey-'tîn] on sekiz; ~**fold** sekiz misli; ~**y** seksen

either ['aydhı] ikisinden biri, her iki; ~ ... **or** ... ya ... yahut ...

ejaculation [icäkyu'leyşın] ünlem

eject [i'cekt] *v/t* dışarı atmak, kovmak

elaborate [i'läbırit] *adj.* dikkatle işlenmiş, özenilmiş; *v/t* incelikle işlemek

elapse [i'läps] *v/i* geçmek

elastic [i'lästik] elastikî, esnek; lastik bant

elbow ['elbuı] *n.* dirsek; *v/t* dirsekle dürtmek

elder[1] ['eldı] *bot.* mürver ağacı

elder[2] daha yaşlı, büyük; ~**ly** yaşlı

elect [i'lekt] *v/t* seçmek; *adj.* seçkin; ~**ion** seçim; ~**or** seçmen

electric [i'lektrik] elektrik (-li); ~**al engineer** elektrik mühendisi; ~**ian** [~'trişın] elektrikçi; ~**ity** [~'trisiti] elektrik

electrify [i'lektrifay] *v/t* elektriklemek

electrocution [ilektrı'kyûşın] elektrikle idam

electron [i'lektrın] elektron

elegan|ce ['eligıns] zarafet, şıklık; ~**t** zarif, şık

element ['elimınt] öğe; unsur; eleman; **~al** [~'mentl] temel, ilkel; **~ary** [~'mentrı] ilk, basit; **~ary school** ilkokul

elephant ['elifınt] *zo.* fil

elevat|e ['elyveyt] *v/t* yükseltmek; **~ion** yükseklik; yüksek yer; **~or** *Am.* asansör; *av.* irtifa dümeni

eleven [i'levn] on bir

eligible ['elicıbl] seçilebilir; uygun

eliminat|e [i'limineyt] *v/t* çıkarmak; bertaraf etm.; **~ion** çıkarma

elk [elk] *bir geyik çeşidi*

ellipse [i'lips] elips

elm [elm] *bot.* karaağaç

elongate [i'longeyt] *v/t* gerip uzatmak

elope [i'lup] âşıkı ile kaçmak

eloquen|ce ['elукwıns] belâgat; **~t** beliğ; dokunaklı

else [els] yoksa; başka; what **~**? bundan başka ne var?; **~where** başka yerde *veya* yere

elu|de [i'luud] *v/t* sakınmak, sıyrılmak *-den*; **~sive** tutulmaz, ele geçmez

emaciated [i'meyşieytid] çok zayıflanmış, sıska

emanate ['emıneyt] çıkmak (**from** *-den*)

emancipat|e [i'mänsipeyt] *v/t* serbest bırakmak; **~ion** serbest bırakma, eşit hakları verme

embalm [im'bâm] *v/t* tahnit etm.

embankment [im'bänkmınt] set, bent; rıhtım

embargo [em'bâgıu] *naut.* ambargo

embark [im'bâk] *v/t* gemiye bindirmek; *v/i* gemiye binmek; girişmek (**in, on** *-e*)

embarras [im'bärıs] *v/t* şaşırtmak; utandırmak; **~ing** utandırıcı; nahoş; **~ment** sıkıntı, sıkılganlık

embassy ['embäsi] *pol.* büyük *veya* orta elçilik; sefarethane

embed [im'bed] *v/t* gömmek, yerleştirmek

embellish [im'beliş] *v/t* süslemek, güzelleştirmek

ember ['embı] kor

embezzle [im'bezl] *v/t* zimmetine geçirmek

embitter [im'bitı] *v/t* acılaştırmak

emblem ['em'blım] sembol, simge

embody [im'bodi] *v/t* temsil etm.   [*med.* amboli]

embolism ['embılizım] }

embrace [im'breyc] *v/t* kucaklamak; benimsemek; *v/i* kucaklaşmak; *n.* kucaklaşma

embroider [im'broydı] *v/t -in* üzerine nakış işlemek; **~y** nakış, işleme

embryo ['embriu] cenin, dölüt

emerald ['emırıld] zümrüt

emerge [i'möc] ortaya çıkmak, (**from** *-den*); **~nce** çıkma, zuhur

emergency [i'mōcınsı] olağanüstü durum, tehlike; ~ **brake** imdat freni; ~ **call** istimdat; ~ **exit** ihtiyat kapı; ~ **landing** av. mecburî iniş

emery ['emırı] zımpara

emigra|nt ['emıgrınt] göçmen; **~te** [~ˌeyt] göçmek; **~tion** göçmenlik

eminen|ce ['emınıns] yükseklik; yüksek rütbe; **~t** yüksek; seçkin; **~tly** adv. pek, gayet

emission [i'mişn] yayma

emit [i'mit] v/t çıkarmak

emotion [i'mouşn] heyecan, his; **~al** duygulu; heyecanlı

emperor ['empırı] imparator

empha|sis ['emfısis] şiddet, vurgu, kuvvet; **~size** v/t önem vermek -e, vurgulamak -i; **~tic** [im'fätik] etkili; vurgulu

empire ['empayı] imparatorluk

employ [im'ploy] v/t kullanmak, istihdam etm.; n. görev, hizmet; **~ee** [employ'î] işçi, müstahdem; **~er** işveren, patron; **~ment** iş verme; memuriyet; **~ment agency** iş ve işçi bulma kurumu

empower [im'pauı] v/t yetki vermek -e

empt|iness ['emptinis] boşluk; **~y** adj. boş; anlamsız; v/t boşaltmak

enable [i'neybl] v/t mukte-

dir kılmak; kuvvet vermek -e

enact [i'näkt] v/t kararlaştırmak; thea. oynamak

enamel [i'nämıl] n. mine; v/t mine ile kaplamak

encase [in'keys] v/t kılıflamak

enchant [in'çânt] v/t büyülemek, teshir etm.

encircle [in'sökl] v/t kuşatmak

enclos|e [in'kluz] v/t kuşatmak; ilişikte göndermek; **~ure** [~jı] çit; ilişik kâğıt

encompass [in'kampıs] v/t -in etrafını çevirmek

encounter [in'kauntı] n. karşılaşma; v/t karşılamak

encourage [in'karic] v/t teşvik etm.; cesaret vermek -e; **~ment** teşvik

encroach [in'krıuç] v/i el uzatmak (**on, upon** -e)

encumber [in'kambı] v/t yüklemek; engel olm. -e

end [end] n. son; amaç, gaye; v/t bitirmek; bit mek; **stand on** ~ tüyleri ürpermek; **to this** ~ bu amaçla

endanger [in'deyncı] v/t tehlikeye düşürmek

endear [in'dii] v/t sevdirmek (**to** -e)

endeavo(u)r [in'devı] n. emek, çaba; çalışmak

end|ing ['endiŋ] son; gr. sonek; **~less** sonsuz

endorse [in'dôs] v/t. ec. ciro etm.; onaylamak; **~ment** ciro; tasvip

endow [in'dau] *v/t* donatmak

endur|ance [in'dyurins]
tahammül; **~e** *v/t* tahammül etm., dayanmak *-e*

enemy ['enimi] düşman,
hasım

energ|etic [en'cetik] ener-
jik, faal; **~y** enerji, gayret

enervate ['enöveyt]*v/t* kuvvetten düşürmek

enfold [in'fuld] *v/t* sarmak

enforce [in'fôs] *v/t* zorla
kabul ettirmek; yürütmek

enfranchise [in'frânçayz]
v/t pol. seçim hakkı vermek
-e

engage [in'geyc] *v/t* hizmete almak, tutmak; *v/i*
meşgul olm. (**in** ile); **be ~d**
nişanlı olm. (**to** ile); **~ment**
söz, vaat; angajman, hiz-
mete alma; nişanlanma;
randevu

engine ['encin] makine,
motor; lokomotif; **~driv-
er** makinist

engineer [enci'niı] makinist; mühendis; **~ing** mü-
hendislik

England ['inglınd] İngil-
tere

English ['ingliş] İngiliz;
İngilizce; **the ~** *pl.* İngiliz-
ler; **~man** İngiliz erkeği;
~woman İngiliz kadını

engrav|e [in'greyv] *v/t* hak-
ketmek, oymak; **~ing** hak-
kâk işi

engross [in'grıus] *v/t* zaptetmek, işgal etm.

enigma [i'nigmı] bilmece

enjoin [in'coyn] *v/t* emretmek, tembih etm.

enjoy [in'coy] *v/t* sevmek;
hoşlanmak *-den;* **~ oneself**
zevk almak; **~ment** eğlence, zevk

enlarge [in'lâc] *v/t* büyült-
mek, genişletmek; *v/i* genişlemek; **~ment** büyü(lt)-
me; ağrandısman

enlighten [in'laytn] *v/t* aydınlatmak; **~ed** aydın

enlist [in'list] *v/t mil.* kaydetmek; *v/i* asker olm.

enliven [in'layvn] *v/t* canlandırmak

enmity ['enmiti] düşmanlık

enormous [i'nômıs] kocaman, iri

enough [i'naf] kâfi, yeter

enquire [in'kwayı] *s.* **inquire**

enrage [in'reyc] *v/t* kızdırmak

enrapture [in'râpçı] *v/t*
kendinden geçirmek

enrich [in'riç] *v/t* zengin-
leştirmek

enrol(l) [in'rul] kaydetmek

enslave [in'sleyv] *v/t* köle
yapmak

ensue [in'syû] *v/i* ardından
gelmek; hâsıl olm., gelmek
(**from** *-den*)

ensure [in'şuı] *v/t* sağlamak

entangle [in'tängl] *v/t* dolaştırmak

enter ['entı] *v/i* girmek
(**into** *-e*); girişmek (*-e*); *v/t*
kaydetmek, deftere geçir-
mek

enterpris|e ['entıprayz] te-

şebbüs, iş; **~ing** girişken,
faal

entertain [entı'teyn] *v/t*
eğlendirmek; misafirliğe
kabul etm.; **~er** prezan-
tatör; **~ment** eğlence;
ağırlama

enthusias|m [in'thyûziä-
zım] coşkunluk; can atma;
~tic [~'ästik] heyecanlı,
coşkun

entic|e [in'tays] *v/t* ayart-
mak; **~ing** ayartıcı

entire [in'tayı] tam, bütün;
~ly *adv.* büsbütün

entitle [in'taytl] *v/t* şekli
vermek -*e*

entity ['entiti] varlık

entrails ['entreylz] *pl.* bağırsaklar

entrance [in'trɛns] giriş,
girme; giriş yeri; **~ fee** gir-
melik, duhuliye

entreat [in'trît] *v/t* ısrarla
rica etm. -*den*; **~y** yalvarma, rica

entrust [in'trast] *v/t* emniyet etm. (**to** -*e*)

entry ['entri] girme, giriş;
kayıt; **~ permit** giriş mü-
saadesi

enumerate [i'nyûmıreyt]
v/t birer birer saymak

envelop [in'velıp] *v/t* sarmak; **~e** ['envılıup] zarf

env|iable ['envibl] gıpta
edilir; **~ious** gıpta eden,
kıskanç

environment [in'vayırın-
ment] muhit, çevre; **~al
pollution** çevre kirlen-
mesi

environs ['environz] *pl.*
civar, etraf

envoy ['envoy] elçi

envisage [in'vizic] *v/t* plan-
lamak; tasavvur etm.

envy ['envi] *n.* gıpta, haset;
v/t gıpta etm., imrenmek -*e*

epic ['epik] destan; destan
gibi

epidemic [epi'demik] (**disease**) *med.* salgın hastalık

epidermis [epi'dömis] üstderi   [sara, tutarak}

epilepsy ['epilepsi] *med.}

epilog(ue) ['epilog] sonsöz

episcopa|l [i'piskıpıl] *rel.*
piskoposa ait; **~te** [~pit]
piskoposluk

episode ['episıud] olay

epitah ['epitäf] mezar kita-
besi

epoch ['îpok] devir, çağ

equal ['îkwıl] *adj.* eşit, denk;
n. eş, emsal; *v/t* eşit olm.
-*e*; **~ity** [î'kwoliti] eşitlik;
~ize *v/t* eşitlemek

equanimity [ekwı'nimiti]
ılım, vakar

equat|ion [i'kweyjın] *math.*
denklem; **~or** *geo.* ekvator

equilibrium [îkwi'libriım]
denge

equip [i'kwip] *v/t* donatmak; **~ment** teçhizat, do-
natım

equity ['ekwiti] insaf, adalet

equivalent [i'kwivılınt] *n.*
bedel, karşılık; *adj.* muadil}
eşit (**to** -*e*)

era ['iırı] devir, çağ

erase [i'reyz] *v/t* silmek,
çizmek

ere [äı] -den önce

erect [i'rekt] v/t dikmek, kurmak; adj. dik, dikili; **.ion** dikme, kurma; bina

erosion [i'rujın] erozyon

erotic [i'rotik] aşka ait; şehvanî

err [ö] v/i yanılmak

errand ['erınd] iş, sipariş

erro|neous [i'runyıs] yanlış, hatalı; **.r** ['eri] hata, yanlışlık

erudition [eru'dişın] âlimlik

erupt [i'rapt] v/i fışkırmak; **.ion** fışkırma; med. kızartı

escalat|ion [eskı'leyşın] artış; **.or** ['..tı] yürüyen merdiven

escape [is'keyp] n. kaçma, kurtuluş; v/i kaçmak, kurtulmak (from -den)

escort [es'kôt] n. muhafız; maiyet; kavalye; [is'kôt] v/t refakat etm. -e

especial [is'peşıl] özel, mahsus; **.ly** adv. özellikle

espionage [espi'nâj] casusluk

essay ['esey] makale, yazı; deneme

essen|ce ['esns] öz, esas, nitelik; chem. esans; **.tial** [i'senşıl] esaslı; elzem

establish [is'tâbliş] kurmak; **~ oneself** yerleşmek; **~ment** kurma; kurum; egemen çevreler, ileri gelenler pl.

estate [is'teyt] mal, mülk, arsa; **~ agency** emlâk bürosu; **~ car** pikap

esteem [is'tîm] n. itibar, saygı; v/t takdir etm.; hürmet etm. -e

estimat|e ['estimit] n. hesap; tahmin; ['estimeyt] v/t tahmin etm.; takdir etm.; **.ion** tahmin; itibar; fikir

estrange [is'treync] v/t soğutmak, uzaklaştırmak

estuary ['estyuıri] geo. nehir ağzı

etern|al [i'tönl] ebedî, sonsuz; ezelî, öncesiz; **.ity** ebediyet, sonsuzluk

ether ['îthı] eter; esir

ethic|al ['ethikıl] ahlâkî; **~s** pl. ahlâk

Ethiopia [îthi'ıupyı] Habeşistan

ethno|graphy [eth'nogrıfi] etnografya; **.logy** [**~**lıci] etnoloji

eucalyptus [yûkı'liptıs] bot. okaliptüs

eunuch ['yûnık] hadım, harem ağası

Europe ['yuurıp] Avrupa; **.an** [**~**'piın] Avrupalı

evacuat|e [i'väkyueyt] v/t boşaltmak; **.ion** boşaltma, tahliye

evade [i'veyd] v/t sakınmak -den

evaporate [i'väpıreyt] v/t buharlaştırmak; v/i buharlaşmak; **.d milk** kondanse süt

evasi|on [i'veyjın] kaçınma; kaçamak; **.ve** [**~**siv] kaçamaklı

eve [îv] arife

even ['îvın] adj. düz, pürüzsüz; tam; denk; *adv.* hatta, bile, dahi; ~ **number** çift sayı; ~ **if**, ~ **though** olsa bile

evening ['ívnin] akşam; **good** ~! iyi akşamlar!

event [i'vent] olay; hal; **at all** ~s her halde; ~**ful** olaylarla dolu

eventual [i'vençul] sonraki; ~**ly** *adv.* ilerde

ever ['evı] daima, her zaman; hiç; **for** ~ ebediyete kadar; **hardly** ~ hemen hemen hiç; ~ **since** *-den* beri; ~**lasting** sonsuz; devamlı

every ['evri] her, her bir; ~ **now and then** arasıra; ~ **other day** günaşırı; ~**body** herkes; ~**day** her günkü; ~**one** s. ~**body**; ~**thing** her şey; ~**where** her yer(d)e

eviden|ce ['evidıns] tanıklık, delil; ~**t** aşikâr, belli, açık

evil ['ívl] fena, kötü; fenalık, kötülük

evoke [i'vıuk] *v/t* uyandırmak [me]

evolution [ívı'luuşın] geliş-ƒ

ewe [yû] *zo.* dişi koyun

ex- [eks-] sabık, eski

exact [ig'zäkt] *adj.* tam, doğru; *v/t* icap etm.; talep etm.; ~**itude** [-ityûd] sıhhat, doğruluk; ~**ly** *adv.* tamamen; aynen; ~**ness** s. ~**itude**

exaggerat|e [ig'zäcıreyt] *v/t* mübalâğa etm., abartmak; ~**ion** mübalâğa

exalt [ig'zôlt] *v/t* yükseltmek; ~**ation** [egzôl'teyşın] heyecan

examin|ation [igzämi'neyşın] sınav, imtihan, muayene, yoklama; ~**e** [-'zämin] *v/t* sınavlamak, yoklamak; teftiş etm.

example [ig'zâmpl] örnek, misal; **for** ~ meselâ, örneğin

exasperate [ig'zâspıreyt] *v/t* kızdırmak

excavat|e ['ekskıveyt] *v/t* kazmak; ~**ion** kazı

exceed [ik'sîd] *v/t* aşmak, geçmek; ~**ingly** *adv.* son derece

excel [ik'sel] *v/t* geçmek, üstün olm. *-den*; ~**lence** ['eksılıns] üstünlük; **His** (*or* **Your**) **Excellency** Ekselans; ~**lent** mükemmel, çok iyi

except [ik'sept] *v/t* hariç tutmak; *prp. -den* başka; ~**ion** istisna; ~**ional** müstesna; olağanüstü

excess [ik'ses] ifrat, aşırılık fazla; ~ **fare** bilet ücretine yapılan zam; ~ **luggage** fazla bagaj; ~ **postage** taksa

exchange [iks'çeync] *n.* değişme, trampa; kambiyo; borsa; *v/t* değiştirmek; **foreign** ~ döviz

exchequer [iks'çeki] *pol.* devlet hazinesi

excite [ik'sayt] *v/t* kışkırtmak; heyecanlandırmak; ~**ment** heyecan; telâş

exclaim [iks'kleym] *v/i, v/t* bağırmak

exclamation [ekskli'mey-şın] ünlem; **~ mark** *gr.* ünlem işareti

exclu|de [iks'kluud] *v/t* hariç tutmak; **~sion** [~jın] hariç tutma; **~sive** [~siv] has; tek; özel

excommunication ['eks-kımyûni'keyşın] *rel.* aforoz

excursion [iks'köşın] gezinti

excuse [iks'kyûs] *n.* özür, mazeret; bahane; [~z] *v/t* affetmek, mazur görmek; **~ me** affedersiniz

execut|e ['eksikyût] *v/t* yapmak; yerine getirmek; idam etm., **~ion** yapma, icra; idam; **~ioner** cellât; **~ive** [ig'zekyutiv] icra eden; idareci, yetki sahibi; **~or** vasiyeti tenfiz memuru

exemplary [ig'zemplıri] örnek verici; ibret verici

exempt [ig'zempt] *adj.* muaf; *v/t* muaf tutmak (**from** -*den*); **~ion** muafiyet

exercise ['eksısayz] *n.* uygulama; idman; egzersiz, alıştırma; *v/t* kullanmak; *v/i* idman yapmak

exert [ig'zöt] *v/t* sarfetmek, kullanmak; **~ oneself** uğraşmak; **~ion** kullanma; çaba

exhale [eks'heyl] *v/t* koku *v.s.* çıkarmak

exhaust [ig'zöst] *n. tech.* egzoz; *v/t* tüketmek, bitir-

mek; **~ion** bitkinlik; **~-pipe** egzoz borusu

exhibit [ig'zibit] *v/t* teşhir etm., sermek, göstermek; *n. jur.* delil olarak ibraz edilen şey; **~ion** [eksi'bi-şın] sergi; burs; **~or** sergiye katılan kimse

exhumation [eksyû'mey-şın] mezardan çıkarma

exile ['eksayl] *n.* sürgün; *v/t* sürmek, sürgüne göndermek

exist [ig'zist] var olm.; bulunmak; yaşamak; **~ence** varlık; hayat; **~ent** mevcut, bulunan

exit ['eksit] çıkış; çıkış yeri; **~ visa** çıkış vizesi

exorbitant [ig'zöbitınt] aşırı [(gelen)]

exotic [eg'zotik] dışarıdan

expan|d [iks'pänd] *v/t* genişletmek, yaymak; *v/i* yayılmaq, açılmak; **~sion** yayılma, genişleme; **~sive** geniş, engin

expect [iks'pekt] *v/t* beklemek; ummak; **~ation** [ekspek'teyşın] bekleme, ümit

expedi|ent [iks'pîdyınt] *adj.* yararlı, uygun; çare, tedbir; **~tion** [ekspi'dişın] acele; sefer; gezi; **~tious** süratli

expel [iks'pel] *v/t* kovmak, çıkarmak

expen|d [iks'pend] *v/t* sarfetmek, harcamak; **~se** [~s] masraf, gider; **at the ~se of** -*in* zararına; **~sive** masraflı, pahalı

experience [iks'piirins] *n.*
tecrübe, deneme, görgü;
v/t görmek, tecrübe etm.;
~d tecrübeli, görgülü

experiment [iks'perimınt]
n. tecrübe, deney; [~mınt]
v/t tecrübe etm., denemek

expert [n.'ekspöt] usta, mahir; uzman, eksper

expir|ation [ekspayı'rey
şın] nefes verme; son; **~e**
[iks'payı] nefes vermek;
ölmek; sona ermek

expl|ain [iks'pleyn] *v/t*
açıklamak, anlatmak; **~anation** [ekspli'neyşın] izah,
açıklama

explicit [iks'plisit] açık,
kesin

explode [iks'plud] *v/i* patlamak; *v/t* patlatmak

exploit [iks'ployt] *v/t* sömürmek

explor|ation [eksplô'rey
şın] araştırma, keşif; **~e**
[iks'plô] *v/t* araştırmak, keşfetmek; **~er** kâşif, bulucu

explosi|on [iks'pluujın] patlama; **~ve** [~siv] patlayıcı
(madde)

export [n.'ekspôt] *n. ec.* ihraç
malı; ihracat; [~'pôt] *v/t*
ihraç etm., **~ation** ihraç;
~er ihracatçı

expos|e [iks'piuz] *v/t* açığa
vurmak; maruz bırakmak;
teşhir etm.; **~ition** [ekspiu'zişın] sergi; **~ure** [iks
'piuji] maruz olma; açığa
vurma; *phot.* poz; **~ure
meter** *phot.* ışıkölçer, pozometre

express [iks'pres] *adj.* açık,
sarih; süratli, hızlı; *n.* ekspres; *v/t* ifade etm.; **~
train** ekspres treni; **~ion**
ifade, deyim; **~ive** anlamlı;
etkileyici; **~way** *Am.* otoyol

expropriation [eksprıupri
'eyşın] kamulaştırma

expulsion [iks'palşın] kovma, çıkarma

exquisite ['ekskwizit] ince,
seçkin

extant [eks'tänt] hâlâ mevcut

exten|d [iks'tend] uzatmak,
genişletmek, yaymak; *v/i*
uzanmak, büyümek; **~sion**
uzatma; uzanma; ek;
munzam telefon; **~sive**
geniş; şümullü; **~t** derece,
had; büyüklük; mesafe; **to
a certain ~t** bir dereceye
kadar

exterior [eks'tiiriı] dış taraf; dış; zâhirî

exterminat|e [eks'tömineyt] *v/t* imha etm.

external [eks'tönl] dış, zâhirî

extinct [iks'tinkt] sönmüş;
nesli tükenmiş

extinguish [iks'tingwiş] *v/t*
söndürmek; **~er** yangın
söndürme aleti

extirpate ['ekstöpeyt] *v/t*
imha etm., yok etm.

extortion [iks'tôşın] zorla
alma, şantaj

extra ['ekstrı] fazla; ekstra;
ilâve, ek, zam

extract ['eksträkt] *n.* özet;

esans; [iks'~] v/t çıkarmak; koparmak; ~ion çıkarma; nesil, soy

extraordinary [iks'trôdnri] olağanüstü; garip

extravagan|ce [iks'trävigıns] israf; aşırılık; ~t tutumsuz; aşırı

extrem|e [iks'trîm] son derece; son; aşırı, müfrit; ~ist aşırı giden kimse; ~ity [~emiti] uç; son; sınır; aşırı tehlike; pl. an. eller, ayaklar

extricate ['ekstrikeyt] v/t kurtarmak [coşkun; bol]
exuberant [ig'zyûbırınt]
exult [ig'zalt] çok sevinmek (at -e)

eye [ay] n. göz; delik, ilik; budak; v/t göz atmak -e; ~ball göz küresi; ~brow kaş; (a pair of) ~glasses gözlük; ~lash kirpik; ~lid göz kapağı; ~shot görüş mesafesi; ~sight görme kuvveti; ~witness jur. görgü tanığı

F

fable ['feybl] masal, efsane
fabric ['fäbrik] yapı; kumaş; ~ate ['~eyt] v/t yapmak, uydurmak
fabulous ['fäbyulıs] efsanevî; inanılmaz
face [feys] n. yüz, çehre; yüzey; kadran, mine; yüzsüzlük; v/t karşılamak; -in karşısında olm.; -in kenarını çevirmek; make ~s yüzünü gözünü oynatmak; ~ value itibarî değer
facilit|ate [fı'siliteyt] v/t kolaylaştırmak; ~y kolaylık; pl. imkânlar, tesisat
fact [fäkt] gerçek; durum; in ~ gerçekten [tilâf)
faction ['fäkşın] grup; ih-)
factor ['fäktı] âmil, sebep; ~y fabrika, imalâthane
faculty ['fäkılti] yetenek; güç; fakülte
fade [feyd] solmak, rengi uçmak

fag(g)ot ['fägıt] çalı demeti
fail [feyl] v/i başaramamak (in -i); yapamamak; zayıflamak; iflâs etm.; v/t bırakmak; **without** ~ mutlaka, elbette; ~ure ['~yı] başarısızlık; iflâs; başarı kazanamıyan insan
faint [feynt] adj. baygın, zayıf; v/i bayılmak
fair¹ [fäı] ec. panayır, fuar
fair² insaflı, doğru; haklı; güzel; sarışın; şöyle böyle; ~ copy temiz kopya; ~ play temiz oyun; tarafsızlık; ~ly adv. oldukça; ~ness dürüstlük; güzellik
fairy ['fäıri] peri; ~tale peri masalı; yalan
faith [feyth] itikat, inanç; güven; vefa; sadakat; ~ful vefalı, sadık; ~less vefasız
fake [feyk] n. taklit; uydurma; şarlatan; v/t uydurmak

falcon

falcon ['fôlkın] *zo.* doğan, şahin

fall [fôl] *n.* düşme, çökme; *Am.* sonbahar; çağlayan; meyil; *v/i* düşmek, dökülmek, azalmak; ~ **asleep** uykuya dalmak; ~ **back** geri çekilmek; başvurmak (**on** -*e*); ~ **in love** âşık olm. (**with** -*e*); ~ **short** ulaşamamak (**of** -*e*); ~**en s. fall**

false [fôls] sahte, yapma; yanlış; yalancı; ~**ness** sahtelik, yalan

falsify ['fôlsifay] *v/t* bozmak, taklit etm.

falter ['fôltı] *v/i* kekelemek, tutuk konuşmak; sendelemek

fame [feym] şöhret

familiar [fı'miliı] bilinen; lâubali, senli benli; alışkın (**with** -*e*), bilen (-*i*); ~**ity** [,fili'âriti] alışkanlık; teklifsizlik

family ['fâmili] aile; soy, cins; *bot.* familya; ~ **name** soyadı

famine ['fâmin] kıtlık

famous ['feymıs] meşhur, tanınmış

fan[1] *n.* yelpaze; vantilatör; *v/t* yelpazelemek

fan[2] meraklı, düşkün

fanatic(**al**) [fı'nâtik(ıl)] mutaassıp, fanatik; ~**ism** [,isizım] taassup

fanciful ['fânsiful] hayalperest, kaprisli

fancy ['fânsi] *n.* hayal, kapris, geçici arzu; *adj.* hayale dayanan; süslü; *v/t* tasav-

vur etm., kurmak; beğenmek; ~**dress** balo kıyafeti; ~**goods** *pl.* fantezi eşya; ~**work** ince el işi

fang [fâŋ] zehirli diş; azıdişi

fantastic [fân'tâstik] hayalî, acayip, garip

far [fâ] uzak; uzun; çok; **by** ~ diğerlerinden çok üstün olmak üzere; ~**away** uzakta

farce [fâs] fars; saçma

fare [fâı] *n.* yol parası; yolcu; yiyecek; *v/i* olmak, yaşamak; ~**well** veda; Allaha ısmarladık! [rakı]

far-fetched yapmacık; zo-]

farm [fâm] *n.* çiftlik; *v/i* çift sürmek; *v/t* işletmek; ~**er** çiftçi

far-reaching geniş kapsamlı; vahim; ~**sighted** geniş görüşlü olan

farther ['fâdhı] daha uzak, daha öte; ~**st** ['_ist] en uzak

fascinate ['fâsineyt] *v/t* büyülemek, teshir etm.; ~**ion** teshir

fashion ['fâşın] *n.* moda, biçim; tarz; *v/t* yapmak; şekil vermek -*e*; ~**able** ['_şnıbl] modaya uygun, zarif

fast[1] [fâst] *n. rel.* oruç; perhiz; *v/i* oruç tutmak; perhiz etm.

fast[2] çabuk, tez, hızlı; ileri (*saat*); sıkı, sabit; ~ **asleep** derin uykuda; ~**en** ['fâsn] *v/t* bağlamak, tutturmak; ~**ener** toka kıskacı; çıtçıt.

fastidious [fɪs'tidiɪs] titiz, kolay beğenmez

fat [fät] yağ; şişman, semiz, yağlı

fatal ['feytl] öldürücü; mukadder; **~ism** ['~lizim] kadercilik, fatalism

fate [feyt] kader, talih

father ['fâdhı] baba; ata; **~hood** babalık; **~-in-law** kaynpeder; **~less** babasız, yetim

fathom ['fädhım] n. kulaç; v/t iskandil etm.; fig. -in içyüzünü anlamak; **~less** dipsiz; anlaşılmaz

fatigue [fɪ'tîg] n. yorgunluk; v/t yormak

fatten ['fätn] v/t semirtmek

faucet ['fôsit] musluk

fault [fôlt] n. kusur, kabahat, hata; **find ~** kusur bulmak (**with** -de); **~less** kusursuz, mükemmel; **~y** kusurlu, hatalı

favo(u)r ['feyvı] n. teveccüh; himaye, taraf tutma; v/t lütuf göstermek -e; -in tarafını tutmak; tercih etm. -i; **do** s.o. **a ~** yardımda bulunmak -e; **in ~ of** -in lehinde; **~able** uygun, müsait; **~ite** ['~rit] en çok beğenilen; gözde

fawn [fôn] zo. geyik yavrusu; açık kahverengi

fear [fiı] n. korku, endişe; v/t korkmak -den; **~ful** korkunç; korkak; **~less** korkusuz

feasible ['fîzıbl] yapabilir, mümkün

feast [fîst] n. ziyafet; bayram; yortu; v/i bol yiyip içmek

feat [fît] hayret verici iş, başarı

feather ['fedhı] n. kuş tüyü; v/t tüy takmak -e

feature ['fîçı] özellik; asıl film; makale; pl. yüz, çehre

February ['februri] şubat (ayı)

fed [fed] s. **feed**

federa|l ['fedırıl] federal, federe; **~tion** [~'reyşın] birlik; federasyon

fee [fî] ücret; vizita

feeble ['fîbl] zayıf, dermansız

feed [fîd] n. yem, gıda; v/t yedirmek, beslemek; v/i otlamak; **be fed up** bıkmak (**with** -den); **~er** sulama kanalı; ana demiryoluna bağlı hat; **~ing bottle** biberon

feel [fîl] n. his, duygu; v/t hissetmek, duymak; yoklamak; **~er** zo. anten, dokunaç; **~ing** his, duygu

feet [fît] pl. s. **foot**

felicitate [fi'lisiteyt] v/t **on** -in ş.ini kutlamak

fell [fel] s. **fall**; v/t yere indirmek

fellow ['felıu] arkadaş, yoldaş; herif, adam; **~-citizen** vatandaş; **~ship** arkadaşlık

felon ['felın] jur. mücrim, suçlu; **~y** cinayet, ağır suç

felt[1] [felt] s. **feel**

felt[2] keçe; fötr

female ['fîmeyl] dişi; kadın

feminine ['feminin] gr. dişil

fen [fen] bataklık

fenc|e [fens] n. çit, parmaklık, tahta perde; v/t -in etrafını parmaklıkla çevirmek; v/i eskrim yapmak; **~ing** çit; eskrim

fend [fend]: **~ for** geçindirmek -i; **~ off** v/t kovmak; **~er** çamurluk

ferment ['fôment] n. mayalanma; maya; [fô'~] v/t mayalamak; v/i mayalanmak; **~ation** mayalanma

fern [fôn] bot. eğreltiotu

ferocious [fı'rıuşıs] yırtıcı, vahşi

ferry ['feri] n. naut. feribot, araba vapuru; v/t nehirden geçirmek; **~boat** feribot

fertil|e ['fôtayl] bereketli, verimli; **~ity** [~'tiliti] verimlilik; **~ize** [~'ilayz] v/t gübrelemek; verimli hale getirmek; **~izer** gübre

fervent ['fôvınt] hararetli, ateşli

festiv|al ['festivıl] bayram, festival; **~e** [~iv] şen, neşeli; **~ity** [~'tiviti] şenlik, eğlenti [mek]

fetch [feç] v/t gidip getir-

fetter ['feti] zincir, köstek

feud¹ [fyûd] kan davası

feud² tımar, zeamet; **~al** ['~dl] derebeyliğe ait; **~alism** ['~dılizm] derebeylik

fever ['fivı] ateş, humma; **~ish** hararetli, ateşli

few [fyû] az; **a ~** birkaç; **quite a ~** birçok

fez [fez] fes

fiancé(e) [fi'ânsey] nişanlı

fib|re, Am. **~er** ['faybı] lif, tel; **~rous** lifli, telli

fickle ['fikl] kararsız

ficti|on ['fikşın] roman; roman edebiyatı; hayal; yalan; **~tious** [~'tişıs] hayalî, uydurma

fiddle ['fidl] n. keman; v/i keman çalmak

fidelity [fi'deliti] vefa

fidget ['ficit] v/t rahat oturamamak; **~y** yerinde durmıyan

field [fîld] tarla, kır; alan, meydan; **~ events** pl. atlama ve atma yarışları; **~ glasses** pl. çifte dürbün sg.; **~-marshal** mil. mareşal

fiend [fînd] iblis, şeytan; fig. tiryaki

fierce [fiıs] vahşi, azgın

fiery [fayıri] ateşli, alevli

fife [fayf] mus. fifre

fift|een ['fif'tîn] on beş; **~y** elli

fig [fig] bot. incir

fight [fayt] n. dövüş, kavga, savaş; v/i savaşmak; dövüşmek; v/t defetmek; yapmak; **~er** savaşçı; av. avcı uçağı

figurative ['figyurıtiv] mecazî

figure ['figı] n. şekil, endam, boy bos; şahsiyet; rakam; mecaz; v/t desenlerle süslemek; temsil etm.; tasavvur etm.; **~ out** v/t hesaplamak

filament ['filımınt] tel, lif

file¹ [fayl] *n. tech.* eğe; *v/t* eğelemek

file² *n.* dizi; dosya, klasör; *v/t* dosyaya koymak, tasnif etm.; *dilekçe v.s.* vermek

filigree ['filigri] telkâri

fill [fil] *v/i* dolmak, kabarmak; *v/t* doldurmak; işgal etm.; ~ **in** *soru kâğıdını* doldurmak; ~ **up** *v/t* tamamen doldurmak

fillet ['filit] fileto; dilim

filling ['filiŋ] doldurma; dolgu; ~ **station** benzin istasyonu

film [film] *n.* zar; film; *v/t* filme geçirmek; zarla kaplamak

filter ['filtı] *n.* süzgeç; *v/t* süzmek; *v/i* sızmak

filth [fildh] kir, pislik; ~**y** kirli, pis

fin [fin] *zo.* yüzgeç

final ['faynl] son; kesin; final, son yarış; ~**ly** *adv.* nihayet, sonunda

financ|e [fay'näns] *n.* maliye; *v/t -in* masraflarını karşılamak; ~**ial** [~şıl] mali; ~**ier** [~sii] sermayedar

finch [finç] *zo.* ispinoz

find [faynd] *n.* bulunmuş şey; keşif; *v/t* bulmak; öğrenmek; rastlamak -*e*; ~ **out** keşfetmek; öğrenmek; ~**ing** bulunan şey; *pl.* sonuç

fine¹ [fayn] *n. jur.* para cezası; *v/t* para cezasına mahküm etm.

fine² ince; güzel, zarif; hoş, nazik; **I am** ~ iyiyim; ~**ry** gösteriş, süslü giyim

finger ['fiŋgı] parmak; ~-**nail** tırnak; ~-**print** parmak izi

finish ['finiş] *n.* son; son iş, rötuş; *v/t* bitirmek, tamamlamak; *v/i* bitmek, sona ermek

Finland ['finlınd] Finlandiya [diyalı]

Finn(ish) [fin(iş)] Finlan-J

fir [fö] *bot.* köknar; ~-**cone** köknar kozalağı

fire ['fayı] *n.* ateş, yangın; *v/t* tutuşturmak, yakmak; patlatmak; işinden çıkarmak; **cease** ~ ateş kesmek; **on** ~ tutuşmuş, yanan; ~-**alarm** yangın işareti; ~-**brigade,** *Am.* ~ **department** itfaiye; ~-**engine** yangın tulumbası; ~-**escape** yangın merdiveni; ~-**extinguisher** yangın söndürme aleti; ~-**man** itfaiyeci; ateşçi; ~-**place** ocak, şömine; ~-**proof** ateşe dayanır, yanmaz; ~-**side** ocak başı; ~-**wood** odun; ~-**works** *pl.* donanma fişekleri

firm [föm] sabit, metin, bükülmez; *ec.* firma; ~**ness** sağlamlık, metanet

first [föst] birinci; *adv.* önce, ilkin; **at** ~ ilk önce; ~ **aid** ilk yardım; ~ **floor** birinci kat; *Am.* zemin kat; ~-**aid box** ilk yardım kutusu; ~-**class** birinci sınıfa ait; ~-**rate** birinci sınıf, en iyi cinsten

fiscal ['fiskıl] mali

fish   274

fish [fiş] *n.* balık; *v/i* balık tutmak; **~bone** kılçık
fisher|man ['fişımın] balıkçı; **~y** balıkçılık
fishing ['fişin] balık avı; **~line** olta; **~rod** olta kamışı; **~tackle** balıkçı takımı
fishmonger ['fişmangı] balıkçı; balık satan
fissure ['fişı] yarık, çatlak
fist [fist] yumruk
fistula [fistyulı] *med.* fistül
fit [fit] *n.* tutarak, hastalık nöbeti; *adj.* uygun, yaraşır; lâyık; hazır; *v/i* uymak, yakışmak; *v/t* yerleştirmek; donatmak; **~ on** *v/t* takmak, prova etm.; **~ out** *v/t* donatmak; **~ness** uygunluk; sağlık; **~ter** boru işlerine bakan kimse; **~ting** uygun; prova; *pl.* tertibat
five [fayv] beş; **~fold** beş misli, beş kat
fix [fiks] *v/t* takmak; yerleştirmek; hazırlamak; tamir etm.; *gözlerini* dikmek (**on** *-e*); *n.* güç durum; **~ up** *v/t* kurmak, düzeltmek; **~ed** sabit; bağlı; **~tures** ['~çız] *pl.* demirbaş eşya
fizz [fiz] *v/i* fışırdamak
flabbergast ['flæbıgaast] *v/t* şaşırtmak
flabby ['flæbi] gevşek
flag [flæg] *n.* bayrak, bandıra; kaldırım taşı; *bot.* süsen, susam; *v/t* bayraklarla donatmak
flail [fleyl] harman döveni

flake [fleyk] *n.* kuşbaşı, lapa; ince tabaka; **~ off** *v/i* tabaka tabaka ayrılmak
flame [fleym] *n.* alev; *v/i* alevlenmek
flank [flænk] *n.* böğür; yan; *v/t* yandan kuşatmak; bitişik olm. *-e*
flannel ['flænıl] fanila
flap [flæp] *n.* sarkık parça, kapak; vuruş; *v/i* kanatlarını çırpmak; *v/t* hafifçe vurmak *-e*
flare [flæı] *v/i* alevlenmek; *fig.* birden hiddetlenmek
flash [flæş] ışıltı, parıltı; *fig.* an; bülten; *v/i* parlamak; birden gelmek; *v/t* (radyo ile) yayımlamak; **~bulb** *phot.* flaş ampulü; **~light** *phot.* flaş; cep feneri
flask [flaask] küçük şişe; termos
flat [flæt] düz, yassı; tatsız, yavan; *mus.* bemol; yüzey; apartman dairesi; **~iron** ütü; **~ten** *v/t* yassılatmak; *v/i* yassılaşmak
flatter ['flætı] *v/t* pohpohlamak, göklere çıkarmak; **~y** dalkavukluk
flavo(u)r ['fleyvı] *n.* tat, lezzet, çeşni; *v/t* tat vermek *-e*; lezzet vermek *-e*
flaw [flô] çatlak, yarık; noksan, kusur; **~less** kusursuz
flax [flæks] *bot.* keten
flea [fli] pire
fled [fled] *s.* **flee**
flee [fli] kaçmak
fleece [flîs] *n.* yapak, yünlü

fluster

post; v/t aldatmak, kazıklamak

fleet [flit] *naut.* donanma, filo; süratli, hızlı

flesh [fleş] et; vücut, ten; **~y** etli, şişman

flew [fluu] *s.* fly

flexible ['fleksıbl] bükülebilir; uysal

flick [flik] v/t hafifçe vurmak *-e*

flicker ['flikı] v/i titremek, oynamak

flight [flayt] uçma, uçuş; firar, kaçış; sıra

flimsy ['flimzi] ince, gevşek

flinch [flinç] v/i sakınmak, kaçınmak

fling [fling] *n.* fırlatma, atma; v/t atmak, fırlatmak

flint [flint] çakmak taşı

flip [flip] *n.* fiske; v/i fiske vurmak

flippant ['flipınt] küstah

flipper ['flipı] balık kanadı

flirt [flöt] v/i flört yapmak; **~ation** flört

flit [flit] v/i geçmek; çırpınmak

float [flaut] *n.* duba, şamandıra; olta mantarı; v/t yüzdürmek; v/i yüzmek, suyun yüzünde durmak; **~ing** yüzen; değişen

flock [flok] *n.* sürü; yün *veya* saç yumağı; v/i toplanmak

floe [flau] buz kitlesi

flog [flog] kamçılamak; dövmek

flood [flad] *n.* sel, seylâp; met, kabarma; v/t taşmak;

su basmak; **~-gate** bent kapağı; **~-light** projektör; **~-tide** met, kabarma

floor [flô] *n.* döşeme; zemin; kat; v/t tahta *veya* parke döşemek *-e*; yere yıkmak *-i*; **~-lamp** ayaklı lâmba

flop [flop] v/i çöküvermek; v/t düşürmek

florist ['florist] çiçekçi

flour ['flaui] un

flourish ['flariş] v/t sallamak; v/i gelişmek, bayındır olm.; *n.* gösterişli hareket; paraf

flow [flıu] *n.* cereyan, akıntı; met, kabarma; v/i akmak; kabarmak

flower ['flaui] çiçek; **~-pot** saksı

flown [flıun] *s.* fly

flu [fluu] grip

fluctuate ['flaktyueyt] v/i değişmek; **~ion** değişme

fluent ['fluınt] akıcı (*söz*)

fluff [flaf] tüy, hav; **~y** tüy gibi yumuşak

fluid ['fluid] akıcı; sıvı madde

flung [flaŋ] *s.* fling

flunk [flaŋk] v/t sınavda bırakmak; v/i başaramamak

flurry ['flari] anî rüzgâr; sağanak; telâş; v/t telâşa düşürmek

flush [flaş] birden akmak; (*face*) kızarmak; v/t akıtmak; kızartmak; *n.* galeyan; akıtma

fluster ['flastı] *n.* telâş; v/t telâşa düşürmek

flute 276

flute [fluut] *mus.* flavta, flüt

flutter ['flʌtı] *v/i* çırpınmak; *n.* çırpınma; telâş

flux [flʌks] akış; değişiklik

fly¹ [flay] sinek

fly² *v/i* uçmak; kaçmak; *v/t* uçurmak; **~ into a rage** öfkelenmek; **~er** pilot; **~ing** uçma; uçan; **~over** üstgeçit; **~weight** sinekağırlı

foal [fiul] *zo.* tay, sıpa

foam [fium] *n.* köpük; *v/i* köpürmek; **~y** köpüklü

focus ['fiukıs] *n.* odak, mihrak; *v/t* ayar etm.

fodder ['fodı] yem

foe [fıu] düşman

fog [fog] sis; **~gy** sisli, dumanlı

foil¹ [foyl] foya, ince yaprak

foil² *v/t* engellemek

fold¹ [fıuld] ağıl; sürü

fold² kat, kıvrım; *v/t* katlamak; *elleri* kavuşturmak; **~er** dosya; **~ing-chair** açılır kapanır sandalye

foliage ['fiuliic] ağaç yaprakları *pl.*

folk [fıuk] halk, ahali; *pl. fam.* aile; **~lore** folklor

follow ['folıu] *v/t* takip etm., izlemek; riayet etm. **-e**; **~er** taraftar

folly ['foli] ahmaklık

fond [fond] seven (**of -i**); düşkün (**-e**); **~le** *v/t* okşamak

food [fuud] yiyecek, yemek, gıda; yem; **~stuffs** *pl.* gıda maddeleri

fool [fuul] *n.* budala, enayi;

v/t aldatmak; **~hardy** delice cesur; **~ish** sersem, akılsız; **~proof** sağlam; kusursuz

foot [fut] *pl.* **feet** [fiit] ayak; kadem (*30,48 cm*); **on ~** yaya; **~ball** futbol; **~hills** *pl.* dağ eteklerindeki tepeler; **~hold** ayak basacak yer; **~ing** ayak basacak yer; durum, hal; **~note** dipnot; **~path** keçi yolu, patika; **~print** ayak izi; **~step** ayak sesi; ayak izi

for [fô, fı] *prep.* için; olarak; zarfında; *-den* beri; yerine; yüzünden; *conj.* zira, çünkü; **~ example**, **~ instance** meselâ, örneğin

foray ['forey] çapul

forbade [fı'bäd] *s.* **forbid**

forbid [fı'bäd] *v/t* yasak etm.; **~den** *s.* **forbid**; yasak; **~ding** nahoş

forbor|e [fô'bô, **~n**] *s.* **forbear**

force [fôs] *n.* kuvvet, kudret; şiddet, zor; *v/t* zorlamak; sıkıştırmak; kırıp açmak; **armed ~s** *pl.* silahlı kuvvetler; **in ~** yürürlükte; **~d** mecburî

ford [fôd] *n.* nehir geçidi, sığ geçit; *v/t* sığ yerden geçmek

fore [fô] ön, ön taraf; **~boding** ['buudin] önsezi; **~cast** *n.* tahmin; *v/t* önceden tahmin etm.; **~finger** işaretparmağı; **~ground** ön plan; **~head** ['forid] alın

foreign ['forin] ecnebi, yabancı; dış; **~ currency** *ec.* döviz; **~ exchange** kambiyo; **2 Office** Dışişleri Bakanlığı; **~trade** dış ticaret; **~er** ecnebi, yabancı

fore|leg önayak, **~man** *jur.* jüri başkanı; işçi başı; **~most** en önde; ilk önce; **~noon** öğleden önceki zaman; *v/t* **~see** önceden görmek; **~sight** basiret, önceden görme

forest ['forist] orman; **~ry** ormancılık

fore|taste önceden alınan tat; **~tell** önceden haber vermek (*sth.* hakkında)

forever [fı'revı] devamlı olarak

foreword önsöz

forfeit ['fôfit] *n.* ceza; *v/t* kaybetmek

forge [fôc] *n.* demirci ocağı; *v/t* demiri işlemek; uydurmak; **~ry** sahte şey; kalpazanlık

forget [fı'get] *v/t* unutmak; **~ful** unutkan; **~menot** *bot.* unutma beni

forgive [fı'giv] *v/t* affetmek, bağışlamak; **~ness** af, bağışlama **[forget)**

forgot, ~ten [fı'got, ~n] *s.)*

fork [fôk] *n.* çatal; bel; *v/i* çatallaşmak

forlorn [fı'lôn] kimsesiz; ümitsiz

form [fôm] *n.* şekil, biçim; kâğıt, formül; form; forma; sınıf (*school*); *v/t* teşkil etm., kurmak; şekil vermek **~e**; *v/i* şekil almak

formal ['fômıl] biçimsel; resmî; **~ity** [~'äliti] usul; formalite

formation [fô'meyşın] teşkil, kurma

former ['fômı] önceki, eski, sabık; **~ly** *adv.* eskiden

formidable ['fômidıbl] heybetli, korkulur

formula ['fômyulı] formül; reçete

formulate ['fômyuleyt] *v/t* açık olarak belirtmek

for|sake [fı'seyk] *v/t* terketmek; vazgeçmek *-den*; **~saken, ~sook** [fı'suk] *s.* **~sake**

fort [fôt] kale

forth [fôth] ileri, dışarı, aşağa; sonra; **~coming** gelecek, çıkacak; **~right** açık; **~with** derhal, hemen

forti|fication [fôtifi'keyşın] tahkim, istihkâm; **~fy** ['~fay] *v/t* kuvvetlendirmek

fortnight ['fôtnayt] iki hafta

fortress ['fôtris] kale

fortunate ['fôçnit] talihli, şanslı; **~ly** *adv.* hamdolsun, çok şükür

fortune ['fôçın] baht; fal; *ec.* servet; **~teller** falcı

forty ['fôti] kırk

forward ['fôwıd] *adv.* ileri (-ye); *adj.* önde, ilerdeki; küstah; *v/t* sevketmek, göndermek (**to** *-e*)

foster ['fostı] *v/t* beslemek; **~child** evlâtlık; **~mother** analık

foul [faul] *adj.* pis, kirli;

found

bozuk; iğrenç; *v/t* kirletmek; dolaştırmak

found[1] [faund] *s.* **find**

found[2] *v/t* kurmak; *tech.* dökmek; **~ation** kurma, tesis; kuruluş; temel; **~er** kurucu; dökmeci; **~ling** sokakta bulunmuş çocuk; buluntu; **~ry** *tech.* dökümhane

fountain ['fauntin] çeşme; memba; fıskiye; **~-pen** dolma kalem

four [fô] dört; **~score** seksen; **~teen** ['~'tîn] on dört

fowl [faul] tavuk; kuş; **~ing piece** av tüfeği

fox [foks] *zo.* tilki

fract|ion ['fräkşın] kır(ıl)ma; parça; *math.* kesir; **~ure** ['~çı] *n.* kırma; kırık; *v/t* kırmak

fragile ['fräcayl] kolay kırılır

fragment ['frägmınt] kırılmış parça, kısım

fragran|ce ['freygrıns] güzel koku; **~t** güzel kokulu

frail [freyl] zayıf, narin; **~ty** zayıflık

frame [freym] *n.* çerçeve, gergef; beden; yapı; *v/t* şekil vermek –e, uydurmak *-i*; çerçevelemek *-i*; **~ of mind** mizaç, hal; **~work** çatı, iskelet

France [frâns] Fransa

franchise ['fränçayz] *pol.* oy verme hakkı

frank [fränk] açık sözlü, samimî

frankfurter ['fränkfıtı] *bir çeşit* sosis [sözlülük}

frankness ['fränknis] açık}

frantic ['fräntik] çılgınca heyecanlanmış

fratern|al [frı'tönl] kardeşçe; **~ity** kardeşlik

fraud [frôd] hile, dolandırıcılık

fray [frey] *v/t* yıpratmak; *v/i* yıpranmak

freak [frîk] kapris; eksantrik kimse

freckle ['frekl] çil

free [frî] *adj.* serbest; parasız; muaf; cömert; *v/t* serbest bırakmak, kurtarmak; tahliye etm.; **~ set ~** *v/t* serbest bırakmak; **~dom** hürriyet, serbestlik; açıklık; **~mason** mason; **~way** *Am.* çevre yolu

freez|e [frîz] *v/i* donmak; *v/t* dondurmak; **~ing-point** donma noktası

freight [freyt] *n.* hamule, navlun; *v/t* yükletmek; **~er** *naut.* yük vapuru, şilep

French [frenç] Fransız; Fransızca; **~ window** balkona *v.s.* giden camlı kapı; **~man** Fransız

frenzy ['frenzi] çılgınlık

frequen|cy ['frîkwınsi] sık sık olma; *phys.* frekans; **~t** *adj.* sık sık olan; [fri'kwent] *v/t* sık sık gitmek *-e*

fresh [freş] taze; yeni; dinç; acemi; **~man** üniversitenin birinci sınıf öğrencisi; **~ness** tazelik; acemilik; **~water** tatlı suda olan

fun

fret [fret] *v/t* rahatsız etm.; *v/i* kızmak

friar ['frayı] rahip

friction ['frikşın] sürtünme; friksiyon, *fig.* uyuşmazlık

Friday ['fraydi] cuma (günü)

fridge [fric] buzdolabı

fried [frayd] kızartılmış

friend [frend] dost, arkadaş, ahbap; *ly* dostça, samimî; *ship* dostluk, arkadaşlık

fright [frayt] dehşet, korku; *en v/t* korkutmak, ürkütmek; *ful* korkunç

frigid ['fricid] soğuk, buzlu

frill [fril] fırfır, farbala

fringe [frinc] saçak; kenar

frisk [frisk] sıçramak, oynamak; *y* neşeli, oynak

fro [fru]: to and *~* öteye beriye

frock [frok] kadın elbisesi, rop; *rel.* rahip cüppesi

frog [frog] *zo.* kurbağa

frolic ['frolik] *n.* neşe; *v/i* oynamak; *some* ['*sım] oynak, neşeli

from [from, frım] -den, -dan; *-den* itibaren

front [frant] ön, yüz; cephe; in *~* of *-in* önünde; *~ door* ön kapı; *~ page* ön sayfa; *~ wheel* ön tekerlek

frontier ['frantiı] sınır

frost [frost] *n.* don, ayaz, kırağı; *v/t* dondurmak; *~-bitten* donmuş; *~ed glass* buzlu cam; *~y* ayazlı; soğuk

froth [froth] *n.* köpük; *v/i* köpürmek

frown [fraun] *v/i* kaşlarını çatmak; hoş görmemek (upon *-i*)

froze, *~n* [friuz, *~n] *s.*

freeze; *~n meat* dondurulmuş et

frugal ['fruugıl] tutumlu, idareli

fruit [fruut] meyva, yemiş; *fig.* verim, sonuç; *~erer* manav, yemişçi; *~ful* verimli; *~less* verimsiz; faydasız

frustrat|e [fras'treyt] *v/t* önlemek, bozmak; hüsrana uğratmak; *~ion* önleme; hüsran

fry [fray] *v/t* tavada kızartmak; *v/i* kızarmak; *~-ing-pan* tava [çiçeği]

fuchsia ['fyûşı] *bot.* küpe

fuel [fyuıl] yakacak, yakıt

fugitive ['fyûcitiv] kaçak, mülteci

fulfil [ful'fil] *v/t* yerine getirmek, yapmak; bitirmek; *~ment* icra, yapma

full [ful] dolu; dolgun; olgun; tam, bütün; tok; *~ moon* dolunay; *~ stop gr.* nokta

ful(l)ness ['fulnis] dolgunluk; olgunluk

full-time tam günlük

fumble ['fambl] *v/i* el yordamiyle aramak (for *-i*)

fume [fyûm] *n.* duman, buhar; *v/t* tütsülemek; *v/i* hiddetlenmek

fun [fan] eğlence; şaka, alay; for *~* şakadan; make *~* alay etm. (of ile)

function

function ['faŋkşın] *n.* görev; tören, merasim; *math.* fonksiyon; *v/i* işlemek, iş görmek; **~ary** görevli

fund [fand] kapital, stok; fon

fundamental [fandı'mentl] esaslı; önemli

funeral ['fyûnırıl] cenaze alayı, gömme

funicular (railway) [fyu-'nikyulı] füniküler, kablolu demiryolu

funnel ['fanl] baca; huni; boru

funny ['fani] eğlenceli; tuhaf, acayip

fur [fö] kürk, post; pas, kir

furious ['fyuırıs] öfkeli; şiddetli

furl [föl] *v/t* sarmak

furnace ['fönis] ocak

furnish ['föniş] *v/t* döşemek, teçhiz etm. **~ed** möbleli, mobilyalı

furniture ['fönıçı] mobilya

furrier ['farı] kürkçü

furrow ['farı] sapan izi; tekerlek izi; *v/t* sabanla açmak

further ['födhı] *adj.* daha fazla, daha öte, yeni; *adv.* ayrıca; *v/t* ilerletmek; **~ more** bundan başka, ayrıca

furtive ['fötiv] sinsi, gizli

fury ['fyuırı] kızgınlık; şiddet

fuse [fyûz] *n. mil.* tapa; *el.* sigorta; *v/t* eritmek; *v/i* erimek

fuselage ['fyûzilâj] *av.* gövde

fusion ['fyûjın] eri(t)me; birleşme

fuss [fas] *n.* telâş; *v/i* meraklanmak, sızlanmak; **make a ~ about** mesele yapmak **~i** [boş]

futile ['fyûtayl] beyhude,

future ['fyûçı] gelecek; gelecekteki

G

gab [gäb] palavra; **gift of ~** konuşkanlık

gable ['geybl] çatı altındaki üç köşeli duvar

gad-fly ['gädflay] *zo.* atsineği

gadget ['gäcit] hünerli alet, cihaz

gag [gäg] ağız tıkacı; şaka

gage [geyc] *s.* **gauge**

gai|ety ['geyiti] neşe, şenlik; **~ly** *s.* **gay**

gain [geyn] *n.* kâr, kazanç;

yarar; artış; *v/t* kazanmak; varmak **-e**; **~say** *v/t* inkâr etm.

gait [geyt] yürüyüş, gidiş; **~er** tozluk, getir

galaxy ['gälıksi] *astr.* gökada; samanyolu

gale [geyl] bora, fırtına

gall [gôl] *an.* safra

gallant ['gälınt] cesur; gösterişli; nazik, kibar

gallery ['gälıri] galeri; üstü kapalı balkon

galley ['gäli] *naut.* kadırga; gemi mutfağı

gallon ['gälın] galon *(4,54 l, Am. 3,78 l)*

gallop ['gälıp] *n.* dörtnala gidiş; *v/i* dörtnala koşmak

gallows ['gäluz] darağacı

gambl|e ['gämbl] *n.* kumar; *v/i* kumar oynamak; **~ing-house** kumarhane

gambol ['gämbl] *n.* sıçrama; *v/i* sıçrayıp oynamak

game [geym] oyun, parti; av; **~keeper** avlak bekçisi

gander ['gändı] *zo.* erkek kaz

gang [gäŋ] güruh, takım, ekip; **~ster** ['~stı] gangster

gangway ['gäŋwey] geçit; *naut.* iskele tahtası

gaol [ceyl] *n.* cezaevi; *v/t* tutuklamak; **~er** gardiyan

gap [gäp] yarık, aralık, boşluk; eksiklik

gape [geyp] *v/i* esnemek; hayretten ağzı açık kalmak; açık olm.

garage ['gäräj] *n.* garaj; *v/t* garaja koymak

garbage ['gaabic] süprüntü; çöp

garden ['gaadn] bahçe; **~er** bahçıvan

gargle ['gaagl] *v/t* gargara etm.

garland ['gaalınd] çelenk

garlic ['gaalik] *bot.* sarmısak

garment ['gaamınt] elbise, giysi

garnet ['gaanit] lâl taşı

garnish ['gaaniş] *v/t* süslemek

garret ['gärıt] çatı arası

garrison ['gärisn] *mil.* garnizon

garrulous ['gärulıs] geveze

garter ['gaatı] çorap bağı; **Order of the ♀ Dizbağı nişanı

gas [gäs] gaz, havagazı; *Am.* benzin; **~burner** havagazı memesi

gash [gäş] uzunca bıçak *v.s.* yarası

gasket ['gäskit] *tech.* conta

gasoline ['gäsılîn] *Am.* benzin

gasp [gaasp] *n.* soluma; *v/i* solumak, soluyarak konuşmak

gate [geyt] kapı; su yolu kapağı; **~way** giriş yeri, kapı

gather ['gädhı] *v/t* toplamak; anlamak, kavramak; *v/i* toplanmak; çoğalmak; **~speed** hızlanmak; **~ing** toplantı

gaudy ['gôdi] zevksizce süslenmiş

gauge [geyc] *n.* ölçü, ayar; çap; *v/t* ayar etm.

gaunt [gônt] zayıf; kasvetli

gauze [gôz] gaz, tül

gave [geyv] *s.* **give**

gay [gey] neşeli, şen; zevk düşkünü; parlak *(renk)*; **~ly** neşe ile

gaze [geyz] dik dik bakmak (at *-e*)

gazelle [gıˈzel] *zo.* ceylan

gear [gii] eşya, giyim; *tech.* dişli takımı; şanjman; vites; **~change** şanjman; **~-lever**, **~-shift** vites kolu

gem [cem] kıymetli taş

gender ['cendı] gr. cins

general ['cenırıl] mil. general; genel; **ize** v/t genelleştirmek; **ly** adv. genellikle

generat|e ['cenıreyt] v/t husule getirmek, doğurmak; **ion** nesil, döl; meydana getirme; **or** el. jeneratör, dinamo

gener|osity [cenı'rositi] cömertlik, âlicenaplık; **ous** cömert, eli açık

Geneva [ci'nıvı] Cenevre

genial ['cînyıl] güleryüzlü, hoş

genitive (case) ['cenitiv] gr. -in hali, tamlayan

genius ['cînyıs] deha; dâhi; cin, ruh

Genoa ['cenıuı] Cenova

gentle ['centl] nazik; yumuşak; kibar; **man** centilmen; **manlike** centilmence; **ness** kibarlık, nezaket

gentry ['centri] küçük derebeylik sınıfı

genuine ['cenyuin] sahih, taklit olmıyan

geo|graphy [ci'ogrıfi] coğrafya; **logy** [~'olıci] jeoloji; **metry** [~'omitri] geometri

Georgia ['côcyı] Kafkasya'da Gürcüstan; A.B.D. de Georgia devleti

germ [côm] mikrop; tohum

German ['cômın] Alman; Almanca; **y** Almanya

germinate ['cômineyt] v/i filizlenmek

gerund ['cerınd] gr. ulaç, gerundium

gesture ['cesçı] hareket, jest

get [get] v/t elde etm., almak, sağlamak, kazanmak; yakalamak; anlamak, kavramak; yaptırmak; **about** v/i yayılmak; dolaşmak; **along** ilerlemek; geçinmek (**with** ile); **away** kurtulmak, kaçmak; **in** içeri girmek; **off** inmek; kurtulmak; **out** dışarı çıkmak; **to varmak** -e; başlamak -e; **to know** v/t tanımak; have got to inf. -meğe mecbur olm.; **together** bir araya gelmek; **up** kalkmak

geyser ['gayzı] geo. gayzer

ghastly ['gaastli] korkunç; ölü gibi

ghost [gıust] hayalet, hortlak; **Holy** ♀ rel. Ruhulkudüs

giant ['cayınt] dev; dev gibi iri

gibbit ['cibit] darağacı

gibe [cayb] v/i alay etm. (**at** ile)

giblets ['ciblits] pl. tavuk sakatatı

giddy ['cidi] başı dönmüş; hoppa

gift [gift] hediye, armağan; Allah vergisi, hüner; **ed** hünerli

gigantic [cay'gäntik] kocaman

glorify

giggle ['gigl] v/i kıkır kıkır gülmek
gild [gild] v/t yaldızlamak
gill [gil] zo. solungaç
gilt [gilt] s. gild; yaldız
gin ['cin] cin, ardıç rakısı
ginger ['cıncı] bot. zencefil; sl. canlılık; ~bread zencefil pastası; ~ly ihtiyatla, dikkatle
gipsy ['cipsi] Çingene
giraffe [ci'râf] zo. zürafa
gird [göd] v/t sarmak, kuşatmak
girder ['gödı] kiriş; direk
girdle ['gödl] kemer; kuşak; korsa
girl [göl] kız; sevgili; ~hood kızlık çağı; ~ish genç kız gibi
girt [göt] s. gird
girth [göth] kolan, çevre
give [giv] v/t vermek, bağışlamak; ~ away v/t vermek; açığa vurmak; ~ in v/i vazgeçmek; ~ rise sebebiyet vermek (to -e); ~ up v/t terketmek; teslim etm.; vazgeçmek -den; ~ way çekilmek; çökmek; ~n s. give; düşkün (to -a)
glacier ['glâsyı] geo. buzul
glad [gläd] memnun (of -den); ~ness memnunluk, sevinç
glam|orous ['glämırıs] göz alıcı; ~o(u)r parlaklık; cazibe
glance [glâns] n. bakış; göz atma; parıltı; v/i bakmak, göz atmak (at -e)

gland [gländ] an. bez, gudde
glare [glâı] n. kamaştırıcı ışık; dargın bakış; v/i parıldamak; ters ters bakmak (at -e)
glass [glâs] cam; bardak; ayna; dürbün; pl. gözlük; ~y cam gibi
glaz|e [gleyz] n. sır, cilâ; v/t cilâlamak; cam geçirmek -e; ~ier camcı
gleam [glîm] n. parıltı; v/i parıldamak
glee [glî] neşe; birçok sesle söylenen şarkı
glen [glen] vadi, dere
glib [glib] süratli konuşan, çevik
glide [glayd] n. kayma; v/i kaymak; av. motoru işletmeden inmek; ~r av. planör
glimmer ['glimı] v/i parıldamak; n. parıltı
glimpse [glimps] n. kısa bakış; v/t bir an için görmek
glint [glint] parlamak
glisten ['glisn] parlamak, parıldamak
glitter ['glitı] n. parıltı, ışıltı; v/i parıldamak
gloat [glut] v/i şeytanca bir zevkle seyretmek (upon, over -i)
globe [glub] küre, top; dünya
gloom [gluum] karanlık; üzgünlük, hüzün; ~y kapanık; kederli, endişeli
glor|ify ['glôrifay] v/t yü-

celtmek, methetmek; **~i-ous** şanlı, parlak; **~y** şan, şeref, ihtişam

gloss [glos] cilâ, perdalı

glossary ['glosırı] ek sözlük

glossy ['glosi] parlak

glove [glav] eldiven

glow [gluu] n. kızıllık; hararet; v/i hararet saçmak, yanmak, parlamak; **~worm** zo. ateşböceği

glue [gluu] n. tutkal; v/t tutkallamak, yapıştırmak

glutton ['glatn] obur; **~ous** obur gibi; **~y** oburluk

gnarled [naald] budaklı, boğumlu

gnash [näş] v/t gıcırdatmak

gnat [nät] zo. sivrisinek

gnaw [nô] v/t kemirmek

go [guu] n. gayret; başarı; v/i gitmek; hareket etm., kalkmak; çıkmak; gezmek; işlemek; olmak; **let ~** v/t bırakmak; **~ by** geçmek; **~ for** -i almaya gitmek; sayılmak -e; **~ in for** -in meraklısı olm.; **~ mad** çıldırmak, delirmek; **~ on** devam etm. (**-ing** -meğe); **~ through** geçmek **-den**; uğramak -e; **~ up** çıkmak, yükselmek

goad [gud] v/t dürtmek

goal [gıul] hedef, gaye; gol, kale; **~keeper** kaleci

goat [gıut] zo. keçi

go-between aracı

goblet ['goblit] kadeh

goblin ['goblin] gulyabani, cin

god [god] tanrı, ilâh; put; ♀

Tanrı, Allah; **~child** vaftiz çocuğu; **~dess** tanrıça, ilâhe; **~father** vaftiz babası; **~less** dinsiz; **~mother** vaftiz anası

goggle ['gogl] v/i şaşı bakmak; n. pl. gözlük sg.

going ['guin] gidiş; **be ~ to** inf. -mek üzere olm.

gold [guld] altın; **~en** altından yapılmış; altın renkli; **~smith** kuyumcu

golf [golf] golf oyunu; **~ course**, **~-links** pl. golf alanı sg. [muş]

gone [gon] s. **go**; mahvol-)

good [gud] adj. iyi, güzel; edepli, nazik; uygun; n. iyilik; fayda, yarar; pl. eşya, mallar; **~ afternoon!** günaydın! (öğleden sonra kullanılır); **~ evening!** iyi akşamlar!, tünaydın!; ♀ **Friday** rel. paskalya yortusundan önceki cuma (İsanın çarmıhta öldüğüne inanılan gün); **~ morning!** günaydın!; **~ night!** iyi geceler!; **~-by(e)!** Allaha ısmarladık!, güle güle!; **~-for-nothing** yaramaz, serseri; **~-natured** iyi tabiatlı, halim; **~ness** iyilik; **thank ~ness!** Allaha şükür!; **~will** iyi niyet, hayırhahlık

goose [guus] pl. **geese** [gîs] zo. kaz; **~berry** ['guzbırı] bot. bektaşiüzümü

gorge [gôc] n. boğaz, dar geçit; gırtlak; v/t yutmak, tıka basa yemek

gorgeous ['gôcıs] parlak, tantanalı

gospel ['gospıl] *rel.* İncil

gossip ['gosip] *n.* dedikodu; dedikoducu; *v/i* dedikodu etm.

got, **~ten** [got, '~n] *s.* get

gourd [guıd] *bot.* kabak

gout [gaut] *med.* gut, nıkrıs

govern ['gavın] *v/t* yönetmek, idare etm.; hâkim olm. *-e*; **~ess** mürebbiye; **~ment** hükümet; idare; **~or** vali

gown [gaun] rop; cüppe

grab [gräb] *v/t* kapmak, ele geçirmek

grace [greys] lütuf; nezaket; rahmet; *ec.* mühlet, vade; *rel.* şükran duası; **~ful** zarif, latif

gracious ['greyşıs] şirin, nazik; inayetkâr; **good ~!** Allah Allah!

grade [greyd] *n.* derece; rütbe; mertebe; sınıf; *v/t* sınıflandırmak; tesviye etm.; **~ crossing** *Am.* hemzemin geçit; **~ school** *Am.* ilkokul

gradient ['greydyınt] yokuş

gradua|l ['grâcuıl] tedrici, derece derece; **~te** ['~cuıt] *n.* mezun, diplomalı; ['~dyueyt] *v/i* mezun olm.; *v/t* diploma vermek *-e*; derecelere ayırmak *-i*; **~tion** [~dyu'eyşın] mezun olma

graft [grâft] *n.* ağaç aşısı; *v/t* aşılamak; *med.* transplante etm.

grain [greyn] tane, habbe; damar; hububat

gramma|r ['grämı] gramer; **~tical** [grı'mätikıl] gramere ait; dilbilgisinin kurallarına uygun

gram(me) [gräm] gram

gramophone ['grämıfıun] gramofon

granary ['gränıri] tahıl ambarı

grand [gränd] büyük; muhteşem, şahane; **~child** ['~nç-] torun; **~daughter** ['~ndô-] kız torun; **~eur** ['~ncı] azamet; **~father** ['~df-] büyükbaba; **~mother** ['~nm-] büyükanne; **~son** ['~ns-] erkek torun; **~stand** tribün

granite ['gränit] granit

granny ['gräni] *fam.* nineciğim

grant [graant] *n.* bağış; hibe; tahsisat; *v/t* vermek, bağışlamak; kabul etm.; **take for ~ed** *v/t* olmuş gibi kabul etm.

granula|r ['grünyulı] taneli; **~te** ['~eyt] *v/t* tanelemek

grape [greyp] *bot.* üzüm; **~fruit** greypfrut, altıntop; **~sugar** dekstroz

graphic ['gräfik] çizgili; canlı

grasp [graasp] *n.* tutma; kavrayış; *v/t* tutmak; kavramak

grass [graas] ot; çimen; çayır; **~hopper** *zo.* çekirge; **~y** çimenlik

grate [greyt] *n.* demir par-

grateful 286

maklık, ızgara; v/t rendelemek; gıcırdatmak
grateful ['greytful] minnettar
grater ['greytı] rende
grati|fication [grätifi'key-
şın] memnuniyet; ~**fy** ['-
fay] v/t memnun etm.
grating ['greytin] parmaklık, ızgara
gratitude ['grätityûd] min-
nettarlık, şükran
gratuit|ous [grı'tyuitıs] be-
dava, parasız; ~**y** bahşiş;
bağış
grave[1] [greyv] ağır, ciddî
grave[2] mezar, kabir
gravel ['grävil] çakıl
graveyard mezarlık
gravit|ation [grävi'teyşın]
phys. yerçekimi; ~**y** ['-ti]
ağırbaşlılık; önem; yerçekimi
gravy ['greyvi] etsuyu, salça
gray [grey] Am. s. **grey**
graze [greyz] v/i otlamak;
v/t otlatmak
greas|e [grîs] n. yağ; [~z]
v/t yağlamak; ~**y** ['-zi]
yağlı
great [greyt] büyük, iri;
şöhretli; 2 **Britain** Büyük
Britanya; ~**coat** palto; ~
-**grandfather** büyük dede; ~**ly** pek çok; ~**ness**
büyüklük; şöhret; önem
Greece [grîs] Yunanistan
greed [grîd] hırs, açgözlü-
lük; ~**y** obur, açgözlü
Greek [grîk] Yunan(lı);
Yunanca; Rum; Rumca

green [grîn] yeşil; ham,
taze; tecrübesiz; çimen; ~
grocer manav, yemişçi;
~**horn** toy, acemi; ~**house**
limonluk
greet [grît] v/t selâmlamak;
selâm vermek -e; ~**ing** selâm
grew [gruu] s. **grow**
grey [grey] boz, gri, kır; ~
hound zo. tazı
grid [grid] ızgara; şebeke;
~**iron** ızgara
grief [grîf] keder, acı
griev|ance ['grîvıns] keder
verici şey, dert; ~**e** v/i ke-
derlenmek, üzülmek; v/t
üzüntü vermek -e; ~**ous**
kederli, acıklı
grill [gril] n. ızgara; v/t ız-
garada pişirmek
grim [grim] haşin; korkunç
grimace [gri'meys] n. yüz
buruşturma; v/i yüzünü
ekşitmek
grim|e [graym] kir, pis; ~**y**
kirli
grin [grin] n. sırıtma; v/i
sırıtmak
grind [graynd] v/t öğütmek,
ufalamak; bilemek; teeth:
gıcırdatmak; ~**stone** bileği
taşı
grip [grip] n. sıkı tutma,
kavrama; kabza; v/t sıkı
tutmak, kavramak; fig. -in
dikkatini çekmek
gripes [graips] pl. med. sancı
gristle ['grisl] an. kıkırdak
grit [grit] çakıl, iri taneli
kum

groan [grıun] *n.* inilti; *v/i* inlemek

grocer ['grıusı] bakkal; **~y** bakkaliye

groin [groyn] *an.* kasık

groom [grum] *n.* seyis; güvey; *v/t* tımar etm.; *bir işe* hazırlamak

groove [gruuv] yiv, oluk

grope [grıup] *v/t*, *v/i* el yordamiyle aramak (**for** *-i*)

gross [grıus] on iki düzine; kaba, şişko, hantal; toptan

grotesque [grıu'tesk] acayip, tuhaf

ground[1] [graund] *s.* **grind**

ground[2] *n.* yer, zemin; toprak, arsa; dip; meydan; neden, sebep; *v/t* kurmak; *el.* toprağa bağlamak; **~ crew** *av.* hava meydanı tayfası; **~ floor** zemin katı; **~less** sebepsiz; **~nut** *bot.* yerfıstığı

group [gruup] *n.* grup; *v/i* grup halinde toplanmak; *v/t* toplamak

grove [grıuv] koru, ormancık

grow [grıu] *v/i* olmak; büyümek, gelişmek; *v/t* yetiştirmek; **~ up** büyümek

growl [graul] *v/i* hırlamak; homurdanmak

grow|n [grıun] *s.* **grow**; **~th** [_th] büyüme, artma, gelişme

grub [grab] *zo.* sürfe, kurt; **~by** kirli, pis

grudge [grac] *n.* kin, garaz; *v/t* esirgemek, kıskanmak

gruel [gruıl] pişirilmiş yulaf ezmesi

gruesome ['gruusım] ürkütücü

gruff [graf] sert; boğuk sesli

grumble ['grambl] mırıldanmak; şikâyet etm. (**at** *-den*) [hırıldamak\

grunt [grant] domuz gibi\

guarant|ee [gärın'tî] *n.* kefalet, garanti, teminat; kefil; *v/t* garanti etm.; **~or** [~'tô] kefil; **~y** ['~ti] garanti, kefalet

guard ['gaad] *n.* muhafız; korucu, bekçi; koruma; *v/t* korumak, beklemek, muhafaza etm.; **~ian** ['~yın] bekçi, muhafız; *jur.* veli, vasi

guess [ges] *n.* zan, tahmin; *v/t* tahmin etm., zannetmek

guest [gest] misafir, davetli; müşteri; **~room** misafir yatak odası

guidance ['gaydıns] rehberlik, yol gösterme

guide [gayd] *n.* rehber, kılavuz; *v/t* yol göstermek *-e*; sevketmek, idare etm. *-i*; **~book** seyahat rehberi; **~line** prensip, tüzük

guild [gild] lonca; **hall** Londra belediye dairesi

guileless ['gaylîıs] saf, riyasız

guilt [gilt] suç, kabahat; **~y** suçlu, mücrim

Guinea ['gini] *geo.* Gine; **2-pig** *zo.* kobay

guitar [gi'tâ] *mus.* gitar

gulf [galf] körfez; uçurum; **2 Stream** *geo.* golfstrim

gull [gal] zo. martı

gullet ['galit] an. boğaz, gırtlak

gulp [galp] n. yudum; v/t yutmak

gum [gam] n. zamk; an. dişeti; v/t zamklamak, yapıştırmak

gun [gan] tüfek; top; Am. tabanca; **~ner** topçu; **~ powder** barut

gurgle ['gögl] v/i fokurdamak

gush [gaş] n. fışkırma; v/i fışkırmak

gust [gast] ani rüzgâr, bora

guts [gats] pl. bağırsaklar; sl. cesaret sg.

gutter ['gatı] oluk, su yolu

guttural ['gatırıl] gırtlaktan çıkarılan (ses)

guy [gay] Am. sl. adam, herif

gymnas|ium [cim'neyzyım] cimnastik salonu; **~tics** [~'nästiks] pl. cimnastik sg.

gyn(a)ecologist [gayni'kolıcist] kadın hastalıkları hekimi, jinekolog

gypsum ['cipsım] alçı taşı

gypsy ['cipsi] s. gipsy

H

haberdasher ['häbıdäşı] tuhafiyeci; Am. erkek giyimi satan mağaza

habit ['häbit] âdet, alışkanlık, huy; **~ation** ev, ikametgâh; **~ual** [hı'bityuıl] alışılmış, âdet olmuş

hack [häk] v/t çentmek, yarmak; **~saw** demir teste-\ re

had [häd] s. have [resi\

haddock ['hädık] zo. mez-\ (g)it balığı

haemorrh|age ['hemıric] kanama; **~oids** [~'roydz] pl. basur sg.

hag [häg] acuze, cadı

haggard ['hägıd] bitkin görünüşlü

Hague [heyg] **the ~** Lâhey

hail[1] [heyl] n. dolu; v/i dolu yağmak

hail[2] v/t çağırmak; alkışlarla karşılamak

hair [häı] saç, kıl, tüy; **~cut** saç kesme; **~do** saç şekli; **~dresser** berber, ku(v)aför; **~pin** firkete; **~y** kıllı, tüylü

half [hâf] yarım; yarı; buçuk; **three and a ~** üç buçuk; **~ past six** saat altı buçuk; **~breed** melez (adam); **~moon** yarımay; **~penny** ['heypni] yarım peni; **~time** haftaym; **~way** yarı yolda

hall [hôl] salon; hol; koridor; resmî bina

hallo! [hä'lou] heyls! alo!

halo ['heylıu] ağıl, hale

halt [hôlt] n. duruş; durak; v/i duraklamak; v/t durdurmak [ipi\

halter ['hôltı] yular; idam\

halve [hâv] v/t yarıya bölmek

ham [häm] jambon

hamburger ['hämbögı] sığır kıyması; köfte; köfteli sandviç

hamlet ['hämlit] küçük köy

hammer ['hämı] n. çekiç; tüfek horozu; v/t çekiçle işlemek

hammock ['hämık] hamak

hamper ['hämpı] n. büyük sepet; v/t engel olm. -e

hand [händ] n. el; akrep; ibre; işçi; v/t el ile vermek; teslim etm.; at ~ yanında; on the other ~ diğer taraftan; on the right ~ sağ tarafta; ~ back geri vermek; ~ over teslim etm. (to -e); ~bag el çantası; ~cuff kelepçe; ~ful avuç dolusu

ɑandi|cap ['händikäp] n. engel; v/t engel olm. -e; ~craft el sanatı [mendil]

handkerchief ['hänkıçif]

handle ['händl] n. sap, kulp, tokmak; v/t ellemek, ele almak, kullanmak; ~-bar gidon

hand|-made elişi; ~rail tırabzan; ~shake el sıkma; ~some ['hänsım] yakışıklı, güzel; ~writing el yazısı; ~y kullanışlı; elverişli

hang [häŋ] v/t asmak, takmak; v/i asılı olm., sarkmak; ~ about avare dolaşmak; ~ out v/t sarkıtmak; ~ up v/t asmak

hangar ['häŋı] av. hangar

hang|man cellât; ~over içkiden gelen baş ağrısı

haphazard ['häp'häzıd] rasgele, gelişigüzel

happen ['häpın] olmak, vuku bulmak; ~ to inf. rasgele olm.; ~ on bulmak -i; ~ing olay

happ|iness ['häpinis] saadet, bahtiyarlık; ~y bahtiyar, talihli; neşeli; yerinde

harass ['härıs] v/t taciz etm., tedirgin etm.

harbo(u)r ['hâbı] n. liman; fig. barınak; v/t barındırmak; beslemek

hard [hâd] sert, katı; zor, güç, ağır; çetin; şefkatsiz; ~ by pek yakın; ~ up eli dar; try ~ çok uğraşmak; ~-boiled haşırlıyıp; fig. pişkin; ~en v/t katılaştırmak, sertleştirmek; v/i sertleşmek, katılaşmak; ~ly adv. hemen hiç; ancak; ~ness sertlik, katılık; ~ship güçlük; sıkıntı; ~ware maâdenî eşya; ~y cesur, dayanıklı

hare [häı] zo. tavşan; ~bell bot. çançiçeği; ~lip tavşandudağı

hark [hâk] v/t dinlemek

harm [hâm] n. zarar; kötülük; v/t vermek -e; ~ful zararlı; ~less zararsız

harmony [hâ'mını] uyum, ahenk

harness ['hânis] n. koşum; v/t horse: koşmak

harp [hâp] mus. harp; ~ on üzerinde durmak

harpoon [hâ'puun] n. zıpkın; v/t zıpkınlamak

harrow 290

harrow ['härıu] *n*. sürgü;
v/t sürgü geçirmek -*e*

harsh [hâş] sert, haşin,
merhametsiz; **~ness** sertlik

harvest ['hâvist] *n*. hasat;
ürün, rekolte; *v/t* ürünü
toplamak; biçmek; **~er**
orakçı; orak makinesi

has [häz] *s*. have

hash [häş] *n*. kıymalı yemek;
v/t doğramak, kıymak

hast|e [heyst] acele; **~en**
['~sn] *v/i* acele etm.; *v/t*
hızlandırmak; **~y** acele,
çabuk, üstün körü

hat [hät] şapka

hatch [häç] *n*. kaporta; üstü
açık kapı; *v/t fig*. kurmak;
v/i yumurtadan çıkmak

hatchet ['häçit] küçük balta

hat|e [heyt] *n*. nefret, kin;
v/t nefret etm. -*den*, kin
beslemek -*e* karşı; **~eful**
nefret verici, iğrenç; **~red**
['~rid] kin

haught|iness ['hôtinis] gu-
rur, kurum; **~y** kibirli,
mağrur

haul [hôl] *n*. çekme; bir
ağda çıkarılan balık mikda-
rı; *v/t* çekmek

haunch [hônç] kalça, but;
sağrı

haunt [hônt] *n*. uğrak; *v/t*
sık sık uğramak -*e*; sık görünmek -*de*; **~ed** perili,
tekin olmıyan

have [häv, hıv] *v/t* malik
olm., sahip olm. -*e*; (yardımcı fiil olarak bileşik fiil
şekillerine katılır); yaptur-
mak -*i*; **~ to** *inf*. -*meğe* mec-

bur olm.; **we had better
finish now** artık bitirsek
iyi olur; **~not** fakir, yoksul

haven ['heyvn] liman; sığınak

havoc ['hävık]: **make ~** çok
zarar vermek (**of** -*e*)

hawk [hôk] *zo*. doğan

hawthorn ['hôthôn] *bot*.
yabanî akdiken

hay [hey] kuru ot; **~ fever**
med. saman nezlesi; **~cock,
~rick, ~stack** ot yığını

hazard ['häzıd] *n*. riziko,
talih; tehlike; *v/t* talihe
bırakmak; **~ous** tehlikeli

haze [heyz] sis, pus

hazel ['heyzl] *bot*. fındık
(ağacı); **~nut** fındık

H-bomb ['eyçbom] hidrojen bombası

he [hî] o (*eril*)

head [hed] *n*. baş, kafa; başkan; şef; baş taraf; *v/t -in*
başında olm.; *v/i* gitmek,
yönelmek (**for** -*e* doğru);
~ache baş ağrısı; **~gear**
başlık, baş örtüsü; **~ing**
serlevha, başlık; **~light** ön
ışık, far; **~line** başlık; **~
long** baş önde; **~master**
okul müdürü; **~mistress**
okul müdiresi; **~quarters**
pl. mil. karargâh *sg*.; merkez; **~way** ilerleme

heal [hîl] *v/t* iyileştirmek;
şifa vermek -*e*; *v/i* iyileşmek; **~ up** *v/i yara*: kapanmak

health [helth] sağlık, sıhhat;
~ resort ılıca; **~y** sağlıklı

heap [hîp] *n.* yığın, küme; *v/t* yığmak

hear [hiı] *v/t* işitmek, duymak, dinlemek; haber almak (**about, from, of** -*den*); ∼**d** [hôd] *s.* **hear**; ∼**ing** dinleme, sorgu; ses erimi; ∼**say** söylenti

hearse [hôs] cenaze arabası

heart [hât] kalp, yürek, gönül; iç; cesaret; *pl.* kupa; **by** ∼ ezber; ∼**breaking** son derece keder verici; ∼**burn** mide ekşimesi

hearth [hâth] ocak

heart|less [hâtlis] kalpsiz, merhametsiz; ∼**y** içten, samimî; bol

heat [hît] *n.* hararet, sıcaklık, ısı; *v/t* ısıtmak; *v/i* ısınmak

heath [hîth] fundalık; *bot.* funda, süpürgeotu

heathen [´hîdhın] dinsiz, kâfir

heat|ing [´hîtin] ısıtma; **central** ∼**ing** kalorifer; ∼**-stroke** *med.* güneş çarpması

heave [hîv] *n.* kaldırma; *v/t* atmak; kaldırmak; *v/i* kabarıp inmek

heaven [´hevn] gök, sema; **for** ∼**'s sake!** Allah aşkına!; **good** ∼**s!** Allah Allah!, aman aman!; ∼**ly** göksel; tanrısal

heav|iness [´hevinis] ağırlık, siklet; ∼**y** ağır; güç; şiddetli; üzgün; ∼**y-weight** ağır siklet(li)

Hebrew [´hîbruu] İbranî, Yahudi; İbranîce

hectic [´hektik] heyecanlı, telâşlı

hedge [hec] çit, çalı; *fig.* mania; ∼**hog** *zo.* kirpi

heed [hîd] *n.* dikkat; *v/t* dikkat etm., kulak vermek -*e*; ∼**less** dikkatsiz

heel [hîl] topuk, ökçe; *sl.* Am. alçak herif; **take to one's** ∼**s** kaçmak

he-goat *zo.* teke, erkeç

heifer [´hefı] *zo.* düve

height [hayt] yükseklik; tepe; ∼**en** *v/t* yükseltmek, artırmak

heinous [´heynıs] iğrenç, kötü

heir [âı] varis, mirasçı; ∼**ess** kadın varis

held [held] *s.* **hold**

helicopter [´helikoptı] *av.* helikopter

hell [hel] cehennem

hello! [he´luı] merhaba!, günaydın!

helm [helm] *naut.* dümen

helmet [´helmit] miğfer, tolga

help [help] *n.* yardım, imdat; yardımcı, hizmetçi; *v/t* yardım etm. -*e*; **not** ∼ -*ing* -*mekten* alamamak; ∼ **yourself!** buyurunuz! (*ye-mek için*); ∼**er** yardımcı; ∼**ful** faydalı, işe yarar; ∼**less** çaresiz, gücü yetmez

helter-skelter [´heltı´skeltı] aceleyle

hem[1] [hem] *n.* kenar; *v/t* -*in* kenarını kıvırıp dikmek

hem² v/i hafifçe öksürmek; sesi tutulmak

hemisphere ['hemisfiı] yarımküre

hemline etek ucu

hemp [hemp] bot. kenevir

hen [hen] zo. tavuk; dişi kuş

hence [hens] buradan; bundan dolayı; **˷forth, ˷forward** bundan sonra

henna ['henı] kına

hen-pecked kılıbık

her [hö] ona, onu; onun (dişil)

herald ['herıld] n. haberci, müjdeci; v/t ilân etm.; **˷ry** armacılık

herb [höb] ot, bitki

herd [höd] sürü; **˷sman** çoban

here [hiı] burada, buraya; **˷ you are!** buyurun alınız!; işte!; **˷after** bundan sonra, gelecekte; **˷by** bu vesile ile

hereditary [hi'reditırı] kalıtsal; **˷y** kalıtım

heresy ['herısi] rel. bir akideye aykırı mezhep

here|upon bunun üzerine; **˷with** bununla

heritage ['heritic] miras, tereke

hermit ['hömit] münzevi

hero ['hiırıu] kahraman; **˷ic** [hi'ruik] kahramanca

heroin ['herıuin] eroin

heron ['herın] zo. balıkçıl

herring ['herin] zo. ringa

her|s [höz] onun(ki) (dişil); **˷self** kendisi (dişil)

hesita|nt ['hezitınt] tereddüt eden, kararsız; **˷te**

['˷teyt] tereddüt etm., duraksamak; **˷tion** tereddüt

heterogeneous ['hetırıu'cinyıs] heterogen, ayrı cinsten

hew [hyû] v/t yontmak, yarmak; **˷n** s. hew

heyday ['heydey] en enerjik çağ

hi! [hay] hey!; Am. merhaba!

hicc|ough, ˷up ['hikap] n. hıçkırık; v/i hıçkırık tutmak

hid [hid] s. hide

hide¹ deri, post

hide² v/t saklamak, gizlemek; v/i saklanmak (from -den)

hideous ['hidiıs] çirkin, iğrenç

hi-fi ['hay'fay] coll. s. high-fidelity

high [hay] yüksek, yukarı; pahalı; şiddetli; kibirli; dolgun; esrarın etkisi altında; n. yüksek basınç bölgesi; **˷ school** lise; **˷ spirits** pl. neşe sg.; **˷ time** tam vakit; **˷ treason** jur. vatan hainliği; **˷brow** fig. fikir adamı; **˷fidelity** sesi çok tabiî şekilde veren; **˷land** dağlık bölge; **˷light** ilgi çekici olay; v/t adv. çok; **˷ness** yükseklik; His (or Your) ♀ness fehametlû; **˷road** anayol; **˷way** karayol

hijack ['haycäk] v/t kuvvet zoru ile çalmak; kaçırmak; **˷er** yolkesici; uçak korsanı

hike [hayk] *v/i* yürümek

hilarious [hi'lâriıs] neşeli ve gürültücü

hill [hil] tepe; yokuş; **~billy** ['~bili] *Am.* orman köylüsü; **~y** tepelik

hilt [hilt] kabza

him [him] onu, ona; **~self** kendisi (*eril*)

hind [haynd] arka; **~ leg** arka ayak

hind|er ['hindı] *v/t* engellemek; mâni olm. *-e*; **~rance** ['hindrıns] engel

hinge [hinc] menteşe, reze

hinny ['hini] *zo. at ile dişi eşekten hâsıl olan* katır

hint [hint] *n.* ima, üstü kapalı söz; *v/i* ima etm., çıtlatmak (at *-i*)

hip [hip] kalça, kaba et.

hippo|drome ['hipıdrıum] hipodrom, at meydanı; **~potamus** [~'potımıs] *zo.* suaygırı

hire ['hayı] *n.* kira; *v/t* kiralamak, ücretle tutmak; **for ~** kiralık, serbest

his [hiz] onun(ki) (*eril*)

hiss [his] *n.* tıslama; *v/i* tıslamak; ıslık çalmak

histor|ian [his'tôrin] tarihçi; **~ical** [~'torikıl] tarihî; **~y** ['~uri] tarih

hit [hit] *n.* vuruş, darbe; isabet; başarı; *v/t* vurmak, çarpmak *-e*; isabet etm. *-e*; rasgele bulmak (**upon** *-i*); **~-and-run** çarpıp kaçan (*şöför*)

hitch [hiç] *n.* çekiş; engel, arıza; *v/t* bağlamak, tak-

mak; *v/i* takılmak; **~hike** otostop yapmak; **~hiker** otostopçu

hither ['hidhı] buraya; **~to** şimdiye kadar

hive [hayv] kovan; arı kovanı gibi kaynaşan yer

hoard [hôd] *n.* saklanan stok; *v/t* biriktirmek, saklamak

hoarfrost ['hô'-] kırağı

hoarse [hôs] boğuk, kısık

hoax [hıuks] *n.* şaka, muziplik; *v/t* aldatmak

hobble ['hobl] *v/i* topallamak; *v/t* kösteklemek

hobby ['hobi] merak

hobgoblin ['hobgoblin] gulyabani

hobo ['hubıu] serseri, aylak

hockey ['hoki] hokey

hoe [hıu] *n.* çapa; *v/t* çapalamak

hog [hog] *zo.* domuz

hoist [hoyst] *n.* kaldıraç; yük asansörü; *v/t* yükseltmek; *bayrağı* çekmek

hold [hıuld] *n.* tutma; dayanak; otorite; *v/t* tutmak, kavramak; dayanmak *-e*; sahip olm. *-e*; içine almak *-i*; işgal etm. *-i*; **get** (**lay, take**) **~ of** *v/t* yakalamak; **~ the line** telefonda beklemek; **~ on** devam etm.; **~ to** *v/t* tutmak; devam etm. *-e*; **~ up** *v/t* tutmak; durdurmak; **~er** sahip, hamil; **~ing** tutma; mülk; *ec.* holding; **~up** gecikme; yol kesme

hole [hıul] delik, çukur

holiday ['holidi] tatil günü; bayram günü

Holland ['holınd] Hollanda, Felemenk

hollow ['holıu] adj. içi boş, oyuk; n. çukur, boşluk; v/t oymak, çukurlatmak

holly ['holi] bot. çobanpüskülü

holy ['huli] kutsal; ♀ **Week** paskalyadan önceki hafta

homage ['homic] biat

home [hıum] ev, aile ocağı; vatan, yurt; yerli; adv. eve; **at ~** evde; **see ~** v/t evine kadar refakat etm. -e; ♀ **Office** pol. İçişleri Bakanlığı; **~ Secretary** İçişleri Bakanı; **~less** evsiz, yurtsuz; **~ly** basit, sade, gösterişsiz; **~made** evde yapılmış; **~sick** yurt hasreti çeken; **~ward** eve doğru

homicide ['homisayd] jur. adam öldürme

homosexual [hum̄u'seksyuıl] homoseksüel

honest ['onist] doğru, dürüst, namuslu; **~y** namusluluk, dürüstlük

honey ['hani] bal; **~moon** bal ayı

honk [honk] v/i klakson

honorary ['onırıri] fahrî

hono(u)r ['onı] n. şeref, onur, namus; v/t şereflendirmek; ec. -in karşılığını ödemek; **have the ~ to** inf. -mek şerefine nail olm.; **~able** şerefli, namuslu; sayın

hood [hud] kukulete; Am. motor kapağı

hoodlum ['huudlım] serseri, kabadayı

hoodwink ['hudwink] v/t aldatmak

hoof [huuf] zo. at v.s. tırnağı

hook [huk] n. çengel, kanca; v/t kancaya takmak; yakalamak

hooligan ['huuligın] serseri, külhanbeyi

hoop [huup] kasnak, çember

hooping-coug ['huupiŋ-] med. boğmaca

hoot [huut] v/i baykuş gibi ötmek; yuha çekmek

hop[1] [hop] bot. şerbetçiotu

hop[2] n. sekme, sıçrama; v/i sıçramak, sekmek

hope [hıup] n. umut, ümit; v/i ümit etm., ummak (**for** -i); **~ful** ümitli, ümit verici; **~less** ümitsiz

horizon [hı'rayzn] çevren, ufuk; **~tal** [hori'zontl] yatay

horn [hôn] boynuz; mus. boru; korna, klakson

hornet ['hônit] zo. büyük sarı arı

horny ['hôni] boynuzdan; boynuzlu; nasırlanmış

horoscope ['hôrıskup] zayiçe

horr|ible ['horibl] dehşetli, korkunç; iğrenç; **~id** ['~id] korkunç; iğrenç; **~ify** ['~i-fay] v/t korkutmak; **~or** dehşet, korku; nefret

horse [hôs] at; **on ~back** ata binmiş; **~power** *tech.* beygir gücü; **~race** at yarışı; **~shoe** at nalı

horticulture ['hôtikalçı] bahçıvanlık

hos|e [hıuz] hortum; çorap; **~iery** ['~iıri] çorap ve iç çamaşırı

hospitable ['hospitıbl] misafirperver

hospital ['hospitl] hastane; **~ity** [~'tâliti] konukseverlik

host [hıust] ev sahibi, mihmandar; otelci; kalabalık; *rel.* takdis edilen fodla

hostage ['hostic] rehine, tutak

host|el ['hostıl] talebe yurdu; **~ess** ['hıustis] ev sahibesi; hostes

hostile ['hostıyl] düşmanca; **~ity** [~'tiliti] düşmanlık

hot [hot] sıcak, kızgın; acı; şiddetli; **~ dog** sıcak sosisli sandviç; **~bed** camlık

hotel [hıu'tel] otel

hot|headed ateşli, kızgın; **~house** camlık

hound [haund] *n.* av köpeği; *v/t* takip etm., izlemek

hour ['auı] saat (60 *dakika*); zaman; **~ly** saatte bir, her saat başı

house [haus] *n.* ev; hanedan; seyirciler *pl.*; ev barındırmak; 2 **of Commons** Avam Kamarası; 2 **of Lords** Lordlar Kamarası; **~hold** ev halkı, aile; eve ait; **~keeper** kâhya ka-

dın; **~warming** *yeni eve taşınanların verdikleri* ziyafet; **~wife** ev kadını

hove [hıuv] *s.* **heave**

hover ['hovı] *v/i* dolaşmak, sallanmak; **~craft** tazyikli hava üzerinde gidebilen taşıt

how [hau] nasıl; **~ are you?**, **~ do you do?** nasılsınız?; **~ much (many)?** nekadar?; **~ever** mamafih, bununla beraber; nekadar ... olursa olsun

howl [haul] *n.* uluma, bağırma; *v/i* ulumak

hub [hab] poyra

hubbub ['habab] gürültü

huddle ['hadl] *v/i* sıkı halde toplanmak; *v/t* toplamak

hue [hyû] renk

hug [hag] *n.* kucaklama; *v/t* kucaklamak

huge [hyûc] pek büyük, kocaman

hull [hal] *n. bot.* kabuk; *naut.* tekne, gövde; *v/t -in* kabuğunu soymak

hullabaloo [halıbı'luu] gürültü

hallo! ['ha'lu] *s.* **hello!**

hum [ham] *v/i* vınlamak, vızıldamak

human ['hyûmın] insana ait; insan; **~ being** insanoğlu; **~e** [~'meyn] insanca, merhametli; **~ity** [~'mâniti] beşeriyet; insanlık

humble ['hambl] *adj.* alçak gönüllü; *v/t -in* kibrini kırmak, aşağılatmak

humbug ['hambag] *n.* şarlatanlık, yalan; v/t aldatmak

humdrum ['hamdram] can sıkıcı, tekdüzen

humid ['hyûmid] rutubetli, nemli; **~ity** [~'miditi] rutubet

humili|ate [hyû'milieyt] v/t küçültmek; _-in_ kibrini kırmak; **~ation** küçültme; **~ty** [~'militi] alçak gönüllülük

humming-bird zo. sinek kuşu

humorous ['hyûmırıs] mizahî, komik

humo(u)r ['hyûmı] mizah, nükte; huy, tabiat; **good-~ed** iyi huylu

hump [hamp] hörgüç; kambur; tümsek

hunch [hanç] kambur; **~back** kambur adam

hundred ['handrıd] yüz; **~weight** (50.8 kilo, Am. 45.4 kilo)

hung [haŋ] s. **hang**

Hungar|ian [haŋ'gäriın] Macar; Macarca; **~y** ['~gıri] Macaristan

hung|er ['haŋgı] n. açlık; v/i şiddetle arzulamak (**after, for** _-i_); **~ry** aç; pek istekli

hunt [hant] n. av; arama; v/t avlamak; **~er** avcı; **~ing** avcılık

hurdle ['hödl] çit, mânia; **~-race** mânialı koşu

hurl [höl] v/t fırlatmak

hurra|h! [hu'râ], **~y!** [~'rey] yaşa!

hurricane ['harıkın] kasırga

hurried ['harid] acele ile, telâşlı

hurry ['hari] n. acele; telâş; v/i acele etm.; v/t aceleleştirmek; **be in a ~** acelesi olm.; **~ up** acele etm.

hurt [höt] n. yara; zarar; v/t yaralamak; incitmek; v/i ağrımak

husband ['hazbınd] koca, eş; **~ry** ziraat, tarım

hush [haş] n. susma, sessizlik; v/i susmak; v/t susturmak; **~ up** v/t örtbas etm.

husk [hask] n. kabuk, kılıf; v/t _-in_ kabuğunu soymak; **~y** kısık, boğuk; dinç, gürbüz

hustle ['hasl] n. itip kakma; falliyet; v/t itip kakmak; v/i itişip kakışmak

hut [hat] kulübe, baraka

hutch [haç] tavşan kafesi; kulübe

hyacinth ['hayısinth] bot. sümbül

hybrid ['haybrid] melez

hydr|ant ['haydrınt] yangın musluğu; **~aulic** [~'drôlik] hidrolik

hydro|- ['haydrıu-] su ile ilgili; **~carbon** hidrokarbon; **~gen** [~'icın] idrojen; **~phobia** med. kuduz

hyena [hay'înı] zo. sırtlan

hygien|e ['haycîn] sağlık bilgisi, hıfzıssıhha; **~ic** sağlıkla ilgili

hymn [him] rel. ilâhi

ill-treat

hyphen ['hayfın] tire, çizgi
hypno|sis [hip'nıusis] ipnoz; **~tic** [~'notik] uyutucu
hypo|crisy [hi'pokrısı] ikiyüzlülük; **~crite** ['hipıkrit]

I [ay] ben
ice [ays] *n.* buz; *v/i* buzlanmak; *v/t* buz ile kaplamak; soğutmak; **~berg** ['~böğ] buzdağ, aysberk; **~breaker** buzkıran; **~cream** dondurma; **2land** İzlanda
ic|icle ['aysikl] buz parçası; **~y** buz gibi, soğuk
idea [ay'di] fikir, düşünce, sanı, tahmin; **~l** *n.* ideal, ülkü; *adj.* ülküsel; **~list** ülkücü, idealist
identi|cal [ay'dentikl] aynı; **~fication** [aydentifi'keyşın] hüviyet; **~fy** [~'dentıfay] *v/t* -*in* hüviyetini göstermek; **~ty** [~'dentiti] aynılık; hüviyet; **~ty card** kimlik cüzdanı
ideology [aydi'olıcı] ideoloji
idiom ['idiım] şive, lehçe; deyim
idiot ['idiıt] anadan doğma deli; aptal; **~ic** [~'otik] ahmak
idle ['aydl] *adj.* aylak, boş; *v/i* vaktini boş geçirmek; boşta çalışmak; **~ness** tembellik
idol ['aydl] put; tapılan kimse; **~ater** [~'dolıtı]

ikiyüzlü; **~thesis** [hay-'pothisis] varsayım, hipotez
hyster|ia [his'tiıri] *med.* isteri; **~ical** [~'terikl] isterik

---

putperest; **~ize** ['~dılayz] *v/t* tapınmak -*e*
idyl|l(l) ['idil] idil; **~lic** [ay'dilik] pastoral; saf ve sevimli
if [if] eğer, şayet; ise; **as ~** sanki, güya
ignition [ig'nişın] ateşleme; marş
ignoble [ig'nıubl] alçak
ignor|ance ['ignırıns] cahillik; **~ant** cahil, bilmez; **~e** [ig'nô] *v/t* önem vermemek -*e*
ill [il] hasta, rahatsız; fena, kötü; uğursuz; kötülük, fenalık; **fall ~, be taken ~** hastalanmak; **~ at ease** huzursuz; **~-advised** tedbirsiz; **~-bred** terbiyesiz
il|legal [i'lıgıl] kanuna aykırı; **~legible** okunmaz; **~legitimate** kanuna aykırı; evlilik dışı
ill-humo(u)red fena huylu; huysuz
il|licit [i'lisit] kanuna aykırı; caiz olmıyan; **~literate** [i'litırit] okuma yazma bilmiyen
ill|ness ['ilnis] hastalık; **~tempered** huysuz; **~timed** zamansız; **~treat** *v/t* kötü davranmak -*e*

illuminate 298

illuminat|e [i'lyûmineyt] aydınlatmak; ~ion aydınlatma, tenvir

illusi|on [i'luujın] hayal, kuruntu, aldanma; ~ve aldatıcı

illustrat|e ['ilıstreyt] v/t tasvir etm., anlatmak, resimlerle süslemek; ~ion resim; izah; örnek

illustrious [i'lastriıs] ünlü, meşhur

imag|e ['imic] şekil, suret; heykel; hayal; ~inary [i'mäcinıri] hayalî; ~ination tasavvur; imgelem; ~inative yaratıcı; ~ine v/t tasavvur etm.; hayal etm.

imbecile ['imbisil] ahmak, budala

imitat|e ['imiteyt] v/t taklit etm., benzetmek; ~ion taklit, yapma

im|maculate [i'mäkyulit] lekesiz; ~material [imı'tiiriıl] önemsiz; ~mature olgunlaşmamış; ~measurable ölçülemez

immediate [i'midyıt] doğrudan doğruya; derhal olan; ~ly derhal, hemen

immense [i'mens] çok büyük, engin

immerse [i'mös] v/t daldırmak

immigra|nt ['imigrınt] göçmen; ~te [~eyt] göçmek; ~tion göçmenlik

imminent ['iminınt] yakında olan

im|mobile [i'mubayl] hareketsiz; ~moderate öl-

çüsüz, ifrata kaçan; ~modest açık saçık; haddini bilmez; ~moral ahlâkı bozuk, ahlâksız

immortal [i'môtl] ölümsüz, ölmez; ~ity [~'täliti] ölmezlik [kımıldamaz]

immovable [i'muuvıbl] immun|e [i'myûn] muaf (from -den); ~ity jur. dokunulmazlık

imp [imp] küçük şeytan

impact [im'päkt] vuruş; etki

impair [im'päı] v/t bozmak

impart [im'pât] v/t vermek; bildirmek; ~ial tarafsız; ~iality ['ʃı'äliti] tarafsızlık

im|passable geçilmez; ~passive duygusuz

impatien|ce sabırsızlık; ~t sabırsız; çok arzu eden (for -i)

impeach [im'piç] v/t suçlamak

impediment [im'pedimınt] mânia, engel

impend [im'pend] v/i asılı olm., vuku bulmak üzere olm.

impenetrable [im'penitrıbl] girilemez

imperative [im'perıtiv] mecburî; ~ (mood) gr. emir kipi

imperceptible hissolunamaz

imperfect [im'pöfikt] eksik, kusurlu; tamam olmayan; ~ (tense) gr. geçmiş zaman

imperial [im'piiriil] şahane; imparatora ait; **~ism** emperyalizm

imperil v/t tehlikeye düşürmek

imperious [im'piiris] zorba; zarurî

impermeable [im'pömyibl] su ve hava geçirmez

impersona|l [im'pösnl] şahsî olmayan; **~te** [~'pösineyt] v/t temsil etm.

impertinen|ce [im'pötinins] küstahlık; **~t** arsız, küstah

imperturbable [impi'töbibl] ağırbaşlı

impetuous [im'petyus] coşkun, atılgan

impinge [im'pinc] v/i çarpmak (**on, upon** -e)

implacable [im'pläkibl] teskin edilemez, amansız

implant v/t dikmek; aşılamak

implement ['implimint] n. alet, araç; v/t yerine getirmek

implicate ['implikeyt] v/t sokmak, karıştırmak

implicit [im'plisit] zimnî, altık [varmak -e]

implore [im'plô] v/t yal-ß

imply [im'play] v/t içine almak; ima etm.

impolite nezaketsiz

import [im'pôt] n. ec. ithal, ithalât; mana; önem; [~'pôt] v/t ithal etm.; belirtmek; **~ance** [~'pôtıns] önem; **~ant** önemli; **~ation** ithal (malı)

importune [im'pötyûn] v/t sıkıştırmak

impos|e [im'pıuz] v/t yüklemek; v/i aldatmak (**on, upon** -i); **~ing** heybetli

impossib|ility olanaksızlık; **~le** imkânsız, olamaz

impostor [im'posti] sahtekâr

impotent ['impıtınt] kudretsiz; med. iktidarsız

impoverish [im'povıriş] v/t fakirleştirmek

impracticable yapılamaz; kullanışsız

impregnate ['impregneyt] v/t döllemek, doyurmak

impress [im'pres] n. basma, damga; v/t basmak; etkilemek; **~ion** basma; izlenim; etki; **~ive** etkili, müessir

imprint n. damga; v/t basmak; etkilemek

imprison [im'prizn] v/t hapsetmek; **~ment** hapis, tutukluluk

improbable [im'probıbl] ihtimal dahilinde olmıyan

improper yersiz, yakışıksız

improve [im'pruuv] v/t düzeltmek; v/i düzelmek; **~ment** ıslah, düzelme

improvise ['imprıvayz] v/t doğaçtan söylemek veya yapmak

imprudent [im'pruudınt] tedbirsiz

impuden|ce ['impyudıns] yüzsüzlük, arsızlık; **~t** arsız, saygısız

impuls|e ['impals] itici

impulsive

kuvvet, tahrik, içtepi; **~ive** itici; atılgan

impunity [im'pyúniti] cezadan muaf olma

impure [im'pyuı] pis, kirli

imput|ation [impyu'teyşın] suçlama; **~e** v/t [~'pyút] itham etm., suçlamak (**to** ile)

in [in] -de, -(y)e; -in içinde, içine; içerde, içeriye; evde

inability ehliyetsizlik

inaccessible [inäk'sesıbl] erişilemez

inaccurate [in'äkyurit] yanlış, kusurlu

inactive hareketsiz

inadequate [in'ädıkwıt] yetersiz

inadvertent [inıd'vötınt] dikkatsiz; kasıtsız

inalienable satılamaz

inalterable değişmez

inanimate [in'änimit] cansız

inappropriate münasebetsiz

inapt beceriksiz; uygun olmıyan

inarticulate anlaşılmaz

inasmuch as [inız'maç -] mademki

inattentive dikkatsiz

inaudible işitilemez

inaugura|l [i'nógyrıl] açılışa ait; **~te** [~eyt] v/t açmak; başlamak -e; **~tion** açılış (töreni)

inborn ['in'bón] doğuştan, fıtrî

incalculable [in'kälkyulıbl] hesap edilemez

incapa|ble [in'keypıbl] yeteneksiz; beceriksiz; **~city** [inki'päsiti] kabiliyetsizlik; yetkisizlik [tecessüm]

incarnation [inkaa'neyşın]∫

incautious düşüncesiz

incendiary [in'sendyırı] kundakçı; yangın çıkarıcı

incense[1] ['insens] buhur

incense[2] [in'sens] v/t öfkelendirmek

incentive [in'sentiv] dürtü, saik

incessant [in'sesnt] sürekli

incest ['insest] *jur.* akraba arasında cinsî temas

inch [inç] pus (2,54 cm)

incident ['insidnt] olay; **~al** [~'dentl] tesadüfî

incinerate [in'sinıreyt] v/t kül etm.

incis|e [in'sayz] v/t oymak, hakketmek; **~ion** [~ijın] yarma, deşme; **~or** an. ön diş

incite [in'sayt] v/t teşvik etm., kışkırtmak

inclin|ation [inkli'neyşın] meyil; istek; **~e** [~'klayn] n. meyil, yokuş; v/i eğilmek, meyletmek (**to** -e); v/t eğmek

inclos|e [in'kluz], **~ure** [~jı] s. **enclose, enclosure**

inclu|de [in'kluud] v/t içine almak; **~sion** [~jın] dahil olma; **~sive** dahil, kapsayan

incognito [in'kognitu] takma adla; takma ad

incoherent anlaşılmaz, manasız

income ['inkam] gelir, irat; **~-tax** ['inkımtäks] gelir vergisi

incomparable emsalsiz

incompatible birbirine uymaz

incompetent ehliyetsiz

incomplete tam olmıyan

incomprehensible anlaşılamaz

inconceivable tasavvur olunamaz

inconsequent mantıksız, birbirini tutmaz

inconsidera|ble önemsiz; **~te** saygısız; düşüncesiz

inconsistent kararsız; uyuşmaz

inconspicuous önemsiz

inconvenien|ce n. zahmet, rahatsızlık; v/t rahatsız etm.; **~t** zahmetli

incorporate [in'kôpıreyt] v/t birleştirmek; v/i birleşmek; **~d** ec. anonim

incorr|ect yanlış; **~igible,** düzelmez

increas|e ['inkrîs] n. çoğalma; [in'krîs] v/i artmak, çoğalmak; v/t artırmak, çoğaltmak; **~ingly** gittikçe artarak

incred|ible inanılmaz; **~ulous** inanmaz; kuşkusu olan

incriminate [in'krimineyt] v/t suçlamak

incubator [in'kyubeytı] kuluçka makinesi

incur [in'kö] v/t uğramak -e, yakalanmak -den

incurable şifa bulmaz

indebted borçlu (**to** -e)

indecen|cy ahlâksızlık; **~t** utanmaz; yüzsüz

indecisi|on kararsızlık; **~ve** kararsız; kesin olmıyan

indeed gerçekten; intj. öyle mi?

indefatigable [indi'fätigıbl] yorulmaz

indefinite belirsiz

indelible [in'delibl] silinmez [suzluk}

indelicacy kabalık, uygun-}

indemni|fy [in'demnifay] v/t -in zararını ödemek; **~ty** tazminat

indent ['indent] n. çentik; [~'dent] v/t çentmek; -in kenarını oymak; **~ure** [in'dençı] sözleşme

independen|ce bağımsızlık; **~t** bağımsız

indescribable [indis'kraybıbl] anlatılmaz

indestructible [indis'traktıbl] yıkılmaz

index ['indeks] n. indeks; fihrist; ibre; işaret; v/t -in indeksini yapmak; **~ (finger)** işaret parmağı

India ['indyı] Hindistan; **~n** Hint, Hintli; (**Red**) **~n** kırmızı derili; **~n corn** bot. mısır; **~n summer** pastırma yazı

indicat|e ['indikeyt] v/t göstermek; **~ion** belirti, delil; **~ive** (**mood**) [in'dikıtiv] gr. bildirme kipi; **~or** [~çeytı] ibre, gösterge

indict [in'dayt] v/t suçlamak; **~ment** jur. iddianame

indifferen|ce aldırmazlık; ~t kayıtsız; orta derecede
indigest|ible hazmolunmaz; ~ion hazımsızlık
indigna|nt [in'dignınt] dargın, öfkeli; ~tion dargınlık, öfke
indirect dolaşık; dolaylı
indiscre|et boşboğaz, düşüncesiz; ~tion boşboğazlık, düşüncesizlik
indiscriminate [indis'kriminit] gelişigüzel
indispensable zarurî
indispos|ed [indis'pıuzd] rahatsız; ~ition rahatsızlık
indisputable ['indis'pyûtıbl] söz götürmez
indistinct iyice görülmez
individual [indi'vidyul] birey, fert, kimse; bireysel, ferdî; ~ist bireyci; ~ity ferdiyet
indivisible bölünmez
indolen|ce ['indılıns] tembellik; ~t tembel
indomitable [in'domitıbl] boyun eğmez
indoor ['indô] ev içinde olan; ~ aerial oda anteni; ~s [in'dôz] ev içinde
indorse [in'dôs] s. endorse
induce [in'dyûs] v/t teşvik etm.; sebep olm. -e
indulge [in'dalc] v/t düşmana maha etm.; v/i düşkün olm., kapılmak (in -e); ~nce müsamaha; düşkünlük; ~nt müsamahakâr
industr|ial [in'dastriıl] sınaî, endüstri ile ilgili; ~ialize v/t sanayileştirmek;

~ious çalışkan; ~y ['indıstri] sanayi, endüstri; çalışkanlık
ineff|ective, ~icient etkisiz
inept [i'nept] yersiz; hünersiz
inequ|ality eşitsizlik; ~table insafsız
inert [i'nöt] hareketsiz; tembel; ~ia [~şyı] atalet
inestimable [in'estimıbl] hesaba sığmaz
inevitable [in'evitıbl] kaçınılmaz
inex|cusable affedilemez; ~haustible tükenmez; ~pensive ucuz; ~perienced tecrübesiz, acemi; ~plicable [~'eksplikıbl] izah edilemez; ~pressible [inks-'presıbl] ifade edilemez; ~pressive anlatımsız; ~tricable sökülemez
infallible [in'fálıbl] yanılmaz; şaşmaz
infam|ous ['infımıs] ahlâkı bozuk, rezil; ~y rezalet
infan|cy ['infınsi] çocukluk, bebeklik; ~t küçük çocuk, bebek; jur. ergin olmıyan kimse; ~tile ['~tayl] çocuğa ait, çocukça; ~tile paralysis med. çocuk felci
infantry ['infıntri] mil. piyade, yaya
infatuate [in'fätyueyt] v/t çıldırtmak; ~d meftun (with -e)
infect [in'fekt] v/t bulaştırmak; ~ion bulaşma; ~ious bulaşık, bulaşıcı
infer [in'fö] v/t anlamak,

çıkarmak; **~ence** ['infırıns] sonuç çıkarma

inferior [in'fıırii] aşağı, alt; ikinci derecede, adî; ast; **~ity** [~'oriti] aşağılık

infernal [in'fönl] cehenneme ait, şeytanca

infest [in'fest] v/t sarmak; zarar vermek -e

infidel ['infidıl] kâfir, imansız

infiltrate ['infiltreyt] v/t girmek -e; v/i süzülmek

infinit|e ['infinit] sonsuz; **~esimal** [infini'tesimıl] bölünemiyecek kadar küçük; **~ive (mood)** [in'finitiv] gr. mastar; **~y** sonsuzluk

infirm [in'föm] zayıf; hastalıklı; **~ary** hastane; **~ity** sakatlık, zayıflık

inflam|e [in'fleym] v/i tutuşmak; v/t alevlendirmek

inflamma|ble [in'flämıbl] tutuşur; **~tion** [~ı'meyşın] med. yangı, iltihap

inflat|e [in'fleyt] v/t şişirmek; **~ion** ec. enflasyon

inflect [in'flekt] v/t gr. çekmek

inflex|ible [in'fleksıbl] eğilmez; sarsılmaz; **~ion** [~kşın] bükülme; gr. çekim

inflict [in'flikt] v/t getirmek, uğratmak (**on** -e); **~ion** [~kşın] ceza; sıkıntı

influen|ce [in'fluıns] n. etki, nüfuz; v/t etkilemek; **~tial** [~'enşıl] sözü geçer, nüfuzlu

influenza [influ'enzı] med. grip, enflüanza

inform [in'föm] v/t haber vermek -e (**of** hakkında), bildirmek (-i); **~al** resmî olmıyan, teklifsiz

information [infı'meyşın] bilgi; danışma; **~ bureau**, **~ office** danışma bürosu

inform|ative [in'fömıtiv] aydınlatıcı; **~er** jurnalcı

infringe [in'frinc] v/t bozmak; **~ment** bozma, ihlâl

infuriate [in'fyuurieyt] v/t çıldırtmak

infuse [in'fyûz] v/t aşılamak; fig. telkin etm.

ingen|ious [in'cinyıs] hünerli; usta; **~uity** [~i'nyuiti] hüner, marifet

ingot ['ingıt] külçe

ingratiate [in'greyşieyt]: **~ oneself** yağcılık yaparcasına sokulmak (**with** -e)

ingratitude [in'grätityûd] nankörlük

ingredient [in'grîdyınt] cüz, parça

inhabit [in'häbit] v/t oturmak, ikamet etm. -de; **~able** oturulabilir; **~ant** oturan, sakin

inhale [in'heyl] v/t içine çekmek

inherent [in'hiırınt] tabiî, doğal

inherit [in'herit] v/t miras almak; **~ance** miras, kalıt

inhibit [in'hibit] v/t engel olm. -e; **~ion** yasak

inhospitable misafir sevmez; barınılmaz

inhuman gaddar, kıyıcı

initia|l [in'nişıl] *n.* ilk harf; büyük harf; *adj.* ilk, baştaki; **~te** [~şieyt] başlamak *-e*; başlatmak *-i*; **~tive** [~şiitiv] öncelicik, inisiyatif

inject [in'cekt] *v/t* şırınga etm.; iğne ile içine sokmak; **~ion** enjeksiyon, iğne yapma

injur|e ['inci] *v/t* zarar vermek, dokunmak *-e*; bozmak *-i*; **~ious** [in'cuiris] zararlı; **~y** ['~iri] zarar; haksızlık; yara

injustice adaletsizlik

ink [ink] mürekkep

inkling ['inklin] ima; seziş

ink-pot mürekkep hokkası

inlaid [in'leyd] kakma

inland ['inlınd] *n.* memleket içi; *adj.* iç, dahilî

inlay ['in'ley] *v/t* kakma ile süslemek

inlet ['inlet] giriş yolu; *geo.* koy

inmate ['inmeyt] oturan

inmost ['inmoust] en içerdeki

inn [in] otel, han

innate [in'neyt] fıtrî, doğuştan olan

inner ['ini] iç; **~ tube** iç lastik; **~most** en içerdeki

innkeeper otelci, hancı

innocen|ce ['inısns] suçsuzluk; **~t** suçsuz, günahsız

innovation [inıu'veyşın] yenilik

innumerable [i'nyûmırıbl] sayısız

inoculat|e [i'nokyuleyt] *v/t* aşılamak; **~ion** aşılama

inoffensive zararsız

inopportune vakitsiz

input ['input] *ec.* girdi

inquest [inkwest] *jur.* resmî soruşturma

inquietude endişe

inquir|e [in'kwayı] *v/t* sormak; *v/i* soruşturmak (**about, after, for** *-i*); araştırmak (**into** *-i*); **~y** sorgu, soruşturma; araştırma

inquisitive [in'kwizitiv] çok sual soran, meraklı

insan|e [in'seyn] deli; **~ity** [in'säniti] akıl hastalığı, delilik

insatia|ble [in'seyşıbl], **~te** [~şiit] doymak bilmez

inscri|be [in'skrayb] *v/t* kaydetmek, yazmak; hakketmek; **~ption** [~ipşın] kayıt; yazıt

insect [insekt] böcek, haşere

insecure emniyetsiz

insensi|ble hissiz, duygusuz; kayıtsız; **~tive** duygusuz

inseparable ayrılmaz

insert [in'söt] *v/t* sokmak, sıkıştırmak; **~ion** ekleme; ilân

inside [in'sayd] *n., adj.* iç; *adv.* içeride, içeriye; *prp. -in* içerisinde, içerisine

insight ['insayt] anlayış

insignificant önemsiz

insincere ikiyüzlü

insinuat|e [in'sinyueyt] *v/t*

intellect

ima etm.; **~ion** ima, üstü kapalı itham [lezzetsiz]

insipid [in'sipid] yavan; tatsız

insist [in'sist] ısrar etm. (**on, upon** üzerinde); **~ent** ısrarlı, inatçı

insolent ['insılınt] küstah, terbiyesiz

insoluble [in'solyubl] erimez; çözülemez

insolvent müflis

insomnia [in'somni] uykusuzluk

insomuch [insu'maç] **that** o kadar ki

inspect [in'spekt] v/t teftiş etm., muayene etm.; **~ion** teftiş, yoklama; **~or** müfettiş; kontrol memuru

inspir|ation [inspi'reyşın] nefes alma; ilham; **~e** [in-'spayı] v/t ilham etm., esinlemek

instability sebatsızlık

instal|(**l**) [in'stôl] v/t yerleştirmek, kurmak; **~lation** [~'leyşın] yerleştirme; tesisat; **~(l)ment** [~'stôlmınt] taksit

instance ['instıns] misal, örnek; **for ~** mesela, örneğin

instant ['instınt] n. an; adj. hemen olan; **~aneous** [~'teynyıs] ani; **~ly** adv. hemen, derhal

instead [in'sted] yerinde, yerine; **~ of** -in yerine

instep ['instep] ayağın üst kısmı

instigat|e ['instigeyt] v/t kışkırtmak; **~or** kışkırtıcı

instinct ['instinkt] içgüdü, insiyak; **~ive** [~'stinktiv] içgüdülü

institut|e ['instityût] n. enstitü; kuruluş; kurum; v/t kurmak; **~ion** kuruluş, müessese

instruct [in'strakt] v/t eğitmek; talimat vermek -e; **~ion** eğitim, talim; pl. emir, direktif sg.; **~ive** öğretici; **~or** eğitmen, okutman

instrument [in'strumınt] alet; mus. çalgı, saz; jur. belge

insubordinate [insı'bôdnit] itaatsiz

insufferable tahammül olunamaz

insufficient eksik

insula|r ['insyulı] adaya ait, adada yaşıyan; **~te** [~'eyt] v/t izole etm., yalıtmak

insult [insalt] n. hakaret; v/t -in şerefine dokunmak

insur|ance [in'şuırıns] sigorta; **~e** [~'şuı] v/t sigorta etm.; sağlamak

insurmountable [insô-'mauntıbl] geçilemez

insurrection [insı'rekşın] ayaklanma

intact [in'täkt] dokunulmamış, eksiksiz

integr|al ['intigrıl] gerekli; tam, bütün; **~ate** v/t tamamlamak, bütünlemek; **~ity** [in'tegriti] bütünlük; dürüstlük

intellect ['intilekt] akıl; an-

intellectual   306

lık; ~ual [~'lektyuıl] akla
ait; bilgili, zekâ sahibi

intellig|ence [in'telicıns]
akıl, anlayış, haber; ~**ence
service** istihbarat dairesi;
~**ent** akıllı, zeki, anlayışlı;
~**ible** anlaşılır

intemperate taşkın; şiddetli

intend [in'tend] v/t niyet
etm., tasarlamak

intens|e [in'tens] keskin,
şiddetli, gergin; ~**ify** [~i-
fay] v/t -*in* şiddetini artırmak; v/i şiddetlenmek;
~**ity** keskinlik, şiddet; ~**ive**
şiddetli

intent [in'tent] n. niyet,
maksat; adj. gayretli; meşgul (**on** ile); ~**ion** niyet,
maksat; ~**ional** kasıtlı

inter [in'tö] v/t gömmek

inter|cede [intı'sîd] aracılık
etm.; ~**cept** [~'sept] v/t
durdurmak; -*in* yolunu
kesmek; ~**cession** [~'seşın]
şefaat, iltimas

interchange [intı'çeync] n.
mübadele; v/t değiştirmek

intercourse ['intıkôs] münasebet   [sak etm.]

interdict [intı'dikt] v/t ya-

interest ['intırist] n. ilgi,
merak; menfaat; ec. faiz;
v/t ilgilendirmek; ~**ed** ilgili (**in** ile); meraklı (-e);
~**ing** ilgi çekici, ilginç

interfere [intı'fiı] karışmak, mâni olm. (**with** -e);
~**nce** karışma, müdahale

interior [in'tiıriı] iç; içerdeki

inter|jection [intı'cekşın]
ünlem; ~**lude** ['luud] ara
faslı

intermedia|ry [intı'mîdyı-
ri] aracı; aracılık eden; ~**te**
[~yıt] ortadaki; aradaki

inter|mission aralık, fasıla;
~**mittent fever** [intı'mi-
tınt -] med. sıtma

intern [in'tön] v/t enterne
etm.; n. Am. stajyer dok-
tor; ~**al** [~'tönl] iç

inter|national uluslararası;
~**pellation** [intöpe'leyşın]
pol. gensoru; ~**pose** v/t
arasına koymak; v/i araya
girmek

interpret [in'töprit] v/t -*in*
manasını açıklamak; ~**a-
tion** yorum, tefsir; ~**er** tercüman, çevirmen

interrogat|e [in'terıugeyt]
v/t sorguya çekmek; ~**ion**
sorgu; **note** (**mark,
point**) **of** ~**ion** gr. soru
işareti; ~**ive** [intı'rogıtiv]
pronoun gr. soru za-
miri

interrupt [intı'rapt] v/t
kesmek; ara vermek -*e*;
~**ion** ara, fasıla

intersect [intı'sekt] v/t iki-
ye bölmek; v/i kesişmek;
~**ion** kesişme, kavşak

interurban [intır'öbın] şehirlerarası

interval ['intıvıl] ara, fasıla;
müddet

interven|e [intı'vîn] araya
girmek; ~**tion** [~'venşın]
araya girme; aracılık

interview ['intıvyû] n. gö-

rüşme, mülâkat; *v/t* görüşmek *b.* ile   [bağırısak)
intestine [in'testin] *an.)*
intima|cy [in'timisi] sıkı
dostluk; **~te** ['~it] *adj.* sıkı
fıkı; içten; ['~eyt] *v/t* üstü
kapalı anlatmak, ima etm.;
~tion ima
intimidate [in'timideyt] *v/t*
korkutmak
into ['intu, 'inti] -e, -*in* içerisine
intolera|ble   tahammül
olunmaz; **~nce** taassup;
~nt hoşgörüsüz
intoxicate [in'toksikeyt] *v/t*
sarhoş etm.
intransitive *gr.* geçişsiz
intrepid [in'trepid] yılmaz
intri|cate [in'trikit] karışık;
~gue [in'trîg] *n.* entrika;
v/i entrika çevirmek
introduc|e [intrı'dyûs] *v/t*
tanıştırmak, tanıtmak (**to**
-*e*); **~tion** [~'dakşın] takdim; önsöz; **~tory** [~'dak-
tıri] tanıtma maksadıyle
yapılan
intru|de [in'truud] *v/t* zorla
sokmak; *v/i* zorla sokulmak
(**into** -*e*); **~der** davetsiz
misafir; zorla sokulan biri;
~sion [~jın] içeri sokulma
intuition [intyu'işın] sezgi,
içine doğma
invade [in'veyd] *v/t* saldırmak, istilâ etm. -*e*; **~r** saldıran
invalid ['invlid] *jur.* hükümsüz; *med.* hasta, sakat;
~ate [~eyt] *v/t* hükümsüz
kılmak

invaluable para biçilmez
invariab|le değişmez; **~ly**
adv. değişmiyerek; her zaman
invasion [in'veyjin] akın,
saldırış, istilâ
invent [in'vent] *v/t* icat
etm.; uydurmak; **~ion**
icat; uydurma; **~or** mucit,
türeten
inver|se [in'vös] ters; **~**
sion ters dönme; ters çevirme; **~t** *v/t* tersine çevirmek; **~ted commas** *pl.* *gr.*
tırnaklar
invest [in'vest] *v/t* *ec.* yatırmak; *authority:* vermek -*e*;
mil. kuşatmak -*i*
investigat|e [in'vestigeyt]
v/t araştırmak; **~ion** araştırma
investment [in'vestmint]
ec. yatırma; yatırılan para
invincible [in'vinsibl] ye-
nilmez
inviolable [in'vayılıbl] do-
kunulmaz; bozulamaz
invisible [in'vizibl] görülmez
invit|ation [invi'teyşın] da-
vet, çağrı; davetiye; **~e**
[in'vayt] *v/t* davet etm.,
çağırmak
invoice ['invoys] *ec.* fatura
invoke [in'vıuk] *v/t* yalvarmak -*e*; çağırmak -*i*
involuntary   tasarlanma-
mış
involve [in'volv] *v/t* sarmak; sokmak, karıştırmak
(**in** -*e*); gerektirmek
invulnerable yaralanamaz

inward ['inwıd] iç; ~(s) içe
doğru

iodine ['ayıudîn] *chem.* iyot

irascible [i'räsibl] çabuk
öfkelenir

Ir|eland ['ayılınd] İrlanda;
~ish [~riş] İrlandalı; İrlanda dili

irksome ['öksım] usandırıcı

iron ['ayın] *n.* demir; ütü;
adj. demirden, demir gibi;
v/t ütülemek

ironic(al) [ay'ronik(ıl)] alay
eden

iron|ing ütüleme; ~mon-ger hırdavatçı; ~works *pl.*
demirhane *sg.*

irony ['ayırıni] alay, istihza

irradiate [i'reydieyt] *v/t*
aydınlatmak

irrational akla uymaz

irreconcilable barıştırıla-maz

irrecoverable geri alına-maz, telâfi edilemez

irredeemable ıslah oluna-maz; *ec.* nakde tahvil olu-namaz

irregular düzensiz, usule
aykırı; *gr.* kural dışı

irrelevant konu dışı

irreparable [i'repırıbl] te-lâfisi imkânsız; tamir olu-namaz

irreplacable yeri doldurula-maz

irresistible karşı konula-maz

irrespective of -e bakmak-sızın

irresponsible sorumsuz,
güvenilemez

irretrievable telâfi edile-mez, bir daha ele geçmez

irreverent [i'revırınt] say-gısız

irrevocable [i'revıkıbl] de-ğiştirilemez, geri alınamaz

irrigat|e ['irigeyt] *v/t* sula-mak; ~ion sulama

irrita|ble ['iritıbl] çabuk
kızan, titiz; ~te [~eyt] *v/t*
gücendirmek, sinirlendir-mek; ~tion sinirlilik, dar-gınlık

is [iz] -dir, -tir

Islam ['izlâm] İslâm, müs-lümanlık; ~ic [~'lämik] İs-lâma ait

island [ay'lınd], **isle** [ayl]
ada

isolat|e ['aysıleyt] *v/t* ayır-mak, tecrit etm.; ~ion ayır-ma, tecrit

Israel ['izreyıl] İsrail

issue ['işuu] *n.* çıkış; akma;
sonuç; döl, zürriyet; ya-yım, dağıtma; *v/i* çıkmak;
v/t çıkarmak, dağıtmak,
yayınlamak

isthmus ['ismıs] *geo.* berzah

it [it] o, onu, ona *(cinssiz)*

Ital|ian [i'tälyın] İtalyan;
İtalyanca; ~y ['itıli] İtalya

itch [iç] *n.* kaşıntı; *v/i* kaşın-mak   [madde]

item ['aytım] parça; fıkra,
madde

itinerary [ay'tınırıri] yol;
yolcu rebberi

its [its] onun(ki) *(cinssiz)*

itself [it'self] bizzat, kendi;
by ~ kendi kendine

ivory ['ayvıri] fildişi

ivy ['ayvi] *bot.* sarmaşık

J

jab [cäb] *v/t* dürtmek, itmek

jack [cäk] *tech.* kriko; bacak, vale (*cards*); *v/t* bocurgat ile kaldırmak

jackal ['cäköl] *zo.* çakal

jack|ass ['cäkäs] erkek eşek; *fig.* ['.kaas] ahmak; **~daw** ['.dö] küçük karga

jacket ['cäkit] ceket; kitap zarfı; kaplama

jack|-knife ['cäk-] çakı; **~pot** *oyunda* pot

jag [cäg] diş, uç; **~ged** ['~gid] dişli, çentik

jail [ceyl] *n.* cezaevi; *v/t* tutuklamak; **~er** gardiyan

jam [cäm] **1.** reçel, marmelat; **2.** *n.* sıkışma, kalabalık; *v/t* sıkıştırmak; *v/i* sıkışmak

janitor ['cänitı] kapıcı

January ['cänyuıri] ocak ayı

Japan [cı'pän] Japonya; **~ese** [cäpı'niz] Japon(yalı); Japonca

jar [câ] kavanoz

jaundice ['côndis] *med.* sarılık

javelin ['cävlin] cirit

jaw [cô] çene; **~bone** çene kemiği

jazz [cäz] caz

jealous ['celıs] kıskanç; **~y** kıskançlık, haset

jeep [cip] cip

jeer [ciı] *a.* alay, yuha; *v/i* yuhalamak (**at** *-i*)

jelly ['celi] *n.* pelte; jelatin

v/t pelteleştirmek; *v/i* pelteleşmek; **~fish** *zo.* denizanası, medüz

jeopardize ['cepıdayz] *v/t* tehlikeye koymak

jerk [côk] *n.* anî çekiş; *v/i* birdenbire çekmek; *v/t* atmak; **~y** sarsıntılı

jersey ['côzi] jarse

jest [cest] *n.* şaka; *v/i* şaka söylemek; **~er** şakacı

Jesu|it ['cezyuit] *rel.* cizvit; **~s** ['cîzıs] Hazreti İsa

jet [cet] meme; tepki; *av.* jet uçağı; *v/i* fışkırmak

jetty ['ceti] dalgakıran; iskele

Jew [cuu] Yahudi

jewel ['cuul] kıymetli taş, mücevher; **~(l)er** kuyumcu; **~(le)ry** kuyumculuk; mücevherat *pl.*

Jew|ish ['cuuiş] Yahudi, Musevî; **~ry** ['~uri] Yahudilik

jiggle ['cigl] *v/i* sallanmak; *v/t* sallamak

jingle ['cingl] *n.* çıngırtı; *v/t* çıngırdatmak

jingo ['cingıu] *pol.* şoven

job [cob] iş, görev; **out of ~** işsiz; **~less** işsiz; **~-work** götürü iş

jockey ['coki] cokey

jog [cog] *v/t* sarsmak; *v/i* yavaş gezinmek

join [coyn] *n.* bitişim noktası; *v/t* birleştirmek, bağlamak; katılmak *-e*; **~er**

joint

doğramacı, marangoz; **~t**
n. ek; *an.* eklem, mafsal;
Am. sl. esrarlı sigara; *adj.*
birleşik, ortaklaşa; **~t-stock
company** *ec.* anonim ortaklık

joke [cıuk] *n.* şaka; *v/i* şaka
yapmak; **~r** oyunda koz,
coker

jolly ['coli] şen, neşeli

jolt [cult] *n.* sarsıntı; *v/t*
sarsmak

Jordan ['côdn] Ürdün

jostle ['cosl] *v/t* itip kakmak

jot [cot] *n.* zerre; **~ down**
v/t yazıvermek

journal ['cônl] gazete; dergi; yevmiye defteri; **~ism**
['~lizım] gazetecilik; **~ist**
gazeteci

journey ['cöni] *n.* yolculuk,
seyahat; *v/i* seyahat etm.;
~man kalfa

jovial ['cıuvyıl] şen, keyifli

joy [coy] sevinç, neşe; **~ful,
~ous** neşeli, sevinçli

jubil|ant ['cuubilınt] büyük
neşe içinde; **~ee** ['~lî] ellinci yıldönümü; neşeli kut-
lama

Juda|ic [cuu'deyik] Yahu-
dilere ait; **~sm** Yahudi-
lik

judg|e [cac] *n.* hâkim, yar-
gıç; hakem; *v/t* yargılamak;
tenkit etm.; karar vermek
(hakkında); **~(e)ment** hüküm, yargı; mahkeme ka-
rarı; 2(e)ment Day *rel.*
kıyamet günü

judic|ial [cu'dişıl] mahke-

meye ait, adlî; **~ious** tedbirli, akıllı

jug [cag] testi, çömlek

juggle ['cagl] *n.* hokkabazlık; *v/i* hokkabazlık yapmak; **~r** hokkabaz

Jugoslav ['yûgu'slâv] Yu-
goslav(yalı); **~ia** [~yı] Yugoslavya

juic|e [cuus] özsu, usare; **~y**
sulu, özlü

juke-box ['cuuk-] otomatik
pikap

July [cu'lay] temmuz

jump [camp] *n.* atlama, sıçrama; *v/i* atlamak, sıçramak; *v/t* atlamak (-den, -i);
~er atlayıcı; **~y** sinirli

junct|ion ['caŋkşın] birleş-
me; kavşak; **~ure** birleşme
yeri; nazik zaman, önemli
an

June [cuun] haziran

jungle ['caŋgl] cengel

junior ['cuunyı] yaşça küçük; ast

junk [caŋk] pılı pırtı, çöp

jur|idical [cu'ridikıl] adlî,
kanunî; **~isdiction** [~ris-
'dikşın] yargılama hakkı;
kaza dairesi; **~isprudence**
['~rispruudıns] hukuk ilmi;
~or ['~rı] jüri üyesi; **~y**
['~rî] jüri

just [cast] *adj.* âdil, insaflı;
haklı; *adv.* sadece; tam;
hemen; ancak; şimdi; **~
now** hemen şimdi

justice ['castis] adalet, insaf; hâkim, yargıç

justif|ication [castifi'key-
şın] haklı çık(ar)ma; mazur

gösterme; **~y** ['.fay] v/t haklı çıkarmak

justly ['castli] adv. haklı olarak

K

kangaroo [kängı'ruu] zo. kanguru

keel [kil] naut. omurga

keen [kin] keskin; canlı; şiddetli; düşkün (**on** -e)

keep [kip] n. geçim; v/t tutmak, korumak; işletmek; sürdürmek; devam etm. (-ing -meğe); v/i kalmak; ~ **away** v/i uzak durmak; v/t uzak tutmak; ~ **off** v/t uzak tutmak (**from** -den); v/i uzak kalmak; ~ **on** v/t çıkarmamak, söndürmemek; devam etm. (-ing -meğe); ~ **up** geri kalmamak (**with** -de); **~er** bakıcı; bekçi; **~ing** koruma; geçim; **in** **~ing** uygun (**with** -e); **~sake** hatıra, andaç

kennel ['kenl] köpek kulübesi

kerb(stone) ['köb(-)] yaya kaldırımının kenar taşı

kerchief ['köçif] baş örtüsü

kernel ['könl] çekirdek

kettle ['ketl] çaydanlık; kazan; **~drum** mus. dümbelek

key [ki] anahtar; tuş; **~board** klavye; **~hole** anahtar deliği; **~note** ana nota; fig. temel, ilke

khaki ['kaaki] toprak rengi, haki

jut [cat]: ~ **out** dışarı çıkmış olm.

juvenile ['cuuvinayl] genç; gençlikle ilgili

khan [kaan] han

kick [kik] n. tekme, tepme; v/t tekmelemek, çiftelemek

kid [kid] n. zo. oğlak; sl. çocuk; v/t takılmak -e; **~nap** ['.näp] v/t zorla kaçırmak

kidney ['kidni] an. böbrek

kill [kil] v/t öldürmek; time: geçirmek; **~er** adam öldüren

kiln [kiln] kireç ocağı, fırın

kilo|gram(me)['kilugräm] kilo(gram); **~metre** Am. **~meter** kilometre; **~watt** kilovat

kilt [kilt] İskoç erkeklerinin giydiği eteklik

kin [kin] akraba

kind [kaynd] n. cins, çeşit; adj. sevimli, nazik

kindergarten ['kindıgaatn] anaokulu

kindle ['kindl] v/t tutuşturmak, yakmak; v/i tutuşmak

kindness ['kayndnis] şefkat, yumuşaklık [akrabalık]

kindred ['kindrid] akraba; J

king [kiŋ] kıral; şah; **~dom** kırallık, kıraliyet; **~size** normalden büyük

kinship ['kinşip] akrabalık

kipper ['kipı] tuzlanmış isli ringa balığı

kiss [kis] n. buse, öpücük; v/t öpmek

kit¹ [kit] avadanlık; takım
kit² yavru kedi
kitchen ['kiçin] mutfak; **~ette** [~'net] ufak mutfak
kite [kayt] uçurtma
kitten ['kitn] yavru kedi
knack [näk] hüner, ustalık
knapsack ['näpsäk] sırt çantası
knave [neyv] herif, düzenbaz; *oyunda* bacak; **~ry** ['~ri] hilekârlık
knead [nîd] *v/t* yoğurmak; masaj yapmak
knee [nî] *an.* diz, **~-cap**, **~-pan** diz kapağı; **~l** [~l] *v/i* diz çökmek
knelt [nelt] *s.* **kneel**
knew [nyû] *s.* **know**
knife [nayf], *pl.* **knives** [~vz] *n.* bıçak; *v/t* bıçaklamak
knight [nayt] silâhşor; şövalye

knit [nit] *v/t* örmek; **~ the eyebrows** kaşlarını çatmak
knob [nob] topuz; pürtük
knock [nok] *n.* vuruş, çalma, darbe; *v/t* vurmak; çarpmak *-e*; *v/i* çalmak (**at** *-i*); **~ down** *v/t* yere sermek; etme; **~er** kapı tokmağı
knoll [nuul] tepecik
knot [not] *n.* düğüm, bağ; küme; güç durum; *v/t* düğümlemek, bağlamak, **~ty** düğümlü; budaklı
know [nuu] *v/t* bilmek; tanımak; **make ~n** *v/t* tanıtmak; bildirmek; **~ing** akıllı, açıkgöz; **~ingly** *adv.* bilerek; **~ledge** ['nolic] bilgi; malumat
knuckle ['nakl] *an.* parmak orta eklemi; **~bone** aşıkkemiği

L

label ['leybl] *n.* etiket, yafta; *v/t* etiketlemek
labo|ratory [lı'borıtırı] laboratuvar; **~rious** [~'bôris] çalışkan; yorucu
labo(u)r ['leybı] *n.* iş, çalışma; emek; işçi sınıfı; *med.* doğum ağrıları *pl.*; zahmet; *v/i* çalışmak, uğraşmak; **Ministry of ♀ Çalışma Bakanlığı**; **forced ~** angarya; **♀ Party İşçi Partisi**; **~ union** işçi sendikası; **~er** işçi, rençper
lace [leys] *n.* bağ, şerit; dan-

tel(a); *v/t* bağlamak; dantel ile süslemek
lack [läk] *n.* noksan, eksiklik; ihtiyaç; *v/i* eksik olm.; *v/t* muhtaç olm. *-e*
lackey ['läki] uşak, hizmetçi
laconic [lı'konik] kısa ve öz
lacquer ['läki] *n.* vernik; *v/t* vernik ile kaplamak
lad [läd] genç, delikanlı
ladder ['lädı] el merdiveni; **~proof** çözülmez (*çorap*)
lad|e [leyd] *v/t* yüklemek; **~en** ['~n] *s.* **lade**; **~ing** yük
ladle ['leydl] kepçe

lady ['leydi] bayan, hanım; asılzade kadın, leydi; **~bird** zo. gelinböceği; **~like** hanıma yakışır

lag [läg] n. geçikme; v/i geri kalmak

lager(beer) ['lâgı(-)] Alman birası

lagoon [lı'guun] geo. deniz kulağı

laid [leyd] s. lay

lain [leyn] s. lie

lair [läı] in, yatak

lake [leyk] göl

lamb [läm] kuzu

lame [leym] adj. topal, ayağı sakat; v/i topallamak

lament [lı'ment] n. iniltı; v/i inlemek; v/t ağlamak için; **~able** ['lämıntıbl] acınacak; **~ation** [lämen'teyşın] ağlayış, inleme

lamp [lämp] lamba; **~post** sokak feneri direği; **~ -shade** abajur

lance [lâns] n. mızrak; v/t deşmek, yarmak

land [länd] n. toprak, kara; ülke; arsa; arazi; v/i karaya çıkmak, yere inmek; v/t karaya çıkarmak; indirmek; **~ed property** arazi, mülk; **~holder** mülk sahibi

landing ['ländin] iniş, karaya çıkma; sahanlık; **~gear** av. iniş takımı; **~stage** naut. iskele

land|lady ['länleydi] pansiyoncu kadın; ev sahibesi; **~lord** ['län-] mal sahibi; **~mark** ['länd-] sınır taşı; **~scape** ['län-] manzara;

peyzaj; **~slide** ['länd-] geo., fig., **~slip** ['länd-] geo. kayşa, heyelân

lane [leyn] dar sokak, dar yol; otomobil yolu

language ['längwic] dil, lisan

langu|id ['längwid] gevşek, cansız; **~ish** v/i gevşemek, zayıf düşmek; **~or** ['~gı] gevşelik, cansızlık

lank [länk] uzun ve zayıf; **~y** sırık gibi

lantern ['läntın] fener

lap [läp] n. diz üstü; kucak; etek; v/t üst üste bindirmek; yalıyarak içmek

lapel [lı'pel] klapa

lapse [läps] kusur; geçme, mürur

larceny ['lâsıni] hırsızlık

lard [lâd] domuz yağı; **~er** kiler

large [lâc] büyük, iri, bol, geniş; at **~** serbest; ayrıntılı olarak; **~-scale** büyük çapta

lark [lâk] zo. tarla kuşu; fig. şaka

larva ['lâvı] zo. kurtçuk, sürfe

larynx ['lärinks] an. hançere, gırtlak

lascivious [lı'siviıs] şehvetli

lash [läş] n. kamçı darbesi; kamçı; kirpik; v/t kamçılamak; iple bağlamak

lass [läs] kız

lassitude ['läsityûd] yorgunluk

last[1] [lâst] son, sonuncu; son defa, son olarak; at **~**

last   314

sonunda; ~ (but) not least
özellikle

last² v/i devam etm., sürmek; dayanmak; ~ing sü-
rekli; dayanıklı

latch [läç] n. mandal, sürgü;
v/t mandallamak

late [leyt] geç; gecikmiş;
ölü, rahmetli; as ~ as ancak; artık; at (the) ~st en
geç olarak; of ~ son zamanlarda; ~ly geçenlerde; ~r
on daha sonra

lath [lâth] lata

lathe [leydh] torna tezgâhı

lather ['lâdhə] n. sabun köpüğü; v/i köpürmek; v/t
sabunlamak

Latin ['lätin] Latin(ce)

latitude ['lätityûd] geo. en-
lem, arz

latter ['lätə] son, sonraki

lattice ['lätis] kafes

laudable ['lôdıbl] övgüye
değer

laugh [lâf] n. gülme, gülüş;
v/i gülmek; alay etm. (at
ile); ~ter gülüş; kahkaha

launch [lônç] v/t naut. kı-
zaktan suya indirmek; at-
mak, fırlatmak; ~ing-pad
atış rampası

laundr|ess ['lôndris] çama-
şırcı kadın; ~y çamaşır; ça-
maşırhane

laurel ['loril] bot. defne

lavatory ['lävıtıri] yıkanma
yeri; tuvalet, helâ

lavender ['lävindı] lavanta

lavish ['läviş] adj. savurgan,
müsrif; v/t bol bol harcamak

law [lô] kanun, yasa; ni-
zam; hukuk; ~ful kanuna
uygun, meşru; ~less kanu-
na aykırı; kanunsuz

lawn [lôn] çimen(lik)

law|suit dava; ~yer ['lôyı]
avukat, dava vekili

lax [läks] gevşek; ihmalci;
~ative ['~ıtiv] med. sürgün)
lay¹ [ley] s. lie   (ilâcı)
lay² rel. layik; işin ehli ol-
miyan

lay³ n. durum; v/t koymak,
yatırmak, yaymak, sermek;
table: kurmak; ~ out yay-
mak; tasarlamak; düzenle-
mek; ~er kat, tabaka

layman ['leymın] meslek
sahibi olmıyan kimse

layout düzen, tertip

lazy ['leyzi] tembel

lead¹ [led] kurşun

lead² [lîd] n. kılavuzluk, ön-
cülük; thea. baş rol; tasma
kayışı; el. ana tel; v/t yol
göstermek -e; kumanda
etm. -i; götürmek -i; idare
etm. -i

leaden ['ledın] kurşun(dan)

leader ['lîdı] önder, lider,
önayak; ~ship önderlik,
liderlik

leading ['lîdiŋ] önde olan,
baş, başlıca

leaf [lîf] pl. leaves [~vz]
bot. yaprak; (door) kanat;
~let ['~lit] yaprakçık; ufak
risale

league [lîg] lig; birlik

leak [lîk] n. delik, akıntı; v/i
sızmak; ~age sızıntı; ~y
sızıntılı

lean¹ [lîn] zayıf

lean² v/t dayamak; v/i dayanmak (**against** -e)

leant [lent] s. **lean²**

leap [lîp] n. atlama, sıçrayış; v/i atlamak, sıçramak; v/t atlatmak; ~t [lept] s. **leap**;
~**year** artık yıl

learn [lön] v/t öğrenmek; ~**ed** [~id] âlim, bilgili; ~**ing** öğrenme, bilgi; ~**t** [lönt] s. **learn**

lease [lîs] n. kira(lama); v/t kiralamak; kiraya vermek

leash [lîş] tasma sırımı

least [lîst] en az, en ufak; **at** ~ hiç olmazsa

leather [ledhı] kösele, meşin

leave [lîv] n. müsaade; izin; v/t bırakmak, terketmek; ayrılmak -den

leaven [levn] maya

Lebanon [lebının] Lübnan

lecture [lekçı] n. konferans; umumî ders; azarlama; v/i konferans vermek, ders vermek; v/t azarlamak; ~**r** konferans veren kimse; doçent

led [led] s. **lead**

ledge [lec] düz çıkıntı; kaya tabakası

leech [lîç] zo. sülük

leek [lîk] bot. pırasa

leer [lii] kötü niyetle bakmak (**at** -e)

left¹ [left] s. **leave**

left² sol, sol taraf; ~**-handed** solak

leg [leg] bacak; but; **pull someone's** ~ takılmak -e

leprosy

legacy [legısi] miras, kalıt

legal [lîgıl] kanunî, meşru; ~**lize** v/t kanunlaştırmak, meşru kılmak

legation [li`geyşın] pol. orta elçilik

legend [lecınd] masal, hikâye; yazı; ~**ary** efsanevî

legible [lecıbl] okunaklı

legion [lîcın] eski Roma alayı; birçok; kalabalık

legislat|ion [lecis`leyşın] jur. yasama; ~**ive** [~`lıtiv] yasamalı; ~**or** [~`leytı] kanun yapan

legitimate [li`citimit] kanuna uygun, meşru

leisure [leji] boş vakit; ~**ly** rahatça

lemon [lemın] limon; ~ **squash** limon suyu; ~**ade** [~`neyd] limonata

lend [lend] v/t ödünç vermek; ~ **help** yardım etm. (**to** -e)

length [lendh] uzunluk; boy; süre; **at** ~ nihayet; ~**en** v/t uzatmak; v/i uzamak; ~**wise** [~`wayz] uzunluğuna

lenient [lînyınt] yumuşak huylu

lens [lenz] phys. mercek, adese

Lent¹ [lent] rel. büyük perhiz

lent² [lent] s. **lend**

lentil [lentil] bot. mercimek

leopard [lepıd] zo. pars

lep|er [lepı] med. cüzamlı; ~**rosy** [~`rısi] cüzam, miskin hastalığı

less [les] daha az, daha küçük; *math.* eksi; **~en** *v/t* küçültmek, azaltmak; *v/i* azalmak; **~er** daha az

lesson ['lesn] ders; ibret

lest [lest] olmasın diye; belki

let [let] *v/t* bırakmak; kiraya vermek; müsaade etm. *-mesine;* **~ alone** şöyle dursun; **~ down** *v/t* indirmek; hayal kırıklığına uğratmak; **~ go** elinden bırakmak

lethal ['liːðhl] öldürücü

lethargy ['leθədʒi] uyuşukluk

letter ['letə] harf; mektup; *pl.* edebiyat; **~box** mektup kutusu; **~head** mektup başlığı

lettuce ['letis] *bot.* salata

leuk(a)emia [ljuː'kiːmiə] *med.* lösemi, kan kanseri

level ['levl] *n.* seviye, hiza; tesviye aleti; *adj.* düz, düzlem; ufkî, yatay; *v/t* düzlemek, tesviye etm.; **~ crossing** *yolun* yolundan aynı seviyede geçmesi

lever ['liːvə] manivela

levity ['leviti] hoppalık

levy ['levi] *n.* toplama, tarh; *v/t* tarhetmek; **~ war** harp açmak (**on** *-e* karşı)

lewd [luːd] şehvet düşkünü

liab|ility [layə'biliti] sorumluluk, mükellefiyet; **~le** ['~bl] sorumlu (**for** *-den*), mükellef (ile); maruz (**to** *-e*)

liar ['layə] yalancı

libel ['laybl] *jur.* iftira

liber|al ['libırıl] serbest düşünceli; *pol.* liberal; **~ate** ['~reyt] *v/t* kurtarmak, özgür kılmak; **~ation** kurtuluş, serbest bırakma; **~ty** ['~ti] hürriyet, serbestlik

librar|ian [lay'breəriən] kütüphane memuru; **~y** ['~briri] kitaplık, kütüphane

lice [lays] *pl., s.* **louse**

licen|ce, Am. ~se ['laysıns] *n.* ruhsat; müsaade; çapkınlık; *v/t* ruhsat veya yetki vermek *-e;* **~see** ['~'siː] ruhsat sahibi; **~tious** ['~'senʃəs] şehvete düşkün

lick [lik] *v/t* yalamak; dayak atmak *-e*

lid [lid] kapak

lie¹ [lay] *n.* yalan; *v/i* yalan söylemek

lie² *v/i* yatmak, uzanmak

lieutenant [lef'tenənt, *naut.* le'tenənt, *Am.* luː'tenənt] *mil.* teğmen; **~-colonel** yarbay; **~-general** korgeneral

life [layf] *pl.* **lives** [~vz] hayat; ömür; **~ assurance, ~ insurance** hayat sigortası; **~ expectancy** ortalama ömür uzunluğu; **~-belt** cankurtaran kemeri; **~-guard** cankurtaran yüzücüsü; **~less** cansız; **~like** canlı gibi görünen; **~time** hayat süresi, ömür

lift [lift] *n.* asansör; kaldırma gücü; *v/t* kaldırmak, yükseltmek; yükselmek; **give** *so.* **a ~** arabasına almak *-i*

literary

liga|ment ['ligimint] *an.*
bağ; **~ture** ['~çu] *med.*
kanı durduran bağ

light¹ [layt] *n.* ışık, aydınlık; *adj.* açık; ~ **(up)** *v/t*
yakmak; aydınlatmak; *v/i*
parıldamak; **give** *so.* **a ~**
ateş vermek *-e*

light² hafif

lighten¹ ['laytn] *v/t* aydınlatmak

lighten² *v/i* hafifletmek

light|er ['laytı] çakmak; **~-
house** fener kulesi; **~ning**
şimşek, yıldırım

lightweight *adj.* hafif; *n.*
tüysüklet

like¹ [layk] *v/t* sevmek, beğenmek

like² gibi; benzer *-e*; **~li-
hood** ['layklihud] ihtimal;
~ly muhtemel; **~ness** benzerlik; **~wise** ['~wayz] dahi, keza [meyil\

liking ['laykiŋ] beğenme,/

lilac ['laylık] *bot.* leylak;
adj. açık mor

lily ['lili] *bot.* zambak; ~ **of
the valley** inciçiçeği

limb [lim] uzuv, örgen; dal

lime [laym] 1. kireç; 2. *bot.*
ıhlamur; **in the ~light** *fig.*
göz önünde, halkın dilinde;
~stone kireç taşı

limit ['limit] *n.* had, sınır;
v/t sınırlamak; hasretmek;
off ~s *Am.* yasak bölge;
~ation tahdit; kayıtlama;
~ed mahdut, sayılı; *ec.*
limitet

limp [limp] *adj.* gevşek, yumuşak; *v/i* topallamak

line [layn] *n.* sıra, dizi; çizgi; satır; hat; ip, olta; *v/t*
dizmek, sıralamak; çizgiler-
le göstermek; astarlamak;
hold the ~ telefonu kapat-
mamak; **stand in ~** kuy-
rukta beklemek

lineament ['liniımınt] yüz
hattı

linear ['liniı] doğrusal

linen ['linin] keten bezi; iç
çamaşır

liner ['laynı] *naut.* transat-
lantik; *av.* yolcu uçağı

linger ['liŋgı] *v/i* gecikmek,
ayrılamamak

linguistics [liŋ'gwistiks]
pl. dilbilim, lengüistik *sg.*

lining ['layniŋ] astar

link [liŋk] *n.* zincir halkası;
fig. bağ; *v/t* bağlamak; *v/i*
bağlanmak

links [liŋks] *pl.* kumullar;
golf oyunu alanı *sg.*

lion ['layın] aslan; **~ess** dişi
aslan

lip [lip] dudak; **~stick** ruj

liquid ['likwid] sıvı, mayi;
~ate ['~eyt] *v/t* tasfiye etm.;
~ity [li'kwiditi] *ec.* likidite

liquor ['likı] içki; sıvı madde

lisp [lisp] peltek konuşmak

list [list] *n.* liste, cetvel; *v/t*
listeye yazmak, kaydetmek

listen ['lisn] dinlemek **(to
-i)**, kulak vermek (-e); **~er**
dinleyici

listless ['listlis] kayıtsız

lit [lit] *s.* light¹

litera|l ['litırıl] harfi har-
fine; sözlü; **~ry** ['~rıri]

edebî; **~ture** ['~riçi] edebiyat

lithe [laydh] esnek

lit|re, *Am.* **~er** ['lîtı] litre

litter ['lîtı] sedye; teskere; *zo.* bir batında doğan yavrular *pl.*; **~ bag** çöp torbası

little ['lîtl] küçük, ufak; az, önemsiz; *n.* ufak miktar, az zaman

live¹ [liv] yaşamak; oturmak, ikamet etm.; geçinmek (**on** ile)

live² [layv] diri, canlı; direkt, doğrudan

live|lihood ['layvlihud] geçim, geçinme; **~liness** canlılık; **~ly** canlı

liver ['livı] *an.* karaciğer

livery ['livırı] hizmetçi üniforması

livestock ['layv-] çiftlik hayvanları *pl.*

livid ['livîd] mavimsi; solgun

living ['livîŋ] hayatta, canlı; yaşayış, geçim; **~-romm** oturma odası

lizard ['lizıd] *zo.* kertenkele

load [lıud] *n.* yük, hamule; *el.* şarj; *v/t* yüklemek; doldurmak

loaf¹ [lıuf], *pl.* **loaves** [~vz] bütün bir ekmek, somun

loaf² *v/i* vaktini boş geçirmek; **~er** haylaz, aylak

loam [lıum] balçık

loan [lıun] *n.* ödünç verme, ödünç alma; *v/t* ödünç vermek

loath [lıudh] isteksiz; **~e** *v/t* iğrenmek, nefret etm. *-den;*

~ing nefret; **~some** iğrenç, nefret verici

lobby ['lobi] koridor; antre; *pol.* kulis yapanlar *pl.*

lobe [lıub] *an.* kulak memesi

lobster ['lobstı] *zo.* ıstakoz

local ['lıukıl] mahallî, yöresel; **~ize** [~'kâliti] yer, yöre; **~ize** *v/t* sınırlamak

locate [lıu'keyt] *v/t* yerleştirmek; bulmak; **be ~d in** *-de* bulunmak

lock [lok] *n.* kilit; yükseltme havuzu; bukle; *v/t* kilitlemek; **~ up** kilit altında saklamak; **~et** ['~it] madalyon; **~-out** lokavt; **~smith** çilingir

locomotive ['lıukımıutiv] lokomotif

locust ['lıukıst] *zo.* çekirge

lodg|e [loc] *n.* kulübe; in; loca; *v/t* yerleştirmek, barındırmak; *v/i* yerleşmek, kirada oturmak; **~er** kiracı; **~ing** kiralık oda; geçici konut

loft [loft] çatı arası; **~y** yüksek; kibirli

log [log] kütük; **~-book** *naut.* rota defteri; **~-cabin** kütüklerden yapılmış kulübe

logic ['locik] mantık; **~al** mantıkî, makul

loin [loyn] bel; fileto

loiter ['loytı] *v/i* gezmek, aylak dolaşmak

loll [lol] *v/i* sallanmak

lonely ['lıunli] yalnız, kimsesiz; tenha

long¹ [loŋ] uzun; çok; **be-**

fore ~ yakında; **so ~!** Allaha ısmarladık!

long² v/i can atmak (**for** -e), çok istemek (**to** inf. -meği)

long-distance şehirlerarası

longing ['loŋiŋ] n. özlem, iştiyak

longitude ['loncityûd] geo. boylam, tul

look [luk] n. bakış, nazar; görünüş, güzellik; v/i bakmak (**at** -e); görünmek; ~ **after** bakmak -e; ~ **for** aramak -i; ~ **forward to** beklemek, ummak -i; ~ **into** araştırmak -i; ~ **out!** dikkat et!; ~ **over** gözden geçirmek -i; ~ **up** yukarıya bakmak; v/t sözlükte aramak; ~**ing glass** ayna

loom¹ [luum] dokuma tezgâhı

loom² v/i hayal gibi görünmek

loop [luup] n. ilmik, düğüm; v/i ilmik yapmak; v/t ilmiklemek

loose [luus] çözük, gevşek; hafifmeşrep, başıboş; ~**n** ['~sn] v/t gevşetmek, çözmek; v/i gevşemek, çözülmek

loot [luut] n. yağma, ganimet; v/i yağma etm.

lop [lop] v/t budamak, kesmek; v/i sarkmak; ~**-sided** bir tarafa yatkın

lord [lôd] sahip; lord; **the** 2 Allah, Tanrı; **House of** 2**s** pol. Lordlar kamarası; ~ **Mayor** Londra belediye başkanı; 2**'s Prayer** rel.

İsa'nın öğrettiği dua; 2**'s Supper** kudas, liturya

lorry ['lori] üstü açık yük arabası; kamyon

lose [luuz] v/t kaybetmek; kaçırmak; ~**r** kaybeden veya yenilen kimse

loss [los] kayıp; zarar; **at a** ~ şaşırmış; zararına

lost [lost] s. **lose**; ~**-property office** kayıp eşya bürosu

lot [lot] hisse, pay; talih; çok miktar; **a** ~ **of** çok; **draw** ~**s** kur'a çekmek

loth [luth] s. **loath**

lotion ['lûşın] losyon

lottery ['lotıri] piyango

loud [laud] (voice) yüksek; gürültülü; (colour) çiğ; ~**speaker** hoparlör

lounge [launc] n. dinlenme salonu, hol; şezlong; v/i tembelce uzanmak; avare dolaşmak

lous|**e** [laus], pl. **lice** bit, kehle; ~**y** bitli; alçak

lout [laut] kaba adam

love [lav] n. sevgi; aşk; sevgili; v/t sevmek; **fall in** ~ **with** âşık olm. -e; **send one's** ~ **to** selâm söylemek -e; ~**ly** sevimli, güzel; ~**r** sevgili; meraklı

low¹ [lu] v/i böğürmek

low² [lu] aşağı; alçak; bayağı; düşük; (voice) yavaş; ~**tide** geo. cezir, inik deniz; ~**er** adj. daha alçak; v/t indirmek, alçaltmak; düşürmek, azaltmak; 2**er House** Avam Kamarası; ~**land** geo. düz-

arazi, ova; ~necked de-
kolte; ~-pressure alçak
basınçlı; ~spirited ke-
derli

loyal ['loyıl] sadık; ~ty sadakat

lozenge ['lozinç] eşkenar
dörtgen; pastil

lubber ['lʌbı] acemi kimse

lubricate ['luubrikeyt] v/t
yağlamak

lucid ['luusid] vazıh, berrak

luck [lʌk] talih, uğur, şans;
bad~ talihsizlik, fena talih;
~y talihli, şanslı

ludicrous ['luudikrıs] gülünç

lug [lag] v/t sürüklemek

luggage ['lagiç] bagaj; ~-
-rack bagaj filesi; ~van
furgon

lukewarm ['luukwôm] ılık;
fig. kayıtsız

lull [lal] v/t uyuşturmak; v/i
uyuşmak; ara, fasıla; ~aby
['lʌbay] ninni

lumbago [lam'beygu] med.
lumbago

lumber ['lambı] lüzumsuz
eşya; kereste

luminous ['luuminıs] par-
lak; açık

lump [lamp] topak, yumru,

küme; in the ~ toptan; ~
sugar kesme şeker

lunar ['luunı] aya ait

lunatic ['luunıtik] deli; ~
asylum tımarhane

lunch [lanç] n. öğle yemeği;
v/i öğle yemeğini yemek;
~eon öğle yemeği; ~hour
öğle tatili

lung [laŋ] an. akciğer

lunge [lanc] v/i ileri atılmak
(at ~e)

lurch [lôç] v/i sallanmak

lure [lyuı] n. cazibe, tuzak;
v/t cezbetmek

lurk [lôk] v/i gizlenmek

luscious ['laşıs] pek tatlı,
nefis

lust [last] şehvet; hırs
lust|re, Am. ~er ['lastı]
perdah; avize

lusty ['lasti] dinç, kuvvetli

lute [luut] mus. ut, lavta

luxate ['lakseyt] med. v/t
mafsaldan çıkarmak

luxur|iant [lag'zyuriint]
bol; ~ious [~riıs] süslü,
tantanalı; ~y ['lakşıri] lüks;
süs

lying ['layiŋ] s. lie¹, lie²

lynch [linç] v/t linç etm.

lynx [liŋks] zo. vaşak

lyric ['lirik] lirik

M

ma'am [mäm, mım] s.
madam

macaroni [mäkı'rıuni] ma-
karna

machine [mı'şîn] makina;
~gun makinalı tüfek; ~

-made makina işi; ~ry
makinalar pl.

mack [mäk] s. ~intosh

mackerel ['mäkrıl] zo. uskumru [yağmurluk)

mackintosh ['mäkintoş]

malevolence

mad [mäd] deli, çılgın; kuduz; öfkeli; **drive ~** v/t çıldırtmak; **go ~** delirmek

madam ['mädim] hanımefendi, bayan

madden ['mädn] v/t çıldırtmak

made [meyd] s. **make**

mad|man deli; **~ness** delilik, çılgınlık

magazine [mägı'zîn] depo; tech. şarjör; dergi

maggot ['mägıt] kurt, sürfe

magic ['mäcik] sihir, büyü; sihirbazlik; **~(al)** sihirli; **~ian** [mı'cişın] sihirbaz

magistrate ['mäcistreyt] sulh yargıcı

magnanimous [mäg'nänimıs] yüce gönüllü, âlicenap

magnet ['mägnit] mıknatıs; **~ic** [~'netik] manyetik; **~ism** manyetizma

magnificen|ce [mäg'nifisns] azamet, ihtişam; **~t** muhteşem

magnify ['mägnifay] v/t büyütmek; **~ing glass** büyüteç, pertavsız

magpie ['mägpay] zo. saksağan

mahogany [mı'hogıni] mahun

maid [meyd] kadın hizmetçi; kız; **old ~** gençliği geçmiş kız; **~en** kız; evlenmemiş; bakir; **~en name** kızlık adı

mail¹ [meyl] zırh

mail² n. posta; v/t posta ile göndermek; **~bag** posta torbası; **~box** Am. mektup kutusu; **~man** Am. postacı; **~order** posta ile sipariş

maim [meym] v/t sakatlamak

main [meyn] asıl, esas, başlıca, ana; **~land** geo. kara; **~ly** başlıca

maint|ain [meyn'teyn] v/t sürdürmek, muhafaza etm.; iddia etm.; **~enance** ['~tınıns] bakım; muhafaza

maize [meyz] bot. mısır

majest|ic [mı'cestik] muhteşem, heybetli; **~y** ['mäcisti] haşmet, azamet; **His (Her)** 2y Majeste

major ['meycı] daha büyük, daha önemli; mus. majör; mil. binbaşı; başlıca konu; **~general** tümgeneral; **~ity** [mı'coriti] çoğunluk

make [meyk] n. şekil; yapı; marka; v/t yapmak; meydana getirmek; teşkil etm.; sağlamak; kazanmak; **~ for** -in yolunu tutmak; **~ out** anlamak, çözmek; yazmak; **~ over** devretmek; **~ up** teşkil etm.; uydurmak; telâfi etm., tamamlamak (**for** -i); **~ up one's mind** karar vermek; **~r** yapan, fabrikatör; **~shift** eğreti; **~-up** makyaj

malady ['mählıdı] hastalık

malaria [mı'läırıı] med. sıtma

male [meyl] erkek

male|diction [mäli'dikşın] lânet; **~factor** ['~fäktı] kötülük eden; **~volence** [mı'levılıns] kötü niyet

malice

malic|e ['mälis] garaz, kötü niyet; **~ious** [mi'lişıs] kötü niyetli

malignant [mi'lignınt] kötü yürekli; *med.* habis

malnutrition ['mälnyu'tri'şın] gıdasızlık

malt [môlt] malt

Malt|a ['môltı] Malta adası; **~ese** ['~'tîz] Maltız

mam(m)a [mı'mâ] *fam.* anne

mammal ['mämıl] *n.* memeli hayvan

man [män, mın], *pl.* **men** *n.* erkek, adam; insan; insan türü; *v/t* kadro koymak *-e*

manage ['mänic] *v/t* idare etm.; kullanmak; *-in* yolunu bulmak; **~able** idare edilebilir; **~ment** idare, yönetim; müdürlük; **~r** müdür, yönetmen

mandate ['mändeyt] vekillik; *pol.* manda

mane [meyn] yele

maneuver [mi'nuuvı] *Am. s.* manoeuvre

manger ['meyncı] yemlik

mangle ['mängl] *n.* ütü cenderesi; *v/t* cendereden geçirmek; *fig.* parçalamak

manhood ['mänhud] erkeklik; mertlik

mania ['meynyı] tutku, mani, manya; **~c** ['~iäk] manyak

manicure ['mänikyuı] manikür

manifest ['mänifest] *adj.* belli, anlaşılır; *v/t* açıkça göstermek; **~ation** gösteri, izhar

manifold ['mänifıuld] *adj.* türlü türlü, çok; *v/t* çoğaltmak

manipulate [mı'nipyuleyt] *v/t* hünerle kullanmak; hile karıştırmak *-e*

man|kind [män'kaynd] insanlık; **~ly** mert, yiğit

mannequin ['mänikin] manken

manner ['mänı] tarz, yol, usul; *pl.* terbiye

manoeuvre [mı'nuuvı] *n. mil.* manevra; düzen, hile; *v/i* manevra yapmak; *v/t* sokmak (**into** *-e*)

manor ['mänı] tımar, malikâne; **~-house** toprak ağası konağı

man|power el emeği; insan gücü; **~servant** erkek hizmetçi

mansion ['mänşın] konak

manslaughter *jur.* kasıtsız adam öldürme

mantelpiece ['mäntlpîs] şömine rafı

manual ['mänyuıl] el ile yapılan; el kitabı

manufacture [mänyu'fäkçı] *n.* imal, yapım; *v/t* imal etm.; **~r** [~] fabrikatör

manure [mı'nyuı] *n.* gübre; *v/t* gübrelemek

manuscript ['mänyuskript] yazma; el yazması

Manx [mänks] Man adasına ait

many ['meni] çok, birçok;

how ~? kaç tane?; **a good**
~, **a great** ~ hayli
map [mäp] *n.* harita; *v/t -in*
haritasını yapmak
maple ['meypl] *bot.* akçaa-
ğaç
marble ['mâbl] mermer;
bilya, bilye
March[1] [mâç] mart ayı
march[2] *n.* marş; yürüyüş;
v/i yürümek
mare [mär] kısrak
margarine [mâcı'rin] margarin
margin ['mâcin] kenar, ara;
kazanç; ~al kenarda olan
marine [mı'rin] denize ait;
deniz kuvvetleri *pl.*; silâh-
endaz; ~r ['mârin] gemici
marionette [märiı'net]
kukla
marital [mı'raytl] evlen-
meğe ait
maritime ['märitaym] de-
nizciliğe ait
mark [mâk] *n.* işaret, alâmet; iz; leke; marka; hedef;
numara, not; *v/t* işaretle-
mek; not vermek -*e*; dikkat
etm. -*e*; ~out -in sınırlarını
çizmek; ~ed işaretlenmiş;
göze çarpan
market ['mâkit] *n.* çarşı;
pazar; piyasa; *v/t* satmak,
satışa çıkarmak; ~ing *ec.*
pazarlama
marksman ['mâksmın] nişancı
marmalade ['mâmıleyd]
portakal marmelatı
marmot ['mâmıt] *zo.* dağ
sıçanı

marqu|ess, ~is ['mâkwis]
marki
marriage ['märic] evlenme; evlilik; ~ **certificate**
evlenme cüzdanı; ~**able**
evlenecek yaşta
married ['mârid] evli
marrow ['märu] ilik, öz
marry ['märi] *v/t* evlenmek
(*so.* ile); evlendirmek (*so.*
to -*i* ile) [Sakıt]
Mars [mârz] *astr.* Merih,]
marsh [mâş] bataklık
marshal ['mâşıl] *n.* polis
müdürü; *mil.* mareşal; *v/t*
dizmek, sıralamak
marshy ['mâşi] bataklık
marten ['mâtin] *zo.* zerdava
martial ['mâşıl] harbe ait;
~ **law** sıkıyönetim
martyr ['mâti] şehit
marvel ['mâvıl] *n.* mucize,
harika; *v/i* hayret etm. (**at**
-*e*); ~(l)**ous** hayret verici,
şaşılacak
mascot ['mäskıt] maskot
masculine ['mäskyulin] er-
keğe ait; erkeksi; *gr.* eril
mash [mäş] *v/t* ezmek; ~**ed
potatoes** patates ezmesi
mask [mâsk] *n.* maske; *v/t*
maskelemek
mason ['meysn] duvarcı; 2
farmason; ~**ry** duvarcılık;
duvarcı işi
mass [mäs] kütle, yığın,
küme; *rel.* kilise ayini; *v/t*
yığmak, bir araya toplamak
massacre ['mäsıkı] *n.* katliam; *v/t* kılıçtan geçirmek
massage ['mâsâj] *n.* ovma,
masaj; *v/t* ovmak

massif

massi|f ['mäsîf] *geo.* dağ kitlesi; ~ve ['~siv] som; kütle halinde

mast [mâst] direk

master ['mâstı] *n.* usta; üstat; öğretmen; amir; kolej rektörü; *v/t* idare etm.; yenmek; ♀ **of Arts** (*edebiyat fakültesi diploması ile doktora arasında bir derece*); ~ful zorba; ustaca; ~ly ustaca; ~piece şaheser; ~ship yönetim; ustalık; ~y üstünlük; maharet

mat [mät] hasır; paspas; altlık; donuk, mat

match¹ [mäç] kibrit

match² denk; eş; maç; *v/t* uymak, denk olm. -e; karşılaştırmak -*i*; ~less eşsiz, emsalsiz; ~maker çöpçatan

mate [meyt] *n.* eş; arkadaş; *v/i* evlenmek; *v/t* çiftleştirmek

material [mı'tiriıl] *n.* madde; malzeme; kumaş; *adj.* maddî; önemli; ~ism materyalizm

matern|al [mı'tönl] anaya ait; ana tarafından; ~ity analık

mathematics [mäthi'mätiks] *pl.* matematik *sg.*

matriculate [mı'trikyuleyt] *v/t* kaydetmek; *v/i* kaydedilmek

matrimony ['mätrimıni] evlilik

matron ['meytrın] ana kadın; amir kadın

matter ['mätı] *n.* madde;

mesele; konu; *med.* irin; *v/i* önemi *olm.*; **no** ~ zararı yok; önemi yok; **what's the** ~? ne var?; **what's the** ~ **with you?** neyiniz var?; ~ **of course** işin tabii gidişi; ~ **of fact** hakikat

mattress ['mätris] şilte

matur|e [mı'tyuı] *adj.* olgun, ergin; reşit; *v/i* olgunlaşmak; vadesi gelmek; *v/t* olgunlaştırmak; ~ity olgunluk, erginlik; vade

mausoleum [môsı'lîım] türbe

mauve [muuv] leylak rengi

maxim ['mäksim] vecize; kural; ~um ['~ım] maksimum; azami

May¹ [mey] mayıs ayı

may² ~-ebilmek, ~-meğe izinli *olm.*; ~-be belki

may-bug *zo.* mayısböceği

mayor ['mäı] belediye başkanı

maze [meyz] lâbirent

me [mî, mi] bana, beni

meadow ['medıu] çayır

meag|re, *Am.* ~er ['mîgı] zayıf, yavan

meal¹ [mîl] yemek

meal² un [alçak]

mean¹ [mîn] bayağı, adî,

mean² orta; *pl.* vasıtalar; gelir, servet *sg.*; **by all** ~s şüphesiz; **by no** ~s asla; **by** ~s **of** vasıtasiyle

mean³ *v/t* düşünmek; demek istemek; kastetmek; demek; ~ing mana, anlam; ~ingless manasız; ~t [ment] *s.* mean

mental

mean|time, ~while bu aralık, bu sırada

measles ['mîzlz] *pl. med.* kızamık *sg.*

measure ['meji] *n.* ölçü; tedbir; ölçme; *v/t* ölçmek; ~ment ölçü; ölçme

meat [mît] et

mechani|c [mi'känik] makinist, makinacı; mekanik, *pl.* mekanika, teknik *sg.*; ~cal makinaya ait, makanik; ~sm ['mekinizm] mekanizma; ~ze *v/t mil.* motorlu taşıtlarla donatma

medal ['medl] madalya

meddle ['medl] *v/i* karışmak (in, with -e)

mediaeval [medi'îvl] *s.* medieval

mediat|e ['îdieyt] *v/i* aracılık etm.; ~ion aracılık; ~or aracı

medic|al ['medikl] tıbbî; ~inal [~'disinl] şifa verici; ~ine ['medsin] ilâç; tıp

medieval [medi'îvl] ortaçağa ait

mediocre ['mîdi'uuk] orta derecede

meditat|e ['mediteyt] *v/i* düşünceye dalmak; *v/t* tasarlamak; ~ion düşünme; dalgınlık; ~ive ['~tutiv] düşünceli

Mediterranean (Sea) [meditı'reynyın(-)] Akdeniz

medium ['mîdyım] orta, ortalama; medyum; ~ wave *tech.* orta dalga

medley ['medli] karışık şey; *mus.* potpuri

meek [mîk] alçak gönüllü, uysal

meet [mît] *v/t* rastlamak -e; karşılamak -i; tanışmak, görüşmek (*so.* ile); ödemek -i; *v/i* toplanmak; uğramak (with -e); rastlamak (-e); ~ing miting, toplantı

melancholy ['melınklii] melankoli, karasevda; karasevdalı

mellow ['meluu] olgun; yumuşak

melod|ious [mi'liudyıs] ahenkli; ~y ['melıdi] melodi, ezgi

melon ['melın] *bot.* kavun

melt [melt] *v/i* erimek; *v/t* eritmek; *fig.* yumuşatmak

member ['membı] üye; organ, uzuv; ~ship üyelik; üyeler *pl.*

membrane ['membreyn] zar

memoirs ['memwâs] *pl.* hatıralar

memor|able ['memırıbl] hatırlanmağa değer; ~andum [~'rändım] *pol.* memorandum; ~ial [mi'môriıl] anıt, abide; hatırlatıcı; ~ize ['memırayz] *v/t* ezberlemek; ~y hafıza; hatıra

menace ['menıs] *n.* tehdit; *v/t* tehdit etm.

mend [mend] *v/t* onarmak, yamamak

menial ['mînyıl] hizmetçiye ait, bayağı

menstruation [menstru-'eyşın] *med.* aybaşı

mental ['mentl] akılla ilgili; zihnî; **~ity** [~'täliti] zihniyet

mention ['menşın] *n.* anma; *v/t* anmak, zikretmek; **don't ~ it!** bir şey değil!; estağfurullah!

mercantile ['mökıntayl] ticarete ait

mercenary ['mösınıri] ücretli; ücretli asker

merchan|dise ['möçındayz] ticaret eşyası, emtia; **~t** ['~ınt] tüccar

merci|ful ['mösiful] merhametli; **~less** merhametsiz

mercury ['mökyuri] *chem.* cıva

mercy ['mösi] merhamet

mere [mii] saf, sade; **~ly** *adv.* sadece, ancak, yalnız

merge [möc] *v/t* birleştirmek; *v/i* birleşmek

meridian [mı'ridiın] *geo.* meridyen

merit ['merit] değer; fazilet; *v/t* lâyık olm. **~e**; **~ori-ous** [~'töriıs] değerli; medhe değer

mermaid ['mömeyd] denizkızı

merriment ['merimınt] neşe

merry ['meri] şen, neşeli; **~ andrew** ['~'ändruu] soytarı; **~go-round** atlıkarınca

mesh [meş] ağ gözü

mess [mes] karışıklık; sofra arkadaşları *pl.*; *v/t* **(up)** kirletmek; karıştırmak

mess|age ['mesic] haber, mesaj; **~enger** ['~ıncı] haberci, kurye

met [met] *s.* **meet**

metal ['metl] maden; metal; **~lic** [mi'tälik] madenî

meteor ['mitiı] *astr.* akanyıldız, meteortaşı; **~ology** [~'rolıci] meteoroloji

meter ['mitu] **1.** sayaç; **2.** *s.* **metre**

method ['methıd] usul, yöntem, metot; **~ical** [mi'thodikıl] yöntemli

meticulous [mi'tikyulıs] çok titiz

met|re *Am.* **~er** ['mitu] metre; vezin

metropoli|s [mi'tropilis] başkent; **~tan** [metrı'politın] başşehre ait

mew [myû] *v/i* miyavlamak

Mexico ['meksikıu] Meksika

miaou, miaow [mî'au] *s.* **mew**

mice [mays] *s.* **mouse**

micro|be ['maykrıub] mikrop; **~phone** ['~krıfıun] mikrofon; **~scope** ['~krıskıup] mikroskop

mid [mid] orta; **~day** öğle

middle ['midl] orta, merkez; **2 Ages** *pl.* ortaçağ *sg.*; **~ class** orta sınıf; **~ weight** orta sıklet; **~aged** orta yaşlı

midge [mic] tatarcık; **~t** ['~it] cüce

mid|night ['midnayt] gece yarısı; **~st: in the ~st of** -*in* ortasında; **~summer** yaz ortası; yaz dönemi; **~**

minute

way yarı yolda; **~wife** ebe

might[1] [mayt] s. **may**

might[2] kuvvet, kudret; **~y** kuvvetli, güçlü

migrate [may'greyt] v/i göçmek   [şak]

mild [mayld] hafif; yumu-

mildew ['mildyû] küf

mildness ['mayldnis] hafiflik, yumuşaklık

mile [mayl] mil (*1,609 km*); **~(e)age** [~lic] mil hesabiyle mesafe; **~estone** kilometre taşı

milit|ant ['militınt] saldırgan; **~ary** [~tıri] askerî; **~ia** [~'şı] milis

milk [milk] n. süt; v/t sağmak; **~man** sütçü **~sop** [~'sop] korkak; **~y** sütlü; **~y Way** astr. samanyolu

mill [mil] n. değirmen; fabrika; v/t öğütmek; tech. frezelemek; **~er** değirmenci

millet ['milit] bot. darı

milli- ['mili-] mili-

milliner ['milinı] kadın şapkacısı

million ['milyın] milyon; **~aire** [~'nâl milyoner

milt [milt] an. dalak

mimic ['mimik] n. taklitçi; v/t taklit etm.

minaret ['minıret] minare

mince [mins] v/t kıymak; **~d meat** kıyma; **~-meat** tatlı börek dolgusu

mind [maynd] n. akıl, beyin; hatır; fikir; istek; v/t dikkat etm., bakmak **-e**;

önem vermek **-e**; karşı çıkmak **-e**; **never ~!** zararı yok!; **out of one's ~** deli; **would you ~ opening the window?** pencereyi açar mısınız?; **~ your own business!** sen kendi işine bak!; **~ful** dikkatli (**of -e**)

mine[1] [mayn] benim(ki)

mine[2] maden ocağı; mil. mayın; v/t kazmak, çıkarmak; **~r** madenci

mineral ['minırıl] maden, mineral; madenli

mingle ['mingl] v/t karıştırmak; v/i karışmak (**in -e**); katılmak (**with -e**)

mini|ature ['minyıçı] minyatür; küçük; **~mal** ['mi-nıml] asgarî; **~mize** [~-nimayz] v/t küçümsemek; **~mum** ['~nimım] minimum; asgarî

minist|er ['ministı] n. rel. papaz; pol. bakan; orta elçi; v/i bakmak (**to -e**); **~ry** bakanlık

mink [mink] zo. Amerika sansarı, vizon

minor ['maynı] daha küçük; önemsiz; ikinci konu; mus. minör; **~ity** [~'noriti] azınlık

minstrel ['minstrıl] halk şairi; zenci şarkıcısı

mint[1] [mint] bot. nane

mint[2] n. darphane; v/t madenî parayı basmak

minus ['maynıs] math. eksi

minute ['minit] dakika; [may'nyût] an; ufak, minimini; pl. tutanak sg.; **to**

miracle

the ~ ['minit] tam zamanında

miracle ['mirıkl] mucize, harika; **~ulous** [~'räkyulıs] mucize gibi

mirage ['mirâj] ılgım, serap

mire ['mayı] çamur, pislik

mirror ['mirı] n. ayna; v/t yansıtmak

mirth [möth] neşe

miry ['mayırı] çamurlu

mis- [mis-] yanlış; kötü

misadventure aksilik, kaza

mis|apply v/t yerinde kullanmamak; **~apprehension** yanlış anlama; **~behaviour** yanlış davranış; **~calculate** v/t yanlış hesap etm.

miscarr|iage başarısızlık; *med.* çocuk düşürme; **~y** başaramamak; çocuk düşürmek

miscellaneous [misi'leynyıs] çeşitli

mischie|f ['misçif] yaramazlık; fesat; **~vous** ['~vıs] yaramaz; zarar verici

mis|conduct kötü davranış; **~deed** kötülük; **~demeano(u)r** *jur.* hafif suç

miser ['mayzı] hasis, cimri

miser|able ['mızırıbl] sefil; **~y** sefalet

mis|fortune talihsizlik, bedbahtlık; **~giving** şüphe; korku; **~government** kötü idare; **~guide** v/t yanlış yola sapmak; **~hap** ['~häp] kaza, aksilik, **~inform** v/t yanlış bilgi vermek *-e*; **~lay** v/t kaybetmek; **~lead** v/t

yanlış yola sevketmek; aldatmak; **~place** v/t yanlış yere koymak; **~print** ['~print] n. baskı hatası; [~'print] v/t yanlış basmak; **~pronounce** v/t yanlış söylemek; **~represent** v/t yanlış anlatmak

miss¹ [mis] bekâr bayan

miss² n. nişanı vuramayış; başarısızlık; v/t vuramamak; kaçırmak

missile ['misayl] mermi

missing ['misin] eksik; kaybolmuş

mission ['mişın] görev; misyon; **~ary** ['~şnırı] *rel.* misyoner

mis-spell v/t yanlış yazmak

mist [mist] sis, duman

mistake [mis'teyk] n. yanlış(lık), hata; v/t yanlış anlamak; benzetmek (**for** *-e*); **by ~** yanlışlıkla; **be ~n** yanılmak

mister ['mistı] bay

mistletoe ['mistltu] *bot.* ökseotu

mistress ['mistris] bayan; metres

mistrust v/t güvenmemek *-e*

misty ['misti] sisli; bulanık

misunderstand v/t yanlış anlamak; **~ing** anlaşmazlık

misuse ['mis'yûs] suiistimal; v/t [~'yûz] suiistimal etm.

mitigate ['mitigeyt] v/t hafifletmek

mitten ['mitn] kolçak, parmaksız eldiven

mix [miks] *v/t* karıştırmak; *v/i* karışmak, birleşmek (**with** -*e*); ~**ed up** karmakarışık; ~**ture** ['~çı] karışım

moan [mıun] *n.* inilti; *v/i* inlemek

moat [mıut] kale hendeği

mob [mob] ayaktakımı

mobil|e ['mıubayl] oynak; seyyar; ~**ize** ['~bilayz] *v/t* seferber etm.

mock [mok] *adj.* sahte, taklit; *v/i* alay etm. (**at** ile); *v/t* taklit etm. ~**ery** alay

mode [mıud] tarz, usul; moda

model ['modl] *n.* örnek, numune, model; *v/t* -*in* modelini yapmak

moderat|e ['modirit] *adj.* ılımlı; ['~eyt] *v/t* hafifletmek; *v/i* azalmak; ~**ion** itidal, ölçülülük

modern ['modın] yeni, modern; ~**ize** *v/t* modernleştirmek

modest ['modist] alçak gönüllü, mütevazı; ~**y** alçak gönüllülük

modif|ication [modifi'keyşın] değişiklik; ~**y** ['~fay] *v/t* değiştirmek

module ['modyûl] *tech.* feza gemisinin kısmı

moist [moyst] nemli, rutubetli; ~**en** ['~sn] ıslatmak; ~**ure** ['~sçı] nem, rutubet

molar (**tooth**) ['mıulı] azı (dişi)

mole[1] [mıul] *zo.* köstebek

mole[2] ben, leke

mole[3] dalgakıran

molekule ['molikyûl] *phys.* molekül

molest [mıu'lest] *v/t* rahatsız etm.

mollify ['molifay] *v/t* yumuşatmak

moment ['mıumınt] an; önem; ~**ary** anî; geçici; ~**ous** [~'mentıs] önemli; ~**um** [~'mentım] *phys.* moment; *fig.* hız

monarch ['monık] hükümdar, kıral; ~**y** kırallık

monastery ['monıstri] manastır

Monday ['mandi] pazartesi

monetary ['manituri] paraya ait

money ['mani] para, nakit; ~ **order** posta havalesi

Mongolia [moŋ'gıulyı] Moğolistan

monk [maŋk] rahip

monkey ['maŋki] *zo.* maymun   [tekeşliklik]

monogamy [mo'nogımi]]

mono|polize [mı'nopılayz] *v/t* tekeline almak; ~**poly** tekel; ~**tonous** [~'tnıs] monoton, tekdüzen; ~**tony** [~'tni] tekdüzenlik

monst|er ['monstı] canavar, dev; ~**rous** canavar gibi; anormal

month [manth] ay; ~**lay** aylık, ayda bir; aylık dergi

monument ['monyumınt] anıt, abide

moo [mıu] böğürmek

mood [mıud] mizaç, ruh haleti; ~**y** dargın, küskün

moon 330

moon [muun] ay, kamer;
~**light** mehtap
moor¹ [muu] kır
moor² naut. v/t palamarla
bağlamak
mop [mop] n. silme bezi;
v/t silip süpürmek, temizlemek
moral ['moril] adj. ahlâkî,
törel; n. ahlâk dersi; pl. ahlâk; ~**e** [mo'râl] maneviyat,
manevî güç; ~**ity** [mı'râliti]
ahlâk
morass [mı'räs] bataklık
morbid ['môbid] hastalıklı
more [mô] daha, daha çok,
fazla; artık; ~**once** ~ bir
daha; ~**over** bundan başka
morgue [môg] morg
morning ['môniŋ] sabah;
good ~! günaydın!
Morocco [mı'rokıu] Fas
morose [mı'rıus] somurtkan
morphi|a ['môfyı], ~**ne** ['~
fîn] chem. morfin
morsel ['môsıl] lokma, parça
mortal ['môtl] ölümlü; öldürücü; insan; ~**ity** [~'täliti] ölümlülük; ölüm oranı
mortar ['môtı] harç; mil.
havan topu
mortgage [n. 'môgic] ipotek; v/t rehine koymak
mortify ['môtifay] v/t alçaltmak
mortuary ['môtyuri] morg
mosaic¹ [mıu'zeyik] mosaik
Mosaic² Musa'ya ait
Moslem ['mozlım] Müslüman

mosque [mosk] cami
mosquito [mıs'kîtıu] zo.
sivrisinek
moss [mos] bot. yosun; ~**y**
yosunlu
most [mıust] en, en çok, son
derecede; en çoğu; **at
(the)** ~ olsa olsa; ~**ly** ekseriya
motel ['mutel] motel
moth [moth] güve; pervane; ~**eaten** güve yemiş
mother ['madhı] anne, ana;
~ **country** anayurt; ~**hood**
analık; ~**in-law** kaynana;
~**of-pearl** sedef
motion ['mıuşın] n. hareket;
önerme; v/t işaret etm. -e;
~ **picture** film; ~**less** hareketsiz
motiv|ate ['mutiveyt] v/t
sevketmek; ~**e** saik, güdü
motor ['mutı] n. motor; v/i
otomobille gitmek; v/t otomobille götürmek; ~**car**
otomobil; ~**coach** otobüs;
~**cycle** motosiklet; ~**ing**
otomobilcilik; ~**ist** otomobil kullanan; ~**ize** v/t motorla donatmak; ~**lorry**
kamyon; ~**scooter** skuter;
~**way** oto yolu   [rola)
motto ['motıu] vecize; pa-
mo(u)ld¹ [muuld] küf
mo(u)ld² n. kalıp; v/t kalıba
dökmek; şekil vermek -e;
~**er** v/i çürümek
mo(u)ldy ['muuldi] küflü
mo(u)lt [mult] tüylerini
dökmek
mound [maund] höyük; tepecik

mount [maunt] *n.* dağ, tepe; binek; *v/t* binmek, çıkmak *-e*; kurmak *-i*; *v/i* artmak, yükselmek

mountain ['mauntin] dağ, tepe; *fig.* dağ silsilesi; **~eer** [~'niı] dağlı; dağcı; **~ous** dağlık

mourn [môn] *v/i* yas tutmak; *v/t -in* matemini tutmak; **~er** yaslı; **~ing** matem, yas; matem elbiseleri *pl.*

mouse [maus] fare

moustache [mıs'tâş] bıyık

mouth [mauth] ağız; **~ful** ağız dolusu; **~piece** ağızlık; *fig.* sözcü; **~-wash** gargara

mov|able ['muuvibl] taşınabilir; *jur.* menkul; **~e** *n.* hareket; tedbir; göç, nakil; *v/i* hareket etm., ilerlemek; taşınmak; *v/t* harekete getirmek, yürütmek; tahrik etm.; önermek; **~e in** eve taşınmak; **~e out** çıkmak; **~ement** hareket; **~ies** ['~ viz] *pl.* sinema *sg.*; **~ing** oynar; *fig.* dokunaklı

mow [mıu] *v/t* biçmek; **~n** *s.* mow

much [maç] çok, hayli; **how ~?** ne kadar?; **make ~** önem vermek (**of** *-e*); **too ~** pek çok, pek fazla

mucus ['myûkıs] sümük

mud [mad] çamur

muddle ['madl] *n.* karışıklık; **~** (**up, together**) *v/t* karıştırmak

mud|dy ['madi] çamurlu; **~guard** çamurluk

muff [maf] manşon; *tech.* boru bileziği

muffle ['mafl] *v/t* sarmak; *voice:* boğmak; **~r** boyun atkısı

mug [mag] maşrapa, bardak

mulberry ['malbıri] *bot.* dut

mule [myûl] *zo.* katır; **~teer** [~li'tiı] katırcı

mullet ['malit], **red ~** *zo.* barbunya

multi|ple ['maltipl] katmerli, çeşitli; **~plication** [~pli'keyşın] *math.* çarpma; çoğalma; **~ply** ['~play] *v/t* çarpmak; çoğaltmak; *v/i* çoğalmak; **~tude** ['~tyûd] kalabalık

mumble ['mambl] *v/t, v/i* mırılda(n)mak

mummy ['mami] mumya

mumps [mamps] *med.* kabakulak

munch [manç] *v/t* kıtır kıtır yemek

municipal [myu'nisipıl] belediyeye ait; **~ity** [~'pâliti] belediye

mural ['myuırıl] duvara ait

murder ['môdı] *n.* katil, adam öldürme; *v/t* öldürmek, katletmek; **~er** katil; **~ous** öldürücü

murmur ['mômı] *n.* mırıltı; *v/i* mırılda(n)mak; homurdanmak (**against, at** *-e* karşı)

muscle ['masl] adale, kas; **~-bound** kas tutukluğu olan

muscular ['maskyulı] adaleli; kuvvetli

muse [myûz] *v/i* düşünceye dalmak

museum [myu'ziim] müze

mush [maş] *Am.* mısır unu lapası

mushroom ['maşrum] *bot.* mantar

music ['myûzik] müzik, musiki; ~al müzikal; müziğe ait; ahenkli; ~hall varyete; ~ian [~'zişın] çalgıcı; ~stand nota sehpası

musk [mask] misk

musket ['maskit] asker tüfeği [man]

Muslim ['muslim] Müslü-}

muslin ['mazlin] muslin

mussel ['masl] midye

must[1] [mast] şıra

must[2] küf (kokusu)

must[3] -meli, -malı; *n.* zorunluk; **I ~ not** izinli değilim

mustard ['mastıd] hardal

muster ['mastı] *v/t* toplamak

musty ['masti] küflü

mute [myût] sessiz, dilsiz

mutilate ['myûtileyt] *v/t* kötürüm etm.

mutin|eer [myûti'niı] isyan eden asker; ~y [\~'ni] *n.* isyan; *v/i* ayaklanmak

mutter ['matı] mırıltı; *v/i* mırıldanmak

mutton ['matn] koyun eti; ~ **chop** koyun pirzolası

mutual ['myûçuıl] karşılıklı; ortak

muzzle ['mazl] *n.* hayvan burnu; zorunsalık; top *veya* tüfek ağzı; *v/t* burunsalık takmak -*e*

my [may] benim

myrtle ['môtl] *bot.* mersin

myself [may'self] ben, kendim

myster|ious [mis'tiırıs] esrarengiz, gizemli; ~y [\~tı-ri] gizem, sır

mysti|cism ['mistisizm] mistisizm; tasavvuf; ~fy *v/t* şaşırtmak

myth [mith] efsane, mit

N

nag [näg] dırlanmak; ~ **at** -*in* başının etini yemek

nail [neyl] *n. tech.* çivi; *an., zo.* tırnak; *v/t* çivilemek, mıhlamak

naive [nä'îv] saf, bön

naked ['neykid] çıplak

name [neym] *n.* isim, ad; nam, şöhret; *v/t* adlandırmak; tayin etm., atmak; **call** *so.* ~**s** sövmek -*e*; ~

less isimsiz; bilinmiyen; ~**ly** yani, şöyle ki; ~**sake** adaş

nanny ['näni] dadı; ~ **(goat)** dişi keçi

nap [näp] şekerleme

nape [neyp] ense

napkin ['näpkin] peçete; kundak bezi

narcissus [nâ'sısıs] *bot.* nergis

narco|sis [nâ'kıusis] narkoz; **~tic** [~'kotik] narkotik, uyuşturucu (ilâç)

narrat|e [nä'reyt] v/t anlatmak; **~ion** hikâye; **~ive** [~ıtiv] rivayet

narrow ['näru] adj. dar, ensiz; v/i daralmak; v/t daraltmak; **~-minded** der fikirli

nasty ['nâsti] pis, fena kokulu, iğrenç; yaramaz

nation ['neyşın] millet, ulus

national ['näşınl] ulusal, millî; n. vatandaş; **~ist** ['~şınlist] milliyetçi; **~ity** [~'näliti] milliyet; vatandaşlık; **~ize** ['~şınlayz] v/t kamulaştırmak

native ['neytiv] yerli; doğma; **~ language** ana dil

natural ['nâçrıl] tabiî, doğal; doğuştan; sunî olmıyan; **~ize** v/t vatandaşlığa kabul etm.

nature ['neyçı] tabiat; mizaç

naught [nôt] sıfır; **~y** yaramaz, haylaz

nausea ['nôsyı] bulantı; iğrenme; **~ting** ['~ieytin] bulandırıcı; iğrenç

nautical ['nôtikıl] gemiciliğe ait; **~ mile** deniz mili

naval ['neyvıl] bahriye ile ilgili; **~ base** deniz üssü

nave [neyv] tekerlek yuvası

navel ['neyvıl] göbek

naviga|ble ['nävigıbl] gidiş gelişe elverişli; **~te** ['~eyt] v/t gemiyi, uçağı: kullanmak; v/i gemi ile gezmek;

~tion denizcilik; dümencilik

navy ['neyvi] deniz kuvvetleri pl.; donanma

nay [ney] hayır; hatta

near [nii] adj. yakın; bitişik; samimî; cimri; adv. yakın(da); v/i yaklaşmak; **~ly** hemen hemen, âdeta; **~-sighted** miyop

neat [nît] temiz; zarif

necess|ary ['nesisıri] gerekli; zarurî; **~itate** [ni'sesiteyt] v/t gerektirmek; **~ity** [ni'sesiti] lüzum, zaruret, ihtiyaç

neck [nek] n. boyun, gerdan; şişede boğaz; v/i sl. öpüşmek; zapaç ['~lis] kolye; **~tie** kravat

née [ney] kızlık adı

need [nîd] n. ihtiyaç, lüzum, gereklik; v/t ihtiyaç olm. -e, istemek -i

needle ['nîdl] iğne; ibre

need|less ['nîdlis] lüzumsuz; **~y** muhtaç

negat|e [ni'geyt] v/t inkâr etm.; **~ion** inkâr

negative ['negıtiv] negatif; olumsuz

neglect [ni'glekt] v/t ihmal etm., savsaklamak; n. ihmal

negligent ['neglicınt] kayıtsız, ihmalci

negotiat|e [ni'gıuşieyt] v/t müzakere etm.; **~ion** müzakere, görüşme

negr|ess ['nîgris] zenci kadın; **~o** ['~ıu] zenci

neigh [ney] n. kişneme; v/i kişnemek

neighbo(u)r ['neybı] komşu; **~hood** komşuluk; civar; **~ing** komşu, bitişik

neither ['naydhı] hiç biri; ne ne de; **~ ... nor ...** ne ... ne de ...

nephew ['nevyu] erkek yeğen

nerve [növ] n. sinir; cesaret; v/t cesaret vermek -e; **~ oneself to** inf. -meğe cesur olm.

nervous ['növıs] sinirli; **~ness** sinirlilik

nest [nest] n. yuva; v/i yuva yapmak; **~le** ['nesl] v/i sokulmak (**to** -e); v/t barındırmak

net[1] [net] ağ, tuzak

net[2] adj. net, safi; v/t kazanmak

Netherlands ['nedhılındz] **the ~** pl. Holanda sg.

nettle ['netl] n. bot. ısırgan; v/t kızdırmak

network ['netwök] şebeke

neurosis ['nyuu'rusis] med. nevroz

neuter ['nyûtı] gr. cinssiz

neutral ['nyûtrıl] yansız, tarafsız; **~ gear** tech. boş vites; **~ity** [~'träliti] tarafsızlık; **~ize** [~'trılayz] v/t etkisiz bırakmak; yansız kılmak

neutron ['nyûtron] nötron

never ['nevı] asla, hiç bir zaman; **~theless** bununla beraber, mamafih

new [nyû] yeni; taze; acemi; **♀ Year** yılbaşı; **~born** yeni doğmuş

news [nyûz] pl. haber sg.; **~cast** haber yayını; **~paper** gazete; **~reel** aktüalite filmi; **~stand** gazete tezgâhı

next [nekst] en yakın; sonraki, gelecek; sonra

nibble ['nibl] v/i kemirmek (**at** -i)

nice [nays] güzel, hoş, sevimli; ince; **~ty** [~iti] incelik

niche [niç] duvarda hücre

nick [nik] n. çentik, kertik; tam zaman; **~el** ['nikl] n. nikel; Am. beş sentlik para; v/t nikel ile kaplamak

nickname ['nikneym] n. takılmış ad; v/t lakap takmak -e

niece [nîs] kız yeğen

niggard ['nigıd] cimri adam

night [nayt] gece; **good ~!** iyi geceler!; **~club** gece kulübü; **~dress, ~gown** gecelik; **~ingale** ['~iŋgeil] zo. bülbül; **~mare** ['~mäı] karabasan, kâbus; **~y** fam. gecelik

nil [nil] hiç, sıfır

nimble ['nimbl] çevik, tez

nine [nayn] dokuz; **~pins** pl. kiy oyunu sg.; **~ty** doksan

nip[1] [nip] n. ayaz; çimdik; v/t çimdiklemek; v/i hızlı gitmek

nip[2] n. azıcık içki; v/t azıcık içmek

nipple ['nipl] meme başı

nit|re, *Am.* **~er** ['naytı] *chem.* güherçile; **~rogen** azot, nitrojen

no [nıu] hayır, öyle değil; hiç (bir); **~ one** hiç kimse

nobility [nıu'biliti] asalet; asılzadeler sınıfı

noble ['nıubl] asıl, soylu; asılzade; **~man** asılzade

nobody ['nıubıdi] hiç kimse

nocturnal [nok'tönl] geceye ait

nod [nod] *n.* baş sallama; *v/i* kabul ifade etmek için başını sallamak; uyuklamak

nois|e [noyz] gürültü, patırdı; **~y** gürültülü

nomad ['nomıd] göçebe

nomina|l ['nominl] sözde; saymaca; **~te** ['~eyt] *v/t* atamak; görevlendirmek; **~tion** tayin, aday gösterme; **~tive** ['~nıtiv] (**case**) *gr.* yalın hal

non|-aggression [non-] *pol.* saldırmazlık; **~alcoholic** alkolsuz; **~commissioned officer** *mil.* erbaş; **~descript** ['~diskript] kolay tanımlanamaz

none [nan] hiç biri

non-existence yokluk, varolmayış

nonsense ['nonsıns] saçma

non-stop doğru giden; aralıksız

noodle ['nuudl] şeriye

nook [nuk] bucak, köşe

noon [nuun] öğle

noose [nuus] ilmik

nor [nô] ne de

norm [nôm] kural, norm, örnek; **~al** normal; düzgülü

north [nôth] kuzey; kuzeye doğru; 2 **Sea** *geo.* Kuzey Denizi; 2 **Star** *astr.* kutup yıldızı; **~east** kuzeydoğu; **~ern** ['~dhın] kuzeye ait; **~ward(s)** ['~wıd(z)] kuzeye doğru; **~west** kuzeybatı

Norw|ay ['nôwey] Norveç; **~egian** ['~'wıcın] Norveçli

nose [nıuz] *n.* burun; uç; *v/t* ~ **into** kokusunu almak; arayıp bulmak *-i*; **~gay** ['~gey] çiçek demeti

nostril ['nostril] burun deliği

not [not] değil; **~ at all** asla

nota|ble ['nıutıbl] tanınmış; dikkate değer; **~ry** ['~tıri] noter; **~tion** [~'tey-şın] not; sistem; kayıt

notch [noç] *n.* çentik, kertik; *v/t* çentmek, kertmek

note [nıut] *n.* not; işaret; *mus., pol.* nota; pusula; *v/t* kaydetmek; **~ down** deftere yazmak; **~d** tanınmış; **~book** not defteri; **~worthy** önemli, dikkate değer

nothing ['nathiŋ] hiçbir şey; sıfır; **say ~ of** bile değil, şöyle dursun

notice ['nıutis] *n.* haber; ilân; dikkat; *v/t -in* farkına varmak; görmek *-i*, dikkat etm. *-e*; **until further ~** yeni bir habere kadar; **without ~** mühlet vermeden; **~able** görülebilir

noti|fication [nιutifi'keyşın] bildirme; ihbar; **~fy** ['~fay] *v/t* ilân etm.; bildirmek

notion ['nιuşın] sanı; zan; *Am.* tuhafiye

notorious [nιu'tôriıs] adı çıkmış; dile düşmüş

notwithstanding [notwith'ständin] -e rağmen

nought [nôt] sıfır

noun [naun] *gr.* isim, ad

nourish ['nariş] *v/t* beslemek; **~ing** besleyici; **~ment** yemek, gıda

novel ['novıl] roman; yeni, tuhaf; **~ist** romancı; **~ty** yenilik

November [nıu'vembı] kasım (ayı)

novice ['novis] çırak

now [nau] şimdi, bu anda; işte; *just* **~** demin(cek), şimdi; **~ and again,** (every) **~ and then** arasıra; **~adays** ['~ıdeyz] bugünlerde

nowhere ['nuwäı] hiçbir yerde

noxious ['nokşıs] zararlı

nozzle ['nozl] *tech.* ağızlık, meme

nuclear ['nyúklıı] nükleer; **~ power plant,** **~ station** nükleer elektrik santralı

nude [nyúd] çıplak; nüd

nudge [nac] *n.* dürtme; *v/t* dirsek ile dürtmek

nugget ['nagit]   (altın) külçe

nuisance ['nyúsns] sıkıcı şey *veya* kimse

null [nal] **(and void)** hükümsüz, geçersiz

numb [nam] uyuşuk, duygusuz

number ['nambı] *n.* sayı; miktar; numara; *v/t* saymak; numara koymak *-e*; **~ plate** plaka; **~less** sayısız

numeral ['nyúmırıl] sayı, rakam; **~ous** birçok

nun [nan] *rel.* rahibe

nuptials ['napşlz] *pl.* düğün, nikâh *sg.*

nurse [nös] *n.* sütnine; hastabakıcı; dadı; *v/t* emzirmek; beslemek; bakmak *-e*

nursery ['nösıri] çocuk odası; fidanlık; **~ school** anaokulu

nursing ['nösin] hastabakıcılık; **~ home** özel sağlık yurdu

nut [nat] fındık, ceviz; *tech.* vida somunu; **drive ~s** *v/t sl.* çıldırtmak; **~cracker** fındıkkıran

nutri|ment ['nyútrimınt] gıda, besin; **~tion** besleme; **~tious** besleyici

nutshell fındık kabuğu; **in a ~** kısaca

nylon ['naylın] naylon

nymph [nimf] peri

O

oak [ɪuk] *bot.* meşe ağacı

oar [ô] kürek; **~sman** kürekçi

oasis [ɪu'eysis] vaha

oat [ɪut] *bot.* yulaf (tanesi)

oath [ɪuth] yemin; küfür; **take an ~** ant içmek

oatmeal yulaf unu

obe|dience [ɪ'bîdyıns] itaat; **~dient** itaatli

obey [ɪ'bey] *v/t* itaat etm. *-e*

obituary [ɪ'bityuiri] ölüm ilânı; anma yazısı

object ['obcikt] *n.* şey; *gr.* nesne; amaç, hedef; *v/i* razı olmamak, itiraz etm. (**to** *-e*); **~ion** itiraz; **~ive** *n. phys.* mercek, objektif; amaç; *adj.* objektif; tarafsız

obligat|ion [obli'geyşın] mecburiyet, yüküm; borç; **~ory** [ɪ'bligıturi] mecburî

oblig|e [ɪ'blayc] *v/t* zorunlu kılmak; minnettar kılmak; **be ~ed** minnettar olm.; mecbur olm. (**to** *inf. -meğe*); **~ing** nazik

oblique [ɪ'blîk] eğri, meyilli

obliterate [ɪ'blitureyt] *v/t* silmek, yoketmek

oblivi|on [ɪ'blivîın] unutma; **~ous** unutkan

oblong ['oblɒŋ] boyu eninden fazla

obscene [ɪb'sîn] açık saçık

obscure [ɪb'skyuı] *adj.* çapraşık; karanlık; *v/t* karartmak

obsequies ['obsikwız] *pl.* cenaze törenleri

observ|ance [ɪb'zövıns] yerine getirme; usul; **~ant** dikkatli; **~ation** gözetleme; gözlem; fikir; **~atory** [~tri] rasathane; **~e** *v/t* yerine getirmek; gözlemek; **~er** gözliyen

obsess [ɪb'ses] *v/t* musallat olm. *-e*; **~ed** musallat (**by, with** *-e*); **~ion** musallat fikir

obsolete ['obsılît] eskimiş

obstacle ['obstıkl] engel, mâni

obstina|cy ['obstinısı] inatçılık; **~te** ['~it] inatçı, dik kafalı

obstruct [ɪb'strakt] *v/t* tıkamak; engel olm. *-e*

obtain [ɪb'teyn] *v/t* bulmak, ele geçirmek; **~able** bulunabilir

obtrusive [ɪb'truusîv] sokulup sıkıntı veren

obvious ['obvîıs] belli, açık

occasion [ɪ'keyjın] *n.* fırsat, vesile; sebep; *v/t* sebep olm. *-e*; **on the ~ of** dolayısiyle; **~al** arasıra olan

occident ['oksidınt] batı; **~al** batı(lı)

occup|ant ['okyupınt] işgal eden; **~ation** işgal; meslek, iş; **~y** ['~pay] *v/t* işgal etm.

occur [ɪ'kö] *v/i* yer bulmak; **~ to** *-in* aklına gelmek; **~rence** [ɪ'karıns] olay

ocean ['iuşın] okyanus, deniz

o'clock [ı'klok] saate göre

October [ok'tıubı] ekim (ayı)

ocul|ar ['okyulı] göze ait; gözle görülür; **~ist** göz doktoru

odd [od] tuhaf, acayip; *math.* tek; seyrek; *pl.* fark, eşit olmayış *sg.*; menfaat; **the ~s are that** ihtimali var ki; at ~s araları açık; **~s and ends** *pl.* ufak tefek şeyler

odo(u)r ['ıudı] koku; *fig.* şöhret

of [ov, ıv] -in; -den; **the city ~ London** Londra şehri; **~ wood** tahtadan

off [of] -den; -den uzak; kesilmiş; kopuk; görev dışında; *intj.* defol!; **be ~** ayrılmak

offen|ce [ı'fens], *Am.* **~se** suç, kabahat; hakaret; hücum; **~d** *v/t* gücendirmek, darıltmak; *v/i* suç işlemek; **~sive** taarruz, saldırı; çirkin; yakışmaz

offer ['ofı] *n.* teklif; sunu; *v/t* sunmak, teklif etmek; **~ing** teklif; *rel.* kurban

offic|e ['ofis] büro, yazıhane; daire; bakanlık; **~er** subay; polis memuru; memur; **~ial** [ı'fişıl] resmî; memur; **~ious** [ı'fişıs] el sokan

off|set *n.* ofset; *v/t* denkleştirmek; **~side** ofsayt; **~spring** döl, ürün

often ['ofn] çok defa, sık sık

oh! [ıu] *intj.* ya!; öyle mi?

oil [oyl] *n.* yağ; petrol; *v/t* yağlamak; **~cloth** muşamba; **~y** yağlı

ointment ['oyntmınt] merhem

O. K., okay ['ıu'key] peki

old [ıuld] eski, köhne; yaşlı; **~age** yaşlılık; **~fashioned** modası geçmiş

oleander [ıuli'ändı] *bot.* zakkum

olive ['oliv] *bot.* zeytin

Olympic games [ıu'limpik -] *pl.* olimpiyat oyunları

omelet(te) ['omlit] omlet, kayguna

ominous ['ominıs] uğursuz

omi|ssion [ı'mişın] atlama, ihmal; **~t** *v/t* atlamak, ihmal etm.

omni|bus ['omnibıs] otobüs; antoloji; **~potent** her şeye kadir

on [on] -*in* üzerine, üzerinde, üstüne, üstünde; -*de,* -*e* doğru; **and so ~** ve saire; **turn ~** *v/t* açmak

once [wans] bir defa; bir zamanlar; **at ~** derhal, hemen

one [wan] bir, tek; biri(si); **~ another** birbirine, birbirini; **the little ~s** *pl.* küçük çocuklar; **~self** kendisi; **~sided** tek taraflı; **~way street** tek yönlü sokak

onion ['anyın] soğan

onlooker ['onlukı] seyirci

only ['ıunli] tek, biricik; yalnız, ancak, sadece

onto ['ontu,'ᴧ] *in* üstün(d)e

onward ['onwıd] ileri

ooze [uuz] *n* sızıntı; balçık; *v/i* sızmak

opaque [ıu'peyk] ışık geçirmez

open ['ıupen] *adj.* açık, meydanda; *v/i* açılmak; *v/t* açmak; başlamak *-e*; **in the ~ air** açıkta; **~e** açacak; **~ing** açıklık; fırsat; münhal görev; **~-minded** açık fikirli

opera ['opırı] opera

operat|e ['opıreyt] *v/i* iş görmek, işlemek; *v/t* kullanmak, işletmek; *med.* ameliyat etm.; **~ion** ameliyat; işleme, işletme; *mil.* hareket *pl.*; **~or** *tech.* operatör; *tel.* telefon memuru

ophthalmic [of'θælmik] göze ait

opinion [ı'pinyın] fikir, düşünce; tahmin

opium ['ıupyım] afyon

opponent [ı'pıunınt] muhalif, karşısı [fırsat]

opportunity [opı'tyûniti]

oppos|e [ı'pıuz] *v/t* direnmek, engel olm. *-e*; karşılaş(tır)mak *-i*; **~ite** ['opızit] karşıda, karşı karşıya; zıt, aksi; *-e* karşı; **~ition** [opı'zişın] muhalefet; zıtlık; *pol.* muhalif parti

oppress [ı'pres] *v/t* sıkıştırmak; zulmetmek; **~ion** baskı; zulüm; sıkıntı; **~ive** ezici; sıkıcı

optic ['optik] görme duyusuna ait; **~al** optikle ilgili; **~ian** [~'tişın] gözlükçü

optimis|m ['optimizım] iyimserlik; **~t** iyimser

option ['opşın] seçme (hakkı)

or [ô] yahut, veya; yoksa; ya; **~ else** yoksa

oral ['ôrıl] sözlü

orange ['orinc] *bot.* portakal; **~ade** ['~'eyd] portakal suyu

orator ['orıtı] hatip, söyleyici

orbit ['ôbit] *n. astr.* yörünge; *v/t -in* etrafında dönmek

orchard ['ôçıd] meyva bahçesi

orchestra ['ôkıstrı] *mus.* orkestra

orchid ['ôkid] *bot.* orkide

ordeal [ô'dîl] büyük sıkıntı

order ['ôdı] *n.* düzen; dizi; emir, sipariş; tabaka, sınıf; *rel.* tarikat; *v/t* emretmek; düzenlemek; ısmarlamak; **in ~ to** *-mek* için; **out of ~** bozuk; düzensiz; **~ly** düzenli; *mil.* emir eri

ordinal number ['ôdinl] *math.* sıra sayısı

ordinary ['ôdnri] *adi;* bayağı

ore [ô] maden cevheri

organ ['ôgın] organ, örgen, uzuv; araç, vasıta; *mus.* org; **~ic** [ô'gänik] organik; canlı

organiz|ation [ôgınay'zeyşın] teşkilât, örgüt; düzen

(-leme) ~e ['~ayz] v/t düzenlemek, örgütlemek
orient ['ôrient] doğu; ~al [~'entl] doğu ile ilgili
origin ['oricin] asıl, köken; soy; ~al [ı'ricinl] aslî, yaratıcı; orijinal; ~ate [ı'ricineyt] v/i meydana gelmek (**from** -den); v/t yaratmak, türetmek
ornament ['ônimınt] n. süs; [~.ment] v/t süslemek; ~al süs kabilinden
orphan ['ôfin] öksüz, yetim; ~age ['~ic] öksüzlük, yetimlik
ortho|dox ['orthdoks] rel. ortodoks; ~graphy [ô'thogrıfi] imlâ
oscillate ['osileyt] v/i sallanmak, sarsılmak
ostrich ['ostriç] zo. devekuşu
other ['adhı] başka, diğer, sair; the ~ day geçen gün; every ~ day her gün aşırı; ~wise [~'wayz] başka türlü; yoksa
Ottoman ['otımın] Osmanlı
ought [ôt] to inf. ~meli
ounce [auns] ons (28,35 g)
our ['auı] bizim; ~s bizimki; ~selves ['selvz] kendimiz
oust [aust] v/t yerinden çıkarmak
out [aut] dışarı, dışarıda; sönmüş; intj. defol!; ~ of -den dışarı; -den yapılmış; -den dolayı; için; daha; ~balance v/t geçmek; ~board motor takma motor; ~break, ~burst patlama, fışkırma;

~cast toplumdan atılmış, serseri; ~come sonuç; ~do v/t üstün gelmek -e; ~door(s) açık havada; ~er dış, dışarıdaki; ~fit gereçler pl.; v/t donatmak; ~grow v/t -den daha çabuk büyümek; ~last v/t -den daha çok dayanmak; ~law n kanun dışı adam; v/t kanun dışı etm.; ~let çıkış (yeri); delik; ~line n. taslak; v/t -in taslağını çizmek; ~live v/t -den fazla yaşamak; ~look görünüş; ~number sayıca üstün gelmek -e; ~put verim
outrage ['autreyç] n. zulüm, zorbalık; v/t kötü davranmak -e; ~ous gaddar, insafsız
out|right büsbütün; açıkça; ~side dış; dış taraf, dış görünüş; ~sider bir grubun dışında olan kimse; ~skirts pl. kenar, civar; ~spoken sözünü sakınmaz; ~standing göze çarpan; (debt) kalmış; ~ward dış; görünüşte; ~weigh v/t -den daha ağır gelmek; ~wit v/t -den daha kurnazca davranmak
oval ['ıuvıl] oval, beyzî
oven ['avn] fırın
over ['ıuvı] karşı tarafa; fazla, artık; bitmiş; -in üstüne, üstünde, üzerine, üzerinde; yukarısında; (all) ~ again bir daha; ~ there karşıda; ~all baştan başa; iş tulumu; ~board gemiden denize; ~burden

v/t fazla yük yüklemek *-e*; **~cast** bulutlu; **~charge** *v/t* aşırı fiat istemek *-den*; *el.* fazla doldurmak *-i*; **~coat** palto; **~come** *v/t* yenmek; **~crowd** *v/t* fazla kalabalık etm.; **~do** *v/t* abartmak; fazla pişirmek; **~draw** *v/t* bankadaki hesabından fazla para çekmek; **~due** vadesi geçmiş; **~estimate** *v/t* fazla tahmin etm.; **~flow** *n.* taşma; *v/t* su basmak; *v/i* taşmak; **~haul** *v/t* elden geçirmek, kontrol etm.; **~head** baştan geçen; yukarıda; **~hear** *v/t* rastlantılı olarak işitmek; **~land** karadan; **~lap** *v/i* üst üste kaplanmak; **~load** *v/t* fazla yüklemek; **~look** *v/t* gözden kaçırmak; yukarıdan bakmak *-e*; **~night** geceleyin; bir gece için; **~rate** *v/t* fazla önem vermek *-e*; **~rule** *v/t* geçersiz kılmak; **~run** *v/t* kaplamak; **~sea(s)** denizaşırı

oversee *v/t* yönetmek; **~r** müfettiş; ustabaşı

over|shadow *v/t* gölgelemek; **~sight** kusur; **~size**

fazla büyük; **~sleep** *v/i* uykuda kaçırmak; **~strain** *v/t* fazla yormak; **~take** *v/t* yetişmek *-e*; **~throw** ['ıuvɪ-θrıu] *n.* devirme; [~'θrıu] *v/t* devirmek; **~time** fazla çalışma süresi; **~top** *v/t -in* tepesini aşmak

overture ['ıuvɪtyuə] teklif; *mus.* uvertür

over|turn *v/t* devirmek; *v/i* devrilmek; **~weight** fazla ağırlık; **~whelm** [ıuvɪ-'welm] *v/t* yenmek; bunaltmak; **~work** *v/i* fazla çalışmak; *v/t* fazla çalıştırmak

ow|e [ıu] borcu olm., borçlu olm. (*so. sth. -e -den* dolayı); **~ing** to sebebiyle, yüzünden

owl [aul] *zo.* baykuş, puhu

own [ıun] *adj.* kendi; özel; *v/t* malik olm., sahip olm.; tanımak, itiraf etm. *-i*; **~er** sahip, mal sahibi

ox [oks], *pl.* **~en** ['~ın] öküz; sığır

oxidation [oksi'deyşın] oksitlenme

oxygen ['oksicın] oksijen

oyster ['oystı] *zo.* istiridye

ozone ['ıuzıun] *chem.* ozon

P

pace [peys] *n.* adım, yürüyüş; *v/t* adımlamak

Pacif|ic Ocean [pı'sifik] *geo.* Büyük Okyanus; 2ist ['päsifist] barışçı; 2y ['päsi-fay] *v/t* yarıştırmak

pack [päk] *n.* bohça; sürü;

(*iskambilde*) deste; balya; *Am.* paket (*sigara*); *v/t* istif etm.; sarmak; **~age** paket; ambalaj; **~et** ['~it] paket; deste; **~ing** bağlama; ambalaj   [leşme]

pact [päkt] anlaşma, söz-}

pad

pad [päd] *n.* yastık; *tech.* rampa; *v/t -in* içini doldurmak

paddle ['pädl] *n.* kısa kürek, pala; *v/i* suda oynamak

padlock ['pädlok] asma kilit

pagan ['peygn] putperest

page[1] [peyc] ulak, uşak

page[2] sayfa

paid [peyd] *s.* **pay**

pail [peyl] kova

pain [peyn] *n.* ağrı, sızı; acı; *v/t* acı vermek *-e*; **take** ~s **to** *inf. -e* özenmek; ~**ful** acı veren, zahmetli; ~**staking** özenli

paint [peynt] *n.* boya; *v/t* boyamak; tasvir etm.; ~**box** boya kutusu; ~**brush** boya fırçası; ~**er** ressam; ~**ing** ressamlık; resim, tablo

pair [pä] *n.* çift; *v/i* çiftleşmek; *v/t* çiftleştirmek

pajamas [pı'cämız] *pl. Am.* pijama *sg.*

palace ['pälis] saray

palate ['pälit] *an.* damak

pale[1] [peyl] kazık

pale[2] *adj.* soluk, solgun; *v/i* sararmak; ~**ness** solgunluk

Palestine ['pälistayn] Filistin

pallor ['pälı] solgunluk

palm[1] [pâm] *bot.* palmiye

palm[2] el ayası

palpitation [pälpi'teyşın] çarpıntı [martmak]

pamper ['pämpı] *v/t* şı-

pamphlet ['pämflit] risale, broşür

pan [pän] tava; ~**cake** gözleme

pane [peyn] pencere camı

panel ['pänl] *n.* kapı aynası; pano; heyet; *v/t* tahta ile kaplamak

pang [päŋ] ani sancı

panic ['pänik] panik, korku

panorama [pänı'râmı] panorama, manzara

pansy ['pänzi] *bot.* hercaî menekşe

pant [pänt] *v/i* solumak

panther ['pänthı] *zo.* pars, panter

pantry ['päntri] kiler

pants [pänts] *pl.* pantolon *sg.*; don

pap [päp] lapa

papa [pı'pâ] baba

papacy ['peypısi] *rel.* papalık

paper ['peypı] *n.* kâğıt; gazete; *pl.* evrak; hüviyet cüzdanı *sg.*; *v/t* duvar kâğıdı ile kaplamak; ~**back** cep kitabı; ~**bag** kese kâğıdı; ~**hanger** duvar kâğıdı yapıştıran; ~**mill** kâğıt fabrikası

paprika [pı'prîkı] kırmızı biber

parachut|**e** ['pärışuut] paraşüt; ~**ist** paraşütçü

parade [pı'reyd] *n.* gösteri, nümayiş; *v/i* gösteriş yapmak; yürümek

paradise ['pärıdays] cennet

paragraph ['pärıgrâf] satır başı; paragraf

parallel ['pärılel] paralel

paraly|**se**, *Am.* ~**ze** ['pärılayz] v/t felce uğratmak; ~sis [pı'rälisis] felç

paramount ['pärımaunt] üstün, en önemli

parasite ['pärısayt] parazit, asalak

parcel ['pâsl] n. paket, koli; parsel; v/t parsellemek

parch [pâç] v/t kavurup kurutmak; ~ment parşömen, tirşe

pardon ['pâdn] n. af, bağışlama; v/t affetmek; I beg your ~ affedersiniz; ~able affolunabilir

pare [pär] v/t yontmak; -in kabuğunu soymak

parent ['pärınt] baba; anne; pl. ana baba, ebeveyn; ~age soy, nesil; ~al [pı'rentl] ana babaya ait

parenthesis [pı'renthisis] gr. parantez, ayraç

parings ['pärinqz] pl. kırpıntı, döküntü sg.

parish ['päriş] rel. cemaat

park [pâk] n. park; otopark; v/t park etm.

parking ['pâkin] park yapma; ~ lot Am. park yeri; ~ meter otopark sayacı

parliament ['pâlimınt] parlamento, millet meclisi; Member of ♀ Am. İngiliz parlamento üyesi; ~ary [~'mentırı] parlamentoya ait

parlo(u)r ['pâlı] oturma odası, salon

parole [pı'rul] şeref sözü

parquet ['pâkey] parke

parrot ['pärıt] zo. papağan

parsley ['pâsli] bot. maydanoz

parson ['pâsn] papaz; ~age papaz evi

part [pât] n. parça, bölüm; pay; taraf; v/t parçalara ayırmak; v/i ayrılmak (with -den); for my ~ bence, bana kalırsa; take ~ katılmak (in -e)

partake [pâ'teyk] v/i katılmak (of -e)

partial ['pâşıl] eksik, tam olmayan; taraflı; ~ity [~şi-'äliti] tarafgirlik; beğenme

particip|ant [pâ'tisipınt] katılan; paylaşan; ~ate [~eyt] v/i katılmak (in -e)

participle ['pâtisipl] gr. ortaç, sıfat-fiil

particle ['pâtikl] cüz, zerre; gr. edat, takı

particular [pı'tikyulı] belirli; özel; titiz; pl. ayrıntılar; ~ity [~'läriti] özellik; titizlik; ~ly adv. özellikle

parting ['pâtin] ayrılma; ayıran, bölen

partisan [pâti'zän] taraftar; partizan, çeteci

partition [pâ'tişın] n. taksim; bölme; v/t bölmek

partly ['pâtli] adv. kısmen

partner ['pâtnı] ortak; eş; dans arkadaşı; ~ship ortaklık

partridge ['pâtric] zo. keklik

part-time yarım günlük

party ['pâti] grup; taraf; parti; toplantı, şölen

pass [pâs] n. geo. boğaz, geçit; pasaport; paso; v/t

geçmek, aşmak; geçirmek;
v/i bitmek; sayılmak (**as, for** olarak); ~ **away** *v/i* ölmek; geçmek; *v/t* geçirmek; ~ **by** *v/i* geçmek; ~ **round** *v/t* elden ele geçirmek; ~**able** geçilebilir; oldukça iyi

passage ['päsic] yol; geçit; pasaj; yolculuk

passenger ['päsıncı] yolcu

passer-by ['pâsı'bay] yoldan gelip geçen

passion ['päşın] ihtiras, tutku; aşk; hiddet; ~**ate** ['-it] heyecanlı, ateşli

passive ['päsiv] eylemsiz, uysal, pasif; *gr.* edilgen

pass|port ['pâspöt] pasaport; ~**word** parola

past [pâst] geçmiş, bitmiş; *-in* yanından; geçmiş zaman (*gr.* ~ **tense**); **quarter** ~ **two** ikiyi çeyrek geçiyor

paste [peyst] *n.* macun; çiriş, kola; *v/t* yapıştırmak; ~**board** mukavva

pasteurize ['pâstırayz] *v/t* pastörize etm.

pastime ['pâstaym] eğlence

pastry ['peystri] hamur işi, pasta

pasture ['pâsçı] *n.* otlak, çayır; *v/t* otlatmak

pat [pät] *n.* el ile hafif vuruş; *v/t* hafifçe vurmak *-e*

patch [päç] *n.* yama; arazi parçası; *v/t* yamamak; ~**work** yama işi

patent ['peytınt] *n.* patent; *v/t -in* patentini almak

patent leather rugan

patern|al [pı'tönl] babaya ait; ~**ity** babalık

path [pâth] keçi yolu, patika

pathetic [pı'thetik] acıklı, dokunaklı

patien|ce ['peyşıns] sabır; ~**t** sabırlı; hasta

patriarch ['peytriâk] *rel.* patrik

patriot ['peytriıt] *n.*, ~**ic** [pätri'otik] *adj.* yurtsever; ~**ism** ['pätriıtizm] yurtseverlik

patrol [pi'trıul] *n.* devriye; *v/t* devriye gezmek

patron ['peytrın] velinimet; patron; ~**age** ['pätrınic] himaye, koruma

patter ['pätı] *v/i* pıtırdamak

pattern ['pätın] örnek, model, nümune, mostra

paunch [pônç] göbek

pause [pöz] *n.* fasıla, mola, teneffüs; *v/i* durmak, duraklamak

pave [peyv] *v/t* kaldırım *v.s.* ile döşemek; *fig. yolu* açmak; ~**ment** kaldırım

paw [pô] *n.* pençe; *v/t* kabaca ellemek

pawn [pôn] *n.* rehin; *v/t* rehine koymak; ~**broker** rehinci

pay [pey] *n.* maaş, ücret; *v/t* ödemek; ~ **for** *b.ş.* için para vermek; *-in* cezasını çekmek; ~ **attention** dikkat etm.; ~ **a visit** görmeğe gitmek (**to** *-i*); ~**able** ödenmesi gereken; ~**day** ücretlerin verildiği gün; **~ee** [~'i] alacaklı; **~ment** ödeme; ücret; **~roll** ücret bordrosu

pea [pî] *bot.* bezelye

pease [pîz] barış, sulh; rahat; **~ful** sakin; uysal

peach [pîç] *bot.* şeftali

peacock ['pîkok] *zo.* tavus

peak [pîk] zirve, tepe; *kaskette* siper; **~ load** azami sıklet

peal [pîl] *n.* gürültü; *v/i* gürlemek

peanut ['pînat] *bot.* American fıstığı, yerfıstığı

pear [pâı] *bot.* armut

pearl [pöl] inci

peasant ['pezınt] köylü

peat [pît] turba

pebble ['pebl] çakıl taşı

peck [pek] *v/i* gaga ile vurmak (**at** *-e*)

peculiar [pi'kyûlyı] özel; tuhaf, garip; **~ity** [~li'äriti] özellik

pedal ['pedl] *n.* pedal; *v/t* ayakla işletmek

pedestal ['pedistl] *arch.* taban; temel

pedestrian [pi'destrın] yaya giden; **~ precinct, ~ zone** yaya bölgesi

pedigree ['pedigrî] şecere; soy

pedlar ['pedlı] seyyar satıcı

peel [pîl] *n.* kabuk; *v/t -in* kabuğunu soymak; *v/i* soyulmak

peep [pîp] *n.* **1.** civciv gibi ötme; **2.** azıcık bakış; *v/i* gizlice bakmak (**at** *-e*)

peer [pîı] eş; asılzade; **~age** [~'rîc] asalet; **~less** eşsiz

peevish ['pîvîş] titiz, densiz

peg [peg] *n.* tahta çivi; askı; *v/t* mıhlamak; *ec. -de* istikrar sağlamak

pelt [pelt] *v/t* atmak; *v/i* üzerine boşanmak

pen¹ [pen] yazı kalemi

pen² [pen] kümes, ağıl

penal ['pînl] cezaya ait; **~ servitude** ağır hapis cezası; **~ty** ['penlti] ceza; penaltı

penance ['penıns] *rel.* kefaret

pence [pens] *pl.* pensler

pencil ['pensl] kurşun kalem; **~ sharpener** kalemtıraş

pend|ant ['pendınt] askı; **~ing** henüz karara bağlanmamış; zarfında, *-e* kadar

penetrate ['penitreyt] *v/t* delip girmek *-e, -in* içine girmek; **~ion** sokuluş; etki

penguin ['pengwin] *zo.* penguen

penholder kalem sapı

penicillin [peni'silin] penisilin

peninsula [pi'ninsyulı] *geo.* yarımada

penitent ['penitınt] pişman, tövbekâr; **~iary** [~'tenşırı] *Am.* hapishane, cezaevi

penknife çakı

penn|iless ['penilis] parasız; **~y** pens, peni

pension ['penşın] pansiyon; emekli aylığı; **~er** emekli

pensive ['pensiv] dalgın, düşünceli

penthouse

penthouse ['penthaus] çatı katı

people ['pîpl] n. halk, ahali; millet, ulus; akrabalar pl.; v/t insanla doldurmak

pepper ['pepı] n. biber; v/t biberlemek; **~mint** nane

per [pö] vasıtasiyle

perambulator ['prämbyu-leytı] çocuk arabası

perceive [pı'sîv] v/t görmek, anlamak

percent [pı'sent] yüzde; **~age** yüzdelik

percept|ible [pı'septıbl] duyulur, farkına varılır; **~ion** idrak, anlayış

perch [pöç] tünek

percussion [pı'kaşın] vurma, çarpma

peremptory [pı'remptırı] kesin, katî

perfect ['pöfikt] adj. tam; kursursuz; n. gr. (**~** tense) geçmiş zaman; [pı'fekt] v/t tamamlamak; **~ion** kusursuzluk; ikmal

perforate ['pöfıreyt] v/t delmek

perform [pı'fôm] v/t yapmak, yerine getirmek; thea. oynamak; **~ance** yerine getirme; thea. temsil, gösteri

perfume ['pöfyûm] n. güzel koku; parfüm, esans; v/t lavanta sürmek -e

perhaps [pı'häps] belki

peril ['peril] tehlike; **~ous** tehlikeli

period ['pirird] çağ, devir, süre; **~ic** [~'odik] belirli

aralıklarla yer bulan; **~ical** belli zamanlarda çıkan; dergi

perish ['periş] v/i ölmek; mahvolmak; **~able** kolay bozulur

perjury ['pöcırı] jur. yalan yere yemin

perm [pöm] coll. perma (-nant); **~anent** sürekli, devamlı; **~anent wave** perma(nant) [çirgen]

permeable ['pömyıbl] ge-]

permi|ssion [pı'mişın] müsaade; ruhsat; **~t** [~t] v/t müsaade etm.; kabul etm.; ['pömit] n. permi, ruhsatname

perpendicular [pöpın'dikyulı] dikey; düşey

perpetual [pı'peçuıl] sürekli, ebedî

persecut|e ['pösikyût] v/t sıkıştırmak; zulmetmek -e; **~ion** zulüm; **~or** zulmelden

persever|ance [pösi'vırıns] sebat; **~e** [~'viı] v/i sebat göstermek (**in** -de)

Persia ['pöşı] İran; **~n** İranlı; Farsça

persist [pı'sist] ısrar etm., sebat etm. (**in** -de); **~ence, ~ency** sebat; ısrar; **~ent** ısrarlı

person ['pösn] şahıs, kimse; **~age** şahsiyet, zat; **~al** özel; şahsî, zatî; **~ality** [~sı'näliti] şahsiyet; **~ify** [~'sonifay] v/t cisimlendirmek; **~nel** [~sı'nel] kadro, takım

perspective [pı'spektiv]
perspektif
perspir|ation [pöspı'rey-
şın] ter(leme); **~e** [pıs-
'payı] v/i terlemek
persuade [pı'sweyd] v/t
kandırmak; **~sion** [~jın]
kandırmak; inanç; **~sive**
[~siv] kandırıcı
pert [pöt] şımarık, arsız
pertain [pö'teyn] ait olm.
(**to** -**e**) [etm.
perturb [pı'töb] v/t altüst/
perus|al [pı'ruuzıl] dikkatle
okuma; **~e** v/t incelemek
pervade [pö'veyd] v/t kaplamak; yayılmak **~e**
perverse [pı'vös] ters, aksi;
sapık
pessimis|m ['pesimizım]
kötümserlik; **~t** ['~mist] n.
kötümser
pest [pest] veba, taun; **~er**
v/t sıkmak, usandırmak
pet [pet] n. evde beslenen
hayvan; sevgili; v/t okşamak
petal ['petl] bot. çiçek yaprağı
petition [pi'tişın] n. dilekçe;
v/t dilekçe vermek -**e** (**for**
için)
petrify ['petrifay] v/t taş
haline getirmek; v/i taş
haline gelmek
petrol ['petrıl] benzin; **~
station** benzin istasyonu
petticoat ['petikut] iç etek-
liği
petty ['peti] küçük, önemsiz
pew [pyû] kilisede oturacak
sıra

phantom ['fäntm] hayal;
görüntü
pharmac|eutic(al) [fâmı-
'syûtıkıl] eczacılığa ait; **~y**
['~si] eczane
phase [feyz] safha, faz
pheasant ['feznt] zo. sülün
philanthropist [fi'länthrı-
pist] hayırsever
philately [fi'lätıli] pul me-
rakı
philology [fi'lolıci] filoloji
philosoph|er [fi'losıfı] filo-
zof; **~y** felsefe
phone [fıun] coll. n. telefon;
v/t telefon etm. -**e**
phon(e)y ['fıuni] sl. sahte,
düzme
photo ['fıutu] n. fotoğraf;
~copy fotokopi
photograph ['fıutıgrâf] n.
fotoğraf; v/t -**in** fotoğrafını
çekmek; **~er** [fı'togrıfı]
fotoğrafçı; **~y** fotoğrafçılık
phrase [freyz] ibare; deyim;
cümle
physic|al ['fizikıl] fiziksel;
maddî; bedene ait; **~ian**
[fi'zişın] doktor, hekim;
~ist ['~sist] fizikçi; **~s** pl.
fizik sg.
physique [fi'zîk] beden
yapısı
piano [pi'änu] mus. piyano
piast|er, ~re [pi'yästı] ku-
ruş
pick [pik] n. sivri kazma;
seçme; v/t gagalamak; kazmak; delmek; toplamak,
koparmak; seçmek; **~ out**
seçmek, ayırmak; **~ up**
kaldırmak, toplamak

picket ['pikit] *n.* kazık; grevciler nöbetçisi; *v/i* nöbet beklemek

pickle ['pikl] *n.* turşu, salamura; *v/t -in* turşusunu kurmak

pick|pocket yankesici; ~up pikap kolu

picnic ['piknik] piknik

pictorial [pik'tôriıl] resimli; resimlerle ilgili; resimli dergi

picture ['pikçı] *n.* resim; tablo; *pl.* sinema; *v/t* tasavvur etm.; *-in* resmini yapmak; tanımlamak; ~ postcard resimli kartpostal; ~sque [~'resk] pitoresk, canlı

pie [pay] börek, turta

piece [pîs] parça, bölüm; by the ~ parça başına; ~meal parça parça; ~work parça başına ücret

pier [piı] *naut.* iskele, rıhtım

pierce [pîs] *v/t* delmek; nüfuz etm. *-e*

piety ['payti] dindarlık

pig [pig] domuz

pigeon ['picin] güvercin; ~-hole *yazı masasında v.s.* göz

pig|-headed inatçı; ~-tail saç örgüsü

pike [payk] *zo.* turna balığı

oile [payl] *n.* yığın, küme; *v/t* yığmak, istif etm.; *v/i* birikmek

pilfer ['pilfı] *v/t* aşırmak

pilgrim ['pilgrim] hacı; ~age hacca gitme

pill [pil] hap

pillar ['pilı] direk, sütun; ~box mektup kutusu

pillory ['pilıri] teşhir direği

pillow ['pilıu] yastık; ~case, ~slip yastık yüzü

pilot ['paylıt] *n.* kılavuz; pilot; *v/t* kılavuzluk etm. *-e*

pimp [pimp] pezevenk

pimple ['pimpl] sivilce

pin [pin] *n.* toplu iğne; çivi; *v/t* iğnelemek

pincers ['pinsız] *pl.* kerpeten, kıskaç *sg.*

pinch [pinç] *n.* çimdik; tutam; sıkıntı; *v/t* çimdiklemek; kıstırmak; *sl.* ele geçirmek

pine¹ [payn] *v/i* zayıflamak; ~ for *-in* hasretini çekmek

pine² *bot.* çam; ~apple ananas

pink [pink] *bot.* karanfil; pembe

pinnacle ['pinıkl] kule; zirve, tepe

pint [paynt] galonun sekizde biri *(0,57 l, Am. 0,47 l)*

pioneer [payı'niı] öncü; *mil.* istihkâm eri

pious ['payıs] dindar

pip [pip] çekirdek

pipe [payp] *n.* boru; çubuk; pipo; künk; *v/t* borularla iletmek; çalmak; *v/i* düdük çalmak; ~line petrol borusu

pira|cy ['payırısi] korsanlık; ~te [~'rıt] korsan

pistachio [pis'tâşiu] *bot.* fıstık

pistol ['pistl] tabanca

piston ['pistın] *tech.* piston

plea

pit¹ [pit] çukur

pit² *Am.* çekirdek

pitch¹ [piç] zift

pitch² *n.* fırlatma; yükseklik; *mus.* perde; derece; *v/t* tenzil: kurmak; atmak, fırlatmak; **high-~ed** *mus.* perdesi ince; **~ed battle** meydan savaşı

pitcher ['piçi] testi

piteous ['pitiis] acınacak

pitfall ['pitfôl] tuzak olarak kazılan çukur; tuzak

pith [pith] *an.*, *zo.*, *bot.* öz, ilik

piti|able ['pitiibl] acınacak; acıklı; **~ful** acınacak; aşağılık; **~less** merhametsiz

pity ['piti] *n.* acıma, merhamet; **it is a ~** yazık

pivot ['pivit] mil; eksen; mihver

placard ['plâkaad] *n.* yafta, duvar ilânı; *v/t* afiş ile bildirmek

place [pleys] *n.* yer; meydan; görev; *v/t* koymak, yerleştirmek; **in ~ of** yerine; **out of ~** yersiz; **take ~** yer bulmak

placid ['plâsid] sakin, halim

plague [pleyg] *n.* veba; belâ, musibet; *v/t* eziyet vermek *-e*

plaice [pleys] *zo.* pisi balığı

plain [pleyn] ova; düz, sade, sarih, süssüz; **~clothes man** sivil polis

plaint [pleynt] şikâyet; **~iff** ['~tif] *jur.* davacı; **~ive** ['~tiv] iniltili, kederli

plait [plât] kırma; örgü; *v/t hair:* örmek

plan [plân] *n.* plan, taslak; niyet; *v/t* tasarlamak

plane [pleyn] *adj.* düz, düzlem; *n. tech.* planya, rende; *av.* uçak; *v/t* rendelemek

planet ['plânit] *astr.* gezegen, seyyare   [kalas]

plank [plânk] uzun tahta,}

plant [plânt] *n.* bitki, nebat; fabrika; *v/t* dikmek, kurmak; **~ation** [plân'teyşın] fidanlık; büyük çiftlik; **~er** ['plântı] ekici; çiftlik sahibi

plaque [plâk] levha

plaster ['plâstı] *n.* sıva; alçı; yakı; *v/t* sıvamak, yakı yapıştırmak *-e*

plastic ['plâstik] *adj.*, **~s** *pl.* plastik

plate [pleyt] *n.* tabak; levha; plaka; fotograf camı; *v/t* kaplamak

platform ['plätfôm] sahanlık; peron; *pol.* parti programı

platinum ['plâtinım] platin

platoon [plı'tuun] *mil.* takım

plausible ['plôzıbl] akla sığan, makul

play [pley] *n.* oyun; piyes; *v/t* oynamak; *mus.* çalmak; **~er** oyuncu; **~fellow** oyun arkadaşı; **~ful** oyunbaz, şakacı; **~ground** oyun sahası; **~thing** oyuncak; **~time** tatil zamanı; **~wright** ['~rayt] *thea.* piyes yazarı

plea [plî] müdafaa; rica; bahane

plead [plîd] v/t ileri sürmek; savunmak; v/i yalvarmak; **~ guilty** suçu kabul etm.

pleasant ['pleznt] hoş, latif

please [plîz] v/t sevindirmek, -in hoşuna gitmek; intj. lütfen; **be ~d** memnun olm. (**with** -den)

pleasure ['pleji] zevk, keyif

pleat [plît] pli

plebiscite ['plebisit] plebisit

pledge [plec] n. rehin; söz, vaat; v/t rehin olarak vermek

plent|iful ['plentiful] bol, çok; **~y** bolluk, zenginlik; **~y of** çok

pleurisy ['plûrisi] med. zatülcenp

pliable ['playıbl] bükülür; fig. uysal

pliers ['playız] pl. kıskaç, pens(e)

plight [playt] kötü durum

plod [plod] ağır yürümek veya çalışmak

plot [plot] n. arsa, parsel; entrika, suikast; plan; v/t -in haritasını çıkarmak; v/i kumpas kurmak

plough, Am. **plow** [plau] saban, pulluk; v/t sabanla işlemek; **~share** saban demiri

pluck [plak] n. cesaret, yiğitlik; v/t koparmak, yolmak; **~y** cesur, yılmaz

plug [plag] n. tapa, tıkaç; el. fiş; buji; v/t tıkamak; **~ in** el. prize sokmak

plum [plam] bot. erik; kuru üzüm; **~ pudding** baharatlı Noel pudingi

plumage ['pluumic] kuşun tüyleri pl.

plumb [plam] n. şakul; v/t iskandil etm.; **~er** lehimci, muslukçu

plume [pluum] gösterişli tüy, sorguç

plump [plamp] adj. şişman, tombul; v/i birdenbire düşmek; oy vermek (**for** -e); yardım etm. (-e)

plunder ['plandı] n. yağma; v/t yağma etm., soymak

plunge [planc] v/t daldırmak; v/i dalmak, atılmak (**into** -e)

pluperfect (tense) ['pluupöfikt] gr. geçmiş zamanın hikâye şekli

plural ['plûrıl] gr. çoğul

plus [plas] ve, ilâvesiyle; math. artı

plush [plaş] pelüş

ply [play] n. kat; v/t eğmek; **~wood** kontrplak

pneum|atic [nyûˈmätik] tech. hava basıncı ile ilgili; **~onia** [ˌ~ˈmuunyı] med. zatürree

poach [puç] v/i gizlice avlanmak; **~er** ruhsatsız avlanan kimse

pocket ['pokıt] n. cep; v/t cebe sokmak; **~book** cep kitabı; **~knife** çakı

pod [pod] kabuk, zarf

poem ['puim] şiir

poet ['puit] şair; **~ic(al)** [ˌ~ˈetik(ıl)] şiire ait; manzum; **~ry** ['puitri] şiir sanatı

poignant ['poynɪnt] acı, keskin

point [poynt] *n.* nokta; uç; puvan; derece; *pl. demiryolunda* makaslar; *v/t* yöneltmek, sivriltmek; *v/i* göstermek (**at** *-i*); silâhı doğrultmak (*-e*); **beside the ~** konu dışında; **on the ~ of** *-ing -mek* üzere; **~ of view** görüş noktası; **~ out** *v/t* belirtmek; **~-blank** doğrudan doğruya; **~ed** uçlu; manalı; **~er** işaret değneği; gösterge

poise [poyz] *n.* denge; istikrar; *v/t -in* dengesini sağlamak; *v/i* sarkmak

poison ['poyzn] *n.* zehir; *v/t* zehirlemek; **~ous** zehirli

poke [pɪuk] *v/t* dürtmek, karıştırmak; **~r** ocak demiri

Poland ['pɪulənd] Polonya

polar ['pɪuli] *geo.* kutba ait; **~ bear** *zo.* kutup ayısı

pole¹ [pɪul] kutup; direk, kazık

Pole² Polonyalı, Lehli

police [pɪ'liːs] polis; **~man** polis memuru; **~-station** karakol

policy ['polisi] siyaset; poliçe   [felçi]

polio ['pɪuliu] *med.* çocuk]

polish¹ ['poliʃ] *n.* cilâ, perdah; boya; *v/t* cilâlamak, parlatmak

Polish² ['pɪuliʃ] Polonyalı; Lehçe

polite [pɪ'layt] nazik, kibar; **~ness** nezaket, kibarlık

political [pɪ'litikl] siyasî; **~ sciences** *pl.* siyasal bilgiler

politics ['politiks] *pl.* siyaset, politika *sg.*

poll [pɪul] *n.* oy; anket; *pl.* seçim bürosu *sg.*

pollut|e [pɪ'luut] *v/t* kirletmek; **~ion** pisletme

polygamy [po'ligəmi] çokkarılılık, poligami

pomegranate ['pomgrænit] *bot.* nar

pomp [pomp] gösteriş, tantana; **~ous** tantanalı, debdebeli

pond [pond] havuz, gölcük

ponder ['pondɪ] *v/i* uzun boylu düşünmek (**on, over** *-i*); *v/t* zihninde tartmak; **~ous** ağır; can sıkıcı

pony ['pɪuni] *zo.* midilli

poodle ['puudl] *zo.* kaniş köpeği

pool [puul] *n.* gölcük, su birikintisi; havuz; ortaya konulan para; toto; *v/t* ortaklaşa toplamak

poor [puı] fakir, yoksul; az; fena; **the ~** *pl.* yoksullar

pop [pop] *n.* pat, çat; patlama sesi; *v/i* patlamak; *v/t* patlatmak; **~ out** *v/i* fırlamak

pope [pɪup] *rel.* papa

poplar ['poplı] *bot.* kavak

poppy ['popi] *bot.* gelincik, haşhaş

popul|ace ['popyulıs] halk, avam; **~ar** halka ait; herkesçe sevilen; **~arity** [~'læriti] halk tarafından tutulma; rağbet; ~ate ['~eyt] v/t şeneltmek; ~ation nüfus, ahali; ~ous nüfusu çok, kalabalık

porcelain ['pôslin] porselen

porch [pôç] kapı önünde sundurma; Am. veranda

porcupine ['pôkyupayn] zo. oklukirpi

pore [pô] n. an. gözenek, mesame; v/i derin düşünmek (over -i)

pork [pôk] domuz eti

pornography [pô'nografi] pornografi, müstehcen yazılar pl.

porous ['pôris] gözenekli

porphyry ['pôfiri] somaki, porfir

porridge ['poric] yulaf lapası

port¹ [pôt] liman

port² naut. lombar

port³ porto şarabı

portable ['pôtibl] taşınabilir, portatif

porter ['pôti] hamal; kapıcı

portion ['pôşin] n. hisse, pay; parça; porsiyon; çeyiz; v/t ayırmak

portly ['pôtli] iri yapılı; heybetli

portrait ['pôtrit] portre, resim

Portug|al ['pôtyugıl] Portekiz; ~uese [~'giz] Portekizli; Portekizce

pose [puuz] n. tavır; duruş; poz; v/i poz almak; taslamak (as -i)

position [pı'zişın] yer; durum, vaziyet

positive ['pozitiv] olumlu; pozitif

possess [pı'zes] v/t malik olm., sahip olm. -e; ~ed deli; düşkün (with -e); ~ion tasarruf; mal, mülk; iyelik; ~ive pronoun gr. iyelik zamiri; ~or mal sahibi

possib|ility [posi'biliti] imkân, ihtimal; ~le ['posibl] mümkün, muhtemel; ~ly adv. belki

post [pıust] n. direk, kazık; görev, memuriyet; posta; v/t postaya vermek; koymak, yerleştirmek; ~age posta ücreti; ~age stamp posta pulu; ~card kartpostal; ~e restante [~'rest-tant] postrestant

poster ['pıustı] poster, afiş

posterity [pos'teriti] gelecek nesiller pl.

post-free posta ücretine tabi olmıyan

post|-graduate üniversite mezunu; ~humous ['postyumıs] ölümden sonra olan

post|man postacı; ~mark posta damgası; ~master postane müdürü; ~(-)office postane; ~(-)office box posta kutusu

postpone [pıust'pıun] v/t ertelemek, sonraya bırakmak

postscript ['pıusskript] derkenar, not

posture ['posçı] duruş, poz

post-war ['pıust'wô] savaş sonrası

posy ['pıuzi] çiçek demeti
pot [pot] n. çömlek, kavanoz; saksı; v/t saksıya dikmek; kavanozda konserve etm.

potato [pı'teytıu] patates; **~es in their jackets** pl. kabuğiyle haşlanan patates
potent ['pıutınt] kuvvetli, etkili; **~ial** güç; potansiyel
potter[1] ['potı] v/i oyalanmak

potter[2] çömlekçi; **~y** çanak çömlek; çömlekçilik
pouch [pauç] kese
poulterer ['pıultırı] tavukçu
poultice ['pıultis] lapa
poultry ['pıultri] kümes hayvanları pl.
pounce [pauns] v/i atılmak (**on** -in üzerine)
pound[1] [paund] libre (454 g); sterlin, İngiliz lirası
pound[2] v/t dövmek; yumruklamak
pour [pô] v/i akmak, dökülmek; v/t dökmek, akıtmak
pout [paut] v/t dudaklarını sarkıtmak; v/i somurtmak
poverty ['povıti] yoksulluk
powder ['paudı] n. toz; pudra; barut; v/t toz veya pudra sürmek -e
power ['pauı] kudret, kuvvet, güç; yetki; **~ful** kuvvetli, kudretli; etkili; **~less** kuvvetsiz; **~plant,** **-station** elektrik santralı
practicable ['präktikıbl] yapılabilir; elverişli; **~al** pratik; kullanışlı; **~ce,** Am.

~se ['~tis] uygulama; alışıklık; pratik; müşteriler pl.; **~se** v/t yapmak; uygulamak; talim etm.; **~tioner** [**~**'tişnı] doktor; avukat
prairie ['präri] Kuzey Amerika'da bozkır
praise [preyz] n. övgü; v/t övmek; **~worthy** övülmeğe değer
pram [präm] çocuk arabası
prank [pränk] kaba şaka, oyun
prattle ['prätl] gevezelik etm.
prawn [prôn] zo. karides, deniz tekesi
pray [prey] v/i dua etm.; yalvarmak (**to** -e); çok rica etm. (**for** -i); **~er** [prä] dua; ibadet
preach [prîç] v/i va'zetmek (**to** -e); **~er** vaiz
preamble [prî'ämbl] önsöz
precarious [pri'käıris] kararsız; tehlikeli
precaution [pri'kôşın] ihtiyat, tedbir
precede [pri'sîd] v/t -den önce gelmek; -in önünden yürümek; **~nce** önce gelme, üstünlük; **~nt** ['presidınt] emsal, örnek
precept ['prîsept] hüküm; kural
precinct ['prîsinkt] bölge, çevre
precious ['preşıs] kıymetli, çok sevilen
precipice ['presipis] uçurum; **~tate** [pri'sipiteyt] v/t zamanından önce meydana

getirmek; hızlandırmak;
[pri'sipitit] *adj.* aceleci;
düşüncesiz; **~tation** [pri-
sipi'teyşın] acelecilik, telâş;
yağış (miktarı); **~tous** [pri-
'sipitıs] dik, sarp

précis ['preysi] özet

precis|e [pri'says] tam; ke-
sin; **~ion** [~'sijın] dikkat;
kesinlik

precocious [pri'kuşıs] vak-
tinden önce gelişmiş

preconception ['prikın-
'sepşın] önyargı

predatory ['predıtıri] yağ-
macılıkla geçinen; yırtıcı

predecessor ['prídisesı] ön-
cel, self

predetermine [pridi'tö-
min] *v/t* önceden tayin etm.

predicament [pri'dikımınt]
kötü durum

predicate ['predikit] *gr.*
yüklem

predict [pri'dikt] *v/t* önceden bildirmek; **~ion** önceden haber

predisposition ['prídıspı-
'zişın] eğilim, meyil

predomina|nt [pri'domi-
nınt] üstün; **~te** [~eyt] *v/i*
hâkim olm.

preface ['prefis] önsöz

prefer [pri'fö] *v/t* tercih
etm. (**to** -*e*); **~able** ['prefi-
rıbl] daha iyi; **~ence** ['prefi-
rıns] öncelik, üstünlük;
~ment [pri'fömınt] terfi,
yükselme

prefix ['prifiks] *gr.* önek

pregnan|cy ['pregnınsi] ge-
belik; **~t** gebe

prejudice ['precudis] *n.* önyargı, peşin hüküm; *v/t*
haksız hüküm verdirmek -*e*
(**against** -*e* karşı)

preliminary [pri'liminıri]
hazırlayıcı, ilk

prelude ['prelyûd] başlangıç, giriş

premature [premı'tyuı]
mevsimsiz, erken

premeditate [pri'mediteyt]
v/t tasarlamak

premier ['premyı] baştaki;
pol. başbakan

premises ['premisiz] *pl.*
mülk, ev ve müştemilâtı *sg.*

premium ['primyım] prim,
mükâfat; ikramiye

preoccupied [pri'okyu-
payd] zihni meşgul

prepar|ation [prepı'reyşın]
hazırlama; hazırlık; **~atory**
[pri'pärıtıri] hazırlayıcı; **~e**
[pri'päı] *v/t* hazırlamak; *v/i*
hazırlanmak

prepay ['pri'pey] *v/t* peşin
ödemek

preposition [prepı'zişın]
gr. edat

prepossess [prípı'zes] *v/t*
lehinde fikir hâsıl ettirmek;
~ing elıcı, cazibeli

preposterous [pri'postırıs]
akıl almaz, mantıksız

Presbyterian [prezbı'tiri-
yın] *rel.* İskoçya Protestan
kilisesine ait

prescri|be [pris'krayb] *v/t*
emretmek; *ilâcı* vermek;
~ption [~'kripşın] *med.* reçete

presence ['prezns] huzur,

primitive

varlık; ~ of mind soğukkanlılık

present[1] ['preznt] hazır; şimdiki; hediye, armağan; ~ (**tense**) *gr.* şimdiki zaman

present[2] [pri'zent] *v/t* sunmak; tanıştırmak; göstermek

presentation [prezen'tey-şın] sunma, takdim; hediye; temsil

presentiment [pri'zentimınt] önsezi

presently ['prezntli] *adv.* derhal; *Am.* şimdi

preserv|ation [prezö'vey-şın] saklama, koruma; ~e [pri'zöv] *v/t* korumak, saklamak; dayandırmak; -*in* konservesini yapmak; *n. pl.* reçel *sg.*

preside [pri'zayd] *v/t* başkanlık etm. -*e*

president ['prezidınt] başkan

press [pres] *n.* baskı; basın; matbaa; mengene; *v/t* sıkmak, sıkıştırmak; basmak; zorlamak; ütülemek; ~*ing* acele; ~**ure** [~şı] basınç; baskı

prestige [pres'tij] ün; nüfuz

presum|e [pri'zyûm] *v/t* tahmin etm.; cesaret etm. -*e*; ~*ing* haddini aşan

presumpt|ion [pri'zamp-şın] farz, tahmin; küstahlık; ~**uous** [~tyus] küstah

preten|ce, *Am.* ~**se** [pri-'tens] bahane; iddia; ~**d** *v/t* yalandan yapmak; taslamak (**to** *inf.* -*i*); *v/i* yapar

gibi görünmek; iddia etm. (**to** -*i*); ~**der** hak iddia eden; ~**sion** hak iddiası; haksız iddia

preterit(e) (**tense**) ['prete-rit] *gr.* geçmiş zaman kipi

pretext ['prîtekst] bahane

pretty ['priti] güzel, sevimli; *adv.* oldukça, hayli

prev|ail [pri'veyl] hâkim olm.; yürürlükte olm.; ~**alent** ['prevılınt] hüküm süren, yaygın

prevent [pri'vent] *v/t* önlemek; durdurmak; ~**ion** önleme; ~**ive** önleyici

previous ['prîvyıs] önceki, sabık; önce (**to** -*den*)

pre-war [prî'wô] savaş öncesi

prey [prey] *n.* av; *v/i* soymak, yağma etm. (**upon** -*i*)

price [prays] *n.* fiat, bedel; *v/t* fiat koymak -*e*; ~**less** paha biçilmez

prick [prik] *n.* iğne *veya* diken batması; *v/t* sokmak, delmek; ~ **up one's ears** kulak kabartmak; ~**le** diken; ~**ly** dikenli

pride [prayd] kibir, gurur, iftihar

priest [prîst] papaz

primary ['praymıri] ilk, asıl; başlıca; ~ **school** ilkokul

prime [praym] birinci; başlıca; olgunluk çağı; ~ **minister** *pol.* başbakan; ~**r** okuma kitabı

primitive ['primitiv] iptidaî, ilkel; basit; kaba

primrose ['primrıuz] *bot.* çuhaçiçeği

prince [prins] prens; hükümdar; **..ss** ['..ses] prenses

princip|al ['prinsipıl] başlıca, en önemli; şef, müdür, patron; sermaye; **..le** ['..pl] prensip, ilke

print [print] *n.* damga; emprime, basma kumaş; matbua, basma; *v/t* basmak; **out of ..** baskısı tükenmiş; **..ed matter** matbua; **..er** başımcı; **..ing** matbaacılık; baskı; **..ing-office** basımevi, matbaa

prior ['prayı] önce (**to** -*den*); **..ity** [..'oriti] öncelik

prison ['prizn] cezaevi, hapishane; **..er** tutuklu; esir; **take ..er** *v/t* esir etm.

privacy ['privısi, 'pray..] özellik; gizlilik

privat|e ['prayvit] özel; şahsî; gizli; *mil.* er; **..ion** [..'veyşın] yoksunluk, sıkıntı

privilege ['privilic] imtiyaz; **..d** imtiyazlı

prize [prayz] *n.* mükâfat, ödül; *v/t* değer vermek -*e*

pro- [prıu-] lehinde, ... tarafları; profesyonel

probab|ility [probı'biliti] ihtimal, **..able** ['..ıbl] muhtemel

probation [prı'beyşın] deneme süresi; *jur.* gözaltı

probe [prıub] *n.* sonda; *v/t* araştırmak

problem ['problım] sorun, mesele

procedure [prı'sîcı] işlem, muamele

proceed [prı'sîd] *v/i* ilerlemek; çıkmak (**from** -*den*); *n. pl.* kazanç, gelir *sg.*; **..ing** muamele, usul

process ['prıuses] *n.* yöntem, metot, işlem; gidiş, gelişme; *jur.* dava; celp-name; *v/t* işlemek; **..ion** [prı'seşın] alay

procla|im [prı'kleym] *v/t* ilân etm.; beyan etm.; **..mation** [proklı'meyşın] ilân; bildiri

procure [prı'kyuı] *v/t* elde etm., tedarik etm.

prodig|ious [prı'dicıs] kocaman, şaşılacak; **..y** ['prodici] olağanüstü şey; dâhi

produce [prı'dyûs] *v/t* meydana getirmek; üretmek; çıkarmak; ['prodyûs] *n.* ürün, mahsul; **..r** [prı-'dyûsı] üretici; *thea.* prodüktör

product ['prodakt] ürün, mahsul; sonuç; **..ion** [prı-'dakşın] imal, üretim; *thea.* sahneye koyma; **..ive** [prı-'daktiv] verimli

profess [prı'fes] *v/t* açıkça söylemek; ikrar etm.; **..ed** açıklanmış; **..ion** meslek; iddia, söz; **..ional** mesleğe ait; meslekî; profesyonel; **..or** profesör

proffer ['profı] *v/t* sunmak

proficien|cy [prı'fişınsi] ehliyet, becereklilik; **..t** ehliyetli, usta

profile ['prıufayl] profil

profit ['profit] *n.* kazanç; yarar; *v/t* kazanç getirmek *-e*; *v/i* yararlanmak (**by, from** *-den*); **~able** kazançlı; faydalı; **~eer** [**~'tɪi**] vurguncu

profound [prɪ'faund] derin, engin

profusion [prɪ'fyûjın] bolluk

progeny ['procini] soy, nesil

prognosis [prog'nɪusis] tahmin, prognoz

program(me) ['prɪugræm] program; düzen

progress ['prɪugres] *n.* ilerleme, gelişme; *v/i* ilerlemek; **~ive** [prɪ'gresiv] ilerliyen; ilerici

prohibit [prɪ'hibit] *v/t* yasak etm.; mâni olm. *-e*; **~ed area** yasak bölge; **~ion** [prɪui'bişın] yasak; içkilerin yasak olması

project ['procekt] *n.* plan, proje, tasarı; *v/t* tasarlamak; perdede göstermek; *v/i* çıkık olm.; **~ion** *phys.* projeksiyon; gösterim; çıkıntı, **~or** projektör; ışıldak

proletaria|n [prɪule'târirin] proleter; **~t** [**~iit**] proletarya

prolog(ue) ['prɪulog] *thea.* prolog, önsöz

prolong [prɪu'loŋ] *v/t* uzatmak

promenade [promi'nâd] gezinti; gezme yeri

prominent ['promɪnınt] tanınmış; çıkıntılı

promiscu|ity [promis-'kyûiti] karışıklık; **~ous** [prɪmıs'kyuus] rasgele cinsel ilişkide bulunan

promontory ['promɪntri] *geo.* gağlık burun

promot|e [prɪ'mɪut] *v/t* ilerletmek; terfi ettirmek; **~ion** terfi

prompt [prompt] *adj.* hemen, çabuk; *v/t* tahrik etm., sevketmek

prong [proŋ] çatal dişi

pronoun ['prɪunaun] *gr.* zamir

pro|nounce [prɪ'nauns] *v/t* söylemek, telaffuz etm.; **~nunciation** [**~**nansi'eyşın] söyleyiş

proof [pruuf] delil; deneme; prova; dayanıklı

prop [prop] *n.* destek; *v/t* desteklemek

propaga|nda [propɪ'gændı] propaganda; **~te** [**~**geyt] *v/i* çoğalmak; *v/t* çiftleştirmek; yaymak; **~tion** [**~**'geyşın] üreme; yayım

propel [prɪ'pel] *v/t* sevketmek; **~ler** *tech.* pervane, uskur

proper ['propı] uygun; özel; yakışıklı; **~ty** mal, mülk; özellik

prophe|cy ['profisi] önceden haber verme; kâhinlik; **~sy** [**~**'say] *v/t* önceden haber vermek (*sth.* hakkında); **~t** peygamber; kâhin

proportion [prɪ'pôşın]

oran(tı), nispet; **~al** orantılı

propos|al [prı'pıuzıl] önerme, teklif; evlenme teklifi; **~e** *v/t* önermek; *v/i* evlenme teklifi yapmak (**to** *-e*); **~ition** [propı'zişın] teklif; mesele

propriet|ary [prı'prayıtırı] *ec.* sicilli, markalı; **~or** sahip

propulsion [prı'palşın] itici güç

prose [prıuz] nesir

prosecut|e [prosikyût] *v/t* takip etm.; kovuşturmak; **~ion** *jur.* takibat; **~or** davacı; savcı

prospect ['prospekt] *n.* manzara, görünüş; ümit; ihtimal; [prıs'pekt] *v/i* araştırmak (**for** *-i*); **~ive** [prıs'pektiv] muhtemel; beklenen; **~us** [prıs'pektıs] prospektüs

prosper ['prospı] *v/i* başarılı olm.; gelişmek; **~ity** [~'periti] refah, gönenç; **~ous** ['~pırıs] bayındır; başarılı

prostitute ['prostityût] fahişe

prostrate ['prostreyt] yere uzanmış; takati kesilmiş

protect [prı'tekt] *v/t* korumak (**from** *-den*); **~ion** koruma; **~ive** koruyucu; **~or** hami, koruyucu

protest [prı'prıutest] *n.* protesto, itiraz; [prı'test] *v/i* protesto etm. (**against** *-i*); *v/t* protesto etm.; iddia etm.;

~ant ['protistınt] *rel.* Protestan; **~ation** [prıutes'teyşın] itiraz

protocol ['prıutikol] tutanak; *pol.* protokol

protract [prı'träkt] *v/t* uzatmak

protrude [prı'truud] *v/i* dışarı çıkmak; *v/t* çıkarmak

proud [praud] kibirli; kıvanç duyan (**of** *-e*)

prove [pruuv] *v/t* tanıtlamak, göstermek; *v/i* çıkmak

proverb ['provôb] atasözü; **~ial** [prı'vôbyıl] herkesçe bilinen

provide [prı'vayd] *v/t* tedarik etm.; donatmak; *v/i* sağlamak (**for** *-i*); **~d** (**that**) *-si* şartiyle

providence ['providıns] *rel.* takdir; basiret

provinc|e ['provins] il, vilâyet; taşra; yetki alanı; **~ial** [prı'vinşıl] taşralı; dar düşünceli

provision [prı'vijın] tedarik; şart, koşul; *pl.* erzak; **~al** geçici

provo|cation [provı'keyşın] kışkırtma; gücendirme; **~cative** [prı'vokitiv] kışkırtıcı; kızdırıcı; **~ke** [prı'vıuk] *v/t* kışkırtmak, tahrik etm.; sebep olm. *-e*

prowl [praul] *v/t* dolaşmak; *v/i* gezinmek

proximity [prok'simiti] yakınlık

proxy ['proksi] vekillik

prude [pruud] fazilet taslayıcı

pruden|ce ['pruudıns] ihtiyat, basiret; **~t** ihtiyatlı, tedbirli

prune [pruun] *n.* kuru erik; *v/t* budamak

pry [pray] burnunu sokmak (**into** *-e*)

psalm [sâm] *rel.* ilâhi

pseudonym ['psyûdınim] takma ad

psych|iatry [say'kayitri] psikiyatri, ruh hekimliği; **~ology** [say'kolıci] psikoloji

pub [pab] birahane

puberty ['pyûbıti] ergenlik çağı

public ['pablik] halk; halka ait; devletle ilgili; alenî; genel; **~ house** lokanta, birahane; **~ school** özel okul; *Am.* resmî okul; **~ Works** *pl.* Bayındırlık İşleri; **~ation** yayım(lama); yayın; **~ity** [~'lisiti] alenîyet; reklam

publish ['pabliş] *v/t* yayımlamak; bastırmak; **~er** yayınlayıcı; **~ing-house** yayınevi

pudding ['pudiŋ] puding

puddle ['padl] su birikintisi

puff [paf] *n.* üfleme, püf; hafif yumuşak börek; pudra pomponu; *v/i* üflemek; püflemek; *v/t* şişirmek; **~y** şişkin

pull [pul] *n.* çekme, çekiş; *v/t* çekmek; koparmak; **~**

down indirmek, yıkmak; **~ out** *v/t* çekip çıkarmak; *v/i* ayrılmak; **~ oneself together** kendine gelmek

pulley ['puli] *tech.* makara

pull-over ['puluvı] kazak, süveter

pulp [palp] meyva *veya* sebze eti; lapa

pulpit ['pulpit] mimber

pulpy ['palpi] etli, özlü

puls|ate [pal'seyt] *v/i* nabız gibi kımıldamak; **~e** nabız

pulverize ['palvırayz] *v/t* ezmek, toz haline getirmek

pump [pamp] *n.* *tech.* tulumba, pompa; iskarpin; *v/t* tulumba ile çekmek; **~ up** pompa ile şişirmek

pumpkin ['pampkin] *bot.* helvacı kabağı

pun [pan] cinas, söz oyunu

punch [panç] *n.* punç; *tech.* zımba; yumrukla vuruş; *v/t* yumruklamak; zımbalamak

Punch [panç] **and Judy** ['cuudi] *İngiliz kukla oyununda iki başfigür*

punctual ['paŋktyuıl] tam zamanında olmuş

punctuat|e ['paŋktyueyt] *v/t* noktalamak; **~ion** *gr.* noktalama

puncture ['paŋkçı] delik, lastik patlaması

pungent ['pancınt] keskin, dokunaklı

punish ['paniş] *v/t* cezalandırmak; **~ment** ceza(landırma)

pup [pap] köpek yavrusu

pupil[1] ['pyûpl] öğrenci, talebe
pupil[2] *an.* gözbebeği
puppet ['papit] kukla
puppy ['papi] köpek yavrusu
purchase ['pôçıs] *n.* satın alma; satın alınan şey; *v/t* satın almak; ~r müşteri
pure [pyuı] saf, halis; temiz
purée ['pyurey, pü're] püre, ezme
purgat|ive ['pôgıtiv] müshil, sürgün ilâcı; ~ory *rel.* araf
purge [pôc] *n. med.* müshil; *pol.* tasfiye; *v/t* temizlemek
puri|fy ['pyurifay] *v/t* temizlemek; 2tan [~tın] Püriten, mutaassıp Protestan; ~ty temizlik, saflık
purloin ['pôloyn] *v/t* aşırmak
purple ['pôpl] mor
purpose ['pôpıs] *n.* maksat, niyet; *v/t* niyet etm.; **on** ~ kasten, istiyerek; **to no** ~ faydasızca; ~**ful** maksatlı; ~**less** manasız; ~**ly** bile bile
purr [pô] *v/t* mırlamak
purse[1] [pô] *n.* para kesesi; *Am.* el çantası; haz(i)ne
purse[2] *v/t dudakları* büzmek
pursu|e [pı'syû] *v/t* takip

etm., kovalamak; ~**it** [~yût] takip, arama; iş, uğraşma
purvey [pô'vey] *v/t* tedarik etm.; ~**or** satıcı
pus [pas] irin
push [puş] *n.* itiş, dürtüş; teşebbüs; *v/t* itmek, dürtmek; saldırmak; ~ **on** devam etm.
puss [pus], ~**y** kedi
put [put] *v/t* koymak, yerleştirmek; ifade etm.; ~ **away** saklamak; ~ **down** indirmek; bastırmak; yazmak; ~ **forth**, ~ **forward** ileri sürmek; ~ **off** sonraya bırakmak; vazgeçirmek; çıkarmak; ~ **on** giymek; açmak; takınmak; ~ **out** söndürmek; çıkarmak; ~ **through** *tel.* bağlamak; ~ **up with** katlanmak ~*e*
putr|efy ['pyûtrifay] *v/i* çürümek; *v/t* çürütmek, bozmak; ~**id** [~id] çürük, bozuk
putty ['pati] çamcı macunu
puzzle ['pazl] *n.* bilmece, bulmaca; mesele; *v/t* şaşırtmak; *v/i* şaşırmak
pyjamas [pı'câmız] *pl.* pijama *sg.*
pyramid ['pirımid] piramit, ehram

Q

quack [kwäk] *n.* ördek sesi; *fig.* doktor taslağı, şarlatan; *v/i* ördek gibi bağırmak
quadr|angle ['kwodrängl]

dörtgen; avlu; ~**ate** [~it] kare; dört köşeli; ~**ipartite** [~i'pátayt] dört taraflı
quadrup|ed ['kwodruped]

dört ayaklı; **~le** *adj.* dört kat, dört misli; *v/t* dört misli çoğaltmak

quail [kweyl] *zo.* bıldırcın

quaint [kweynt] tuhaf, garip ve hoş

quake [kweyk] *n.* titreme, deprem; *v/i* titremek; **2r** Kuveykır mezhebinin üyesi

qualif ication [kwolifi'keyşın] ehliyet; **~ied** ['~fayd] ehliyetli; nitelik; **~y** ['~fay] *v/t* nitelendirmek; sınırlamak; hafifletmek; *v/i* ehliyet göstermek

quality ['kwoliti] nitelik; kalite

qualm [kwâm] azap; bulantı

quantity ['kwontiti] nicelik, miktar   [karantina]

quarantine ['kworıntîn]ʃ

quarrel ['kworıl] *n.* kavga; *v/i* kavga etm., çekişmek; **~some** kavgacı, huysuz

quarry[1] ['kwori] av

quarry[2] taş ocağı

quart [kwôt] galonun dörtte biri *(1,136 l, Am. 0,946 l)*

quarter ['kwôtı] *n.* dörtte bir, çeyrek; üç aylık süre; etraf, semt; aman, hayatını bağışlama; *mil. pl.* kışla, ordugâh *sg.*; *v/t* dörde ayırmak; *mil.* yerleştirmek; **a ~ past** *-i* çeyrek geçe; **a ~ to** *-e* çeyrek kala; **~ly** üç ayda bir

quartet(te) [kwô'tet] *mus.* kuartet

quaver ['kweyvı] *v/i* titremek *(ses)*

quay [kî] rıhtım, iskele

queen [kwîn] kıraliçe

queer [kwiı] acayip, tuhaf

quell [kwel] *v/t* bastırmak

quench [kwenç] *v/t* söndürmek; soğutmak

querulous ['kwerulıs] şikâyetçi

query ['kwiri] *n.* soru; *v/t* sormak *-e*; şüphelenmek *-den*

quest [kwest] arama

question ['kwesçın] *n.* soru; mesele; şüphe; *v/t* sual sormak *-e*; şüphe etm. *-den*; sorguya çekmek *-i*; **be out of the ~** olamamak; **~able** şüpheli; **~-mark** *gr.* soru işareti; **~naire** [~stü-'näı] soru kâğıdı

queue [kyû] bekliyen halk dizisi, kuyruk; **~ up** *v/i* kuyruğa girmek

quick [kwik] çabuk, tez, süratli; keskin; çevik; **~en** *v/t* canlandırmak; çabuklaştırmak; *v/i* hızlanmak; **~ness** çabukluk, sürat; **~sand** bataklık kumu; **~silver** civa; **~witted** çabuk anlıyan

quid [kwid] *sl.* bir sterlin

quiet ['kwayıt] *adj.* sakin, sessiz; gösterişsiz; *n.* sessizlik; *v/t* susturmak; **~ness**, **~ude** ['~ityûd] sessizlik, rahat

quill [kwil] tüy kalem; kirpi dikeni

quilt [kwilt] yorgan

quince [kwins] *bot.* ayva

quinine [kwi'nin] *chem.* kinin [luk ağırlık]

quintal ['kwintl] yüz kilo- [luk ağırlık]

quit [kwit] *v/t* terketmek, bırakmak; *adj.* serbest

quite [kwayt] tamamen; gerçekten; hayli

quiver ['kwivı] *n.* ok kılıfı; titreme; *v/i* titremek

quiz [kwiz] *n.* sorgu, test; *v/t* sorguya çekmek

quota ['kwıutı] hisse, pay, kota

quotation [kwıu'teyşın] aktarma; *ec.* fiat; ~ **marks** *pl. gr.* tırnaklar

quote [kwıut] *v/t* (aktarma yolu ile) söylemek

R

rabbi ['räbay] *rel.* haham

rabbit ['räbit] *zo.* adatavşanı

rabble ['räbl] ayaktakımı

rabid ['räbid] kudurmuş; öfkeli; ~es ['reybiz] *med.* kuduz

race[1] [reys] ırk, soy; nesil

race[2] *n.* yarış; koşu; akıntı; *v/i* yarışmak, koşmak

racial ['reyşıl] ırksal

racing ['reysin] yarış; yarışlara ait

rack [räk] *n.* parmaklık; raf; yemlik; *v/t* yormak, işkence etm.; ~ **one's brains** kafa patlatmak

racket ['räkit] raket; velvele, gürültü; haraçcılık; ~eer [~ı'tiı] şantajcı, haraçcı

racy ['reysi] canlı; açık saçık

radar ['reydı] radar (aygıtı)

radiance ['reydyıns] parlaklık; ~nt parlak; ~te [~ieyt] *v/i* ışın saçmak; *v/t* yaymak; ~tion yayılma; ~tor radyatör

radical ['rädikıl] kökten, radikal; köksel

radio ['reydiıu] *n.* radyo;

telsiz telgraf; *v/t* yayımlamak; ~activity radyoetkinliği; ~therapy radyoterapi

radish ['rädiş] *bot.* turp

radius ['reydyıs] yarıçap; *fig.* çevre

raffle ['räfle] piyango

raft [räft] sal; ~er kiriş

rag [räg] paçavra; değersiz şey

rage [reyc] *n.* öfke, hiddet; düşkünlük (**for** -*e*); *v/i* kudurmak, köpürmek

ragged ['rägid] yırtık; pürüzlü

raid [reyd] *n.* akın, baskın; *v/t* baskın yapmak -*e*

rail[1] [reyl] sövüp saymak

rail[2] *n.* tırabzan, parmaklık; *tech.* ray; *v/t* parmaklıkla çevirmek; **run off the ~s** raydan çıkmak; ~ing parmaklık; ~road *Am.*, ~way demiryolu

rain [reyn] *n.* yağmur; *v/i* yağmur yağmak; *v/t* yağmak; ~bow alkım, gökkuşağı; ~coat yağmurluk; ~y yağmurlu

raise [reyz] *v/t* kaldırmak, yükseltmek, artırmak; *parayı* toplamak; yetiştirmek, büyütmek; ileri sürmek

raisin ['reyzn] kuru üzüm

rake [reyk] *n.* tarak, tırmık; sefih adam; *v/t* taramak, tırmıklamak

rally ['räli] *n.* toplama; ralli; *v/i* düzene girmek; *v/t* düzeltmek, canlandırmak

ram [räm] *n.* koç; *tech.* şahmerdan; *v/t* vurmak; vurarak yerleştirmek

ramble ['rämbl] *n.* gezinme; *v/i* boş gezinmek

ramify ['rämifay] *v/i* dallanmak; *v/t* kollara ayırmak

ramp [rämp] rampa; **~art** ['.ât] sur

ran [rän] *s.* **run**

ranch [ränç] *Am.* hayvan çiftliği; büyük çiftlik; **~er** çiftlik sahibi

rancid ['ränsid] ekşimiş, kokmuş

ranco(u)r ['ränkı] kin, hınç

random ['rändım]: **at ~** boş gezinmek

rang [räng] *s.* **ring** [rasgele]

range [reync] *n.* sıra, dizi; erim, menzil; uzaklık; alan; mutfak ocağı; atış yeri; *Am.* otlak; *v/t* sıralamak, dizmek; dolaşmak; *v/i* uzanmak; yetişmek; **~r** korucu

rank [ränk] *n.* rütbe, derece; sıra, dizi; *v/t* sıralamak, tasnif etm.; saymak; *v/i* katılmak (**among, with** -*e*); *adj.* uzun büyümüş; komuş

ransack ['ränsäk] *v/t* araştırmak; yağma etm.

ransom ['ränsım] *n.* fidye, kurtulmalık; *v/t* fidye ile kurtarmak

rap [räp] *n.* hafif vuruş; *v/t* hafifçe vurmak *-e*

rapacious [rı'peyşıs] haris, açgözlü

rape [reyp] *n.* ırzına geçme; *v/t -in* ırzına geçmek

rapid ['räpid] çabuk, hızlı; *n. pl. geo.* ivinti yeri *sg.*; **~ity** [rı'piditi] sürat, hız

rapt [räpt] dalgın, esri(k); **~ure** ['.çı] esrilik, vecit

rar|e [rä] seyrek, nadir; az bulunur; **~ity** nadirlik; kıymetli şey

rascal ['räskıl] çapkın, serseri

rash[1] [räş] *med.* isilik

rash[2] sabırsız, düşüncesiz

rasp [räsp] *n.* raspa, kaba törpü; *v/t* törpülemek; *v/i* törpü gibi ses çıkarmak

raspberry ['räzbıri] *bot.* ahududu

rat [rät] *zo.* sıçan

rate [reyt] *n.* nispet, oran; fiyat; ücret; belediye vergisi; sürat; sınıf, çeşit; *v/t* saymak; değerlendirmek; *v/i* sayılmak; **at any ~** her halde; **~ of exchange** *ec.* kambiyo sürümdeğeri; **~ of interest** faiz oranı

rather ['râdhı] oldukça, tersine; **~ than** -*den* ziyade

ratif|ication [rätifi'keyşın] tasdik; **~y** ['.fay] *v/t* tasdik etm., onaylamak

ration ['räşın] *n.* pay; tayın; miktar; *v/t* karneye bağlamak; **~al** ['~ɔnl] akıl sahibi; akıllı; **~alize** ['~şnılayz] *v/t* akla uydurmak; ölçülü şekle sokmak

rattle ['rätl] *n.* takırtı, çıtırtı; çıngırak; *v/i* takırdamak; *v/t* takırdatmak; **~snake** *zo.* çıngıraklı yılan

ravage ['rävic] *v/t* tahrip etm.

rave [reyv] *v/i* çıldırmak; bayılmak (**about, of** *-e*)

raven ['reyvn] *zo.* kuzgun; kuzgunî; **~ous** ['rävnıs] haris, doymak bilmez

ravine [rı'vîn] çukur

ravish ['räviş] *v/t* esritmek

raw [rô] ham, çiğ; *fig.* acemi, tecrübesiz; **~ material** hammadde

ray [rey] ışın, şua

rayon ['reyon] suni ipek

raz|e [reyz] *v/t* temelinden yıkmak; **~or** ustura; tıraş makinesi

re- ['ri-] geri(ye)

reach [riç] *n.* uzatma; alan; menzil; erim; *v/t* varmak, yetişmek, ulaşmak *-e*; uzatmak *-i*; **out of** *-e* erişilmez; **within** *-e* erişilebilir

react [ri'äkt] *v/i* tepkimek; etkilemek (**to** *-i*); **~ion** tepki; reaksiyon; *pol.* gericilik; **~ionary** [~şnıri] gerici; **~or** reaktör

read [rîd] *v/t* okumak; göstermek; **~able** okunaklı; **~er** okuyucu

readi|ly ['redili] seve seve; **~ness** hazır olma

ready ['redi] hazır (**to do sth.** *-i* yapmağa); istekli; **get ~** hazırlanmak; **~money** hazır para, nakit; **~-made** hazır

real [riıl] gerçek; asıl; **~ estate** *jur.* gayri menkul mal, mülk; **~ism** gerçekçilik, realizm; **~istic** gerçeğe uygun; **~ity** [~'äliti] gerçeklik, realite; **~ization** farketme; gerçekleştirme; *ec.* paraya çevirme; **~ize** *v/t* anlamak, *-in* farkına varmak; gerçekleştirmek *-i*; *ec.* paraya çevirmek *-i*; **~ly** *adv.* gerçekten

realm [relm] kırallık; alan

realty ['riılti] mülk, gayri menkul mal

reap [rîp] *v/t* biçmek, toplamak; **~er** orakçı; biçerdöver

reappear ['rîı'piı] *v/i* tekrar görünmek

rear[1] [riı] *v/t* dikmek; yetiştirmek; *v/i* yükselmek; şahlanmak

rear[2] geri, arka; **~ view mirror** dikiz aynası; **~ admiral** *naut.* tuğamiral; **~-lamp, ~-light** arka feneri

rearmament ['rî'âmımınt] silâhlandırma

reason ['rîzn] *n.* akıl, idrak; sebep; mantık; *v/t* düşünmek; uslamlamak, muhakeme etm.; *v/i* kandırmağa çalışmak (**with** *-e*); **by ~ of**

sebebiyle; **~able** akla uygun, makul

reassure [ri:'ʃuə] v/t tekrar güven vermek -e

rebel ['rebl] adj., n. isyan eden, ayaklanan; [ri'bel] v/i isyan etm., ayaklanmak; **~lion** [~'beljən] isyan, ayaklanma; **~lious** [~'beljəs] serkeş

rebound [ri'baund] v/i geri tepmek

rebuff [ri'baf] ters cevap

rebuild ['ri:'bild] v/t tekrar inşa etm.

rebuke [ri'bju:k] n. azar, paylama; v/t azarlamak

recall [ri'kɔ:l] n. geri çağırma; v/t geri çağırmak; hatırlamak; feshetmek

recede [ri'si:d] v/i geri çekilmek

receipt [ri'si:t] reçete; alındı; pl. gelir sg.

receive [ri'si:v] v/t almak; kabul etm.; **~r** alıcı; ahize

recent ['ri:snt] yeni (olmuş); **~ly** adv. son zamanlarda, geçenlerde

reception [ri'sepʃn] alma; kabul; resepsiyon; **~ist** resepsiyon memuru

recess [ri'ses] arch. girinti; Am. paydos, teneffüz; pl. iç taraf sg.; **~ion** ec. durgunluk

recipe ['resipi] yemek tarifi; reçete

recipient [ri'sipiənt] alıcı

reciprocal [ri'siprikl] karşılıklı

recital [ri'saitl] ezberden

okuma; mus. resital; **~e** v/t ezberden okumak; anlatmak   [pervasız]

reckless ['reklis] dikkatsiz,

reckon ['rekən] v/t hesap etm., saymak; tahmin etm.; v/i güvenmek (**on** -e); hesaba katmak (**with** -i); **~ing** ['~kniŋ] hesaplama

reclaim [ri'kleym] v/t geri istemek; elverişli hale koymak

recline [ri'klayn] v/i uzanmak; dayanmak

recogni|tion [rekəg'niʃn] tanıma; **~ze** v/t tanımak

recoil [ri'koyl] v/i geri çekilmek; geri tepmek

recollect [rekɪ'lekt] v/t hatırlamak; **~ion** hatırlama

recommend [rekɪ'mend] v/t tavsiye etm.; **~ation** tavsiye

recompense ['rekɪmpens] v/t mükâfatlandırmak; telâfi etm.

reconcil|e ['rekɪnsayl] v/t barıştırmak; mutabık kılmak; **~iation** [~sili'eyʃn] barışma, uzlaşma

reconsider ['ri:kɪn'sidɪ] v/t tekrar düşünmek

reconstruct ['ri:kɪn'strakt] v/t yeniden inşa etm.; yinelemek; **~ion** tekrar inşa; yeniden kalkınma

record ['rekɔ:d] kayıt; sicil; tutanak; rekor; plak; [ri-'kɔ:d] v/t kaydetmek, yazmak; plaka almak; **~er** kayıt aygıtı; **~-player** pikap

recourse

recourse [ri'kôs]: have ~ to başvurmak -e

recover [ri'kavı] v/t tekrar ele geçirmek; geri almak; v/i iyileşmek; kendine gelmek; ~y geri alma; iyileşme; kendine gelme

recreation [rekri'eyşn] dinlenme, eğlence

recruit [ri'kruut] n. mil. acemi asker; v/t toplamak

rect|angle ['rektängl] dik dörtgen; tatil; ~ify ['~ifay] v/t düzeltmek

rector ['rektı] rel. papaz; rektör; ~y papaz evi

recur [ri'kö] v/i tekrar dönmek (to -e); tekrar olmak; ~rent [ri'karınt] tekrar olan

red [red] kızmızı, kızıl, al; ♀ Crescent Kızılay; ♀ Cross Kızılhaç; ~ tape kırtasiyecilik; ~den v/t kırmızılaştırmak; v/i kızıllaşmak, kızarmak

redeem [ri'dîm] v/t fidye vererek kurtarmak; yerine getirmek; rel. halâs etm.; ♀er rel. Kurtarıcı, Halâskâr

redemption [ri'dempşn] halâs; kurtar(ıl)ma

red|-handed jur. suçüstü; ~hot kızgın; ~letter day yortu günü; önemli gün

redouble [ri'dabl] v/t tekrarlamak; v/i iki misli olm.

reduc|e [ri'dyûs] v/t azaltmak, indirmek, küçültmek; ~tion [~'dakşın] azaltma, indirme

reed [rîd] kanış, saz

re-education ['riedyu'key-şın] yeniden eğitme

reef [rîf] kayalık, resif

reek [rîk]: ~ of, with -in kokusunu yaymak

reel [rîl] n. makara; v/t makaraya sarmak; v/i sendelemek; dönmek

re|-elect ['ri:'lekt] v/t pol. tekrar seçmek; ~enter v/t tekrar girmek -e; ~establish v/t yeniden kurmak

refer [ri'fö] v/t göndermek (to -e); v/i göstermek (to -i); ilgili olm. (ile); ~ee [refı'rî] hakem

reference ['refrıns] ilgi; başvuruş; referans; bon-servis; with ~ to -e gelince

refill [ri'fil] n. yedek takım; ['~'fil] v/t tekrar doldurmak

refine [ri'fayn] v/t tasfiye etm.; inceleştirmek; incelmek, zarifleşmek; ~ment incelik, zariflik; ~ry rafineri; şeker fabrikası

reflect [ri'flekt] v/t yansıtmak; v/i düşünmek (on, upon -i); ~ion yansıma; düşünme; fikir

reflex ['rifleks] refleks, tepke, yansı; ~ive [ri'fleksiv] gr. dönüşlü

reform [ri'fôm] n. reform, ıslah; v/t ıslah etm., düzeltmek; v/i iyileşmek; ♀ation [refı'meyşn] rel. Reformasyon, dinsel devrim; ~er reformcu

refract [ri'fräkt] v/t ışınları kırmak; ~ory inatçı

refrain¹ [ri'freyn] *mus.* nakarat

refrain² *v/i* çekinmek, sakınmak (**from** *-den*)

refresh [ri'freş] *v/t* canlandırmak; **~ oneself** dinlenmek; **~ment** canlan(dır)ma; canlandırıcı şey

refrigerator [ri'fricıreytı] buzdolabı, soğutucu

refuel ['ri'fyuıl] *v/t* yakıt doldurmak

refuge ['refyûc] sığınak, barınak; **~e** [~'ci] mülteci

refund [ri'fand] *v/t* parayı geri vermek

refus|al [ri'fyûzıl] ret, kabul etmeyiş; **~e** *v/t* reddetmek; istememek; ['refyûs] *n.* süprüntü

refute [ri'fyût] *v/t* yalanlamak

regain [ri'geyn] *v/t* tekrar ele geçirmek

regal ['rîgıl] krala ait

regard [ri'gaad] *n.* bakış, nazar; saygı; *v/t* dikkatle bakmak *-e*; dikkat etm. *-e*; saymak *-i* (**as** ...); **as ~s** hakkında, hususunda; **~s** *pl.* saygılar; selâmlar; **with ~ to** *-e* gelince; **~ing** hakkında, *-e* gelince; **~less of** *-e* bakmayarak

regent ['rîcınt] saltanat vekili

regiment ['recimınt] *mil.* alay

region ['rîcın] bölge; **~al** bölgesel

regist|er ['recistı] *n.* kütük; sicil; fihrist; *v/t* kaydetmek; taahhütlü olarak göndermek; *v/i* kaydolunmak; **~ered** taahhütlü; kaydolunmuş; **~ration** kayıt, tescil

regret [ri'gret] *n.* teessüf; pişmanlık; *v/t* teessüf etm., acınmak *-e*; pişman olm. *-e*; **~table** acınacak

regular ['regyulı] kurallı, düzenli; *mil.* nizamî; **~ity** [~'lâriti] düzen, intizam

regulat|e ['regyuleyt] *v/t* düzenlemek; ayar etm., yoluna koymak; **~ion** düzen, nizam; *pl.* kurallar; tüzük *sg.*

rehears|al [ri'hösıl] *thea.* prova; **~e** *v/t* prova etm., tekrarlamak

reign [reyn] *n.* hükümdarlık (devri); *v/i* hüküm sürmek

rein [reyn] dizgin

reindeer ['reyndiı] *zo.* ren

reinforce [riin'fôs] *v/t* kuvvetlendirmek; **~d concrete** betonarme

reiterate [ri'itıreyt] *v/t* tekrarlamak

reject [ri'cekt] *v/t* reddetmek; atmak; **~ion** ret, reddedilme

rejoic|e [ri'coys] *v/i* sevinmek (**at** *-e*); *v/t* sevindirmek; **~ing** sevinç; şenlik

rejoin ['ri'coyn] *v/t* tekrar kavuşmak *-e*; [ri'coyn] cevap vermek *-e*

relapse [ri'läps] *n.* eski hale dönme; *v/i* tekrar fenalaşmak; tekrar sapmak (**into** *-e*)

relate 368

relate [ri'leyt] *v/t* anlatmak; *v/i* ilgili olm. (**to** ile); **~d to** *-in* akrabası olan

relation [ri'leyşın] ilişki; ilgi; akraba; hikâye; *pl.* ilişkiler; **in ~ to** *-e* gelince; **~ship** akrabalık; ilişki

relative [re'lıtiv] göreli, nispî; bağlı, ilişkin (**to** *-e*); akraba; ~ (**pronoun**) *gr.* ilgi adılı; **~ly** *adv.* nispeten

relax [ri'läks] *v/t* gevşetmek; *v/i* gevşemek; dinlenmek

relay ['ri'ley] *n.* değiştirme atı; *el.* düzenleyici; *v/t* nakletmek, yaymak; ~ **race** bayrak koşusu; ~ **station** *el.* ara istasyonu

release [ri'lîs] *n.* kurtarma, salıverme; *phot.* deklanşör; *v/t* kurtarmak; serbest bırakmak; harekete geçirmek

relent [ri'lent] *v/i* yumuşamak; **~less** merhametsiz

relevan|ce, **~cy** ['relivıns, ~si] ilgi; uygunluk; **~t** uygun, ilgili

relia|ble [ri'layıbl] güvenilir; **~nce** güven, itimat

relic ['relik] kalıntı; *rel.* mukaddes emanet

relie|f [ri'lîf] yardım, imdat; nöbet değiştirme; ferahlama; rölyef, kabartma; **~ve** [~v] *v/t* rahatlatmak; yardım etm. *-e*; kurtarmak *-i*

religi|on [ri'licın] din; **~ous** dinî, dinsel; dindar; dikkatli

relinquish [ri'linkwiş] *v/t* terketmek; vazgeçmek *-den*

relish ['reliş] *n.* tat, lezzet; çeşni; *v/t* hoşlanmak *-den*

reluctant [ri'laktınt] isteksiz, gönülsüz

rely [ri'lay] güvenmek (**on**, **upon** *-e*)

remain [ri'meyn] *v/i* kalmak; durmak; *n. pl.* kalıntılar; cenaze *sg.*; **~der** kalıntı; artan

remand [ri'mând] *v/t* geri göndermek; *n. jur.* tutukevine geri gönderme

remark [ri'mâk] *n.* söz; mülâhaza; *v/t* söylemek, demek; **~able** dikkate değer

remedy ['remidi] *n.* çare; ilâç; *v/t* düzeltmek; *-in* çaresini bulmak

rememb|er [ri'membı] *v/t* hatırlamak; anmak; **~rance** hatırlama; andaç

remind [ri'maynd] *v/t* hatırlatmak *-e* (**of** *-i*); **~er** hatırlatma

reminiscent [remi'nisnt] hatırlayan, hatırlatan (**of** *-i*)

remit [ri'mit] *v/t* affetmek, bağışlamak; havale etm.; **~tance** para gönderme

remnant ['remnınt] artık

remodel [ri'modl] *v/t -in* şeklini değiştirme

remonstrate ['remınstreyt] *v/i* protesto etm. (**against** *-i*); *v/t* itiraz etm. (**that** *-e*)

remorse [ri'môs] pişmanlık, nedamet; **~less** merhametsiz

remote [ri'miut] uzak

remov|al [ri'muuvıl] kaldır(ıl)ma; yol verme; taşınma; *~e* v/t kaldırmak; uzaklaştırmak; v/i taşınmak; *~er* leke v.s. giderici; nakliyeci [Rönesans]

Renaissance [ri'neysıns]/

rend [rend] v/t yırtmak; v/i yırtılmak

render ['rendı] v/t kılmak, yapmak; geri vermek; teslim etm.; tercüme etm., çevirmek (**into** -e)

renew [ri'nyû] v/t yenile(ş-tir)mek; *~al* yenile(n)me

renounce [ri'nauns] v/t terketmek; vazgeçmek -den; reddetmek -i

renovate ['renuveyt] v/t yenileştirmek

renown [ri'naun] şöhret, ün; *~ed* ünlü

rent¹ [rent] s. **rend**; yırtık, yarık

rent² n. kira; v/t kiralamak

reorganize ['rî'ôgınayz] v/t düzenlemek

repair [ri'pâı] n. tamir, onarım; v/t tamir etm., onarmak; **in good** ~ iyi halde; ~ **shop** tamir evi

reparation [repı'reyşın] tazminat pl.

repartee [repâ'tî] hazırcevap sözlerle konuşma

repatriation ['rîpâtri'ey-şın] kendi vatanına dönme

repay [ri'pey] v/t ödemek; -in karşılığını vermek

repeat [ri'pît] v/t tekrarlamak

repel [ri'pel] v/t püskürtmek, defetmek; *~lent* uzaklaştırıcı

repent [ri'pent] v/t pişman olm. -e; *~ance* pişmanlık

repetition [repi'tişın] tekrarla(n)ma

replace [ri'pleys] v/t tekrar yerine koymak; ödemek; -in yerini almak; *~ment* yerine geçen şey

replenish [ri'pleniş] v/t tekrar doldurmak

reply [ri'play] n. cevap, karşılık; v/i cevap vermek (**to** -e)

report [ri'pôt] n. rapor; not karnesi; söylenti; patlama sesi; v/t anlatmak; bildirmek; söylemek; *~er* muhabir, muhbir

repose [ri'piuz] n. rahat, istirahat; v/t yatırmak; v/i yatmak; dayanmak (**on** -e)

represent [repri'zent] v/t göstermek; temsil etm.; *~ation* temsil; göster(il)-me; itiraz; *~ative* temsil eden, nümune olan; pol. milletvekili; **House of** 2a-tives Am. Temsilciler Meclisi

repress [ri'pres] v/t bastırmak

reprieve [ri'prîv] geçici olarak erteleme

reprimand ['reprimând] n. azar, paylama; v/t azarlamak

reprint ['rî'print] yeni baskı

reproach [ri'priuç] n. ayıp

(-lama); v/t azarlamak; **~ful** sitem dolu

reproduc|e [ri:prɪˈdjūs] v/t kopya etm.; tekrar meydana getirmek; v/i çoğalmak, üremek; **~tion** [ˈ~ˈdakşın] üreme; kopya

reproof [ri'pruuf] azar, paylama

reprove [ri'pruuv] v/t ayıplamak

reptile ['reptayl] sürüngen; yılan

republic [ri'pablik] cumhuriyet; **~an** cumhuriyete ait; cumhuriyetçi

repudiate [ri'pyūdieyt] v/t tanımamak

repugnan|ce [ri'pagnıns] nefret, tiksinme; **~t** iğrenç, çirkin

repuls|e [ri'pals] n. kovma; ret; v/t püskürtmek, kovmak; **~ive** iğrenç

reput|able ['repyutbl] saygıdeğer; **~ation** ün, şöhret; **~e** [ri'pyût] ad, şöhret

request [ri'kwest] n. dilek; rica; v/t rica etm., dilemek **(from** -den); **by ~ on ~** istenildiği zaman; **~ stop** ihtiyarî durak

require [ri'kwayı] v/t istemek; muhtaç olm. -e; **~ment** gerek, ihtiyaç

requisite ['rekwizit] gerekli, elzem (şey)

requite [ri'kwayt] v/t mükâfatlandırmak; -in karşılığını vermek

rescue ['reskyû] n. kurtuluş, kurtarış; v/t kurtarmak

research [ri'söç] araştırma; **~er** araştırıcı

resembl|ance [ri'zemblıns] benzeyiş; **~e** v/t andırmak; benzemek -e

resent [ri'zent] v/t gücenmek -e; **~ful** gücenik; **~ment** gücenme

reserv|ation [rezı'veyşın] yer ayırtma, rezervasyon; jur. ihtiraz kaydı; pol. yerlilere ayrılmış bölge; **~e** [ri'zöv] n. yedek olarak saklanan şey; ağız sıkılığı; v/t saklamak; ayırtmak; hakkını muhafaza etm.; **~ed** ağzı sıkı; mahfuz; **~oir** ['~vwâ] su haznesi; havza

reside [ri'zayd] v/i oturmak, ikamet etm.; **~nce** ['rezidıns] ikamet(gâh); **~nce permit** ikamet tezkeresi; **~nt** oturan, sakin

residue ['rezidyû] artık

resign [ri'zayn] v/t bırakmak; vazgeçmek -den; **~ oneself to** baş eğmek -e; **~ation** [rezig'neyşın] istifa, çekilme; uysallık; **~ed** baş eğmiş

resin ['rezin] sakız, reçine

resist [ri'zist] v/t karşı durmak -e; dayanmak -e; **~ance** direniş; phys. direniş, rezistans; **~ant** direnen **(to** -e)

resolut|e ['rezıluut] kararlı, cesur; **~ion** kararlılık; pol. önerge

resolve [ri'zolv] v/t çözmek; kararlaştırmak **(to** inf. -i);

v/i tasarlamak, kararlaştırmak (**on, upon** -*i*)

resonance ['reznıns] yankılama

resort [ri'zôt] *n.* dinlenme yeri; barınak; *v/i* sık sık gitmek (**to** -*e*); başvurmak (-*e*)

resound [ri'zaund] *v/i* çınlamak

resource [ri'sôs] kaynak, çare; *pl.* imkânlar, olanaklar; ~ful becerikli

respect [ris'pekt] *n.* münasebet; saygı, itibar; *v/t* saygı göstermek -*e*; riayet etm. -*e*; **in** ~ **to, with** ~ **to** -*e* gelince; ~able namuslu; epeyce; ~ful saygılı; ~ing bakımından, -*e* gelince; ~ive ayrı ayrı, kendisinin olan; ~ively sırası ile

respiration [respı'reyşın] nefes (alma); soluk

respite ['respayt] mühlet; geçici erteleme

resplendent [ris'plendınt] parlak, göz alıcı

respond [ris'pond] *v/i* cevap vermek (**to** -*e*); ~ent *jur.* savunan

respons|e [ris'pons] cevap; ~ibility sorumluluk; ~ible sorumlu, mesul (**for** -*den*, **to** -*e*)

rest[1] [rest] *v/i* dinlenmek; yatmak; oturmak; dayanmak (**on, upon** -*e*); *v/t* dayamak, koymak (**on** -*e*); *n.* rahat; istirahat; dayanak

rest[2] geri kalan, artan

restaurant ['restırôn] restoran, lokanta

rest|ful rahat (verici); ~ **house** dinlenme evi; ~less yerinde durmaz; uykusuz

restor|ation [restı'reyşın] yenileme; eski haline getirme; restore etme; ~e [ris'tô] *v/t* geri vermek; eski haline koymak; restore etm.; ~e **to health** iyileştirmek

restrain [ris'treyn] *v/t* zapt tutmak; sınırlamak; ~t sınırlılık; çekinme

restrict [ris'trikt] *v/t* kısıtlamak, sınırlamak; ~ion sınırlama, kısıtlama

result [ri'zalt] *n.* sonuç; son; *v/i* meydana gelmek (**from** -*den*); sonuçlanmak (**in** -*i*)

resum|e [ri'zyûm] *v/t* yeniden başlamak -*e*; geri almak -*i*; ~ption [~'zampşın] yeniden başlama

resurrection [rezı'rekşın] yeniden diril(t)me

retail ['rîteyl] *n. ec.* perakende satış; [~'teyl] *v/t* perakende olarak satmak; ~er [~'t-] perakendeci

retain [ri'teyn] *v/t* alıkoymak; tutmak

retaliat|e [ri'tälieyt] *v/t* dengiyle karşılamak; *v/i* intikam almak (**upon** -*den*); ~ion misilleme

retard [ri'tâd] *v/t* geciktirmek [latmak

retell ['rî'tel] *v/t* tekrar an-]

retention [ri'tenşın] alıkoyma

retinue ['retinyû] maiyet, heyet

retire [ri'tayı] v/i çekilmek; emekliye ayrılmak; v/t geri çekmek; **~d** emekli; münzevi; **~ment** emeklilik; inziva

retort [ri'tôt] sert cevap vermek

retrace [ri'treys] v/t -*in izini* takip ederek kaynağına gitmek

retract [ri'träkt] v/t geri çekmek; geri almak

retreat [ri'trît] v/i geri, çekilmek; n. geri çek(il)me

retribution [retri'byûşın] karşılıkta bulunma; ceza

retrieve [ri'trîv] v/t tekrar ele geçirmek; bulup getirmek

retrospect ['retruspekt] geçmişe bakış; **~ive** geçmişi hatırlayan; önceyi kapsayan

return [ri'tön] n. geri dönüş; tekrar olma; resmî rapor; ec. kazanç, kâr; v/i geri dönmek; cevap vermek; v/t geri vermek; geri göndermek; **by ~** hemen; **in ~** karşılık olarak; **~ match** revanş maçı; **~ ticket** gidiş dönüş bileti; Am. dönüş bileti

reunion [ri'yûnyın] yine birleşme

revaluation [rivälyu'eyşın] yeniden değerlendirme

reveal [ri'vîl] v/t açığa vurmak; göstermek

revel ['revl] v/i eğlenmek;

mest olm. (**in** -*de*); n. şenlik, eğlenti

revelation [revi'leyşın] açığa vurma; rel. ilham, vahiy

revenge [ri'venc] n. öç, intikam; revanş; intikam almak (**on** -*den*); **~ful** kinci

revenue ['revinyû] gelir; **~ office** maliye tahsil şubesi

revere [ri'vîı] v/t saymak; saygı göstermek -*e*; **~nce** ['rivırıns] n. saygı, hürmet; v/t yüceltmek; saygı göstermek -*e*; **~nd** ['rivırınd] muhterem (*papazın lakabı*)

reverse [ri'vös] n. ters; arka taraf; aksilik; adj. ters; aksi; v/t tersine çevirmek; jur. iptal etm.; **~ gear** geri vites; **~ side** ters taraf

review [ri'vyû] n. resmî teftiş; geçit töreni; eleştiri; dergi; v/t yeniden incelemek; teftiş etm.; eleştirmek; tekrar gözden geçirmek; **~er** eleştirici

revise [ri'vayz] v/t tekrar gözden geçirip düzeltmek; değiştirmek; **~ion** [~ijın] düzeltme, tashih

reviv|al [ri'vayvıl] yeniden canlanma; **~e** v/t canlandırmak; v/i yeniden canlanmak

revocation [revı'keyşın] geri alınma, iptal

revoke [ri'vıuk] v/t geri almak, iptal etm.

revolt [ri'vıult] v/i ayaklanmak; fig. tiksinmek (**against**, **at** -*den*); n. isyan, ayaklanma

revolution [revi'luuşın]
dönme, devir; *pol.* devrim,
inkılâp; ihtilâl; **~ary** dev-
rimci; ihtilâlci; **~ize** *v/t*
tamamen değiştirmek

revolve [ri'volv] *v/i* dönmek; **~r** revolver, altıpatlar

reward [ri'wôd] *n.* mükâfat,
ödül; *v/t* mükâfatlandırmak

rheumati|c [ruu'mätik] ro-
matizmalı; **~sm** ['~mıti-
zım] romatizma

rhubarb ['ruubâb] *bot.* ravent

rhyme [raym] *n.* kafiye;
şiir; *v/t* kafiyeli olarak yazmak

rhythm ['ridhım] ritim;
vezin; **~ic(al)** ahenkli,
ritmik

rib [rib] *an.* kaburga kemiği

ribbon ['ribın] kurdele;
şerit

rice [rays] *bot.* pirinç

rich [riç] zengin; verimli,
bol; dolgun (*ses*); **the ~** *pl.*
zenginler; **~es** ['~iz] *pl.*
zenginlik, servet *sg.*; **~ness**
zenginlik

rickets ['rikits] *pl. med.* ra-
şitizm *sg.*

rid [rid] *v/t* kurtarmak; **get
~** başından atmak (**of** *-i*)

ridden ['ridn] *s.* **ride**

riddle¹ ['ridl] bilmece, bulmaca

riddle² kalbur

ride [rayd] *n.* binme; gezinti; *v/t* binmek **~e**; sürmek
-i; **~ out** *fig.* atlatmak; **~r**
atlı, binici

ridge [riç] sırt; çatı sırtı

ridicul|e ['ridikyûl] *n.* alay;
v/t alay etm. (*so.* ile); **~ous**
['~dikyulıs] gülünç

rifle ['rayfl] tüfek

rift [rift] yarık, açıklık

right [rayt] *n.* sağ (taraf);
hak; yetki; *adj.* doğru; sahih; haklı; insaflı; *adv.*
hemen; doğruca; **all ~** iyi;
intj. peki; **be ~** haklı olm.;
put ~, set ~ *v/t* düzeltmek;
turn ~ *v/i* sağa dönmek; **~
angle** dik açı; **~ away** hemen; **~ of way** önden
geçme hakkı; **~eous** dürüst; **~ful** haklı

rig|id ['ricid] eğilmez, sert;
~orous ['~ırıs] sert, şiddetli; **~o(u)r** sertlik, şiddet

rim [rim] kenar; jant

rind [raynd] kabuk

ring¹ [riŋ] yüzük, halka;
çember; ring

ring² *n.* zil sesi, çan sesi;
çınlama; *v/i* çalmak, çınlamak; *v/t* çalmak; **~ up**
telefon etm. *-e*; **~leader**
elebaşı

rink [riŋk] patinaj alanı

rinse [rins] *v/t* çalka(la)mak

riot ['rayıt] *n.* kargaşalık,
ayaklanma; *v/i* kargaşalık
yapmak; **~ous** gürültülü

rip [rip] *n.* yarık; sökük
dikiş; *v/t* sökmek; yarmak

ripe [rayp] olgun(laşmış);
yetişmiş; **~n** *v/i* olgunlaş-
mak, *v/t* olgunlaştırmak

ripple ['ripl] *n.* ufacık dalga; *v/i* hafifçe dalgalanmak

rise [rayz] *n.* yükseliş, artış;

risen

çıkış; v/i kalkmak, yüksel-mek, artmak; kabarmak; ayaklanmak; ~n ['rizn] f. **rise**

rising ['rayziŋ] yükselen; yükseliş; ayaklanma

risk [risk] n. tehlike, riziko; v/t tehlikeye koymak, göze almak; ~y tehlikeli

rite [rayt] rel. ayin, tören

rival ['rayvıl] n. rakip; v/t rekabet etm., çekişmek (so. ile); ~ry rekabet

river ['rivı] nehir, ırmak

rivet ['rivit] n. perçin; v/t perçinlemek

rivulet ['rivyulit] dere, çay

road [rıud] yol, şose; ~ **sign** trafik işareti [zinmek]

roam [rıum] dolaşmak, ge-J

roar [rô] n. gürleme, gümbürtü; v/i gürlemek, gümbürdemek

roast [rıust] adj. kızarmış; v/t kızartmak; kavurmak; ~ **beef** rozbif

rob [rob] v/t soymak; çalmak; ~**ber** hırsız, haydut; ~**bery** hırsızlık; soyma

robe [rıub] rop; kaftan, üstlük giysi

robin (**redbreast**) ['robin] zo. kızıl gerdan (kuşu)

robot ['rıubot] makine adam, robot

robust [rıu'bast] dinç, kuvvetli

rock[1] [rok] kaya

rock[2] v/i sallanmak, sarsılmak; v/t sallamak

rocket ['rokit] roket; havaî fişek

rocking-chair salıncaklı koltuk

rocky ['roki] kayalık

rod [rod] çubuk, değnek

rode [rıud] s. **ride**

rodent ['rıudınt] zo. kemirgen

roe[1] [rıu] balık yumurtası

roe[2] (**deer**) karaca

rogu|**e** [rıug] çapkın; dolandırıcı; ~**ish** çapkın; kurnaz

rôle, role [rıul] rol

roll [rıul] n. makara, silindir; tomar; sicil, kayıt; küçük ekmek; v/t yuvarlamak, tekerlemek; sarmak; v/i yuvarlanmak; dalgalanmak; ~ **film** makaralı film; ~ **up** v/t sarmak, sıvamak; ~**call** yoklama; ~**er** silindir; ~**er-skate** tekerlekli paten; ~**ing-mill** haddehane

Roman ['rıumın] Romalı

roman|**ce** [rıu'mäns] macera; aşk macerası; macera romanı; ~**tic** romantik

Rome [rıum] Roma

romp [romp] v/i gürültü ile oynamak; ~**er(s** pl.) çocuk tulumu

roof [ruuf] n. dam, çatı; v/t çatı ile örtmek

room [ruum] yer; oda; **make** ~ yer açmak (**for** -e); ~**y** geniş

rooster ['ruustı] horoz

root [ruut] n. kök; v/t kökleştirmek; v/i köklemek; ~ **out** v/t kökünden sökmek

rope [rıup] n. halat; ip; v/t

halatla bağlamak; ~ **off** ip çevirerek sınırlamak

ros|ary ['ruzıri] tesbih; **~e¹** [ruz] gül

rose² s. **rise**

rosy ['ruzi] gül gibi; *fig.* ümit verici

rot [rot] *n.* çürüme; *v/i* çürümek; *v/t* çürütmek

rota|ry ['rutıri] dönen, dönel; **~te** [~'teyt] *v/i* dönmek; *v/t* döndürmek; **~tion** dönme

rotor ['rutı] rotor; helikopter pervanesi

rotten ['rotn] çürük, bozuk

rotund [ru'tand] yuvarlak; dolgun (*ses*)

rough [raf] pürüzlü; kaba; sert; ~ **copy** taslak, müsvedde; **~ness** kabalık, sertlik

round [raund] *adj.* yuvarlak, toparlak; *prp. -in* etrafın(d)a; *n.* parti; devriye; dönem; ravnt; *v/t* yuvarlak hale getirmek; dönmek *-den*; *v/i* yuvarlaklaşmak; ~ **trip** gidiş dönüş, tur; ~ **up** *v/t* bir araya toplamak; **~about** dolambaçlı; dolaşık; **~table conference** yuvarlak masa konferansı

rouse [rauz] *v/t* uyandırmak, canlandırmak; *v/i* uyanmak

rout|e [ruut] yol; rota; **~ine** [~'tin] usul, iş programı

rove [ruuv] dolaşmak, gezinmek

row¹ [rau] kavga, patırtı

row² [ruu] sıra, dizi

row³ [ruu] *v/i* kürek çekmek; *v/t* kürek çekerek götürmek

rowdy ['raudi] külhanbeyi

rowing-boat ['ruuiŋ -] kayık, sandal

royal ['royıl] kırala ait; şahane; **~ty** hükümdarlık, kırallık; *ec.* kâr hissesi

rub [rab] *v/t* sürtmek, ovmak; *n.* ovalama, sürt(ün)me; ~ **in** ovarak yedirmek; ~ **out** silmek

rubber ['rabı] lastik, kauçuk; silgi

rubbish ['rabiş] süprüntü, çöp; saçma

rubble ['rabl] moloz

ruby ['ruubi] yakut, lâl

rucksack ['ruksäk] sırt çantası

rudder ['radı] dümen

ruddy ['radi] kırmızı yanaklı

rude [ruud] kaba; terbiyesiz; **~ness** kabalık

ruffian ['rafyın] kavgacı, gaddar

ruffle ['rafl] *v/t* buruşturmak; rahatsız etm.; *n.* kırma, farbala

rug [rag] halı, kilim; **~ged** ['~id] engebeli; sert

ruin [ruin] *n.* harabe; yıkım; perişanlık; *v/t* yıkmak, tahrip etm.; perişan etm.; **~ous** yıkıcı; yıkık

rul|e [ruul] *n.* kural; usul; yönetim; cetvel; *v/t* idare etm., yönetmek; *v/i* saltanat sürmek; ~ **out** *v/t* çıkarmak, silmek; **~er** cetvel;

hükümdar; **~ing** yönetim; *jur.* yargı; çizme, çizgi
rum [ram] rom
Rumania [ru'meynyı] Romanya; **~n** Romanyalı; Romen(ce)
rumble ['rambl] *n.* gümbürtü; *v/i* gümbürdemek
ruminant ['ruuminınt] *zo.* gevişgetiren
rummage ['ramic] *v/t* araştırmak
rumo(u)r ['ruumı] şayia, söylenti
run [ran] *v/i* koşmak; akmak; gitmek; *tech.* işlemek, çalışmak; adaylığını koymak (**for** için); *v/t* işletmek; yönetmek; sürmek; *n.* koşu; rağbet; sıra; süre
in the long ~ eninde sonunda; **~ across** rast gelmek *-e*; **~ down** *v/i* bitmek; *v/t* kötülemek; **~ into** rast gelmek, çarpmak *-e*; **~ out** bitmek, tükenmek; **~ short of** *sth. -si* azalmak, tükenmek; **~ up to** erişmek *-e*
rung[1] [ran] *s.* ring
rung[2] portatif merdiven basamağı

runner ['ranı] koşucu; kızak ayağı; **~-up** ikinciliği kazanan
running koşu; sürekli; akan; **~-board** marşpiye
runway ['ranwey] pist
rupture ['rapçı] kır(ıl)ma; kesilme
rural ['ruırıl] köye ait; tarımsal
rush [raş] *n.* namle, saldırış; sıkışıklık; *v/i* koşmak; saldırmak (**at** *-e*); *v/t* acele ettirmek; püskürtmek
Russia ['raşı] Rusya; **~n** Rus(yalı); Rusça
rust [rast] *n.* pas; *v/i* paslanmak
rustic ['rastik] köye ait; kaba; köylü
rustle ['rasl] *n.* hışırtı; *v/i* hışırdamak; *v/t* hışırdatmak
rusty ['rasti] paslı
rut[1] [rat] *n.* kösnüme
rut[2] tekerlek izi
ruthless ['ruuthlis] merhametsiz
rutty ['rati] tekerlek izleriyle dolu
rye [ray] *bot.* çavdar

S

sable ['seybl] *zo.* samur
sabotage ['sabıtâj] *n.* sabotaj; *v/t* baltalamak
sabre ['seybı] kılıç
sack [säk] *n.* çuval, torba; yağma; *v/t* yağma etm.; işinden çıkarmak
sacr|ament ['säkrımınt]

rel. Hıristiyanlıkta kutsal ayin; **~ed** ['seykrid] kutsî, kutsal; **~ifice** ['säkrifays] *n.* kurban; fedakârlık; *v/t* kurban etm.; feda etm.
sad [säd] kederli, üzgün; acınacak; **~den** *v/i* acınmak; *v/t* kederlendirmek

377   sardine

saddle ['sädl] n. eyer; sırt; v/t eyerlemek; ~r saraç
sadness ['sädnis] keder, üzgünlük
safe [seyf] emin (from -den); sağlam; kasa; ~guard n. koruma; v/t korumak
safety ['seyfti] güvenlik; emniyet; ~belt emniyet kemeri; ~pin çengelli iğne
saffron ['säfrın] bot. safran
sag [säg] v/i sarkmak; çökmek
sagacity [sı'gäsiti] akıllılık
said [sed] s. say
sail [seyl] n. yelken; naut. yola çıkmak; ~ing-ship yelkenli; ~or gemici, denizci
saint [seynt] rel. aziz, evliya
sake [seyk]: for the ~ of -in hatırı için
salad ['säld] salata
salary ['sälıri] maaş, aylık
sale [seyl] satış; for ~ satılık; ~sman satıcı; ~s-woman satıcı kadın
salient ['seylyınt] göze çarpan
saliva [sı'layvı] salya, tükürük
sallow ['sälu] soluk yüzlü
sally ['säli] v/i dışarı fırlamak
salmon ['sämın] som balığı
saloon [sı'luun] salon; bar; Am. meyhane
salt [sôlt] n. tuz; v/t tuzlamak; ~cellar tuzluk; ~y tuzlu
salutation [sälyu'teyşın]

selâm (verme); ~e [sı'luut] v/t selâmlamak; n. selâm
salvage ['sälvic] tahlisiye (ücreti)
salvation [säl'veyşın] kurtuluş, kurtarma; 2 Army selâmet ordusu
salve [sâv] merhem
same [seym] aynı, tıpkı; all the ~ bununla beraber
sample ['sâmpl] örnek, numune; mostra
sanatorium [sänı'tôrium] sanatoryum
sanct|ify ['sänktifay] v/t kutsallaştırmak; ~ion n. tasdik, tasvip; v/t uygun bulmak; ~uary ['~tyuıri] tapınak; sığınak
sand [sänd] kum
sandal ['sändl] çarık, sandal
sandwich ['sänwic] sandviç; ~man sırtında ve göğsünde reklam yaftaları dolaştıran adam
sandy ['sändi] kumlu; kumsal
sane [seyn] aklı başında, akıllı; makul
sang [säŋ] s. sing
sanit|ary ['sänitri] sıhhî; ~ation hıfzıssıhha; sağlık işleri pl.; sıhhî tertibat; ~y akıl sıhhati
sank [säŋk] s. sink
Santa Claus [säntı'klôz] Noel baba
sap [säp] bot. özsu, usare
sapling ['säpliŋ] fidan
sarcasm ['säkäzım] dokunaklı alay
sardine [sâ'dîn] sardalya

sash [säş] kuşak; ~ **window** sürme pencere

Satan ['seytın] *rel.* İblis, şeytan

satchel [säçıl] okul çantası

satellite ['sätılayt] *astr.*, *pol.* peyk

satin ['sätin] saten, atlas

satir|e ['sätayı] hiciv, yergi; ~**ical** [sı'tirikıl] hicivli

satis|faction [sätis'fäkşın] hoşnutluk; tarziye; tazmin; ~**factory** tatmin edici; memnunluk verici; ~**fy** ['~fay] *v/t* memnun etm.; tatmin etm.; tazmin etm.

Saturday ['sätudi] cumartesi

sauce [sôs] salça; ~**r** fincan tabağı; ~**pan** uzun saplı tencere

saucy ['sôsi] arsız, saygısız

saunter ['sôntı] gezinmek

sausage ['sosic] sucuk, salam; sosis

savage ['sävic] vahşî, yabani; yırtıcı

sav|e [seyv] *v/t* kurtarmak; biriktirmek, tasarruf etm.; *prp. -den* başka; ~**ings** *pl.* biriktirilen paralar

savio(u)r ['seyvyı] kurtarıcı, halâskâr; 2 Hazreti İsa

savo(u)r ['seyvı] *n.* tat, lezzet, çeşni; *v/i* andırmak (**of** *-i*); ~**y** lezzetli

saw[1] [sô] *s.* **see**

saw[2] *n.* testere, bıçkı; *v/t* testere ile kesmek; ~**dust** bıçkı tozu; ~**mill** kereste fabrikası; ~**n** *s.* **saw**[2]

Saxon ['säksn] Sakson(yalı)

say [sey] *v/t* söylemek, demek; beyan etm.; **he is said to** *inf.* onun -*diği* söyleniyor; **that is to** ~ yani; **have a** ~ **in** -*de* söz sahibi olm.; ~**ing** söz; atasözü; **it goes without** ~**ing** kendisinden anlaşılır

scab [skäb] yara kabuğu

scaffold ['skäfıld] yapı iskelesi

scald [skôld] *v/t* kaynar su ile haşlamak; kaynatmak

scale[1] [skeyl] *n.* balık pulu; *v/t* pullarını çıkarmak

scale[2] terazi gözü; ölçek; ıskala; ölçü; derece

scalp [skälp] *n.* kafatasını kaplayan deri; *v/t -in* başının derisini yüzmek

scan [skän] *v/t* incelemek; gözden geçirmek

scandal ['skändl] rezalet; dedikodu; ~**ous** ['~dılıs] rezil, iftiralı

Scandinavia [skändi'neyvyı] Skandinavya; ~**n** Skandinav

scant (**y**) ['skänt(i)] az, kıt, dar

scapegoat ['skeypgıut] başkalarının suçlarını yüklenen kimse

scar [skaa] *n.* yara izi; *v/t -in* üstünde yara izi bırakmak

scarce [skäıs] az bulunur, nadir, seyrek; kıt; ~**ely** *adv.* ancak, hemen hemen hiç; ~**ity** azlık kıtlık

scare [skäı] *v/t* korkutmak, ürkütmek; **be** ~**d** korkmak, ürkmek (**of** -*den*); ⁀**crow** bostan korkuluğu

scarf [skaaf] boyun atkısı; eşarp

scarlet ['skaalit] al, kırmızı; ⁀ **fever** *med.* kızıl hastalığı

scarred [skaad] yara izi olan

scathing ['skeydhiŋ] sert; yakıcı

scatter ['skätı] *v/t* saçmak, dağıtmak; *v/i* dağılmak, yayılmak

scavenger ['skävıncı] çöpçü

scene [sîn] sahne; dekor; manzara; ⁀**ry** manzara, dekor

scent [sent] *n.* güzel koku; iz; *v/t* -*in* kokusunu almak; koku ile doldurmak -*i*

sceptic ['skeptik] *n.*, ⁀**al** *adj.* şüpheci, septik

schedule ['şedyûl] *n.* liste, program; *Am.* ['skecûl] tarife; *v/t* -*in* listesini yapmak; tarifeye geçirmek -*i*

scheme [skîm] *n.* plan, proje, tasarı; entrika; *v/t* tasarlamak

scholar ['skolı] âlim, bilgin; ⁀**ship** burs

school [skuul] *n.* okul; mezhep; balık sürüsü; *v/t* alıştırmak; ⁀**fellow** okul arkadaşı; ⁀**ing** terbiye; ⁀**master** öğretmen; ⁀**mate** *s.* ⁀**fellow**; ⁀**mistress** kadın öğretmen

scien|ce ['sayıns] ilim, bilgi, bilim; fen; ⁀**tific** [⁀'tifik] ilmî; bilimsel, fennî; ⁀**tist** ilim adamı; fen adamı

scissors ['sizız] *pl.* makas *sg.*

scoff [skof] alay etm. (**at** ile)

scold [skuld] *v/t* azarlamak; paylamak

scoop [skuup] *n.* kepçe; *v/t* kepçe ile çıkarmak

scooter ['skuutı] trotinet; küçük motosiklet

scope [skıup] saha, alan; faaliyet alanı

scorch [skôç] *v/t* kavurmak, yakmak

score [skô] *n.* sıyrık, kertik; hesap; puvan sayısı; yirmi; *mus.* partisyon; *v/t* çentmek; hesap etm.; *puvanları* saymak; *puvan* kazanmak

scorn [skôn] *n.* küçümseme; tahkir; *v/t* küçümsemek; ⁀**ful** tahkir edici

scorpion ['skôpyın] *zo.* akrep

Scot [skot] İskoçyalı

Scotch [skoç] İskoçya ile ilgili; ⁀**man** İskoçyalı

Scotland ['skotlınd] İskoçya; ⁀ **Yard** Londra Emniyet Müdürlüğü

Scots|man İskoçyalı; ⁀**woman** İskoçyalı kadın

scoundrel ['skaundrıl] kötü adam, herif

scour ['skauı] *v/t* ovalayarak temizlemek

scout [skaut] *n.* izci; *v/t* keşfetmek, taramak

scowl [skaul] *v/i* kaşlarını çatıp bakmak; *n.* tehditkâr bakış

scrabble ['skräbl] v/t sıyırmak; acele ile yazmak

scramble ['skrämbl] v/t tırmanmak -e; karıştırmak -i; ~d eggs pl. karıştırılıp yağda pişirilmiş yumurtalar

scrap [skräp] parça; döküntü, kırıntı

scrape [skreyp] n. kazıma, sıyırma; kazımak, sıyırmak; ~ away, ~ off kazıyarak silmek

scrap-iron hurda demir

scratch [skräç] n. çizik, sıyrık; v/t kaşımak, tırnaklamak

scrawl [skrôl] v/t acele ile yazmak; n. dikkatsiz yazı

scream [skrîm] n. feryat, çığlık; v/i feryat etm.

screech [skrîç] s. scream

screen [skrîn] n. paravana, bölme; perde; v/t gizlemek, korumak; elemek, kalburdan geçirmek

screw [skruu] n. vida; pervane; v/t vidalamak; ~driver tornavida

scribble ['skribl] n. dikkatsiz yazı; v/t dikkatsiz yazmak

script [skript] yazı; thea. senaryo; ~ure ['~pçı] rel. Kutsal Kitap

scroll [skruul] tomar

scrub [skrab] n. çalılık, fundalık; v/t fırçalıyarak yıkamak

scrup|le ['skruupl] vicdan; tereddüt; endişe; ~ulous ['~pyulıs] dikkatli, titiz

scrutin|ize ['skruutinayz] v/t incelemek; ~y tetkik, inceleme

scuffle ['skafl] v/i çekişmek, dövüşmek

sculpt|or ['skalptı] heykeltıraş; ~ure ['~çı] n. heykeltıraşlık; heykel; v/t oymak, hakketmek

scum [skam] pis köpük; fig. ayaktakımı

scurf [sköf] kepek, konak

scurvy ['skövi] med. iskorbüt

scuttle ['skatl] kömür kovası

scythe [saydh] tırpan

sea [sî] deniz; yüksek dalga; **at** ~ denizde, gemide; ~faring denizcilikle uğraşan; ~gull zo. martı

seal[1] [sîl] zo. fok

seal[2] n. mühür; v/t mühürlemek; kapatmak, tıkamak

seam [sîm] dikiş (yeri)

seaman ['sîmın] denizci

seamstress ['semstris] dikişçi kadın

sea|plane deniz uçağı; ~port liman

search [söç] n. arama, araştırma; v/t aramak, araştırmak, yoklamak; ~light ışıldak, projector

sea|shore sahil; ~sick deniz tutmuş; ~side sahil

season ['sîzn] n. mevsim; zaman; v/t çeşnilendirmek, kurutmak; alıştırmak; v/i kurumak; **in** ~ zamanında, kullanılabilir; ~able tam vaktinde olan, uygun; ~al mevsimlik; **~ing** çeşni veren şey

seat [sīt] *n.* oturulacak yer, iskemle, sandalya; *thea.* koltuk; merkez; *v/t* oturtmak; **take a ~** oturmak; **be ~ed!** oturunuz!; **~-belt** emniyet kemeri

seaweed yosun

secession [si'seşın] ayrılma

seclu|de [si'kluud] *v/t* ayırmak, tecrit etm.; **~sion** [~jın] inziva

second ['sekınd] saniye; ikinci; **~ary** ikinci derecede, ikincil; **~ary school** ortaokul, lise; **~class** ikinci sınıf; **~hand** kullanılmış, elden düşme; **~rate** ikinci derecede

secre|cy ['sikrisi] gizlilik, ketumiyet; **~t** gizli, mahrem; sır, gizli şey

secretary ['sekrıtri] sekreter, kâtip; **2 of State** *Am.* Dışişleri Bakanı

secret|e [si'krīt] *v/t med.* salgılamak, ifraz etm.; **~ion** salgı, ifraz

sect [sekt] *rel.* mezhep; **~ion** ['~kşın] kesme, kesilmiş şey; kısım, parça; bölge; şube; *math.* kesit; **~or** bölge

secular ['sekyulı] layik; dünyevî

secur|e [si'kyuı] *adj.* emin, emniyetli, sağlam; *v/t* sağlamak; bağlamak; elde etm.; **~ity** emniyet, güven; rehin; *pl. ec.* tahviller, senetler

sedan [si'dän] kapalı otomobil; **~ (chair)** sedye

sedative ['seditiv] teskin edici, yatıştırıcı (ilâç)

sediment ['sedimınt] tortu, telve

sedition [si'dişın] ayaklanma(ya teşvik)

seduc|e [si'dyûs] *v/t* baştan çıkarmak, ayartmak; **~tive** [~'daktiv] çekici

see [si] *v/t* görmek; anlamak, kavramak; bakmak -*e*; **~ home** eve götürmek; **~ off** uğurlamak; **~ to** bakmak -*e* meşgul olm. ile

seed [sīd] tohum

seek [sīk] *v/t*, *v/i* (**after, for**) aramak -*i*

seem [sīm] görünmek, gelmek (**like** gibi); **~ing** görünüşte; **~ly** yakışır, münasip

seen [sīn] *s.* **see**

seep [sīp] *v/i* sızmak

seesaw ['sîsô] tahterevalli

segment ['segmınt] parça, kısım

segregat|e ['segrigeyt] *v/t* ayırmak; *~ion* ayırma

seismic(al) ['sayzmik(ıl)] depremsel

seiz|e [sīz] *v/t* yakalamak, tutmak; kavramak; müsadere etm.; **~ure** ['sîjı] müsadere, el koyma

seldom ['seldım] nadiren, seyrek

select [si'lekt] *adj.* seçme, güzide; *v/t* seçmek; **~ion** seçme (şeyler *pl.*)

self [self] zat, kişi; kendi;

kendi kendine; ~-com-
mand kendini tutma, nef-
sini yenme; ~-confidence
kendine güven; ~-con-
scious utangaç, sıkılgan;
~-control kendini yenme;
~-defence nefsini koruma;
~-evident aşikâr, belli; ~-
-government özerklik,
muhtariyet; ~ish bencil,
hodbin; ~-made kendini
yetiştirmiş; ~possession
kendine hâkim olma; ~-
-reliant kendine güvenir;
~-respect onur, öz saygısı;
~-service selfservis

sell [sel] v/t satmak; v/i
satılmak; ~ out bütün stoku
satmak; ~er satıcı

semblance ['semblıns] benzerlik

sem|ester [si'mestı] sö-
mestr; ~icolon ['semi'kiu-
lın] noktalı virgül

Semitic [si'mitik] Samî

senat|e ['senit] senato; ~or
['~ıtı] senatör

send [send] v/t yollamak,
göndermek; ~ for çağır-
mak, getirtmek -i; ~er
gönderen

senior ['sinyı] yaşça büyük;
kıdemli

sensation [sen'seyşın] his,
duygu; heyecan uyandıran
olay .

sense [sens] n. mana; his,
duyu; anlayış; akıl; v/t sezmek; anlamak; ~less bay-
gın; duygusuz; manasız

sensi|bility [sensi'biliti]
duyarlık; seziş inceliği;

~ble hissedilir; aklı başında; be ~ble of sezmek -i;
~tive hassas, içli, duygulu
sensual ['sensyuıl] şehvanî
sent [sent] s. send
sentence ['sentıns] n. gr.
cümle; jur. hüküm, karar;
v/t mahkûm etm.
sentiment ['sentimınt] his,
duygu; düşünce; ~al
['~mentl] hisli, duygusal,
içli
sentry ['sentri] nöbetçi
separa|ble ['sepırıbl] ayrı-
labilir; ~te ['~eyt] adj. ayrı;
v/t ayırmak; v/i ayrılmak;
~tion ayırma, ayrılma
September [sep'tembı] ey-
lül
septic ['septik] med. bulaşık, mikroplu
sepulchre, Am. ~er ['se-
pılkı] kabir, mezar
seque|l ['sikwıl] devam;
sonuç; ~nce sıra; ardıllık
seren|ade [seri'neyd] mus.
serenat; ~e [si'rin] sakin;
açık
serf [söf] serf, köle
sergeant ['sâcınt] mil. çavuş; polis komiseri mua-
vini
seri|al ['sirııl] seri halinde
olan; tefrika; ~es ['~rîz]
sg., a. pl. sıra, seri
serious ['siırıs] ciddî
sermon ['sömın] vaız
serpent ['söpınt] yılan
serv|ant ['sövınt] hizmetçi,
uşak; ~e v/t hizmet etm.
-e; sofraya koymak -i; yerine getirmek -i; yaramak

-e; v/i işini görmek; ~e out
v/t dağıtmak

service ['sövis] hizmet;
servis; görev; yarar; *mil.*
askerlik; *rel.* ayin, tören; ~
station benzin istasyonu;
~able işe yarar, faydalı

session ['seşın] oturum,
celse

set [set] *n.* takım; koleksiyon; seri; cihaz; grup; v/t
koymak, yerleştirmek, dikmek, kurmak; düzeltmek,
tanzim etm.; v/i katılaş-
mak; *sun:* batmak; *adj.* belirli; düzenli; değişmez; ~
about başlamak (-*ing* -e);
~ **free** birini serbest bırakmak;
~ **off** yola çıkmak; ~ **to**
başlamak -e; ~ **up** v/t dikmek, kurmak; ~**back** aksilik

settee [se'tî] kanepe

setting ['setin] yuva; batma
(*güneş*); ortam

settle ['setl] v/i oturmak,
yerleşmek; durulmak; v/t
yerleştirmek; kararlaştırmak; halletmek; *account:*
görmek, ödemek; *quarrel:*
yatıştırmak; ~ **down** yerleşmek; ~**ment** yerleş(tir)-
me; sömürge; yeni iskân
edilmiş yer; *ec.* hesap görme, tasfiye; halletme; ~**r**
yeni yerleşen göçmen

seven ['sevn] yedi; ~**teen**
['.'tîn] on yedi; ~**ty** yetmiş

sever ['sevı] v/t ayırmak,
koparmak; v/i ayrılmak

several ['sevrıl] birkaç;
çeşitli

sever|e [si'viı] şiddetli, sert;
~**ity** [.eriti] şiddet, sertlik

sew [sıu] v/t dikiş dikmek

sew|age ['syuic] pis su; ~**er**
lağım

sex [seks] cins; cinsiyet;
~**ual** ['.yuul] cinsî, cinsel

shabby ['şäbi] kılıksız; alçak

shack [şäk] kulübe

shade [şeyd] *n.* gölge; siper;
abajur; renk tonu; v/t ışık-
tan korumak; gölgelemek

shadow ['şädu] *n.* gölge;
v/t gölgelemek; gizlice gözetlemek; ~**y** [şüpheli]

shady ['şeydi] gölgeli; *fig.)*

shaft [şäft] sap; sütun; şaft;
maden kuyusu

shaggy ['şägi] kaba tüylü

shake [şeyk] v/t silkmek,
sallamak, sarsmak; v/i sallanmak, titremek; *n.* çalka-
lanmış şey; sarsıntı; ~
hands el sıkışmak; ~**n** *s.*
shake; sarşılmış

shaky titrek; zayıf

shall [şäl] -ecek; -meli

shallow ['şälu] sığ; üstünkörü; sığyer

sham [şäm] yapma; v/t yalandan yapmak

shame [şeym] *n.* utanç; rezalet; v/t utandırmak; ~**ful**
utandırıcı, ayıp; ~**less**
utanmaz, arsız

shampoo [şäm'puu] *n.*
şampuan; v/t baş yıkamak

shank [şänk] *an.* incik, baldır

shape [şeyp] *n.* şekil, biçim;
v/t şekil vermek -e; düzen-

shapeless 384

lemek -*i*; **~less** biçimsiz, şekilsiz; **~ly** yakışıklı

share¹ [şäı] saban demiri

share² *n.* pay, hisse; *ec.* hisse senedi, aksiyon; *v/t* paylaşmak; katılmak -*e*; **~holder** hissedar

shark [şäk] *zo.* köpek balığı

sharp [şâp] keskin, sivri; ekşi; sert; zeki; tam; **~en** *v/t* bilemek, sivriltmek; *v/i* keskinleşmek; **~ener** ['~pnı] kalemtıraş; **~ness** keskinlik, sivrilik; şiddet; **~-witted** zeki

shatter ['şätı] *v/t* kırmak, parçalamak; *v/i* kırılmak

shav|e [şeyv] *n.* tıraş; *v/t* tıraş etm.; sıyırıp geçmek; *v/i* tıraş olm.; **~en** *s.* **shave**; **~ing** tıraş; *pl.* talaş *sg.*

shawl [şôl] omuz atkısı; şal

she [şi] o (*dişil*); dişi

sheaf [şif] demet

shear [şiı] *v/t* kırkmak, kesmek; **~s** *n. pl.* büyük makas *sg.*

sheath [şîth] kın, kılıf, zarf

shed¹ [şed] *n.* baraka, kulübe

shed² *v/t* dökmek, akıtmak; dağıtmak

sheep [şîp] koyun(lar *pl.*); **~ish** sıkılgan, utangaç

sheer [şiı] halis, saf; tamamiyle

sheet [şît] çarşaf; yaprak, tabaka; levha; **~ iron** saç; **~ing** çarşaflık bez

shelf [şelf] raf; *geo.* şelf, sığlık

shell [şel] *n.* kabuk; top

mermisi; *v/t* kabuğundan çıkarmak; **~fish** *zo.* kabuklu hayvan

shelter ['şeltı] sığınak, barınak, siper; *v/t* barındırmak

shepherd ['şepıd] çoban

sherbet ['şôbıt] şerbet; dondurma

sheriff ['şerif] *ilce veya bucakta* polis müdürü

shield [şîld] *n.* kalkan; siper; *v/t* korumak

shift [şift] *n.* değiş(tir)me; nöbet; çare; hile; *v/t* değiştirmek; *v/i* değişmek; **~y** hilekâr

shilling ['şilin] şilin

shin(-bone) ['şin(-)] *an.* incik kemiri

shine [şayn] *n.* parlaklık; *v/i* parlamak; *v/t* parlatmak

shingle ['şingl] padavra, tahta kiremit

shiny ['şayni] parlak

ship [şip] *n.* gemi; *v/t* gemiyle sevketmek, yollamak; **~ment** gemiye yükleme; hamule; **~ping** gemiye yükleme; deniz nakliyesi; **~wreck** gemi enkazı; deniz kazası; **~yard** tersane işçisi; tersane

shire ['şayı] kontluk

shirk [şôk] *v/t* kaçınmak -*den*

shirt [şôt] gömlek; **~-sleeve** gömlek kolu

shiver¹ ['şivı] ufak parça

shiver² *n.* titreme; *v/i* titremek

shock [şok] *n.* sarsma, sarsıntı; darbe; *v/t* sarsmak; iğrendirmek; **~absorber** *tech.* amortisör; **~ing** korkunç; iğrenç; **~proof** sarsıntıya dayanır

shoe [şuu] *n.* kundura, ayakkabı; nal; *v/t* nallamak; **~maker** ayakkabıcı; **~string** ayakkabı bağı; **on a ~string** az pata ile

shone [şon] *s.* **shine**

shook [şuk] *s.* **shake**

shoot [şuut] *n.* atış; filiz; *v/t* atmak; silâhla vurmak; öldürmek; filme almak; *v/i* fışkırmak; filiz sürmek; **~ at** ateş etmek *-e*; **~ down** düşürmek; **~er** nişancı; **~ing** atış; avcılık; **~ing star** *astr.* göktaşı

shop [şop] dükkân, mağaza; fabrika; **talk ~** iş konusunda konuşmak; **~keeper** dükkâncı; **~lifter** dükkân hırsızı; **~ping** alışveriş; **~window** vitrin

shore [şô] kıyı, sahil

shorn [şôn] *s.* **shear**

short [şôt] kısa; bodur, kısa boylu; az; ters; *pl.* spor, kısa pantolon *sg.*; **~ cut** kestirme yol; **in ~** kısaca; **~ of** adv. *-den* başka; **be ~ of** *-si* eksik olm.; **~age** yokluk, kıtlık; **~circuit** kısa devre; **~coming** kusur, noksan; **~en** *v/t* kısaltmak; *v/i* kısalmak; **~hand** stenografi; **~ness** kısalık, eksiklik; **~sighted** miyop; *fig.* kısa görüşlü; **~term** kısa vadeli; **~winded** nefes darlığı olan

shot [şot] atış; gülle; erim; silâh sesi; *s.* **shoot**; **big ~** *pop.* önemli şahıs; **~gun** saçma tüfeği

should [şud] *s.* **shall**

shoulder ['şuldı] *n.* omuz; *v/t* omuzlamak; **~ blade** *an.* kürek kemiği

shout [şaut] *n.* bağırma; *v/t* bağırmak

shove [şav] *v/t* itmek, dürtmek

shovel ['şavl] *n.* kürek; *v/t* kürelemek

show [şu] *n.* gösteriş; *thea.* temsil, oyun; sergi; *v/t* göstermek; sergilemek; tanıtlamak; *v/i* görünmek; **~off** gösteriş yapmak; **~ up** *v/i* gözükmek

shower ['şau] *n.* sağanak; duş; *v/i* sağanak halinde yağmak; *v/t* bol vermek; yağdırmak   [gösterişli]

show|n [şun] *s.* **show**; **~y**

shrank [şränk] *s.* **shrink**

shred [şred] *n.* dilim, paçavra; *v/t* parçalamak

shrewd [şruud] kurnaz, becerikli

shriek [şrik] *n.* feryat, yaygara; *v/i* çığlık koparmak

shrill [şril] keskin sesli

shrimp [şrimp] *zo.* karides

shrink [şrink] *v/i* ürkmek; çekinmek, büzülmek; *v/t* daraltmak

shrivel ['şrivl] *v/i* büzülmek

Shrovetide ['şruvtayd] *rel.* etkesimi, apukurya

shrub 386

shrub [ʃrab] küçük ağaç; çalı; **~bery** çalılık

shrug [ʃrag] *n.* omuz silkme; *v/t* omuzlarını silkmek

shrunk [ʃrʌŋk] *s.* shrink; **~en** büzülmüş

shudder [ʃadı] *n.* titreme; *v/i* ürpermek, titremek

shuffle [ʃafl] *v/t* karıştırmak; *v/i* ayak sürümek

shun [ʃan] *v/t* sakınmak, kaçınmak *-den*

shut [ʃat] *v/t* kapa(t)mak; *v/i* kapanmak; **~ down** *v/t* işyerini kapamak; **~ up!** *intj.* sus!; **~ter** kepenk; *phot.* kapak

shuttle [ʃatl] mekik

shy [ʃay] *adj.* korkak, ürkek; *v/i* ürkmek; **~ness** çekingenlik

sick [sik] hasta; midesi bulanmış; bıkmış (**of** *-den*); **~en** *v/i* hastalanmak; *v/t* bıkturmak

sickle [sikl] orak

sick-leave hastalık izni; **~ness** hastalık; kusma

side [sayd] yan, taraf; kenar; **~** *with -in* tarafını tutmak; **~board** büfe; **~-car** yan arabası, sepet; **~walk** *Am.* yaya kaldırımı; **~ways** yandan; yan [ʃatma]

siege [siːc] muhasara, ku- ʃ

sieve [siv] *n.* kalbur, elek; *v/t* elemek

sift [sift] *v/t* kalburdan geçirmek, elemek; *fig.* incelemek; ayırmak

sigh [say] *n.* iç çekme; *v/i* iç çekmek

sight [sayt] *n.* görme; manzara; *v/t* görmek; **at first ~** ilk görüşte; **know by ~** *v/t* yüzünden tanımak; **~-seeing** seyredecek yerleri görmeğe gitme, gezme

sign [sayn] *n.* işaret, alâmet; iz, belirti; levha; *v/t* imzalamak; işaret etm. *-e*

signa|l [signl] *n.* işaret; ihtar; *v/t* işaretle bildirmek; **~tory** [ʌnıtıri] imza eden; **~ture** [ʌniçi] imza

signboard tabela, afiş

significa|nce [sig'nifikıns] mana; önem; **~nt** manalı; önemli; **~tion** mana

signify [signifay] *v/t* belirtmek

signpost işaret direği

silen|ce [saylıns] *n.* sessizlik; *v/t* susturmak; **~t** sessiz, sakin

silk [silk] ipek; **~en** ipekli; **~y** ipek gibi

sill [sil] eşik; denizlik

silly [sili] budala, aptal

silver [silvı] *n.* gümüş; *v/t* gümüş kaplamak *-e*; **~y** gümüş gibi, parlak

similar [similı] benzer (**to** *-e*), gibi; **~ity** [ʌlâriti] benzerlik

simmer [simı] *v/i* yavaş yavaş kaynama

simpl|e [simpl] basit, sade, kolay; sadfil; **~icity** [ʌ'plisiti] sadelik; saflık; **~ify** [ʌlifay] *v/t* kolaylaştırmak; **~y** *adv.* sadece, sırf, ancak

simulate [simyuleyt] *v/t*

yalandan yapmak; ... gibi görünmek

simultaneous [siml'teynyis] aynı zamanda olan, eşzamanlı

sin [sin] n. günah; v/i günah işlemek

since [sins] *prp. -den* beri; mademki, zira, çünkü

sincer|e [sin'siı] samimi, içten; **Yours ~ely** saygılarımla; **~ity** [~'seriti] samimiyet, içtenlik

sinew ['sinyû] kiriş; **~y** kiriş gibi; *fig.* kuvvetli, dinç

sing [sin] v/t şarkı söylemek; ötmek; v/t söylemek, okumak

singe [sinc] v/t yakmak

singer ['sinı] şarkıcı

single ['singl] tek, bir; yalnız; tek kişilik; bekâr; ~ **out** v/t seçmek, ayırmak; **~-handed** tek başına

singular ['singyulı] acayip; tek; eşsiz; *gr.* tekil; **~ity** [~'lâriti] özellik

sinister ['sinistı] uğursuz

sink [sink] n. musluk taşı, bulaşık oluğu; v/i batmak, düşmek, inmek; v/t batırmak

sinner ['sinı] günahkâr

sip [sip] v/t azar azar içmek

siphon ['sayfın] sifon

sir [sö] beyefendi, efendim; ♀ sör (*bir asalet unvanı*)

siren ['sayırın] canavar düdüğü

sirloin ['söloyn] sığır filetosu

sister ['sistı] kızkardeş,

hemşire; abla; **~-in-law** görümce, baldız, yenge, elti

sit [sit] v/i oturmak; ~ **down** (yerine) oturmak; ~ **up** dik oturmak; yatmamak

site [sayt] yer, mahal

sitting ['sitin] oturum; **~room** oturma odası

situat|ed ['sityueytid]: **be ~ed** bulunmak (**in** *-de*); **~ion** yer; durum

six [siks] altı; **~teen** ['~'tîn] on altı; **~ty** altmış

size [sayz] hacim, oylum; büyüklük

sizzle ['sizl] v/i cızırdamak

skat|e [skeyt] paten; **~er** patinaj yapan; **~ing** patinaj

skeleton ['skelitn] iskelet; çatı

sketch [skeç] n. kroki, taslak; skeç; v/t -in taslağını çizmek

skewer ['skyûı] kebap şişi

ski [skî] n. kayak; v/i kayak yapmak

skid [skid] n. takoz; kayma; v/i yana kaymak

ski|er ['skîı] kayakçı; **~ing** kayakçılık

skil|ful ['skilful] hünerli, mahir; **~l** hüner, ustalık; **~led** tecrübeli; kalifiye; **~l-ful** *Am. s.* **skilful**

skim [skim] v/t -in köpüğünü almak; *fig.* göz gezdirmek *-e*; **~(med) milk** kaynağı alınmış süt

skin [skin] n. deri; post; kabuk; v/t yüzmek, -in kabuğunu soymak; **~-deep** sathî, yüzeysel; **~ny** sıska

skip [skip] *n.* sekme, zıplama; *v/i* zıplamak; *v/t* atlamak

skipper ['skipi] kaptan

skirmish ['skömiş] *mil.* hafif çarpışma

skirt [sköt] *n.* etek(lik); kenar; *v/t* -*in* kenarından geçmek [nu *sg.*]

skittles ['skitlz] *pl.* kiy oyu-*i*

skull [skal] kafatası

sky [skay] gök; **~jacker** ['~câki] hava korsanı; **~lark** *zo.* tarlakuşu, toygar; **~light** dam penceresi, kaporta; **~scraper** gökdelen

slab [släb] kalın dilim, tabaka

slack [släk] gevşek; kayıtsız; *pl.* pantolon; **~en** *v/i* gevşemek; *v/t* gevşetmek

slain [sleyn] *s.* slay

slake [sleyk] *v/t* thirst: gidermek; *lime:* söndürmek

slam [släm] *v/t* çarpıp kapamak; yere vurmak

slander ['slândı] *n.* iftira; *v/t* iftira etm. -*e*

slang [släŋ] argo

slant [slânt] *n.* eğim; meyilli düzey; *v/i* eğilmek; *v/t* eğmek

slap [släp] *n.* şamar, tokat; *v/t* avuçla vurmak -*e*; **~stick** *thea.* güldürü; gürültülü

slash [släş] *n.* uzun yara; yarık; kamçı vuruşu; *v/t* yarmak; kamçılamak

slate [sleyt] arduvaz, kayağantaş

slattern ['slätın] pasaklı kadın

slaughter ['slôtı] *n.* kesim, katliam; *v/t* kesmek, boğazlamak; **~house** mezbaha

slave [sleyv] *n.* köle, esir; *v/i* köle gibi çalışmak; **~ry** kölelik, esirlik

slay [sley] *v/t* öldürmek

sled(ge) [sled (slec)] *n.* kızak; *v/i* kızakla gitmek

sledge-hammer balyoz

sleek [slik] *adj.* düzgün, parlak; *v/t* düzlemek

sleep [slip] *n.* uyku, *v/i* uyumak; **go to ~** yatağa yatmak; **~ on, ~ over** *v/t* ertesi güne bırakmak; **~er** uyuyan kimse; yataklı vagon; travers; **~ing-bag** uyku tulumu; **~ing-car** yataklı vagon; **~less** uykusuz; **~walker** uyurgezer; **~y** uykusu gelmiş

sleet [slit] sulu sepken kar

sleeve [sliv] yen, elbise kolu; *tech.* manşon, kol, bilezik

sleigh [sley] *n.* kızak; *v/i* kızakla gitmek

slender ['slendı] ince, zayıf, az

slept [slept] *s.* sleep

slew [sluu] *s.* slay

slice [slays] *n.* dilim, parça; balık bıçağı; *v/t* dilimlemek

slick [slik] kaygan; kurnaz

slid [slid] *s.* slide

slide [slayd] *v/i* kaymak; *v/t* kaydırmak; *n.* kayma; *tech.* sürme; diyapozitif; **~-rule** hesap cetveli

slight [slayt] *adj.* zayıf,

önemsiz; *v/t* önem vermemek *-e*, küçümsemek *-i*
slim [slim] *adj.* ince, zayıf; *v/i* incelmek
slime [slaym] sümük; balçık; *~y* sümüksü, pis
sling [sliŋ] *n.* sapan; askı; *v/t* sapanla atmak; askı ile kaldırmak
slip [slip] *n.* kayma; söz kaçırma; hata; kâğıt, pusula; yastık yüzü; *v/i* kaymak; kaçmak; *v/t* kaydırmak; **~on** *v/t* giyivermek; **~out** *v/i* ağzından kaçmak; **~per** terlik; **~pery** kaygan, kaypak
slit [slit] *n.* kesik, yarık; *v/t* yarmak
slogan ['sluıgın] parola, slogan
sloop [sluup] *naut.* şalopa
slop [slop] *n.* sulu çamur; *v/t* dökmek; **~over** *v/i* taşmak
slope [slıup] *n.* bayır; meyilli düzey; *v/t* meyletmek
sloppy ['slopi] çamurlu; *fig.* şapşal
slot [slot] delik, kertik
sloth [sluuth] tembellik
slot-machine oyun makinası
slough [slau] bataklık
sloven ['slavn] hırpani, şapşal
slow [slıu] *adj.* ağır, yavaş; geri kalmış; aptal; **~down** *v/t* yavaşlatmak; *v/i* ağırlaşmak; **~motion** yavaşlatılmış hareket; **~ness** ağırlık, yavaşlık

sluggish ['slagiş] tembel, cansız
sluice [sluus] savak
slum [slam] teneke mahallesi
slumber ['slambı] *n.* uyku, uyuklama; *v/i* uyumak, uyuklamak
slung [slaŋ] *s.* sling
slush [slaş] eriyen kar; çamur
slut [slat] pasaklı kadın
sly [slay] kurnaz, şeytan gibi
smack¹ [smäk] *n.* şapırtı; şamar; *v/t* şaplatmak
smack² hafif çeşni; **~of** *-in* çeşnisi olm.
small [smôl] küçük, ufak, az; **~change** bozuk para; **~hours** *pl.* gece yarısından sonraki saatler; **~talk** önemsiz sohbet; **~pox** *med.* çiçek hastalığı
smart [smât] şık, zarif; akıllı; kurnaz; çevik; şiddetli
smash [smäş] *v/t* ezmek, parçalamak; *v/i* ezilmek; **~ing** *fig.* çok güzel
smattering ['smätırıŋ] çat pat bilgi
smear [smiı] *n.* leke; *v/t* bulandırmak, lekelemek; sürmek
smell [smel] koku; *v/t* *-in* kokusunu almak; *v/i* kokmak
smelt¹ [smelt] *s.* smell
smelt² *v/t* eritmek
smile [smayl] *n.* gülümseme, tebessüm; *v/i* gülümsemek

smith [smith] demirci, nalbant

smitten ['smitn] çarpılmış;
fig. vurgun (**with** -*e*)

smock [smok] iş kıyafeti

smog [smog] dumanlı sis

smok|e [smuuk] *n.* duman;
v/i tütmek; *v/t* tütsülemek;
cigarette, etc.: içmek; **~er**
tütün içen; tütün içenlere
mahsus vagon; **~ing** tütün
içme; **~ing-car(riage)** tütün içenlere mahsus vagon;
~y dumanlı, tüten

smooth [smuudh] düz, düzgün, pürüzsüz; akıcı; na-
zik; *v/t* düzlemek, yatıştırmak

smother ['smadhı] *v/t* boğmak; *v/i* boğulmak

smo(u)lder ['smuuldı] alev-
siz yanmak

smudge [smac] *n.* leke; *v/t*
kirletmek

smuggle ['smagl] *v/t* kaçırmak; **~r** kaçakçı

smut [smat] is, kurum; pis
laf

snack [snäk] çerez, hafif yemek

snail [sneyl] *zo.* salyangoz

snake [sneyk] *zo.* yılan

snap [snäp] *n.* ısırma; çatırtı, şıkırtı; gayret, enerji;
v/i ısırmak, kopmak (**at** -*i*);
çatırdayıp kırılmak; *v/t*
kırmak; **cold ~** soğukluk
dalgası; **~py** çevik, çabuk;
~shot enstantane fotoğraf

snare [snää] tuzak, kapan

snarl [snâl] *v/i* hırlamak; *n.*
hırlama

snatch [snäç] *v/t* kapmak,
koparmak; *n.* kapma; parça

sneak [snîk] *v/i* sinsi sinsi
dolaşmak

sneer [snıı] *n.* alay, istihza;
v/i küçümsemek (**at** -*i*),
alay etm. (ile)

sneeze [snîz] *n.* aksırma; *v/i*
aksırmak

sniff [snif] *v/i* burnuna hava
çekmek; burnunu buruş-
turmak; *v/t* koklamak; **~le**
['~fl] nezle

snipe [snayp] *zo.* çulluk; **~r**
pusuya yatan nişancı

snivel ['snivl] *v/i* burnu akmak; burnunu çekerek ağ-
lamak

snob [snob] snop, züppe

snoop [snuup] burnunu so-
kan

snooze [snuuz] *n.* şekerleme; *v/i* kısaca uyumak

snore [snô] *n.* horlama; *v/i*
horlamak

snort [snôt] at gibi horuldamak

snout [snaut] *zo.* burun,
hortum

snow [snou] *n.* kar; *v/i* kar
yağmak; **~ball** kar topu;
~-drift kar yığıntısı; **~-
drop** *bot.* kardelen; **~y** karlı, kar gibi

snub [snab] *v/t* küçümsemek; *n.* hiçe sayma; **~
nose** ucu kalkık burun

snuff [snaf] enfiye

snug [snag] rahat, konforlu;
~gle ['~gl] *v/i* yerleşmek,
sokulmak

so [sıu] öyle, böyle; bu kadar; bundan dolayı; **~ far** şimdiye kadar; **~ long!** hoşça kalın!

soak [sıuk] v/t ıslatmak; v/i ıslanmak

so-and-so filanca

soap [sıup] n. sabun; v/t sabunlamak

soar [sô] yükselmek

sob [sob] n. hıçkırık; v/i hıçkıra hıçkıra ağlamak

sober ['sıubı] adj. ayık; ağırbaşlı; v/i ayılmak

so-called diye anılan, sözde

soccer ['sokı] futbol

sociable ['sıuşıbl] girgin; nazik

social ['sıuşıl] hoş sohbet; toplumsal, sosyal; **~ insurance** sosyal sigorta; **~ism** sosyalizm; **~ist** sosyalist; **~ize** v/t kamulaştırmak

society [sı'sayıti] kurum; ortaklık; sosyete

sociology [sıusi'olıci] sosyoloji

sock [sok] kısa çorap, şoset

socket ['sokit] sap deliği, oyuk; yuva

sod [sod] çimen parçası

soda ['sıudı] soda; soda suyu

sofa ['sıufı] kanepe

soft [soft] yumuşak; uysal; (voice) yavaş; **~ drink** alkolsuz içki; **~en** ['sofn] v/t yumuşatmak; v/i yumuşamak; **~ness** yumuşaklık

soil [soyl] n. toprak; v/t kirletmek; v/i kirlenmek

sojourn ['socön] v/i kalmak; n. konukluk

solar ['sıulı] güneşe ait

sold [sıuld] s. **sell**

soldier ['sıulcı] asker, er

sole[1] [sıul] n. taban, pençe; v/t pençe vurmak -e

sole[2] zo. dilbalığı

sole[3] yalnız, biricik

solemn ['solım] törenli; ağırbaşlı

solicit ['lisit] v/t istemek, rica etm.; **~or** avukat; **~ous** endişeli; istekli

solid ['solid] sağlam; katı; som; **~arity** [.'därıti] dayanışma, tesanüt; **~ity** katılık

solit|ary ['solituri] tek, yalnız; tenha; **~ude** ['.tyûd] yalnızlık

solo ['sıulu] solo; **~ist** solist

solstice ['solstis] astr. gündönümü

solu|ble ['solyubl] eriyebilir, çözülebilir; **~tion** [sı-'luuşın] erime; çözüm; çare

solve [solv] v/t halletmek, çözmek; v/i çözebilir; **~nt** ec. borcunu ödeyebilir

somb|re, Am. **~er** ['sombı] loş, karanlık

some [sam] bazı, birkaç; biraz; **~body** ['.bıdi] biri (-si); **~how** nasılsa; **~one** biri(si)

somersault ['samısôlt] taklak

some|thing bir şey; **~times** bazan, arasıra; **~what** bir dereceye kadar; **~where** bir yer(d)e

son [san] oğul

song [soŋ] şarkı; ötme; **~-bird** ötücü kuş

sonic ['sonik] sesle ilgili

son-in-law damat

soon [suun] biraz sonra; hemen; erken; **as ~ as -ince**; **no ~er ... than** -ir -mez

soot [suut] *n.* is, kurum; *v/t* ise bulaştırmak

soothe [suudh] *v/t* yatıştırmak, teskin etm.

sophisticated [sı'fistikeytid] hayata alışmış; kültürlü; yapmacık

soporific [sopı'rifik] uyutucu ilâç

sorcer|er ['sôsırı] büyücü, sihirbaz; **~y** büyü(cülük)

sordid ['sôdid] alçak, sefil; kirli

sore [sô] acı veren; kırgın; şiddetli; **~ throat** boğaz ağrısı

sorrow ['sorıu] keder, acı; **~ful** kederli, elemli

sorry ['sori] üzgün; pişman; **be ~** acımak, üzülmek (**for** -e)

sort [sôt] *n.* çeşit, nevi; *v/t* sınıflandırmak, ayıklamak

sought [sôt] *s.* **seek**

soul [sıul] ruh, can

sound[1] [saund] sağlam; emin

sound[2] *geo.* boğaz

sound[3] *v/t* iskandil etm.

sound[4] *n.* ses; *v/i* ses vermek; gelmek, görünmek (**like** gibi); *v/t* çalmak; **~-proof** ses geçirmez; **~-wave** *phys.* ses dalgası

soup [suup] çorba

sour ['sauı] ekşi(miş); somurtkan, asık

source [sôs] kaynak

south [sauth] güney; **~east** güney doğu

souther|ly ['sadhılı] güneye doğru; **~rn** güneyde olan; **2ner** *Am.* güneyli

south|ward(s) ['sauthwıd(z)] güneye doğru; **~west** güneybatı

souvenir ['suuvınii] hatıra, andaç

sovereign ['sovrin] hükümdar; **~ty** ['~rınti] egemenlik

Soviet Union ['sıuviet ~] Sovyetler Birliği

sow[1] [sau] *zo.* dişi domuz

sow[2] [sıu] *v/t* ekmek; **~n** *s.* **sow**[2]

soya, soybean ['soyı] *bot.* soya (fasulyesi)

spa [spâ] ılıca, kaplıca

space [speys] alan, yer; uzay; **~craft**, **~ship** uzay gemisi [engin)

spacious ['speyşıs] geniş,}

spade [speyd] bel; maça

Spain [speyn] İspanya

span[1] [spän] *n.* karış; süre; *arch.* açıklık; *v/t* ölçmek; boydan boya uzatmak

span[2] *s.* **spin**

spangle ['spängl] *n.* pul; *v/t* pullarla süslemek

Spani|ard ['spänyıd] İspanyol; **~sh** İspanyol(ca)

spank [spänk] *v/t -in* kıçına şaplak vurmak; **~ing** şaplak atma

spanner ['spänı] somun anahtarı

spare [späı] *adj.* dar; boş; yedek; *v/t* esirgemek; vazgeçmek *-den*; tutumlu kullanmak *-i*; ~ **part** *tech.* yedek parça; ~**room** misafir odası; ~ **time** boş vakit

spark [spåk] *n.* kıvılcım; *v/i* kıvılcım saçmak; ~(**ing**)-**plug** *tech.* buji; ~**le** *n.* kıvılcım; parlayış; *v/i* parıldamak

sparrow [späru] *zo.* serçe

sparse [spås] seyrek

spasm [späzm] *med.* ıspazmoz; ~**odic** [~'modik] ıspazmoz kabilinden

spat [spät] *s.* **spit**

spatter ['spätı] *v/t* serpmek

spawn [spón] balık yumurtası

speak [spîk] *v/i* konuşmak (**to** ile); bahsetmek (**about, of** *-den*); *v/t* söylemek; ~ **out, ~ up** açıkça söylemek; ~**er** sözcü

spear [spiı] *n.* mızrak; *v/t* mızrakla vurmak *-e*

special ['speşıl] özel; mahsus; özellik; ~**ist** uzman, mütehassıs; ~**ity** [~i'äliti] özellik; ~**alize in** *-in* ihtisas sahibi olm.; ~**ty** özellik

species ['spîşîz] tür, çeşit

speci|fic [spi'sifik] has, özgü; özel; belirli; ~**fy** *v/t* belirtmek; ~**men** ['spesimin] örnek, numune

specta|cle ['spektıkl] manzara; *pl.* gözlük *sg.*; ~**cular** [~'täkyulı] görülmeğe değer; ~**tor** [~'teytı] seyirci

speculat|e ['spekyuleyt] *v/i*

ec. borsada oynamak; düşünmek, mütalâa etm. (**on, upon** *-i*); ~**ion** spekülasyon; kurgu

sped [sped] *s.* **speed**

speech [spîç] dil; söz, söylev; ~**less** dili tutulmuş

speed [spîd] *n.* hız, sürat, çabukluk; *v/i* hızla gitmek; *v/t* hızlandırmak; ~**limit** azami sürat; ~**ometer** [spi'domitı] hızölçer; ~**y** çabuk, hızlı

spell [spel] nöbet; süre

spell *v/t* hecelemek; belirtmek

spell büyü; ~**bound** büyülenmiş

spelling ['spelin] imlâ, yazım

spelt [spelt] *s.* **spell**[2]

spend [spend] *v/t* harcamak, sarfetmek, israf etm.; *time:* geçirmek

spent [spent] *s.* **spend**

sperm [spöm] sperma, belsuyu

sphere [sfiı] küre; alan, saha

spic|e [spays] *n.* bahar; *v/t* çeşni vermek *-e*; ~**y** baharatlı; *fig.* açık saçık

spider ['spaydı] örümcek

spike [spayk] *bot.* başak; uclu demir, çivi

spill [spil] *v/t* dökmek; *v/i* dökülmek

spilt [spilt] *s.* **spill**

spin [spin] *v/t* eğirmek; döndürmek; *v/i* dönmek

spinach ['spinic] *bot.* ıspanak

spinal ['spaynl] *an.* belkemiğine ait; **~ column** omurga, belkemiği; **~ cord** omurilik

spindle ['spindl] iğ, eğirmen; mil

spine [spayn] *an.* omirga, belkemiği; diken

spinning eğirme; **~-wheel** çıkrık

spinster ['spinstı] kalık, yaşı geçmiş kız

spiny ['spayni] dikenli

spiral ['spayırıl] helis, helezon; helezonî

spire ['spayı] kule tepesi

spirit ['spirit] ruh; cin, peri; canlılık; alkol; ispirto; **high ~s** *pl.* keyif, neşe; **low ~s** keder, gam; **~ed** cesur, canlı; **~ual** ['~tyuıl] ruhanî; ruhî; *mus.* Amerikan zencilerine has ilâhi

spit¹ [spit] kebap şişi

spit² *n.* tükürük; *v/i* tükürmek (**on** -*e*); *cat:* tıslamak

spite [spayt] kin, garaz; **in ~ of** -*e* rağmen; **~ful** garazkâr

spittle ['spitl] salya, tükürük

splash [splâş] *n.* zifos; *v/t* zifos atmak, su sıçratmak -*e*; *v/i* suya çarpmak; **~ down** suya inmek

spleen [splîn] *an.* dalak; *fig.* terslik; kin

splend|id ['splendid] parlak, gösterişli; mükemmel; **~o(u)r** parlaklık; tantana

splint [splint] *med.* cebire, süyek; **~er** *n.* kıymık; *v/i* parçalanmak

split [split] *n.* yarık, çatlak

v/t yarmak, bölmek, ayırmak; *v/i* yarılmak, ayrılmak; **~ting** şiddetli, keskin

splutter ['splatı] *v/t* fışkırtmak

spoil [spoyl] *n.* yağma, çapul; *v/t* bozmak; şımartmak; **~-sport** oyunbozan; **~t** *s.* spoil

spoke¹ [spuuk] tekerlek parmağı

spoke² *s.* speak; **~sman** sözcü

sponge [spanc] *n.* sünger; **~ away, ~ off** *v/t* silmek

sponsor ['sponsı] *n.* *rel.* vaftiz babası; *jur.* kefil; *v/t* desteklemek

spontaneous [spon'teynyıs] kendiliğinden olan

spook [spuuk] hayalet

spool [spuul] *n.* makara; *v/t* makaraya sarmak

spoon [spuun] kaşık; **~ful** kaşık dolusu

sporadic [spı'rädik] arasıra olan

sport [spôt] *n.* spor; eğlence; alay; *v/i* takılmak (**at, over** -*e*); *v/t* övünmek ile; **~sman** sporcu, sportmen

spot [spot] *n.* nokta, benek; yer; *v/t* beneklemek; görmek, bulmak; **on the ~** yerinde; derhal; **~less** lekesiz; **~light** projektör ışığı

spouse [spauz] eş, koca, karı

spout [spaut] *n.* oluk ağzı, emzik; *v/t* fışkırtmak; *v/i* fışkırmak

sprain [spreyn] *n.* burkulma; *v/t* burkmak

sprang [spräŋ] s. **spring**

sprawl [spröl] yerde uzanmak

spray [sprey] n. serpinti;
püskürgeç; v/t serpmek,
püskürtmek

spread [spred] n. yayılma;
örtü; v/t yaymak, sermek;
sürmek; v/i yayılmak

sprig [sprig] ince dal

sprightly ['spraytli] canlı,
şen

spring [spriŋ] (ilk)bahar;
tech. yay, zemberek; kay-
nak; sıçrayış; v/i fırlamak,
sıçramak; çıkmak (**from**
-den); v/t sıçratmak;
sıçrama tahtası; **~time** ilk-
bahar

sprinkle ['spriŋkl] v/t serpmek; **~r** serpme makinası

sprint [sprint] v/i koşmak;
n. kısa koşu; **~er** kısa mesafe koşucusu

sprout [spraut] n. filiz; v/i
filizlenmek

spruce [spruus] şık

sprunk [spraŋ] s. **spring**

spun [span] s. **spin**

spur [spö] n. mahmuz; fig.
saik; güdü; v/t kışkırtmak
(**into** -e)

sputter ['spatı] v/t saçmak;
v/i tükürük saçmak

spy [spay] n. casus; hafiye;
v/i gizlice gözetlemek (**on**
-i); [ga etm.)

squabble['skwobl]v/ikav-}

squad [skwod] takım

squall [skwöl] bora, kasırga

squander ['skwondı] v/t
israf etm., savurmak

square [skwäı] n. dördül,
kare; meydan; adj. dürüst,
doğru; eşit; pop. eski kafalı;
v/t math. -in karesini almak; doğrultmak -i; öde-
mek -i; **~ mile** mil kare
(259 hektar)

squash[1] [skwoş] n. ezme;
v/t ezmek; bastırmak

squash[2] bot. kabak

squat [skwot] v/i çömelmek;
boş topraklara yerleşmek

squeak [skwîk] cırlamak;
gıcırdamak

squeal [skwîl] domuz gibi
ses çıkarmak

squeamish ['skwîmiş] çabuk tiksinen; titiz

squeeze [skwîz] v/t sıkmak,
sıkıştırmak

squint [skwint] şaşı bakmak; yan bakmak

squire ['skwayı] asılzade;
kavalye

squirm [skwöm] kıvranmak

squirrel ['skwiril] zo. sincap

squirt [skwöt] v/t fışkırtmak

stab [stäb] n. bıçak yarası;
v/t bıçaklamak

stability [stı'biliti] denge;
sağlamlık; **~ze** ['steybilayz]
v/t dengelemek; saptamak

stable[1] ['steybl] sağlam,
sabit

stable[2] ahır

stack [stäk] n. tınaz; yığın;
v/t yığmak

stadium ['steydyım] stadyum

staff [stâf] n. değnek, asa;

personel, kadro; *mil.* kurmay

stag [stäg] *zo.* erkek geyik

stage [steyc] *n.* sahne; tiyatro; merhale; konak; safha; *v/t* sahneye koymak; **~ coach** menzil arabası

stagger ['stägı] *v/i* sendelemek, sersemlemek

stagna|nt ['stägnınt] durgun; **~tion** durgunluk

stain [steyn] *n.* leke, boya; *v/t* lekelemek; **~ed** lekeli; renkli; **~less** leksesiz; paslanmaz

stair [stäı] basamak; **~case**, **~way** merdiven

stake [steyk] *n.* kazık; kumarda ortaya konan para; *v/t* tehlikeye koymak; **be at ~** tehlikede olm.

stale [steyl] bayat

stalk [stók] *n.* sap; *v/i* azametle yürümek

stall [stól] *n.* kulübe; ahır bölmesi; *thea.* koltuk; *v/t* durdurmak; *v/i* durmak

stallion ['stälyın] aygır, damızlık at

stalwart ['stólwıt] kuvvetli; sadık

stammer ['stämı] *n.* kekemelik; *v/i* kekelemek

stamp [stämp] *n.* damga; posta pulu; *v/t* damgalamak; pul yapıştırmak *-e*; ayağını vurmak *-e*

stanch [stánç] *s.* **staunch**

stand [ständ] *n.* duruş; ayaklık; tezgâh; *v/i* durmak; ayakta durmak; *v/t* dayanmak *-e*; **~ by** hazır

beklemek; **~ for** manası olm.; **~ (up)on** *-in* üzerinde ısrar etm.; *-in* tarafını tutmak; **~ up** ayağa kalkmak; taraftarı olm. **(for** *-in)*

standard ['ständıd] **1.** bayrak; **2.** standart; ayar; mikyas, ölçü; seviye; **~ize** *v/t* belirli bir ölçüye uydurmak

standing ayakta duran; şöhret; süreklilik; **of long ~** eski

stand|point görüş noktası, bakım; **~still** durma

stank [stäŋk] *s.* **stink**

star [stá] yıldız; *v/i fig.* birinci rolü oynamak

starboard ['stábıd] *naut.* sancak (tarafı)

starch [stáç] *n.* nişasta; kola; *v/t* kolalamak

stare [stä] *n.* sabit bakış; *v/i* dik bakmak **(at** *-e)*

starling ['stálıŋ] *zo.* sığırcık

start [stát] *n.* başlangıç; kalkış; sıçrama; *v/i* hareket etm., yola çıkmak; ürkmek; *v/t* başlamak *-e*; çalıştırmak *-i*; *xer tech.* marş

startl|e ['státl] *v/t* ürkütmek, korkutmak; **~ing** şaşırtıcı

starv|ation [stá'veyşın] açlık(tan ölme); **~e** *v/i* açlıktan ölmek; *v/t* açlıktan öldürmek

state [steyt] *n.* durum, hal; *pol.* devlet; *v/t* beyan etm., belirtmek; **2 Department** *Am.* Dışişleri Bakanlığı;

∼ly haşmetli; heybetli; **∼ment** ifade; demeç; rapor; **∼room** naut. tek kişilik kamara; **∼sman** devlet adamı

static ['stätik] phys. statik

station ['steyşın] n. yer; makam, rütbe; istasyon; karabol; v/t yerleştirmek; **∼ary** sabit; **∼ery** kırtasiye; **∼-master** istasyon müdürü

statistics [stı'tistiks] pl. istatistik sg.

statue ['stäcuu] heykel

status ['steytıs] durum, hal

statute ['stätyût] kanun; kural

staunch [stônç] adj. sadık; kuvvetli; v/t durdurmak

stay [stey] n. kalış, ikamet; destek; v/i durmak, kalmak; v/t durdurmak; **∼ away** gelmemek; **∼ up** yatmamak

stead [sted]: **in his ∼** onun yerine; **∼fast** sabit, sarsılmaz; **∼y** adj. devamlı, düzenli; sabit, sarsılmaz; v/t sağlamlaştırmak; v/i yatışmak

steak [steyk] fileto; kontr-} [file}
steal [stîl] v/t çalmak, aşırmak; v/i gizlice hareket etm.

stealth [stelth]: **by ∼** gizlice; **∼y** sinsi, gizli

steam [stîm] n. buhar, istim; v/i buhar salıvermek; v/t buharda pişirmek; **∼engine** buhar makinesi; **∼er**, **∼ship** vapur

steel [stîl] çelik; **∼works** pl. çelik fabrikası sg.

steep [stîp] n. dik, sarp; v/t suya batırmak

steeple ['stîpl] çan kulesi; **∼chase** engelli yarış

steer[1] [stıı] boğa; öküz

steer[2] v/t dümenle idare etm., yönetmek; **∼ing-gear** dümen donanımı; **∼ing-wheel** direksiyon

stem [stem] sap; gövde

stench [stenç] pis koku

stenography [ste'nogrıfi] stenografi

step[1] [step] n. adım; basamak; kademe, derece; v/i adım atmak; basmak (**on -e**)

step[2] üvey; **∼father** üvey baba; **∼mother** üvey ana

steppe [step] bozkır

steril|e ['sterayl] kısır; verimsiz; **∼ize** ['-ilayz] v/t kısırlaştırmak; sterilize etm.

sterling ['stölin] sterlin; değerli

stern [stön] sert, haşin; naut. kıç; **∼ness** sertlik

stew [styû] n. güveç; v/t hafif ateşte kaynatmak

steward ['styuıd] kâhya; naut. kamarot; **∼ess** hostes

stick [stik] n. değnek, sopa; baston; v/t saplamak; yapıştırmak; v/i yapışmak, takılmak (**to -e**); **∼y** yapışkan

stiff [stif] katı, sert; bükülmez; alkolü çok; **∼en** v/i

stifle

katılaşmak; *v/t* katılaştırmak

stifle ['stayfl] *v/t* boğmak;
v/i boğulmak

still [stil] *adj.* sakin, durgun; *v/t* durdurmak; ya-
tıştırmak; *adv.* hâlâ, henüz;
mamafih; **~born** ölü doğmuş

stimula|nt ['stimyulınt]
uyandırıcı (ilâç); **~te**
['~eyt] *v/t* uyarmak; **~tion**
uyarım, teşvik

sting [stin] *n.* sokma; iğne;
v/t sokmak, yakmak; *v/i*
acımak

stingy ['stinci] cimri

stink [stink] pis koku; **~ of**
-in kokusunu çıkarmak

stipulat|e ['stipyuleyt] *v/i*
şart koymak; *v/t* anlaşmak
-de; **~ion** şart (koyma)

stir [stö] *v/i* harekete geçmek; *v/t* karıştırmak; harekete geçirmek; **~rup**
['stirıp] üzengi

stitch [stiç] *n.* dikiş; ilmik;
v/t dikmek

stock [stok] *n.* soy; çiftlik
hayvanları *pl.*; *ec.* stok;
kapital; sermaye hisseleri
pl.; *v/t* yığmak; **in ~** mevcut; **out of ~** mevcudu
tükenmiş; **♀ Exchange**
borsa; **~breeder** büyük-
baş yetiştiren çiftçi; **~-
broker** borsacı; **~holder**
hissedar

stocking ['stokin] (uzun)
çorap

stock|-market borsa; **~y**
bodur

stole [stuul], **~n** *s.* **steal**

stomach ['stamık] *n.* mide;
karın; *v/t* hazmetmek

ston|e [stuun] *n.* taş; çekir-
dek; *v/t* taşlamak; **~in** çe-
kirdeğini çıkarmak; **~y**
taşlık; taş gibi

stood [stud] *s.* **stand**

stool [stuul] iskemle, tabure; *med.* büyük aptes

stoop [stuup] *v/i* eğilmek;
alçalmak

stop [stop] *n.* dur(dur)ma;
durak; engel; nokta; *v/t*
durdurmak, önlemek, kes-
mek, engellemek; tıkamak;
v/i durmak, kesilmek; **~
over** yolculukta mola vermek; **~page** durdurma,
kes(il)me; *ec.* stopaj; **~per**
tapa, tıkaç; **~ping** *med.*
dolgu

storage ['stôric] depoya
koyma; ardiye (ücreti)

store [stô] *n.* depo, ambar;
Am. dükkân, mağaza; stok;
v/t saklamak; ambara koymak; biriktirmek; **~house**
ambar, depo

storey ['stôri] bina katı

stork [stôk] *zo.* leylek

storm [stôm] *n.* fırtına;
mil. hücum; *v/t* hücumla
zaptetmek; **~y** fırtınalı

story[1] ['stôri] *s.* **storey**

story[2] hikâye, masal; roman

stout [staut] sağlam; şişman

stove [stuv] soba; fırın

stow [stu] *v/t* saklamak, istif etm.; **~away** kaçak yolcu

stripe

straggle ['strägl] v/i yoldan sapmak; ~r arkada kalan

straight [streyt] doğru; dürüst; saf; ~ away, ~ off hemen; ~ ahead, ~ on doğru; ~en v/t doğrultmak, düzeltmek; v/i doğrulmak; ~forward doğru sözlü, dürüst

strain [streyn] n. ger(il)me, gerginlik; med. burkulup incinme; v/t germek, zorlamak; süzmek; v/i çabalamak; süzülmek; ~er süzgeç

strait [streyt] geo. boğaz; sıkıntı; ~en v/t sıkıştırmak; ~-laced tutucu

strand [ständ] n. sahil; halat kolu; v/i karaya oturmak

strange [streync] yabancı; tuhaf, acayip; ~r yabancı

strangle ['strängl] v/t boğmak

strap [sträp] n. kayış; atkı; v/t kayışla bağlamak

strateg|ic [strı'tîcîk] stratejik; ~y ['strätici] strateji

straw [strô] saman; ~berry bot. çilek

stray [strey] adj. başı boş; v/i yoldan sapmak

streak [strîk] n. çizgi; iz; v/t çizgilemek; ~y çizgili

stream [strîm] n. çay, dere; ırmak; akıntı; v/i akmak; dalgalanmak

street [strît] sokak, cadde; ~car Am. tramvay

strength [strenth] kuvvet,

güç; ~en v/t kuvvetlendirmek; desteklemek

strenuous ['strenyuıs] faal, gayretli

stress [stres] n. baskı; tazyik; gayret; gr. vurgu; v/t vurgulamak

stretch [streç] n. uzanma; geniş yer; süre; v/t germek, uzatmak; v/i gerilmek, uzanmak; ~er teskere, sedye

strew [struu] v/t serpmek, dağıtmak; ~n s. strew

stricken ['strikn] uğramış (with -e); s. strike

strict [strikt] sıkı; kesin

strid|den ['stridn] s. stride; ~e [strayd] v/i uzun adımlarla yürümek; n. uzun adım

strife [strayf] çekişme

strike [strayk] n. vurma; grev; v/i grev yapmak; çalmak; v/t vurmak, çarpmak -e; flag: indirmek -i; match: çakmak -i; coin: kesmek -i; oil, etc.: bulmak -i; ~ off, out v/t listeden çıkarmak; ~r grevci

striking ['straykin] göze çarpan, şaşılacak

string [strin] n. ip, sicim, kordon; dizi; tel; v/t dizmek; tel takmak -e; ~-bean fasulye; ~y ['~nî] liflî; kılcıklı

strip [strip] n. şerit; v/t soymak, sıyırmak; v/i soyunmak

stripe [strayp] n. çizgi, kumaş yolu; v/t çizgilemek

strive

strive [strayv] uğraşmak, çalışmak (**for** -_meğe_); **∼n** ['strivn] _s._ **strive**

strode [strud] _s._ **stride**

stroke [struk] _n._ vuruş, çarpma; çizgi; _med._ inme; _v/t_ okşamak

stroll [strul] _v/i_ gezinmek; _n._ gezme

strong [stroŋ] sağlam; kuvvetli; şiddetli; **∼hold** kale; _fig._ merkez; **∼-room** hazine odası

strove [struv] _s._ **strive**

struck [strak] _s._ **strike**

structure ['strakçı] yapı; yapılış

struggle ['stragl] _n._ savaş; çaba; _v/i_ çabalamak; uğraşmak (**against** ile)

strung [straŋ] _s._ **string**

strut [strat] _v/i_ baba hindi gibi gezmek

stub [stab] kütük

stubble ['stabl] anız; uzamış tıraş

stubborn ['stabın] inatçı; sert

stuck [stak] _s._ **stick**

stud [stad] _n._ çivi; düğme; _v/t_ çivilerle süslemek

stud|ent ['styudınt] öğrenci; araştırıcı; **∼io** ['∼diıu] stüdyo; **∼ious** ['∼dyıs] çalışkan; dikkatli; **∼y** ['stadi] _n._ tahsil, öğrenim; tetkik; çalışma; çalışma odası; _v/t_ tahsil etm.; araştırmak

stuff [staf] _n._ madde; malzeme; kumaş; boş laf; _v/t_ doldurmak; **∼ing** dolma (içi); **∼y** havasız, küf kokulu

stumble ['stambl] _n._ sürçme; hata; _v/i_ sürçmek; rastlamak (**across, upon** -_e_)

stump [stamp] _n._ kütük; _v/i_ tahta ayaklı gibi yürümek

stun [stan] _v/t_ sersemletmek

stung [staŋ] _s._ **sting**

stunk [staŋk] _s._ **stink**

stunning ['staniŋ] hayret verici

stunt [stant] hüner gösterisi; **∼ man** dublör

stupefy ['styupifay] _v/t_ sersemletmek

stupid ['styupid] budala, akılsız; **∼ity** aptallık

stupor ['styupı] uyuşukluk

sturdy ['stödi] kuvvetli

stutter ['statı] _n._ kekeleme; _v/i_ kekelemek

sty[1] [stay] domuz ahırı

sty[2] _med._ arpacık

styl|e [stayl] tarz, üslûp; moda; **∼ish** zarif, modaya uygun

suave [swâf] tatlı, nazik

sub- [sab, sıb] ast, alt; **∼conscious** ['sab-] bilinçaltı

subdivision ['sab-] parselleme; alt bölüm

subdue [sıb'dyû] _v/t_ zaptetmek; hafifletmek

subject ['sabcikt] _n._ konu; _pol._ uyruk, tebaa; _gr._ özne; _adj._ tabi, bağlı (**to** -_e_); [sıb'cekt] _v/t_ maruz kılmak (**to** -_e_); **∼ion** [sıb'cekşın] hüküm altına alma

subjunctive (**mood**) [sıb-'cantiv] _gr._ şart kipi

sublime [sı'blaym] yüce, ulu

submarine [sab-] *naut.* denizaltı

submerge [sub'mȫc] *v/t* batırmak; *v/i* batmak

submissi|on [sıb'mişın] boyun eğme; ~**ve** uysal, boyun eğen

submit [sıb'mit] *v/t* teslim etm. (**to** -*e*); sunmak (-*e*); *v/i* boyun eğmek, itaat etm. (**to** -*e*)

subordinate [sı'bôdnit] ikincil; ast memur; ~**clause** *gr.* bağımlı cümlecik

subpoena [sıb'pînı] *jur.* mahkemeye davet

subscribe [sıb'skrayb] *v/t* imzalamak; bağışlamak; *v/i* abone olm. (**to** -*e*); ~**r** abone (olan)

subscription [sıb'skripşın] imza; abone; üye aidatı

subsequent ['sabsikwınt] sonra gelen; ~**ly** sonradan

subsid|e [sıb'sayd] *v/i* inmek; yatışmak; ~**iary** [sıb-'sidyıri] yardımcı; bağlı; ~**ize** ['sabsidayz] *v/t* para vermek -*e*; ~**y** ['sabsidi] para yardımı

subsist [sıb'sist] *v/i* beslenmek (**on** ile); ~**ence** geçinim; nafaka

substance ['sabstıns] madde, cevher; öz

substantial [sıb'stänşl] gerçek; önemli; zengin

substantive ['sabstıntiv] *gr.* isim, ad

substitut|e ['sabstityût] *n.* bedel; vekil; *v/t* yerine koymak (**for** -*in*); *v/i* yerine geçmek; ~**ion** ikame, yerine koyma

subterrane|an, ~ous [sab-tı'reynyın, ~yıs] yeraltı; gizli

subtle ['satl] ince; kurnaz

subtract [sıb'träkt] *v/t* *math.* çıkarmak

suburb ['sabȫb] varoş, banliyö; ~**an** [sı'bȫbın] banliyö ile ilgili

subvention [sıb'venşın] para yardımı

subversi|on [sab'vȫşın] devirme; ifsat; ~**ve** yıkıcı

subway ['sabwey] tünel; *Am.* yaraltı metro

succeed [sık'sîd] *v/i* başarmak (**in** -*i*); vâris olm. (**to** -*e*), (-*in*) yerine geçmek

success [sık'ses] başarı; ~**ful** başarılı; ~**ive** ardıl, müteakıp; ~**or** halef, ardıl

succumb [sı'kam] dayanamamak (**to** -*e*)

such [saç] böyle, öyle; bu gibi; ~ **as** gibi; örneğin

suck [sak] *v/t* emmek, içine çekmek; ~**le** *v/t* emzirmek; meme vermek -*e*; ~**ling** memede çocuk

sudden ['sadn] ani, birden; **all of a** ~, ~**ly** birdenbire, ansızın

suds [sadz] *pl.* sabun köpüğü *sg.*

sue [syû] *v/i* istemek (**for** -*i*); *v/t* dava açmak (*so.* -*in* aleyhine)

suède [sweyd] (podü)süet
suet ['syuıt] iç yağı
suffer ['safı] v/t katlanmak
-e; v/i tutulmuş olm. (**from**
-e); **~ance** müsamaha;
~ing acı, ıstırap
suffic|e [sı'fays] kâfi gel-
mek, yetmek; **~ient** ['~'fi-
şınt] kâfi, yeterli
suffix ['safiks] gr. sonek
suffocate ['safıkeyt] v/t
boğmak; v/i boğulmak
suffrage ['safric] oy kullanma (hakkı)
sugar ['şugı] n. şeker; v/t
şeker katmak -e; **~cane**
şekerkamışı
suggest [sı'cest] v/t telkin
etm.; ileri sürmek; öner-
mek; **~ion** teklif; ima; **~ive**
manalı; müstehcen
suicide ['syuisayd] intihar;
kendini öldüren kimse
suit [syût] n. takım; erkek
elbisesi; tayyör; jur. dava;
v/t uygun gelmek, yaramak
-e; **~able** uygun, elverişli
(**for, to** -e); **~case** bavul,
valiz; **~e** [swît] maiyet; oda
takımı; **~or** ['syûtı] jur.
davacı; âşık
sulk [salk] somurtmak; **~y**
somurtkan
sullen ['salın] asık yüzlü,
somurtkan; kapanık
sulphur ['salfı] chem. kükürt   [cu; tutkulu)
sultry ['saltri] sıcak, boğu-)
sum [sam] tutar; yekün;
miktar; **~ up** v/t özetlemek;
hüküm vermek (so. b. hak-
kında)

summar|ize ['samırayz] v/t
özetlemek; **~y** özet, hulâsa
summer ['samı] yaz; **~ resort** sayfiye
summit ['samit] zirve, do-
ruk
summon ['samın] v/t çağırmak; **~s** ['~z] pl. jur.
celpname, çağrı
sumptuous ['samtyus]
tantanalı
sun [san] n. güneş; v/t gü-
neşlendirmek; v/i güneş-
lenmek; **~bath** güneş
banyosu; **~beam** güneş
ışını; **~burn** güneşten yanma; **~day** ['~di] pazar
(günü)
sundry ['sandri] çeşitli
sunflower bot. ayçiçeği
sung [san] s. **sing**
sun-glasses pl. güneş göz-
lüğü sg.
sunk [sank] s. **sink**; **~en**
gömülmüş; çökmüş
sun|ny ['sani] güneşli; neşe-
li; **~rise** gün doğuşu; **~set**
güneş batması; **~shine**
güneş ışığı; **~stroke** güneş
çarpması
super|- ['syûpı-] üst; fazla;
~abundant bol
superb [syu'pöb] muhteşem
super|ficial [syûpı'fişıl]
sathî, üstünkörü; **~fluous**
['~'pöfluıs] fazla, lüzumsuz;
~highway Am. oto yolu;
~human insanüstü; **~in-
tend** v/t kontrol etm.;
~intendent müfettiş; müdür

superior [syu'piiri:] üstün,
daha iyi; üst, âmir; **~ity**
[~'oriti] üstünlük

superlative [syu'pölitiv] *gr.*
enüstünlük

super|man üst insan; **~**
market büyük mağaza;
~natural doğaüstü; **~**
scription yazıt; adres;
başlık; **~sonic** *phys.* sesten
hızlı; **~stition** [~'stişn]
boş inan, hurafe; **~stitious**
boş şeylere inanan; **~vise**
['~vayz] *v/t* nezaret etm. -*e*;
idare etm. -*i*; **~visor** murakıp, denetçi

supper ['sapı] akşam yemeği; **the Lord's ♀** *rel.* kudas

supple ['sapl] kolayca eğilir;
uysal

supplement ['saplimınt] *n.*
ek, zeyil; ['~ment] *v/t* eklemek; **~ary** eklenen; bütün-
leyici **[yalvarış]**

supplication [sapli'keyşn] *n.*

supply [sı'play] *n.* gereç,
malzeme; *ec.* arz, sunu; *v/t*
sağlamak (*sth. -i*; *so.* **with**
-*e -i*)

support [sı'pôt] *n.* dayanak, destek; yardım; ge-
çim; *v/t* desteklemek; -*i*
beslemek -*i*

suppos|e [sı'puuz] *v/t* far-
zetmek, zannetmek; **~ition**
[sapı'zişn] farz; varsayım,
ipotez

suppress [sı'pres] *v/t* bastırmak; **~ion** bastırma;
baskı

suppurate ['sapyureyt] *v/i*
cerahat bağlamak

supra- [syûprı] üst; öte

supremacy [syu'premısi]
üstünlük; egemenlik; **~e**
[~'prîm] en yüksek

surcharge ['söcâc] *n.* sürşarj; [~'çâc] *v/t* fazla yüklemek, fazla doldurmak; sürşarj basmak -*e*

sure [şu] emin (**of** -*den*);
sağlam; muhakkak; **make**
~ kanaat getirmek (**of**,
that -*e*); **~ly** elbette; **~ty**
['~ırti] kefil; rehine

surf [söf] çatlayan dalgalar
pl.

surface ['söfis] yüz, düzey;
görünüş

surge [söc] *n.* büyük dalga;
v/i dalgalanmak

surg|eon ['söcın] cerrah,
operatör; **~ery** cerrahlık;
~ical cerrahî

surly ['söli] gülmez, ters

surmise [sö'mayz] *n.* zan,
sanı; [~'mayz] *v/t* sanmak,
zannetmek

surmount [sö'maunt] *v/t*
üstün gelmek -*e*

surname ['söneym] soyadı

surpass [sö'pâs] *v/t* geçmek; üstün olm. -*e*

surplus ['söplıs] fazla, artık

surprise [sı'prayz] *n.* sürpriz; hayret; *v/t* hayrete
düşürmek, şaşırtmak

surrender [sı'rendı] *n.* teslim, feragat; *v/t* teslim
etm.; *v/i* teslim olm. (**to** -*e*)

surround [sı'raund] *v/t* kuşatmak; **~ings** *pl.* çevre,
muhit *sg.*

surtax ['sötäks] ek vergi

survey ['sövey] *n.* teftiş; gözden geçirme; mesaha; [~'vey] *v/t* teftiş etm.; yoklamak; mesaha etm.; ~or [~'v~] mesaha memuru

surviv|al [sı'vayvıl] kalım; hayatta kalma; ~e *v/i* hayatta kalmak; *v/t* fazla yaşamak -*den*; ~or hayatta kalan, kurtulan

susceptible [sı'septıbl] has sas, alıngan

suspect ['saspekt] *adj.*, *n.* şüpheli; [sıs'pekt] *v/t* şüphelenmek, kuşkulanmak -*den*

suspend [sıs'pend] *v/t* asmak; ertelemek; geçici olarak durdurmak; tart etm.; ~ed asılı, muallak; ~er çorap askısı; *Am.* pantolon askısı

suspens|e [sıs'pens] muallak kalma; merak; asma; (*of payment*) tatil, durdurma

suspici|on [sıs'pişın] şüphe; ~ous şüpheli; şüphe verici

sust|ain [sıs'teyn] *v/t* desteklemek; beslemek; kallanmak -*e*; kuvvet vermek -*e*; ~enance ['sastinıns] besleme, gıda, geçim

swagger ['swägı] caka satmak, horozlanmak

swallow¹ ['swolu] *zo.* kırlangıç

swallow² *v/t* yutmak, em-[mek]

swam [swäm] *s.* **swim**

swamp [swämp] *n.* bataklık; *v/t* batırmak

swan [swon] *zo.* kuğu

swarm [swôm] *n.* sürü; küme; *v/i* toplanmak; kaynaşmak

swarthy ['swôdhi] esmer

swathe [sweydh] *v/t* sarmak

sway [swey] *n.* sallanma; nüfuz; *v/i* sallanmak; *v/t* sallamak; etkilemek

swear [swä] *v/i* yemin etm.; küfretmek (**at** -*e*); ~**in** *v/t* yeminle işe başlatmak

sweat [swet] *n.* ter; *v/i* terlemek; *v/t* terletmek; ~er kazak

Swed|e [swed] İsveçli; ~en İsveç; ~ish İsveçli; İsveççe

sweep [swip] *n.* süpürme; alan; ocakçı; *v/t* süpürmek, temizlemek; taramak; geçmek; ~er sokak süprücü; çöpçü; ~ing genel, şümullü; ~ings *pl.* süprüntü *sg.*

sweet [swit] tatlı, şekerli; hoş; *pl.* tatlılar, bonbonlar; ~en *v/t* tatlılaştırmak; ~heart sevgili; ~ness tatlılık

swell [swel] *v/i* şişmek, kabarmak; *v/t* şişirmek, kabartmak; *Am. adj.* güzel, âlâ; ~ing kabarık, şişlik

swept [swept] *s.* **sweep**

swerve [swöv] yoldan sapmak

swift [swift] çabuk, hızlı; ~ness çabukluk, hız

swim [swim] *v/i* yüzmek; *head:* dönmek; ~mer yüzücü; ~ming-pool yüzme havuzu

swindle ['swindl] *n.* dolan-

dırıcılık; *v/t* dolandırmak;
~r dolandırıcı
swine [swayn] domuz
swing [swiŋ] *n.* sallanma;
salıncak; *v/i* sallanmak,
salınmak; dönmek; *v/t* sallamak; **~door** iki tarafa
açılır kapanır kapı
swirl [swöl] girdap
Swiss [swis] İsviçreli
switch [swiç] *n. el.* düğme;
şalter; anahtar; (*rail*) makas; ince değnek; *v/t* çevirmek; **~ off** *el.* kapamak; **~
on** *el.* açmak; **~board** *el.*
anahtar tablosu [İsviçre]
Switzerland ['switsılınd]∫
swivel ['swivl] fırdöndü; **~
chair** döner iskemle
swollen ['swuuln] *s.* **swell**
swoon [swuun] *n.* bayılma;
v/i bayılmak
sword [sôd] kılıç
swor|e [swô], **~n** *s.* **swear**
swum [swam] *s.* **swim**
swung [swaŋ] *s.* **swing**
syllable ['silıbl] hece
symbol ['simbl] sembol,
simge; **~ic(al)** ['~bolik(ıl)]
sembolik, simgesel

symmetry ['simitri] simetri, bakışım
sympath|etic [simpı'thetik] sempatik, sevimli; **~ize**
yakınlık duymak (**with** *-e*);
~y sempati
symphony ['simfıni] *mus.*
senfoni
symptom ['simptım] alâmet, belirti
synagogue ['sinıgog] *rel.*
havra
synchronize ['siŋkrınayz]
v/t aynı zamana uydurmak
synonym ['sinınim] *gr.*
eşanlam, anlamdaş kelime;
~ous ['~nonimıs] anlamdaş
syntax ['sintäks] *gr.* sözdizimi, sentaks
synthe|sis ['sinthisis] bireşim, sentez; **~tic** ['~thetik]
sentetik
syphilis ['sifilis] *med.* frengi
Syria ['siri] Suriye; **~n**
Suriyeli
syringe ['sirinc] şırınga
syrup ['sirıp] şekerli sos
system ['sistim] sistem,
usul; **~atic** ['~mätik] sistemli, usule göre

T

tab [täb] askı; etiket
table ['teybl] masa; sofra;
liste, cetvel; tarife; **~land**
geo. plato, yayla; **~spoon**
yemek kaşığı
tablet ['täblit] komprime,
tablet; levha
tacit ['täsit] zımnî; **~urn**
['~ôn] az konuşur

tack [täk] *n.* pünez; teyel
dikişi; *v/t* teyellemek
tackle [täkl] *n.* takım, cihaz;
tech. palanga; *v/t* uğraşmak
(*sth.* ile)
tact [täkt] incelik, nezaket;
~ful ince(likli); **~ics** *pl.*
taktik *sg.*; **~less** nezaketsiz,
kaba

tadpole

tadpole ['tädpıul] *zo.* iribaş

tag [täg] *n.* etiket; *v/t* etiketlemek; *v/i* takılmak (after *-e*)

tail [teyl] kuyruk; arka; son; ~coat frak

tailor ['teylı] terzi

taint [teynt] *n.* leke; kusur; *v/t* lekelemek, bozmak

take [teyk] *v/t* almak; kabul etm.; götürmek; yapmak; sürmek; uğramak *-e*; ihtiyacı olm. *-e*; ~ **account** hesaba katmak (of *-i*); ~ **advantage** faydalanmak (of *-den*); ~ **care** bakmak (of *-e*); ~ **hold** tutmak (of *-i*); ~ **in** *v/t* almak; daraltmak; *pop.* aldatmak; ~ **off** *v/t* çıkarmak; *v/i* av. havalanmak; ~ **pains** uğraşmak (with *ile*); ~ **place** vuku bulmak; ~ **to** kendini vermek *-e*, hoşlanmak *-den*; ~ **n** *s.* take; ~**off** *av.* havalanma

tale [teyl] masal, hikâye

talent ['tälınt] kabiliyet, yetenek; ~**ed** kabiliyetli, hünerli

talk [tôk] *n.* konuşma; görüşme; laf; *v/i* konuşmak (to *ile*); *v/t* söylemek, konuşmak; ~ **big** övünmek; ~**ative** ['..ıtiv] konuşkan

tall [tôl] uzun (boylu); yüksek

tallow ['tälıu] donyağı

talon ['tälın] *zo.* pençe

tame [teym] *adj.* evcil, ehli; uysal; *v/t* alıştırmak

tamper ['tämpı] karışmak (with *-e*), karıştırmak *-i*

tan [tän] *n.* güneş yanığı; *adj.* açık kahverengi; *v/t* tabaklamak; karartmak

tang|ent ['täncınt] *math.* teğet; ~**ible** dokunulur; gerçek

tangerine [täncı'rîn] *bot.* mandalina

tangle ['tängl] *n.* karışıklık; *v/t* karıştırmak

tank [tänk] *mil.* tank; depo, sarnıç

tankard ['tänkıd] içki maşrapası

tanner ['tänı] tabak, sepici

tantalize ['täntılayz] *v/t* hayal kırıklığına uğratmak

tantrum ['täntrım] hiddet (nöbeti)

tap [täp] *n.* musluk; fıçı tapası; hafif vuruş; *v/t* hafifçe vurmak *-e*; akıtmak *-i*

tape [teyp] şerit, bant, kurdele; ~ **recorder** teyp; ~ **recording** teype alma; ~ **-measure** mezür, mezura

taper ['teypı] ~ **off** *v/i* sivrilmek

tapestry ['täpistri] *n.* goblen

tapeworm bağırsak kurdu

tar [tâ] *n.* katran; *v/t* katranlamak

tare [tä] *ec.* dara

target ['tâgit] hedef, nişangâh

tariff ['tärif] gümrük tarifesi; fiat listesi

tarnish ['täniş] *v/i* donuklaşmak; *v/t* donuklaştırmak

tart [tât] ekşi; keskin; turta

task [tâsk] ödev; görev; **take to** ~ v/t azarlamak

tassel ['tâsıl] püskül

taste [teyst] n. tat, lezzet, çeşni; zevk; v/t -in tadına bakmak; denemek -i; ~**ful** lezzetli; zevkli; ~**less** tatsız; zevksiz

tasty ['teysti] tatlı; zevkli

tatter ['tätı] paçavra

tattoo [tı'tuu] n. dövme; mil. yat borusu; v/t dövme yapmak -e

taught [tôt] s. **teach**

taunt [tônt] n. hakaret, alay; v/t alay etm. ile

tavern ['tävın] meyhane

tax [täks] n. vergi, resim; v/t vergi koymak -e; ~**ation** vergi tarhı

taxi(-**cab**) ['täksi(-)] taksi; ~-**driver** taksi şoförü

tax|**payer** vergi mükellefi; ~-**return** vergi beyannamesi

tea [tî] çay

teach [tîç] v/t öğretmek, okutmak; ders vermek -e; ~**er** öğretmen

team [tîm] takım, ekip; ~**work** takım halinde çalışma

teapot çaydanlık

tear[1] [tiı] gözyaşı

tear[2] n. yırtık; v/t yırtmak, koparmak; v/i yırtılmak

tease [tîz] v/t tedirgin etm.; takılmak -e

teaspoon çay kaşığı

teat [tît] meme, emcik

techni|cal ['teknikıl] tek-

nik; resmî; kurallara uygun; ~**cian** [~'nişın] teknisyen, teknikçi; ~**que** [~'nîk] teknik, yapma usulü

tedious ['tîdyıs] usandırıcı, can sıkıcı

teen|**ager** ['tîneycı] on üçten on dokuz yaşlar arasındaki kimse, delikanlı; ~**s** [~z] pl. on üç ile on dokuz arasındaki yaşlar

teeny ['tîni] ufak

teetotal(l)**er** [tî'tuutlı] içki içmiyen kimse

tele|**gram** ['teligräm] telgraf(name); ~**graph** ['~grâf] n. telgraf; v/i telgraf çekmek

telephone ['telifoun] n. telefon; v/t telefon etm. -e; ~ **call** telefon çağırması; ~ **exchange** santral

tele|**printer** ['teliprintı] teleks; ~**scope** [~'skıup] teleskop; ~**vision** [~'vijın] televizyon

tell [tel] v/t söylemek, anlatmak, bildirmek (so. -e); ~**er** veznedar; ~**tale** dedikoducu; belli eden

temper ['tempı] n. tabiat; huy, mizaç; öfke; v/t ayarlamak, hafifletmek; tech. tavlamak; **lose one's** ~ hiddetlenmek; ~**ament** ['~rımınt] mizaç, tabiat; ~**ance** ölçülülük; içkiden kaçınma; ~**ate** ['~rit] ılımlı; içkiden kaçınan; ~**ature** ['~prıçı] sıcaklık; ısı derecesi

tempest ['tempist] fırtına,

bora; **~uous** [~'pestyuıs] fırtınalı

temple¹ ['templ] *rel.* mabet, tapınak

temple² *an.* şakak

tempor|al ['tempırıl] geçici; *rel.* dünyevî; **~ary** geçici

tempt [tempt] *v/t* baştan çıkarmak, ayartmak; **~a-tion** günaha teşvik; **~ing** çekici

ten [ten] on

tenacious [ti'neyşıs] inatçı, vazgeçmez

tenant ['tenınt] kiracı

tend [tend] *v/t* bakmak -e; *v/i* meyletmek, yönelmek (**to** -*e*); **~ency** meyil, eğilim

tender¹ ['tendı] tender

tender² *n.* teklif; *v/t* sunmak

tender³ nazik, şefkatli; **~loin** fileto; **~ness** şefkat

tendon ['tendın] *an.* veter, kiriş

tendril ['tendril] *bot.* asma filizi

tenement ['tenimınt] apartman; kiralık daire

tennis ['tenis] tenis; **~court** kort, tenis alanı

tenor ['tenı] gidiş; yön; *mus.* tenor

tens|e [tens] gergin, gerili; *gr.* fiil zamanı; **~ion** gerginlik; *el.* gerilim

tent [tent] çadır

tentacle ['tentıkl] *zo.* kavrama uzvu

tentative ['tentıtiv] deneme, tecrübe

tepid ['tepid] ılık

term [töm] *n.* terim; süre; şart; sömestr; dönem; *v/t* adlandırmak; **bring to ~s** *v/t* razı etm.; **on good ~s** araları iyi

termin|al ['töminl] son; terminal; **~ate** ['~eyt] *v/t* bitirmek; sınırlamak; **~a-tion** son, bitirme; **~us** ['~nıs] terminal

terrace ['teris] taraça, teras

terri|ble ['terıbl] korkunç, dehşetli; **~fic** [tı'rifik] korkunç; *pop.* çok güzel; **~fy** ['terifay] *v/t* korkutmak, dehşete düşürmek

territor|ial [teri'töriıl] karaya ait; belirli bir bölgeye ait; **~y** ['~turi] ülke; bölge; arazi

terror ['terı] korku, dehşet; **~ism** tedhişçilik; **~ist** tedhişçi

test [test] *n.* deney, tecrübe; test; *v/t* denemek, prova etm.; imtihan etm.

testament ['testimınt] vasiyetname

testify ['testifay] *v/i* şehadette bulunmak; *v/t* kanıtlamak

testimon|ial [testi'mıunyıl] bonservis; belge; **~y** ['~mını] tanıklık, şahadet

testy ['testi] ters, hırçın

text [tekst] metin; konu; **~book** ders kitabı

text|ile ['tekstayl] dokuma; tekstil; *pl.* mensucat; **~ure** ['~çı] doku; örgü; yapı

than [dhän, dhın] *-den* daha

thorny

thank [thänk] v/t teşekkür
etm. -e; ~ **God** Allaha
şükür; ~s pl. teşekkür; şükür; ~s **to** sayesinde; I'm
minnettar; ♀giving **Day**
Am. şükran yortusu

that [dhät, dhıt] şu, o; ki; ~
is yani

thatch [thäç] n. dam örtüsü
olarak kullanılan saman
veya saz; v/t sazla kaplamak

thaw [thô] n. erime; v/t
eritmek; v/i erimek

the [dhı, dhi] (belirtme edatı); ~ ... ~ ne kadar ... o kadar

theat|re, Am. ~er ['thıtı]
tiyatro

thee [dhi] seni; sana

theft [theft] hırsızlık

their [dhär] onların; ~s [~z]
onlarınki

them [dhem, dhım] onları,
onlara

theme [thîm] konu

themselves [dhım'selvz]
kendileri (ni, -ne, -nde)

then [dhen] ondan sonra; o
zaman; şu halde; **by** ~ o
zamana kadar; ~**ce** oradan;
bundan dolayı

theology [thi'olıci] ilâhiyat,
teoloji

theor|etic|al [thiı'retik(ıl)]
kuramsal, nazarî; ~y ['~ri]
teori, kuram

therapy ['therıpi] med. tedavi

there [dhär] ora(sı); orada;
oraya; ~ **is**, pl. ~ **are** vardır; ~**about(s)** o civarda;

~**after** ondan sonra; ~**by**
o suretle; ~**fore** onun için,
bundan dolayı; ~**upon**
bunun üzerine; ~**with** onun-
la

therm|al ['thömıl] sıcağa
ait; termal; ~**ometer** [thı-
'momitı] termometre; ~**os**
['thömos] (**bottle, flask**)
termos

these [dhîz] bunlar

thesis ['thîsis] tez; dava

they [dhey] onlar

thick [thik] kalın; sık; kesif;
~**en** v/t kalınlaştırmak; v/i
kalınlaşmak; ~**et** ['~it] çalılık; ~**ness** kalınlık; sıklık

thief [thîf] hırsız

thigh [thay] an. uyluk, but

thimble ['thimbl] yüksük

thin [thin] adj. ince, zayıf,
az; v/t inceltmek; v/i incelmek

thing [thin] şey, nesne

think [think] v/i düşünmek
(**about** -i); v/t düşünmek;
zannetmek; tasavvur etm.;
~ **of** hatırlamak -i; saymak
-i; ~ **over** v/t -in üzerinde
düşünmek   [bir\

third [thöd] üçüncü; üçte\

thirst [thöst] n. susuzluk;
v/i susamak (**after, for** -e);
~**y** susuz, susamış

thirt|een ['thö'tîn] on üç;
~**y** otuz

this [dhis] bu

thistle ['thisl] bot. devedi-
keni

thither ['dhidhı] oraya

thorn [thôn] diken; ~**y** dikenli

thorough ['thʌrı] tam, mükemmel; ~**bred** saf kan, soylu; ~**fare** cadde; geçit

those [dhuz] şunlar, onlar

thou [dhau] sen

though [dhu] gerçi, her ne kadar, ~**diği** halde; **as ~ ~miş** gibi

thought [thôt] düşünme; düşünce; fikir; s. **think**; ~**ful** düşünceli; saygılı; ~**less** düşüncesiz; dikkatsiz

thousand ['thauzınd] bin

thrash [thräş] v/t dövmek; dayak atmak -e; ~**ing** dayak

thread [thred] n. iplik, tire; *tech.* yiv; v/t ipliğe dizmek; yol bulup geçmek; ~**bare** eskimiş, yıpranmış

threat [thret] tehdit; tehlike; ~**en** v/t tehdit etm.; ~**ening** tehdit edici

three [thrî] üç; ~**fold** üç misli; ~**score** altmış

thresh [threş] v/t harman dövmek; ~**er**, ~**ing-machine** harman dövme makinası

threshold ['threşhuld] eşik

threw [thruu] s. **throw**

thrice [thrays] üç kere

thrifty ['thrifti] tutumlu, idareli

thrill [thril] n. titreme; heyecan; v/t heyecanlandırmak; v/i heyecanla titremek; ~**er** heyecanlı kitap *veya* piyes

thrive [thrayv] iyi gitmek, gelişmek; ~**n** ['thrivn] s. **thrive** [lak]

throat [thrıut] boğaz, gırt-√

throb [throb] v/i çarpmak; titreşmek

throne [thrıun] taht

throng [throŋ] n. kalabalık; v/i toplanmya

throstle ['throsl] zo. ardıç-kuşu

throttle ['throtl] v/t boğmak; kısmak; ~**(-valve)** *tech.* kısma valfı; kelebek

through [thruu] arasında, içinden; bir yandan öbür yana; baştan başa; bitirmiş; ~ **carriage** direkt vagon; ~**out** -*in* her tarafında; baştan başa

throve [thrıuv] s. **thrive**

throw [thruu] n. atış; v/t atmak, fırlatmak; ~ **off** çıkarmak, üstünden atmak; ~ **up** yukarı atmak; kusmak

thrush [thraş] zo. ardıçkuşu

thrust [thrast] n. itiş; hamle; v/t itmek, dürtmek

thud [thad] n. gümbürtü; v/i güm diye ses çıkarmak

thumb [tham] başparmak; v/t aşındırmak; ~ **a ride** ototsop yapmak; ~**tack** *Am.* pünez

thump [thamp] n. vuruş; ağır düşüş; v/t vurmak -e; v/i hızla çarpmak

thunder ['thandı] n. gök gürlemesi; v/i gök gürlemek; ~**storm** gök gürültülü yağmur fırtınası; ~**struck** *fig.* hayrete düşmüş

Thursday ['thözdi] perşembe

thus [dhas] böyle(ce), bu suretle

thwart [thwôt] v/t bozmak, önlemek

thy [dhay] senin

thyme [taym] bot. kekik

tick[1] [tik] zo. kene

tick[2] n. tıkırtı; v/i tıkırdamak; **~ off** v/t işaretleyerek saymak

tick[3] kılıf

ticket ['tikit] n. bilet; aday listesi; etiket; v/t etiketlemek; **~-office** Am., **~-window** bilet gişesi

tickl[e ['tikl] v/i gıdıklanmak; v/t gıdıklamak; **~ish** gıdıklanır; fig. nazik

tid[al ['taydl] geo. gelgite bağlı; **~e** [tayd] gelgit, met ve cezir; fig. akış

tidy ['taydi] temiz, düzenli; pop. epey; **~ up** v/t düzeltmek

tie [tay] n. bağ; kravat; travers; v/t bağlamak

tier [tiı] sıra, kat

tiger ['taygı] zo. kaplan

tight [tayt] sıkı; su geçirmez; müşkül; pop. sarhoş; **~en** v/t sıkıştırmak; v/i sıkışmak; **~rope** sıkı gerilmiş ip; **~s** pl. sıkı giysi sg.; külotlu çorap

Tigris ['taygris] Dicle

tile [tayl] n. kiremit; çini; v/t kiremit kaplamak

till[1] [til] e kadar, -e değin

till[2] para çekmecesi

till[3] v/t toprağı işlemek

tilt[1] [tilt] tente

tilt[2] n. devrilmek; v/t eğmek

timber ['timbı] kereste; kerestelik orman

time [taym] n. vakit, zaman; süre; defa; mus. tempo; v/t ayarlamak; uydurmak; ölçmek; **for the ~ being** şimdilik; **in ~** vaktinde; **in no ~** bir an evvel; **on ~** tam zamanında; **~ly** uygun, yerinde; **~table** tarife

tim[id ['timid], **~orous** ['~ırıs] sıkılgan, ürkek

tin [tin] n. teneke; kalay; teneke kutu; v/t kalaylamak; kutulara doldurmak

tinge [tinc] n. hafif renk, iz; v/t hafifçe boyamak

tingle ['tiŋgl] sızlamak

tinkle ['tiŋkl] v/i çınlamak; v/t çıngırdatmak

tint [tint] n. hafif renk; v/t hafif boyamak

tiny ['tayni] ufak, minicik

tip [tip] n. uç; ağızlık; bahşiş; tavsiye; v/t bahşiş vermek -e; eğmek -i; v/i devrilmek; **~ off** v/t imada bulunmak -e

tipsy ['tipsi] çakırkeyf

tiptoe ['tiptou] ayak parmağının ucu; **on ~** ayak parmaklarının ucuna basarak

tire[1] ['tayı] s. **tyre**

tire[2] v/t yormak; usandırmak; v/i yorulmak; **~d** yorgun; bıkmış (of -den); **~some** yorucu

tissue ['tişuu] doku; ince kâğıt

tit[1] [tit] baştankara

tit[2]: **~ for tat** kısasa kısas

titbit ['titbit] lezzetli lokma

title ['taytl] unvan; isim; hak

titmouse ['titmaus] *zo.* baştankara

to [tuu, tu, tı] **1.** (*mastar edatı*); **2.** -e (-a, -ye, -ya); -mek için; ~ **and fro** öteye beriye

toad [tuud] *zo.* kara kurbağa

toast[1] [tuıst] *n.* kızartılmış ekmek; *v/t* ekmek kızartmak

toast[2] *n* sıhhatine içme; *v/t* -*in* şerefine içmek

tobacco [tı'bæku] tütün; ~-**nist** [~kınist] tütüncü

toboggan [tı'bogın] kızak

today [tı'dey] bugün

toe [tuu] ayak parmağı; uç

together [tı'gedhı] birlikte; aralıksız

toil [toyl] *n.* zahmet; *v/i* zahmet çekmek

toilet ['toylit] tuvalet, aptesane; ~-**paper** tuvalet kâğıdı

token [tı'tukın] belirti; hatıra

told [tuıld] *s.* **tell**

tolera|ble ['tolırıbl] dayanılabilir; ~**nce** müsamaha, ~**nt** müsamahakâr; ~**te** ['~eyt] *v/t* müsamaha etm. -*e*; katlanmak -*e*; ~**tion** müsaade; hoşgörü

toll[1] [tuul] *v/i*, *v/t* çalmak

toll[2] yol *veya* köprü parası; resim; ~-**bar**, ~-**gate** bariyer

tomato [tı'mâtu] domates

tomb [tuum] kabir, türbe; ~**stone** mezar taşı

tomcat ['tom'kæt] erkek kedi

tomorrow [tı'moru] yarın

ton [tan] ton (*1016 kilo, Am. 907 kilo*)

tone [tuun] ses; *mus.* ton

tongs [tonz] *pl.* maşa *sg.*

tongue [taŋ] dil, lisan

tonic ['tonik] ilâç, tonik

tonight [tı'nayt] bu gece

tonnage ['tonic] tonilato, tonaj

tonsil ['tonsil] *an.* bademcik; ~**itis** [~si'laytis] *med.* bademcik iltihabı

too [tuu] dahi, keza; (haddinden) fazla

took [tuk] *s.* **take**

tool [tuul] alet

tooth [tuuth] diş; ~**ache** diş ağrısı; ~**brush** diş fırçası; ~**paste** diş macunu; ~**pick** kürdan

top [top] *n.* üst, zirve, tepe; en yüksek nokta; *v/t* kapamak; üstün gelmek -*den*, -*in* birincisi olm.; **on** (**the**) ~ **of** -*in* üstünde; ~ **secret** çok gizli

topic ['topik] konu

topple ['topl] *v/i* devrilmek; *v/t* devirmek

topsy-turvy ['topsi'tövi] alt-üst; karmakarışık

torch [tôç] meşale; cep feneri

tore [tô] *s.* **tear**[2]

torment ['tôment] *n.* cefa, eziyet; *v/t* eziyet etm. -*e*

torn [tôn] *s.* **tear**[2]

tornado [tô'neydıu] kasırga

torpedo [tô'pidıu] *n.* torpil; *v/t* torpillemek

torpid ['tôpid] uyuşuk

torrent ['torınt] sel

tortoise ['tôtıs] *zo.* kaplumbağa
torture ['tôçı] *n.* işkence; *v/t* işkence etm. *-e*
Tory ['tôri] *pol.* tutucu parti üyesi
toss [tos] *n.* atma, fırlatma; *v/t* atmak, fırlatmak; ~ **about** *v/i* çalkanmak
total ['tıutl] *n.* tutar, yekûn; *adj.* tam, bütün; *v/t* toplamak; tutmak; ~**itarian** [~täli'tärıın] *pol.* totaliter
totter ['totı] sendelemek
touch [taç] *n.* dokunma; temas; iz; *v/t* dokunmak *-e*, ellemek *-i*; ~ **down** *v/i* inmek; ~**ing** dokunaklı; ~**y** alıngan; titiz
tough [taf] sert; çetin; dayanıklı
tour [tuı] *n.* gezi; tur; *v/i, v/t* gezmek; ~**ism** ['~rizım] turizm; ~**ist** turist; ~**nament** ['~nımınt] turnuva, yarışma
tousle ['tauzl] *v/t saçı* karıştırmak
tow [tıu] *n.* yedekte çek(il)me; *v/t* çekmek; **have, take in** ~ *v/t* yedekte çekmek
toward(s) [tı'wôd(z)] *-e* doğru; *-e* karşı
towel ['tauıl] havlu
tower ['tauı] *n.* kule, burç; *v/i* yükselmek
town [taun] şehir, kasaba; ~ **hall** belediye binası
tow-rope yedek halatı
toy [toy] *n.* oyuncak; *v/i* oynamak
trace [treys] *n.* iz; *v/t* izlemek; kopya etm.
track [träk] *n.* iz; pist; yol; ray; *v/t* izlemek; ~ **down,** ~ **out** izliyerek bulmak; ~**-and-field** atletizm
tract [träkt] risale; bölge; alan
tract|ion ['träkşın] çekme; ~**or** traktör
trade [treyd] *n.* ticaret; meslek, iş; *v/i* ticaret yapmak (**in** ile); ~**mark** alâmeti farika, marka; ~**r** tüccar; ~ **union** sendika; ~**-unionist** sendıkacı
tradition [trı'dişın] gelenek, anane; ~**al** geleneksel
traffic ['träfik] *n.* gidişgeliş, trafik; ticaret, trampa; *v/i* ticaret yapmak; ~ **jam** trafik tıkanıklığı; ~ **sign** trafik işareti
trag|edy ['trăcidi] trajedi; facia; ~**ic(al)** feci; acıklı
trail [treyl] *n.* kuyruk; iz; yol; *v/t* peşinden sürüklemek; izlemek; *v/i* sürüklenmek; ~**er** römork; treyler
train [treyn] *n.* tren; maiyet; sıra; yerde sürünen uzun etek; *v/t* öğretmek, alıştırmak; talim etm.; ~**er** antrenör; ~**ing** talim; antrenman
trait [trey] özellik
traitor ['treytı] hain
tram(-car) [träm(-)] tramvay (vagonu)
tramp [trämp] *n.* serseri; *naut.* tarifesiz işliyen yük gemisi; avare gezme; ağır

trample

adım ve sesi; *v/i* avare dolaşmak; *v/t* ayak altında çiğnemek; **~le** *v/t* çiğnemek, ezmek

tramway tramvay

tranquil ['trăŋkwil] sakin, asude; **~(I)ity** sükûn; **~(I)izer** yatıştırıcı (ilâç)

transact [trăn'zăkt] *v/t* bitirmek, iş görmek; **~ion** iş, muamele

trans|alpine ['trănz'ălpayn] *geo.* Alplerin ötesinde bulunan; **~atlantic** Atlantik aşırı; **~continental** kıtayı kateden

transcribe [trăns'krayb] *v/t* kopya etm.

transcript ['trănskript] ikinci nüsha, kopya; **~ion** transkripsiyon

transfer ['trăns'fö] *n.* nakil; transfer; aktarma bileti; [~'fö] *v/t* nakletmek; devretmek; havale etm.; *v/i* aktarma yapmak; **~able** [~'föribl] devredilebilir

transform [trăns'fôm] *v/t* başka kalıba sokmak; *-in* şeklini değiştirmek; tahvil etm. *-i*; **~ation** dönüş(tür)üm; şekil değişmesi; **~er** *el.* transformatör

transfus|e [trăns'fyûz] *v/t* aktarmak; **~ion** [~jın] aktarma; *med.* kan nakli

transgress [trăns'gres] *v/t* bozmak; çiğnemek; aşmak; **~ion** haddi aşma; suç; **~or** tecavüz eden

transient ['trănziınt] geçici; kısa zaman kalan misafir

transistor [trăn'sıstı] *el.* transistor

transit ['trănsit] geçme; *ec.* transit; **~ion** [~'sijın] geçiş; **~ive** *gr.* geçişli

translat|e [trăns'leyt] *v/t* çevirmek, tercüme etm.; **~ion** çeviri, tercüme; *v/t* çevir(m)en [yarı şeffaf]

translucent [tră nz'luusnt]

transmission [trănz'mişın] nakil; intikal; yayım

transmit [trănz'mit] *v/t* geçirmek; göndermek; yayımlamak; **~ter** yayım istasyonu

transparent [trăns'păırınt] şeffaf, saydam

transpire [trăns'payı] *v/i* terlemek; *fig.* duyulmak, sızmak

transplant [trăns'plânt] *v/t* başka yere dikmek *veya* yerleştirmek; **~(ation)** nakil

transport [trăns'pôt] *v/t* götürmek, nakletmek, taşımak; [~'.] *n.* nakil; taşınma; taşıt; ulaştırma; **~ation** nakil; taşıt

trap [trăp] *n.* tuzak; kapanca; *v/t* tuzağa düşürmek, yakalamak; **~-door** kapak şeklinde kapı; **~per** tuzakçı

trash [trăş] değersiz şey, süprüntü; değersiz adam; ayaktakımı

travel ['trăvl] *n.* yolculuk, seyahat; *v/i* seyahat etm.; *v/t* dolaşmak, **~(I)er** yolcu; **~(I)er's cheque** (*Am.* **check**) seyahat çeki

traverse ['trävös] *v/t* karşıdan karşıya geçirmek; ka-
tetmek

trawl [tröl] *n.* tarak ağı; *v/i*
tarak ağı ile balık tutmak

tray [trey] tepsi; tabla

treacher|ous ['treçırıs]
hain, güvenilmez; ~y hainlik   [mezi]

treacle ['trikl] şeker pek-
tread [tred] *n.* ayak basışı;
v/i ayakla basmak (**on** -*e*);
çiğnemek (-*i*); ~le pedal;
~mill ayak değirmeni; *fig.*
sıkıcı iş

treason ['trîzn] hainlik

treasure ['treji] *n.* hazine;
v/t biriktirmek; değerli
tutmak; ~r haznedar

treasury ['trejiri] hazne; ♀
Department *Am.* Maliye
Bakanlığı

treat [trît] *n.* zevk; ikram;
v/t ikram etm. -*e* (**to** *sth.*
-*i*); muamele etm. -*e*; tedavi etm. -*i*; *v/i* bahsetmek
(**of** -*den*); ~ise ['~iz] risale;
~ment muamele; tedavi;
~y antlaşma

treble ['trebl] üç kat, üç
misli; *v/i* üç misli olm.; *v/t*
üç kat etm.

tree [trî] ağaç

trefoil ['trefoyl] *bot.* yonca

trellis ['trelis] kafes işi

tremble ['trembl] titremek
(**with** -*den*)

tremendous [tri'mendıs]
kocaman; heybetli

trem|or ['tremı] titreme;
sarsıntı; ~ulous ['~yulıs]
titrek; ürkek

trench [trenç] hendek, siper

trend [trend] yön, eğilim
(**towards** -*e*)

trespass ['trespıs] *n.* günah,
suç; *v/i* tecavüz etm. (**on**,
upon -*e*), bozmak (-*i*)

tress [tres] bukle; saç örgüsü

trestle ['tresl] sehpa

trial ['trayıl] deneme, tecrübe; *jur.* muhakeme, du-
ruşma

triang|le ['trayäŋgl] üçgen;
~ular ['~äŋgyulı] üçgen
şeklinde

tribe [trayb] kabile, aşiret

tribulation [tribyu'leyşın]
keder, sıkıntı

tribun|al [tray'byûnl] mah-
keme; ~e ['tribyûn] 1. halkı
savunan; 2. tribün

tribut|ary ['tribyutıri] ne-
hir kolu; ~e ['~yût] haraç,
vergi; takdir

trick [trik] *n.* oyun, hile,
düzen; *v/t* aldatmak; **play
a** ~ oyun oynamak (**on** -*e*)

trickle ['trikl] *v/i* damla
damla akmak; *v/t* akıtmak

tricky ['triki] hileli

trifl|e ['trayfl] *n.* önemsiz
şey; az miktar; *v/i* oynamak; ~ing önemsiz

trigger ['trigı] tetik

trill [tril] *n.* ses titremesi;
v/i sesi titretmek

trillion ['trilyın] trilyon;
Am. bilyon

trim [trim] *adj.* biçimli, şık;
v/t düzeltmek; süslemek;
kısaltmak; denkleştirmek

Trinity ['triniti] *rel.* teslis

trinket 416

trinket ['triŋkit] değersiz süs

trip [trip] *n.* gezinti, kısa seyahat; tur; *v/i* sürçmek; hata yapmak

tripe [trayp] işkembe

triple ['tripl] üç misli; üçlü; ~ts ['~its] *pl.* üçüzler

tripod ['traypod] sehpa

Tripoli ['tripıli] Trablusgarp; Trablusşam

triumph ['trayımf] *n.* zafer, galebe; zafer alayı; *v/i* yenmek (**over** -*i*); **~ant** galip, muzaffer

trivial ['triviıl] ufak tefek, önemsiz

trod [trod], **~den** *s.* **tread**

troll(e)y ['troli] yük arabası; tekerlekli servis masası; troleybüs

troop [truup] *n.* takım, sürü; *pl.* askerler; *v/i* bir araya toplanmak

trophy ['trıufi] ganimet; hatıra

tropic ['tropik] *geo.* tropika, dönence; *pl.* sıcak ülkeler; **~al** tropikal

trot [trot] *n.* tırıs; *v/i* tırıs gitmek; koşmak

trouble ['trabl] *n.* sıkıntı, zahmet; dert, keder; rahatsızlık; *v/t* rahatsız etm.; sıkmak; *v/i* zahmet çekmek; **ask for ~** belâ aramak; **~maker** kendine çıkaran; **~some** zahmetli, sıkıntılı

through [truf] tekne, yalak

trousers ['trauzız] *pl.* pantolon *sg.*

trousseau ['truusıu] çeyiz

trout [traut] *zo.* alabalık

truant ['truınt] dersi asan

truce [truus] ateşkes, mütareke

truck[1] [trak] el arabası; üstü açık yük vagonu; kamyon

truck[2] *Am.* sebze

trudge [trac] zahmetle yürümek

true [truu] doğru, gerçek; sahih; halis; sadık; **come ~** gerçekleşmek

truly ['truuli] *adv.* gerçekten; samimi olarak

trump [tramp] *n.* koz; *v/i* koz çıkarmak

trumpet ['trampit] *mus.* boru; boru sesi

truncheon ['trançın] polis sopası

trunk [traŋk] bavul; gövde; *zo.* hortum; *tel.* ana hat; *Am.* kısa don; erkek mayosu; **~call** şehirlerarası telefon

trust [trast] *n.* güven; emanet; *ec.* tröst; *v/t* güvenmek -*e*; emanet etm. -*e* (**with** -*i*); **~ee** [~'ti] mutemet, vekil; **~ful**, **~ing** güvenen; **~worthy** güvenilir

truth [truuth] doğruluk, hakikat; **~ful** doğru; gerçek

try [tray] *v/t* denemek, tecrübe etm.; *jur.* yargılamak, muhakeme etm.; *v/i* uğraşmak; *n.* deneme, tecrübe; **~ing** yorucu

tub [tab] tekne; fıçı; küvet

tube [tyûb] boru; tüp; iç lastik; yeraltı metro

tuberculosis [tyubökyû'lusis] tüberküloz, verem

tuck [tak] *v/t* sokmak, sıkıştırmak; **~ up** sıvamak

Tuesday ['tyûzdi] salı

tuft [taft] küme; sorguç; püskül

tug [tag] *n.* kuvvetli çekiş; *naut.* römorkör; *v/t* şiddetle çekmek

tuition [tyû'işın] öğretim

tulip ['tyûlip] *bot.* lâle

tumble ['tambl] *v/i* düşmek, devrilmek; *v/t* düşürmek; **~r** bardak

tummy ['tami] *fam.* karın; mide

tumo(u)r ['tyûmı] *med.* tümör, ur

tumult ['tyûmalt] kargaşalık, gürültü; **~uous** [~'maltyuıs] gürültülü

tun [tan] fıçı

tuna ['tuunı] *zo.* ton balığı, orkinos

tune [tyûn] *n.* nağme, melodi; akort; *v/t* akort etm.

tunnel ['tanl] tünel

turban ['töbın] sarık

turbine ['töbin] türbin

turbulent ['töbyulınt] serkeş; çalkantılı

turf [töf] *n.* çimen(lik); hipodrom; *v/t* çimen döşemek **-e**

Turk [tök] Türk

Turkey[1] ['töki] Türkiye

turkey[2] *zo.* hindi

Turkish ['tökiş] Türk; Türkçe; **~ delight** lokum

turmoil ['tömoyl] kargaşa, gürültü

turn [tön] *n.* dönme; devir; nöbet; viraj; tarz; sıra; yön; *v/i* olmak; dönmek; sapmak, yönelmek (**to -e**); *v/t* döndürmek, çevirmek; **take ~s** sıra ile yapmak (**at -i**); **~ back** *v/i* geri dönmek; *v/t* geri çevirmek; **~ down** *v/t* indirmek; reddetmek; **~ off** *v/t* kapatmak, kesmek; **~ on** *v/t* açmak; çevirmek; **~ out** *v/t* kovmak; *v/i* meydana çıkmak (**to inf. -diği**); **~ up** *v/i* çıkmak; görünmek; *v/t* yukarı çevirmek; **~coat** *pol.* dönek adam; **~er** tornacı; **~ing** dönen; dönüş

turnip ['tönip] *bot.* şalgam

turn-out *ec.* ürün, verim; **~over** devrilme; *ec.* satış; **~pike** *Am.* geçiş parası alınan yol; **~stile** turnike

turquoise ['tökwâz] firuze

turret ['tarit] küçük kule; *mil.* taret

turtle ['tötl] *zo.* kaplumbağa; **~dove** kumru

tusk [task] *zo.* fildişi; azıdişi

tutor ['tyûtı] öğretmen; *jur.* vasi

tuxedo [tak'sidiu] smokin

twang [twäŋ] *n.* tıngırtı; genizden çıkan ses; *v/i* tıngırdamak; genizden konuşmak

tweed [twid] tüvit

tweezers ['twîzız] *pl.* cımbız *sg.*

twelve [twelv] on iki

twenty ['twenti] yirmi

twice [tways] iki kere, iki defa [dürmek]

twiddle ['twidl] v/t dön-

twig [twig] ince dal

twilight ['twaylayt] alaca karanlık

twin [twin] ikiz; çift, çifte

twine [twayn] n. sicim; v/t bükmek, sarmak; v/i sarılmak

twinkle ['twinkl] n. pırıltı; v/i pırıldamak; göz kırpıştırmak

twirl [twöl] n. dönüş; kıvrım; v/i fırıldanmak

twist [twist] n. bük(ül)me; burma; dönüş; ibrişim; v/t bükmek, burmak; v/i bükülmek, burulmak

twitch [twiç] v/i seğirmek; v/t seğirtmek

twitter ['twiti] cıvıldamak

two [tuu] iki; ~fold iki kat; ~pence ['tapıns] iki pens; ~-way iki taraflı; iki yollu

type [tayp] n. çeşit, tip; model; basma harf; v/t daktilo ile yazmak; ~writer yazı makinesi, daktilo

typhoid (fever) ['tayfoyd] med. tifo

typhoon [tay'fuun] tayfun

typhus ['tayfıs] med. tifüs

typical ['tipikıl] tipik

typist ['taypist] daktilo(da yazan)

tyrann|ic(al) [ti'ränikl] zalim, gaddar; ~y ['~rıni] istibdat, zulüm

tyrant ['tayırınt] zalim, zorba

tyre ['tayı] dış lastik

U

udder ['adı] zo. inek memesi

ugly ['agli] çirkin; korkunç

ulcer ['alsı] med. ülser, karha

ultimat|e ['altimit] son, nihaî; ~um [~'meytım] pol. ültimatom

ultra- ['altrı] aşırı, son derece

umbrella [am'brelı] şemsiye

umpire ['ampayı] hakem

un- [an-] -siz, gayri

un|abashed küstah, arsız; ~able gücü yetmez; beceriksiz; ~acceptable kabul edilemez; ~accountable anlatılmaz; olağanüstü; ~affected etkilenmemiş; samimî; ~alterable değişmez

unanim|ity [yûnı'nimiti] oy birliği; ~ous [~'nänimıs] aynı fikirde

un|approachable yanına varılamaz; ~armed silâhsız; ~asked sorulmamış, davetsiz; ~assuming gösterişsiz; ~authorized yetkisiz; ~avoidable kaçınılmaz; ~aware ['anı'wäı] habersiz; ~balanced dengesiz; ~bar v/t -in sürgü-

sünü açmak; ~bearable
dayanılmaz; ~becoming
yakışıksız; ~believable
inanılmaz; ~bending sabit, eğilmez; ~bias(s)ed
tarafsız; ~bidden davetsiz;
~born henüz doğmamış;
~bounded sınırsız; ölçüsüz; ~breakable kırılamaz;
~broken kırılmamış; sürekli; ~button v/t -in düğmelerini çözmek; ~called-for lüzumsuz, yersiz; ~canny [~'käni] tekin olmayan; ~cared-for bakımsız; ~ceasing durmıyan, aralıksız; ~certain şüpheli; kararsız, belirsiz;
~changing değişmez; ~checked durdurulmamış, serbest; ~civil nezaketsiz;
~civilized medenileşmemiş; ~claimed sahibi çıkmamış

uncle ['aŋkl] amca, dayı;
teyze veya halanın kocası
un|clean pis, kirli; ~comfortable rahatsız (edici);
~common olağanüstü; nadir; ~communicative az
konuşur; ~complaining
şikâyet etmiyen; ~compromising uzlaşmaz, eğilmez; ~concerned ilgisiz;
kayıtsız; ~conditional
şartsız; ~confirmed doğrulanmamış; ~conscious
bilinçsiz; baygın; ~constitutional anayasaya aykırı; ~conventional göreneklere uymayan; ~couth
[an'kuuth] kaba; ~cover

v/t -in örtüsünü kaldırmak;
~damaged zarar görmemiş; ~decided kararsız;
kararlaştırılmamış; asıda;
~deniable inkâr olunamaz
under ['andı] -in altın(d)a;
-den aşağı, -den eksik; ~carriage şasi; av. iniş
takımı; ~clothes pl., ~clothing iç çamaşır; ~developed az gelişmiş; ~do v/t gerektiğinden az pişirmek; ~estimate v/t gerektiğinden az değer vermek -e; ~fed gıdasız; ~go
v/t katlanmak, uğramak -e;
~graduate üniversite öğrencisi; ~ground yeraltı;
metro; ~line v/t -in altını
çizmek; -in önemini belirtmek; ~mine v/t -in temelini çürütmek; ~most en
alttaki; ~neath -in altın(d)a; ~privileged imkânları kıt olan; ~rate s.
~estimate; ~shirt iç gömleği, fanila; ~signed imza
sahibi; ~sized normalden
küçük; ~stand v/t anlamak, kavramak; ~standing
anlayış; anlaşma; anlayışlı;
~statement olduğundan
hafif gösteren ifade; ~take
v/t üzerine almak; ~taker
cenaze işleri görevlisi; ~taking iş, teşebbüs; ~value s. ~estimate; ~wear s. ~clothes; ~world
ölüler diyarı; kanunsuzlar
âlemi
un|deserved lâyık olmıyan;
~developed gelişmemiş;

~**diminished** azalmamış; ~**disputed** karşı gelinmemiş; ~**disturbed** karıştırılmamış, rahatsız edilmemiş; ~**do** v/t açmak; çözmek; telâfi etm.; bozmak; ~**dreamt-of** akla gelmeyen; ~**dress** v/i elbiselerini çıkarmak, soyunmak; ~**due** aşırı; kanunsuz; uygunsuz; ~**dying** ölmez; ~**earth** v/t topraktan çıkarmak; ~**easy** huzursuz; ~**educated** okumamış

unemploy|ed işsiz; ~**ment** işsizlik [tükenmez] **unending** sonsuz, bitmez] **unequal** eşit olmıyan; ~(l)ed eşsiz; üstün

un|erring yanılmaz; ~**even** düz olmıyan; *math.* tek; ~**eventful** olaysız; ~**expected** beklenilmedik; ~**failing** tükenmez; şaşmaz; ~**fair** haksız; hileli; ~**familiar** iyi bilmiyen (with -i); alışılmamış (-e); ~**fasten** v/t çözmek, açmak; ~**favo(u)rable** müsait olmıyan; elverişsiz; ~**feeling** hissiz; merhametsiz; ~**finished** bitmemiş, tamamlanmamış; ~**fit** uymaz (for -e); ehliyetsiz; ~**fold** v/t açmak, yaymak; v/i açılmak; ~**foresee** beklenmedik; ~**forgettable** unutulmaz; ~**forgiving** uzlaşmaz

unfortunate talihsiz, bahtsız; ~**ly** adv. maalesef, yazık ki

un|founded temelsiz, asılsız; ~**friendly** dostça olmıyan; ~**furl** v/t açmak; ~**furnished** mobilyasız; ~**gainly** hantal, biçimsiz; ~**governable** yönetilmez; ~**gracious** nezaketsiz; ~**grateful** nankör; ~**happy** kederli; şanssız; ~**harmed** zararsız; ~**healthy** sıhhate zararlı; ~**heard-of** işitilmemiş

unheed|ed aldırış edilmiyen; ~**ing** dikkat etmiyen

un|hesitating tereddüt etmiyen; ~**hurt** zarar görmemiş

uni|fication [yûnifi'keyşn] birleş(tir)me; ~**form** ['yûnifôm] üniforma, resmî elbise; tekdüzen, yeknesak; ~**fy** ['yûnifay] v/t birleştirmek; ~**lateral** ['yûni'lätırıl] tek taraflı

un|imaginative yaratma kabiliyeti olmıyan; ~**impaired** zarar görmemiş; ~**important** önemsiz; ~**inhabited** oturulmamış, ıssız; ~**intelligible** anlaşılmaz; ~**intentional** istemiyerek yapılan; ~**interrupted** aralıksız

union ['yûnyın] birleşme; birlik; anlaşma; sendika; 2 **Jack** İngiliz bayrağı; ~**ist** sendikacı

unique [yû'nîk] tek, biricik **unison** ['yûnizn] birlik, ahenk

unit ['yûnit] birlik; ünite;

~e [~'nayt] v/i birleşmek; v/t birleştirmek; ~ed Kingdom Britanya Krallığı; ~ed Nations pl. Birleşmiş Milletler; ~ed States pl. of America Amerika Birleşik Devletleri; ~y birlik, birleşme

univers|al [yûni'vôsıl] genel; evrensel; ~e [~'ôs] evren, kâinat; ~ity [~'vôsiti] üniversite

un|just haksız; ~kempt taranmamış; ~kind dostça olmıyan, sert; ~known bilinmez; yabancı; ~lace v/t -in bağlarını çözmek; ~ lawful kanuna aykırı; ~ learn v/t öğrendiğini unutmak

unless [ın'les] -medikçe, meğerki

unlike -e benzemiyen, -den farklı; ~ly umulmaz, olasısız

un|limited sınırsız; sayısız; ~load v/t boşaltmak; ~lock v/t -in kilidini açmak; ~ loose(n) v/t çözmek; ~ lucky talihsiz, bahtsız; ~manageable idare edilemez; ~manly erkekçe olmıyan; ~married evlenmemiş; ~mistakable açık, belli; ~moved sarsılmaz; ~natural tabiata aykırı; anormal; ~necessary lüzumsuz; ~noticed, ~observed gözden kaçmış; ~ obtrusive göze çarpmaz; alçak gönüllü; ~occupied boş, serbest; ~offending

kusursuz, zararsız; ~official resmi olmayan; ~ pack v/t boşaltmak; açmak; ~paid ödenmemiş; ücretsiz; ~paralleled essiz, emsalsiz; ~pardonable affedilemez; ~perturbed ['~pô'tôbd] sakin, soğukkanlı; ~pleasant nahoş; ~ polished parlatılmamış; fig. kaba; ~popular rağbet görmeyen; gözden düşmüş; ~practical elverişli olmayan; ~precedented emsali görülmemiş; ~prejudiced tarafsız; ~prepared hazırlıksız; ~principled karaktersiz, ahlâksız; ~productive verimsiz

unprovided yoksun (with -den); ~ for ihtiyacı karşılanmamış

un|qualified ehliyetsiz; şartsız; ~questionable şüphe götürmez

unreal gerçek olmıyan, hayali; ~istic gerçekçi olmayan

un|reasonable makul olmayan; aşırı; ~recognizable tanınmaz; ~refined tasfiye edilmemiş; incelilksiz; ~reliable güvenilmez; ~reserved sınırlanmamış; samimî; ~rest kargaşa, rahatsızlık; ~restrained frenlenmemiş; ~restricted sınırsız; ~ripe ham; erken gelişmiş; ~rival(l)ed essiz, rakipsiz; ~roll v/t açmak; v/i açılmak; ~ruly azılı, itaatsiz; ~safe emniyetsiz;

tehlikeli; **~satisfactory** memnuniyet vermeyen; tatmin etmiyen; **~screw** v/t -in vidalarını sökmek; çevirerek açmak -i; **~scrupulous** vicdansız; prensipsiz; **~seemly** yakışıksız; **~seen** görülmemiş; gizli; **~selfish** kendini düşünmiyen; **~settled** kararlaştırılmamış; belirsiz; boş; ödenmemiş [mış] **unshave|d, ~n** tıraşı uzamış **unshrink|able** çekmez, büzülmez; **~ing** çekinmesiz **un|sightly** çirkin; **~skilled** becerisiz; ehliyetsiz; **~sociable** çekingen, konuşmayan; **~sophisticated** saf, sade; **~sound** sağlam olmıyan; hastalıklı; **~spoiled** bozulmamış; şımarmamış; **~stable** sağlam olmıyan; kararsız; **~steady** oynak; kararsız; **~successful** başarısız; **~surpassed** eşsiz **unsuspect|ed** şüphelenilmiyen; **~ing** saf, masum **un|thinkable** düşünülemez, akla gelmez; **~tidy** düzensiz; **~tie** v/t çözmek **until** [un'til] -e kadar, -e değin **un|timely** vakitsiz; uygunsuz; **~tiring** yorulmak bilmez; **~told** hesapsız; **~touched** dokunulmamış; **~tried** denenmemiş; yargılanmamış; **~true** yalan, doğru olmıyan; **~trustworthy** güvenilmez

unus|ed ['an'yûzd] kullanılmamış; **~ual** nadir; olağandışı **un|utterable** ağza alınmaz, söylenmez; **~veil** v/t -in örtüsünü açmak; **~wanted** istenilmez; **~warranted** [~'worıntld] haksız; **~wholesome** sıhhate zararlı; **~willing** isteksiz; **~wind** v/t çözmek; v/i açılmak; **~wise** akılsız; **~worthy** yakışmaz; lâyık olmıyan (of -e); **~wrap** v/t açmak, çözmek; **~yielding** boyun eğmez

up [ap] yukarı(ya); yukarıda; **~ to** -e kadar; be ~ to -e bağlı olm., -in işi olm.; be **~ to** inf. -mekte olm.; **~ and about** hastalıktan kurtulmuş; **~s and downs** pl. iniş çıkışlar, iyi ve kötü günler

up|bringing yetiş(tir)me; **~heaval** karışıklık; devrim; **~hill** yokuş yukarı; **~hold** v/t tutmak; desteklemek; **~holstery** döşemecilik; **~keep** bakım; bakım masrafı

upon [ı'pon] s. on

upper ['api] üst; üstteki; yukarıdaki; **~ class** zenginler sınıfı; 2 **House** pol. Lortlar kamarası; **~most** en üst

up|right dik, dikey; dürüst; **~rising** ayaklanma; **~roar** şamata; **~set** v/t devirmek, altüst etm.; v/i devrilmek; adj. altüst; **~side-down**

valentine

altüst; **~stairs** yukarıya; yukarıda; üst kat; **~start** türedi, sonradan görme; **~stream** akıntıya karşı; **~to-date** modern, asrî; **~ward(s)** ['~wıd(z)] yukarıya doğru

uranium [yu'reynyım] uranyum

urban ['öbın] şehre ait

urbane [ö'beyn] nazik, kibar

urchin ['öçin] afacan çocuk

urge [öc] v/t ileri sürmek; sevketmek; sıkıştırmak; **~ncy** acele; **~nt** acele olan

urine ['yuurin] an. idrar, sidik

urn [ön] (ayaklı) kap; semaver

us [as, ıs] bizi; bize

usage ['yûsic] kullanış; usul; âdet

use [yûs] n. fayda; kullanma; âdet; [yûz] v/t kullanmak; yararlanmak *-den*; he

~d [yûst] to *inf.* eskiden -erdi; **~ up** v/t tüketmek; **~d** [yûzd] kullanılmış; alışık (to *-e*); **~ful** faydalı, yararlı; **~less** faydasız

usher ['aşı] n. mübaşir; kapıcı; *thea.* yer gösteren kimse; v/t yol gösteren *-e*

usual ['yûjuıl] her zamanki, olağan; **~ly** adv. çoğunlukla

usurer ['yûjırı] tefeci

usurp [yü'zöp] v/t gaspetmek, zorla almak

usury ['yûjıri] murabaha

utensil [yu'tensil] yarar(lık); kamu hizmeti; **~ze** v/t kullanmak; faydalanmak *-den*

utili|ty [yu'tiliti] yarar(lık); kamu hizmeti; **~ze** v/t kullanmak; faydalanmak *-den*

utmost ['atmust] en uzak; son derece

utter ['atı] adj. tam; sapına kadar; v/t ağza almak, söylemek; **~ance** ifade; söz

uvula ['yûvyulı] an. küçük dil

V

vacan|cy ['veykınsi] boşluk; boş yer; **~t** boş; açık; münhal

vacat|e [vı'keyt] v/t boş bırakmak; boşaltmak; **~ion** tatil

vaccinat|e ['väksineyt] v/t aşılamak; **~ion** aşı(lama)

vacuum ['väkyum] boşluk, vakum; **~ bottle** termos; **~ cleaner** elektrik süpürgesi [seri, avare]

vagabond ['vägibond] ser-

vagary ['veygıri] kapris

vagina [vı'caynı] an. dölyolu, mehbil

vague [veyg] belirsiz, müphem

vain [veyn] boş, nafile; kendini beğenmiş; **in ~** adv. boşuna, beyhude (yere)

vale [veyl] vadi, dere

valentine ['välıntayn] sevgili; **Saint 2's Day** 14 şubat

valerian [vɪ'lɪırin] *bot.* kediotu

valiant ['välyınt] yiğit, cesur

valid ['välid] yürürlükte olan, geçerli

valise [vɪ'lîz] valiz, bavul

valley ['väli] vadi, dere

valo(u)r ['väli] yiğitlik, cesaret

valu|able ['välyuıbl] değerli; değerli şey; **~ation** değer biçme; **~e** [˗ˌû] *n.* değer; *v/t* takdir etm.; değer vermek **-e**

valve [välv] *tech.* supap, valf; radyo lambası

vamp [vämp] *pop.* fındıkçı kadın; **~ire** ['˗ˌayı] vampir, hortlak

van [vän] üstü kapalı yük arabası; furgon

vane [veyn] yelkovan, fırıldak; pervane kanadı

vanilla [vɪ'nilı] vanilya

vanish ['väniş] gözden kaybolmak

vanity ['väniti] nafilelik; kendini beğenme; **~ bag, ~ case** makyaj çantası

vanquish ['vänkwiş] *v/t* yenmek

vantage ['vântic] üstünlük

vap|orize ['veypırayz] *v/t* buharlaştırmak; *v/i* buharlaşmak; **~orous** buharlı; **~o(u)r** buhar

variable ['väırıbl] değişken; kararsız

variance ['väırıns] değişiklik; ayrılık; **at ~** aykırı (**with** **-e**)

varia|nt ['väırıınt] farklı; varyant; **~tion** değişme; değişiklik

varicose ['värikus] (**vein**) *med.* varisli (damar)

varie|d ['väırid] çeşitli, türlü; **~ty** [vɪ'rayıti] değişiklik; varyete (*birkaç*)

various ['väırıs] çeşitli

varnish ['vâniş] *n.* vernik; *v/t* verniklemek

vary ['väıri] *v/t* değiştirmek; *v/i* değişmek; farklı olm. (**from** *-den*)

vase [väz] vazo

vast [vâst] engin, geniş, vâsi

vat [vät] tekne, fıçı

vault [vôlt] *n.* tonoz; kemer; kasa; atlayış; *v/t* atlamak

veal [vîl] dana eti

vegeta|ble ['vecitıbl] bitkilere ait; bitki; sebze; **~rian** [˗'tärin] et yemez kimse; **~tion** bitkiler *pl.*

vehemen|ce ['vîimıns] şiddet; **~t** şiddetli

vehicle ['vîikl] taşıt; vasıta

veil [veyl] *n.* peçe, duvak; örtü; *v/t* örtmek; *v/i* örtünmek

vein [veyn] damar

velocity [vi'losıti] hız, sürat

velvet ['velvit] kadife

venal ['vînl] satın alınır

vend [vend] *v/t* satmak; **~er, ~or** satıcı

venera|ble ['venırıbl] muhterem, saygıdeğer; **~te** ['˗eyt] *v/t* saygı göstermek **-e**; tapmak **-e**

venereal [vi'niırıl] *med.* zührevî

Venetian ['vɪ'nɪʃɪn] Venedikli; ~ **blind** jaluzi

vengeance ['vencɪns] öç, intikam; **with a** ~ son derecede

Venice ['venɪs] Venedik

venison ['venzn] geyik *veya* karaca eti

venom ['venɪm] zehir; *fig.* düşmanlık; ~**ous** zehirli

vent [vent] delik, menfez; kıç; **give a** ~ **to** -*i* açığa vurmak

ventilat|e ['ventɪleyt] *v/t* havalandırmak; ~**ion** havalandırma; ~**or** vantilatör

ventr|al ['ventrl] karna ait; ~**iloquist** ['~'trɪlıkwıst] vantrlok

venture ['vençı] *n.* tehlikeli iş, şans işi; *v/t, v/i* (**to** *inf.*) tehlikeye atmak -*i*; ~**some** atılgan; tehlikeli

Venus ['vɪnıs] *rel.* Venüs; *astr.* Çulpan, Venüs

veranda(h) [vɪ'rændı] veranda, çamlı taraça

verb [vöb] *gr.* fiil; ~**al** *gr.* fiile ait; sözlü; harfiyen

verdant ['vödınt] yeşil, taze

verdict ['vödıkt] *jur.* jüri kurulu hükmü; karar

verdure ['vöcı] yeşillik

verge [vöc] *n.* kenar; sınır; *v/i* yaklaşmak (**on** -*e*)

verif|ication [verifi'keyşın] tahkik; ~**y** ['~'fay] *v/t* doğrulamak; tahkik etm.

vermicelli [vömi'seli] *pl.* tel şehriye *sg.*

vermiform ['vömiföm] **appendix** *an.* apandis

vermin ['vömin] haşarat

vernacular [vɪ'nækyulı] bölgesel; günlük dil

vers|atile ['vösıtayl] çok iş bilen; ~**e** [vös] mısra; beyit; ~**ed** iyi bilen (**in** -*i*); ~**ion** tercüme; okunuş tarzı; ~**us** -*e* karşı

vertebra ['vötıbrı] *an.* omur(ga kemiği)

vertical ['vötıkıl] dikey, düşey

very ['veri] çok, pek; tam; aynı; bile; **this** ~ **day** bugünkü gün

vessel ['vesl] kap; gemi; *an.* damar

vest [vest] iç gömleği; *Am.* yelek

vestige ['vestic] iz

vestry ['vestri] *rel.* giyinme odası; yönetim kurulu

vet [vet] *pop.* veteriner

veteran ['vetırın] kıdemli, emekli; emekli asker

veterinary (surgeon) ['vetırinri] veteriner, baytar

veto ['vɪtu] *n.* veto; *v/t* reddetmek, veto etm.

vex [veks] *v/t* incitmek, kızdırmak; ~**ation** kızma; sıkıntı; ~**atious** gücendirici; aksi

via ['vayı] yolu ile

viaduct ['vayıdakt] *arch.* köprü, viyadük

vibrat|e [vay'breyt] *v/i* titremek, sallanmak; ~**ion** titreşim

vicar ['vıkı] *rel.* papaz; vekil; ~**age** papazın evi

vice[1] [vays] kötü huy; leke

vice² mengene, sıkmaç
vice versa ['vaysi'vösı] tersine
vice|-admiral [vays-] koramiral; ~consul konsolos yardımcısı; ~president başkan yardımcısı
vicinity [vi'siniti] civar, çevre
vicious ['vişıs] kötü; ahlâkı bozuk
victim ['viktim] kurban; mağdur kimse
victor ['viktı] galip; ✛ian [~'tôrin] Kıraliçe Viktorya zamanına ait; ~ious galip, muzaffer; ~y zafer
victuals ['vitlz] pl. yemekler, erzak
Vienna [vi'enı] Viyana
view [vyû] n. bakış; manzara; görüş; ✛f bakmak -e; tetkik etm. -i; düşünmek -i; in ~ of -in karşısında; point of ~, ~point bakım, görüş noktası
vigil ['vicil] gece nöbet tutma; ~ance uyanıklık; ~ant uyanık
vigo|rous ['vigırıs] dinç, kuvvetli; ~(u)r kuvvet, dinçlik
vile [vayl] kötü, iğrenç; pis
village ['vilic] köy; ~r köylü
villain ['vilın] alçak veya çapkın adam; ~ous çirkin, habis; ~y kötülük, rezalet
vindicat|e ['vindikeyt] v/t -in doğruluğunu ispat etm.; korumak -i; ~ion koruma
vindictive [vin'diktiv] kinci

vine [vayn] asma (çubuğu); ~gar ['vinigı] sirke; ~yard bağ
vintage ['vintic] bağ bozumu; kaliteli şarap
violat|e ['vayıleyt] v/t bozmak; tecavüz etm. -e; ~tion ihlâl; tecavüz
violen|ce ['vayılıns] zor; şiddet; ~t şiddetli, sert
violet ['vayılit] bot. menekşe; mor
violin [vayı'lin] mus. keman
viper ['vaypı] zo. engerek; yılan
virgin ['vöcin] kız, bakire; bakir; ~ity kızlık, bakirelik
viril|e ['virayl] erkeksi; ~ity [~'riliti] erkeklik
virtual ['vötyuıl] gerçek kuvveti olan; ~ly adv. gerçekte
virtue ['vötyû] fazilet, iffet; by ~ of -e dayanarak
virtuous ['vötyuıs] iffetli
virus ['vayırıs] virüs
visa ['vîzı] vize
viscount ['vaykaunt] vikont
vise [vays] s. vice²
visib|ility [vizi'biliti] görüş; görünürlük; ~le görünebilir; belli
vision ['vijın] görme; görüş; hayal, kuruntu
visit ['vizit] n. ziyaret; vizita; v/t ziyaret etm., görmeğe gitmek; pay a ~ to -i ziyaret etm.; ~or ziyaretçi, misafir
visual ['vizyuıl] görmekle ilgili; görülebilir; ~ize v/t gözünde canlandırmak

vital ['vaytl] hayatî; esaslı, zarurî; **~ity** [~'täliti] dirilik; canlılık

vitamin ['vitmin] vitamin

viv|acious [vi'veyşıs] canlı, neşeli; **~id** ['~vid] canlı; parlak

vocabulary [vıu'käbyuhri] sözlük; kelime bilgisi

vocal ['vıukıl] sesle ilgili; sesli; **~ist** şarkıcı

vocation [vıu'keyşın] davet; meslek; **~al** meslekle ilgili

vogue [vıug] moda; rağbet

voice [voys] ses; gr. etken veya edilgen şekil, çatı; **~d** sesli

void [voyd] boş; hükümsüz; mahrum (**of** -den)

volcan|ic [vol'känik] volkanik; **~o** [~'keynıu] volkan, yanardağ

volley ['voli] yaylım ateş; yağmur; (tennis) topa yere değmeden geri vurma

volt [vıult] el. volt; **~age** voltaj, gerilim

voluble ['volyubl] konuşkan; çenebaz

volum|e ['volyum] hacim, oylum; cilt; **~inous** [vı'lyúminıs] büyük, hacimli

volunt|ary ['volınturi] is-

temli, ihtiyarî, gönüllü; **~eer** [~'tiı] n. gönüllü; v/t kendi isteği ile teklif etm.; v/i gönüllü yazılmak (**for** -e)

voluptuous [vı'lapçuıs] şehvetli

vomit ['vomit] v/i kusmak; v/t kusturmak

voodoo ['vuuduu] zenci büyücü

voracious [vı'reyşıs] doymak bilmez

vote [vıut] n. oy (hakkı); v/i oy vermek (**for** lehine); v/t seçmek; **~r** seçmen

voting ['vıutin] seçme; seçim; **~-paper** oy pusulası

vouch [vauç] temin etm. (**for** -i); kefil olm. (için); **~er** belgit, tanıt; **~safe** [~'seyf] v/t ihsan etm.

vow [vau] n. adak, yemin; v/t yemin etm. -e; adamak, nezretmek -i

vowel ['vauıl] gr. sesli harf

voyage ['voyic] yolculuk, seyahat

vulcanize ['valkınayz] v/t vulkanize etm.

vulgar ['valgı] kaba; bayağı

vulnerable ['valnırıbl] kolayca yaralanır

vulture ['valçı] zo. akbaba

W

wad [wod] n. tıkaç; tampon; v/t pamukla beslemek; **~ding** pamuk v.s. kaplaması, vatka [yürümek] **waddle** ['wodl] badi badi

wade [weyd] su içinde yürümek

wafer ['weyfı] bisküvit, kâğıt helvası; rel. mayasız ince ekmek

wag [wäg] v/t sallamak; v/i
sallanmak

wage¹ [weyc]: ~ war savaşmak (on ile)

wage², pl. ~s ['weyciz] ücret;
~-earner ['~önı] ücretli
kimse

wager ['weycı] n. bahis; v/i
bahis tutuşmak

wag(g)on ['wägın] yük arabası

wail [weyl] n. çığlık; v/i ha-
yıflanmak (over -e)

wainscot ['weynskıt] tahta
kaplama

waist [weyst] an. bel; ~coat
['weyskuot] yelek; ~line
bel yeri

wait [weyt] v/i beklemek
(for -i); hizmetçilik yapmak (on -e); ~er garson;
keep ~ing v/t bekletmek;
~ing-room bekleme salo-
nu; ~ress kadın garson

waive [weyv] v/t vazgeç-
mek, feragat etm. -den

wake¹ [weyk] dümen suyu;
fig. değende

wake² : ~ (up) v/i uyanmak;
v/t uyandırmak; ~n s.
wake²

walk [wôk] n. yürüyüş; gezinti; v/i yürümek; a. v/t
gezmek; terk etm. (on -i);
~ out pop. grev
yapmak; terk etm. (on -i);
~er gezen; yürüyücü; ~e-
-talkie ['wôki'tôki] portatif
telsiz telefon; ~ing-stick
baston; ~out grev

wall [wôl] n. duvar; sur; v/t
duvarla çevirmek; ~ up
duvarla kapamak

wallet ['wolit] cüzdan

wallpaper duvar kâğıdı

walnut ['wôlnat] bot. ceviz
(ağacı)

walrus ['wôlrıs] zo. mors

waltz [wôls] n. vals; v/i
vals yapmak

wan [won] solgun, soluk

wand [wond] değnek, çu-
buk

wander ['wondı] v/i dolaşmak, gezmek; sayıklamak;
~er ['~rı] gayesizce dolaşan

wane [weyn] v/i moon:
küçülmek; azalmak

want [wont] n. yokluk; ihtiyaç; zaruret; v/t istemek;
gereksemek; gerektirmek;
~ed aranan; ~ing eksik;
yoksun (in -den)

war [wô] savaş; ♀ Depart-
ment Am. Milli Savunma
Bakanlığı

warble ['wôbl] v/i ötmek,
şakımak

ward [wôd] vesayet; vesa-
yet altında bulunan kimse;
koğuş; bölge; ~ off v/t sa-
vuşturmak; ~en, ~er bekçi;
müdür

wardrobe ['wôdruob] giysi
dolabı, gardırop; elbiseler
pl.

ware [wä] mal, emtia; ~-
house ambar

war|fare ['wôfä] savaş;
~like savaşçı; savaşla ilgili

warm [wôm] adj. sıcak;
hararetli; v/t ısıtmak; v/i
ısınmak; ~th [.th] sıcaklık

warn [wôn] v/t ihtar etm.
(of -i); ~ing ihtar; ihbar

warp [wôp] *v/t* eğriltmek;
v/i eğrilmek

warrant ['worınt] *n.* yetki;
ruhsat; tevkif müzekkeresi;
garanti; *v/t* temin etm.;
izin vermek. -e; kefil olm.
-e; **~y** kefalet, garanti

warrior ['woriı] savaşçı

wart [wôt] siğil

wary ['wäiri] uyanık, ihti-
yatlı

was [woz, wız] *s.* **be**

wash [woş] *v/t* yıkamak;
wave: yalamak; *v/i* yıkan-
mak; *n.* yıkama; çamaşır;
~ up *v/t* bulaşık yıkamak; **~**-
basin, *Am.* **~bowl** lavabo;
~ed-out soluk; **~er** yıkama
makinesi; **~ing** yıkama; çamaşır

wasp [wosp] *zo.* yabanarısı

waste [weyst] *n.* savurma;
boş arazi; çöp; *adj.* boş,
ıssız; *v/t* boşuna sarfetmek;
harap etm.; **~ away** *v/i*
eriyip gitmek; **~paper-
basket** kâğıt sepeti; **~-
pipe** kılok

watch [woç] *n.* gözetleme;
nöbet; gözetlemek *veya*
kol saati; *v/t* gözetlemek;
bakmak -e; *v/i* beklemek
(**for** -i); **~** ile *v/t* dikkat
etm.; **~dog** bekçi köpeği;
~ful uyanık; **~maker** saat-
çi; **~man** bekçi

water ['wôtı] *n.* su; *v/t* sula-
mak, sulandırmak; **~ buf-
falo** manda; **~-closet** ap-
teshane; **~-colour** sulu
boya (resim); **~fall** çağlayan; **~ing-can** emzikli ko-

va, sulama ibriği; **~-level**
su seviyesi; **~-melon** karpuz; **~proof** su geçirmez;
yağmurluk; **~-ski** su kaya-
ği; **~works** *pl.* su dağıtım
tesisatı; **~y** sulu

watt [wot] *el.* vat

wave [weyv] *n.* dalga; sallama; *v/i* dalgalanmak; sallanmak; *v/t* sallamak

waver ['weyvı] *v/i* kararsız-
lık göstermek; sallanmak

wavy ['weyvi] dalgalı

wax[1] [wäks] *n.* balmumu;
v/t mum sürmek -e

wax[2] *v/i* büyümek, artmak

way [wey] yol; yön, cihet;
mesafe; tarz, usul; çare,
vasıta; **by the ~** sırası değiş-
mişken; **by ~** of yolu ile;
give ~ geri çekilmek; öncelik vermek (**to** -e); **on the ~**
yolunda; **out of the ~** sapa;
yerinde olmayan; **~ of life**
yaşama tarzı; **~lay** *v/i* -in
yolunu kesmek; **~side** yol
kenarı; **~ward** ['~wıd] ters,
inatçı

we [wi, wi] biz

weak [wik] zayıf; dayanık-
sız; **~en** *v/t* zayıflamak; *v/t*
zayıflatmak; **~ness** kuvvet-
sizlik

wealth [welth] bolluk, servet; **~y** zengin

wean [wîn] *v/t* sütten kesme

weapon ['wepın] silâh

wear [wäı] *v/t* giymek, takınmak; taşımak; takmak;
dayanmak -e; *n.* giysi, elbise; **~** aşınma; **~ (away,**

down, off, up) v/t aşındırmak; v/i aşınmak; ~ **out** v/t tüketmek

wear|isome ['wiirisım] usandırıcı; yorucu; ~**y** adj. yorgun; yorucu; v/t yormak

weasel ['wîzl] zo. gelincik

weather ['wedhı] n. hava; v/t aşındırmak; v/i aşınmak, solmak; ~ **out** v/i geçiştirmek; ~**beaten** fırtına yemiş; yanık; ~**cock** yelkovan; ~**forecast** hava raporu

weave [wîv] v/t dokumak; *basket:* örmek; ~**r** dokumacı, çulha

web [web] ağ; doku; örgü

wed [wed] evlenmek (*so. b.* ile); ~**ding** evlenme, düğün, nikâh; ~**ding-ring** nikâh yüzüğü

wedge [wec] *n.* kama, takoz; v/t sıkmak, sıkıştırmak

wedlock ['wedlok] evlilik

Wednesday ['wenzdi] çarşamba

weed [wîd] *n.* yabanî ot; v/t ayıklamak, temizlemek

week [wîk] hafta; ~**day** iş günü; ~**end** hafta sonu; ~**ly** haftalık, haftada bir

weep [wîp] ağlamak; ~**ing willow** *bot.* salkımsöğüt

weigh [wey] v/t tartmak; ölçünmek; ağırlığı olm.; ~ **r** ağırlık, sıklet; ~**t-lifting** haltercilik; ~**ty** ağır; önemli

welcome ['welkım] *n.* karşılama; v/t hoş karşılamak; hoş geldiniz demek *-e;*

(you are) ~! Bir şey değil!

weld [weld] v/t kaynak yaparak birleştirmek

welfare ['welfâı] refah; (yoksullara) yardım; ~ **state** refah devleti

well¹ [wel] kuyu

well² iyi, iyice, tamamiyle; işte; neyse; **as** ~ dahi, bile; **as** ~ **as** hem ... hem de ...; **I am not** ~ rahatsızım; ~ **off** varlıklı; ~**being** saadet, refah; ~**known** tanınmış, meşhur; ~**mannered** terbiyeli; ~**timed** zamanlı; ~**to-do** hali vakti yerinde; ~**worn** eskimiş; bayatlamış

Welsh [welş] Gal dili; ~**man** Galli; ~ **rabbit,** ~ **rarebit** [.'râbit] kızarmış ekmeğe sürülen peynir

wench [wenç] kız

went [went] *s.* **go**

wept [wept] *s.* **weep**

were [wö] *s.* **be**

west [west] batı, batıya doğru; ~**erly,** ~**ern** batıya ait; ~**ward(s)** [.'~wıd(z)] batıda; batıya

wet [wet] *adj.* ıslak, rutubetli; v/t ıslatmak; ~**through** sırs klam; ~**nurse** sütnine

whack [wâk] *n.* şaklama; v/t dövmek

whale [weyl] *zo.* balina

wharf [wôf] iskele, rıhtım

what [wot] ne; nasıl; hangi; ~ **for?** niçin?; ~**(so)ever** her ne, her hangi

wheat [wît] buğday

wheel [wîl] *n.* tekerlek; çark; *v/i* dönmek; *v/t* döndürmek; tekerlekli bir taşıtla götürmek; ~**barrow** tekerlekli el arabası; ~**chair** tekerlekli sandalye

whelp [welp] *zo.* enik

when [wen] ne zaman?; -*diği zaman; iken; ~**ever** her ne zaman

where [wäî] nerede?; nereye?; -*diği yerde; ~**about(s) nerelerde; ~**as** halbuki; ~**by** vasıtasiyle; mademki; ~(**up**)**on** bunun üzerine; ~**ver** her nereye; her nerede

whet [wet] *v/t* bilemek

whether ['wedhı] -ip -me-diğini

which [wiç] hangi(si); ki; ~(**so**)**ever** her hangi(si)

whiff [wif] esinti; püf

Whig [wig] *pol.* İngil. liberal partisi üyesi

while [wayl] müddet, zaman, süre; *conj.* iken, -*diği halde

whim [wim] geçici istek, heves

whimper ['wimpı] *v/i* ağlamak, inlemek

whimsical ['wimzikıl] tuhaf, kaprisli

whine [wayn] *v/i* sızlanmak

whip [wip] *n.* kırbaç, kamçı; *v/t* kamçılamak; çalkamak; ~**ped cream** kremşanti

whirl [wöl] *n.* hızla dönme; *v/i* hızla dönmek; *v/t* hızla döndürmek; ~**pool** burgaç, girdap

whir(r) [wö] *v/i* vızlamak

whisk [wisk] *n.* yumurta teli; tüy süpürge; *v/t* çalkamak

whiskers ['wiskız] *pl.* favori, bıyık

whisk(e)y ['wiski] viski

whisper ['wispı] *n.* fısıltı; *v/i* fısıldamak

whistle ['wisl] *n.* ıslık; düdük; *v/i* ıslık çalmak

white [wayt] beyaz, ak; 2 **House** *Am.* Beyaz Saray; ~**lie** zararsız yalan; 2**hall** *Londra'da resmi dairelerin bulunduğu cadde; ~**n** *v/t* beyazlatmak; *v/i* beyazlanmak, ağarmak; ~**ness** beyazlık; ~**wash** *n.* badana; *v/t* badana etm.; *fig.* temize çıkarmak

Whitsun (**day**) ['witsn; 'wit'sandi] *rel.* pantekot yortusunun pazar günü; ~**tide** *rel.* pantekot

whiz(z) ['wiz] *v/i* vızıldamak

who [huu] kim?; o ki, onlar ki; ~**dunit** [~'danit] *sl.* dedektif romanı; ~**ever** kim olursa olsun

whole [huul] bütün, tam; tam şey; toplam; **on the** ~ genellikle; ~**sale** *ec.* toptan; ~**some** sıhhate yararlı

wholly ['hulli] büsbütün

whom [huum] kimi?; ki onu

whoop [huup] *n.* bağırma; *v/i* bağırmak; ~**ing cough** *med.* boğmaca öksürüğü

whore [hö] fahişe, orospu

whose [huuz] kimin?

why [way] nicin?, niye?
wick [wik] fitil
wicked ['wikid] fena, kötü; **~ness** kötülük; günahkârlık
wicker ['wikı] hasır; sepet işi; **~ chair** hasır koltuk
wicket ['wikit] ufak kapı; *krikette* kale
wide [wayd] geniş, enli; açık; **~ awake** tamamen uyanık; **~n** v/t genişletmek; v/i genişlemek; **~spread** yaygın
widow ['widıu] dul kadın; **~er** dul erkek
width [width] genişlik, en (-lilik)
wife [wayf] karı, eş
wig [wig] peruka, takma saç
wild [wayld] yabani; vahşi; şiddetli; **run ~** v/i yabanileşmek; **~cat** zo. yaban kedisi; *fig.* düzensiz; **~erness** ['wildınis] kır, sahra; **~ness** ['wayldnis] yabanilik, vahşet
wil(l)ful ['wilful] inatçı; kasıtlı
will [wil] *n.* istek, arzu; vasiyet(name); *(auxiliary verb)* istemek; -ecek; **~ing** razı, hazır (to *inf.* -*meğe*)
willow ['wilıu] *bot.* söğüt
wilt [wilt] v/i solmak
win [win] v/t kazanmak
wince [wins] v/i birdenbire ürkmek
wind¹ [wind] *n.* rüzgâr, yel; hava; osuruk; nefes; v/t -*in* kokusunu almak
wind² [waynd] v/t çevir-

mek, dolamak; v/i bükülmek; dolaşmak; **~ up** v/t *watch:* kurmak; **~ing** dolambaç(lı) [ırgat]
windlass ['windlıs] *tech.*}
windmill ['winmill] yeldeğirmeni
window ['windıu] pencere; vitrin; **~pane** pencere camı; **~shop** v/i vitrin gezmek
wind|pipe *an.* nefes borusu; **~screen**, *Am.* **~shield** ön cam; **~screen wiper** silgiç; **~y** rüzgârlı
wine [wayn] şarap
wing [win] kanat; kol
wink [wink] *n.* göz kırpma; v/i göz kırpmak; gözle işaret vermek (at -*e*)
winn|er ['winı] kazanan; **~ing** kazanma; kazanan
wint|er ['wintı] *n.* kış; v/i kışlamak; **~ry** ['~tri] kış gibi, pek soğuk
wipe [wayp] v/t silmek, silip kurutmak; **~ off** silip gidermek; **~ out** silip yoketmek
wire ['wayı] *n.* tel; *pop.* telgraf; v/t telle bağlamak; v/i telgraf çekmek; **~less** telsiz; radyo
wiry ['wayıri] tel gibi
wisdom ['wizdım] akıl(lılık), hikmet; **~ tooth** akıl dişi
wise [wayz] akıllı; tedbirli; tecrübeli
wish [wiş] *n.* istek, arzu; v/t istemek, arzu etm.
wistful ['wistful] hasretli; dalgın

wit [wit] akıl; anlayış; nükte; nükteci; **be at one's ~'s end** tamamen şaşırmak

witch [wiç] büyücü kadın; **~craft, ~ery** büyücülük

with [widh] ile; **-e** karşı; **-den** dolayı; **-in** yanında

withdraw [widh'drô] v/t geri almak; v/i çekilmek **(from -den); ~al** geri çek(il)me

wither ['widhı] v/i kurumak, solmak; v/t kurutmak

with|hold [widh'huld] v/t tutmak; vermemek; **~in** [~'dhin] -in içinde; içeride; **~out** [~'dhaut] -siz, -in dışında; **~stand** v/t dayanmak -e

witness ['witnis] n. tanık, şahit; delil; şahitlik; v/t şahit olm. -e; şehadet etm. -e; **~box**, Am. **~stand** jur. tanık kürsüsü

witty ['witi] nükteci; nükteli

wizard ['wizıd] büyücü, sihirbaz

wobble ['wobl] v/i sallanmak; titremek

woe [wıu] keder, dert; **~begone, ~ful** kederli

woke [wuk], **~n** s. **wake**

wolf [wulf] kurt

woman ['wumın] kadın; **~ doktor** kadın doktoru; **~hood** kadınlık; **~kind** kadınlar pl.; **~ly** kadına yakışır

womb [wuum] an. rahim, dölyatağı

won [wan] s. **win**

wonder ['wandı] n. harika, şaşılacak şey; hayret; v/i hayrette kalmak, hayran olm.; merak etm. **(if, whether** -ip -mediğini); **~ful** hayret verici, şaşılacak

won't [wıunt] = **will not**

wont [wıunt] âdet; alışmış **(to inf. -meğe)**

woo [wuu] v/t kur yapmak -e

wood [wud] orman; odun, tahta; **~cutter** baltacı; **~ed** ağaçlı; **~en** tahtadan yapılmış, ahşap; **~pecker** zo. ağaçkakan; **~work** doğrama(cılık), dülgerlik; **~y** ormanlık; ağaç; cinsinden

wool [wul] yün; **~(l)en** yünden, yünlü; **~(l)y** yünlü; yumuşak

word [wöd] n. kelime; söz; laf; haber; v/t ifade etm.; **~ing** yazılış tarzı

wore [wö] s. **wear**

work [wök] n. iş, çalışma; emek; eser; pl. fabrika sg.; mekanizma; v/i çalışmak, uğraşmak; işlemek; v/t çalıştırmak; işletmek; zorlamak **(into -e); at ~** iş başında; **out of ~** işsiz, boşta; **public ~s** pl. bayındırlık sg.; **~able** işlenebilir; pratik; **~day** iş günü; **~er** işçi, amele

working iş gören, çalışan; işliyen; **~class** işçi sınıfı; **~hours** pl. iş saatleri

workman işçi; **~ship** usta işi

workshop atelye

world ['wöld] dünya, cihan, âlem; evren; uzay; **~ war** dünya savaşı; **~ly** dünyevî; **~-wide** âlemşümul, dünyaya yaygın

worm [wöm] kurt, solucan; **~-eaten** kurt yemiş

worn [wôn] s. wear; **~-out** bitkin; eskimiş

worried ['warid] endişeli; **~y** n. üzüntü, endişe, merak; v/i üzülmek, tasalanmak (about -e)

worse [wös] daha fena, daha kötü; **~n** v/i fenalaşmak; v/t fenalaştırmak

worship ['wöşip] n. tapınma, ibadet; v/t tapmak, tapınmak -e; **~(p)er** tapan, ibadet eden

worst [wöst] en fena, en kötü

worsted ['wustid] yün ipliği

worth [wöth] n. değer, kıymet; adj. değer, lâyık (-ing -e); **~ seeing** görmeğe değer; **~less** değersiz; **~ while** (zahmetine) değer; faydalı; **~y** ['.dhi] değerli; lâyık (of -e)

would [wud] -ecek(ti); istedi **~ rather** inf. -meyi tercih edecekti

wound[1] [wuund] n. yara; v/t yaralamak; -in gönlünü kırmak

wound[2] [waund] s. wind[2]

wove [wuuv], **~n** s. weave

wrangle ['räŋgl] n. kavga, ağız dalaşı; v/i kavga etm., çekişmek

wrap [räp] n. örtü; atkı; v/t sarmak, örtmek; **~ up** v/t sarmak (in -e); **~ped up** sarılmış (in -e); **~per** sargı; **~ping** ambalaj

wrath [roth] öfke, hiddet

wreath [rîth] çelenk

wreck [rek] n. gemi enkazı pl.; kazaya uğrama; harap olmuş kimse; v/t kazaya uğratmak; yıkmak; **~age** enkaz pl.; **~ing service** Am. yedeğe alma servisi

wren [ren] zo. çalıkuşu

wrench [renç] n. burk(ul)ma; tech. İngiliz anahtarı; v/t burkmak

wrest [rest] v/t zorla elde etm.

wrestle ['resl] v/i güreşmek; uğraşmak; **~er** pehlivan; **~ing** güreş

wretch [reç] herif; **~ed** ['.id] alçak, sefil; bitkin

wriggle ['rigl] v/i kıvranmak, sallanmak

wring [riŋ] v/t burup sıkmak

wrinkle ['riŋkl] n. kırışık; v/t kırıştırmak; v/i kırışmak

wrist [rist] an. bilek; **~ watch** kol saati

writ [rit] yazı; ferman

write [rayt] v/t yazmak; **~ out** yazıya dökmek; **~r** yazar

writhe [raydh] v/i kıvranmak

writing ['raytiŋ] yazı; el yazısı; **~-paper** yazı kâğıdı

written ['ritn] s. write

wrong [roŋ] *adj.* yanlış;
ters; *n.* haksızlık; *v/t* haksız
muamele etm. **-e;** *-in* hak-
kını yemek; **be** ~ yanılmak;
yanlış olm.

wrote [rɪut] *s.* **write**
wrought [rôt] işlenmiş; ~
iron dövme demir
wrung [raŋ] *s.* **wring**
wry [ray] çarpık, eğri

X

Xmas ['krısmıs] = **Christ-**
mas

X-ray ['eks'rey] *n.* röntgen
ışını; *v/t* röntgen ışınları
ile muayene etm.

Y

yacht [yot] *naut.* yat; ~**ing**
kotracılık
Yank(ee) ['yäŋki] Amerikalı; A.B.D.'nin kuzey
eyayetlerinde oturan kimse
yap [yäp] havlamak
yard[1] [yâd] yarda *(0,914 m)*
yard[2] avlu
yarn [yân] iplik; *pop.* hikâye, masal
yawn [yôn] *n.* esneme; *v/i*
esnemek
yeah [yey] evet
year [yō] yıl, sene; ~**book**
yıllık; ~**ly** yıllık, yılda bir
yearn [yôn] *v/i* çok istemek
(for *-i)*
yeast [yîst] maya
yell [yel] *n.* çığlık, bağırma;
v/i çığlık koparmak
yellow ['yelıu] sarı
yelp [yelp] kesik kesik havlamak
yes [yes] evet
yesterday ['yestıdi] dün
yet [yet] henüz, daha, hâlâ;
bile; **as** ~ şimdiye kadar
yew [yû] *bot.* porsukağacı

yield [yîld] *n.* mahsul, ürün;
v/t vermek, meydana çıkarmak; *v/i* razı olm., teslim
olm. **(to** *-e)*; ~**ing** yumuşak, uysal
yoke [yɪuk] *n.* boyunduruk;
çift; *v/t* boyunduruğa koşmak
yolk [yɪuk] yumurta sarısı
yonder ['yondı] ötedeki;
ötede
you [yû, yu] sen; siz; sana,
seni; size, sizi
young [yaŋ] genç; yavru;
~**ster** ['~stı] çocuk; delikanlı
your [yô] senin; sizin; ~**s**
[~z] seninki; sizinki; ~**self**
kendin(iz); ~**selves** kendi-
niz
youth [yûth] genç, delikanlı; gençlik; ~ **hostel** gençlik yurdu, hostel; ~**ful**
genç, dinç
Yugoslav ['yûgu'slâv] Yu-
goslav(yalı); ~**ia** ['~'slâvyı]
Yugoslavya

zeal 436

Z

zeal [zîl] gayret; **~ous** ['ze-
lıs] gayretli
zebra ['zîbrı] *zo.* zebir; **~
crossing** çizgili yaya geçidi
zenith ['zenith] *astr.* başu-
cu; *fig.* zirve
zephyr ['zefı] hafif rüzgâr,
meltem
zeppelin ['zepılın] *av.* zeplin
zero ['zîırıu] sıfır
zest [zest] tat, lezzet; zevk
zigzag ['zigzäg] zikzak

zinc [zîŋk] çinko, tutya
Zionis|m ['zayınızım] siyo-
nizm; **~t** siyonist
zip [zip] vızıltı; **~ code** *Am.*
posta bölgesi numarası; **~
fastener, ~per** fermuar
zodiac ['zııudiäk] *astr.* zod-
yak
zone [zıun] bölge
zoo [zuu], **~logical garden**
[zıu'locikıl -] hayvanat
bahçesi; **~logy** [zıu'olıcı]
zooloji, hayvanlar bili-
mi

British and American Abbreviations

İngilizce'de Kullanılan Kısaltmalar

A.D.	anno Domini = Christian era *Milâttan sonra*
a.m.	ante meridiem = before noon *öğleden önce*
AP	Associated Press (*Amerikan haber ajansı*)
B.A.	Bachelor of Arts *edebiyat fakültesi diploması, başölyelik*
BBC	British Broadcasting Corporation *İngiliz Radyo Kurumu*
B.C.	Before Christ *Milâttan önce*
Bros.	Brothers *ec. Kardeşler*
CIA	Central Intelligence Agency (*A.B.D. istihbarat bürosu*)
CID	Criminal Investigation Department (*İngiliz cinayet zabıtası*)
Co.	company *ec. ortaklık, şirket*
c/o	care of *eliyle*
COD	cash (*Am.* collect) on delivery *teslimde ödenecek, ödemeli*
Dept.	Department *kısım, şube; bakanlık*
doz.	dozen *düzine*
E	east *doğu*
Ed., ed.	edition *baskı;* edited *hazırlanmış;* editor *hazırlayan*
E(E)C	European (Economic) Community *Avrupa (Ekonomik) Topluluğu*
e.g.	exempli gratia = for instance *örneğin*
encl.	enclosed *ilişikte*
Esq.	Esquire (*isimden sonra*) *Bay*

438

F	Fahrenheit *fahrenhayt*
FBI	Federal Bureau of Investigation (*A.B.D. cinayet zabıtası örgütü*)
ft	foot, feet *kadem*
GB	Great Britain *Büyük Britanya*
GMT	Greenwich Mean Time *Greenwich orta saati*
GP	General Practitioner *pratisyen hekim*
GPO	General Post Office *merkez postanesi*
HMS	His (Her) Majesty's Ship (*İngiliz donanmasına ait gemi*)
hr.	hour(s) *saat(ler)*
i.e.	id est = that is to say *yani*
IMF	International Monetary Fund *Uluslararası Para Fonu*
Inc.	Incorporated *ec. anonim*
£	pound sterling *İngiliz lirası, sterlin*
lb.	pound(s) *yarım kilo, libre*
Ltd.	limited *ec. limitet*
M.A.	Master of Arts *edebiyat fakültesi yüksek diploması*
M.D.	Doctor of Medicine *tıp doktoru*
MP	Member of Parliament *parlamento üyesi*; Military Police *askeri inzibat*
m.p.h.	miles per hour *saatte ... mil*
Mr	Mister *Bay*
Mrs	Mistress *Bayan*
Ms	miss *Bayan*
Mt.	Mount *geo. dağ*
N	north *kuzey*
NE	northeast *kuzeydoğu*
NW	northwest *kuzeybatı*
oz, oz.	ounce(s) *ons*
p	new penny (pence) *yeni pens*
Ph.D.	Doctor of Philosophy *felsefe* (= *edebiyat*) *doktoru*
p.m.	post meridiem = after noon *öğleden sonra*
PO	Post Office *postane*; Postal Order *posta havalesi*
POB, POBox	Post Office Box *posta kutusu*

RAF	Royal Air Force (*İngiliz hava kuvvetleri*)
Rd	Road *cadde*
S	south *güney*
$	dollar *dolar*
SE	southeast *güneydoğu*
Sq	Square *meydan, alan*
St	Saint *rel. aziz, sen*; Street *cadde, sokak*
SW	southwest *güneybatı*
TV	television *televizyon*
UK	United Kingdom *Britanya Kırallığı*
UN	United Nations *Birleşmiş Milletler*
UPI	United Press International (*Amerikan haber ajansı*)
US(A)	United States (of America) *Amerika Birleşik Devletleri*
V.A.T.	value-added tax *ec. katma değer vergisi*
W	west *batı*

Turkish Abbreviations

Türkçe'de Kullanılan Kısaltmalar

AA	Anadolu Ajansı *Anatolian News Agency*
ABD	Amerika Birleşik Devletleri *United States of America*
AET	Avrupa Ekonomik Topluluğu *European Economic Community*
A.O.	anonim ortaklık *joint stock company*
AP	Adalet Partisi *Justice Party*
Apt.	apartman *apartment (house)*
A.Ş.	anonim şirket *joint stock company*
As.	Askerî *Military*
A.Ü.	Ankara Üniversitesi *University of Ankara*
B.	Bay *Mr*; batı *west*
bkz.	bakınız *see*
Blv.	Bulvar(ı) *Boulevard*
B.M.M.	Büyük Millet Meclisi *Grand National Assembly*
Bn.	Bayan *Mrs*; *Ms*
Bşk.	başkan *president*
Cad.	cadde(si) *Street, Road*
CHP	Cumhuriyet Halk Partisi *Republican People's Party*
D.	doğu *east*
DDY	Devlet Demiryolları *Turkish State Railways*
DİSK	Devrimci İşçi Sendikaları Konfederasyonu *Federation of Revolutionary Labourers' Unions*
doğ.	doğumlu *born*
Dz.	Deniz(i) *Sea*
G.	güney *south*
Gn.Kur.	Genelkurmay *General Staff*
İÖ	İsa'dan önce *before Christ*
İS	İsa'dan sonra *Christian era*
İTÜ	İstanbul Teknik Üniversitesi *Technical University of Istanbul*
İ.Ü.	İstanbul Üniversitesi *University of Istanbul*

K.	kuzey *north*
krş.	kuruş *piaster*; karşılaştırınız *compare*
Mah.	Mahalle(si) *quarter*; Mahkeme(si) *jur. Court*
MC	Milliyetçi Cephe *Nationalist Front*
Md.	Müdür(ü) *Director*; Müdürlü(~ğü) *Directorate, Head Office*
MÖ, M.Ö.	Milâttan önce *before Christ*
MS, M.S.	Milâttan sonra *Christian era*
MSP	Millî Selâmet Partisi *National Salvation Party*
msl.	meselâ *for instance*
ODTÜ	Orta Doğu Teknik Üniversitesi *Middle East Technical University*
ölm.	ölümü *died*
PK, P.K.	posta kutusu *Post Office Box*
PTT	Posta Telgraf Telefon (İdaresi) *Post, Telegraph and Telephone (Administration)*
s.	sayfa *page*
Sok.	soka|k (~ğı) *Street*
SSCB, S.S.C.B.	Sovyet Sosyalist Cumhuriyetler Birliği *Union of Soviet Socialist Republics*
TAO	Türk Anonim Ortaklığı *Turkish Joint Stock Company*
TAŞ	Türk Anonim Şirketi *Turkish Joint Stock Company*
TBMM	Türkiye Büyük Millet Meclisi *Turkish Grand National Assembly*
T.C.	Türkiye Cumhuriyeti *Republic of Turkey*
TCDD	Türkiye Cumhuriyeti Devlet Demiryolları *Turkish State Railways*
TDK	Türk Dil Kurumu *Turkish Language Association*
TİP	Türkiye İşçi Partisi *Turkish Labourers' Party*
TTK	Türk Tarih Kurumu *Turkish Historical Association*
THY	Türk Havayolları *Turkish Airlines*
TL, T.L.	Türk lirası *Turkish lira*
T.M.	Türk malı *Turkish product*
TRT	Türkiye Radyo ve Televizyon Kurumu *Turkish Radio and Television Institution*
vb.	ve benzeri *and the like*
vd.	ve devamı *and so on*
Vet.	veteriner *veterinary*, *Am. veterinarian*
vs., v.s.	ve saire *and so on*

Irregular English Verbs

İngilizce' deki Kuralsız Fiiller

(*) işaretli kuralsız fiil biçimlerinin yerlerine kurallı fiil
· biçimleri kullanılabilir.

abide (*kalmak*) – abode* –
abode*

awake (*uyan[dır]mak*) –
awoke – awoke*

be (*olmak*) – was – been

bear (*taşımak; doğurmak*) –
bore – taşı(n)mış: borne –
doğmuş: born

beat (*vurmak*) – beat –
beaten

begin (*başlamak*) – began –
begun

bend (*bük[ül]mek*) – bent –
bent

bereave (*çalmak*) – bereft* –
bereft*

bet (*bahse girmek*) – bet* –
bet*

bid (*emretmek*) – bade, bid –
bid(den)

bind (*bağlamak*) – bound –
bound

bite (*ısırmak*) – bit – bitten

bleed (*kanamak*) – bled –
bled

blend (*karış[tır]mak*) –
blent* – blent*

blow (*üflemek, esmek*) –
blew – blown

break (*kır[ıl]mak*) – broke –
broken

breed (*üretmek*) – bred –
bred

bring (*getirmek*) – brought –
brought

build (*inşa etm.*) – built –
built

burn (*yakmak; yanmak*) –
burnt* – burnt*

burst (*patla[t]mak*) – burst –
burst

buy (*satın almak*) – bought –
bought

cast (*atmak*) – cast – cast

catch (*yakalamak*) – caught –
caught

choose (*seçmek*) – chose –
chosen

cleave (*yar[ıl]mak*) – cleft,
clove* – cleft, cloven*

cling (*yapışmak*) – clung –
clung

clothe (*giydirmek*) – clad* –
clad*

come (*gelmek*) – came –
come

cost (*fiatı olm.*) – cost – cost

creep (*sürünmek*) – crept –
crept

crow (*ötmek*) – crew* – crowed
cut (*kesmek*) – cut – cut
deal (*uğraşmak*) – dealt – dealt
dig (*kazmak*) – dug – dug
do (*yapmak*) – did – done
draw (*çekmek*) – drew – drawn
dream (*rüya görmek*) – dreamt* – dreamt*
drink (*içmek*) – drank – drunk
drive (*sürmek*) – drove – driven
dwell (*oturmak*) – dwelt – dwelt
eat (*yemek*) – ate, eat – eaten
fall (*düşmek*) – fell – fallen
feed (*yedirmek*) – fed – fed
feel (*duymak*) – felt – felt
fight (*savaşmak*) – fought – fought
find (*bulmak*) – found – found
flee (*kaçmak*) – fled – fled
fling (*fırlatmak*) – flung – flung
fly (*uçmak*) – flew – flown
forbid (*yasak etm.*) – forbade – forbidden
forget (*unutmak*) – forgot – forgotten
forsake (*vazgeçmek*) – forsook – forsaken
freeze (*don[dur]mak*) – froze – frozen
get (*elde etm.*) – got – got, Am. gotten
gild (*yaldızlamak*) – gilt* – gilt*

gird (*kuşatmak*) – girt* – girt*
give (*vermek*) – gave – given
go (*gitmek*) – went – gone
grind (*öğütmek*) – ground – ground
grow (*büyümek; yetiştirmek*) – grew – grown
hang (*asmak; asılı olm.*) – hung – hung
have (*sahip olm.*) – had – had
hear (*işitmek*) – heard – heard
heave (*kaldırmak*) – hove* – hove*
hew (*yontmak*) – hewed – hewn*
hide (*sakla[n]mak*) – hid – hid(den)
hit (*vurmak*) – hit – hit
hold (*tutmak*) – held – held
hurt (*yaralamak*) – hurt – hurt
keep (*tutmak*) – kept – kept
kneel (*diz çökmek*) – knelt* – knelt*
knit (*örmek*) – knit* – knit*
know (*bilmek*) – knew – known
lay (*yatırmak*) – laid – laid
lead (*yol göstermek*) – led – led
lean (*daya[n]mak*) – leant* – leant*
leap (*atlamak*) – leapt* – leapt*
learn (*öğrenmek*) – learnt* – learnt*
leave (*ayrılmak*) – left – left
lend (*ödünç vermek*) – lent – lent
let (*bırakmak*) – let – let

lie (*yatmak*) – lay – lain
light (*yakmak*) – lit* – lit*
lose (*unutmak*) – lost – lost
make (*yapmak*) – made – made
mean (*kastetmek*) – meant – meant
meet (*rastlamak*) – met – met
mow (*biçmek*) – mowed – mown*
pay (*ödemek*) – paid – paid
put (*yerleştirmek*) – put – put
read (*okumak*) – read – read
rend (*yırt[ıl]mak*) – rent – rent
rid (*kurtarmak*) – rid* – rid
ride (*binmek*) – rode – ridden
ring (*çalmak*) – rang – rung
rise (*kalkmak*) – rose – risen
run (*koşmak*) – ran – run
saw (*testere ile kesmek*) – sawed – sawn*
say (*demek, söylemek*) – said – said
see (*görmek*) – saw – seen
seek (*aramak*) – sought – sought
sell (*satmak*) – sold – sold
send (*göndermek*) – sent – sent
set (*koymak*) – set – set
sew (*dikmek*) – sewed – sewn*
shake (*sallamak*) – shook – shaken
shave (*tıraş etm. veya olm.*) – shaved – shaven*
shear (*kırkmak*) – sheared – shorn

shed (*dökmek*) – shed – shed
shine (*parla[t]mak*)– shone – shone
shoot (*ateş etm.*) – shot – shot
show (*göstermek*) – showed – shown*
shred (*parçalamak*) – shred* – shred*
shrink (*daral[t]mak*) – shrank – shrunk
shut (*kapa[t]mak*) – shut – shut
sing (*şarkı söylemek*) – sang – sung
sink (*bat[ır]mak*) – sank – sunk
sit (*oturmak*) – sat – sat
slay (*öldürmek*) – slew – slain
sleep (*uyumak*) – slept – slept
slide (*kaymak*) – slid – slid
sling (*sapanla atmak*) – slung – slung
slit (*yarmak*) – slit – slit
smell (*kokmak; kokusunu almak*) – smelt* – smelt*
sow (*ekmek*) – sowed – sown*
speak (*konuşmak*) – spoke – spoken
speed (*hızlan[dır]mak*) – sped* – sped
spell (*hecelemek*) – spelt* – spelt*
spend (*harcamak*) – spent – spent
spill (*dök[ül]mek*) – spilt* – spilt*
spin (*eğirmek*) – spun, span – spun

spit (*tükürmek*) – spat – spat

split (*yar[ıl]mak*) – split – split

spoil (*bozmak*) – spoilt* – spoilt*

spread (*yay[ıl]mak*) – spread – spread

spring (*sıçramak*) – sprang – sprung

stand (*durmak*) – stood – stood

steal (*çalmak*) – stole – stolen

stick (*yapış[tır]mak*) – stuck – stuck

sting (*sokmak*) – stung – stung

stink (*koku çıkarmak*) – stank, stunk – stunk

strew (*serpmek*) – strewed – strewn*

stride (*yürümek*) – strode – stridden

strike (*vurmak*) – struck, struck, stricken

string (*dizmek; germek*) – strung – strung

strive (*uğraşmak*) – strove – striven

swear (*yemin etm.*) – swore – sworn

sweat (*terlemek*) – sweat* – sweat*

sweep (*süpürmek*) – swept – swept

swell (*şiş[ir]mek*) – swelled – swollen

swim (*yüzmek*) – swam – swum

swing (*salla[n]mak*) – swung – swung

take (*almak*) – took – taken

teach (*öğretmek*) – taught – taught

tear (*çekmek*) – tore – torn

tell (*söylemek*) – told – told

think (*düşünmek*) – thought – thought

thrive (*gelişmek*) – throve* – thriven*

throw (*atmak*) – threw – thrown

thrust (*dürtmek*) – thrust – thrust

tread (*basmak, çiğnemek*) – trod – trodden

wake (*uyan[dır]mak*) – woke* – woke(n)*

wear (*giymek*) – wore – worn

weave (*dokumak*) – wove – woven

weep (*ağlamak*) – wept – wept

wet (*ıslatmak*) – wet* – wet*

win (*kazanmak*) – won – won

wind (*dola[ş]mak*) – wound – wound

work (*çalışmak*) – wrought* – wrought*

wring (*burup sıkmak*) – wrung – wrung

write (*yazmak*) – wrote – written

Numbers

Sayılar

Cardinal Numbers — Asıl sayılar

0 nought, zero, cipher *sıfır*	22 twenty-two *yirmi iki*
1 one *bir*	23 twenty-three *yirmi üç*
2 two *iki*	30 thirty *otuz*
3 three *üç*	40 forty *kırk*
4 four *dört*	50 fifty *elli*
5 five *beş*	60 sixty *altmış*
6 six *altı*	70 seventy *yetmiş*
7 seven *yedi*	80 eighty *seksen*
8 eight *sekiz*	90 ninety *doksan*
9 nine *dokuz*	100 a (one) hundred *yüz*
10 ten *on*	101 a hundred and one *yüz*
11 eleven *on bir*	*bir*
12 twelve *on iki*	572 five hundred and sev-
13 thirteen *on üç*	enty-two *beş yüz yet-*
14 fourteen *on dört*	*miş iki*
15 fifteen *on beş*	
16 sixteen *on altı*	1,000 a (one) thousand *bin*
17 seventeen *on yedi*	1,000,000 a (one) million
18 eighteen *on sekiz*	*bir milyon*
19 nineteen *on dokuz*	1,000,000,000 a (one) milli-
20 twenty *yirmi*	ard (*Am.* billion) *bir*
21 twenty-one *yirmi bir*	*milyar*

Ordinal Numbers — Sıra sayıları

1st first *birinci*	7th seventh *yedinci*
2nd second *ikinci*	8th eighth *sekizinci*
3rd third *üçüncü*	9th ninth *dokuzuncu*
4th fourth *dördüncü*	10th tenth *onuncu*
5th fifth *beşinci*	11th eleventh *on birinci*
6th sixth *altıncı*	12th twelfth *on ikinci*

13th thirteenth *on üçüncü*
14th fourteenth *on dördüncü*
15th fifteenth *on beşinci*
16th sixteenth *on altıncı*
17th seventeenth *on yedinci*
18th eighteenth *on sekizinci*
19th nineteenth *on dokuzuncu*
20th twentieth *yirminci*
21st twenty-first *yirmi birinci*
22nd twenty-second *yirmi ikinci*

23rd twenty-third *yirmi üçüncü*
30th thirtieth *otuzuncu*
40th fortieth *kırkıncı*
50th fiftieth *ellinci*
60th sixtieth *altmışıncı*
70th seventieth *yetmişinci*
80th eightieth *sekseninci*
90th ninetieth *doksanıncı*
100th (one) hundredth *yüzüncü*
101st hundred and first *yüz birinci*
1000th (one) thousandth *bininci*

Fractional and Other Numbers

Kesirli ve diğer sayılar

$1/_2$ one (a) half *yarım*

$1^1/_2$ one and a half *bir buçuk*

$1/_4$ one fourth, one (a) quarter *çeyrek, dörtte bir*

$1/_3$ one (a) third *üçte bir*

$2/_3$ two thirds *üçte iki*

$1/_{10}$ one tenth *onda bir*

$3/_7$ three sevenths *yedide üç*

2.8 two point eight *iki, onda sekiz*

$3 + 6 = 9$ three and six are nine *üç artı altı eşit dokuz; üç, altı daha dokuz eder*

$8 - 5 = 3$ eight minus five are three *sekiz eksi beş eşit üç*

$5 \times 10 = 50$ five times ten are fifty *beş çarpı on eşit elli*

$60 : 6 = 10$ sixty divided by six make ten *altmış bölü altı eşit on*